The 11th North Carolina
Infantry in the Civil War

ALSO BY WILLIAM THOMAS VENNER

*The 7th Tennessee Infantry in the Civil War:
A History and Roster* (McFarland, 2013)

The 11th North Carolina Infantry in the Civil War

A History and Roster

William Thomas Venner

McFarland & Company, Inc., Publishers
Jefferson, North Carolina

LIBRARY OF CONGRESS CATALOGUING-IN-PUBLICATION DATA

Venner, William Thomas, 1950–
The 11th North Carolina Infantry in the Civil War : a history and roster / William Thomas Venner.
    p.   cm.
Includes bibliographical references and index.

ISBN 978-0-7864-9515-3 (softcover : acid free paper) ∞
ISBN 978-1-4766-2089-3 (ebook)

1. Confederate States of America. Army. North Carolina Infantry Regiment, 11th.
2. North Carolina—History—Civil War, 1861–1865—Regimental histories.
3. United States—History—Civil War, 1861–1865—Regimental histories.
4. United States—History—Civil War, 1861–1865—Campaigns.   I. Title.

E573.511th .V46 2015   973.7'456—dc23   2015025560

BRITISH LIBRARY CATALOGUING DATA ARE AVAILABLE

© 2015 William Thomas Venner. All rights reserved

No part of this book may be reproduced or transmitted in any form or by any means, electronic or mechanical, including photocopying or recording, or by any information storage and retrieval system, without permission in writing from the publisher.

Front cover photograph "Three Unidentified Confederate Soldiers" (courtesy of Tom Linjenquist Collection, Library of Congress); back cover photograph "Assault of Brockenbrough's Confederate Brigade" (Robert U. Johnson and Clarence C. Buel, *Battles and Leaders of the Civil War*, 1887, Vol. 3; 278)

Printed in the United States of America

*McFarland & Company, Inc., Publishers
Box 611, Jefferson, North Carolina 28640
www.mcfarlandpub.com*

To the men of the 11th North Carolina Infantry and their families.
We must not let their memories fade.

Table of Contents

Introduction — 1

1. Big Bethel: The Regiment Gets Its Name — 5
2. The Bethel Regiment Forms — 17
3. Defending North Carolina's Coastline — 28
4. The Fight at White Hall, North Carolina, December 16, 1862 — 39
5. The 11th North Carolina Joins Pettigrew's Brigade — 47
6. Heth's Division: The Army of Northern Virginia — 61
7. Gettysburg: July 1, 1863 — 75
8. Gettysburg: July 3, 1863 — 90
9. Falling Waters, July 14, 1863 — 102
10. Bristoe Station, October 14, 1863 — 115
11. Winter 1863-1864 — 126
12. The Wilderness and Spotsylvania, May 5–May 20, 1864 — 133
13. Summer 1864 — 151
14. Late Summer 1864, August to Mid-September — 163
15. Fall 1864, Jones Farm and Burgess Mill — 175
16. Winter 1864-1865 — 190
17. The End: April 1865 — 203

11th North Carolina Infantry Casualties — 221
11th North Carolina Infantry Roster — 258

Chapter Notes — 331
Bibliography — 352
Index — 357

Introduction

I began my senior year at Southern Utah State College in the fall of 1972. My degree was to be in American history, with a minor in Southwest archaeology. One weekend in early October I convinced my cousin and his friend to camp out in the Wasatch Mountains and assist me in an archaeological project: the digging of an Anasazi pit house. The three of us spent Saturday excavating a hole four feet deep and eight feet square. Sunday morning we rested, drinking coffee and talking about future aspirations.

Our camp was two hundred yards away from a lightly used highway and a hundred feet in elevation above that road. As we relaxed, a pickup truck pulled off the road directly below us and a man got out of the vehicle, carrying a hunting rifle. He gazed up at our camp, which was easy to see, as my cousin's tent was a day-glow orange. Then, this fellow raised his rifle and studied us with his weapon's scope. Suddenly, flame belched from the rifle's muzzle and a bullet smacked into the branches of a fir tree a couple feet above our heads. I honestly don't remember hearing that first gunshot. He fired again. That report I did hear, as well as the cracking sound of a bullet passing nearby. This time, though, I did not see the rifle's flash, as my face was pressed against the floor of my excavation. My instincts had taken over and had dived into that hole. There might have been a third shot but I wasn't registering bullet passage or impact; instead, I remained communing with the good earth.

When I looked up I could see my cousin's friend. He sat motionless, white-faced and alone. My cousin had disappeared, having run away seconds after the first shot. Finally, my cousin's friend fled into the stand of trees behind us. Fear gripped me. I did not want to be left alone, so I scrambled out of the hole and chased after my companions. I raced through the trees until I reached a cliff face that prevented further retreat. Here, also stopped in flight, were my cousin and his friend. We could not believe what had just happened, and jabbered incoherently for some time before regaining our composure. Then, we moved to a location where we could view the highway and saw that the truck and its shooter were gone. We cautiously returned to our campsite, there to find a bullet hole had been punched through my cousin's tent.

The three of us broke camp and returned to Southern Utah's dorms, shocked by the morning's events. Later, we discussed the incident. Remarkably, we remembered this episode differently, and, of course, each one of us had reacted uniquely: my cousin chose flight, his friend froze, and I dove for cover. The only thing we shared in common was our total lack of understanding as to why this individual had decided he would shoot at us, and to this day, over forty years later, I still have no clue.

Why am I beginning this book's introduction with a "so there I was," story?

I have not served in the military, so I cannot have any idea what it is like to be in harm's way. However, there was that one insane moment when a bullet zipped past, not far from my head, and from that occurrence I have been able to see how people can perceive a perilous event. I have taken this incident and its aftermath as a lesson in how individuals respond in crisis situations, and I am attempting to apply that wisdom in the writing of this Civil War regimental history.

Each young man who enlisted into the 11th North Carolina entered the unit possessing his own set of experiences, talents, and expectations and these characteristics dictated the manner in which he would comprehend the war's horrendous events. The Bethel Regiment's volunteers in 1861 saw the world through different eyes than did the soldiers of 2014, and today's historians are mistaken in their views when they project modern, twenty-first-century mindsets upon those Civil War recruits. I believe we must guard against interpreting historic behaviors by present-day attitudes, as our experiences and expectations vary greatly from those of the boys of 1861. But how do we bridge this chasm? How do we translate historic thought and action into today's language?

Fortunately, most of the young men filling combat ranks in the Civil War could read and write, and even more fortuitously, a substantial treasury of their letters, journals, articles, and diaries remain for historians to examine. We are able to study these written expressions and catch a glimpse about what our ancestors thought and how they reacted to war's experiences. However, we must also do this with caution, as each soldier, whether wearing blue or gray, wrote from a singular lens shaded by his own experiences. His reaction to what was happening around him could be as different from that of the fellow standing at his shoulder as the differences my cousin, his friend, and I experienced. Our responses were not false, but were rather how each one of us reacted to the situation. Individually, our actions are sentences on a blank sheet of paper; collectively, we create a complete narrative.

Aware of this distinction between fragment and entirety, I have attempted to construct the history of the 11th North Carolina by listening to as many of those resolute Tar Heels as time's arbitrariness has granted voice. In effect, my ambition has been to create, if you will, an environment in which a group of Carolinian soldiers have gathered together to hash out recent experiences, each man contributing what he saw, heard, felt, and did; just as my cousin, his friend and I did. Ultimately, these combined accounts will create a more inclusive description of what happened. And yet, our Tar Heels' story remains incomplete if they are the only conversationalists. It is also important to hear from the men our Carolina boys fought against, as the soldiers wearing blue wool also have much to contribute. Their words should dovetail with Southern statements because they saw the same events from a different point of view. All of these individual experiences, much like single strokes of a paintbrush, can combine to fashion a complete work of art and fuse together a more fully rendered chronicle of the 11th North Carolina Infantry. That is my goal.

Today's historians are blessed by the advent of the Internet, and as a writer with a Web site, I have been fortunate to encounter many descendants of the 11th North Carolina's original riflemen. These individuals have shared their ancestors' worlds by providing letters, journals, and even photographs, all of which has greatly enriched this regimental chronicle. I wish to recognize some of these contributors, as their generosity has greatly enhanced the depth of this story's narrative: Pam Kiser Whitesides, whose forebear Pvt. Hiram Kiser was forced to decide when and where he would eat his three hardtack crackers, David Hartline, whose ancestor was shot in the foot and kept that bullet on his mantelpiece for the rest of his life, Kelly Lassiter honors his great-great-grandfather by reenacting as a soldier in the 11th North Carolina. Kelly wrote that Pvt. George Lassiter "made it through Pickett's Charge without a scratch." And Tom McAnear's family's oral history tells this simple story about their forefather: "He went off north to fight the Yankees and we never heard from him again."

I must also include Lamont Wade, whose ancestor was in the 7th Tennessee Infantry and survived having a tree fall upon him. Lamont has created a blog in which he posts what happened each day to Pvt. Jeremiah Turner and his fellow soldiers of 150 years ago. And finally, there is Michael Black, the great-great-grandson of a sergeant in Company D. Michael's first letters posed serious questions about Sgt. Samuel Black, as he sought to separate truth from myth. His questions forced me to cut deeper and carve the regiment's documents with a sharper scalpel than I had anticipated using. Michael Black's last e-mail arrived within minutes of my completing the book's final paragraph. His words were so appropriate: "Thank you for reaching out and giving families like mine a platform for our stories to be shared. In this way, our ancestors will be understood by future generations."

Chapter 1

Big Bethel: The Regiment Gets Its Name

Barely an hour after sunrise on June 10, 1861, vigilant pickets from Cpt. John Bridgers' company observed a column of troops approaching. These advancing men, soldiers from the 7th New York Infantry, warily drew near the Confederate skirmish line and deployed into line of battle, some 900 yards away.[1] The Confederate pickets, untested volunteers of Company A, 1st North Carolina Infantry, gripped their muskets tightly and waited anxiously. They had been with their regiment almost two months now and until this morning had never seen their enemy. Today, these untried Tar Heels would get their first taste of blood: in the first infantry battle of the Civil War.

Captain John Bridgers' skirmishers, men from counties just east of Raleigh, North Carolina, called themselves the Edgecombe Guards, and were one of ten companies mustered into the 1st North Carolina Infantry.[2] They were part of Col. Daniel H. Hill's regiment, the first formation from North Carolina to leave the Old North State in support of the Southern cause. Hill's volunteers had arrived in Richmond two weeks before and had been met with bands, fervent crowds, and enthusiastic patriotism.[3] It had been a marvelous sight, those thousand Tar Heels marching through Richmond's streets, who were gloriously described by a *Richmond Examiner* reporter: "As almost spectral in its appearance ... as they moved down Main street, in perfect order, their polished muskets glistening in the moonlight."[4]

But now, Col. Hill's uneasy riflemen watched as Yankee infantrymen faced them, just over a half-mile away. Colonel Daniel Harvey Hill was familiar with war. The 39-year-old South Carolinian was a West Point graduate and had served in the Mexican War, earning two brevets for gallantry. When the war ended, he resigned from the military and for a dozen years taught at Washington College and Davidson College, and most recently had served as the superintendent of the North Carolina Military Institute, located in Charlotte, North Carolina.[5] Then, when the war against the North became a reality, Professor Hill put away his books and became commandant of North Carolina's camp of instruction at Raleigh. Thus, he was the perfect choice as leader of North Carolina's first volunteer infantry regiment.

Colonel Hill's field-grade officers also possessed a strong military background. Hill's second-in-command, Lt. Col. Charles C. Lee, was a West Point graduate and had served as a lieutenant of ordnance before resigning his commission to join Hill as a professor at the North Carolina Military Institute.[6] Lee was 29 years old, ambitious, and anxious to lead Tar Heels into battle. Daniel Hill's third-in-command, Maj. James H. Lane, a graduate of the Virginia Military Institute, was a professor of mathematics and military tactics at VMI. When Lane arrived at Raleigh's camp of instruction, Hill immediately assigned the 27-year-old as the Tar Heel's drillmaster and adjutant.[7]

Knowing Maj. Lane's assignment was to train the volunteers, Col. Daniel Hill directed his efforts towards procuring the materials of war: uniforms, accouterments, and weapons. Daniel Hill discovered North Carolina's manufacturing industries were primed to supply his needs, and soon martial equipment flowed into the military encampment. Hill also contacted the state arsenal at Fayetteville and wagonloads of smoothbore Springfield muskets were shipped to the Raleigh camp of instruction. Half of Hill's riflemen received "buck and ball" ammunition, while the rest loaded musket balls into their cartridge boxes.[8]

Meanwhile, Maj. James Lane struggled to train the hundreds of Tar Heel volunteers assembled at Raleigh's war camp. These men were eager to fight the Yankees but adamantly uninterested in learning how. Many of the recruits were displeased by their sudden introduction to military life. One dismayed soldier, 19-year-old Pvt. Louis Leon (Co. C), wrote, "When we got [here] our company was given quarters, and, lo and behold! Horse stables with straw for bedding is what we got." Rifleman Leon continued: "I know we all thought it a disgrace for us to sleep in such places with our fine uniforms—not even a washstand, or any place to hang our clothes."[9] Another indifferent volunteer, 41-year-old Sgt. Thomas Parks (Co. G), wrote, "We drill about 4 hours a day and answer to our names 5 times a day."[10] Even the officers were unhappy. Nineteen-year-old Cpt. Egbert Ross (Co. C) complained about price gouging by local merchants and the regiment's vast distance from the seat of war, writing, "We are still in this detestable hole."[11] Nonetheless, a patriotic Raleigh newspaper glossed over these training deficiencies when a beat-writer noted, "The drilling is energetically, though not laboriously conducted."[12]

This resistance to learning drill and its inherent safety measures quickly developed into a dangerous situation—rowdy young men armed with lethal weapons. Corporal Lewis Warlick (Co. G) noted, "One of the Buncombe rifle men was accidently shot in the left arm.... [I]t penetrated his arm about halfway between the elbow and the hand."[13] The 27-year-old NCO also reported, "One of the privates in the Randalsburg Riflemen from Mecklenburg shot his Capt. ... through the thigh."[14]

Fortunately, most of the volunteers were not

Daniel H. Hill was the superintendent of the North Carolina Military Institute before being commissioned as colonel of the 1st NC Inf. (Miller and Lanier, 1910).

bothered by these martial restrictions and relished the opportunity to flirt with the young women flocking to their camp. Captain Egbert Ross remarked, "I must admit that the ladies are very kind ... to us. They come to cheer us with their smiles and when they leave in the evening you can hear a simple 'God bless them' escape from the lips of our men."[15] Private Louis Leon (Co. C) added, "The ladies showered us with flowers ... cheering us."[16] Corporal Warlick (Co. G) noted, "We have lively times in the camp. A fiddle and banjo are going all day."[17] Indeed, many of the boisterous young Tar Heels were enjoying themselves too much, causing a visiting minister to caution the soldiers "against the vices of the camp."[18]

Colonel Daniel H. Hill's regiment was formally mustered into Confederate service as the 1st North Carolina Volunteer Infantry on May 11, 1861, with requirements that "the service of this regiment will not exceed six months" and the "gray or blue blouse ... [be] recognized as a suitable uniform."[19]

Once the regiment was mustered into service Daniel Hill called for officer elections and the newly organized regiment was given an official commencement date of May 15, 1861. North Carolina's governor, John W. Ellis, on that same day received a telegram from President Abraham Lincoln demanding North Carolina provide two regiments in defense of the Union. John Ellis instantly replied: "You [will] get no troops from North Carolina." Ellis continued: "I regard the levy of troops made by the administration for the purposes of subjugating the States of the South as in violation of the Constitution and a usurpation of power."[20]

Five days later North Carolina representatives met in Raleigh and voted to secede, announcing: "The union now subsisting between the State of North Carolina and the other States under the title of the United States of America, is hereby dissolved, and that the State of North Carolina is in the full possession and exercise of all those rights of sovereignty which belong and appertain to a free and independent State."[21] Colonel Hill then met with Governor Ellis and discussed moving the 1st NC to Richmond. The formation's first three companies (F, H, and K) immediately boarded a train and departed for Richmond.

1st North Carolina Infantry
Col. Daniel H. Hill
Lt. Col. Charles C. Lee
Maj. James H. Lane

Co. A	The Edgecombe Guards	Cpt. John L. Bridgers
Co. B	The Hornets' Nest	Cpt. Lewis S. Williams
Co. C	Charlotte Grays	Cpt. Egbert A. Ross
Co. D	Orange Light Infantry	Cpt. Richard J. Ashe
Co. E	Buncombe Riflemen	Cpt. William Wallis
Co. F	Lafayette Light Infantry	Cpt. Joseph B. Starr
Co. G	Burke Rifles	Cpt. Clark M. Avery
Co. H	Fayetteville Independent Light Inf.	Cpt. Wright Huske
Co. I	Enfield Blues	Cpt. David B. Bell
Co. K	Southern Stars	Cpt. William J. Hoke

The remaining seven companies loaded onto a train on May 21, 1861. A reporter for Charlotte's *Western Democrat* described the scene: "A large number ... assembled at the Raleigh depot to see the regiment off.... There were thirty patriotic Raleigh ladies who showered bouquets into the ranks of the soldiers and cheered with all their might." The correspondent noted, "The gallant soldiers all seemed to have lighter hearts than their friends who bid them farewell. There were tears in the eyes of many of the spectators, but not one in the eye of a soldier." The writer recorded the soldiers "left firmly resolved to do their duty, and every man appeared anxious to get nearer the scene of war."[22] But for the family members left behind, the horrors of loss loomed enormous. One distraught woman recorded, "I have some hope yet that [they] will stop short of a real battle."[23] Another wrote, "We were blue, blue, blue!... May God stand by them in their trials."[24] And even some of the young soldiers were affected; one thoughtful volunteer penned his girl, "Shall we be spared to meet again? I hope and trust we will."[25]

The Tar Heels arrived in Richmond that evening and received a wondrous reception. One newsman wrote, "The remainder of the First Regiment of the North Carolina Volunteers, numbering seven companies and over 700 men, reached this city ... about 8 o'clock." The writer remarked, "We must say that this is the best equipped regiment which has yet made its route through our city."[26] The North Carolinians were equally impressed by what they saw; for many of the young volunteers, this train ride was their first experience from home—Richmond was a huge city to take in all at once. Corporal Lewis Warlick (Co. G) recorded, "We were met by large crowds and especially by the ladies, who presented us with many bouquets [and] cakes." The noncom mused, "I have to laugh at part of our company.... They look at everything ... their fingers pointed at every curiosity.... [I]t shows ... they never traveled."[27]

Colonel Hill consolidated his command and boarded the men onto a train, heading towards Yorktown, Virginia, where they arrived on May 25, 1861. This journey, which also included passage on the steamboat *Logan*, produced the regiment's first fatality. Private Julius Sadler, a 21-year-old in Company B, fell asleep while riding a train car and toppled off and was run over by the train.[28] The Tar Heels were shocked by Sadler's gruesome death. One was recorded as saying, "This is not playing soldier now; it is a stern reality."[29] Julius Sadler was buried and then Col. Hill put his soldiers to work; they became excavators, much to their dismay. Private Leon (Co. C) groused, "The day after we got here our company was sent out with spades and shovels to make breastworks." The unhappy soldier added, "To think of the indignity.... I never thought that this was work for soldiers."[30] Other Tar Heels accustomed to the heavy manual labors involved in farming took their new employment in stride. Corporal Warlick wrote, "We are building a fortification around our encampment. Some of the compan[ies] are at work all the while day and night." Warlick added, "This place suits me first rate as I can get plenty of oysters and fish. I go down to the river and eat oysters raw."[31]

However, a week later, June 6, 1861, the regiment was ordered away from their Yorktown fortifications and marched nearly ten miles. The weather was cool and drizzly and the neophyte soldiers had much to learn. One Tar Heel recorded, "It was a trying [march], as it was made in heavy marching order, with knapsacks, haversacks, canteens, loaded cartridge boxes, often a Bible in the knapsack, and an extra pair of shoes."[32] That night was the first time the novice volunteers slept on wet ground and prepared their meals in the field. The next morning the soldiers were given shovels and ordered to dig more fortifications. They grumbled as they prepared more earthworks, Pvt. Leon complaining, "[We] again commenced making breastworks."[33] Another wrote, "We have had a good deal of hard work to do.... Throwing up embankments and digging ditches."[34] Their commander, though, worried his soldiers would not be able to construct their defenses quickly enough, recorded, "We only had 25 spades, 6 axes, and 3 picks, but these were busily plied all day and night."[35] Regardless of their officer's worry, 21-year-old Pvt. Joseph Saunders (Co. D) noted, "A spade comes as natural to me as a musket and in fact more so; the boys call it gopher drill."[36] Fortunately for Col. Hill, a fresh supply of tools arrived on June 9, 1861, and he implored his Tar Heels to work vigorously.

The Union high command received word of Col. Hill's fortifications at Bethel Church and assembled a force to attack the Confederates. On the night of June 9, 1861, Maj. Gen. Benjamin Butler ordered his Yank forces to march at midnight, following two roads, with the plan these forces would converge on the Confederate position, "timed that the attack should be made just at daybreak."[37] He ordered his soldiers to make their march "rapid but not hurried."[38] One force consisted of Col. Hiram Duryea (5th NY), with his 850 men, and Col. John Bendix (7th NY), and his 750 troops. The other column, led by Col. Frederick Townsend (3rd NY), and his 650 soldiers departed a couple hours later along a different road. Colonel Townsend's volunteers wore grey, while Duryea's Zouaves sported distinctive red and blue uniforms, forcing Butler to order his troops to put white armbands on their left arms in order to identify friend from foe.[39] General Butler, knowing his troops were untested and uniformed differently, directed everyone to know a common watchword, "Boston," "to be shouted when unrecognized troops should approach."[40]

General Butler's worries came to fruition; his two columns of inexperienced soldiers collided in the darkness several hours into the march at a point where the two roads converged.[41] Here, Col. Bendix's New Yorkers heard troops approaching, and as his unproven volunteers peered through the darkness, they believed they saw soldiers wearing gray uniforms. The New Yorkers immediately opened fire. Colonel Bendix recorded, "Not expecting friends from that quarter ... my men fired first."[42] The soldiers receiving this volley, Col. Townsend's 3rd NY, scattered to both sides of the road, leaving behind a tangle of casualties. Colonel Townsend wrote, "A heavy and well-sustained fire ... was opened upon the regiment while it was marching in a narrow road ... in route step, and wholly unsuspicious of an enemy."[43] Townsend's troops rallied and returned fire. The two Union forces shot at each other for fifteen minutes before the 3rd NY's line officers were able to pull their shocked men out of danger. Colonel Bendix, thinking his troops had just beaten the enemy, pushed forward a screen of skirmishers. He wrote, "[I] directed one company ... to go out in the field ... and find out where the enemy [was] situated."[44] Bendix's men rapidly came into contact with Townsend's rear guards. The two sides hollered at each other and discovered the unsettling news; they had been shooting at friends. Colonel Townsend noted, "The result of the fire upon us, two mortally wounded (one since dead), three dangerously, and four officers and 12 privates [wounded], making a total of 21."[45]

This Union disaster in the darkness alerted vigilant Confederate pickets. Corporal Lewis Warlick (Co. G) recorded, "The long roll was sounded and the whole camp was in arms in three minutes."[46] Colonel Hill formed his companies, his battle strength numbering nearly 800 men, at 3:00 a.m. and sent them forward towards the sounds of gunfire. Hill's excited North Carolinians advanced over three miles before running into the Federals' leading elements. The Tar Heel commander wrote, "We learned that the foe, in large force, was within a hundred yards of us."[47] The Confederate regiment turned around and hurried back to their entrenchments. Daniel Hill ordered a strong force posted and had the rest of the men stand down. He also directed Cpt. John Bridgers (Co. A) to take his 80 riflemen forward and deploy them as skirmishers. Bridgers' riflemen moved out of the entrenchments and advanced nearly a thousand yards south of the fortifications.[48] Behind this observant screen the rest of the Tar Heels were supposed to rest but the men were too wound up to sleep. Instead the soldiers crowded along the firing line, hoping to be the first to catch a glance of the enemy. One soldier recalled, "The very prospect set every heart to beating fast."[49] Later, by 6:00 a.m., when most of the men had calmed down, they cooked breakfast.[50] Two hours later Cpt. Bridgers' Tar Heels guessed the Yankees were near. One soldier noted, "Soon the drum-beats of the enemy were heard—so faint at first as to be hardly distinguishable, but clearer and clearer as the enemy drew nearer."[51]

The approaching troops were Duryea's Zouaves, now re-formed and determined to make this costly march worthwhile. The Yanks were tired. Many already had consumed the water in their canteens, and they were hungry. But the New Yorkers were staunch in their desire to defeat the Secessionists. The Zouaves were given the order to deploy into a battle line, protected by a thick screen of skirmishers.[52] Meanwhile, the North Carolinians waited anxiously, and one recorded afterwards, "What soldier does not remember his first battle?... The early morning breakfast, the silence and seriousness that took possession of the troops.... I will never forget this one."[53]

The Federal skirmishers opened fire upon Cpt. Bridgers' picket line and the outnum-

Bethel Church, Virginia. Sketch made April 1862 (Johnson and Buel, 1887).

bered Carolina riflemen scampered backward 200 yards. Then, Duryea and Townsend deployed their forces into a line of battle behind a small stand of trees. The two regiments were formed to the right and left of the main road at a distance of just over a half-mile from the Confederate entrenchments, while three artillery pieces were brought up and unlimbered. It was now 9:00 a.m.[54] The morning's calm was about to be shattered, but for a few more quiet minutes the untested soldiers of both sides waited silently. One Confederate wrote, "What a feeling takes possession of a man when he is crouched down behind earthworks [anticipating] the approach of the enemy."[55]

The Zouaves, anxious to display their drilling expertise, marched forward onto the road and advanced company by company as each unit reached the point of execution. Major George Randolph, a 43-year-old Virginian in charge of the Confederate's artillery pieces, personally sighted one of the guns and fired that cannon at the New Yorkers. Randolph recorded, "[The] shot ... struck the center of the road a short distance in front of the column, and probably did good execution in its ricochet."[56] The Zouaves hurried off the road and formed. The Union artillery crews opened fire upon the Confederate positions. Corporal Lewis Warlick (Co. G) exclaimed, "The balls, grape, canister, and shell sung around us."[57] Not long after the bombardment began, the Tar Heels suffered their first casualty; Pvt. Peter Poteat (Co. G) was wounded by shrapnel.[58] Once over the initial shock of hearing cannon shells scream past, the rest of the Carolinians realized, as one soldier noted, "his artillery, fir[ed] briskly but wildly."[59]

The two forces' artillery pounded away at each other while Townsend's and Duryea's troops inched forward through the trees. Though the bombardment was furious and loud, neither sides' guns were accurate; nearly all the shells flew beyond their intended targets. After the battle, Maj. Randolph reported the fuses for his Parrot Rifles' shells were "fixed ... the shortest being cut for four seconds. The consequence was that the shells burst far in the rear of the enemy."[60] Major Edgar Montegue, whose men held the western side of Col. Hill's fortifications, wrote, "Fortunately for my command ... the major part of the enemy's shot had sufficient elevation to pass over our heads."[61] Unaware their cannons' firing was mostly ineffective, the Northern infantrymen halted at the edge of the tree line and watched as artillery rounds impacted into the Southern earthworks. A New Yorker in Col. Duryea's regiment recalled, "We answered [the] discharges by a cheer and continued to advance, clearing all before us, till we reached a point just on the edge of the woods."[62] Suddenly, the Confederate cannon, barely 600 yards away from the New Yorkers, went silent. Believing the gun had been struck by a Union shell the Yanks rose up and moved out into the open.

Inside the Confederate earthworks, the gunners were frantic; their piece had been disabled—not by a Federal projectile; rather, the priming wire broke within the gun's vent, thus preventing the cannon from firing. The crew withdrew, dumping their gun into a ravine. The 200 Virginia infantrymen manning this forward earthwork, their responsibility to protect that cannon concluded and over 1,500 Union infantry approaching, fell back from their position. One Virginian wrote, "[They] retired in order through the swamp to the second position ... to the left of the church."[63] Captain Clark Avery, commanding Company G and also holding a portion of this earthwork, realized his sixty rifles were all that remained. He pulled his men out.

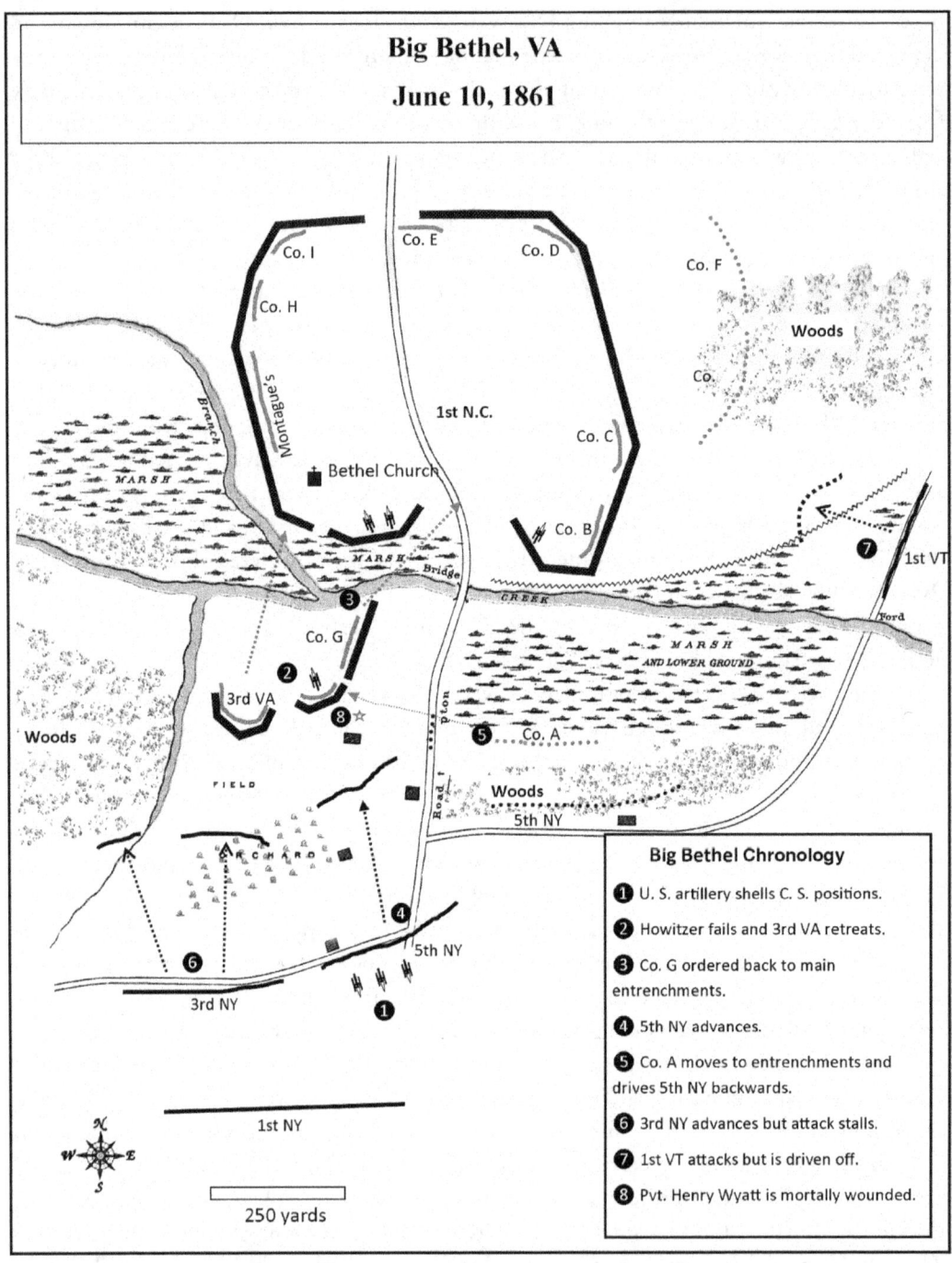

The New Yorkers moved forward cautiously, taking fire from the Confederate cannon hidden in the main earthworks, as well as from musketry of infantry supporting those guns. A Zouave remarked, "The fire was ... hot and heavy."[64] Colonel Daniel Hill realized the forward earthworks were completely undefended. He ordered Cpt. John Bridgers (Co. A) to swing his unit around and retake the position. Hill also commanded Cpt. Egbert Ross (Co.

C) to move his unit across the creek and support Bridgers' movement. Captain Ross's troops raced forward. One Carolinian remarked, "[We] came back like maddened tigers."[65]

The two Tar Heel infantry companies, 150 riflemen at the most, struck the cautious New Yorkers across the front and along their right flank. The Northern advance stalled as the untested Yanks halted to fire upon the Carolinians. The distance between the two forces was less than 200 yards in some places and the musketry became hot. Private Council Rodgers (Co. A) received a serious wound, as did Pvt. Charles Williams (Co. A).[66] But the Tar Heel riflemen were even more accurate. Captain Judson Kilpatrick (5th NY) wrote, "The enemy's fire at this time began to tell upon us with great effect. Men were falling one after the other."[67] The New Yorkers backed up and the small number of Yanks who had taken possession of the gun works retreated when they saw Ross's riflemen racing towards them. Private Luis Leon (Co. C) bragged, "We gave them a good reception."[68]

Twenty-two-year-old Pvt. John Thorpe (Co. A) was a rifleman in Cpt. Egbert Ross's company that retook the earthworks (Clark, 1901).

Colonel Townsend's regiment had not moved forward; instead that formation held its position in the woods for a quarter of an hour before stepping forward. Then, they advanced on the left of the Zouaves without suffering much from the Confederate fire and were still moving forward when the 5th New York fell back. Soon, though, Townsend's men stumbled into their own problems. Colonel Townsend recorded, "A company of my regiment had [become] separated from the regiment by a thickly-hewed ditch."[69] As this solitary unit attempted to keep abreast with the main formation it entered a thick stand of underbrush. Later, when Townsend's riflemen looked in that direction, it appeared as if the company had vanished, and when gunfire was heard, the Yankees "immediately concluded that the enemy [was] outflanking [them]."[70] The 3rd NY had already been ambushed by a hidden force during the night; Col. Townsend was not going to allow it to happen again. He wrote, "[I] conceived it to be my duty immediately to retire and repel that advance."[71] Col. Duryea, seeing Townsend's force falling back, ordered his retreating men to withdraw.

The 3rd and 5th NY regiments nestled back into the protection of the trees, and the Union artillery resumed pounding the Confederates who had retaken the earthworks. Again, the Federal artillery was ineffective, though one close-by burst sent shrapnel into the position, striking 1st Lt. J.W. Ratchford in the head, causing a "contusion in [his] forehead."[72] Another shell, this one way off from its mark, impacted into the northern portion of Hill's fortifications, and among the men of Company D. Private Samuel Patterson (Co. D) was slightly wounded. The musketry died away once the New Yorkers were out of range. One soldier wrote, "[It was] about 11:00 a.m. ... [when] the [U.S.] troops had gone to the shelter of the woods."[73] The artillery from both sides kept up a slow and deliberate bombardment for the next hour, though both sides' guns did little damage. One Yank officer noted, "The rebels were sending their shells in among us at the rate of one per minute."[74]

During this lull in infantry fighting, two more New York regiments approached the battlefield, the 1st NY, Col. William Allen, and 2nd NY, Col. Joseph Carr. They found the weary and battered men of the 3rd and 5th New York in disarray. Joseph Carr recorded, "For at least one mile from the scene of the action the men and officers were scattered singly and in groups, without form or organization, looking far more like men enjoying a huge picnic than soldiers awaiting battle."[75] The two fresh Yank regiments pushed through the worn-out formations and formed into a battle line, but did not move forward into musket range. Colonel Carr wrote, "Our troops soon sought the shelter of the woods."[76] Meanwhile, the men of the 3rd and 5th New York collected their wounded and began withdrawing from the battlefield.

Another Yank force arrived, 300 men of the 1st Vermont and 300 men of the 4th Massachusetts, under the command of Lt. Col. Peter Washburn. One Vermont soldier, recalled, "[We] marched towards the ... sounds of battle."[77] Lt. Col. Washburn conferred with the officers of the New York regiments and concluded a frontal assault was not advisable. A scout located a road running to the east of the Confederate fortifications. This path crossed the creek at a ford and appeared to be unprotected. Washburn ordered his force to march in that direction. He soon discovered a small Confederate force guarding the ford. These Southerners had tied white strips to their caps as a way of identifying themselves to their comrades, as some of the Carolinians wore gray while others were outfitted in blue. Washburn ordered his lead unit to tie white cloth to their caps.[78] The Yanks reached the ford and a Vermont soldier wrote, "[They held] up their cartridge boxes from the water, there about waist deep, they went through it, and straight forward across the open marsh."[79]

Washburn's ruse worked. The platoon of Tar Heels from Company B tasked with protecting the ford did not hinder the attackers, assuming they were friends. When they realized their mistake these Carolinians retreated to the fortifications with news of an enemy formation's approach. Colonel Daniel Hill shifted men from the west side of his fortifications to bolster 1st Lt. William Owens' Company B and notified Cpt. William Hoke, whose riflemen in Company K were deployed as pickets in the woods northeast of the fortifications.[80] The Tar Heels were ready; when the Vermont and Massachusetts battalions advanced, the Northerners were met by a tremendous volley. The Federals fell back and sought shelter behind the creek's embankment. One Yank wrote, "They announced [their] presence by a fire of musketry, so sharp and continuous that for twenty minutes hardly a man ... ventured to show his head."[81] The Vermont unit suffered seven casualties, including Maj. Theodore Winthrop, who was killed.[82] The Federals did shoot back, and 21-year-old Pvt. William White (Co. K) was wounded during this exchange.[83]

When Lt. Col. Peter Washburn received word the New Yorkers were retreating from the battlefield, he pulled his men back across the creek. The Vermont riflemen felt betrayed; their attack had been a waste. One wrote, "The fact is that while we were fighting the other regiments were withdrawing from the field."[84] Once the battlefield became quiet, Col. Daniel Hill ventured out to the advance breastworks, now firmly held by Companies A and C, along with reinforcements from Companies G and H.[85] There were still a few New York skirmishers taking an occasional potshot at the Confederates, forcing the Carolinians to keep their heads down behind the earthworks. Some of these Yanks were hiding behind a building 150 yards away. Hill turned to Cpt. Bridgers saying, "Can't you have that house burned?"[86] Bridgers called for volunteers and instantly five of his riflemen came forward, including 21-year-old John Thorpe and 19-year-old Henry Wyatt. The five were given matches and a hatchet and they scrambled over the earthen works. Private Thorpe described what happened: "A volley was fired at us ... from the road to our left.... [A]ll of us instantly dropped to the ground [but] Wyatt [was] mortally wounded. He never uttered a word or groan, but lay limp on his back ... a clot of blood on his forehead as large as a man's fist."[87] The other four retreated to the entrenchments and then a cannon was directed to fire upon the structure. An artillerist wrote, "After ... five or six shots a shell entered a window of the house ... and soon broke out a blaze."[88]

Nineteen-year-old Pvt. Henry Wyatt (Co. A) was mortally wounded near the end of the fight. He died a few hours later that evening (Library of Congress).

The last shots dwindled away over the next hour and the battlefield grew silent. Confederate skirmishers cautiously moved out from the earthworks and discovered the Federals were gone. Private Wyatt was recovered from the field and taken by an ambulance to Yorktown. He died later that night, the first Confederate soldier to die in an infantry battle.[89]

The Carolinians ventured out onto the battlefield, curious to see the effects of musket and artillery. One noted, "The ground [was] completely strewn with the Yankee dead."[90] Colonel John Magruder reported, "Eighteen dead were found on the field."[91] Private Luis Leon (Co. C) wrote, "After the fight some of the boys and myself went over the battlefield, and we saw several of the Yankee dead—the first I had ever seen, and it made me shudder."[92] Another soldier, sickened by what he saw, wrote, "I came across one of Duryea's red-breeches Zouaves, killed by an artillery shot."[93] And finally, Cpl. Lewis Warlick (Co. G), who did not explore the battlefield, penned, "After the battle was over some of our men went on the ground occupied by the enemy and they report that they found a [large] quantity of blood."[94]

That evening the excited Tar Heels, now veterans of their first battle, buzzed with exhilaration. Each man had his story to tell. They laughed at their colonel's antics, describing how he had shouted at the Yankees after being showered with dirt from close-by cannon shot, "You dogs! You missed me that time!"[95] Corporal Lewis Warlick (Co. G) penned his girl, "I had the but of my gun shot off in my hands."[96] Captain Egbert Ross (Co. C) boasted, "I saw six Zouaves take deliberate aim at me and fire but fortunately they missed."[97] And 1st Lt. Ben Huske (Co. H) recalled, "How the balls showered around us.... You can form no idea how they hissed and struck."[98] However, later, once the young men calmed down, they agreed, as Pvt. Luis Leon (Co. C) exclaimed, "From now on I will never again grumble about digging breastworks. If it had not been for them many of us would not be here now."[99]

By Civil War standards, the fight at Bethel Church was really not much more than a drawn-out skirmish. But for the un-fired-upon soldiers this first battle was the "fight of their lifetime." Though the Federals had over 5,000 men they never committed more than one formation at a time in an uncoordinated series of assaults. One Confederate reported, "There was no concert of action between [their] troops. A regiment would come up, fire a volley or two ... get stung by our return fire, and ... fall back; then another would repeat the performance." The writer continued: "It reminded me more of a lot of boys fighting a bumblebee nest.... [O]ne would rush upon the nest of bees ... get stung, run back, and another would take his place."[100] The Northerners lost 76 soldiers: 18 killed, 53 wounded, and 5 missing.[101] Meanwhile, the Confederates, who as one Southerner reported, "[never] had more than 300 of the 1,400 Confederates engaged simultaneously," lost 10 men: seven in the 1st NC and three in the artillery.[102]

Back home in North Carolina, the battle's outcome produced enthusiastic accolades. On June 17, 1861, the North Carolina state representatives passed a resolution authorizing the 1st NC Infantry to call themselves the Bethel Regiment, and, "to inscribe the word 'Bethel' upon their regimental colors."[103] This flag, brought to the formation by the company from Asheville, would fly over the 1st NC and its successor, the 11th NC, for the entire war.[104]

Chapter 2

The Bethel Regiment Forms

Colonel Hill pulled his regiment out of the Bethel entrenchments that evening, marching his swaggering battle veterans past arriving reinforcements. The exuberant Tar Heels marched back to their fortifications at Yorktown. Private Louis Leon (Co. C) bragged, "We returned the same night to Yorktown, full of glory."[1] The regiment's defense at Big Bethel quickly became the fodder for patriotic writings, and Southern scribes boasted, "This little victory over a vastly superior force ... indicate[s] the future and final success of the cause."[2] Corporal Lewis Warlick (Co. G) added, "Our boys ... have been rejoicing considerably over their victory."[3]

Accolades flooded into Colonel Hill's residence, but he remained humble, writing, "I have to thank God for a great and decided victory." He added a personal note: "I escaped with a slight contusion of the knee."[4] Hill immediately assumed command of Yorktown's defenses and put his cocky Carolinians to work improving the area's fortifications, as he staunchly believed "spades were instruments of defensive, bayonets of offensive warfare, and whether the emergency demanded the use of the one or the other, it was to be done with might and main."[5] The fight at Bethel had proved him correct, and his riflemen, no longer so opposed to digging earthworks, went to work fortifying Yorktown. Corporal Lewis Warlick (Co. G) penned his girl, "Today I have been cutting down timber about a mile from the quarters so we can see the Yankees at a long distance."[6]

The regiment settled into a schedule revolving around drill and digging. At first, Hill's men accepted this program; however, as the summer's heat bore down upon them, they began to complain about their living conditions. Captain Egbert Ross (Co. C) wrote, "It is very hot and [there are] mosquitoes by the millions. [I] cannot sleep [because of] them at night."[7] First Lieutenant Whitnel Lloyd (Co. A), concerned about his volunteers' inability to escape the sun's ravages, requested Sibley tents, writing that his men "had arrived without quarters."[8] And the Rev. William Willis, visiting from home, was appalled by the soldiers' sanitation regulations.

The Tar Heel rifleman also griped about their food, a condition caused by the Confederate high command's decision to focus on supplying the troops defending Richmond rather than those at Yorktown. Corporal Lewis Warlick (Co. G) wrote, "We have hard biscuits ... so hard I have to soften them in coffee."[9] Captain Egbert Ross (Co. C), displeased with the camp food, groused to his parents, "Why in the world don't you send me something to eat? I am nearly starving."[10] And Pvt. Louis Leon (Co. C) noted how he dealt with the paltry rations: "We took a long walk away from camp and saw several [young pigs]. We ran one down ... [and] killed it, cut it into small pieces, put it in our knapsacks, [and] returned to camp, where we shared it with the boys."[11]

Sadly for the Carolinians billeted at Yorktown, the combination of lack of protection from the sun, poor food, mosquitoes, and inadequate sanitation proved to be disastrous, and sickness devastated the regiment. Measles broke out among the young volunteers, striking a few at first but quickly spreading through the crowded tents. Corporal Warlick (Co. G) tracked the epidemic, writing on June 23, 1861, "There are a great many cases of measles in the army," and two months later, remarking, "We report 370 sick."[12] He also admitted he, too, had fallen victim, scribbling, "I had chills and fever, I tell you they pulled me down in a hurry.... [T]hey make a person feel awfully mean and sick at times."[13] At its worst, more than half of the regiment was sick, and at one point Cpt. Egbert Ross (Co. C) recorded the regiment had over 500 ill.[14] Lewis Warlick (Co. G) was fortunate his ailment did not grow serious. By the time the sickness had run its course through the regiment 52 soldiers died.[15]

Just as Col. Daniel Hill had begun to deal with the disease problem he was detached from the regiment; on July 10, 1861, he was promoted to brigadier general. He left, handing the formation to Lt. Col. Charles Lee and Maj. James Lane. The two officers campaigned to get the regiment moved from its unhealthy campsite and on August 22, 1861, the formation marched to Ship Point, Virginia, a location described by one of the Tar Heels: "Our camp is in a beautiful grove of pines where we can get a sea breeze all the while."[16] The regimental sick-call lists did decline, especially once the summer's heat subsided.

Also at this time the regiment's numbers increased when two independent North Carolina companies were assigned to its roster, the "Bertie Volunteers" and the "Dixie Rebels." The unit from Bertie County was designated as Company L, and the "Dixie Rebels," a unit from Chowan County, became Company M, giving the regiment a paper strength of nearly 1,200. Not long after this, the Bethel Regiment was ordered to shift to a location six miles from Yorktown.

In September 1861, Charles Lee was commissioned colonel of the regiment and Cpt. Joseph Starr (Co. F) was elected lieutenant colonel, much to Maj. James Lane's dismay. However, even before the new leaders could get acquainted with their command they were faced with a serious problem: the invasion of the North Carolina coast. Union forces commanded by Maj. Gen. Benjamin Butler had assembled a force of battleships and infantry and attacked North Carolina's Outer Banks forts on Cape Hatteras. Several Carolina fortifications succumbed to Butler's assaults and the Tar Heels defending the region were forced to the brink of disaster.[17] Colonel Charles Lee's shocked soldiers clamored to be allowed to return home and defend their state. Private Henry Huske (Co. H) exclaimed, "Our camp has been thrown into great consternation by hearing that troops had landed in North Carolina."[18] Corporal Lewis Warlick (Co. G) remarked, "When we heard it every man was anxious to strike tents and go at once."[19] Private Huske noted, "Maj. Lane is going to Richmond ... to see if our Regt. will be allowed to go there."[20]

Richmond refused to release the Bethel Regiment, forcing Maj. James Lane to turn to his state's governor. But the governor of North Carolina had just been elected to office and held little sway with the Confederate high command. North Carolina's original war-time governor, John Ellis, died in July 1861 and the state did not have a lieutenant governor. Ellis's position was filled by North Carolina's speaker of the senate, Henry T. Clark, a 53-year-old planter from Edgecombe County. Clark passionately wrote to Richmond: "We are threatened with an expedition of 15,000 men.... We feel very defenseless here without arms.... We see ... three North Carolina regiments [in] ... our lines in Virginia ... who are not allowed to come to the defense of their homes."[21]

Richmond rebuffed the provisional governor and scoffed at his petitions, leaving Clark to scramble for men to defend the state. In time, Governor Clark recorded, "We have now collected in camps about three regiments without arms, and our only reliance is the slow collection of shotguns and hunting rifles."[22] Clark eventually was able to assemble a battalion, armed with a ragtag assortment of weapons and send them to eastern North Carolina. A Tar Heel noted, "A regiment armed with squirrel rifles and fowling pieces, and carving knives in place of bayonets, was transported to Roanoke island."[23] Clark's patched-together force was defeated by Butler's troops and over 2,600 men surrendered.[24] Following this debacle, a Carolinian reported, "The landing at Hatteras and capture of the forts [has brought] the war to our doors with a vengeance."[25]

Meanwhile, Maj. James Lane, who had failed at his mission to get the 1st NC reassigned to the Old North State's defenses, remained in Raleigh. Lane, displeased that he had been passed over for promotion in the Bethel Regiment, petitioned for a unit to command. Governor Clark designated him as colonel of the 28th NC Infantry. Corporal Lewis Warlick (Co. G) recorded, "[Major] Lane is going to leave us as he has been elected Col. of the [28th] regiment."[26] Second Lieutenant Robert Hoke (Co. K), a 24-year-old, was elected major. But now the regiment was near the end of its six-month enlistment; the regiment's senior officers began the process to disband the unit.[27]

The Tar Heels had mixed feelings about their regiment's mustering-out. Many of the men were eager to cast aside their uniforms and weapons and go home. One of these, Lewis Warlick (Co. G), wrote his girl, "We will all go home to see our sweethearts and friends." Warlick also added, "I expect to get married when I get home if I can get any one to have me."[28] Others though, wanted to keep soldiering. A Bethel rifleman recorded, "There is some talk of reorganizing the 1st Regiment in a month or two after it is disbanded, which I hope will be done."[29] And nearly all of the formation's officers made plans to acquire new commissions in other Carolina regiments; in fact, by war's end, the 1st North Carolina would supply the Confederate army with over 130

Maj. James Lane was promoted to Colonel of the 28th NC (Special Collections and Archives at Auburn University).

officers.[30] The 1st North Carolina Regiment was mustered out of service on November 12, 1861.

Just as the Bethel unit's books were being closed, other formations were being created as men from prominent families assembled companies and maneuvered for officer commissions. These ambitious men brought their volunteers to Camp Mangum, North Carolina's recruitment center located a few miles outside Raleigh. Camp Mangum consisted of several hundred acres of woods and grassland, crossed by two creeks, and earned its name from a soldier killed at the battle of Manassas.[31]

Upon arrival at Camp Mangum, these aspiring leaders and their recruits climbed down from their train cars and were assigned quarters. Some of the new volunteers went into log structures. Pvt. Louis Leon, who again was returning to military life, recorded, "We ... were shown our hut. We were surprised to find it without a floor, a roof half off and 'holey' all over."[32] Other soldiers were given tents; one Tar Heel noted, "There were 113 in our Company. We had 19 tents, 6 men to sleep in one tent; all had to sleep together, all lying one way and wedged so tight against each other that when one turned over, the whole six had to do like wise."[33]

Once the volunteers were housed, they were given uniforms and some equipment. One new recruit wrote, "We drew our grey uniforms, blankets, knapsack, haversacks, and canteens."[34] Another noted that he "received a dress uniform, a suit of fatigues, an overcoat, two shirts, two pairs of drawers, and two pairs of shoes."[35] The soldiers were disappointed to learn they would not be issued weapons; instead, they were supplied with spears. One Tar Heel remarked, "[We] trained with a spear, called the 'Confederate Pike,' which had a ten-foot wooded handle with a steel dagger-shaped blade."[36] Another soldier noted sarcastically that these spears, "if not used in the Crusades certainly did good service in the wars of Queen Anne."[37]

The new recruits trained, enduring seemingly endless hours of close-order drill. One Carolinian volunteer recorded Camp Mangum's training schedule: "Roll call about daylight, squad-drill from seven to eight, company drill from nine to eleven, [and] battalion drill from one to three." He finished his daily report, writing, "dress parade at sundown, and roll-call again at night."[38] Men who failed to show at roll call or caused problems during the day were burdened with onerous tasks. A volunteer noted "two men who had gotten in trouble [are] digging stumps up."[39] Another North Carolinian tolerated the seemingly endless drill and fatigue duties and wrote, "[The] purposes for ... drill: To keep the men from enjoying a little rest ... [and] to exasperate the men beyond the endurance of patience."[40]

In Camp Mangum, personnel organizers grouped the various companies into battalions and, once these organizations had sufficient numbers of men, designated them with regimental identifications. All of the six-month units were now defunct, but some of the existing regiments already formed had been given numbers the same as the old six-month formations. This created confusion, so a new numbering system was created to resolve this difficulty; the number ten was added to all the units' numbers. Thus, the new regiment slated to replace the 1st NC, which had been the Bethel Regiment, would now be numbered as the 11th North Carolina.[41]

The Camp Mangum officials held the extinct Bethel Regiment's name in high esteem;

after all it had suffered the first Confederate casualty in the war. Therefore, when a group of officers from that old organization petitioned to be assembled together, their request was easy to approve. Ten company structures were configured together, all of them commanded by leaders from the old 1st NC. In fact, in these ten companies, of the thirty line officers, twenty-four came from the original unit.[42] The company formations were also composed of veterans from the 1st NC. One company had 37 old hands, another a total of 25, and a third 15.[43] This battalion was given the designation of 11th North Carolina, and the unit was allowed to keep the name Bethel Regiment. The senior officer of this group was Cpt. Egbert Ross; his volunteers, men from the Charlotte area, were assigned as Company A. The other nine companies' officers were stocked by men from the First with previous ranks as lieutenants, sergeants, corporals, and a couple privates. The 11th North Carolina Infantry was mustered into service on March 31, 1862.[44]

Twenty-year-old Cpt. Egbert Ross (Co. A) led the regiment in the early months of 1862 until the field-grade officers arrived (Library of Congress).

Captain Egbert Ross, a 20-year-old military student from Charlotte, was awarded a brevet position as major and assumed temporary command of the regiment, to lead until field-grade officers were presented and elected. One of Ross's first orders was to detail Sgt. Francis Gilliam (Co. C) as the assistant to the provost marshal.[45] Sergeant Gilliam, a 22-year-old medical student from Plymouth, North Carolina, was the son of a prominent attorney and was greatly respected by his fellow Tar Heels.[46]

11th North Carolina Infantry
March 31, 1862

Unit	Commander	Company Location	Men
Co. A	Cpt. Egbert Ross	Mecklenburg Co.	105
Co. B	Cpt. Mark Armfield	Burke, Wilkes, & Caldwell Co.	107
Co. C	Cpt. Francis Bird	Bertie Co.	92
Co. D	Cpt. Calvin Brown	Burke Co.	77
Co. E	Cpt. John Nichols	Mecklenburg & Iredell Co.	72
Co. F	Cpt. Edward Small	Chowan, Hertford, & Perquimans Co.	109
Co. G	Cpt. James Jennings	Orange & Chatham Co.	93
Co. H	Cpt. William Grier	Mecklenburg Co.	61
Co. I	Cpt. Albert Haynes	Lincoln & Gaston Co.	109
Co. K	Cpt. James Young	Buncombe Co.	69

The volunteers filling the ranks of the Bethel Regiment came from all across North Carolina. There were men of the coastal plain region coming from the towns of Edenton, Windsor, Hertford, and Plymouth; there were recruits from the piedmont hailing from Charlotte, Raleigh, Lincolnton, Durham, and Chapel Hill; and there were volunteers from the Appalachian Mountains to the west, from Morganton, Swannanoa, and Asheville. They were mostly farmers and mainly single, though some were married, and a handful owned slaves. A few were merchants and clerks, teachers, and lawyers. There was a smattering of overseers, doctors, blacksmiths, and shoemakers. Finally, the battalion contained enough students to fill a good-sized classroom.

The oldest volunteer among the 11th's rank-and-file was Matthew Hubbert (Co. I), a 64-year-old, part-time day laborer from Catawba County's Jacob's Ford. Rifleman Hubbard was married, had a handful of children, and lived on a small farm owned by one of his sons.[47] He, along with five other volunteers, was over fifty years old. The youngest recruit, 14-year-old William Powell, talked his way into Company D. Private Powell, who was taller than many adults, stood 5 feet, 7¾ inches. Before the war, he had helped his father with farm chores on the family farm near Morganton, in Burke County.[48] Young William Powell was not the only youngster; the regiment's ranks also contained a trio of 15-year-olds and nearly two dozen 16-year-olds. One of these 16-year-old youths, Lambert Bristol (Co. B), had run away from home and fibbed his way into the regiment. When the youth's mother contacted her son's commanding officer, Cpt. Mark Armfield, and let him know William's real age, the officer promised to look out for the boy and keep him out of danger. Armfield assigned Powell duties as mail boy.[49]

Some of the recruits were highly educated and came from families with money, such as William Benbury (Co. F). However, the 20-year-old, the son of a prestigious family from Chowan County's Edenton, cast aside the advantages available to him and enlisted as a rifleman, first with the 1st NC, and once that unit had been disbanded, with the 11th NC.[50] Another volunteer, 24-year-old Henry Bazemore (Co. C), also came from a clan possessing wealth and substance. Henry Bazemore's prewar education had earned him a job as a physician's assistant in Windsor; however, just like Pvt. Benbury, Henry Bazemore wanted to serve in the ranks, carry a weapon, and shoot the enemy.[51]

Another volunteer from a family of distinction was Lewis Warlick (Co. B). The 28-year-old had served as a corporal in Company G, 1st NC, but dragged his feet before reenlisting, and thus entered Cpt. Armfield's unit as a rifleman. Lewis Warlick's family farm was well known for its corn-raising: "Stories [were] told of the Warlick's raising more corn than anyone else in the area and of the big corn shuckings with the potpie feasts, the games and fun that came when the corn-pile, that was about a fourth of a mile long, was shucked."[52]

Standing in the ranks near Pvt. Lewis Warlick was another educated rifleman, 28-year-old Elisha Walker (Co. B). He had been a member of the Burke Rifles of the 1st NC, and then reenlisted into the 11th NC, again as a private. Elisha Walker, from Morganton, had lived on his widowed mother's farm, though he earned his livelihood as a teacher.[53] Walker, like many of the Tar Heels who had signed their names to the 11th NC's rolls, left their loved ones behind, believing "it is hard for me to leave ... but I consider I am doing rightly.... I think my first duties are to my country."[54]

But the regiment was not composed solely of educated young men. Most of the Eleventh's rank-and-file earned their keep working on farms. They enlisted, happy to be free of the tedious monotony of farm chores and anxious for adventure. The formation also contained the sons of dirt-poor farmers, young men with no education. In fact, every company had a handful of recruits unable to sign their own names to the company muster roles.

The 20-year-old brevet-major, Egbert Ross, gathered the battalion's company officers together and they began planning how to integrate the old hands with the neophyte recruits. Ross had worked with some of these freshly minted captains in the 1st NC: Frank Bird (Co. C) had been a 2nd lt. in the Enfield Blues; Calvin Brown (Co. D) was a 1st lt. in the Burke Rifles; Edward Small (Co. F) was a 2nd lt. in the Southern Stars; and James Jennings (Co. G) had been a 1st lt. in the Orange Light Infantry. The rest of the regiment's company commanders had been NCO's for the 1st NC. Ross, with the other captains' support, announced the Bethel Regiment's training schedule.[55] He also posted, "For those troops not sufficiently advanced for Company and Battalion Drill there will also be squad drill from 11:00 to 12:00 Noon, and 3:00 to 4:00 p.m."[56] The temporary commander, once the battalion's schedule had been established, awaited the arrival of their senior officers.

Reveille	At daybreak
Breakfast	At 6:30 a.m.
Sick Call	At 7:00 a.m.
Guard Mounting	At 7:30 a.m.
Squad Drill	From 8:00 to 9:00 a.m.
Company Drill	From 10:00 to 12:00 Noon
Orderly Call	At 12:00 Noon
Dinner Call	At 12:30 p.m.
Battalion Drill	From 3:00 to 4:30 p.m.
Dress Parade	At 5:30 p.m.
Tattoo	At 8:00 p.m.
Taps	At 8:30 p.m.

On April 10, 1862, the first field-grade officer to arrive was Lt. Col. William A. Owens, who immediately; "having reported for duty ... assume[d] command of the regiment." He immediately sent Cpt. Ross back to his company.[57] William A. Owens, a 29-year-old calling Charlotte his home, had earned a law degree from the University of North Carolina and practiced law. When the war began, William Owens helped organize a company in Charlotte and he, along with the unit's leader, Lewis Williams, took their volunteers to Camp Mangum. Eventually their formation was designated as Company B of the 1st NC, with Williams as captain and Owens first lieutenant. In September 1862, before the fight at Big Bethel, Cpt. Lewis Williams resigned and Owens was promoted. He had commanded his company until the regiment was mustered out.[58]

William Owens returned to Charlotte and was elected as the city's mayor in January 1862, receiving nearly 60 percent of the vote.[59] However he served for only a few weeks before being appointed to the rank of major in the 34th NC. His new regiment was sent to Hamilton, North Carolina, to guard positions along the Roanoke River, where the soldiers stated "they were playing war."[60] One Carolinian officer wrote, "Up to this time we thought we had seen something of this war, crossing swamps and streams where there were no bridges, but we found out later how little we knew."⁶¹ Major Owens' regiment was sent to Goldsboro, North Carolina, and assumed more security roles. Then, the 34th NC was ordered north to Fredericksburg, Virginia, but just before their movement Maj. William Owens was detached from the regiment to assume command of the 11th NC with the rank of lieutenant colonel.⁶²

A few days later, William J. Martin, the regiment's new major, arrived. William J. Martin a 31-year-old, had been a professor at the University of North Carolina in Chapel Hill before the war. Martin, a Virginian by birth, was well educated, having attended the University of Virginia and earned a degree in chemistry and natural science.⁶³ The professor, having observed the success the Bethel Regiment's leaders had achieved, put out the word he was interested in command. Martin began recruiting among his students for a company he called "The Guards of Southern Independence."⁶⁴ Immediately, hopeful young men contacted Martin, requesting positions within his unit. One such suitor wrote, "I was very pleased to learn from the Gov. that you intended ... raising a company.... [W]ould you like to have me as one of your lieutenants?"⁶⁵ Another ambitious officer candidate, a former student of Martin's, wrote, "[I am] very desirous to get a commission ... and I would much prefer [it] being [from some] one I am acquainted."⁶⁶ The ambitious ex-pupil had his father contact Professor Martin. Richard Sterling wrote, "My son Edward Sterling ... requests me to ask you ... would you give him a commission as Lieutenant?"⁶⁷ And a third applicant, an NCO in a South Carolina unit stationed at Fort Macon, penned, "[I am] interested to serve under you provided [I] could obtain a Lieutenant's commission."⁶⁸

Professor William Martin brought his volunteers to the enlistment center at Camp Mangum, and they joined the other prospective formations, all actively soliciting new recruits. His company was mustered into the 28th North Carolina with him as captain. The 28th was then transported east and billeted near Wilmington with duties to protect the state's east coast. The men of Cpt. Martin's Company G lived in roughly made wooden barracks, ate well, and were in decent health. But his troops were poorly armed with muskets from the Fayetteville arsenal, flintlocks altered to take percussion caps.⁶⁹ They performed guard duties, carried out incessant work details, and drilled constantly. As Captain Martin listened to news of battles and skirmishes coming from Virginia he was disappointed. He kept in contact with political friends in Raleigh as new regiments were being formed. He had his sights set upon a field command: the result—his appointment as major in the 11th North Carolina.

Thirty-one-year-old William J. Martin was a professor at UNC (Chapel Hill) before the war (Clark, 1901).

On April 19, 1862, the regiment's colonel arrived, the 46-year-old Collett Leventhorpe.⁷⁰ The formation's new commander, Collett Leventhorpe was an Englishman and a veteran, having served in several different British regiments. He had begun his military career with the 14th Regiment of Foot as an ensign, serving in Ireland and then in the British West Indies. Leventhorpe obtained the rank of lieutenant when he was 20 and then spent a year in Canada. He was promoted to captain and transferred to the 18th Regiment of Foot. Then, in 1842, at the age of 27, he cashed out his position and immigrated to South Carolina. Leventhorpe operated a British-based business in Charleston for several years and in his commercial travels met Louise Bryan, a 21-year-old from a prominent Rutherford, North Carolina, family. Her

Forty-seven-year-old Collett Leventhorpe assumed command of the 11th NC on April 19, 1862 (Clark, 1901).

father, Gen. Edmund Bryan, was a veteran of the Red Stick War (Creek War) in 1814. Louise Bryan recalled, "[Collett Leventhorpe] was a gentleman by birth and by nature, with a generous heart, high intellect ... [and] a handsome man ... nearly 6 1/2 feet in height."⁷¹ They married in 1849. Leventhorpe then attended Charleston's medical college and earned a physician's license, though he never did practice medicine. Doctor Leventhorpe and his wife settled in Rutherford, and he operated a lucrative business providing supplies to the area's gold mining operations. Collett Leventhorpe became a U.S. citizen in 1849, and when the war began he secured a commission as colonel in the 34th NC Infantry. However, when the 34th NC found itself mired in eastern North Carolina he grew disenchanted with the fledgling Confederate armed services. Leventhorpe wrote his wife, "We are ... not well armed.... I suppose they will give us some sort of tools if they mean us to fight."⁷² He wanted to be where the action was, in Virginia, and he secured his new position with the Bethel Regiment in hopes this unit would be sent where there was the best chance for earning battle laurels.⁷³

Colonel Leventhorpe moved into the regiment's headquarters and immediately evaluated the condition of his formation. He discovered that the young brevet-major Ross had done the best he could to lead the regiment but had not been able to establish any military discipline. Leventhorpe, a veteran of the harsh British martial system, quickly issued orders, tightening control. Leventhorpe declared, "The practice of sending Officers and men to the city before their leaves and furloughs are granted ... must be stopped at once."⁷⁴ Following this, the veteran military executive cracked down on lax security measures by walking through the regiment's camp and inspecting company procedures. Colonel Leventhorpe demonstrated the seriousness of his intentions with harsh penalties against offenders. He made an example of Pvt. Reuben Yaunts (Co. E), who was discovered sleeping on guard duty. The 28-year-old rifleman was "court-martialed ... [and] Confined at the guard tent to wear ball and chain for six months."[75]

Colonel Leventhorpe also examined the regiment's sanitation conditions and was horrified. The ex-physician immediately took steps to improve his men's health as well as changing the locations of the camp's privies and ordering new wells dug. He issued a decree that "soldiers must repair the sinks ... and not wander in the woods, which constitute a nuisance in the neighborhood of a camp."[76] Leventhorpe also commanded that "on Saturday afternoon a cleansing of the whole person shall be practiced."[77] He added that the soldiers' "tents [were] to be opened and raised ... and bedding aired ... unless raining."[78]

Finally, Col. Leventhorpe took complete control over the unit's drillmastery. He required at least four hours of drill each day and demanded his riflemen train with a serious earnestness. Leventhorpe expected all company officers to lead their units.[79] He insisted each company be drilled by squad (led by sergeants) and platoon (led by lieutenants), and then by company (led by captains). Leventhorpe also stipulated that company commanders would take their proper positions in battalion drill—he would not let captains turn their commands over to lieutenants. In time the ex–British officer would write, "There is no doubt this is the best drilled regiment in service. " He also added, "[The men] ... look quite spiffy."[80]

Collett Leventhorpe's second-in-command, Lt. Col. William A. Owens, was an ambitious individual and he chafed beneath Leventhorpe's authority. The ex-lawyer maneuvered among the state's political leaders, chasing a command of his own. Owens succeeded in his efforts, obtaining a commission as colonel of the 53rd NC. He resigned from the Bethel Regiment on May 6, 1862, and left for his new regiment.[81] Leventhorpe instantly endorsed Maj. Martin to fill Owens' old position, and then promoted the 20-year-old Cpt. Egbert Ross to major. Both men accepted their new roles on the same day Owens departed. A Tar Heel pundit recorded the Bethel Regiment was now led by "a physician, a professor, and a boy."[82]

Even though Col. Leventhorpe had worked hard to improve the regiment's health conditions, sickness festered among the Carolinians' camp. Hundreds of young men had come from isolated hamlets with little outside contact, arriving defenseless against the world's diseases and with paltry knowledge about decent sanitation. These guileless young men were crowded together in tents and small cabins, and soon an explosion of contagious illnesses occurred, overwhelming the army's unprepared doctors. Three Bethel Regiment volunteers died within days of arriving at Camp Mangum: Pvt. J.H. Walker (Co. E) died first, just five days after enlisting. He was buried so quickly his records weren't even completed. Then 18-year-old Thaddeus C. Stewart (Co. C) fell to "brain fever" a few days later. When Pvt. Stewart's mother, Sarah Stewart, learned of his death, she traveled to Raleigh and collected her son's effects, which included three pairs of socks, eight pairs of pants, one vest, seven shirts, two blankets, and a single set of drawers.[83] Three days after Stewart died, 36-year-old James C. Castellaw (Co. C) perished due to fever. Fearing contagion, the Carolina physicians interred Castellaw's body immediately and his things were "thrown away." Therefore, when his wife, Sarah Castellaw, arrived, there was nothing remaining for her to take back home.[84] She also learned her husband had already spent his $50 signing bonus, meaning she would receive no extra funds from the regiment. Sarah Castellaw returned to her home in Windsor, brokenhearted.

Camp Mangum's poor sanitation conditions produced ghastly results in April 1862; fifteen Tar Heels succumbed to typhoid fever, measles, meningitis, or pneumonia.[85] Most of these victims were young, including 15-year-old George Patton (Co. B). Almost all were farm boys or small-plot farmers. Regrettably, three of the dead soldiers were relatives, all from Burke County's Company D: Alexander, James, and Stanhope Whisenhunt. They died from the "fever" and pneumonia.[86] Another of the fallen soldiers was 26-year-old John Williams (Co. B), from Burke County. Private Williams had joined the regiment leaving behind a wife and young child. He contracted typhoid fever and pneumonia and died April 20, 1862, in the general hospital in Raleigh. His remains and clothing were taken home to Morganton "under charge of Private W.L. Griffin [Co. B]."[87] Then, when the regimental paymaster discovered Pvt. Williams had not been paid the Confederate bounty and back-pay, a check for $79.33 was sent to the deceased's wife, 21-year-old Jane Williams.[88] Eventually, Col. Leventhorpe's health measures, along with the volunteers' acquired sanitation awareness, began to improve conditions and diminish disease's consequences. Seven Tar Heels died in May and early June 1862.[89]

On June 13, 1862, as the Bethel Regiment recovered from sickness, Col. Leventhorpe received orders to move the regiment. But his boys were not going to Virginia as he had hoped; instead, the 11th NC was directed to travel east and become part of the Carolina coastline defenses.[90]

Chapter 3

Defending North Carolina's Coastline

Colonel Collett Leventhorpe's Bethel Regiment arrived in Wilmington, North Carolina, on June 16, 1862, and marched seven miles to Camp Holmes. His Carolinians were unhappy. They had been expecting to be sent north, to Virginia; going east meant they were being relegated to the backwaters, far from the war's center. Company C's Captain Francis "Frank" Bird's comment summed up many of the Tar Heel feelings: "We were very much disappointed when ordered here having expected to [go to] Richmond.[1] The unimpressed Cpl. Lewis Warlick (Co. B) noted, "I [am] … down in the … sand where the staple production is peanuts and tallow-faced women."[2]

The 11th NC was brigaded with two other North Carolina formations, the 43rd NC (Col. Thomas Kenan) and the 51st NC (Col. John Cantwell).[3] These three Tar Heel regiments were tasked with providing infantry support for the region's coastal defenses. Wilmington had become a vital Confederate shipping port once Abraham Lincoln's naval blockade of the Southern states began to constrict shipping access. The city was perfectly suited for blockade runners, located 28 miles up the Cape Fear River, though only seven miles from the Atlantic Ocean's waters. Wilmington was crucial as an important Confederate port city due to its being much closer to Virginia than was either Charleston or Savannah; and once military goods were unloaded, the reliable Wilmington and Weldon Railroad provided transport to Richmond in less than two days.[4] In addition, Wilmington was 675 miles from Bermuda, making it a quick journey from that island. This proximity meant blockade runners could accurately time their arrival on North Carolina's coast at night, making it easier to slip past Union gunboats.[5]

These adventurous blockade runners who glided past the Federal ships were then protected by Confederate naval guns from two strong fortifications, Forts Fisher and Caswell. Both fortresses were modern structures built of sand, a material proving to be most effective at resisting artillery fire. Fort Fisher consisted of a series of sand-mounded palisades extending for nearly a mile and containing dozens of heavy artillery pieces. These guns were capable of shelling any enemy ship attempting to approach long before that vessel's cannon could get into range.

Leventhorpe's regiment had barely set up their tents on these sandy fields when word reached the unit that Yankee troops were preparing to disembark from their ships and invade Carolina soil. The regiment was ordered to the beach, two miles away, to repel the expected

Fort Fisher's sand construction easily thwarted Federal artillery (*Photographic History of the Civil War*, 1911).

incursion. The Tar Heels responded quickly, excited at the news they were immediately going into action. Colonel Leventhorpe wrote, "[We] expected an attack as boats [came] in the neighborhood." Later, when the fervent Carolinian riflemen realized they had responded to a false rumor, Leventhorpe noted, in light of the fighting taking place outside Richmond, "The supposition is that Burnside has gone to Virginia. I do not think Burnside will attack here until the Richmond matter is settled."[6]

Once the men were settled back in camp, Col. Leventhorpe put them back to work, continuing their education in the school of the soldier. He mandated four or more hours of drill every day, with "company drill at 6 a.m. ... squad drill at 9 a.m., battalion drill at 11 a.m., company drill again at 1 p.m., battalion drill again at 3 p.m., and dress-parade at 5."[7] Lieutenant Edward Outlaw (Co. C) later wrote the regiment "had undergone the severest drilling that any troops ever underwent in all America."[8] The men knuckled under Leventhorpe's agenda and gradually became proficient at drill. The regiment was able to complete its maneuvers almost like "a machine." Captain Frank Bird (Co. C) wrote, "Our regiment is becoming well drilled.... I become daily more pleased."[9] Colonel Leventhorpe, however, though satisfied with his men's progress, noted they were "not quite as proficient as British regulars."[10] The soldiers' morale soared even more when the Bethel Regiment received brand new Enfield rifles from England on the ship *Nashville*.[11] A jubilant Tar Heel wrote his wife, "Don't trouble yourself about me for I am doing well."[12]

Colonel Leventhorpe continued his stringent discipline policies, though he did allow his men to earn passes out of camp. Wilmington, with a population near 11,000 citizens, was adept at providing diversions; after all, the city was a seaport and had been entertaining sailors for over one hundred years. The area's merchants were expert at providing ways to separate boisterous mariners and deckhands from their hard-earned cash. The city boasted a dozen saloons, many restaurants, tattoo parlors, and brothels, with the focus of activity along Water and Market streets. One such well-visited hotspot, Mantague's Billiard and Eating Saloon, advertised "the best of everything is kept at this house."[13] The young men from the Bethel Regiment quickly discovered these pleasures. One wrote home, "I have had a very pleasant time."[14] Another bragged, "I have been enjoying myself with the ladies ... as good as I ever did."[15] It did not take long before the regiment's surgeon, Dr. John Wilson, began to identify men with cases of gonorrhea and syphilis at morning sick call. Regrettably, one of these men would die from gonorrhea.[16]

The city's nearness and allurements tempted some of the men to attempt sneaking past the camp guards. At first the pickets were not adept at countering the cleverness of the absconders and these adventurous fellows snuck back into camp with great tales. One young fellow crowed, "[We] went over ... the other day and George got tite ... [but] none of my tent mates or mess mates has got in the guard house yet."[17] Others, though, were not as lucky and Col. Leventhorpe handed down severe penalties. Pvt. William Cates (Co. G) was found guilty of leaving the camp without permission and sentenced to "thirty-nine lashes."[18]

The regiment's closeness to Wilmington also assured the men a reliable postal system, as well as a good supply of food. One soldier informed his wife, "We have plenty to eat.... [W]e have meat, flour, Breadrise and sugar."[19] Private Franklin Dellinger (Co. I) gratefully received from his father a letter promising to "send you some brandy ... also ... one bottle of whiskey."[20] These notes from home helped stave off bouts of homesickness. One of these lonely soldiers, Pvt. Lewis Warlick (Co. B), wrote his girl, "You very well know that it [was] hard for me to leave you."[21] Another desolate Tar Heel scratched to his family, "I want to see you all again but there is no chance now."[22]

Towards the end of June 1862 the regiment received orders to march to Camp Wyatt, a location not far from Fort Fisher. Colonel Leventhorpe was to take "command of all the forces stationed there and at Zeke's Island."[23] The men of the Bethel Regiment, now 1,050 strong, had been told they were going to be housed in the fort's barracks but once Collett Leventhorpe inspected the accommodations he ordered his men away from the facility and directed them to set up their tents among the dunes not far from the beach. Private Lewis Warlick (Co. B) wrote, "We marched fifteen miles ... and we came here with the intention of going into the barracks ... but we found the place covered with fleas and our Colonel said we should not take quarters there."[24] Captain Frank Bird (Co. C) noted, "Fort Fisher is two miles below us.... Our place is uncomfortable on account of the deep sand."[25]

The soldiers adjusted to their new locality and began to explore their surroundings. Many were intrigued by what they saw. One Tar Heel wrote, "We can see the Yankee ships all the time. The other day one came so close that I could see the Captain and Steerman.... [I]t was really a pretty sight to see a large three masted Steamer in full sail, she had taken her smoke stack down and looked like a sail ship."[26] Captain Bird (Co. C) wrote, "Fort Fisher is ... tolerably fortified.... The boats of the enemy have fired into it Several times, the

Federal blockade ships patrol the waters beyond the range of Fort Fisher's guns (*Harper's Weekly*, 1864).

shells not causing any damage." The 32-year-old officer also recorded, "They have also shelled all along the beach where we are now."[27]

Captain Frank Bird's viewing of cruising Federal gunships and their bombardment of Fort Fisher underscored the seriousness of the situation. Abraham Lincoln's shipping blockade strategy had been a joke for the Southerners at first, but the situation changed once the Federal navy developed a policy and collected enough seagoing vessels to enforce the strategy. The foundation of the blockade system required two approaches: (1) Only the waters near Southern seaports would be blockaded, and (2) the seaports to be guarded needed a tactic involving layers of defense—there would be three lines of ships. The outer layer comprised quick-sailing ships patrolling miles off the coast, tasked with the job of sighting incoming blockade runners and relaying this information to the second line. This next line, composed of gunships, prepared to place themselves in position to sink or apprehend the blockade runners. The third line sailed right at the mouth of the inlets, just out of the Confederate fortifications' artillery range. If a runner succeeded in getting past the middle line, this third line of gunships would be in place to sink or run them aground.[28] In time, over a stretch of twelve months, the Federal ships were able to capture 50 ships out of 310 blockade runners attempting to reach Wilmington.[29]

At 4:00 a.m. on June 27, two Federal ships, the *Cambridge* and the USS *Stars and Stripes* sighted an approaching blockade runner, the *Modern Greece*. The Union vessels immediately went to battle stations and opened fire in the predawn light. The *Modern Greece* raised her British colors and fled towards the Carolina coast, getting to within a half-mile of Fort Fisher before running aground. The *Cambridge* moved in and shelled the *Modern Greece* before being driven off by the fort's heavy guns. Then, a lull occurred for several hours, during which time the *Cambridge* crew ate breakfast and the *Modern Greece*'s sailors boarded small boats and abandoned ship. Following this, the *Cambridge* moved in and shelled the *Modern Greece* until again being driven away by Fort Fisher's artillery.[30]

Captain Albert Haynes, whose Company I was on duty as infantry support at Fort Fisher, brought his men down to the beach, secured a boat, and ventured out to the battered blockade runner. Haynes and his men broke open a few boxes and brought away shoes.[31] Then he returned to the beach and sent a message to the regiment, describing the bounty lying so close to the beach. Captain William Hand (Co. A) and his company arrived next. Hand took boats out to the *Modern Greece* and "went clandestinely into the cabin ... and by his presence encouraged and did not restrain certain Enlisted men ... from pilfering."[32] He was able to get back to the beach before the military police arrived. Later, men from the Bethel Regiment, now under strict supervision, unloaded much of the ship's cargo, which consisted of "1,000 tons of gun powder, some rifled cannon and other arms and equipment ... together with bales of clothing and spirituous liquors."[33] Major Egbert Ross remarked, "Our boys worked hard but had quite a lively time of it drinking Champaign, wine, etc., smoking cigars, eating pine apples, raisins and other fruits."[34] Colonel Leventhorpe dutifully remarked to a *Wilmington Journal* reporter; that his men retrieved "and landed a large quantity of arms," and, "if the weather continues favorable during the day, [the men] ... will be able to save all the cargo."[35] Corporal Lewis Warlick (Co. B) noted, "The steamer is a total wreck and only about two thirds of the cargo (900 tons) was saved. When the ship's stores were unloaded, Col. Leventhorpe wrote up William Hand and Albert Haynes for court-martial. Both captains were tried in a court-martial but eventually acquitted.

The Bethel Regiment remained at their station two miles from Fort Wagner as the summer's heat increased. The Tar Heels discovered that the sweltering heat was only one problem; they were also tormented by sand fleas and mosquitoes. Corporal Lewis Warlick (Co. B) described how bad the fleas were: "You might take up a bucket of sand at night and by the next morning it would be all jumped out."[36] Another Tar Heel expressed his irritation with the mosquitoes, penning to his lady, "[Of] all the nights I ever spent in the neighborhood [the] mosquitoes last night was the worst.... No sleep visited my weary eyes until very late."[37]

The heat, the insects, and the ability of Leventhorpe's men to get passes and visit nearby establishments proved to be hazardous for the young Carolinians; sickness again swept through the ranks. In fact, Cpl. Lewis Warlick (Co. B), stunned by the weather, wrote, "Never have I experienced such scorching weather.... It has been so extremely hot .... That it made me so uncommonly lazy I could scarcely do anything."[38] At first, the regiment's surgeon, Dr. John Wilson, was able to deal with the men's symptoms. However, once the sick flooded into his field hospital and overwhelmed his quarters, he had the sick transported back to Camp Davis. Then Dr. Wilson's patients began to die, with 20-year-old Pvt. John Causby (Co. D) succumbing first to the mumps.[39] He was rapidly followed by seven others in June, then 19 in July, and a dozen more in August.[40]

Typhoid fever was the big killer. The field hospital at Camp Davis was swamped and the Bethel Regiment's overworked medical staff began sending patients to Wilmington's health facilities. The city had three; the Seaman's Home, the Marine Hospital, and the Naval Hospital. Most of Leventhorpe's sick went to the Seaman's Home, a hospital rented by the Confederate government.[41] It was a four-story brick building with enough space for over 200 beds and was considered, "one of the best in the State, even to the point of supplying mosquito netting in the summer."[42] The infirmary's name was changed to the Confederate Military General Hospital No. 4, and it became the last place on earth for three dozen of Collett Leventhorpe's boys.

One of these fatalities was Pvt. David Kerr (Co. H). The 18-year-old farm boy from the west side of Charlotte contracted typhoid fever and was transported to General Hospital No. 4, where he soon succumbed to his sickness. His father, Thomas Kerr, arrived, purchased a coffin from a local supplier, and took his dead son home.[43] Thomas Kerr also brought back his son's personal possessions: "1 coat, 1 pair pants, 1 pair shoes, 2 shirts, 2 pairs drawers, 1 cap, [and] 1 knapsack."[44] Another Carolinian to die, 22-year-old Cpl. John Means (Co. E), was also killed by typhoid fever. Corporal Means was buried in Wilmington's Oakdale cemetery. Then, when his father, William Means, arrived, all that remained of his son was a notation that the army owed Pvt. Means $63.12 in back pay. William Means returned to his son's home in Charlotte with nothing except a check payable in Confederate dollars.[45]

Even though many more young men died during the typhoid fever scourge in Wilmington's hospitals, others succumbed apart from the regiment. One of these men, 31-year-old Jesse Jennings, the captain of Company G, came down with yellow fever symptoms in early September 1862. Captain Jennings, who had owned a restaurant in Chapel Hill before the war, had initially enlisted into the 1st NC and because of his past military experience—he had been in private in the Mexican War—was commissioned a lieutenant. Not long after the 1st NC mustered out, Jennings had organized a company and was elected captain. But now, when Jesse Jennings took sick, he sent a telegram to his mother—he was an only child and his mother a widow—to let her know he was coming home to recuperate. Jennings boarded a train but died before reaching Chapel Hill. The railroad workers, panicked by his dangerous symptoms, hastily built a coffin and stuffed him into it. When the train arrived at the station, there was nothing for his mother except a corpse in a wooden box.[46]

Another Tar Heel, 33-year-old Pvt. J. Franklin Gilbert (Co. I), was a farmer from the Lincolnton area of Lincoln County who had been assigned to the Military General Hospital in Wilmington. Private Gilbert had enlisted into Cpt. Albert Haynes' company

Twenty-two-year-old Sgt. Francis Gilliam (Co. C) was assigned to the Wilmington hospital as a nurse in 1862 (Clark, 1901).

as a rifleman but his prewar experience as a veterinarian was recognized and soon he was assisting at the regiment's medical tent. Then, when the typhoid fever epidemic devastated the unit, Pvt. Gilbert was transferred to the Confederate Military General Hospital No. 4 as a nurse. Franklin Gilbert tended his suffering brothers for several months until he, too, became a victim. Nurse Franklin Gilbert died of yellow fever on October 23, 1862.[47] He was interred in Oakdale Cemetery, his body placed in a wooden coffin for which the regiment paid eight dollars, a fee charged to the 11th NC every time a soldier was entombed in one.[48]

In August 1862, the Bethel Regiment was rotated back to Camp Davis as another Carolina regiment assumed its duties at Fort Fisher. Colonel Leventhorpe was ordered to send four companies to a defensive position on the Carolina coast, east of Wilmington. Leventhorpe assigned Maj. Egbert Ross to command this battalion, and the men of Companies A, B, I, and K marched out to Topsail Inlet.[49] For these men under Maj. Ross, whose ideas about discipline differed from his colonel's, this coastal guard duty became a near lark. One Tar Heel recalled, "I am here ... enjoying our beautiful country camp vastly, and sea bathing.... I ... bathe every afternoon [in] a pretty little bay ... [with] thousands of fishes jumping about all around us."[50] Meanwhile, for the men stationed at Camp Davis, fears caused by the yellow fever epidemic dampened everyone's spirits. One frightened soldier wrote his wife, "If I never get home I want you to raise the children as well as you can."[51]

Another Carolinian remarked, "The black pall of smoke from the burning tar barrels added solemnity to the deadly silence of the streets ... [and] it seemed more like ... a somber emblem of mourning."[52] A Wilmington resident noted, "You cannot imagine the distress and gloom here.... Coffins have had to be brought both from Fayetteville & Charleston. It is a sad sight indeed to see and hear the dray loads of them daily going through the streets."[53]

Free of Wilmington's malaise, Maj. Egbert Ross's command remained on the coast until September 13, 1862, when the entire regiment was rousted in response to a possible Federal raid near Pollocksville, North Carolina, some 50 miles north of Wilmington.[54] The Bethel Regiment formed at Camp Davis and marched several miles north from Camp Davis before being ordered to halt. The next day they were told to return to their summer's campground. Corporal Lewis Warlick (Co. B) wrote in disgust, "I was in hopes when we left Topsail we were then on our way to old 'Stonewall' in Maryland.... I wish we could get to go to Maryland. I believe the whole regiment would like to do so as we are doing nothing here."[55]

The regiment remained at Camp Davis and with the yellow fever epidemic ravaging Wilmington Col. Leventhorpe refused to allow any of his Bethel boys to venture into the city. Instead, he put his soldiers to work constructing defenses. First Sergeant Elam Bristol (Co. B) wrote, "We are throwing up batteries ... and covering them with railroad irons so it is impossible to batter them down with the heaviest siege guns."[56]

General Thomas Clingman, who commanded all of the Confederate forces from his headquarters in Wilmington, fled from the city and turned over operations to Col. Leventhorpe. The annoyed colonel wrote, "Genl. Clingman retired to some point and left [me] to come daily ... into that pestilential air and send off all dispatches."[57] Wilmington was basically under siege from the disease. A reporter for the *Journal Office* reported, "The physicians report 86 new cases of Yellow Fever today. Few make reports of deaths.... [T]he deaths yesterday ... will not differ much from those of the two days last preceding them,—say 15 or 16."[58] In all, by the time the epidemic had run its course through Wilmington, 446 died.[59]

Elsewhere in North Carolina as fall softened the days' temperatures the state changed leadership. The temporary governor, Henry Clark, served out John Ellis's term and new elections were scheduled for September 1862. Two candidates emerged as serious contenders: William J. Johnston and Zebulon Vance. William Johnston, the

Zebulon Vance was 32 when elected governor of North Carolina in 1862 (Library of Congress).

Democrat, favored wholehearted support of Jefferson Davis's policies and argued North Carolina should give up some of its state's rights in defense of the Confederate cause. This platform labeled the Democrat supporters as the Confederate Party. Zebulon Vance, on the other hand, championed the notion that all the state's civil liberties should be vigorously protected. Neither candidate campaigned; instead, both let others speak for them. Johnson was the owner of one of North Carolina's railroads and too busy to campaign, and Vance was colonel of the 26th NC Infantry and involved in the regiment's actions during the summer and fall battles in Virginia.[60] The election results were not close; Zebulon Vance collected over 54,000 votes while Johnston garnered only 24,500.[61] Vance resigned his commission with the 26th NC and was sworn into office on September 8, 1862.

On October 1, 1862, Col. Leventhorpe received orders to move the Bethel Regiment out of Camp Davis and travel north. The excited Tar Heels climbed aboard a train and cheered as Wilmington was left behind. Several days later they moved into their new location, Camp Wilson, not far from Franklin, Virginia, and 230 miles away from Wilmington. Corporal Lewis Warlick (Co. B) scribbled to his girl, "This place is on the Seaboard & Roanoke Rail Road 21 miles from Suffolk where the road crosses the Blackwater river."[62] Colonel Leventhorpe was tasked with defending the bridges and fords of the Blackwater River along a length of two dozen miles. He spread the regiment's companies out along this expanse, directing his units to patrol the river's banks, and guard the crossings. Captain Frank Bird (Co. C) wrote of this assignment: "The line to be guarded was so long, and the troops to guard it so few, that forced marches were of constant occurrences."[63] Soon, the Bethel soldiers, who hustled along the river's banks, began to refer to themselves as "foot cavalry."

Occasionally squads of Carolinians exchanged fleeting shots with Yank soldiers who watched from across the Blackwater, but for the most part, the Northerners stayed on their side of the river. Corporal Warlick (Co. B) noted, "The river here is narrow but very deep.... [I have] been out on picket all night, and one day on a scout ... [and] since that time it has rained nearly all the time." Warlick continued: "We are not living as well as we did at camp Davis. The only thing we get is cracklins.... I was quite cold last night. I ... haven't got any overcoat and a good many of us are nearly barefoot."[64] Not long after Warlick wrote his letter to his sweetheart, Pvt. John Keith (Co. D) seriously injured himself with an "accidental discharge of his gun." The 19-year-old from Burke County died from his wounds two months later.[65]

Reinforcements arrived and these additional Confederate battalions were placed under Col. Leventhorpe's command. He immediately arranged these units to better defend the Blackwater River position. Collett Leventhorpe, now that these new formations strengthened his defensive line and alleviated the crisis facing his men, had time to grumble. He commanded four infantry regiments and two cavalry squadrons, and yet his rank was only colonel. Leventhorpe wrote, "I see two more Brigadier [generals were] made in North Carolina; [James] Lane and [Stephen] Ransom.... I have a large Brigade and most dangerous post." Leventhorpe was especially galled by the fact James Lane had served under him but now was a general. The vexed colonel wrote, "I am considered an experienced officer but the honors are reserved for others. I presume it is owing to my being a foreigner."[66]

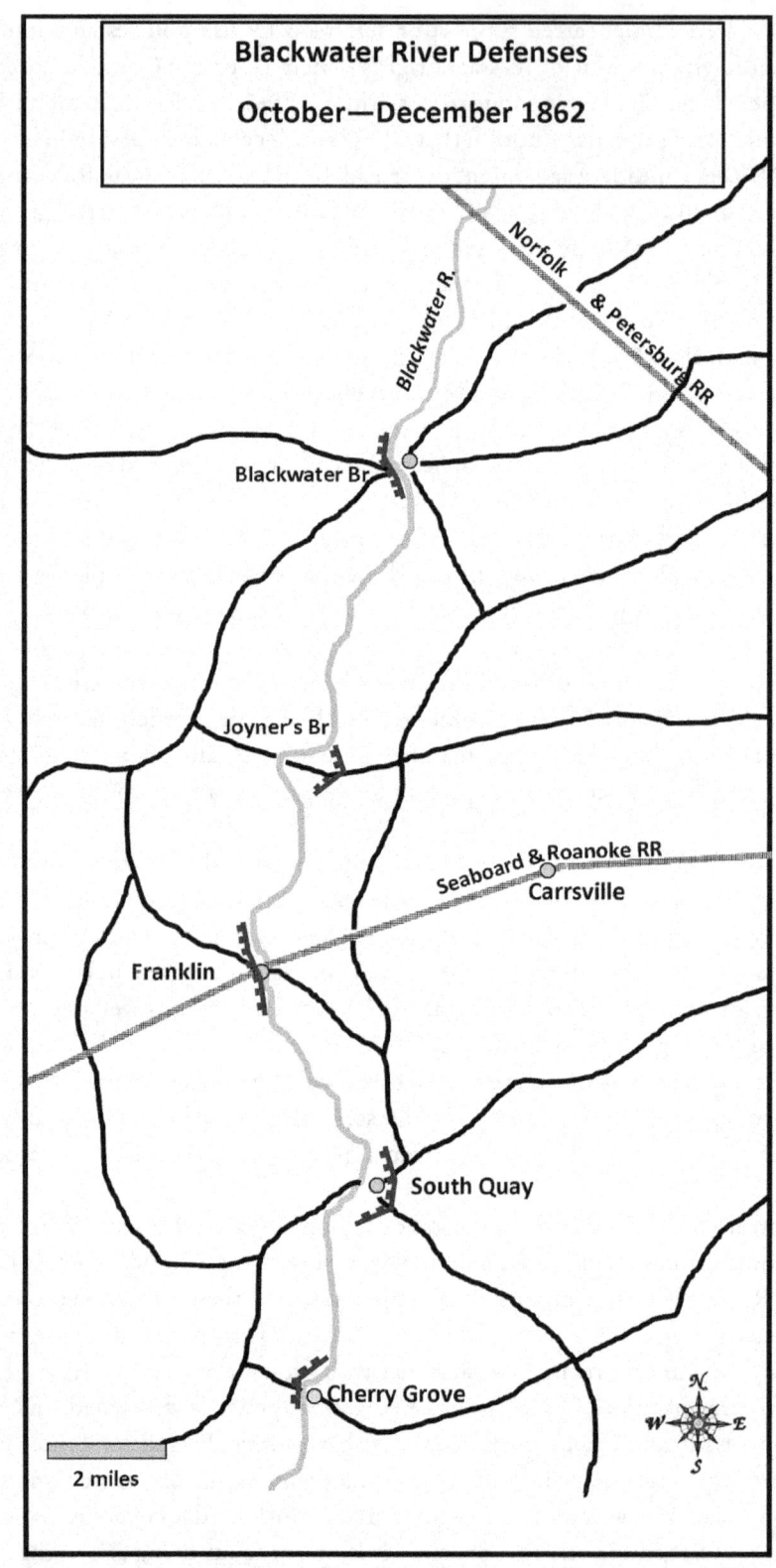

On November 18, 1862, a Northern force pushed against one of the Bethel Regiment's positions at Blackwater Bridge, a dozen miles north of Franklin. The 11th NC had two companies on the east side of the river (A and G) deployed as skirmishers, with other companies occupying the western side. Pickets from Cpt. William Hand's Company A reported Union forces within two miles of their position. Corporal Lewis Warlick (Co. B) described Col. Leventhorpe's response: "The Col. told us ... that they had a very heavy force ... [of] four brigades." Warlick reported that Leventhorpe said, "I am determined to hold the place at all hazards." Leventhorpe's speech to his men continued: "He hoped the Bethel Regiment would still retain the reputation she had for valor."[67]

The Tar Heel riflemen remained in their positions until noon, when the advancing Federals opened fire upon the 11th NC's skirmishers. The two lines exchanged rifle fire for several minutes before Union artillery started shooting at the Carolinians. The pressure increased on William Hand's (Co. A) and John Freeland's (Co. G) men, but they were dug in and fought back aggressively. The Federal commander recorded, "[It was] a brisk skirmish.... [Their] strong guard offered much resistance ... [and] they kept up a sharp fire upon our dismounted skirmishers."[68] The Northerners surged forward with more riflemen, firing as they advanced. Private Isaac Frazier (Co. A) was severely wounded at this time.[69] Frazier's comrades carried the 20-year-old away from the skirmish line while the rest held their positions. Several more Carolinians were injured before the companies fell back. Corporal Warlick (Co. B) noted, "The yanks commenced shelling our scouts ... which was a shade too hot for them."[70] Company A suffered two severely wounded and Company B had three minor injuries. The two companies retreated and crossed the bridge, to take refuge behind the regiment's positions on the western side.

Confederate artillery opened fire once the Carolinians were safely across the river. Union cannon returned fire, pounding the Confederates. Corporal Lewis Warlick (Co. B) recorded, "When each side opened I tell you there was a thundering for two hours almost equal to the Bethel fight."[71] The Southerners' defenses were well constructed, and the Union cannon fire was ineffective, but this fact did not prevent the Tar Heels from close calls. Corporal Warlick (Co. B) recalled, "I would fall flat on the ground and then I would lie for some time and I would rise—here would come the shell, down I would go again." Eventually the shelling died down and silence replaced the angry sounds as the bluecoats withdrew. Corporal Warlick finished his letter about the fight, writing, "I am thankful I came out unhurt."[72]

Following this skirmish the men in the Bethel Regiment became concerned with the approaching winter; the November nights were cold and though the Carolinians had tents many wanted more permanent shelter. A worried Pvt. George Erwin (Co. B) wrote, "The Yankees say that they do not intend building winter quarters but will make an active campaign all this winter. This will compel us to do the same."[73] Corporal Lewis Warlick (Co. B) also mentioned their situation, writing, "O how cold it is this morning—frost deep enough to track a rabbit." Warlick continued, "I wouldn't be surprised now if we stayed here this winter ... [as] we could live in our tents ... all of them ... having chimneys ... with a good fire."[74]

Colonel Collett Leventhorpe's brigade command was given to Brig. Gen. Roger Pryor on December 4, 1862, by order of General Robert E. Lee. Leventhorpe wrote, "Genl. Pryor has relieved me.... I am glad of it, you have no idea of the care and responsibility of such a post as this." However, as Leventhorpe prepared to vacate his brigade headquarters and return to regimental command, Gen. Pryor surprised him. The Bethel Regiment's senior officer noted, "I had my things packed today to go to my Regt., when Genl. Pryor ordered me to command the post and to remain here [Franklin]. He put his Head Quarters probably 4 miles in the rear."[75] It now appeared as if Col. Leventhorpe and his Tar Heels would be protecting the Blackwater River defense line all winter. Leventhorpe ordered the further strengthening of the Franklin fortifications, writing, "I had ... an iron battery constructed.... I do not think they [Federal troops] can hurt it much, or the men."[76] Corporal Warlick (Co. B) added, "We have been ... throwing up breastworks and covering it with railroad iron, putting it on double to protect the cannoneers."[77] Colonel Leventhorpe was quite pleased with his soldiers' defensive positions, writing, "They are as perfect as circumstances admit."[78] Two weeks later, the regiment was ordered to move to Kingston, North Carolina.[79]

Chapter 4

The Fight at White Hall, North Carolina, December 16, 1862

The 11th NC camped two miles from Franklin for only a couple days before marching again. This movement was hurried, pushed along by news the Yankees were attempting to capture Kinston. Lieutenant Colonel William Martin recorded, "We were ordered to Kinston, N.C. but before we reached it the enemy had taken the town."[1] The Bethel Regiment then received orders to get to White Hall, North Carolina, as the Union troops were headed toward that town, and its important river crossing.

White Hall was a community of several hundred residents with many of its businesses focused on the waters of the Neuse River. The town had a sizeable shipyard and blacksmith shop, plus a buggy factory, turpentine distillery, and brickworks.[2] Steamboats could safely traverse the Neuse River as far as White Hall, enabling the nearby plantations to use the town's docks for shipping their agricultural products. Also, finished European goods could be unloaded at White Hall's docks. Finally, the town was on the main road between Goldsboro and Kinston that ran south of the Neuse River and was not far from a station on the Wilmington and Weldon Railroad.

White Hall's river and road connections, combined with a substantial pool of skilled ironworkers, made this the perfect locality for the construction of a Confederate ironclad. The shipbuilding firm Howard and Ellis began work on this ship, the CSS *Neuse*, in the fall of 1860. The *Neuse* was 139 feet long and 34 feet wide and there were plans to cover the hull with 4 inches of wrought iron, making it a dangerous river ship to support the Southern cause, but by December little more than the hull had been completed.[3]

On December 15, 1862, Federal cavalrymen, riding ahead of the main Union formation marching toward White Hall, scouted out the town and noticed the *Neuse*'s existence. The ironclad sat in the shipyard on the north side of the river, not far from the bridge connecting the town to the northern part of the county. This news was an unexpected bonus for Maj. Gen. John Foster, commanding the Federal forces, and he urged his troops forward, wanting to capture or destroy the ship.

Meanwhile, Confederate forces, including the Bethel Regiment, hurried toward White Hall. Corporal Lewis Warlick (Co. B) noted, "We ... marched 16 miles ... to White Hall bridge on the Neuse River."[5] The 11th North Carolina was part of a contingent of South-

**11th North Carolina Infantry
White Hall
December 16, 1862**[4]

F & S	Col. Collett Leventhorpe	5
Co. A	Cpt. William Hand	102
Co. B	Cpt. Mark Armfield	92
Co. C	Cpt. Francis Bird	72
Co. D	Cpt. Calvin Brown	68
Co. E	Cpt. William Kerr	60
Co. F	Cpt. Edward Small	84
Co. G	Cpt. John Freeland	83
Co. H	1st Lt. James Lowrie	50
Co. I	Cpt. Albert Haynes	103
Co. K	Cpt. James Young	53
	Noncombatants	9
		781

erners commanded by Brig. Gen. Beverly Robertson patched together to stop the Northerners' advance. Colonel Collett Leventhorpe had nearly 800 men, all anxious to burn powder against the Yankees.[6] Very few of Leventhorpe's men had battle experience—only the veterans of the 1st NC who had been at Big Bethel and those involved in the skirmish along the Blackwater. The rest anxiously awaited their first test. Colonel Leventhorpe had trained his troops extensively; the Tar Heels were armed with newly imported Enfields, and they were conscious of all the fighting their Carolina brothers had been enduring in the Virginia and Maryland battles. The Bethel Regiment was ready for a fight. Corporal Lewis Warlick (Co. B) noted, "When I hear of our brothers doing so much in Virginia and Maryland it makes me want to be with them."[7]

The Tar Heel regiment hustled towards White Hall from the north, racing to protect the river crossing. Private John Warlick (Co. I) recalled, "We beat the enemy to the bridge ... by a forced march ... [arriving] at dusk."[8] Colonel Leventhorpe sent out Cpt. Albert Haynes' company to secure the bridge. The 24-year-old officer hustled his two platoons across the Neuse River Bridge and they fanned out in skirmish formation through the town's northern streets. They soon came in contact with Northern soldiers; dismounted cavalrymen commanded by Maj. Jeptha Garrard.[9] Shots were exchanged and the bluecoats pushed the Confederates back to the river. Captain Haynes, realizing he could not hold the bridge, informed Col. Leventhorpe, and his commander ordered him to destroy the bridge. Albert Haynes kept one platoon as a rear guard and detailed the other to haul barrels of pitch onto the bridge. Private John Warlick (Co. I) recorded, "[We] barely had time to knock the barrels of rosin to pieces and apply the torch."[10] The Tar Heels retreated to the north side of the river as the bridge burned.

Major Garrard brought artillery pieces forward and bombarded the river's northern shoreline. Corporal Lewis Warlick (Co. B) wrote, "We took a light shelling on Monday night [December 15, 1862]."[11] Colonel Leventhorpe pulled his troops back to a position beyond danger and men of the Bethel Regiment, once they were out of the Yank artillery fire, bivouacked and ate their dinners. Private John Warlick (Co. I) recorded, "Our supper that night was roasted sweet potatoes."[12] The Union artillerymen, not knowing the Confederates had withdrawn, continued shelling the area until they noticed the CSS *Neuse* by the light of the burning bridge. They shifted their guns to fire at the ship. Brigadier General Beverly Robertson wrote, "They [U.S. artillery] shelled the woods until late at night, [nearly] destroying the gunboat."[13] Major Garrard wanted the gunship completely demolished; he ordered a small team of Northerners to finish the task. They, as one Federal recorded, "stripped off, swam the river and [were] in the act of setting the gunboat on fire, when ... discovered and fired upon, and had to dive into the river, leaving [their] work undone."[14]

The Confederate forces assembled during the night; the 31st NC, the 63rd NC, and the 59th NC accompanied Leventhorpe's Carolinians, along with 600 dismounted cavalry and two pieces of artillery.[15] General Robertson, commanding the Confederate force, positioned the 31st NC to guard the destroyed bridge. The 31st NC, led by Col. John Jordan, already had a storied history. Formed in Wilmington in late 1861, the regiment had been sent to Roanoke Island in February 1862, and when the Confederate line collapsed in the battle on February 9, 1862, the entire unit surrendered.[16] The 31st NC had been exchanged and were now placed under Robertson's command. Colonel Jordan's men were still smarting from their humiliating performance, and Brig. Gen. Robertson chose this time to provide them with the opportunity to redeem their honor. General Beverly Robertson wrote, "I placed them [31st NC] in position as much sheltered as circumstances would permit."[17]

The next morning, December 16, 1862, Maj. Gen. Foster ordered the 9th New Jersey forward, supported by a battery of artillery; he wanted to take control of the river crossing and construct a pontoon bridge to support his continued advancement.[18] At 9:00 a.m., the 9th NJ, also veterans of the fight at Roanoke Island, deployed in line of battle behind a screen of skirmishers and moved down from the higher ground, south and east of White Hall. They closed upon a thin line of Tar Heel pickets from the 31st NC. The two forces shot at each other and the Jersey lead quickly overwhelmed Col. Jordan's men. A reporter from *Harper's Weekly* recorded, "Heavy skirmishing immediately ensued between the Ninth New Jersey and ... [the] rebels."[19] The Southerners bolted for the river and crossed, leaving the southern shore to the Federals. Colonel James Ledlie (3rd NY Light Artillery) wrote, "The skirmish lasted but a few minutes."[20]

At 9:30 a.m., Maj. Gen. Foster sent forward several batteries of artillery and they unlimbered on the heights above White Hall. The guns commenced firing, directing their shells at the 31st NC's position and at the Confederate cannon. Captain Edwin Jenney (3rd New York Light Artillery) noted, "I was ordered forward and opened fire ... [at] about 1,000 yards."[21] The Union guns damaged the Confederate artillery piece and then concentrated their fire upon the 31st NC. Some of their shells fell upon the Bethel Regiment posted more than a half-mile away. Private John Warlick (Co. I) wrote, "A bombshell bounced over and landed just in the rear of the company.... Sergt. William Jetton [Co. I] ... threw it into a pond of water just to our rear."[22] As more Union artillery came up and aimed their tubes at Jordan's men his soldiers began to grow rattled. The 9th NJ pushed forward across an open field and began firing volleys. The 31st NC's morale crumbled and the men abandoned their earthworks. General Robertson wrote, "The Thirty-first Regiment withdrew from their position without instructions."[23]

Robertson immediately turned to Col. Leventhorpe, telling him to send his Bethel "boys" forward. The 11th NC formed line of battle and surged into the fray. General Robertson had noted "the alacrity with which the order was obeyed by his men gave ample proof of their gallant bearing."[24] The New Jersey riflemen unloaded a volley into the advancing Tar Heels and the first of Col. Leventhorpe's riflemen fell. Pvt. Benjamin Walker (Co. E) was killed, Pvt. Charles Morris (Co. K) was struck in the head and left arm, and Pvt. Jefferson Thrower (Co. H) was severely wounded.[25] Lieutenant Colonel William Martin noted, "The regiment had its first real baptism of fire. Posted along the river bank, from which another regiment had just been driven."[26] Collett Leventhorpe's Tar Heels settled in among piles of logs and returned fire upon the 9th NJ. Private John Warlick (Co. I) recorded, "We went into action on the bank of the river near a steam mill, where hundreds of pine saw logs had been rafted and rolled up on the bank ... affording us splendid protection."[27] The Carolinian musketry smacked into the 9th NJ. The 11th's fire was so severe the New Jersey's shocked leader, Col. Charles Heckman (9th NJ), recorded, "On arriving near the bridge, shell canister, and musketry were opened upon the Ninth."[28]

Colonel Leventhorpe's men took advantage of every hiding place they could find and from their shelters poured musket balls into the New Jersey formation. The range between the two regiments was 250 yards, but the Jersey fellows were out in the open and standing shoulder to shoulder. The Confederates pummeled the blue line. The New Jersey regiment shuddered; this fight was turning out to be much different than their battle at Roanoke Island. They were accustomed to the Rebels firing a few volleys and then running away; the 11th North Carolina men were different. Major Adam Zabriskie (9th NJ) wrote, "Our loss was heavy."[29]

A number of energetic young Tar Heels climbed up into the trees and shot at the bluecoats from their lofty positions. One Federal soldier complained, "They had a number of sharpshooters in the treetops.... [W]e could not see them, but they could see us, and picked off many of our poor fellows."[30] Even so, the New Jersey regiment stood its ground, firing continuously for nearly two hours and taking the punishment from the Carolinians. Most of the Jersey bullets smacked into the trees above the heads of the Tar Heels. Though the Yanks were on higher ground than Col. Leventhorpe's men, the Neuse River created an illusion making the Confederates' position appear at the same elevation.[31] Thus, New Jersey volleys fired at the level aim meant their bullets passed above the Southerners' heads. Still, New Jersey lead struck Carolina flesh. Second Lt. William Means (Co. E) was killed, as was Pvt. Noah Roundtree (Co. F).[32] Private Michael Craft (Co. I) was struck in the shoulder, Pvt. Samuel Query (Co. A) hit in the legs, and Pvt. William Bazemore (Co. C) injured in the left hand.[33]

When the 9th NJ's ammunition ran low, Col. Heckman ordered his men to fall back. They gave ground grudgingly, leaving behind a line of dead and wounded soldiers. Major Zabriskie noted, "The whole regiment was deployed along the banks of the river, kept up a brisk fire for about two hours, and ... our ammunition being expended ... were at last relieved." Abram Zabriskie also recorded his unit suffered 3 killed and 42 wounded.[34] Corporal Lewis Warlick (Co. B) wrote, "We held the enemy in check for two hours."[35] Brigadier Gen. Beverly Robertson complimented Collett Leventhorpe and his men, writing, "No veteran soldiers ever fought better or inflicted more terrible loss upon the enemy."[36]

Major General John Foster was not finished; he wanted his men across the Neuse River.

4. *The Fight at White Hall, North Carolina, December 16, 1862* 43

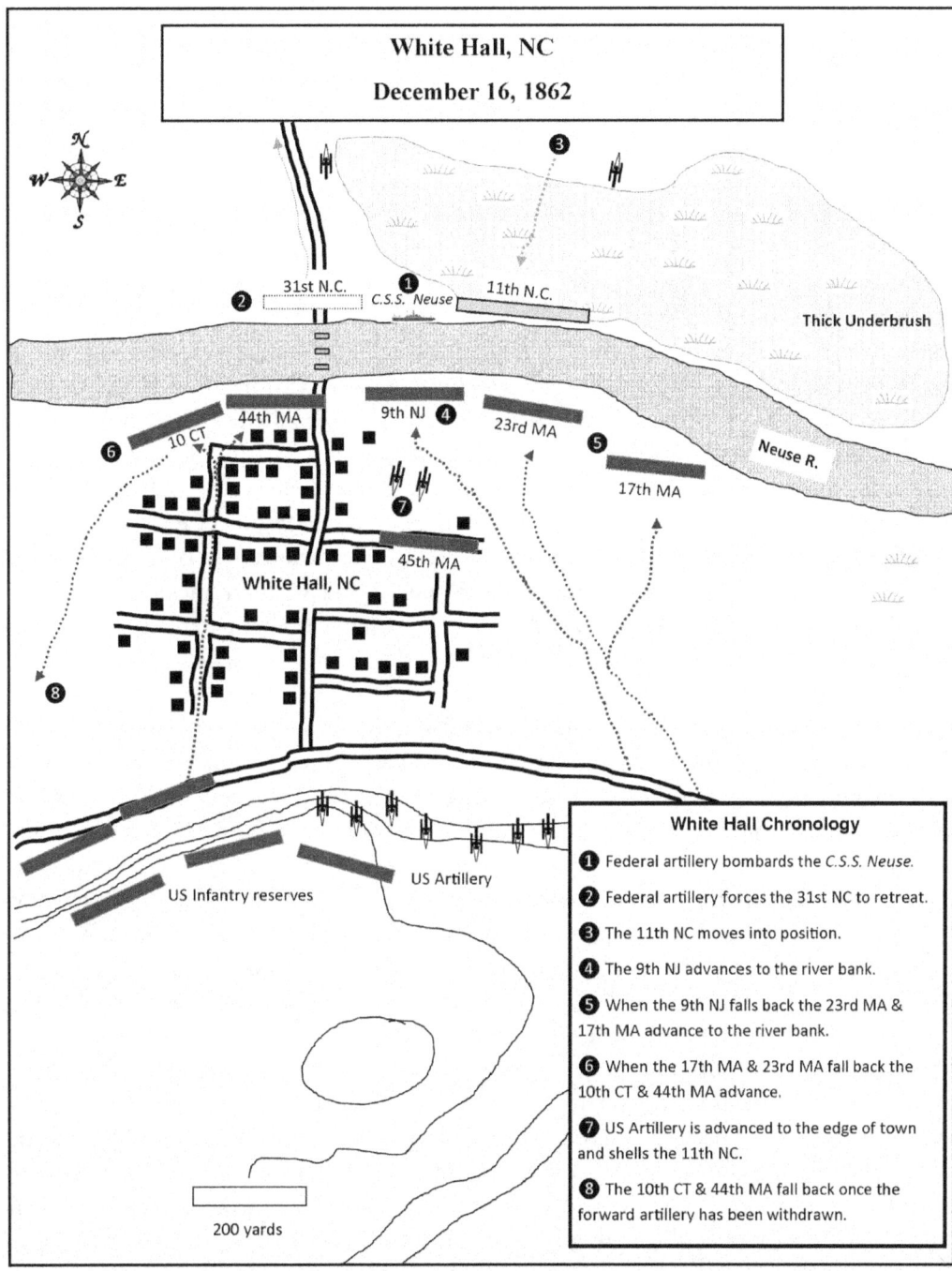

Foster sent forward the 23rd Massachusetts and the 17th Massachusetts, two units totaling nearly 1,300 soldiers. They marched down from the heights behind the town and onto the open fields east of the burned bridge, the 17th MA on the right and the 23rd MA, the left. The Tar Heels opened fire on these new targets. Major John Chambers (23rd MA) recorded, "My regiment was ... ordered forward. I marched it through a small swamp under heavy fire and came to the edge of the river.... [T]he enemy were on the opposite bank, secreted behind trees and stumps."[37] An officer in the 17th MA wrote, "The Seventeenth was ordered down to the river bank ... and got into a hornet's nest." He also remarked, "[Their] bullets made the air vocal with their insinuating whizzing."[38] Both Federal regiments fired volleys into the Eleventh's positions. Corporal Lewis Warlick (Co. B) noted, "The only thing that saved us from all being killed was the heaps of logs on the river bank."[39]

The fight between the two Massachusetts formations and the lone Carolina regiment continued for another thirty minutes before both Northern commanders saw no point in remaining: they were not going to be able to cross the river, and they were standing out in the open taking a beating from a concealed enemy. One wrote, "I think [we] must have [wasted] a great deal of lead."[40] But not all their shooting was in vain. Seventeen-year-old Pvt. James Gault (Co. I) was killed, and so was Pvt. Walter Duckworth (Co. B).[41] Corporal Lewis Warlick (Co. B) wrote, "When Walter Duckworth was killed he fell over Pinks [A. Pinkney Warlick (Co. B)] leg and bled a considerable amount.... [P]oor fellow was shot in the head."[42] Colonel Leventhorpe's riflemen were much more effective; the 17th MA suffered 44 casualties.[43] The 17th MA was ordered to withdraw, and the regiment fell back to a protected position where the men were ordered to lie down. Meanwhile, their Bay State brothers on their left were also being hammered by the Bethel Regiment's marksmen. Major Chambers (23rd MA) recorded, "We continued until we had expended about 40 rounds of ammunition, when we were ordered out."[44] The 23rd MA slipped out of danger, having lost 16.[45]

General Foster still wouldn't give up on his desire to secure the bridgehead; he moved forward the 10th Connecticut, the 44th MA, and 45th MA, another 1,600 Union infantrymen, using them to protect several batteries of artillery, which he ordered to advance to blank-point range. Lieutenant Col. Robert Leggett (10th CT) reported, "We formed line of battle and advanced to the river on the left of the bridge."[46] The 44th MA stepped forward, to the right of the 10th CT. A Bay Stater in the 44th MA wrote, "We marched through the open wood, receiving a heavy fire on our flank ... and formed line along a rail fence at the edge of the woods bordering the river."[47] Both regiments were a distance downriver from the Tar Heels, forcing their riflemen to aim at the right-oblique. The Massachusetts officer noted, "We received the fire [from] .... the sharpshooters who were posted in the trees across the river, but with little opportunity ourselves to make any effective return."[48]

Meanwhile, the 45th MA marched forward to the right of the road, its task to cover the same field of fire protected by the 17th MA and 9th New Jersey. But their commander was not about to sacrifice his men needlessly. Colonel Charles Codman (45th MA) wrote, "This regiment was ordered .... to form upon the White Hall road ... [and] the men were directed to lie down."[49] There were now three Federal regiments arrayed against the 11th North Carolina, masking the Yank artillery shifting into position.

Captain Edwin Jenney's gun crews (3rd NY Light Artillery) rolled their cannon to within 200 yards of Leventhorpe's men and began blasting the Carolinians. A Federal, watching the Union shells tear into the Confederates' protections, noted, "The wooded bank of the river ... was ... becoming dangerous from the fire of our artillery, which ripped through the trees and drove the splinters about in all directions."[50] Corporal Lewis Warlick (Co. B), on the receiving end of this bombardment, recalled, "I was behind a big stump on my knees ... and a cannon ball went into the root of it, which made the dirt and chips fly."[51] There was nothing Col. Leventhorpe's men could do about the Union artillery except keep their heads down and wait out this metal storm. His riflemen held their ground and would not be budged. The Union gunners trained their cannon on the trees above them. Private John Warlick (Co. I) groused, "The artillerymen began shooting off the cypress trees midway to the tops, thinking they could kill or scare us out."[52]

Finally, after another hour of furious shelling the Union batteries lessened their fire and pulled back. Captain Jenney (3rd NY Light Artillery) recorded, "I kept up a continuous fire until my ammunition was exhausted, when I retired." He then reported, "Six men wounded and 8 horses killed."[53] And Col. Ledlie (3rd NY Light Artillery) wrote, "The action terminated a little after 12." Colonel Ledlie totaled up his artillery's losses, noting 21 casualties and "loss in horses very heavy."[54]

General John Foster, realizing his troops were not able to force their way across the Neuse River, ordered his infantry to pull back. The 45th MA slipped away, taking twenty casualties with them.[55] The 10th CT followed soon after, leaving the Neuse River's southern bank, as did the 44th MA, its troops carrying away 21 casualties. A Carolinian wrote triumphantly, "Our troops cleared the river bank of the enemy."[56] Corporal Lewis Warlick (Co. B) scribbled to his girl, "The old Bethel stood its ground and the Yanks had to skedaddle with a considerable loss."[57] General Foster posted an infantry company among White Hall's houses and they occasionally fired at the Southerners, preventing them from crossing the river. Foster remarked, "A few sharpshooters were left behind to keep the Confederates occupied." He then ordered his army to shift towards the west, following the road along the southern flank of the Neuse River. Foster wrote about the day's fighting: "After making a strong feint as if to rebuild the bridge and cross the Neuse River [I] moved on towards Goldsboro."[58]

Brigadier General Beverly Robertson was pleased with the Eleventh's performance,

White Hall, North Carolina, facing towards the north. The bridge has been destroyed (North Carolina Collection, University of North Carolina at Chapel Hill, Chapel Hill Library).

writing, "The conduct of this regiment reflects the greatest credit upon its accomplished and dauntless commander." He continued his praise, describing the Bethel Regiment's commander: "The soldierly qualities displayed by Colonel Leventhorpe on the march and during the action, to which I can bear witness, strongly recommend him to the favorable consideration of the authorities."[59] Later that night, the men gathered around campfires, and once the battle-weary Tar Heels had calmed down and buried their dead, they talked about what had taken place. Later, many wrote home. One shaken soldier wrote to his girl: "They throw[e]d bums [sic] all around us and I tell you they shuck [sic] the ground and I thought at that time I would never see you again."[60] Corporal Lewis Warlick (Co. B), also stunned by the Yank artillery fire, wrote, "Leventhorpe [said] ... that we never would be exposed to such another fire during the war."[61]

While the exhausted Tar Heels bedded down for the night, one rifleman, 16-year-old Lambert Bristol (Co. B), wrestled with his emotions as he gazed at his elder brother's watch. Lambert Bristol's brother, 1st Sgt. Elam Bristol (Co. B), a 20-year-old college student from Morganton, had been buried that evening. The distraught young man wrote his mother: "You don't know how much I miss Elam. I hope he is in a better world than this."[62] First Sergeant Elam Bristol was one of seven Carolinians killed that day, along with 27 wounded.[63] The Federals suffered nearly 150 casualties.[64]

Chapter 5

The 11th North Carolina Joins Pettigrew's Brigade

Colonel Collett Leventhorpe led his regiment back to New Bern, North Carolina, the men shaken and quiet, stunned by the effect of burying their comrades killed at White Hall. That battle had been their first real fight and many of the Carolinians were shocked by the ghastly violence steel and lead could do to their friends and neighbors. A battle-weary young man wrote his family, "A batel [sic] is much harder than I thought.... I cannot tell what a soldier has to go through and ... if I get back home again I never will."[1]

Once they returned Col. Leventhorpe put his Carolinians right back to work, having them prepare winter quarters and continuing their school of the soldier. He also dealt with the personnel changes caused by White Hall's casualties. Lieutenant William Means' (Co. E) death meant his company needed a new second lieutenant. The company's third lieutenant, 22-year-old William Rozzell, was promoted to fill Means' position, and 22-year-old Sgt. William Turner was jumped up to take Rozzell's old slot.[2] In Company B, with the death of 1st Sgt. Elam Bristol, the 21-year-old student from Morganton, Sgt. George Phifer Erwin, was promoted.[3] And to fill Erwin's shoes, Cpl. Lewis Warlick was awarded sergeant's stripes. The newly minted sergeant wrote his girl: "Phifer Erwin has been promoted to Orderly [Sergeant] and I to 3rd Sergeant."[4]

A few days later, on December 22, 1862, the Bethel Regiment was ordered to travel to Weldon, North Carolina. The Tar Heels packed up their gear and marched to Kingston, where a train awaited them. The regiment climbed onto the cars and then sat in frustration because the train never left the station. Eventually Col. Leventhorpe discovered another train blocked his regiment's passage. He pressured that train's engineers to move, but when it did, the 11th NC's train collided with another. Sergeant Lewis Warlick (Co. B) wrote, "Crash went our engine into the [train] lifting the rear car on top of the engine, carrying away the smoke stack and running back nearly as far as the tender before we stopped."[5] Fortunately, none of the soldiers were injured, though the Carolinians spent the rest of the night cleaning up the mess. The next day another engine was attached to the troop cars and they hauled the regiment to Weldon.

Colonel Leventhorpe's staff set up the 11th North Carolina's camp, as he met with his superiors and was informed his Bethel Regiment had been assigned to the brigade commanded by Brig. Gen. James J. Pettigrew.[6] This brigade consisted of the 11th NC, 26th NC (Col. Burgwyn), 44th NC (Col. Singletary), 47th NC (Col. Rogers), and the 52nd NC (Col. James Marshall), a force totaling over 4,000. Collett Leventhorpe met with his new commander and came away impressed. Leventhorpe wrote, "By every account, he is one of the most brilliant men of the day."[7]

Brig. Gen. James J. Pettigrew was 34 when the 11th NC joined his brigade (Library of Congress).

James Johnston Pettigrew was 34 years old, the son of a wealthy Tyrrell County, North Carolina, planter. Pettigrew had entered the University of North Carolina at Chapel Hill when he was fourteen and graduated four years later as valedictorian. He then was appointed professor at the United States Naval Observatory by President James Polk, who had attended the graduation ceremony and was impressed by Pettigrew's valedictory address. Pettigrew served for eight months at the Naval Observatory, where, as a reporter recorded, "his reputation for ability and extraordinary proficiency, especially in the severe Mathematical Sciences, was fully sustained."[8] Then James Pettigrew resigned and began studying law. Following his passing the bar, he traveled to Europe and lived there for several years, studying civil law at the University of Berlin.[9] He learned to speak French, German, Spanish, Italian, Hebrew, and Arabic. He also published several books before returning to the States, where he served in the South Carolina house of representatives, and became distinguished for his speech against reopening the African slave trade.[10] Pettigrew was not reelected following this speech, and in 1859 he returned to Italy and offered his services to the Italians in their struggle against the Austrians.[11]

When James Pettigrew returned from Italy he became the chief military aid to South Carolina's governor. But when shells began to fly at Ft. Sumter, he volunteered his services as a rifleman in the Hampton Legion. Pettigrew was quickly commissioned colonel of the 22nd NC Infantry. He took his Tar Heel regiment to Richmond to help build the city's defenses, and immediately impressed President Jefferson Davis, who recommended him for promotion to brigadier general. The unpretentious colonel turned down the honor, replying, "Not yet. Too many men are ahead of me who have earned their promotion in the field. I will come after them, not before. So far I have done nothing to merit reward."[12] One of Pettigrew's Richmond ladyfriends, Mary Chestnut, wrote, "Modest merits just now [are] at a premium."[13]

The needs of the Confederate army overrode Pettigrew's concerns and he was promoted to brigadier general in March 1862, taking command of a brigade composed of volunteers from North Carolina, Arkansas, Georgia, and Virginia. He trained his riflemen and they went into the battle at Seven Pines. Pettigrew was severely wounded within the first few minutes of the fight when "a rifle ball sliced through his throat and shoulder."[14] His brigade was driven backwards, Pettigrew was left behind, and in the confusion that followed he was injured again by a Union soldier who bayonetted him in the leg. The badly wounded officer was captured and taken to the home of a Gaines's Mill doctor, who nursed him back to health. Eventually, he was sent to the prison at Ft. Delaware, near Baltimore. Pettigrew was confined as a prisoner for two months, during which time he requested that his rank be reduced so that he could be more easily exchanged.[15]

James Pettigrew was exchanged in August 1862 and clamored to be returned to his brigade, but Brig. Gen. William Pender had commanded the formation through all the summer's battles and had earned the right to keep his position. Pettigrew was given command of a Tar Heel brigade consisting of the 44th NC, 47th NC, and 52nd NC. Not long after this, the 26th NC was added to Pettigrew's command, and finally, on December 22, 1862, the Bethel Regiment was attached.[16] Sergeant Lewis Warlick (Co. B), following his first sighting of the regiment's new general, was not as impressed as Col. Leventhorpe. Warlick simply noted, "We have been brigaded ... under the command of Gen. Pettigrew, he had us out on brigade review yesterday."[17]

General Pettigrew's brigade wintered near Weldon, North Carolina, the Carolinian volunteers enduring the season's cold temperatures and heavy rains sheltered in tents or canvas-covered log huts. Private William Elliott (Co. A) growled, "It is the coldest weather out here I ever felt.... I haven't got two hours sleep in the past two nights."[18] Sergeant Lewis Warlick (Co. B) wrote, "We haven't got our tents yet ... [because] they went to Goldsboro and are there yet. We have little huts made of split logs and dirt, something like a potato house."[19] Private Peter Dellinger (Co. I) wrote of his privations: "I must tell you something about camp life. Well ... [it] is a harde life ... [and] we have to suffer a grate deal of colde."[20] Another soldier recorded, "I was ordered on picket duty about a mile and a half from camp.... It was raining ... and it rained without intermission all night."[21] Sergeant Lewis Warlick (Co. B) remarked, "It is so cold I can't write away from the fire and when I go to the fire it smokes me so I can't [see]."[22] Another unhappy Tar Heel noted, "We just had to stand up and take it."[23]

The young men wrote home constantly and their letters were concerned primarily with three subjects: food, clothing, and furloughs.[24] The Carolinians might have been filled with patriotism for their cause; however the Confederate government was not effective in supporting its citizen-soldiers. One Tar Heel complained, "Rations are scarce. A small slice of beef and a few hard crackers for a days' rations and many a man ate all they drew at once."[25] Another grumbled, "We took snow, put it in our kettles, and made coffee. When I say coffee I mean Confederate coffee—parched corn."[26] This shortage of food forced the young men to forage for themselves. One enterprising volunteer found a way to benefit from this problem. He wrote his wife: "I want you to send some pies and butter ... [as] small pies sells at a dollar a piece and apples 25 cents a piece."[27] But for most of the men, rations were short. Sergeant Lewis Warlick (Co. B) succinctly summed up their problem, recording, "got nothing but hard bread and raw bacon."[28]

While food shortages plagued the Carolinians, the men also were dogged by inadequate clothing. Private Dellinger (Co. I) recorded, "None of us has any overcoats ... [so] we rap [*sic*] up in our blankets and do the best we can."[29] He continued: "I want you to ... send me them socks and sewing thread."[30] Private William Elliott (Co. A) wrote to his parents, "I want you to send me a good woolen pair of pants and a good piece of hard soap and some thread and a couple of needles."[31] William Elliott also added, "I want two pare of socks for some rascal stole [mine]."[32] Another soldier, luckier than Dellinger or Elliott, thanked his girl, writing, "[Y]ou ... fulfilled your promise—to make me a pair of stockings.... The socks are not only a very handsome present but a useful present."[33] Sergeant Lewis Warlick (Co. B) remarked, "Was three nights without blankets."[34] And Private Peter Dellinger (Co. I) noted, "Most of us has nearly worn out shoos."[35]

These privations ate at the young men's resolve, and since the war seemed to be on hold for the winter, they pleaded to be able to visit their families at home. Colonel Leventhorpe attempted to satisfy their petitions, causing Sgt. Lewis Warlick (Co. B) to express the emotion everyone in the regiment felt when he wrote, "There is great excitement in camps now about furloughs, arose from the fact that there was an order for each company to furlough one man out of every twenty-five."[36] Private William Elliott (Co. A) wrote, "We have to draw tickets, it is like the lottery—uncertain."[37] The homesick Pvt. Peter Dellinger (Co. I) remarked, "I would love to come home but I donte recon [*sic*] I will get to come."[38] Another lovesick young man penned his love, "I had much rather see you now than any body on the earth."[39] These Carolina volunteers suffered through their miseries, hopeful for the chance to earn a furlough and making the best of their situation, but as one wrote, "I do not like camp life.... [W]e have lively times occasionally but it is counterbalanced by poor times."[40]

Some of the Carolinians could not tolerate these continual deprivations and took matters into their own hands—and deserted. Private William Elliott (Co. A) recorded, "I think ... [many are] getting tired of the army [al]ready."[41] Though the 11th NC had a number of runaways, the Bethel Regiment was not as badly affected by desertion as some of the other formations in Pettigrew's Brigade. The AWOL calamity reached crisis levels, forcing Gen. Pettigrew to smash down on the men with a heavy fist by ordering whippings. One Tar Heel recorded, "Yesterday Private D.B. Thompson ... received 39 lashes on his bare back in the presence of the brigade for desertion."[42] Unfortunately, floggings did not curtail the desertions, driving Pettigrew to increase the penalty—deserters could be shot. The horrified Carolinians were forced to witness an execution, a deed impressing many. Private Frederick Dellinger (Co. I) wrote, "We have to witness a powerful thing tomorrow in our brigade. There's a man to be shot ... and the whole brigade has to see it."[43] Sergeant Lewis Warlick (Co. B) also wrote about the incident: "Tomorrow our brigade will be ordered out to witness the execution by shooting of a member of the 26th N.C. for desertion. I understand there has been about 50 desertions in that regiment, perhaps by shooting one now ... it will put a stop to their leaving."[44] The deserter was "ordered to kneel while blindfolded beside his freshly dug grave. The firing squad was at 'ready' when a pardon ... arrived."[45] Warlick noted, "[T]o the satisfaction of the assembly he was relieved by the commanding general."[46]

Amid all these difficulties, a final difficulty afflicted the Tar Heels in Pettigrew's Brigade—smallpox. The first cases of this disease appeared at the end of December 1862 and the sickness quickly spread. Colonel Collett Leventhorpe realized the disease's focal point was the town of Weldon, North Carolina, and he ordered his soldiers to stay away, writing, "All intercourse with that place ... is positively interdicted." The ex-physician also noted, "Those men selected for ... duties [at Weldon] must ... be vaccinat[ed]."[47] Collett Leventhorpe then ordered his regiment's medical staff to immunize everyone under his command. Sergeant William Parker (Co. C), once he recovered from his inoculation, wrote his wife: "I send you a scab I took off a man's arm. Take a lancet or knife and make a hole in the arm and put a piece of the scab in [it]."[48] Sadly, a handful of Leventhorpe's Tar Heels died; one of these victims, Sgt. William Hoggard (Co. C), was vaccinated with a syringe and developed erysipelas. He died within a few days.[49] Hoggard was buried in a small cemetery along with Pvt. Eli Goodwin (Co. F), Pvt. Ezekiel Ratchford (Co. A), Pvt. William Cates (Co. G), and Pvt. William Bazemore (Co. C), all casualties of smallpox.[50] In some of the other regiments the numbers of those killed by smallpox was so high that record keeping became muddled, causing painful confusion among the soldiers' families. One distraught woman, having not heard from her husband for some time and tortured by rumors of his death, wrote his commanding officer. The Carolinian lieutenant sadly replied, "As you requested me to write you about your dear husband.... I am sorry to inform you that he is certainly dead."[51]

The Confederate high command, struggling to support the Carolinian troops through all of these problems, nonchalantly recorded, "It was a rigorous winter."[52] Meanwhile, Col. Collett Leventhorpe kept his volunteers busy with daily fatigue duties and constant drill, in addition to the frequent brigade dress parades. Leventhorpe required his company commanders to drill their men several hours each day, both in close-order drill and in skirmish drill. He detached Pvt. Duncan Waddell from Company G and made the 18-year-old Chapel Hill student the regiment's skirmish drillmaster.[53] Sergeant Lewis Warlick (Co. B) recorded in one of his letters to his sweetheart, "I will quit [now] and go on drill as the company is now called out for skirmish drill."[54] The Burke County NCO also observed, "There was quite a large turnout of ladies at dress parade last evening."[55]

Leventhorpe's relentless drilling of his men molded them into an efficient-moving formation that easily performed the most complicated battalion maneuvers. His volunteers knew they were good, and this knowledge gave them great pride in their accomplishments. Sergeant Lewis Warlick (Co. B) wrote, "We have the praise of being the best drilled regiment in the service, which makes us feel proud."[56] Colonel Leventhorpe even admitted his troops were good, writing, "There is no doubt this is the best drilled Regt.... I am glad to be able to say it. Yesterday I drilled them and they moved like regulars. Their manual of arms is the admiration of everyone who sees it."[57] Brigadier General James Pettigrew was fond of regimental drill competitions; however, following complaints from the colonels of the other formations, he eventually barred Leventhorpe's boys from contending.[58]

On January 18, 1863, the 11th North Carolina was ordered to move to Magnolia, North Carolina, a town about halfway between Goldsboro and Wilmington, news which angered the enlisted men. Private William Elliott (Co. A) grumbled, "We have to deliver up our tents this morning and then we will have to lie out like hogs."[59] Lieutenant Lemuel Hoyle (Co. I) growled, "I knew it.... I told you when you commenced building that chimney you'd have to move…. It won't do for soldiers to fix up so well, for they're bound to move."⁶⁰ The regiment arrived in Magnolia two days later at 3:30 a.m.⁶¹ The Tar Heels quickly prepared to defend against a Yank advance, with Col. Leventhorpe writing, "My Regiment is in … fine spirits, and if they are called on, they will make their mark once more."⁶² Soon, though, they learned the bluecoats' movements were nothing more than rumors. The Bethel Regiment settled in near Magnolia, with little for the men to do. Bored, a number of soldiers snuck out of camp and bothered the citizens of Magnolia, forcing Gen. Pettigrew to issue an order "establish[ing] a camp guard sufficiently large to see … [that] no enlisted man will be allowed to leave camp."⁶³ Sergeant Lewis Warlick (Co. B), shrugging off the confinement, wrote, "We amuse ourselves now-a-days by playing [base]ball."⁶⁴

The weather turned extremely cold and the Tar Heels were buried by a heavy snowfall. One Carolinian, unfortunately caught out on picket duty during the storm, wrote, "It is very cold, snow nine inches deep…. We marched eight miles without resting. We then fixed our bed in the snow and stole fodder for a bed and rails to make a fire."⁶⁵

One of the Bethel Regiment's officers, Lt. Col. William Martin, did not suffer during this cold snap; instead, his days were filled with warmth. Martin, a widow and thus highly sought-after bachelor, had met a young woman in Wilmington when the regiment was at Camp Davis. Letitia Costin was 21 years old and the daughter of Miles Costin, a wealthy import-export merchant. Miles Costin had entertained at his home such notables as Daniel Webster and President Millard Fillmore, and when he invited Collett Leventhorpe and William Martin to visit, the eligible bachelor and Costin's young daughter became close friends.⁶⁶ William Martin and Letitia Costin were married February 9, 1863, and the next day he brought his young bride to the Eleventh's camp at Magnolia for a celebration. A regimental historian recorded, "The regiment threw a gala ball to honor the couple … [where] the regimental band played waltzes and lively polkas [and] the gallant soldiers and local ladies danced until four the next morning."⁶⁷ Sergeant William Parker (Co. C) described the party's aftermath: "[The officers] … looked worse than our gard did. I think they must be very stiff."⁶⁸

Twenty-one-year-old Letitia Costin married Lt. Col. William Martin in February 1863 (courtesy Davidson College Archives).

Two weeks later, on February 22, 1862, Gen. Pettigrew directed his brigade to travel to Tarboro, North Carolina, some ninety miles north of Magnolia. Pettigrew could not get rail transport for his troops, so the Tar Heels had to march. Private William Elliott (Co. A) wrote, "We left Magnolia … and after two days marching we got … [to] Dudley Station, 8 miles from Goldsboro."⁶⁹ Once at the station, the weary infantrymen loaded onto trains and traveled to Tarboro. Elliott described what happened next: "We got off then and we had to march 8 miles below Tarboro. We are stationed out in the old field[.] We have no tents with us and it has been raining five days."[70]

The brigade marched southwards beneath sullen, rainy skies, the soaked Carolinians grinding out mile after mile until reaching a campsite along the Tar River, just outside Greenville, North Carolina. Private William Elliott (Co. A) penned his father, "We had to march 32 miles in two days. It rains nearly all the time.... I am nearly drouned [sic]."[71] Sergeant William Parker (Co. C) remarked, "I have march[ed] as hard as I ever marched and my feet is sore ... both is blistered."[72] The tired soldiers then received news their efforts were wasted; Pettigrew's anticipated campaign had been canceled.

As the footsore Tar Heels rested Brig. Gen. James Pettigrew received orders to shift his force eastward and attack the Union forces in the New Bern area. Pettigrew gave his brigade orders to march on March 9, 1863, but commanded Col. Leventhorpe to keep the Bethel Regiment at Greenville to protect the city. Collett Leventhorpe, unhappy his men were not going to be involved in action against the Federals, grumbled. He struggled with this slight, along with the Confederate high command's refusal to reward him with a promotion; after all, there were a number of officers who had been junior to him now wearing general's stars. An irritated Leventhorpe wrote, "I feel very keenly the injustice done me about promotion. I am always given posts of danger and the command of brigades but the honors are reserved for others."[73] Regardless of his frustrations, Col. Leventhorpe put his troops to work augmenting the defenses around Greenville. His riflemen, now veterans with axe, pick, and shovel, were becoming adept at constructing earthworks. Leventhorpe recorded, "I am fortifying down river ... and shall get the work done this week."[74]

Pettigrew and his four regiments slopped their way through muddy swamps and attempted to capture the Union position at New Bern. The weather, terrain, and stiff Federal opposition forced Pettigrew to back off. After suffering two dozen casualties he withdrew and wrote off his campaign as a failure.[75] Pettigrew's soldiers then shuffled back to Kinston, North Carolina.

On March 15, 1863, Col. Leventhorpe's regiment was ordered to capture Plymouth, North Carolina, some sixty miles to the northeast. He led the Bethel battalion away from its entrenchments, following a troop of Virginia cavalry. Leventhorpe's men hiked only a few miles before bogging down in the low swamp country. A Confederate remarked, "Our march today has been the wateriest I ever knew, the mud and slush being rarely shallow enough for us to see our shoes."[76] A Virginian cavalryman wrote, "Our route lay through a vast wilderness ... [and] the narrow road has been chopped out—resembling a deep canal."[77] William Elliott (Co. A), not wanting to lose his brogans in the deep mud, noted, "I march [with] my shoos [off]."[78]

The next day, conditions remained dismal. The Virginia horseman complained, "Worse, worser, worsest! Rain still falling, water still rising; land still sinking!" He continued, griping, "Today we had done little else than wade ... long columns of men, wading in water nearly to their arm-pits, holding their firearms above their heads."[79] Regardless of their difficulties, on March 18, 1863, the dog-tired Tar Heels bivouacked only a mile from Plymouth. The Virginia cavalry skirmished with Union outposts, and artillery was brought up to shell the Federal works. Colonel Leventhorpe's exhausted men seemed surprised to have actually reached their destination. Private William Elliott (Co. A) remarked, "We had a hard time of it for it rained three days and nights on us and we had no place to shelter. We had to wade [through] mud and water ... sometimes the water was waste [sic] deep."[80] Another waterlogged and sapped Tar Heel, Pvt. Henry Hill (Co. A), grumbled, "We ... have had to wade creeks and branches for three days and we are all broke down."[81]

The Yanks, now aware a Confederate force was nearby, hid within the earthworks protecting Plymouth. Colonel Leventhorpe posted his men to watch the bluecoats, but he refused to make a frontal assault against a fortified position. Meanwhile, Confederate quartermasters filled the formation's wagons with corn and pork. The Virginian cavalryman recorded, "We [got] three months' supplies ... 600 bushels of corn and ... 1000 pounds of hog-meat."[82]

The weather turned colder, but at least the rain ceased. The miserable Carolinians built fires and tried to dry out their clothing. Then, on March 21, 1863, a storm roared over the wretched soldiers, with wind-driven rain and the next day hail and snow. A despondent Confederate wrote, "Ground white with hail, our hands and feet red with cold.... I spent two nights seated at the root of a tree ... wrapped in my blanket, cross, cold, and miserable."[83] That afternoon the glum soldiers were ordered to march; they formed into a column and began the long slog to the west. They fought their way back through the swampy land and struggled into Greenville three days later. Colonel Leventhorpe's soldiers were exhausted and woeful, and many were sick, but the Confederate high command was ecstatic. The entire haul of forage astounded the officers. Sergeant William Parker (Co. C) recorded, "100,000 pounds of bacon [gathered]."[84] Colonel Leventhorpe was horrified at the reaction of his region's overall commander, Maj. Gen. Daniel Hill, to the expedition. The Confederate railed in anger, "The authorities are so pleased with the results that they are organizing an expedition to repeat the process."[85] Shuddering at the thought of slogging back through more swamps, Leventhorpe agreed with one of his Tar Heels who wrote, "I am getting tired of Eastern NC. I had Rather be any whear [sic] Els [sic]."[86] One soldier recorded, "There are some changes and movements on hand, but of what character or importance remains among the impenetrable secrets of our Generals."[87]

Soon, orders arrived; the Carolinians were commanded to take part in a campaign to capture the town of Washington, North Carolina, a prominent city resting on the banks of the Pamlico River. Washington boasted nearly 4,000 citizens, as well as a number of important wharfs and warehouses. The town had been described as "a flourishing place ... situated on the head of the Pamlico Sound, at the mouth of the Tar River.... It drives a smart trade in the staples of the State—turpentine, cotton, and lumber."[88] It was a pretty town, with "modest white wooden houses ... a few steeples peering out from a thick grove ... [and] at the end of the main street ... the principal hotel ... with beautifully-improved grounds."[89]

Federal troops occupied the town, having moved in with sixteen companies of infantry, an artillery battery, and a small contingent of cavalry, a total of 1,200 soldiers.[90] The Confederate high command felt a combined force of infantry and artillery could capture the town, as well as the Yank soldiers and the fortifications they had constructed. The roads between Greenville and Washington were decent; the gray column covered the thirty miles

Washington, North Carolina, in April 1863, from *Frank Leslie's Illustrated Newspaper*, 16 May 1863 (North Carolina Collection, Uiversity of North Carolina at Chapel Hill Library).

and reached Washington's outskirts in two days. Colonel Collett Leventhorpe recorded on April 2, 1863, "[We are] bivouac[ked] at a camp 4 miles below Washington, N.C."[91]

Major General Daniel Hill shifted his regiments to conquer the town, quickly taking the heights above the southern banks of the Tar River. He posted men from the 26th NC to hold the gun emplacements at Rodman's Point. More Tar Heels swarmed along the southern shores of the Pamlico River, filling another battery's fortifications at Hill's Points. Cannon were hauled into these two positions, allowing the Southerners to shell the town's works and control any boat movement on the Pamlico River. More Confederate troops approached Washington from the north, encircling the Union position. Small skirmishes broke out, but the Confederate leadership felt no desire to make infantry assaults against the Northerners' entrenchments. General Hill decided to besiege the position, knowing his forces could prevent any provisions or reinforcements from reaching Washington.[92] One Confederate wrote, "We now have Washington surrounded, and old Hill says he can take the place without the loss of a man."[93]

Colonel Leventhorpe, with his 700 Tar Heels and 500 men from the 26th NC, was assigned the task of blocking the two main roads leading into Washington from the south. Knowing that Union reinforcements were stationed at New Bern, barely 35 miles away, Leventhorpe sent the 26th NC to guard the New Bern-Washington road at the Swift Creek river crossing. He then positioned his Carolinians to shield the Confederates should Union forces be transported by ship and landed so as to make an attack along the southern region of the Pamlico River. Leventhorpe ordered his soldiers to dig in on the west bank of Blount's Creek. He recorded, "I have command of the lowest point, with 2 Regts. and artillery.... I am at Blount's Creek Mill Bridge 11 miles below Washington, to keep off reinforcements from New Bern."[94]

The Bethel boys went to work creating entrenchments. The men were now experienced at this task, and their successes at White Hall and along the Blackwater River had taught them the value of their labors. A Carolinian rifleman scribbled to his wife, "We have been working day and night on breast works. We have gotten this place tolobly [sic] well fortified."[95] The 11th's fortifications were "dug in the ground and partly thrown up."[96] The Bethel Regiment's flanks were protected by the terrain—to the south—a deeply congested swamp—and to the north, a thick forest and the widening of Blount's Creek which required water-

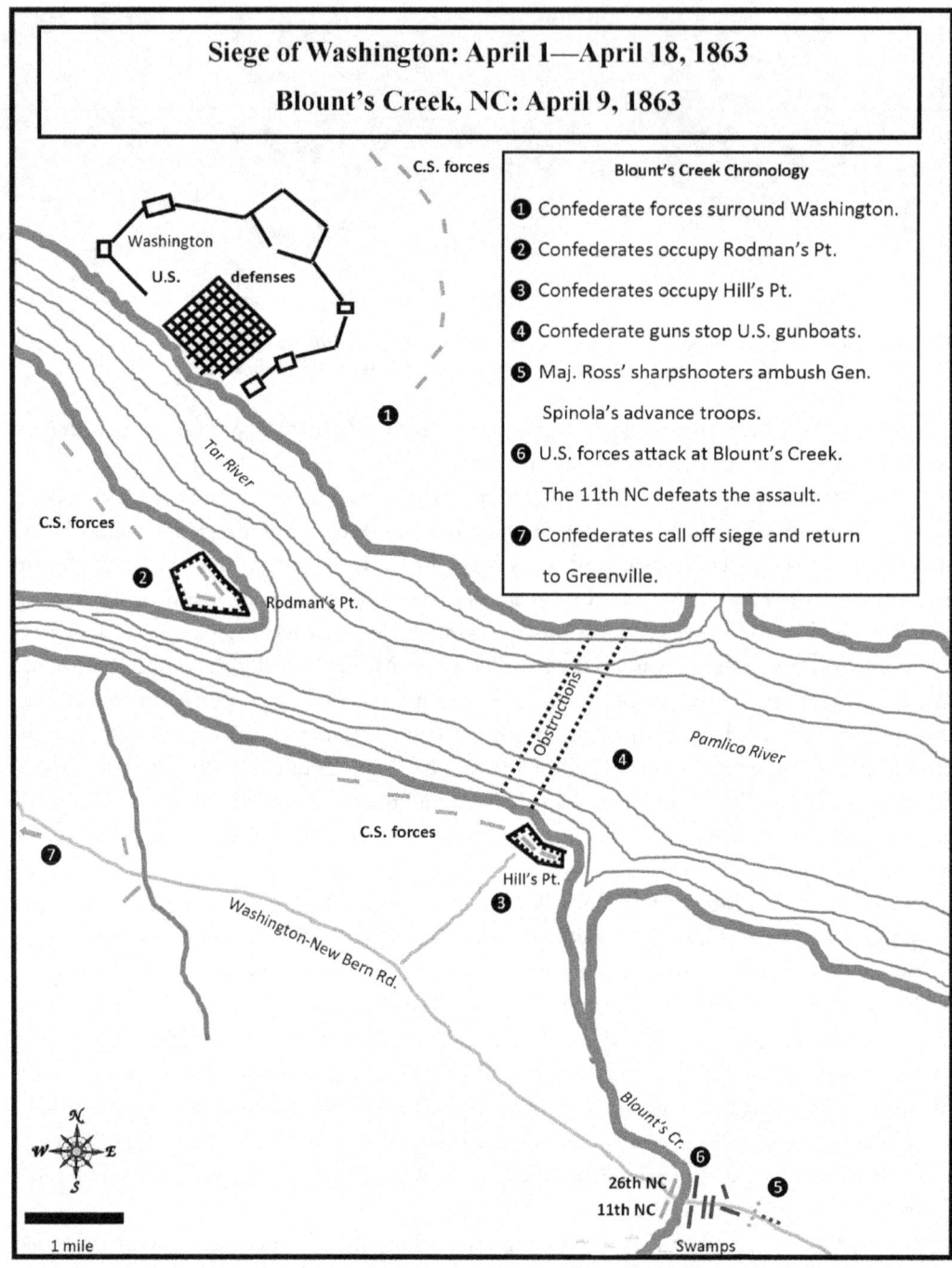

craft for crossings. A bridge spanned the creek in front of Leventhorpe's riflemen. He directed his men to disable the bridge rather than destroy it; his Tar Heels removed the planks, thus restricting passage. Carolinian details could cross single file, but no attacking force would be able to use the bridge. Leventhorpe was pleased with their situation, noting, "The position is better than White Hall."[97]

The soldiers could hear the artillery rumbling from batteries along the Pamlico River. The Confederates at Rodman's Point bombarded the Union positions around Washington daily, and the Northerners returned fire. Neither side's artillery had much military effect, though many of Washington's houses were damaged. One of the town's citizens wrote, "The firing began at dawn and ended at sunset." This woman continued, "A cannon ball crash[ed] through the front of the house, into the bedroom and scarcely missing [my] ... three year [son] before passing through the back wall and landing in the backyard."[98]

Federal gunships attempted to run past the Confederate batteries, an extremely difficult undertaking, as the Southern guns easily controlled the river with accurate fire and a barrier had been placed across the Pamlico River. A Northern officer reported, "The barricade consists of a double row of piles cut off two feet under water." The Federal noted, "Our vessels made a passage through it 60 feet wide, and marked it with buoys [but] the enemy destroyed the buoys."[99] Everyone realized Union ships trying to reach Washington could not do so without considerable danger. However, on April 1, 1863, the gunship *Commodore Hill* attempted to run past the batteries. The ship was struck 89 times before running aground.[100]

Colonel Leventhorpe's men waited impatiently behind their entrenchments, bothered by an early-season heatwave, flies and mosquitoes, and the tension of not knowing when they would be required to place themselves in danger. Private William Elliott (Co. A) wrote his parents: "Our artillery men has been shooting at the gun boats all the time."[101] Sergeant Lewis Warlick (Co. B) remarked, "We do nothing here.... I can form no ideas as to whether there will be a big battle."[102] The regiment's riflemen, not privy to what was taking place just a few miles away, wallowed in the heat, and as Pvt. Elliott (Co. A) noted, "We have been expecting a fight every day but we have not got in it yet."[103]

The Federal gunboat *Ceres* ran past the batteries on April 4, 1863, taking many hits but not being seriously damaged. It was able to deliver a supply of ammunition to the besieged defenders. The next day Federal soldiers were escorted by the *Ceres* in an attack upon Rodman's point. The Confederate guns pounded the *Ceres* until it ran aground, thwarting the assault.[104] General Hill ordered his artillery to increase their bombardment of Washington's defenses. First Sergeant George Erwin (Co. B) noted, "Firing has been going on all the time except at night." He also expressed his worry that the siege was taking too long, writing; "Nothing in the world could be gained by delay.... More gunboats and Yankees [can] ... be expected if we wait."[105]

Sergeant Erwin's concerns proved correct, Federal forces were being readied into a relief force at New Bern. Two brigades of infantry, plus artillery and cavalry, over 7,000 troops were organized under the command of Brig. Gen. Francis Spinola.[106] He wrote, "It is my intention to ... engage the enemy there [Blount's Creek] and drive them, if possible beyond the battery on Hill's Point."[107] He set out on April 8, 1863, with his force, covering fifteen miles before bivouacking for the night. His troops covered another fifteen miles before running into Leventhorpe's advance pickets at 3:00 p.m.; 200 sharpshooters commanded by Maj. Egbert Ross. The 21-year-old officer waited in ambush, and as was reported, "they kept their fire till the enemy was close, and then poured in several volleys."[108] The Union soldiers were demoralized and scampered back towards the main column. Spinola reinforced his skirmishers and slowly drove Maj. Ross's small force back to the main defenses at Blount's Creek.

Brigadier General Francis Spinola moved the 3rd NY cavalry—the troopers dismounted—against the Southerners to determine their strength. Colonel Leventhorpe's Tar Heels were dug in comfortably within their entrenchment, confident in their defensive preparations and certain of the coming results. After all, they had fought this way twice before; the Carolinians knew what to expect, and they understood what their musketry could do to an attacking force. The cavalry inched forward and was met by a hail of bullets. The Union commander concluded "the enemy's position [was] almost impregnable."[109]

Colonel Leventhorpe's precise earthworks placement hemmed in Spinola's ability to maneuver. The deep swamps to the Federal left prevented any movement in that direction, and the rapid widening waters on the right prohibited thoughts of shifting in that direction. General Spinola had room to send only two regiments forward, side by side. He ordered the 17th MA and the 49th MA, almost 1,300 men forward.[110] The two Union regiments advanced, the soldiers scurrying from tree to tree. The Tar Heels poured volley after volley into the Yanks. Lieutenant Colonel William Martin recorded, "Our position was a very strong one.... [W]e were well entrenched.... [It was] hopeless [for] Spinola's command."[111] Brigadier General Francis Spinola recorded, "We were unable to drive them from their position [and] ... it was equally impossible to enfilade their works or to cross or ford the creek at any other point.[112] Colonel Silas Richmond (3rd MA) added, "[The] enemy's [riflemen] were excellently aimed ... causing some loss on our side."[113]

For the next ninety minutes the two sides shot at each other and during this time the well protected Carolinians suffered only a couple casualties. One of these, 58-year-old Pvt. Patrick Black (Co. K) from Swannanoa, Buncombe County, was seriously wounded.[114] Meanwhile, the Northern troops suffered enough losses to destroy their morale. Finally, the frustrated Francis Spinola called for a mass charge to cross the bridge. The commander of the unit chosen for this mission studied the artillery pieces covering the bridge, as well as the secure Carolinian infantry, and talked Spinola out of ordering the assault. Francis Spinola wrote, "We were unable to charge the enemy.... I was obliged to return, and did so at 5 o'clock."[115] Spinola left behind a screen of rear guards and marched his troops back to New Bern. Colonel Leventhorpe crowed, "They disgracefully retreated ... fell[ing] trees on the road and withdrew in the night."[116] First Sergeant George Erwin (Co. B) noted, "They did not come near us."[117] Once things calmed down, Leventhorpe recorded, "Several of my men were hit but none badly hurt or killed.... I devoutly praise God for ... our victory."[118] The Union casualties were over sixty.[119]

The 11th North Carolina remained by the bridge at Blount's Creek for several more days, waiting for renewed Union attacks, but none came. Instead, the Federals forced two small schooners past the Confederate gunners and resupplied the Yank garrison with ammunition and rations.[120] This action gave the Northerners confidence in their ability to withstand the siege. On April 13, 1863, the gunboat *Escort*, with hay bales stacked on its decks as protection, fought its way past the Southern artillery, bringing with it two more schooners loaded with supplies—the siege was collapsing.[121] General Daniel Hill gave up; he ordered his brigades to pull back. Colonel Leventhorpe received his orders to return to Greenville on April 15, 1863. He took his unhappy troops westward towards Greenville. Sergeant Lewis Warlick (Co. B) grumbled, "We were all disappointed at leaving Washington in the hands of the enemy."[122] The march took several days and upon arrival, Sergeant Warlick recorded, "You may guess that we were ... fatigued."[123]

A week later, on April 25, 1863, Brigadier General James Pettigrew, who was hearing rumors his formation might be leaving North Carolina, began contingency preparations. He contacted his regimental leaders, directing them "at once [to] send to [his] HQ Qtrs. a statement of the number of shoes needed in their commands."[124] He also tried to deal with the excessive number of desertions, sending out teams of dependable soldiers to apprehend and bring back the missing men. Private Reuben Branch (Co. B) was one of these responsible soldiers. Sergeant Lewis Warlick (Co. B) wrote of the 19-year-old rifleman, "Yesterday there was a detail of 50 men from the brigade sent to Randolph and Chatham [counties] to hunt up deserters. Reuben Branch was detailed from our company. They were offered fifty dollars and a furlough for every one they catch."[125]

Colonel Leventhorpe received orders to march his regiment to Hookerton, North Carolina. His troops made the 25-mile hike but were dismayed to learn their supplies did not follow. Sergeant Lewis Warlick grumbled, "Our tents have been sent to Wilson together with all heavy baggage, don't suppose we will get our tents any more."[126] And 43-year-old Sgt. William Parker (Co. C) growled, "We have not slept in a tent but one night since the 9th of March."[127]

Not only did Leventhorpe's soldiers have to attempt sleeping beneath drippy skies, the Confederate army did little to supply rations. Sergeant Warlick (Co. B) noted, "We have not drawn but one days rations of flour since we came to Greenville."[128] Private Elliott (Co. A) noted, "Our Regt gets one pound of meal a day and half pound of meat ... we have to bake our bread on boards before the fire."[129] And the hungry Sgt. Warlick added, "I would give considerable now for some nice biskets [sic] and butter. And wouldn't object to having a little honey sprinkled over it."[130] William Elliott (Co. A) summed up their condition, scribbling to his father, "This army is a hard place to be."[131] Colonel Collett Leventhorpe, frustrated at the way the Confederate army was treating his men, struggled to keep their morale strong. He also attempted to keep them attuned to wartime discipline by requiring routine inspections. Private William Elliott (Co. A) recorded, "There is going to be a regimental inspection this evening ... [so] we bin [sic] cleaning up our guns all day."[132]

On April 27, 1863, the 11th North Carolina was ordered to march to Kinston, North Carolina. The Tar Heels began the fifteen mile march but soon were ordered to turn around and return to Hookerton. Two days later, April 29, 1863, again they received a directive to hike to Kinston. The Bethel Regiment completed the march, arriving at the town that evening. Private William Elliott (Co. A) remarked, "We are in camp one mile and a half from Kinston.... We [got] some crackers."[133]

Then, on May 1, 1863, Brig. Gen. James Pettigrew was given the order to transport his brigade to Virginia. His five North Carolina regiments would be joining the Army of Northern Virginia. This news invigorated the Tar Heels who wanted to take part in the real war and frightened others—those who disliked what they had been doing but feared even more what they imagined could come. Private William Elliott (Co. A) penned his mother, "You sed you had give out ever seeing me again. You must not get out of hart."[134] Colonel Collett Leventhorpe, on the other hand, was thrilled at the prospect of leaving the swamps and mud of eastern North Carolina behind. He wrote, "My regiment is in magnificent order.... I somehow feel hopeful that the hour of our deliverance from so many troubles is at hand."[135]

Chapter 6

Heth's Division: The Army of Northern Virginia

Colonel Collett Leventhorpe got his regiment loaded onto a train at Kinston and the cars pulled out of the station that evening. North Carolina's rail system had been able to respond to war's demands admirably well at the start of the war. In 1861, Carolina-based locomotives hauled their loads with considerable speed; a soldier could expect to travel from Goldsboro to Charlotte, a distance of 225 miles, in less than 15 hours, an average of 15 miles per hour.[1] This route, which included 23 station stops, meant at times the trains were reaching speeds as high as 30 to 40 miles per hour.[2] However, as the war's pressures increased, these thin lines of steel began to show signs of wear. As the heavy use mistreated steel rails, railroads began to struggle to keep their degrading lines repaired, especially since replacement steel was no longer available. All the state's available iron was being used in the construction of warships and in fortifications. Besides the declining quality of railway steel, locomotives and rolling stock began to break down as many of the mechanics who had maintained these vehicles now shouldered muskets. And finally, experienced telegraph operators, conductors, and engineers were also being drawn into the military, eroding the railroad's proficiency. These growing deficiencies would hamper the Carolinians in their trek to Virginia.

The Bethel Regiment's cars trailed another train, this one transporting the 26th NC. The two trains rolled north from Kinston to Weldon, covering a hundred miles during the night. Then, in the early morning hours, as the 26th NC's train pulled out of Kinston, it was directed to stop in order to allow a mail train to pass. The Eleventh's train steamed along at a good speed and quickly caught up with the 26th's car. Communications failed between the two trains and the Bethel Regiment's locomotive crashed into the halted train's rear cars. Private William Elliott (Co. A) wrote, "The trains run together and kill[ed] one man ... and wounded a good man very bad." He continued: "The man that got kill[ed] got his head mash[ed] all to peaces between the coaches."[3] The 26th NC had another soldier whose hips were crushed, and ten others were slightly hurt.[4] There were four Bethel Regiment soldiers injured, all from Company A: Lt. William Hand, Pvt. Alfred Johnson, Pvt. John King, and Pvt. Tom Johnson.[5] A Tar Heel in the 26th NC recorded, "Such a mashup I never saw in my life."[6] Private Pvt. Cyrus McLure (Co. E), shaken by the near disaster, quickly wrote his wife: "I set my self to let you know that I am well."[7]

The men from the two regiments helped clear up the mess, and then the 26th NC proceeded on to Petersburg, Virginia. Colonel Leventhorpe's regiment was forced to wait for a new locomotive. Sergeant William Parker (Co. C) remarked, "We lay over at Halifax till Saturday evening [May 2] and [then] a train came."[8] This new locomotive arrived driven by a cautious crew, and Leventhorpe's men were slowly transported the final miles to Petersburg. They reached the city at 11:00 a.m. on May 3, 1863.[9] From here, the men marched to another train station and boarded cars bound for Richmond. The 11th NC reached the Confederate capital at 3:30 that afternoon.[10] Leventhorpe's riflemen unloaded themselves and hiked through the city. Corporal Jacob Bartlett (Co. K) recalled, "As the 11th Regiment marched through Richmond the old citizens gathered on the sidewalks and asked whose brigade it was. The answer was 'It ain't anybody's brigade it's the 11th North Carolina Regiment.'" Jacob Bartlett continued: "The old gentlemen would sigh and say 'It's a fine regiment, but boys you'll never all get back.'"[11]

The men in the Bethel Regiment had hardly settled into their camp when a frantic message reached Col. Leventhorpe; his regiment was needed to drive off a Yank cavalry force. He quickly got his soldiers into battle formation. Lieutenant Colonel William Martin recorded, "We were hurried ... to meet Stoneman's raid."[12] The Carolinians hustled out to confront this threat, ready to defend Richmond from an invasion, but the menace evaporated. Sergeant William Parker (Co. C) wrote, "We got orders to go to intercept the yanks but did not get more than a mile before we got orders to come back."[13] The information about a Federal attack had been greatly exaggerated. Private William Elliott (Co. A) noted, "We were expecting a fight ... yesterday ... but ... the Yankees ... turn[ed] back."[14]

The next day, May 5, 1863, Brig. Gen. James Pettigrew took the 11th NC and 26th NC away from Richmond, his brigade having been ordered to protect the railroad bridges spanning the North and South Anna rivers. His Tar Heels reached Hanover Junction and settled into regimental camps. The battle of Chancellorsville had just ended and as the defeated Union army stumbled away from Lee's forces the Carolinians guarding the river bridges found themselves in a cocoon of limited danger and few responsibilities. For the Tar Heels with nothing to do, the only concern was food. Private William Elliott (Co. A) complained, "I like this place first rate but we only get a quarter of a pound of meat a day ... and a pound of loaf to the man."[15] William Elliott also noted an event which, as time went on, greatly affected their future: "General Jackson, he got wounded in his arm."[16]

When Lt. Gen. Thomas "Stonewall" Jackson died on May 10, 1863, Robert E. Lee was forced to reorganize the Army of Northern Virginia. Lee's Confederate army had been structured to be around two large corps, one commanded by Jackson and the other by Lt. Gen. James Longstreet. But with Jackson's death Lee understood there was no one who could replace the brilliant leader. Lee concluded it was best to re-form his army into three corps, with Longstreet having the first corps and two newly promoted leaders taking command of the second and third corps. Eventually Robert E. Lee settled upon Richard Ewell to lead the second corps and Ambrose Powell A.P. Hill the third. Upon Lee's recommendation, Richmond's military leadership promoted both Ewell and Hill to lieutenant general. Lee then organized the army so that each corps was comprised of three large infantry divisions.

Meanwhile, while Gen. Lee was dealing with the dramatic restructure of his army, the young volunteers in the 11th North Carolina struggled with the day-to-day problems of surviving away from home. Sergeant Lewis Warlick (Co. B) wrote, "Camp life has gone pretty hard ... especially the eatables, not so good ... [and] clothing getting thin."[17] Captain Frank Bird (Co. C) noted, "My life in camp is very dull and boring."[18] And, Pvt. William Elliott (Co. A) groused, "You must over look my short letter for paper is ... four dollars and a half ... [and] envelopes two dollars and a half [per] pack."[19]

Also, during this period of inactivity, Col. Collett Leventhorpe left the regiment and visited home, and when he returned Lt. Col. William Martin was forced to take a medical leave.[20] However, for the enlisted men, furloughs were unavailable. The homesick Pvt. William Elliott (Co. A) wrote, "The furloughs has stop[ped] while we stay in Virginia." He added, "I dreamp last night that I was at home.... I want you to rite me all the news and how [the] wheat looks and how you are getting along with your crop." Elliott finished his letter to his parents: "This is the meanest place.... I ever saw."[21]

General Robert E. Lee completed his army's reorganization by the middle of May 1863, with his staff finalizing all the details—all the way down to regimental level. Colonel Collett Leventhorpe's 11th North Carolina remained within the Carolina brigade commanded by Brig. Gen. James Pettigrew. This brigade was one of four brigades now part of the division led by Maj. Gen. Henry Heth, and Heth's division was included in Lt. Gen. A.P. Hill's third corps.[22]

Major General Henry "Harry" Heth was 37 years old, a Virginian and a graduate of the 1847 West Point class. He came from a family with a military background, as his grandfather had been a colonel during the Revolutionary War. Henry Heth had also participated in the Mexican War. He then served out West, fighting against Sioux Indians, and earned acclaim for leading a successful flanking maneuver against them in the battle of Ash Hollow in 1855.[23] Heth also wrote the army's first marksmanship manual, *A System of Target Practice*. With the coming of the war he distinguished himself and rose quickly from colonel to brigadier general. Some said Harry was a member of the tightly knit "Old Boys Club" of professional officers known for their fighting tendencies.[24] However, there was no one who would deny Harry was always ready for a brawl. Heth, a cousin of Maj. Gen. George Pickett, was also socially charming and had the finest elements of character. General Lee appreciated Heth's qualities; Henry Heth was the "one general officer whom Lee called by his first name."[25]

Maj. Gen. Henry Heth was 37 years old when he took command of the division (Library of Congress).

Major General Henry Heth's immediate

Lt. Gen. Ambrose P. Hill was 38 years old when he took command of the Army of Northern Virginia's Third Corps (Library of Congress).

boss, Lt. Gen. Ambrose P. Hill, a 38-year-old Virginian, was also a graduate of West Point's 1847 class. He had served in the Mexican War and then battled against the Seminole Indians in Florida. Unfortunately, during this time he contracted yellow fever, typhoid fever, and malaria, sicknesses which would plague him for the rest of his life. When the Civil War began, Hill received a commission as colonel of the 13th Virginia. Ambrose P. Hill earned his promotion to brigadier general in February 1862 and took command of James Longstreet's brigade. Brigadier General A.P. Hill led his brigade skillfully during the Seven Days' battles, which convinced Robert E. Lee to announce, "I think Hill the best soldier of his grade." General Lee promoted Hill to major general and put him in charge of a 10,000-man division, to operate as Stonewall Jackson's shock troops. Hill provided Jackson with a crucial punch whenever Stonewall needed a swift movement or attack, and Hill's formation became known as "the Light Division." Sadly, in the incident in which Stonewall Jackson was mortally wounded, A.P. Hill also was struck, taking a bullet to his leg. Then, following Hill's recovery, Gen. Lee elevated him to corps command.[26]

Brigadier General James Pettigrew collected his Carolina regiments in the vicinity of Hanover Junction, Virginia, and began upgrading his formations' equipment and supplies. He also worked to develop communications between his regimental commanders, as well as instill pride in the brigade. One of Hill's approaches to implant brigade distinctiveness was through regimental drill competitions, an activity Col. Leventhorpe undertook with great confidence, as he knew his soldiers were well trained. Colonel Leventhorpe wrote, "We had a review of Pettigrew's Brigade yesterday evening. Five very large Regts.... My Regt. is in magnificent order."[27] Another Tar Heel in the brigade, not as impressed as Leventhorpe, remarked, "Marched in review for Pettigrew.... The dust was very disagreeable."[28]

For the common soldier, the month of May 1863 remained an interval of quiet times, scant danger, and endless fatigue duties. Sergeant William Parker (Co. C) noted, "There [are] no expectations of a fight here as our pickets and the enemy exchange papers every day." Parker continued, "I saw a yankee swim the river ... and brought some papers with him and got some papers in return. He sat with us for some time and talked."[29] Colonel Leventhorpe rotated his companies in drill, camp work details, and picket duties. Sergeant Lewis Warlick (Co. B), recorded, "I have just returned from picket duty.... My health is good ... wish I had some ... butter and salad."[30] Private William Elliott (Co. A), suffering severe homesickness, pleaded with his family for news from home, writing, "You sed you had the best water melon patch for the time of year you ever saw." He also added, "I was glad to heare of you having such good luck with the bees."[31] And Sgt. Lewis Warlick (Co.

B) wrote his cousin: "I got that picture you have been asking me for ... and an ugly thing it is too."[32]

Colonel Collett Leventhorpe remained adamant he was due a promotion to brigadier general. The frustrated officer received news he was being considered for command of a Tar Heel cavalry brigade. He wrote his wife: "I had another letter yesterday from an officer of the Cavalry ... telling me that a meeting had been held in which 4 out of 5 Regts ... were settling down on me, as the one, whom they desired for their Brig. Gen." Leventhorpe remarked, "I am an infantry soldier, both in knowledge and by preference.... I wrote ... declining the position."[33] However, before the Eleventh's commander had more time to dwell on his exasperating situation, commands arrived, ordering him to prepare the regiment for a summer campaign.

Colonel Leventhorpe issued Gen. Heth's divisional directives to his soldiers, forcing them to strip down to the barest of essentials. Major General Henry Heth planned to reduce the number of wagons each regiment could possess; a regiment was now allowed only one wagon per company, one vehicle for the regimental staff, one for the colonel, two to four to hold animal fodder, and two for the surgeons—a total of 16 to 18.[34] This meant the riflemen "could only carry a blanket, canteen, haversack, cartridge box, and a rifle."[35] Sergeant William Parker (Co. C) complained, "I have to throw away my clothes.... I only have one change now of underclothes and ... socks."[36] The men were then ordered to cook three days' rations, and to load three more days' rations onto their company wagons. Sergeant Lewis Warlick (Co. B) recorded, "Our orders in camp are to have every thing in readiness to move at a moment's warning."[37] The 11th North Carolina regiment's veterans figured they were going to fight General Hooker's Yankee army. Private Peter Dellinger (Co. I) informed his family, "[I am] ... expecting to go to Maryland."[38] Sergeant Warlick (Co. B) penned his girl, "We are pretty well assured there will be some hard fighting ... and I expect the old Bethel will be a participant."[39] Sergeant William Parker (Co. C) told his wife, "I hope this one will end the war."[40] And Pvt. William Elliott (Co. A), uneasy about the upcoming campaign, simply wrote his parents, "I want you all to remember me."[41]

The 11th North Carolina left its camp at 3:30 a.m. on June 16, 1863, with the head of the column marching in a westward direction. Colonel Leventhorpe's men trekked 18 miles, suffering terribly beneath a brutal sun and temperatures close to the century mark. None of the Tar Heels were prepared for this punishment and scores of men fell out of the ranks, disabled by the heat. A Carolinian officer recorded, "I could see hundreds of men that was compeld [sic] to fall out of ranks ... [and] it looked hard to see so many men lying on the side of the road all most smothering with heat."[42] The Virginia roads' dry clay became pulverized by thousands of boots, shoes, and bare feet and turned the highway into a choking tunnel of dust. That night one exhausted rifleman scratched a simple note to his loved ones: "The days are so hot that it almost kild [sic] men."[43] It took the regiment's stragglers many hours of limping in the darkness before they were able to rejoin their companies.

The next morning, June 17, 1863, the brigade broke camp hours before dawn and resumed its westward journey, as the Southern commanders wanted to get their formations' marching distances well covered before the season's first heat wave scorched their soldiers. Pettigrew's regiments reached Culpepper, Virginia, by 10:00 a.m. and Leventhorpe's Tar

Heels were informed they were finished for the day, having moved along the road eleven miles.[44] The tired and footsore men scrambled for shade and waited out the day's heat while their regimental supplies were given one last examination. From this point on the Confederate infantry would only have three days' rations in their haversacks, and after that they would have to look out for themselves.

On June 18, 1863, the Carolinians were rousted from their one-blanket beds in the predawn darkness and soon the column formed on the road. They marched all day, taking 20-minute breaks every now and then to rest and to search the countryside for edibles. A Tar Heel officer recorded, "The men are in good spirits." He also observed, "We have had little or no rain which makes the roads exceedingly dusty and the hot sun makes a long march the most disagreeable thing."[45] The brigade forded the Hazel River and passed through Sperryville, Virginia. Later that afternoon a drenching thunderstorm soaked the men, but brought relief from the choking heat and dust. That evening, the tired and footsore soldiers bedded down not far from Gaines' Crossing, Virginia, having covered twenty-three miles. One weary Southerner scribbled, "We lie down at night upon a single blanket and have a biscuit or two and piece of ham."[46]

Again, the next morning, June 19, 1863, the men of the Bethel Regiment were shaken from their bedrolls before sunrise and soon on the highway, traveling north and west. The long, gray column hiked among a set of switchbacks as the road climbed the eastern slopes of the Blue Ridge Mountains. Then they passed through the mountain's ridge at Chester Gap. The brigade remained near Chester Gap, the Tar Heels bivouacking among the lush vegetation of the mountain's top after having marched twelve miles. The soldiers enjoyed the break from the valley's smoldering heat and were subjected to a series of summer showers. One Confederate, not bothered by the rain, wrote, "The scenery along the route was exceedingly beautiful—in some places wild." He also added, "We were struck with the luxuriant riches of the country."[47]

On June 20, 1863, Col. Collett Leventhorpe was visited by staff officers and presented with an Army of Northern Virginia battle flag. Leventhorpe noted he "signed for it while in the field."[48] The ANV battle flag was made of cotton, with the blue crossed arrangement holding thirteen white stars against a red background. Colonel Leventhorpe formed up the 11th North Carolina and formally handed the new battle flag to the regiment's color company, Company C, commanded by Capt. Frank Bird. Leventhorpe then instructed the color guard to retire the Bethel flag, as Army of Northern Virginia regulations prohibited any unit from using any other form of colors besides the red, battle flag.[49] Then, the Carolinians shouldered their gear and muskets, marched down out of the clouds shrouding Chester Gap and descended into the Shenandoah Valley. They reached the town of Front Royal, Virginia, at noon. One infantryman remarked, "You cannot imagine how delighted the Valley people are at our appearance.... The ladies wave their handkerchiefs from every little farmhouse we pass and cheer us onward."[50] The soldiers responded with joyous yelling and salutes. One Front Royal resident recorded, "The men were in splendid condition and high spirits."[51]

The 11th North Carolina regiment left Front Royal behind, heading north, and forded both forks of the Shenandoah River. The bridges spanning these waters had been destroyed, but fortunately the rivers, though wide, were shallow. The men splashed across, most taking off just their footwear, while others stripped completely. They bedded down late that night in a stand of trees a few miles south of Berryville, Virginia, having hiked 28 miles.[52]

The exhausted riflemen did not march on Sunday, June 21, 1863. Instead, they lounged in the shade of the trees and soaked their blistered feet in a nearby stream. The next morning the Bethel soldiers were rousted from their slumbers at 4:00 a.m., ate their morning meals, and formed into marching formation, only to stand there for some time before word reached them to "stand down." The men grumbled but were relieved to be free from another day's marching. This second day of rest gave some of Col. Leventhorpe's soldiers time to think about what lay ahead. Most of the men were convinced of their cause and looked forward to taking the war to the Yankees. Lieutenant William Taylor (Co. A) proclaimed, "I hope [we will] ... devastate the territory and give the enemy a taste of the horrors of war."[53] Others, though just a small number, differed in their feelings about striking into Union territory. They questioned why they should be part of an invading force. That night a few deserted, bringing the 11th North Carolina's AWOL total since the regiment had left Hanover Junction to two dozen.[54]

Colonel Collett Leventhorpe did not have time to send a posse out after the missing men. On June 23, 1863, he roused his troops at 3:00 a.m. and oversaw the distributions of three days' rations of fresh beef and hardtack. Then the Carolinians were back on the march, heading northward. The column trekked through Berryville and were entertained by a young woman who approached them, wrapped in a Confederate flag and shouting, "Hurrah for the rebels!" The local girl hollered for such a long time she had to admit, "I'm all out of breath."[55] The Tar Heels left Berryville and the patriotic woman behind and marched into the expanses of the Shenandoah Valley. One Confederate, enthralled by the area's landscape, wrote, "I have had the pleasure of viewing some of the most beautiful and picturesque scenery I have beheld in my life."[56] They covered eighteen miles before darkness halted their travel.

On June 24, 1863, again the brigade was up early and on the road. The dusty, butternut-colored line of men continued northward, passing through Charlestown, Virginia, the city where John Brown had been tried and executed, and within two miles of Shepherdstown, Virginia, a distance of fourteen miles. Collett Leventhorpe's men were awakened at 4:30 a.m. the next morning and on the road before sunrise. They tramped through Shepherdstown and down to the banks of the Potomac River. The bridges crossing the river no longer existed but there was a well-known ford not far away. The Carolinians followed the column of Confederate soldiers, and prepared to traverse the Potomac. The river was almost 200 yards wide at this point, possessing a firm, rocky bottom, and from knee to armpit in depth. Most of the men took their clothes off and strung all they owned on their rifles, which they held high above their heads as they splashed through the chilly water. They laughed and shouted as they struggled against the water's current. One Confederate noted, "Taking off our shoes, socks, pants, and drawers, we made a comical looking set of men."[57] Someone began singing "Maryland, My Maryland" and soon thousands of men joined in, creating a throaty chorus. The Confederates gave out a roaring Rebel yell when they reached Maryland's shore and staggered up out of the water.[58] Colonel Leventhorpe's officers and NCOs watched as their boisterous, wet soldiers dried off and dressed again as men of war. Following this, the column continued northward, hiking for another five hours before halting on the bluffs just south of Hagerstown, Maryland, having marched eighteen miles.

On June 26, 1863, the men were allowed a couple extra hours of sleep. The morning sky was thick with clouds and it was drizzling. The column returned to the road at 8:30 a.m., just as the misting moisture turned to rain. The Maryland highway was quickly churned into a muddy trough, resisting the soldiers' efforts and forcing them to consume four hours to cover less than ten miles. The sodden Confederates quietly crossed the border into Pennsylvania and halted near Greencastle, Pennsylvania, having struggled for thirteen miles. This was the first night the Confederate soldiers were spending on alien land—Pennsylvania. They immediately ignored orders and slipped out of their camps, fanning out to strip nearby farms of their poultry and fresh vegetables.[59] One Carolinian rifleman crowed, "I am in Yankeedom faring finely."[60]

The men were up before sunrise again, on June 27, 1863, and on the road by 4:30 a.m. They tramped through Greencastle, Pennsylvania, the first enemy town to be visited. The Tar Heels were surprised by how impressed they were by what they saw. One rifleman noted, "They live in substantial brick or stone dwellings ... [and] a more magnificent country I never saw. It looks like a well cultivated garden."[61] The Pennsylvanians gawked at the Confederates, some with dismay, others in sullen anger. One Keystone State citizen remarked, "Now the Southerners were in the Union after all."[62] Another local inhabitant, after studying the Confederates' worn-out uniforms, taunted, "What rags and tatters." This jeer produced a derisive retort: "But we always put on our worst duds when we start out to butcher."[63] That night Pettigrew's brigade bivouacked a few miles from Fayetteville, Pennsylvania, after a march of seventeen miles.

Southern Pennsylvania completely enthralled the Tar Heel farm boys; many had not seen a land of such abundance. One wrote, "I have never yet seen any country in such a high state of cultivation."[64] Another recorded, "We are in Yankeedom ... for certain, and a beautiful and magnificent country it is."[65] A third Carolinian observed, "The farms on this road are all fenced with well built fences.... The barns ... are built ... of Blue Limestone ... all very large and capacious, none of them less than one hundred feet in length."[66]

Colonel Collett Leventhorpe's farm boys, now veterans of over a year as riflemen in the Confederate army, looked upon the Pennsylvania landscape with farmers' eyes, as well as a touch of homesickness. A Carolina writer remarked, "Stretching before [us] were seemingly endless fields of wheat, oats, and hay ... cornfields, apple orchards, vegetable gardens and trees of ripened cherries."[67] One infantryman noted, "More luxuriant fields of wheat cannot be imagined."[68] However, another mused in irritation, "The war has not hurt them like it had us."[69] Most of the Tar Heels, who had experienced Eastern North Carolina's disruptions and the horrible destruction in Virginia, were not hesitant in turning the tables on the Northerners; the Confederates called it "flanking." One ecstatic rifleman recorded, "We had not been many hours in bivouac until turkeys, ducks, chickens, crocks of milk, butter, apple butter, and various delicacies began to make their appearance in almost every mess."[70]

The Pennsylvanian farmers' reactions to the Confederate soldiers varied; some ignored

6. Heth's Division: The Army of Northern Virginia   69

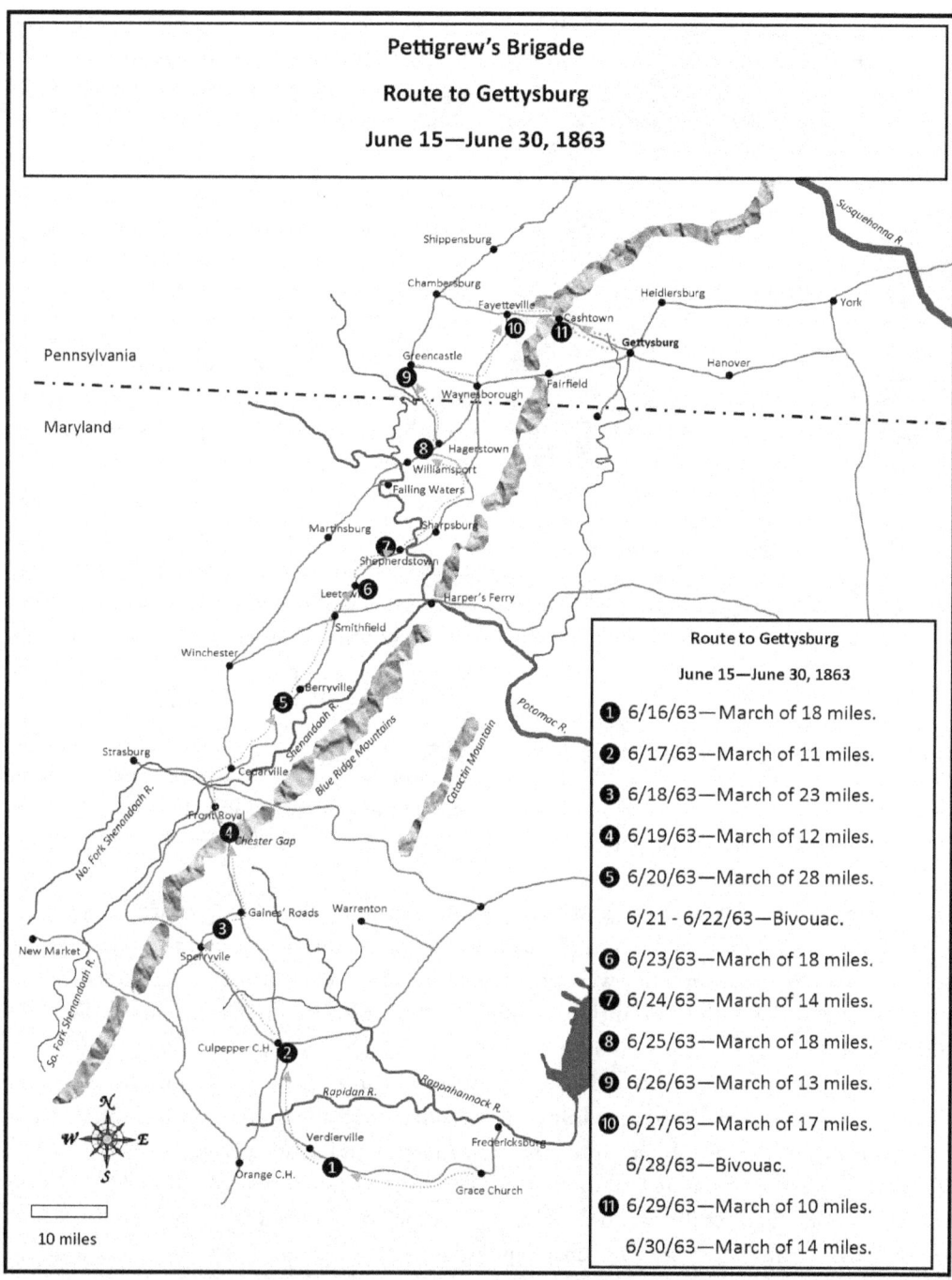

the gray-clad men, while others were alarmed. The Tar Heels responded to the Northerners with equal divergence. One wrote, "The farmers along our line of march were quietly reaping and housing their grain."[71] A second soldier noted, "The people here expected much harsher treatment from our troops than they received."[72] And a third observed, "The citizens are terrified out of their wits."[73] Regardless of the Pennsylvanian reactions to the Confederates,

Twenty-four-year-old 2nd Lt. Lemuel Hoyle (Co. I) was amazed by Pennsylvania's bounty (Clark, 1901).

their farm products quickly vanished as the Southerners moved through the state. One soldier, possibly with a sense of guilt, recorded, "Most of the soldiers seem to harbor a terrific spirit of revenge and steal and pillage in the most sinful manner."[74] Another Carolina rifleman, not bothered by remorse, remarked as he entered his regiment's camp, "The boys certainly lived high now.... To have heard the squealing of pigs, the cackling of chickens, and the quacking of ducks ... one for the instant might have supposed himself on some market square."[75] And not only were the Confederates "liberating" Pennsylvania's foodstuffs; the regimental quartermasters scoured the countryside, collecting livestock. A Southerner commented, "The harvest machines were lying idle in the fields in the very spots our scouts unhitched the horses and drove them away."[76] Another reported, "We gathered up thousands of beeves in Pennsylvania—enough to feed our army until cold weather."[77]

The 11th North Carolina remained in its bivouac on June 28, 1863. This became a day for the men to attend to their personal welfare; they washed their clothes and mended what rips and tears could be repaired. They also fanned out and brought back more Pennsylvania larder, with honey, apple butter, and cherry wine becoming highly sought-after items. The soldiers ate confiscated food and discussed their final destination, a concern they all possessed. No one knew where they were going or where the Federal forces were, and this ignorance provided the fuel for countless rumors. One puzzled Confederate stated, "We hear nothing of Hooker's army."[78] His queries were overshadowed by those who pronounced "Baltimore was the new target."[79] This speculation was argued down by comrades believing they were headed to Harrisburg, while others championed a march on Philadelphia.[80] The Tar Heels, regardless of which rumor they felt most accurate, all agreed, as one remarked, "General Lee knows what he is about. This is certainly a grand move of his and if any man can carry it out successfully he can."[82] Colonel Leventhorpe met with Brig. Gen. Pettigrew and discussed their situation. Leventhorpe wrote, "I ... converse[d] with him about the movement, the exact object of which was, of course, known only to Gen. Lee; and upon remarking that I thought our rear was exposed and that the trains bringing supplies of ammunition might be endangered, he replied 'We have no rear.'"[83]

Colonel Collett Leventhorpe had little time to concern himself with their army's destination; he was required to make sure his regiment was as well-equipped and armed as possible for whenever General Lee brought his army up against the Federals. Leventhorpe, after

**11th North Carolina Infantry
Shoe Requisitions**[81]
30 June 1863

Unit	Commander	Strength	Need shoes
Co. A	Cpt. William Hand	104	59
Co. B	Cpt. Mark Armfield	80	31
Co. C	Cpt. Frank Bird	54	27
Co. D	1st Lt. William Kincaid	68	46
Co. E	Cpt. William Kerr	56	20
Co. F	Cpt. Edward Small	78	48
Co. G	Cpt. John Freeland	71	51
Co. H	Cpt. William Grier	48	20
Co. I	Cpt. Albert Haynes	96	32
Co. K	Cpt. James Young	70	31
Regt.	Col. Collett Leventhorpe	725	365

taking stock of his soldiers' weapons and ammunition, ordered his company officers to inspect the men and report their footwear issues. The company commanders quickly presented Leventhorpe with a near-crisis problem; the past days' marching had severely damaged the men's shoes, and half the men in the regiment did not have adequate brogans or shoes.[84]

The 11th North Carolina's men were rousted from their slumbers at 3:00 a.m. on June 29, 1863. They formed on the road in brigade column, in the predawn light; rumors abounding—the brigade was heading east. There seemed seriousness to the orderlies and messengers racing up and down the long line of riflemen that had not been present before. The "Baltimore is our destination" crowd claimed their easterly position proved them correct, and the fact their officers' attitudes had grown somber indicated that was where the Yankees waited.[85] But the column did not move; instead the annoyed men stood in formation for several hours until, at 11:00 a.m., finally they stepped forward. The sky was heavy with clouds and the humidity high as the men marched eastward. Rumors swept the ranks; the Yankees were on the other side of the mountains they could just barely see in the summer's haze.

The column passed through Cashtown, Pennsylvania, and then worked its way up the mountain's western slopes. A Tar Heel officer wrote his wife, "The scene around us was very different from what we had just passed through. Instead of the enticing fields and lovely landscape, we had now around us that which was rugged,

Twenty-one-year-old Cpt. William Hand (Co. A) reported his company needed 59 new pairs of shoes (Clark, 1901).

grand and towering."[86] The brigade halted that afternoon, up in the mountains, after a day's march totaling ten miles. The Confederate officer continued: "Our stopping place was in a basin of the mountains which was very fertile and contained a few very excellent and highly cultivated farms."[87] General Pettigrew had guards posted around all the farms, preventing the men from foraging, and the soldiers were ordered to "cook one day's rations and have it in haversacks and be ready to march [early] next morning."[88] The Confederate riflemen took this as an omen—tomorrow they would be fighting the bluecoats.

Confederate Military Pay—1863[89]

Rank	Monthly pay
Private	$ 11
Corporal	$ 13
Sergeant	$ 17
1st Sergeant	$ 20
2nd Lieutenant	$ 80
1st Lieutenant	$ 90
Adjutant	$100
Captain	$130
Major	$150
Lieutenant Col.	$170
Colonel	$195

The Confederates awoke on June 30, 1863, aware something was going to happen. Colonel Colett Leventhorpe informed his company commanders that Maj. Gen. Henry Heth had given orders for Pettigrew's brigade to make a reconnaissance in force. General Heth recalled, "I ordered Brigadier-General Pettigrew to take his brigade to Gettysburg, search the town for army supplies (shoes especially, and return the same day."[90] The men in the 11th North Carolina, most of them veterans of nearly fifteen months in the regiment, realized they might be fighting—not from behind prepared entrenchments—but advancing forward, attacking an unknown enemy. This was a different and much more dangerous situation than they had ever faced before, and this prospect sobered even the most enthusiastic youth. The anxious soldiers formed into column, but frustratingly for the men, marching orders did not come. Later, the soldiers were pleased to learn they were being mustered for pay. Then, at 6:30 a.m., commands swept the brigade: "the men were ordered to leave their knapsacks behind, and soldiers too weak to make a forced march were [to be] left at the bivouac."[91] Brigadier General James Pettigrew gave directives, commanding the 11th, 26th, and 47th NC to march east, accompanied by three cannon. The three regiments moved quickly under sodden skies, the riflemen knowing they were heading to Gettysburg with orders to procure shoes. Word spread among the ranks; there were Yankees in Gettysburg, but they most likely were militia and not worth any worry.

The Confederates reached Seminary Ridge three hours later, having covered seven miles in the morning's light rain. The Tar Heel column rested, the front ranks about 1,200 yards from Gettysburg's outskirts. To those who could see, all appeared quiet and peaceful. General Pettigrew sent out brigade skirmishers, riflemen from the 11th NC, under the command of Maj. Egbert Ross. This thin screen of Tar Heels advanced 300 yards closer toward Gettysburg's brick and stone homes. Major Ross's skirmishers cautiously worked their way into the outermost houses of the town. A few shots punctuated the morning's quiet.[92] The

Bethel Regiment's skirmishers rounded up a doctor and this captive was immediately sent to Leventhorpe. The colonel pummeled the Pennsylvanian with questions, the most important being, "Have you seen any Union soldiers?" The citizen replied there were several thousand bluecoats in the town.[93] Collet Leventhorpe took this news to Gen. Pettigrew.

Brigadier General Pettigrew was growing agitated; his scouts, and those officers who owned field glasses could also see bluecoated troops. Pettigrew had received a report that, "Buford's Division of cavalry—estimated at 3,000 strong—had arrived that day and was holding the town."[94] Pettigrew's scouts were certain the town was occupied by regular Union cavalry, and Maj. Ross and his lieutenants agreed. The figures seen moving around in the distance were not home guards; they were an advance unit of the Yankee army. General Pettigrew sent a messenger to Heth, informing him of the Federal's presence but the division commander was not impressed, again repeating what General Lee's staff officer had told him: "He might find the town in possession of a home guard which he would have no difficulty in driving away."[95] Harry Heth scoffed at Pettigrew's concerns; there was nothing in Gettysburg to worry about. General Heth restated his orders: "Go to Gettysburg and procure supplies."[96] He also repeated Gen. Hill's perplexing directive, preventing Pettigrew from any kind of an engagement with the enemy. The conflicted Pettigrew could see the Union cavalrymen before him; they had dismounted and taken up a defensive position. The Yanks appeared ready to fight and moved with the confidence of veterans who knew reinforcements were not far away. General Pettigrew remarked, "The cost of the stores when gotten would have been dear."[97] Finally, Pettigrew made a decision; he gave the command that there would be no collection of shoes—he was turning his brigade around and they were marching back to the division bivouac.[98]

Major Egbert Ross's skirmishers covered the brigade's rear as Pettigrew led his soldiers away from Gettysburg's outskirts. A unit of Federal cavalry dogged along behind the retreating Confederates. A Southern officer from Pettigrew's staff recorded, "I ... remained in the rear to watch ... the movements of the approaching column. Whenever it would come within 300 or 400 yards of us we [Maj. Ross's rearguard] would make our appearance." The staff officer continued: "The [enemy] column would halt until we retired. This was repeated several times."[99]

Pettigrew's three regiments returned to the brigade's camp outside Cashtown and the harried brigadier general met with his boss, Maj. Gen. Heth, to report his Gettysburg findings. Harry Heth shrugged off Pettigrew's analysis, still convinced only militia occupied that Pennsylvania town. James Pettigrew refused to back down and the briefing turned into an argument. Heth maintained there were only militia in Gettysburg and insulted Pettigrew by suggesting he had run from home guards. Their disagreement raged until Lt. Gen. Ambrose Hill arrived. Heth described their dispute and Hill quickly sided with his division commander. Henry Heth recorded, "Hill said, as I had done, that he did not believe that there was any force in Gettysburg, except possibly a small cavalry vidette."[100] Pettigrew made one last effort to convince his superiors they were in error; he brought in Cpt. Louis Young, one of his staff officers. Captain Young at one time had served on A.P. Hill's staff, and because of this, Gen. Pettigrew hoped the 30-year-old officer's observations would hold weight with Gen. Hill. But Hill and Heth refused to change their opinions. Captain Young wrote, "Blindness in part seemed to have come over our commanders, who, slow to believe in the presence of an organized army of the enemy, thought there must be a mistake in the report ... by Pettigrew."[101] The meeting ended after Gen. Heth received permission from A.P. Hill, to, as Heth announced, "march my division tomorrow, go to Gettysburg and secure those shoes."[102]

Chapter 7

Gettysburg: July 1, 1863

The soldiers in the Bethel Regiment were rousted from their blankets before sunrise on July 1, 1863. The Carolinians hurried through morning duties and breakfast, knowing this day was going to be different from anything they had ever experienced before in their first fifteen months of service. Many of the men were quiet, not knowing what to expect, and afraid to let their comrades know they were frightened. Others expressed their anxiety with loud boasts and taunting of those around them. A few dreaded the coming day's events, believing they were going to die in the coming fight. One of these Tar Heels with this intuition was Pvt. William Elliott (Co. A), who, late the evening before, sought out his cousin, Cyrus Allen (Co. A), and "gave [him] his pocket comb and New Testament ... and said, 'Take these to Ma because I'll die tomorrow.'"[1] Another Carolinian feeling the same way was 1st Lt. John Clanton (Co. E), who "seemed to have premonitions that his end was on hand."[2]

11th North Carolina Muster
July 1, 1863[3]

Unit	Commander	Strength
F & S	Col. C. Leventhorpe	4
Co. A	Cpt. William Hand	95
Co. B	1st Lt. Thomas Parks	79
Co. C	Cpt. Frank Bird	45
Co. D	1st Lt. William Kincaid	62
Co. E	Cpt. William Kerr	55
Co. F	Cpt. Edward Small	64
Co. G	Cpt. James Freeland	66
Co. H	1st Lt. James Lowrie	38
Co. I	1st Lt. David Coon	93
Co. K	Cpt. James Young	64
Total		665

Colonel Collett Leventhorpe could not concern himself with the fears his nervous men harbored; Gen. Pettigrew wanted him to have the regiment ready to fight. Collett Leventhorpe's regiment numbered just over 650, the numbers unevenly divided between the companies. Some of his formations had nearly full company complements with close to one hundred, while other units were shrunken to the forties or fifties. Colonel Leventhorpe's second-in-command, Lt. Col. William Martin, still had not returned to the regiment, meaning Maj. Egbert Ross took charge of the unit's right wing, and the senior captain, Mark Armfield (Co. B), was moved up to lead the left wing. Colonel Leventhorpe and his adjutant, Lt. Henderson Lucas, organized the companies to account for officer seniority and to balance out the numbers. Major Ross's right wing consisted of Companies A, D, F, and I, a force of just over 300. The left wing had B, E, G, H, and K, also totaling around 300. Captain Frank Bird's Company C was the color company, and his 45-man unit would occupy the regiment's center. Colonel Leventhorpe reviewed his men and came away pleased. He wrote [they were] "superbly disciplined, full of martial order and ... magnificien[t] in their array."[4]

A cool drizzle fell upon the troops as Maj. Gen. Henry Heth's division formed on the Chambersburg Pike. General Heth laid out the order of march, with Archer's brigade in the lead, followed by Davis, then Brockenbrough, and finally Pettigrew. Henry Heth remained displeased with Pettigrew and pointedly placed Brig. Gen. Archer at the front and Pettigrew in the rear. James Archer was a tough, hard-talking, and enigmatical soldier. Archer possessed battle experience and a number of generals familiar with his ways had dubbed him the "Little Game Cock." Henry Heth held the aggressive Archer in the highest regard and wanted him to lead the division into Gettysburg, brush away any militia holding that town, and get first crack at the shoes. By doing so, he would humble the well-educated but combat-inexperienced James Pettigrew.[5] General Heth was looking for a fight and ordered his brigades to move in light-marching order, with the men leaving their knapsacks in regimental wagons. Colonel Leventhorpe detailed one man per company in his regiment to protect his soldiers' personal articles.[6] Then, Archer's lead elements, Alabama troops, stepped off just after 6:00 a.m.[7] The North Carolinian riflemen stood in position for some time until all the other formations had joined the column and marched eastward. One writer noted, "The Tar Heels tagged along in the rear."[8]

The trek to Gettysburg took only a couple hours, Archer's lead unit crested the rise of Herr's Ridge, two miles west of the town, around 9:00 a.m. General Heth was surprised when his soldiers were immediately fired upon. Heth deployed Archer's Brigade to the right of Chambersburg Pike and Davis's brigade to the left and sent them forward with orders to press the screen of men slowing down his march to Gettysburg. Both brigades pushed the bluecoats eastward, and during these first few minutes of contact Archer and Davis quickly realized they were fighting Regulars—dismounted Federal cavalry. Davis and Archer advanced for a short distance before both brigades were hammered by a brutal fist—veteran Union infantry from the Army of the Potomac's First Corps.

Brigadier General Joseph Davis's 2,300 men had run into the soldiers of I Corps, about 2,000 troops commanded by Brig. Gen. Lysander Cutler.[9] This veteran Federal formation, supported by well-executed artillery barrages, quickly stalled Davis's advance, causing massive casualties. Meanwhile, James Archer's 1,200 men smacked up against Brig. Gen. Solomon Meredith's Iron Brigade, nearly 1,900 tough-fighting men with a reputation for crushing whatever Confederate force was unfortunate enough to get in their way.[10] The Iron Brigade, its men wearing distinctive tall, black hats, flanked Archer's men and rolled over the brigade, capturing Archer and breaking his regiments into crushed pieces.

Oblivious of Archer's and Davis's disaster, Col. Leventhorpe's Bethel boys stood uselessly in column formation west of Herr Ridge. They could not see what was taking place and could only listen to the rumble of artillery and the oppressive noises of massed infantry fire. It was plain to them James Pettigrew had got it right; Gettysburg was defended by more than just home guards. Later, Gen. Heth wrote, "It was evident that the enemy was in the vicinity of the town in some force."[11]

The morning rain showers had passed overhead and the hot summer sun sapped the Tar Heel's energy. The men stood in line, sweating as the temperature rose. Canteen details scrounged the area for water but little could be found.[12] Then orderlies rushed towards Pettigrew, informing him Gen. Heth wanted Pettigrew to deploy his brigade in battle formation. Unfortunately, Heth's directives were unclear, and a Tar Heel recorded, "We deployed to the left of the pike, but soon crossed over to the right." He continued: "We took up our position in rear of our batteries after we moved to the right.[13] Then, the brigade was shifted again, taking up a position in a stand of woods near the top of Herr Ridge. A Carolinian officer recorded, "We moved forward about a half mile, and halted in a skirt of woods ... bordered by a fence."[14]

The 11th North Carolina was tucked in between the 26th NC on its left and the 47th NC to the right, with the 52nd NC farther to the right.[15] Brigade skirmishers were thrown out in front and then the Carolinians settled down in the shade to view the spectacle before them. An officer in the 26th NC wrote, "In our front was a wheat-field about a fourth of mile wide; then came a branch, with thick underbrush and briars skirting the banks. Beyond this was again an open field [and] ... a wooded hill directly in front."[16] The sounds of the fighting had begun to diminish, though the fields in front of the Tar Heels were dotted with frantic, retreating soldiers. Archer's desperate survivors swarmed towards Pettigrew's brigade, the panicked men running for their lives, leaderless, and completely shattered. General Heth, watching the collapse of his two brigades, admitted, "I was ignorant what force was at or near Gettysburg."[17] A staff officer overhead Heth mutter, "This was not supposed to happen."[18]

One of the Tennessee survivors called out as he passed the Tar Heels, "[It's] those damned blackhatted fellows.... It ain't no militia."[19] Henry Heth notified Pettigrew and Brockenbrough to ready their men for an immediate counterattack. General Heth sent a message to his boss, Lt. Gen. A.P. Hill, requesting permission to throw his Carolina brigades at the Yankees, but Hill could not be found. General Hill was ill, felled by a recurring bout of the sicknesses that had plagued him since his early days as an officer. Eventually General Robert E. Lee met up with Heth, and later the ailing Hill joined them. Lee informed Heth he wanted to consolidate his division and strike with both the Second and Third corps at the same time. General Lee told his harried division commander, "Wait awhile, I will send you word when to go in."[20] For the riflemen in the 11th North Carolina who were not privy to Lee and Heth's conversations, the day's heat and humidity wore on them as they watched the black-hatted fellows move about in the woods, just over a half mile away. A Tar Heel wrote, "We remained in line of battle until 2 p.m."[21]

The Carolinian riflemen surveyed the ground between them and the bluecoats. One noted, "[The] woods possessed all the advantage of a redoubt."[22] Another remarked, "Every private in the ranks well knew the nature of the task that lay before [them]."[23] And a Carolina officer recalled, "[We] became quite impatient ... keeping our men as quiet and comfortable as possible, sending details to the rear for water, and watching the movements of the enemy."[24] Colonel Leventhorpe walked along his regiment's battle line, calm and composed. He was a big man, standing over six-feet tall, and wherever he went his men surged forward to share a moment with their respected commander. One officer described Leventhorpe as "conspicuous by his great height, for like Saul, he towered over his fellows from the shoulders up."[25] His soldiers called out, "When do we attack?" and he answered, "When General Lee wants us to!" Then Leventhorpe moved down the regimental line, repeating his words to the next company.

Finally, word rippled down the brigade battle line: they were going to advance. Those with time pieces noted it was almost 3:00 p.m.[26] Colonel Leventhorpe's men stood up, grabbed their muskets, adjusted their gear, and formed a "parade-perfect" battalion front. The Carolina farmhands and shopkeepers had been waiting for this moment since the day they signed their names onto company enlistment rolls. Leventhorpe's riflemen had seen what had happened to Archer's veterans, and they, as one jotted down, "well knew the desperateness of the charge."[27] Company C's color guards measured out their steps in front of the regiment, their new Army of Northern Virginia battle flag hanging limply in the humid air. Colonel Leventhorpe took his position at the regiment's center, with Maj. Egbert Ross standing behind the right wing and Cpt. Mark Armfield with the left.

The 26th NC moved forward on the Bethel Regiment's left; Gen. Pettigrew wanted his units to advance by echelon.[28] Colonel Leventhorpe waited until the 26th was a hundred yards ahead, and then he gave the order to advance.[29] The 11th North Carolina left the safety of the trees and stepped out into the wheat, crushing the ready-to-harvest crop beneath 600 pairs of footwear. Artillery fire had already begun to eat into the 26th NC's lines, but for the first few precious minutes, the Bethel formation moved forward without harm. Colonel Leventhorpe did not look back; nevertheless, he expected the 47th NC to follow the Bethel Regiment, marching in echelon, a hundred yards behind them, off their right flank.

Federal cannoneers redirected some of their pieces towards Leventhorpe's line. The first rounds did not find the thin line of advancing Southerners, but the Yank gunners knew their trade. Soon explosions wracked Leventhorpe's line. An eruption near Company C killed Pvt. Joseph Casper and shrapnel sliced through Pvt. Andrew Pritchard, shredding his right arm, right knee, and right hip.[30] But the line did not falter; the Tar Heels stepped forward in a measured cadence covering one hundred yards per minute. Another blast sent burning metal ripping through Pvt. Jerry Tripp's (Co. G) breast and left shoulder. It also shattered Pvt. Benjamin Coffey's (Co. H) left leg and destroyed his right eye.[31]

By now, the regiment had covered 300 yards and was barely a minute's march from the small creek with its wild foliage, when Union soldiers wearing black hats popped up from the thick underbrush. There were no more than fifty or so Yankees, and their spacing indicated this was the Federal skirmish line. The black-hatted soldiers began shooting slowly as skirmish partners alternated their fire.[32] This first fusillade of musketry did little damage. One Carolinian remarked, "The enemy ... opened fire ... but their aim was too high to be very effective."[33] The Tar Heels moved forward, marching as if on parade. An officer noted, "All kept the step and made as pretty and perfect a line as ... every man endeavor[ed] to keep dressed on the colors."[34]

The 11th North Carolina continued its advance, Leventhorpe's men gritting their teeth and marching, shoulder to shoulder. Union rifled balls started slamming into Carolina flesh. A minié bullet shattered Sgt. John Duval's (Co. B) thigh.[35] Another struck Pvt. Daniel Haynes (Co. I) and knocked him to the ground, mortally wounded.[36] First Lieutenant John McDade (Co. G) dropped to the ground, dead, and Pvt. William Gregory's (Co. C) foot was "shot off."[37] A Carolinian officer observed, "They killed a great many of our men before we could get at them."[38] The 11th North Carolina finished that last hundred yards to the stream known as Willoughby's Run. The Confederates crowded into the narrow animal passages winding through the wild roses and underbrush. A Tar Heel noted, "[The regiment] advanced through a quarter-mile wide field [and into] Willoughby Branch—enshrouded in thick brush and briars."[39] And at the same as the Carolinians forced their way through the packed brushwood, the black-hatted skirmishers ceased shooting and, "scurried back to the safety of their line."[40]

A massive volley struck the 11th North Carolina, as hundreds of minié bullets slashed into the men, starting on their left and rippling to the right. Dozens of Tar Heels fell. One wrote, "When nearing the branch ... the enemy poured a galling fire into the left of the [regiment]."[41] For the men of Company E, on the 11th's far left flank, this was a disaster. First Lieutenant John Clanton (Co. E) was flung backwards by a bullet, mortally wounded. He died four weeks later, killed just as he had predicted. Sergeant John Goodman (Co. E) was killed, and Cpl. William Cathey's (Co. E) "left arm was shattered."[42]

Many of the Tar Heels were still tangled up in the nearly impassable foliage. One Confederate noted, "We reached the branch ... [and] the briers and underbrush made it difficult to pass."[43] Meanwhile, the Yanks continued shooting at the mob of men trying to get through the brambles. Private Ezekiel Helms (Co. E) was dropped in his tracks, killed by a Federal bullet, one of many to be struck in this confusion.[44] A Southern writer reported, "The brush and the water slowed many."[45] The Federals continued to pummel the Carolinians with heavy fire, causing a wall of "dense ... sulphurous [sic] smoke [to] rise above the tree tops."[46]

The 11th North Carolina and the 26th NC were now deep in the killing zone of two hard-core Federal regiments. Colonel Leventhorpe's men were facing the 19th Indiana, while the 26th NC was matched up against the 24th Michigan, both veteran Federal formations with tough reputations. The 24th MI possessed nearly 500 riflemen, arrayed in a well-thought-out battle line and protected by a stand of trees growing on a low ridge known as McPherson's Woods.[47] Their commander, Col. Henry Morrow, had spent all morning posting his riflemen, knowing the Confederates were going to attack his front. Thus, when Col. Henry Burgwyn's 800 Tar Heels came within range, the Michigan troops blistered them with fire. The 26th NC may have outnumbered the Northern regiment facing them; however, the terrain Col. Morrow selected forced the Carolinians to break their battle formation as the soldiers bunched together to cross Willoughby's Run. In effect, the 26th NC's ranks stacked up, preventing many in the rear from firing. This stacked mass of advancing Confederates made an easy target for the defenders. Colonel Burgwyn's Tar Heels suffered horrible casualties as they pushed closer to the Michigan regiment.

Colonel Collett Leventhorpe's men re-formed on the east side of Willoughby's Run.

They were now less than a hundred yards from the Hoosier regiment. The 19th Indiana, led by Col. Samuel Williams, had just over 300 soldiers. This regiment was smaller because it had suffered heavy casualties in a number of battles and had not received replacements. Nevertheless, the 300 riflemen and officers remaining were all stalwart and knew their business.[48] They poured deadly lead into the Bethel Regiment's ranks, their fire being most lethal among the men in Cpt. William Kerr's Company E. One of Cpt. Kerr's men to fall was Pvt. Reubin Yaunts, the sleepy young soldier sentenced to wear a ball and chain a year earlier.[49]

Willoughby's Run meandered in front of the 19th Indiana. The stream generally ran north-south, but in front of the 19th's center, the brook angled to the east, a circumstance forcing several of the 19th Indiana's companies to bulge forward. Then, the watercourse trailed off to the southeast. In all, the 300 black-hats, arrayed two-ranks deep, covered a front of about one hundred yards. As the 11th North Carolina approached the Hoosiers's right, the Carolinian left wing received most of the Indianan fire, with the focus being mainly on the 11th's far-left companies. Captain William Kerr and his 55 Tar Heels suffered first. Then, as the Bethel Regiment closed upon Willoughby's Run, the Hoosier fire began to sweep the companies to Kerr's right.

The 19th Indiana's volleys stunned Col. Leventhorpe's left wing, stopping those companies as the men scrambled across the water. To many of the Carolinians, that first Hoosier volley sounded "like a giant door slamming shut."[50] One Tar Heel remarked, "After crossing Willoughby Run the firing became very heavy."[51] First Sergeant Frank Harris's (Co. H) left arm was destroyed, Pvt. Daniel Powell (Co. A) was killed, and Pvt. Philip Anthony (Co.

The Iron Brigade defends against the 11th and 26th NC's attack (Coffin, 1902).

B) tumbled to the ground, his leg shattered, to name only a few who suffered at this time.⁵² But the Carolinian riflemen recovered, and pushed by their sergeants and company officers, they, as a Tar Heel reported, "went ... across the branch ... driving ... to the second line."⁵³ A Union soldier remarked, "They came on ... yelling like demons."⁵⁴

Captain Mark Armfield's five companies closed to within fifty yards of the Indiana line. Both forces stood in packed lines and slugged it out, each side's riflemen loading and shooting as quickly as they could—now 250 Hoosier soldiers facing off against about 275 Carolinians. It was a brawl in which both sides dealt the other continuous, lethal blows. The riflemen on both sides were skilled; every man could load and fire their weapons at least twice each minute.⁵⁵ Now it became a simple exercise in mathematics—every minute at least 500 bullets swept through the Carolina ranks, and maybe 550 Tar Heel bullets struck trees and Hoosiers. First Lieutenant Tom Cooper (Co. C) was knocked down when a musket ball punched through his leg. With help he stood back up and shouted encouragement until another bullet sliced through his bowels.⁵⁶ Other Carolina boys went down, including Pvt. James Clark (Co. E), who was killed, Pvt. John Cook (Co. B) was hit in the leg, and Pvt. Baxter King (Co. G) was struck in the hip.⁵⁷ An Indiana soldier said it best: "The slaughter in our ranks now became frightful beyond description."⁵⁸

Twenty-two-year-old 1st Lt. Thomas Cooper (Co. C) was killed on July 1, 1863 (Clark, 1901).

The Bethel Regiment's left wing shuffled forward a few more feet, narrowing the distance between the two forces to forty yards.⁵⁹ But then the battered Tar Heels could advance no farther. Indiana bullets impacted into Carolinian bodies, the sounds too horrible to hear. A Confederate penned, "The line hesitate[d]; the crisis [was] reached; the colors must advance."⁶⁰ Officers and NCO's stepped out in front to lead their men forward but quickly were shot and fell to the ground. Second Lieutenant Nathan Tenney (Co. G) was killed, 1st Sgt. Craige Clingman (Co. C) seriously wounded, Sgt. Walter McGrimsey (Co. B) struck in the knee, and Pvt. Thomas Burnett (Co. K) killed.⁶¹

Colonel Collett Leventhorpe was desperate to keep his troops moving forward, for he knew if they did not advance the Hoosier fire would push them backwards. He called his two wing commanders together. Captain Mark Armfield could do nothing more to encourage his riflemen; the soldiers in his five companies were taking a horrendous beating. Their advance had stalled. Major Egbert Ross, however, had a different take on the fight; his wing had done nothing. While Mark Armfield's wing covered the entire Indiana front, Ross's soldiers had no one to shoot. His men had maintained the regiment's battle line, but since there was nothing but empty landscape before them, they had hunkered down to stay out of the way of errant bullets. Major Ross suggested he could flank the Hoosier line. Leventhorpe and Armfield quickly agreed: the faster the maneuver was completed the better.

Captain Frank Bird's Company C was being slaughtered. It may have been an honor to carry the colors; unfortunately, though, when the bullets started to fly, it was a death sentence to be part of the eight men who protected the regimental battle flag. This first fifteen minutes of shooting had resulted in over half the color guard being shot down. The flag had dropped several times as injured bearers, no longer able to hold it upright, gave it up to someone else. After yet another color-carrier tumbled to the ground, the Bethel Regiment's adjutant, Lt. Henderson Lucas, snatched the ensign and raised it. A Carolinian remarked, "Adj't Lucas was the seventh man who bore the flag; six had fallen, either killed or wounded."[62] Moments later a swarm of Indiana lead thudded into the 23-year-old soldier. A Southerner commented, "[Lucas] was shot down, but rose again, waving the colors and urging on his men. [Again] he was brought down, but still supported the [flag] with his left arm until that arm was shot through." Someone else gathered up the battle emblem as Lt. Lucas groaned, "Boys, I have played out, go on to victory."[63]

The butchery continued. Carolinian bullets ripped through Hoosier bodies with such violence the Northerners fell, forming a straight line of dead and wounded. One Indiana farm boy-turned-soldier wrote, "Men dropped like chopped wheat." Another added, "[We] fell like grass before the scythe."[64] Regardless of their massive casualties, the Hoosier fire never slackened; they savaged the Carolinian ranks with musketry. Corporal Jeter Snipes (Co. G) had a bullet smash through his lungs; Pvt. Thomas Peele (Co. C) was shot dead; Sgt. James Rayner's (Co. C) left leg ripped apart, and Pvt. Joseph Creaseman (Co. K) was killed.[65] A Tar Heel wrote, "The bullets were as thick as hail stones in a storm."[66] Another Confederate summed up the slaughter; "The dead on both sides, which were thickly strewn on this hotly contested field attests to the resolute character of ... the contestants."[67] Captain Albert Sidney Haynes (Co. I), whose company was in the right wing and in little danger, had been able to watch the destruction. He coldly recorded, "[Those who] fall forward ... [that] mean[s] shot dead.... [T]hose falling backwards are only wounded.[68]

Colonel Collett Leventhorpe made his way back to his position at the rear of the regiment's center. As Leventhorpe passed behind the body-strewn area where Cpt. Bird and his color company stood a bullet shattered his left arm. The impact spun him around just as another bullet slammed into his hip. The Eleventh's colonel tumbled to the ground. Captain Bird quickly organized a detail to carry their wounded leader to the rear. An officer recorded, "Leventhorpe [was] bourn to the rear, severely wounded in arm and side."[69] A message was sent to Maj. Egbert Ross, who worked to get his men moved. Captain Egbert Ross realized the terrain's hidden gullies and patches of thick underbrush prevented his four companies from neatly completing a "left wheel" without his companies' having to waste precious minutes re-dressing back into a battle line, so he gave the directive for a "Change Front Forward on Fourth Company." When Maj. Ross learned he now commanded the regiment he turned the right wing over to Cpt. Edward Small (Co. F). Then as, one Tar Heel noted, "Ross dashed to [Leventhorpe's] place to lead his men."[70]

Captain Edward Small gave leadership of Company F to 1st Lt. Stephen Roberts and shouted out the order. The fourth company moved forward a few paces and then wheeled

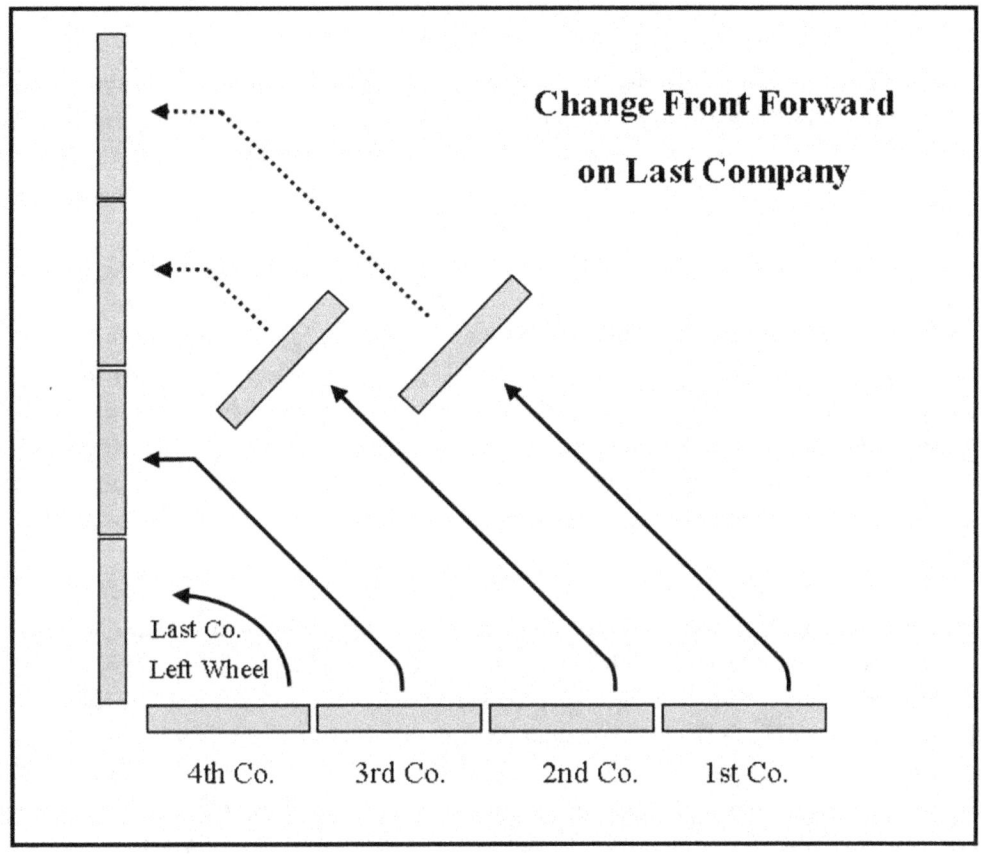

Illustration of "Change Front Forward on Fourth Company" (Casey, *Infantry Tactics*, 1862).

left. The third company left obliqued until they had cleared the right flank of fourth company, and then left-wheeled in line. The second and first companies also were obliquing and wheeling into line. The wing maneuver was accomplished in less than two minutes. The riflemen in Cpt. Small's wing now stared at a thin Yankee line stretched out to protect the Hoosier left flank. The Tar Heels checked their weapons and leaned forward, anticipating Cpt. Small's command and anxious to crush the 19th Indiana's exposed men.

The fighting raged even while the right wing maneuvered and more Carolinian farm boys were shot down. A Tar Heel wrote, "We were pouring volleys into each other at short distance."[71] Among the casualties, Pvt. Levi Crow (Co. K) "was wounded several times; arm, shoulder, and the back of [his] neck."[72] Private James Christy (Co. E) was downed by a bullet to his leg, and Cpl. Lucius Gash's (K) foot was shattered.[73] Third Lieutenant William Taylor (Co. A) experienced two close calls. He wrote that "a bullet hit his sword scabbard, [and] another went through his sock without injuring him."[74] First Sgt. James Triplett (Co. K) was struck by a bullet and dropped to the ground, to die within a few minutes.[75] One Confederate noted, "Lots of men were throwing up their arms and falling to the ground."[76]

Captain Edward Small gave the command to the men in his wing, and as one Tar Heel recalled, "The order to charge with bayonets was given, and we started with a yell."[77]

Companies A, D, F, and I, 300 Carolinians who had not been brutalized by this slaughter, surged towards the thin line of Hoosiers. The black-hats knelt calmly and took aim at the screaming Southerners. Then, they unleashed a volley and one Tar Heel recorded, "Such a rattle of musketry I never heard surpassed."[78] Carolina men fell. First Lt. Stephen Roberts (Co. F) was hit in the shoulder. First Sergeant George McDowell (Co. F) suffered bullets to his hip and foot.[79] Sgt. Samuel Black (Co. D) was knocked unconscious when a musket ball glanced off his forehead.[80]

Meanwhile, just as Cpt. Small's wing unleashed its first volley into the Hoosier left flank, their division commander, Maj. Gen. Henry Heth, was knocked from his horse, wounded. Henry Heth later recalled, "I was struck by a Minié ball on the head which passed through my hat and the paper my clerk had placed there, broke the outer coating of my skull and cracked the inner coating, and I fell senseless."[81] Henry Heth a few days earlier had been looking for a new hat. One was procured for him but it turned out to be too large. Heth's aid stuffed the headband with paper and this additional cushion saved the general's life. Brigadier General James Pettigrew, the division's senior officer, was elevated to command in place of Heth.[82]

As the Tar Heels pressed the 19th Indiana on their left, the rest of the Hoosier line shivered. Word quickly passed down the line; their left flank was being attacked. The Indiana riflemen had known for hours their left was hanging, unprotected. They had even tried to get their brigade commander to bring up reinforcements or allow them to bend line. But all their efforts were rebuffed. Word came back to the 19th Indiana: "Hold the woods at all costs."[83] The stoic veteran Hoosiers shook their heads and, as one Indiana soldier remarked, "We were to simply obey orders and do our duty."[84] Now, the Confederates were exploiting this mistake; it took only a couple minutes for them to crush the lone company protecting the 19th Indiana's left flank.

Major Egbert Ross saw the Union left crumble; he knew now was the time to exhort the bruised left wing one more time. He jumped out in front and shouted at his Carolinians. The color-bearer now carrying the flag was Pvt. Duncan Waddell (Co. G). The 18-year-old student from Durhamsville, North Carolina, started after Maj. Ross, hoping the men would follow. He was immediately joined by Pvt. William Ivey (Co. G).[85] Then Pvt. Robert Porter (Co. H) rushed up to them, and, finally, the entire Carolina left wing pushed into the thick gunsmoke and pressed forward.[86] The Hoosier line did not budge, and the Yanks fired furiously, shredding the Tar Heel line. A Carolinian wrote, "The enemy stubbornly resisted until the two lines were pouring volleys into each other at a distance not greater than 20 paces."[87] Another noted, "The roar ... was incessant and appalling."[88] Major Egbert Ross was flung to the ground. Lieutenant William Taylor (Co. A) remarked, "Ross ... was shot ... in the right side, and [the bullet] went ... through him ... [creating a hole] about the size of an egg."[89] Another bullet slashed through Pvt. Robert Porter's (Co. H) right thigh.[90] Private William Duckworth (Co. B) was killed, and Pvt. Martin Branch (Co. B) went down, his left knee destroyed.[91] A Confederate observed, "The whole field was covered with gray suits soaked in blood."[92]

The Tar Heel right wing surged over the Hoosier flank and slammed into the bluecoat's main line. The Indianan formation collapsed like a row of falling dominoes. One writer

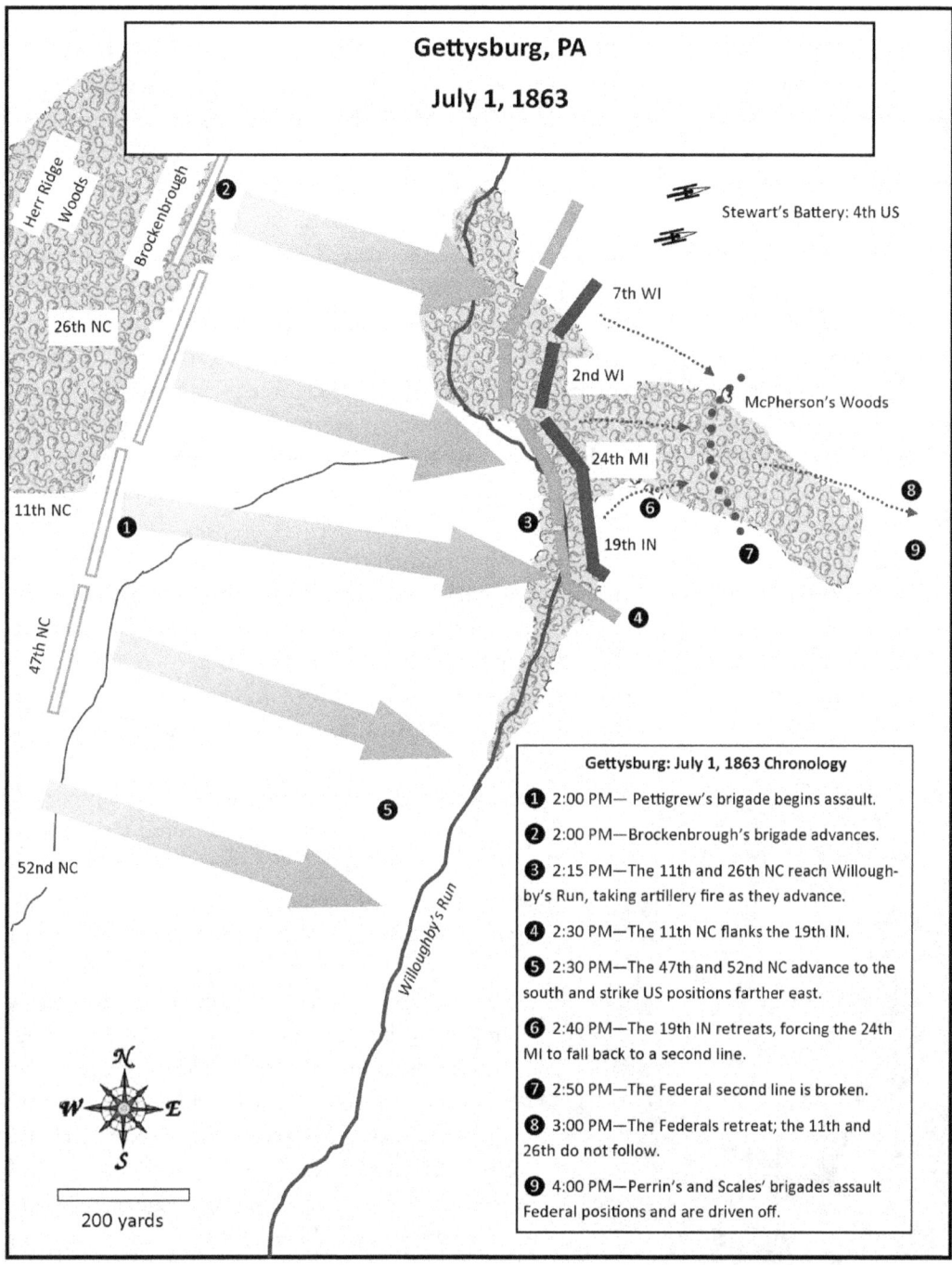

noted, "The 19th Indiana was overwhelmed."[93] The Hoosiers' left evaporated as the survivors fled towards the northeast. Other black-hats retreated into the companies still fighting against the 11th NC's left wing, causing confusion and spreading panic. Then, the entire 19th Indiana line broke and the bluecoats retreated towards the north and east. A Tar Heel recorded, "At last the enemy were compelled to give way."[94]

However, this was not a rout; the veteran Iron Brigade riflemen fell back, darting from tree to tree, loading and firing as they moved. The 19th Indiana's resolute officers and NCO's rallied the regiment and they fought back. A Tar Heel remarked, "They again made a stand in the woods."[95] Private Duncan Waddell (Co. G) had carried the colors for fifty yards and then was shot through the right lung.[96] First Lieutenant James Lowrie (Co. H) was killed, Pvt. Hiram Kiser's (Co. I) face was sliced open by a bullet, and Pvt. James Galloway (Co. A) was struck in the breast.[97]

The Bethel Regiment no longer had an overall commander, yet the Carolinian riflemen sensed the Hoosier weakness and pushed towards them, clots of comrades clustering together around a sergeant or lieutenant, loading and firing and screaming the Rebel yell. The Bethel boys pressed forward and the Hoosiers slowly gave ground, but each yard's advance was paid for in blood. Private Sidney Giles' (Co. D) right leg was punched through by a bullet, Pvt. William Goodrum's (Co. A) intestines were ripped apart, Cpl. William Cathey's (Co. E) left arm was shattered, and Pvt. Daniel Powers (Co. A) was killed instantly.[98] A shocked Confederate scribbled that "volleys of musketry [were] fast thinning out those left."[99]

The Indianans backed up some more but refused to quit. The 11th North Carolina's remaining officers still led from the front, urging their exhausted and battered riflemen forward. Captain William Hand (Co. A), facing his comrades and shouting for them to advance, was wounded in the back.[100] Not far from him, Pvt. David Settlemire (Co. D) went down, his stomach chopped to pieces by a musket ball.[101] And Cpt. Francis Bird (Co. C) watched as 2nd Lt. Edward Rhodes (Co. C) was "shot through the head."[102]

Twenty-one-year-old 2nd Lt. Edward Rhodes (Co. C) was killed in the attack against the Iron Brigade (Clark, 1901).

Finally, though, the Union resistance collapsed; the bluecoats turned and ran. The shattered Carolinians inched forward through the trees, finding "the Federal line which was marked by their dead."[103] Lieutenant William Taylor (Co. A) bragged, "They had to give way and when they did ... we drove them like sheep."[104] Another Confederate, greatly impressed by the Iron Brigade's fierce fighting, wrote, "The Federal forces fought desperately, inflicting so heavy a loss that too few [of us] were left for a successful bayonet charge."[105] General James Pettigrew walked among the bullet-pocked trees and recorded, "Neither language nor pen can describe the scene. The enemy was strewn in piles [and] ... in rows."[106]

The Eleventh's senior officer, Cpt. Mark Armfield, struggled to get the stunned Carolinians organized; the Yankees were still nearby, a couple hundred yards to the east. But the Bethel Regiment was no longer a battle-ready formation; it was now just a collection of shaken and exhausted men. Many were out of ammunition, and most did not have water. They could not advance another step. One officer wrote, "The enemy was driven back to his entrenchments just outside of town. We had too few left."[107] As the regiment's surviving officers and NCO's slowly regained control of the worn-out men Cpt. Armfield surveyed the Union position; it was, "immediately west of the seminary [where] the men took advantage of a barricade of fence railings."[108] Captain Armfield shook his head and agreed when a nearby soldier announced, "I don't want to fight them again."[109] He was greatly relieved when one of Gen. Pettigrew's staff officers told him to take his regiment from the battlefield; Gen. Pender's division was going to pass over them and continue the attack. Armfield looked at his watch; it was now 4:00 p.m.[110]

Later, Col. James Marshall (52nd NC), now in command of the brigade, led the shattered 11th NC and 26th NC regiments back to Herr's Ridge. The other two units, the 47th NC and 52nd NC had also suffered in the fighting that afternoon. Their movements on the brigade's right sent them against another brigade of Union infantry and heavy fighting battered both units. The 46th NC and 52nd NC soon joined the 11th NC and 26th NC on Herr's Ridge. All that could be done now was to find out who was still in the ranks and the names of those missing. A brigade officer recorded, "That night the brigade bivouacked in the woods they had occupied before the charge."[111]

Once the 11th North Carolina's company commanders had compiled muster rolls, they released their men to return to the battlefield. Everyone was frantic to locate their relatives and friends and learn what had happened to them. That night there was a full moon, helping the survivors see, but what they found horrified even the most jaded soldier. One wrote in revulsion, "They were lying on won [sic] another ... the [men's] arms and legs and head[s] shot off." Another penned his family, "Some were all shot to peases [sic]."[112] And, sadly, the soldiers quickly discovered every dead man and many of the seriously wounded had been robbed. One horrified Confederate remarked, "The battlefield robbers had been there plundering the dead."[113] Another disgusted rifleman added, "Their pockets had been slit open ... their money was gone, as were watches, rings, and jewelry."[114]

The shocked Carolinians, stunned by the ghastly evidence of what bullets and artillery could do to human flesh, were also dismayed by the sounds the wounded made. A Southerner noted, "The wounded cried piteously for water."[115] An officer shuddered as he wrote, "My attention was attracted by the dreadful ... howls of some of the wounded." He continued: "I approached several with the purpose of calming them.... I found them foaming at the mouth as if mad."[116] Private George Erwin (Co. A) summed up every man's experience when he scratched out to his parents, "[We have] been looking [for] our wounded and a more sorrowful thing I never saw."[117]

The miserable Carolinians carried their wounded comrades to the regimental hospital. There, surgeons John Wilson and James McCombs and a collection of volunteers attempted to deal with the onslaught of over 150 men needing medical attention. Another Carolinian doctor remembered, "When I arrived at the hospital my ears were greeted by the cries of the wounded."[118] Doctors Wilson and McCombs immediately had to triage the wounded, often dismaying those bringing in the injured. Private Erwin (Co. A) recorded, "The doctors don't examine a wound unless amputation is necessary."[119] The men who brought Adj. Henderson Lucas into the field hospital saw the medical burdens overloading the surgeons and sought permission to immediately take him to the Confederate hospital in Winchester, Virginia. With permission granted they loaded Lucas in an ambulance and he began the three-day trip. Adjutant Lucas did not make it to Winchester. Instead, as a *Fayetteville Observer* writer reported, "[Lucas] travel[ed] three days and nights without a mouthful to eat or having his wounds dress."[120] He died three weeks later.

Major Egbert Ross died later that afternoon. Lieutenant William Taylor (Co. A) recorded, "He lived about four hours and we buried him.... I got a piece of plank, put his name on it with his rank for a head board."[121] General Daniel H. Hill, who was a cousin to Egbert Ross's mother, informed her of her son's death. He added, "I hope that you can look more calmly at the event as being ordered by a wise and merciful God.... He had to die at some time, and surely he could not die more nobly."[122] Others were more fortunate; the bullet in Pvt. David Hartline's (Co. E) foot was removed and he mailed the chunk of lead home. This reminder of Hartline's injury would remain on his mantle until his death many years later.[123]

The doctors worked tirelessly throughout the night. One physician recalled, "I went to work and did not rest until next morning after daylight."[124] However, once the exhausted soldiers left their wounded friends at the hospital, they straggled back to the regimental bivouac and attempted to sleep. A gloom had settled over the men, and as one explained, "Sleep was not possible ... [as] the air was heavy with the stench of death."[125] The next morning the men were faced with the grim task of burying the dead and retrieving the equipment strewn all over the battlefield.

11th North Carolina Casualties[126] July 1, 1863

Unit	Commander	Casualties*
F & S	Col. Collett Leventhorpe	3
Co. A	Cpt. William Hand	24
Co. B	1st Lt. Thomas Parks	31
Co. C	Cpt. Frank Bird	16
Co. D	1st Lt. William Kincaid	15
Co. E	Cpt. William Kerr	27
Co. F	Cpt. Edward Small	9
Co. G	Cpt. James Freeland	20
Co. H	1st Lt. James Lowrie	9
Co. I	1st Lt. David Coon	37
Co. K	Cpt. James Young	10
Total		201

*For a complete listing of July 1, 1863, casualties, see Appendix A, Gettysburg Casualties.

The Bethel Regiment's fight on July first had taken less than forty-five minutes. During those furious moments when the 11th North Carolina came to grips with the 19th Indiana, 200 Tar Heels had fallen. The left wing, which had fought the knuckles-to-knuckles fight, suffered heavier losses—113, while the right wing, which had little to do until it flanked the 19th IN, lost 85.

The Carolinians also demolished the Hoosier regiment; the 19th IN lost over 200 men. That regiment would never be able to successfully mount an attack for the rest of the war. Regardless of their destruction of the 19th Indiana, for the Carolinians their company muster rolls were shattered, officers and NCO's missing and large numbers of riflemen no longer present for roll call. Captain Mark Armfield spent July 2, 1863, reorganizing the unit. This was a completely different regiment than had existed 24 hours before. The Bethel Regiment would never be the same again.

Chapter 8

Gettysburg: July 3, 1863

On the morning of July 2, 1863, Cpt. Mark Armfield, the 56-year-old railroad agent from Morganton, watched as the men of the 11th North Carolina went about the business of starting the day. He was now in command of the regiment, an honor he did not want. Yesterday's fight had swept 200 men from the regiment, slicing away one-third of their comrades in the span of forty-five minutes. They had never experienced anything like this before; war in the Army of Northern Virginia was so much different than the activities they had all complained about in eastern North Carolina. This morning, everyone moved as if they carried huge weights on their shoulders—and they did: the searing memory of yesterday's incredible violence.

11th North Carolina Muster[1]
July 3, 1863

Unit	Commander	Strength
F & S	Cpt. Mark Armfield	3
Co. A	Cpt. William Hand	71
Co. B	1st Lt. Thomas Parks	47
Co. C	Sgt. William Todd	27
Co. D	1st Lt. William Kincaid	51
Co. E	Cpt. William Kerr	29
Co. F	Cpt. Edward Small	54
Co. G	Cpt. John Freeland	46
Co. H	2nd Lt. James Saville	29
Co. I	Cpt. Albert Haynes	56
Co. K	Cpt. James Young	53
Total		466

Captain Armfield and his second-in-command, Cpt. Frank Bird, had already met with the brigade's new leader, Col. James Marshall of the 52nd NC. James Marshall was the only surviving colonel in the brigade. Colonel Marshall informed them Gen. Pettigrew, now the division's senior officer, told him Gen. Lee was going to keep the division in reserve.[2] Their priorities today involved reorganizing and resupplying the battered regiment and burying the dead. Details were sent out to find and identify the Bethel Regiment's dead—there were 37—and inter them in a dignified manner.[3] Then Mark Armfield and Frank Bird met with their existing company commanders. The regiment's leaders had suffered seriously; sixteen officers were gone, as were twenty sergeants and nine corporals. However, Cpt. Albert S.

Haynes (Co. I) had arrived late the night before, having just caught up with the regiment. He had been home on sick leave but now was there to take charge of company.[4] Captain Haynes, along with the other unit commanders, now had to appoint temporary NCO's and familiarize them with their responsibilities. Captain Armfield was thankful the brigade had been given a reprieve, but Col. Marshall had warned him the 11th North Carolina needed to be ready at a moment's notice.

July 2, 1863, passed quickly and the night even faster. The brigade was aroused hours before sunrise and ordered to march toward Gettysburg. Captain Armfield's regiment lined up in the brigade's column as the last unit. They hiked over the trashed wheat field, across Willoughby's Run, and through the bullet-shredded trees of McPherson's Woods. One Tar Heel wrote, "Over hills, across branches, through thickets, we slowly wended our way." As they moved through yesterday's battleground they passed scores of wounded Yanks who called out, "For God's sake don't tread on me ... [and] please give me some water."[5]

As the sun began to rise above the heights to the east, the Confederate column reached Seminary Ridge and turned right. The brigade marched for a short spell towards the south and then halted. The regiments were faced to the east and told to stack their arms and rest. The men in the Bethel Regiment saw they were in a shallow depression just west of a stand of trees. Farmers' rock walls fenced in fields and lined dirt roads, and a few houses and a barn or shed were all they could see. The 26th NC regiment, now barely 200 men, relaxed to their right, and then another brigade's-worth of men arrived and stacked arms to their left. Captain Armfield soon learned this new brigade was Brig. Gen. Joseph Davis's unit and their regiment that abutted up against the Eleventh's left was the 55th NC.[6]

The 11th North Carolina's position was out in the open, a fact which began to cause suffering as the July sun bore down on them. A Tar Heel grumbled, "The 11th halted in the open without benefit of shade."[7] Another recalled, "We were lying down in an open field with nothing to protect us except a small ditch; and the sun was coming down on us pretty hot."[8] Colonel Marshall called his regimental commanders together and informed them they would be part of a massive assault against the Yankee lines. This was to be Gen. Lee's great gamble to punch through the bluecoats' center and break their army. James Marshall went on to tell them Confederate artillery would pulverize the Union position before they attacked.

Captain Armfield returned to the regiment and passed the word to his company commanders. Not surprisingly, most of the riflemen already knew the news; rumors had already swept through the enlisted men's ranks. Curious line officers and NCO's stole through the trees and peered out from the edge of the wood's eastern side to study the ground they would be covering. One officer recorded, "The ground over which we had to pass was perfectly open." He continued: "Numerous fences ... were formidable impediments in our way.... The position of the enemy was all he could desire."[9] Another wrote, "We could see the mouths of the gaping cannon waiting for us."[10] These men returned to their units, grim-faced and shaking their heads; the assault would be across a mile of open ground against a fortified enemy position. A rifleman summed up their situation: "All knew that victory ... was to be at a fearful cost."[11]

The men waited quietly all morning as the summer's heat boiled the humid air. Then,

The Confederate infantry waits out the artillery barrage before Pickett's charge (Johnson and Buel, *Battles and Leaders*, vol. 3, 1887).

at 1:00 p.m., two Confederate artillery pieces fired, signaling the bombardment's commencement. A Tar Heel noted, "The signal gun ... spoke the call to death."[12] Immediately, all the Southern guns opened fire. Not far from the 11th North Carolina, a four-gun battery—the Fredericksburg battery—went into action. The gunners' precise movements fascinated the Tar Heel riflemen.[13] These cannoneers quickly reloaded and fired again, to the cheers of the Carolinians.

Then, Federal artillery answered and shells crashed into the trees in front of the Bethel Regiment. Captain Armfield's riflemen dove for the ground as explosions shook the earth and spewed dirt and hot metal in all directions. Hundreds of projectiles pummeled the trees all along the Confederate positions, filling the air with horrid noise and lethal danger. A Carolinian remarked, "The best writer in the universe could not give the faintest idea of the horrible conflict."[14] And another wrote, "It seemed as if all the Demons in Hell were let loose, and were howling through the air."[15]

Fortunately, Yank shells did not strike among the 11th North Carolina's prone ranks. The men cowered on the ground, shivering as shells exploded close by and wondering if the next detonation would get them. The 55th NC was not as lucky. Several shells impacted into the 55th North Carolina, disgorging a spray of blood, body parts, and shrill screams. A Carolinian recorded, "Seventy cannon ... were pouring forth upon our devoted ranks every missile that human ingenuity could invent for our destruction."[16] Another noted,

"The roar of the artillery ... and the wild terrific scream of the shells as they whizzed through the air was really the most appalling."[17]

A Federal round struck one of the Fredericksburg Battery's caissons, exploding in its ammunition chest. An infantryman described the scene: "All at once the earth trembled with a deafening shock louder than the report of a gun or shell; a thick, hot, white ring shot straight up, into the air as if the mouth of a bottomless pit had opened before us." The rifleman continued: "Shapeless fragments of wood and iron were hurled high above the trees.... The limber of the nearest caisson was a wreck [and] its ammunition chest had disappeared."[18] A single artilleryman responded to the explosion and rushed to the burning remnants, fearing the fire would spread to nearby caissons. He calmly ladled out water from a bucket into the blaze. The Confederate recorded, "[He] coolly and carefully ... remain[ed] at his perilous post until the last spark went out in hissing steam."[19]

The Carolinians huddled on the ground, quaking each time they felt the ground shake. A few steady NCO's went among their men, making sure everyone had water. They sent back canteen details to the rear, both to get some of the white-eyed young men out of this terrifying location and to keep everyone drinking water in the summer's heat. One rifleman, the noise and fear eating at his courage, tried to mentally withdraw from the horror around him. He scribbled into his journal, "Small birds flew about in confusion."[20] Then, after nearly ninety minutes, the cannons fell silent. The Bethel men, their ears ringing, glanced at each other nervously; they knew what came next.

Orders rippled down the brigade's line: "Form up." The Tar Heels hastily brushed the dirt from their uniforms, buckled on their accouterments, and moved into their regiment's battle line. The smoke and dust settled as officers faced their riflemen. One wrote, "Never were men more conscious of the difficulty imposed upon them by duty."[21] Word was given and the regiment moved forward into the shattered trees and out onto the open ground. The 11th North Carolina dressed on the 26th NC to their right, and moments later the 55th NC of Davis's brigade formed to the Bethel left. The riflemen could see a long line of Confederate infantry stretching both right and left. Those who said they knew informed their comrades that Heth's entire division was attacking all at once. They also added that to their right, behind a tongue of trees blocking their view, Gen. George Pickett's division was also in on the assault, a total mass of at least 13,000 Confederates.

General James Pettigrew rode his horse up to his old brigade and stopped. He called out to Col. Marshall, "Colonel, for the honor of the good old North State, forward."[22] Brigade commands were shouted out and the North Carolinian formation, four Carolina regiments strong, moved forward. The Tar Heels strode quietly across a farmer's pasture, the riflemen knowing, as one said, "It will be hot for us."[23] They marched, as the commander of the 26th NC noted, "in as magnificent a style as I ever saw, the lines perfectly formed."[24] An infantryman wrote, "We advanced, marching with deliberation."[25] And Cpt. Albert Haynes (Co. I) recorded, "We were ordered to go at common time."[26] This meant the Tar Heel regiment was closing upon the Union lines at the rate of 100 yards each minute. They had 1,200 yards to go—the Federals would have twelve minutes to inflict as much damage as they could before the Confederates arrived. It was a long way to travel and the afternoon heat and humidity were intense. One soldier wrote, "Even as [we] began moving some of the men fainted from the heat."[27]

Captain Mark Armfield looked to his right and could see the small Tennessee brigade leading the way. The soldiers there were all that remained of Gen. Archer's formation, and with his capture Col. Birkett Fry now was their leader. Mark Armfield glanced to his left, and he noticed his left wing commander, Cpt. John Freeland (Co. G), frowning. Captain Freeland could see that Davis's brigade had not advanced; instead, Davis's regiments lingered at the edge of the trees. General Pettigrew soon realized this fact and quickly dispatched a rider, who raced towards the motionless unit. Moments later, Davis's men were hurrying to catch up.

The Carolina brigade passed beyond the tongue of trees to their right and soon the Tar Heels were able to see the massive ranks of Pickett's division. The Virginia formation stretched off towards the south, covering a front of nearly a half mile. It was a fantastic panorama, all those perfectly aligned gray-clad ranks, bayonets glistening and adorned by dozens of red battle flags. Pickett's left flank joined up with Pettigrew's right, creating a sweeping battle front extending a mile across. A Tar Heel wrote, "With their flags proudly held aloft, waving in the air, with polished muskets and swords gleaming and flashing in the sunlight, they presented an inexpressibly grand and inspiring sight."[28]

The Federal artillerymen were not impressed. Union batteries vanished in boiling clouds of smoke, and shells began detonating among Pickett's men. A Confederate recorded in horror, "Their graceful lines underwent an instantaneous transformation; in a cloud of dense cloud of smoke and dust, arms, heads, blankets, guns, and knapsacks were tossed in the air."[29] The Carolinians watched as their Virginia brothers were ripped apart by Northern steel; their reactions were horrified, and yet filled with admiration. One noted, "When gaps were made in the line the ranks closed up of their own accord, and continued to advance."[30]

As the Bethel Regiment stepped forward the pasture gave way to a field of wheat, demarked by a farmer's fence. The Confederates reached this fence at different times, as the post-and-rail barricade angled across their advance. Parts of the fence collapsed easily when shoved by the soldiers; other portions seemed better built, and resisted. One company was able to move at a steady pace and the one next to it was delayed as its men were forced to get past this impediment. Then another line of fences had to be overcome, destroying their alignment even more. Bunching became a problem as the units drifted into each other and the regiments' lines became scrambled. General Pettigrew ordered a halt in a depression just west of the Bliss farm. Here, in this dip, protected by both terrain and the drifting smoke arising from the farm's burned structures, Pettigrew had his commanders realign their formations. Unfortunately, there was not room for everyone to complete an orderly alignment, and the brigade's left half had to assemble behind the right. Then Pettigrew gave the order to advance. One Southerner recalled, "A great many of the 11th North Carolina and the 26th North Carolina on the left of Marshall's line remained behind, while the right wing (the 47th and 52nd North Carolina) charged toward the front."[31]

The brigade moved up out of the depression, onto the top of a swale and into an apple orchard. Union gunners could see the Confederate formation now and aimed their gun tubes at the Carolinians. The first artillery shots were long, screaming above the Tar Heels' heads and ripping into the trees a quarter-mile behind them. The next rounds were better placed; a shell exploded among Cpt. William Hand's Company A, spitting out slashing metal, tearing through Pvt. Nathan Harris's right shoulder, cleaving Pvt. Alexander Newell's left shoulder, and gashing Pvt. John Smith's face.[32] William Hand's formation staggered briefly before sergeants stiffened their men's resolve, then it continued forward, trailing behind a number of comrades who stopped to help the wounded. A Southerner recorded, "The trouble of crowding was soon remedied by the thinning of the ranks, done by shot and shell."[33]

Another round exploded close to Gen. James Pettigrew, sending metal chunks thudding into his hand and breaking bones. Aides rushed to his side, but he waved away their calls for him to go to the rear. Instead, he agreed to have his hand wrapped and his arm placed in a sling, and then he advanced, along with his Carolinians. A shell erupted near Company G, knocking Pvt. John Clements to the ground, his right hip a mess.[34] Others also went down. A Tar Heel wrote, "Files fell to rise no more as the enemy's shot plunged through."[35] An explosion ripped into Company F; Pvt. Isaac Byrum's (Co. F) left leg was shattered, and 2nd Lt. William Rea (Co. F) was bloodied by shrapnel to his left hip and right foot.[36] Pvt. Anderson Ward (Co. F) had his "ear blown off."[37]

The stalwart Confederates continued to move forward, their long lines easy targets for the veteran Federal artillerymen. The Carolinians could not hide; they could only go forward. Every yard closer to the Yanks was marked by blood. Colonel James Marshall was knocked from his horse by the concussion of a blast. He scrambled to his feet and climbed back up onto his mount. He then rode forward, intent on leading.[38] Second Lieutenant Lemuel Hoyle (Co. I) had steel rip into three parts of his body, and Cpt. William Kincaid (Co. D) was struck in the left knee.[39] Both officers were gently carried to the rear.[40] More soldiers fell. One soldier described the carnage, focusing on a single man and writing, "A soldier gutted by shrapnel had time to write a letter before he died."[41] Another summed up their situation, penning, "Human valor was powerless."[42]

The Carolina regiments finally reached the fence bordering Emmitsburg Road. This structure was, as one Confederate said, "a post and rail, and a post and plank fence of considerable obstruction."[43] Union infantry, now 250 yards away, rose up from behind a stone wall and unleashed a massive volley.[44] The effect was devastating. Private David Glenn's (Co. A) right arm was nearly blown from his shoulder, and 2nd Lt. Patrick Warlick (Co. B) was struck in the left arm.[45] Private John Finger's (Co. E) neck was ripped open, 1st Sgt. Frank Harris's (Co. H) left arm was shattered, and Pvt. William Smith (Co. F) was killed.[46]

The Confederates tried to push the fence down. The rails collapsed in some places, allowing the Southerners to pass through the gaps and seek shelter in the sunken Emmitsburg Road. But most of the fence was too firmly built for the frantic soldiers to knock it down. The riflemen had to climb over the obstruction to reach the safety of Emmitsburg Road. One Tar Heel wrote, "The time it took to climb to the top of the fence seemed an age of suspense."[47] Private Esau Garrett (Co. G) was hit in the lungs as he made it to the top of the fence. He spilled forward and tumbled onto the hard-packed road's surface, bleeding heavily.[48] Sergeant Andrew Haynes (Co. I) "was seen to fall forward." He lurched off the fence and dropped to the road, dying within minutes.[49] A Union soldier described this slaughter, writing, "The men dropped from the fence as if swept by a gigantic sickle."[50]

Once past Emmitsburg Road's first fence, the desperate Tar Heels scrambled about, crawling toward the road's eastern fence line. Here they were sheltered by the two-foot-deep sunken road. Others screamed in pain, and blood splattered about in ever-growing pools. Many of the Carolinians were stunned by the violence and huddled among the wounded and the dead. It was complete pandemonium. First Lieutenant Edward Outlaw (Co. C) remarked, "A perfect storm of musketry ... made it a slaughter-pen."[51] The regiment's NCO's scurried about, trying to organize the shaken soldiers. Sergeant Major James McCorkle raised himself up to embolden those around him, only to be struck down.[52] Colonel James Marshall, still on his mount, yelled at the Tar Heels, encouraging them to advance, and took a pair of musket balls to his forehead. He slumped from his horse, dead.[53] First Lieutenant David Coon (Co. I) was riddled by bullets. A Tar Heel explained Coon's injuries: "He was shot through the right foot, through the right leg, just above the ankle, through the thigh twice, in the left leg twice, in the left side, and in the head."[54] Private Lee Johnson's (Co. I) jaw was shattered, and Pvt. John Pittman (Co. K) was hit in the shoulder.[55]

The Tar Heels' assault had stopped. One Southerner wrote, "The Confederate advanced seemed to stagger."[56] Another recalled, "Rifle fire and canister pattered the rails like rain striking a roof in a down pour."[57] And someone else noted, "Th[e] road was filled with their dead, the ditch was piled up with them."[58] Reinforcements crashed into the first fence, and more Confederates spilled into the chaotic road—men from Col. John Lane's brigade. Lane's men crowded up next to the Carolinians and this pressure pushed them forward. Major John Jones (26th NC), now the Tar Heel brigade's senior officer, shouted for them to advance.[59] Captain Mark Armfield stood up and hollered at the Bethel boys and immediately was shot down. Captain Frank Bird (Co. C) now had command of the regiment. The 33-year-old ex-lawyer climbed over the fence and bellowed at his comrades. A Carolinian wrote, "His clothes were struck by balls in several places and his thigh grazed ... although he ... [was] not hurt."[60] Many courageous Tar Heels ascended the fence and joined Cpt. Bird in a ditch on the eastern side of Emmitsburg Road.

Brave men from the Tennessee brigade also trickled over the fence, and soon a compact mass of Southerners had assembled in the drainage. Men carrying battle flags stepped ahead, and the Confederates advanced, howling as they leaned forward almost as if pushing against a stiff wind. They also began to fire their muskets, moving towards the Yank lines, loading as they stepped closer to a low, stone wall crowded with Yank infantrymen. The 12th New Jersey stood behind that critical line of piled stone, over 450 Northerners armed with .69 caliber muskets and buck-and-ball ammunition. Knowing their weapons were not the most accurate at long distances, the 12th NJ's men waited until the Tar Heels were only a couple hundred feet away. Then they released a tremendous volley. Sergeant William Jetton (Co. I) was killed and eight Bethel Regiment color guards shot down in quick succession.[61] Dozens of others also were felled, including Pvt. Peter Dellinger (Co. I), who had a musket ball slice through his stomach.[62] A Confederate wrote, "We met a perfect hail storm of lead."[63]

The Carolinians and Tennesseans pressed forward into the hurricane of bullets. One officer wrote "the smoke was so dense at times [he] could scarcely distinguish [his] own men."[64] Captain Frank Bird (Co. C) glanced back at the Emmitsburg fences and recognized scores of 11th North Carolina men remaining. If he had been given the time to count how many Bethel boys accompanied him beyond the pike the number would not have reached one hundred.[65] Another officer noted "there seem[ed] to be no way to motivate ... many men to leave the protection of the roadbed."[66]

New Jersey buck-and-balls slashed through Frank Bird's riflemen. Private Joseph Long's (Co. F) left leg and arm were hit, Pvt. Taylor Wright (Co. A) was struck in the back, and 3rd Lt. George Kincaid (Co. D) was killed.[67] One soldier observed, "Officers and men were ... mowed down so rapidly."[68] Another added "they seemed to sink into the earth."[69] Captain Albert Haynes (Co. I) fell, struck in the leg. He recalled, "I was shot down ... and insensible for a time."[70] Haynes continued: "[Private] Jake Bisaner [Co. I] was pulling off my boot [and] was shot.[71] Then, Cpt. Haynes was hit again, this time in the shoulder.[72]

A final cluster of Bethel men pushed even closer to the stone wall, now barely 150 feet away. Not far off to their right, the stone wall jutted forward over one hundred feet and then angled to the south. A clump of Confederates spilled over the corner of this angle. At least one Tar Heel was in that group: Cpl. Robert Hennessee (Co. B), who had become separated from the Carolina brigade and was now moving with a group of Tennesseans.[73] The soldiers in this cluster of Southerners were soon all shot down or overwhelmed and captured. But for the last remnants of the 11th North Carolina, New Jersey buck-and-ball, and minié bullets from the 14th slaughtered them. Sergeant Hugh Tate (Co. D) fell, bleeding from a wound to his right thigh; Pvt. Angus Wingate (Co. A) was killed; Sgt. Benjamin Carter (Co. C) was struck dead; and Pvt. Daniel Dulin (Co. A) was hit in the left hip.[74] Third Lieutenant Oliver Ramsaur (Co. I) fell, Cpl. Joseph Clay (Co. D) was struck in the face, causing him the loss of an eye, Cpl. Robert Briscoe (Co. F) dropped, his leg mutilated, and Pvt. James McQuay (Co. E) was killed.[75] A Tar Heel wrote, "It was murder ... hog butchering back home."[76]

One Carolinian soldier noted, "I was shot down within about fifty yards of the enemy's works, and the ground ... where I lay ... was thickly strewn with killed and wounded."[77] Another wrote, "It [was] folly to stand."[78] All the remaining survivors dropped to the ground, seeking protection from the sheets of lead scything through the air. One of these soldiers recorded, "[We] laid down ... on the crest of the hill near the stone fence."[79] The Federals continued shooting, their vision

Twenty-three-year-old Sgt. Benjamin Carter (Co. C) was killed within 150 feet of the stone wall (Clark, 1901).

hampered by the clouds of smoke their muskets created, and most of their bullets ripped through the air above the Tar Heels' heads. Some Northern lead did impact among the prone Confederates. One Southerner wrote, "While I was lying there on the ground, the Yankees kept shooting.... I expected every minute to be shot."[80] Private Cyrus Allen (Co. A), already wounded in the arm, slowly crawled forward and used the base of the stone wall as protection.[81] He was accompanied by another Bethel rifleman, Pvt. William Suggs (Co. G). Both Carolinians would soon become prisoners of war.[82]

Finally, it was over. The Confederates who still had fight in their hearts were either shot down or stopped shooting at the Yanks. At first a few fellows began to wave white handkerchiefs in surrender, but quickly scores and eventually hundreds of white cloths flitted above the battle-scarred riflemen. The Federals stopped shooting and the area grew quiet save the cries and moans of wounded soldiers. Immediately, ambitious bluecoats jumped across the stone wall and raced out to capture Confederate battle flags. A number of Carolinians and Tennesseans crawled away, heading for the safety of Emmitsburg Road. Captain Frank Bird (Co. C) snatched the 11th North Carolina's emblem and, with 1st Lt. Edward Outlaw (Co. C) crowding next to him in support, slipped away. Lieutenant Outlaw later recorded, "Captain Bird ... [brought] off the flag and the stub of the staff."[83]

The assault had collapsed. Now those who could skulked back towards the Confederate lines. One Tar Heel wrote, "The men retreated in squads."[84] Union artillery shot at the clumps of men, as did some infantry units. Another Confederate, contemplating this retreat, penned, "I saw plainly that it meant death to retreat across the open field a half mile or more.... It was death or surrender to remain. It seemed death to retreat.... We chose the latter alternative ... [and] we sped through the open field expecting every moment to be shot to the ground."[85] Private George Lassiter (Co. F) crawled for a while and then ran as fast as he could, reaching the Confederate lines having survived this assault without a scratch. He considered himself incredibly lucky.[86]

For the rest of the Tar Heels lying wounded and terrified in front of the stone wall, fortune would not be their friend. Yank soldiers prowled among the Confederates rousting up all the uninjured and marching them away. One of these Bethel boys, Pvt. Francis Ostwalt (Co. E), was captured near the wall. His family remembered "he went off to fight the Yankees and we never heard from him again."[87] Francis Ostwalt was one of nearly three dozen unhurt 11th North Carolina soldiers captured in the next couple hours.[88] Another of these Carolinians, Pvt. William Suggs (Co. G), recalled, "I was [captured] and returning to the ground which we passed near the stone wall.... I looked and saw Wm E.

Thirty-nine-year-old Pvt. Francis Ostwalt (Co. E) was captured near the stone wall (Thomas McAnear collection).

8. Gettysburg: July 3, 1863

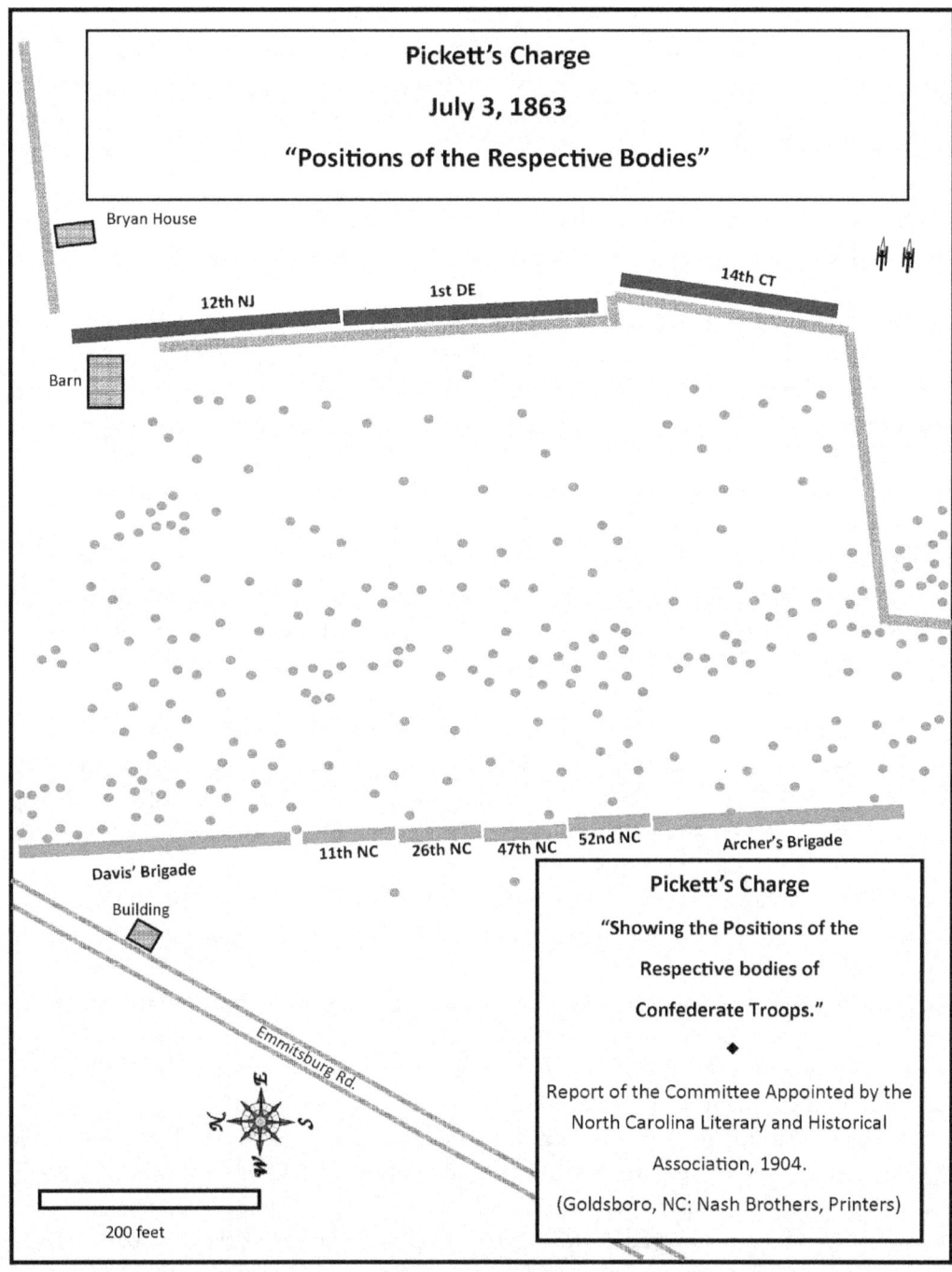

Crabtree [28th NC] of Chapel Hill lying on the ground.... I asked him where he was wounded, he pulled his shirt and showed me a wound in the point of the belly that must have gone through his bowels." William Suggs continued: "He asked me to help him to the rear.... I carried him twenty yards when he asked me to put him down. I did so and he ... died there."[89]

The battlefield was horrendous. A Federal soldier wrote "dead and dying were everywhere ... some crawling on their hands and knees."[90] A second rifleman added, "The wounded lay scattered over the ... field, writhing in pain."[91] A third watched as "a soldier was trying to stuff grass into his head wound."[92] A fourth wrote he saw "a young [soldier] crying and looking for a doctor, holding his bowels in his hands."[93] One Confederate summed up the scene, recording, "You never saw anything like it."[94] Years later, once rain and time had washed away the blood clotting upon the field, a Southerner would write "of the gallant and brave troops ... and the glorious courage of the unknown rank and file whose bones now lie under the edge of the stone wall."[95]

Back at the Confederate lines among the trees on Seminary Ridge the shocked survivors milled around in stunned devastation. General Pettigrew struggled to get his surviving officers to regain control of his broken division, but there were so few remaining that little could be done. One Carolinian noted, "It was a sight too fearful to behold."[96] General Lee rode by and ordered Pettigrew to mount a defense behind the Confederate artillery. Lee's presence heartened enough soldiers to their responsibilities that the disorderly mob of incoherent men was shoved into a defensive line. But Pettigrew's regiments were wrecked. The men were despondent and miserable. They sat appalled, gazing out across the field where their comrades lay dead or dying, cut down in a senseless assault. One Tar Heel officer wrote, "The charge was grand, but that is all it was." He grumbled that "some one blundered."[97] Another complained, "Alas! The reaper death cut down the fair plant of promise.... I could not but think it was a ... pleasant way to die."[98]

Captain Frank Bird scurried around searching for Bethel Regiment riflemen but he could not find many. Lieutenant Edward Outlaw (Co. E) wrote, "The regiment found itself reduced to a mere handful."[99] Frank Bird had someone tie the bullet-shredded battle flag to a pole and he used it as a rallying point. A few Bethel boys saw the emblem and drifted to it and after a few minutes a small clump of comrades clustered together near their flag. Captain Bird could locate only Cpt. John Freeland (Co. G) and 1st Sgt. John Watson (Co. E), but soon Cpt. William Kerr (Co. E) and 2nd Lt. Lewis Elias (Co. D) arrived.[100] This small cadre of leadership moved among the muddled and shambolic throng of dazed soldiers, pulling together men from their regiment. It was almost impossible to record any type of accurate muster; too many men were unaccounted for. First Sergeant George Erwin (Co. B) noted there were "not more than 80 men left and they are worn out."[102] A Tar Heel moaned, "Our regiment is ruined forever."[103]

The Carolina riflemen were placed along a section of a stone wall and told to wait for the expected Yankee counterattack. General A.P. Hill wrote, "[Our] attack failed ... [but] the enemy made no attempt to pursue."[104] Realizing the Federals had not mounted an attack, the weary Carolinians slumped at their posts, sleeping fitfully. But they knew, as 1st Sgt. George Erwin (Co. B) wrote, "the battle is apt to be decided tomorrow."[105] Lieutenant Lemuel Hoyle (Co. I) scribbled a note to his parents: "We have at last had to pass through the ordeal of fire and blood."[106]

Soldiers slowly filtered back from the battlefield all afternoon and evening. Once darkness stilled the battlefield, more Carolinians found their way back to the 11th North Carolina's ranks. Captain Albert Haynes (Co. I) recorded, "I crawled ... [for] hours ... and

8. Gettysburg: July 3, 1863

11th North Carolina Casualties[101]
July 3, 1863

Unit	Commander	Casualties*
F & S	Cpt. Mark Armfield	2
Co. A	Cpt. William Hand	33
Co. B	1st Lt. Thomas Parks	12
Co. C	Sgt. William Todd	5
Co. D	1st Lt. William Kincaid	15
Co. E	Cpt. William Kerr	9
Co. F	Cpt. Edward Small	25
Co. G	Cpt. John Freeland	10
Co. H	2nd Lt. James Saville	5
Co. I	Cpt. Albert Haynes	30
Co. K	Cpt. James Young	10
Total		156

*For a complete listing of July 3, 1863, casualties, see Appendix A, Gettysburg Casualties.

reached our lines at 11 p.m."[107] A few Bethel Regiment men staggered out onto the battlefield, hunting comrades. One soldier recorded of this sad journey that "[he] slowly crept back on to the field of battle searching for the body of his brother."[108] All night long, men came and went, and Cpt. Frank Bird struggled to record the regiment's health. Major John Jones (26th NC), still commanding the brigade, continually sent messengers asking for muster totals. The brigade commander worked feverishly to understand his formation's battle strength and to resupply the regiments in anticipation of tomorrow's fighting. But Jones was disheartened at the brigade's condition. He wrote, "Our brigade is in a bad fix."[109]

Chapter 9

Falling Waters, July 14, 1863

Captain Frank Bird worked continuously and by sunrise on July 4, 1863, had determined a way to keep the regiment organized and functioning. All night long Bethel Regiment soldiers had trickled into the 11th North Carolina's area, and night-duty Tar Heels reunited them with their comrades. Captain Bird mustered the men for roll call and the numbers were much better than those of twelve hours earlier. Frank Bird's formation now totaled 290.[1] Unfortunately for Bird, the regiment severely lacked experienced leadership. With Cpt. James Freeland acting as second-in-command, only four line officers and a first sergeant remained to command the companies. Captain Bird was forced to reorganize the men, combining the units into five composite companies.

11th North Carolina Muster[2]
July 4, 1863

Unit	Commander	Strength
F & S	Cpt. Frank Bird	2
Co. A	3rd Lt. William Taylor	36
Co. B	Cpl. H. Galloway	32
Co. C	Sgt. William Todd	22
Co. D	2nd Lt. Lewis Elias	36
Co. E	Cpt. William Kerr	16
Co. F	Sgt. Nathanial Mardre	28
Co. G	1st Sgt. Jones Watson	32
Co. H	Sgt. Stephen Blankenship	20
Co. I	Sgt. William Ramseur	24
Co. K	Cpt. James Young	41
Total		289

The men's morale was dismal. Captain Bird's riflemen gazed out at the body-strewn field and shook their heads in sadness. One wrote of yesterday's assault, "It was a second Fredericksburg, only the wrong way."[3] Another remarked, contemplating their missing comrades, "How painful indeed it must be to the parents and friends of [those] so young and promising, to hear that life's brittle thread has been cut."[4]

For the wounded Carolinians who lay out on the battlefield, the night had been filled with agony and terror. One of these injured soldiers, Pvt. Isaac Byrum (Co. F), recalled "He tried to drag himself [to safety] … but couldn't for all the other wounded and dead laying around." Isaac Byrum's story continued: "Flies were beginning to light on his wound, so he tore a piece of his army shirt off and wrapped it around the wound."⁵ Another Tar Heel, this one more fortunate than Pvt. Byrum, was 1st Lt. David Coon (Co. I). Lieutenant Coon, who suffered from multiple injuries, "[had] received such extensive wounds that he was left on the field to die in the muck and blood." Coon's "cries for help were answered by a Union soldier who covered him with his own coat and gave him coffee."⁶

As Cpt. Frank Bird was reporting his regiment's strength to the brigade commander, Maj. John Jones (26th NC), he could sense their army was about to go into motion. Rumors already had passed through the ranks, informing the riflemen: Lee had ordered a retreat. When Frank Bird attempted to verify this gossip he was told instructions had already been given to ready the casualties for travel. The wounded were to be loaded into wagons and ambulances. Since there were more casualties than vehicles to transport them, Gen. Lee's medical director had dictated "all sick and wounded soldiers who can accompany or closely follow" were to be allowed to accompany the wagons and ambulances filled with injured.⁷

Thirty-three-year-old Cpt. Francis "Frank" Bird (Co. C) commanded the regiment after Pickett's Charge (Clark, 1901).

The 11th North Carolina's wounded had been taken to a large complex of regimental and brigade field hospitals not far from the Samuel Lohr farm, two miles west of Herr Ridge. Here, there were over 1,500 injured soldiers being tended to by medical staff. One writer described this site, reporting it as "a great sea of white tents."⁸ A Gettysburg resident recalled, "Nothing before in my experience had ever paralleled the sight we ... beheld. They were groaning and crying, the struggling and dying, crowded side-by-side, while attendants sought to aid and relieve them."⁹ Another pronounced the site a horrid place "marked by a red flag attached to a stick planted in the ground ... [and] with a large collection of apple butter pots filled with water to be used for the wounded."¹⁰

The 11th North Carolina's hospital held nearly 225 men.¹¹ Doctors John Wilson and James McCombs had toiled all night, along with the assistance of the regiment's band members, doing the best they could to patch up their men. But the field hospital, like every medical station about Gettysburg, was overflowing with hurt soldiers. Men lay prostrate with wounds gouged through every conceivable part of the human body. Among these battered Tar Heels was the regiment's colonel, Collett Leventhorpe. He was seriously injured; his shattered arm bones needed to be amputated but he refused to allow this to happen. Doctor Wilson had warned Leventhorpe about the possibilities of gangrene but the colonel was willing to gamble his life in the hopes he could keep his arm.¹²

When Dr. Wilson received the orders to organize his wounded for travel he was immediately faced with a horrible dilemma; there were not enough vehicles to carry all the regiment's patients. Doctor Wilson had to decide which men could survive the rigors of travel and which would have to be left behind, a heart-wrenching situation. Unfortunately Dr. Wilson was not alone. This same scene occurred at each regimental hospital in the division, as there was travel space for only half the number of wounded soldiers.[13] A Carolinian wrote, "The wounded, not able to be hauled, were left in [the] hospital near the town with surgeons and nurses to attend their wants."[14]

John Wilson slowly made his way among the 11th North Carolina's suffering men and identified eighty to be abandoned[15] (see the appendix for a list of those left behind). Wilson also designated a number of volunteers to stay with the hurt soldiers, because, as Cpt. Albert Haynes (Co. I) noted, "We were allowed one man to a company to wait on the wounded." Captain Haynes continued: "I kept Fred Wash Dellinger in my company ... in that capacity."[16] The wounded quickly realized what Dr. Wilson was doing, and they all clamored to be included among those to be approved for transport to Virginia. They feared being captured by the Yankees and were uneasy about what kind of medical attention they would receive. Assistant surgeon James McComb offered to remain behind to direct the ten volunteers; sadly, there was nothing more which could be done. Those selected for travel were carried to the brigade's wagon train, where the 11th North Carolina's vehicles were the first in line, as the Bethel Regiment's wagons were slotted to lead the division's convoy. Doctor Wilson's unit had only two ambulances. One was filled by Col. Leventhorpe, 2nd Lt. Lemuel Hoyle (Co. I), and another officer. The other ambulance received more officers. The enlisted men were crammed into a dozen regimental wagons, with most of the men being forced to lie on the wooden floorboards, as little straw could be gathered to soften their ride. The last of the 11th's wounded were packed into the wagons as the gray skies above them began to leak rain, and soon this drizzle exploded into a full-fledged summer downpour. An officer wrote, "Canvas was no protection against its fury, and the wounded men lying upon the naked boards of the wagon-bodies were drenched."[17] Finally, at 4:00 p.m., word was given and the wagon train began to roll towards the west; there were over 12,500 wounded men riding in, or hobbling alongside, over 1,200 vehicles.[18] The morning's rain continued, soaking the Pennsylvania landscape and softening the roads. The wagon train extended for seventeen miles, and the vehicles' thousands of steel wheels quickly chewed up the saturated roads, causing many vehicles to sink into the mud and slow travel speed.

As the rain pounded the battlefield, Cpt. Bird and his regiment manned their position behind a stone wall, ever vigilant against a Northern assault. The morning's heat had attacked the corpses strewn out before them. One soldier wrote, "The dead are not buried yet, and as the weather is very hot, the bodies are turning black, swelling and bursting, which make them smell very strong."[19] Though the men knew the wounded were being transported away, no word had arrived for them to move. So they hunched their shoulders and sat, soaked by the afternoon's rain. Most were miserable. One remarked, "[We] had done very hard fighting, lost a lot of men, and yet have failed to accomplish anything."[20] Their brigade commander, Maj. John Jones (26th NC), recorded, "We remained in position."[21]

Later that afternoon, Maj. John Jones gave the word for the regiments to prepare to march once the sky was sufficiently dark to mask their movements. Captain Frank Bird got his men into marching formation and had stalwart NCO's make sure no one was left behind. Unfortunately there were nearly three dozen Bethel soldiers still lying out on the battlefield, wounded. There was no way their distraught comrades could retrieve them, so they would be abandoned. One of these soldiers, 1st Lt. David Coon (Co. I), "lay in a grove near the field, eleven days with only an awning stretched above him."[22]

Then the Confederates went into motion, heading west toward Hagerstown. They slogged forward all night, stumbling and falling frequently in the rain-filled darkness. A waterlogged soldier recalled, "The road was muddy and slippery ... the night dark, rainy, dreary, and dismal."[23] Another recorded, "The rain fell in sheets and [the night was] ... so dark we could not see our hand an inch from our eyes when there was no lightning."[24]

The next day, July 5, 1863, found the long wagon train inching its way towards Greencastle, Pennsylvania. During the early morning, aggressive Union cavalry commanders had swung around Gettysburg's battlefield with the goal of attacking the Confederate supply trains. Instead, what they found was this massive convoy of wounded. General Lee had anticipated a possible Northern incursion against these wounded and detailed Brig. Gen. John Imboden and his independent cavalry brigade to protect the wagon train. Imboden had nearly 2,000 men. He placed the 18th VA at the head of the wagons, and then spread out the remaining troopers along the long column.[25] Seventeen miles of wagons and ambulances was an immense length to shield; it took Brig. Gen. Imboden hours to travel from one end to the other. He wrote, "For four hours I hurried on my way to the front, and in all that time I was never out of hearing of the groans and cries of the wounded and dying."[26] All Imboden could do was hope his units of horsemen would be enough to keep the Yanks at bay.

Two hundred cavalrymen from the 1st NY and the 12th PA commanded by Cpt. Abraham Jones (1st NY) struck the wagon train at dusk that evening. Captain Jones had sent a detachment to fight against the nearest Confederate cavalry squadron to occupy them while he sent the rest of his troops to capture a segment of the convoy. By pure bad luck for the Bethel Regiment's wounded, the Federals struck the front of Heth's division; led by Pettigrew's brigade and the vehicles of the 11th North Carolina. A Tar Heel described what happened: "I looked back and saw that a small squad of cavalry had dashed into the road ... striking the front of Heth's train [and] captured several teams, wagons and ambulances, the first ambulance having Col. Leventhorpe."[27]

Lieutenant Lemuel Hoyle (Co. I), who was riding beside Leventhorpe, was able to slip out of the ambulance and slither away into the weeds during the initial confusion; however, Col. Leventhorpe was snagged. He and six other Carolina wounded and five teamsters were hauled away as captives.[28] Colonel Leventhorpe would be eventually sent to the prison at Ft. McHenry, Maryland, and from there to Pt. Lookout, Maryland, where he remained until being exchanged in March 1864. Collett Leventhorpe's injury became infected with gangrene and the Union doctors decided amputation was the only solution. Leventhorpe wrote, "This [I] refused to allow, and as an alternative [I] was informed that ... [an application] of acid was advisable. [I] refus[ed] chloroform ... and submitted to this most agonizing pain as the liquid fire burnt its way into sore swollen flesh." Collett Leventhorpe continued, saying "he closed his lips and submitted to the ordeal without a moan ... [and] would have died rather than let the enemy see that a Confederate officer could not endure."[29]

Early, before sunrise on July 6, 1863, the head of the wagon train reached Williamsport, Maryland, and by the end of the day, over 4,000 wagons and ambulances clogged the canal town's streets.[30] The past few days' heavy rains had swollen the Potomac River, making it impossible to cross at the ford; suddenly there was no place for the vehicles to go. The town became a madhouse of wagons and ambulances stuffed with injured men. Soon it was decided to remove the wounded men from their vehicles and place them in barns, warehouses, churches, and houses. One citizen wrote "the cries and moanings of the wounded rebels could be heard for more than a mile."[31] Another noted everything stank: "The foul body odors, coupled with the smell of offal and rotting human ... flesh ... [were] indescribable."[32]

Meanwhile, the infantrymen slowly slopped their way westward, struggling in the mud and rain, without sleep, and lacking rations. One Tar Heel recorded, "July 5: march of ten miles today.... July 6: we crossed the South Mountains at Monterey Gap."[33] The soldiers were exhausted and coated with mud. A Confederate wrote, "[We] were all wet and many of them muddy ... from having fallen down.... [We] looked as if [we] had been wallowing in a mud hole."[34] The Southerners were also hungry. Every farm they passed was stripped of anything edible. One infantrymen recalled, "Two soldiers went off somewhere and killed a large sheep, stole it ... [as] we could not stand on formalities for a hungry soldier would steal anything that he could eat." He continued: "It did not take 22 men as hungry as we were long to eat a sheep weighing about 75 pounds."[35]

The next day, July 7, 1863, the 11th North Carolina reached Hagerstown, Maryland, and Cpt. Frank Bird's weary men slumped down in the mud and slept. General Henry Heth returned to duty as division commander and Brig. Gen. James Pettigrew took over brigade leadership, sending Maj. Jones back to the 26th NC.[36] Heavy rains continued to drench the landscape, turning every bottomland into a swamp, which the soldiers' passage quickly turned into a muddy morass. The Potomac River remained way too high to ford, trapping the Confederate army. Army of Northern Virginia engineers contacted Richmond, and materials for pontoon boats were being hurried to aid the cornered Confederates. But for now, the infantry had to face east and prepare themselves against Union assaults. Supplies and ammunition were handed out to the riflemen. The Bethel Regiment's commander, Cpt. Frank Bird, as he struggled to get rations and supplies to his soldiers, discovered he enjoyed working closely with Brig. Gen. James Pettigrew. Frank Bird wrote, "Since the fight [Gettysburg] I have in some way made a very warm friend of him."[37] The soldiers remained in place and one tired infantryman recorded, "July 8: we are having a very much needed rest."[38]

Meanwhile, while Gen. Lee's exhausted infantry did little his engineers feverishly worked to complete a set of entrenchments just east of Williamsport. By midday, July 10, 1863, Lee's engineers had finished the fortifications and word went out to the divisions to move. The earthworks stretched for nine miles and were so well planned that, as one officer boasted, "Lee could have held them against any attack of the Army of the Potomac."[39] The defenses consisted of two lines of trenches. The first line was for skirmishers, constructed of "forward bastions made of packed earth and, at places, wheat sheaves covered with earth."

The second line was much stronger, built with "fence rails, rocks, and packed earth—described by one eyewitness as a 'very strong line of gopher holes and rifle pits.'"[40] The Carolinians moved into their portion of the entrenchments. A Tar Heel wrote, "We moved 4½ miles on the other side of town and [into the] fortified position."[41]

General Pettigrew's brigade occupied a section of entrenchments not far from the brick structures making up St. James College. The infantrymen quickly spread out and devoured any food they could find and hauled off anything they could use to improve their earthworks.[42] A nearby farmer complained: "He lost seven of his best horses and all of his cattle ... [plus] all his bacon—he knew he had 17 hams, shoulders, and sides ... [and] all his corn."[43] The Confederate riflemen were not bothered by these local deprivations; instead they prepared for the expected Yank attack. One infantryman recorded, "We lay under arms all night."[44]

Union probes began on July 12, 1863, but the Federal soldiers could see the well-prepared defenses and had no interest in making frontal assaults. A Tar Heel noted "skirmishing ... [to] our left and centre."[45] Meanwhile, Confederate engineers and men from the Pioneer Corps frantically worked to build a pontoon bridge over the Potomac at a place called Falling Waters (MD) a dozen miles southwest of the earthworks. A number of men from Pettigrew's brigade worked in this endeavor. One wrote that "he worked from July 7 to 12 carrying planks on his shoulders for a half-mile to accumulate material to make pontoons."[46] Finally, on July 13, 1863, the pontoon bridge was completed, the wounded were loaded back into vehicles, and the injured were transported across the Potomac.

Then Gen. Lee's army went into motion. Lieutenant General Richard Ewell's Second Corps abandoned their portion of the lines and forded the now-safe-to-wade Potomac River just west of Williamsport. Lieutenant General James Longstreet's First Corps slipped out of the earthworks and hiked to the Falling Waters pontoon bridge. Longstreet's soldiers, artillery, and supply trains escaped to Virginia, leaving only Lt. Gen. Ambrose Hill's Third Corps holding the entrenchments. General Lee ordered two of Hill's divisions across the Potomac at Falling Waters and retained Henry Heth's formation as the army's rear guard. Major John Jones (26th NC) recorded, "We remained there [in the entrenchments] until the night of the 13th."[47] The Tar Heels were unhappy and their morale dangerously low, especially since they had received word Vicksburg had fallen.[48] The return of more rain, along with watching everyone else pull out, did little to sustain the men's spirits. One soaked and distraught Confederate wrote, "Such a rain I thought I never before knew to fall."[49] Another scribbled, "I am worn out with exposure and hardships.... I have not been able to change my clothing for ten days."[50] And a third complained, "Seems like the lice will devour us."[51]

Later that night orders came directing Henry Heth to pull his men out of the earthworks. Davis's brigade marched away, followed by Brockenbrough's men. Once those two formations were gone, Brig. Gen. James Pettigrew, now in charge of both his Carolinians and Archer's Tennesseans, gave the command to withdraw.[52] His riflemen had built up all their campfires in hopes this subterfuge would fool the Yanks and buy them some time; in addition, a thin screen of butternut-clad cavalry filed into the trenches to cover Pettigrew's departure.

The men in the 11th North Carolina stumbled southward toward the Falling Waters pontoon bridge, staggering blindly in the night's darkness, fighting the deep mud, and tripping over abandoned military equipment. General Henry Heth recorded, "The night was entirely dark and the roads in dreadful condition, the entire distance ... being ankle-deep in mud."[53] One of Heth's rifleman wrote, "We started our retreat at dark and marched ... through mud and slush.... We [walked] in fours and linked arms for protection, two tall men generally taking the outside."[54] Another scribbled, "It appeared to me that at least half of the road was a quagmire."[55] The march was cruelly slow, with many halts for unknown lengths of time forcing the exhausted men to wallow in the deep mud awaiting the next order to march. Major General Heth wrote, "The division was twelve hours accomplishing seven miles."[56]

By sunrise on July 14, 1863, Henry Heth's division was within two miles of Falling Waters, but the traffic jam of soldiers, vehicles, and artillery pieces up ahead forced them to stop. General Lee ordered Heth to turn his men around and form a defensive line. The exhausted soldiers about-faced along the crest of a ridge. They stared out from their position with sleep-deprived eyes into the thick morning mists. Heth placed Davis's brigade on the far right, then Brockenbrough, and finally Pettigrew in charge of Archer's and his own brigade, a battle line extending for a mile.[57] Major General Henry Heth noted, "On reaching an elevated and commanding ridge of hills one mile and a half ... from Falling Waters, I ... put my division in line of battle on either side of the road."[58] One of his Tar Heels recorded, "After traveling all night in the mud and rain, about 8 o'clock ... we took position ... as a portion of the rear guard, while the rest of the troops crossed the river at the pontoon bridge."[59]

Brigadier General James Pettigrew's half of the division consisted of 1,300 men; his brigade totaled 800; Archer's 500. The two units were anchored by Archer's Tennesseans just north of the Falling Waters Road, near the farm of Daniel Donnelly.[60] Sometime in the past couple of days, Confederate engineers had created half a dozen artillery emplacements, and these works were filled by Archer's men. The North Carolinians stretched out to the left of the Tennesseans, Pettigrew's four regiments extending over a quarter of a mile. The riflemen moved slowly, almost as if they were intoxicated. One wrote, "We were wet to the skin and ... exhausted through hunger, fatigue, and marching."[61] Another recorded they were "tired, foot-sore, wet, hungry, and literally frazzled out."[62] The commander of the 26th NC wrote, "The men stacked arms, and most of them [fell] asleep, feeling ... secure, as [we had been told] our cavalry were out in front."[63]

Brigadier General James Pettigrew met with Henry Heth and the two studied the division's placement. The four infantry brigades were well positioned to defend against any frontal attack. Henry Heth observed, "In our front was an open space, with the view unobstructed for half to three-quarters of a mile."[64] However, neither general was satisfied as two problems went unaddressed: first, the division's battle line could be flanked on either end by a fast-moving enemy; and second, Gen. Lee refused to provide the position with any artillery. General Pettigrew grumbled, "Did you ever hear of a rear guard of a retreating army without artillery?"[65] With no good answer to this question about artillery support, Pettigrew returned to his Tar Heels and ordered a skirmish line to extend all the way to a canal bordering the Potomac River. A company of disheveled riflemen stumbled down the ridge's slope and spread out in a thin line, fifty men covering nearly 300 yards. This small force was the only unit sent out as an advance precaution along the entire battle line. One Confederate wrote, "We had no pickets out; there was no fear or concern ... [as] we supposed that Stuart's Cavalry was in our front."[66]

Unknown to Heth's men, there were no Southern cavalry screening them from the Federals; Stuart's troopers were elsewhere. The vacuum behind Heth's retreating division had been filled by aggressive Union cavalrymen commanded by Brig. Gen. Hugh Judson Kilpatrick. His troopers had followed up on hints the Confederate lines may have been empty with quick forays during the night of July 13, 1863. Now, as the morning sun struggled with the thick ground fog, Kilpatrick's squadrons were racing along the road Heth's men had taken only hours before. Kilpatrick's horsemen halted in the woods, about a mile west of Heth's battle line, and the determined general (whose nickname was "Kill-cavalry") studied the Confederates. Kilpatrick recorded "the enemy was found in large force, drawn up in line of battle, on the crest of a hill commanding the road on which I was advancing. His left was protected by earthworks." Kilpatrick also noted "the enemy was, when first seen ... with arms stacked."[67]

General Kilpatrick immediately ordered an attack and turned to Brig. Gen. George Custer, who quickly deployed the 6th MI for a dismounted assault. Kilpatrick was not satisfied with Custer's cautious decision and countermanded the deployment. Instead, Kilpatrick ordered Maj. Peter Weber (6th MI) to lead a frontal attack with two companies.[68] Major Weber placed nearly 150 troopers into a column and moved them onto the Falling Waters Road, heading toward the Confederate-held heights.

Generals Heth and Pettigrew were together when they observed this body of advancing cavalry. The horsemen's identity was difficult to determine because of the shrouding mists. Henry Heth wrote, "A small body of cavalry ... made their presence known in our front ... [and] they galloped up the road, and halted some 175 yards from my battle line." Heth continued: "From their maneuvering and the smallness of numbers, I concluded it was a party of our own cavalry."[69] Pettigrew was also puzzled; the horsemen and their mounts were covered with mud, making their uniforms indistinguishable. The cavalry unit did possess a Federal pennant but Heth believed it must be a trophy Stuart's men had captured.[70]

First Lieutenant Edward Outlaw (Co. C) was with Cpt. Frank Bird as they watched this column of horsemen gallop towards them. Edward Outlaw wrote, "The men being mostly asleep—a small body of cavalry ... made its appearance, and ... was allowed to approach within 175 yards unmolested."[71] An officer nearby observed with horror and recorded, "I saw a sight that for a moment paralyzed me. A ... line of blue rapidly forming in shape for a charge."[72] The Federal cavalry wheeled from a column into a battle line and charged, the troopers wielding their sabers. Quickly reacting, Confederate officers and NCO's hollered and kicked at their sleeping men. A few pickets fired their muskets but Henry Heth ordered them to quit shooting, as he was convinced they were Confederate cavalry.[73] But the NCO's knew otherwise. One wrote, "I fairly flew toward my comrades, lying stretched out in sleep ... yelling at the top of my voice: 'Lookout! Look out! The Yankees!'"[74]

Major Weber's cavalry covered that last 150 yards so fast the Confederates had time to let loose only a single, ragged volley from the muskets that had not been fouled by the night's rain and mud.[75] The Union cavalry rode over and through the hastily assembled line of Confederates, knocking some down and brushing the rest aside. One Southerner remarked, "The Yankee cavalry came bursting in among us in full tilt, shouting as they waved their carbines: 'Surrender!'"[76] Another recalled, "They struck ... cutting right and left, and riding over our men while asleep, breaking arms and legs and trampling some to death."[77] A Confederate noted, "The next thing I knew I was wide awake, with rifles cracking around me. I sprang to my feet.... Men on horses were amongst us—blue men with drawn sabers."[78] The bluecoats swung their horses around and came back at the Southerners, many of whom still did not have their weapons. One rifleman wrote, "Our men scattered in every direction, most of them leaving their guns in the stack."[79]

The Union attack cut through Archer's men, bewildering the confused Tennesseans. The cavalrymen swung to the north, clawing at the Tennesseans and heading towards the Tar Heels, but now the Confederates were reacting like ants when their anthill has been disturbed. A Southerner wrote, "The men clubbed their guns and knocked Yankees off of their horses. One man knocked one off with a fence rail and another killed a Yankee with an ax."[80] Pettigrew's North Carolinians retrieved their rifles and began to fire at the Northerners, and companies of men from Brockenbrough's brigade joined into the melee. One writer noted "they were engaged in a brutal hand to hand fight."[81]

Brigadier General James Pettigrew's horse became frightened by this sudden onslaught of screaming cavalrymen and started to buck. Pettigrew, who was hampered by one of his arms being bound in a sling, was thrown to the ground. A Confederate wrote, "Rising, [Pettigrew] drew his pistol, and was about to take part in the skirmish."[82] Pettigrew ran into the thick of the fighting among the Tennesseans and, as he approached a Yank crouched near a barn, the Northerner shot him. Pettigrew fell to the ground, and a horrified soldier wrote, "A bullet hit Pettigrew in the lower abdomen just to the left of the navel and passed out through the base of the spine."[83] Then the last of the Yanks were downed and the fight was over. Lieutenant Edward Outlaw (Co. C) recorded, "They madly charged our lines, and were annihilated."[84] Henry Heth remarked, "In less than three minutes they were all killed or captured."[85] The Northerners had lost 40 killed and 85 wounded.[86] The Confederate losses were less than a couple dozen; however, Brig. Gen. James Pettigrew was severely hurt. Captain Frank Bird was worried about his friend, and wrote, "Pettigrew [was] badly wounded in the bowels, I fear mortally."[87] General Heth called for Maj. John Jones (26th NC) and informed him that he, once again, was in charge of Pettigrew's brigade.[88]

Union Brig. Gen. Kilpatrick was not deterred by this rash assault's failure. He quickly ordered a brigade-sized frontal attack, this time with his troopers advancing as dismounted soldiers. They moved forward against Brockenbrough.[89] General Henry Heth wrote, "A large body of dismounted cavalry ... made a vigorous attack on Brockenbrough's brigade.... Brockenbrough repelled the attack, and drove the enemy back into the woods."[90] A Federal officer wrote, "The enemy's rear guard made an obstinate resistance."[91] Brockenbrough's Confederates pushed forward and pursued the Northerners before running into more bluecoats. The Southerners backed up but not before Kilpatrick sent Custer's entire brigade

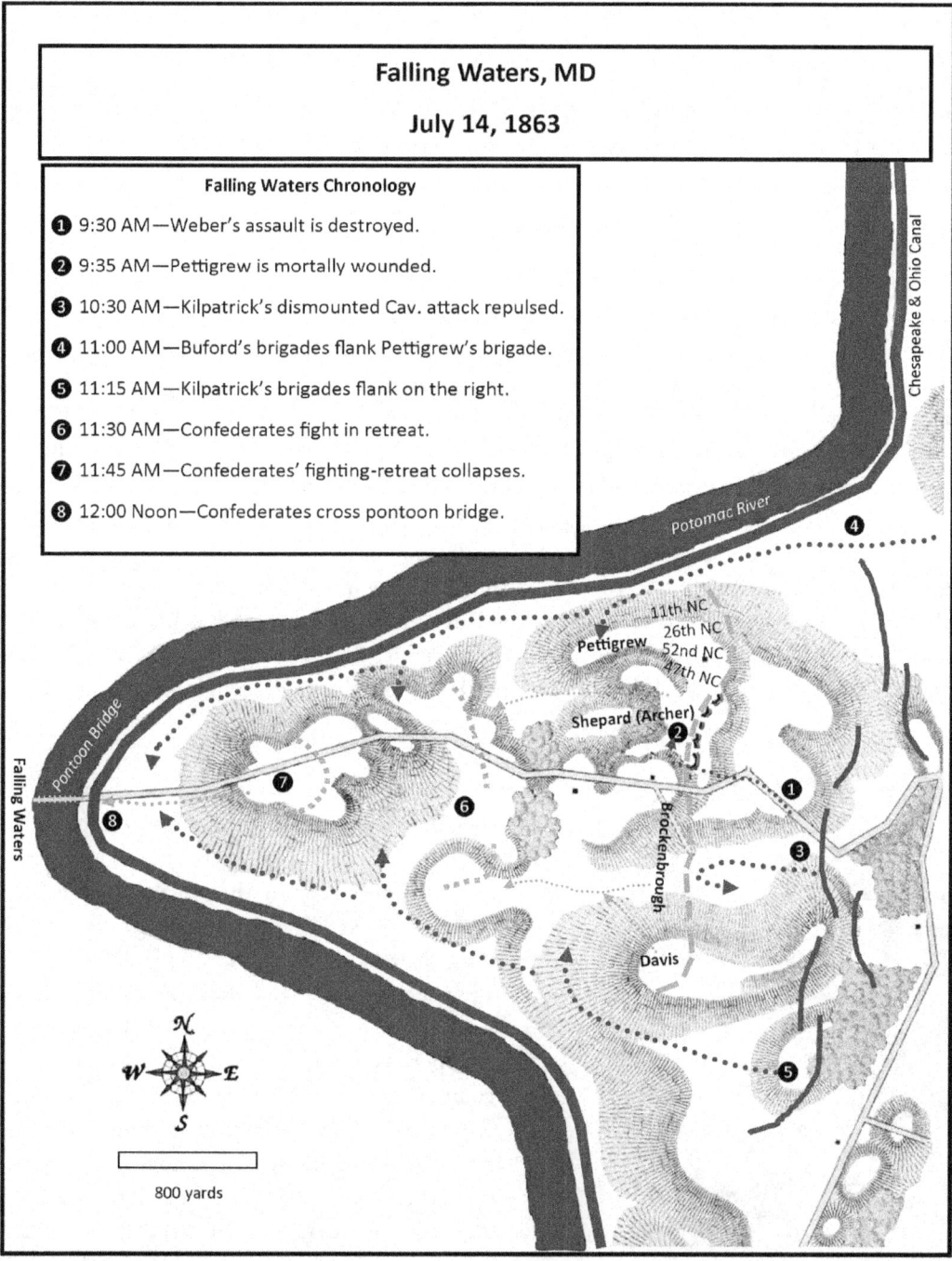

forward, again as dismounted riflemen, and they struck Brockenbrough.[92] The Confederates were sent reeling, placing Davis's men in jeopardy and forcing them to backpeddle to keep from being flanked.

As these actions developed on Heth's right flank, the situation on his left flank also grew ominous. Brigadier General John Buford, commanding two brigades of cavalry, some

4,000 veterans, had now reached the field. Buford's horsemen emerged from the northeast, following the Chesapeake and Ohio Canal's towpath, and pressed against the 11th North Carolina's skirmish line. General Heth recorded, "The enemy appeared on my left flank in force."[93] Captain Frank Bird's skirmish line was quickly overrun and these Tar Heels scattered, leaving behind a wounded Cpl. James Adams (Co. C).[94] Most were able to escape back to the Bethel Regiment's main line, but some, like Pvt. Joseph King (Co. C) were captured. There was nothing Cpt. Frank Bird could do to stop this horde of bluecoats.[95] His Tar Heels had to fall back. Heth wrote, "Seeing the attack was becoming serious.... I sent a message to [A.P. Hill] requesting that artillery be sent to me ... [but instead] Hill directed me to withdraw my command as speedily as possible."[96]

General Heth gave the word to his brigade commanders to conduct a fighting retreat. Major John Jones and Lt. Col. Samuel Shepard (commanding Archer's brigade) worked as a pair, one unit holding their position while the other fell back. Then the rear brigade covered the other as it retreated. Major Jones recorded, "I received orders to fall back gradually to the river. I did so, fighting the enemy."[97] Both brigades were able to leapfrog backwards for nearly three-quarters of a mile. Lieutenant Colonel Shepard (7th TN) wrote, "We kept our lines pretty well organized."[98] Buford's cavalrymen pushed hard against the Tennesseans and Tar Heels, pressing with troopers at their front, while others tried to get past their flank. But, as yet, the Confederates had been able to keep pulling back just before the Yanks could break their defense. More Carolinians were hit; Pvt. Thomas Pearson (Co. B) was slightly wounded and Pvt. John Cook (Co. D) had a ball slice through his cheek.[99] One rifleman recalled, "It was shoot, run and load, halt, shoot, and run again, with no let up."[100]

Nineteen-year-old Pvt. Joseph King (Co. C) was captured when the 11th NC was flanked (Clark, 1901).

Heth's other two brigades were also fighting to maintain cohesiveness against the pressure applied by Kilpatrick's bluecoats. They were able to withdraw over a half-mile, keeping the Northerners at bay. But now their withdrawal opened up clear terrain along their right flank. A Southern noted, "Only a few minutes elapsed before the large fields to our right ... were uncovered."[101] Kilpatrick's troopers swarmed around the Confederates' right and raced to get behind them and cut off their retreat. Davis and Brockenbrough's veterans fled to the rear, stampeding to reach the pontoon bridge. The Federals began to corner groups of trapped Confederates. One Southerner wrote, "The enemy pressed our retreat, and many fell by the wayside from exhaustion."[102]

General Buford's troopers eventually were able to swing past Cpt. Frank Bird's Carolinians and gallop ahead of them. The Tar Heels turned and raced towards the pontoon bridge.

9. Falling Waters, July 14, 1863

One wrote, "They ... had overlapped both wings of our small force."[103] A Federal officer crowed, "After a fight of two hours and a half, we routed the enemy at all points."[104] A Confederate scribbled, "Our command was running for dear life in the direction of the Potomac River."[105] Captain Frank Bird angrily remarked, "Lee was willing to sacrifice our brigade to save the army but I tell you we had no notion of being taken."[106]

The Confederates ran for the pontoon bridge, tossing aside anything which slowed their flight, but the Northerners were mounted and able to travel faster. The Yanks herded clumps of Southerners together and gathered them up as prisoners. Rifle fire crackled in the late morning's air as bluecoats fired upon Confederates who refused to surrender. Sergeant William Todd (Co. C) was struck in the thigh and Pvt. Joseph Boyles (Co. I) hit in the left arm.[107] A cluster of Tar Heels from Company D sought shelter in a ravine, only to find themselves surrounded. The bluecoats fired a volley at the encircled men, striking Pvt. Thomas Benfield (Co. D) in the thigh and wounding Pvt. William Williams (Co. D) slightly. First Sergeant Joseph Brittain (Co. D) and Sgt. Samuel Black (Co. D) realized their men would be slaughtered if they resisted further, and they threw down their weapons. Over a dozen Burke County men surrendered. A Federal officer from the 53rd PA wrote, "In a ravine, a number of prisoners were captured."[108] General John Buford recorded, "The division succeeded in getting the road, and attacking the enemy in flank and rear, doing him great damage, and scattering him in confusion through the woods and ravines."[109]

The Confederates in Brockenbrough's and Davis's brigades scurried towards the pontoon bridge. Kilpatrick's horsemen thundered after them, netting played-out Southerners. An officer in Brockenbrough's brigade wrote, "As we were scattered upon the field and the squadrons came charging among us, a group of men gathered about me asking, 'Captain, what shall we do?' 'Stand still,' I replied, 'and cast down your muskets.'"[110] Others though, kept running and dodging and made their way to the pontoon bridge.

General Henry Heth's survivors reached the pontoon bridge and hurried across. A Confederate battery on the heights above the west side of the Potomac opened fire on the pursuing Federals and the bluecoats backed away, giving the Southerners a few precious minutes. One of these fortunate Confederates wrote, "We had arrived in sight of the Virginia bluffs ... when ... a couple of pieces of artillery planted on the bluff opened fire upon the enemy." The rifleman continued:

Thirty-five-year-old Sgt. Samuel Black (Co. D) was captured within a half mile of the pontoon bridge (Michael Black and Virginia Barlow collection).

"The bursting of the shell in the enemy's line, followed rapidly by other shots, stopped their advance ... [and] the sound of these guns was to us the sweetest music that ever fell upon our ears."[111]

11th North Carolina Casualties[112]
July 14, 1863

Unit	Commander	Casualties*
F & S	Cpt. Frank Bird	0
Co. A	3rd Lt. William Taylor	8
Co. B	Cpl. H. Galloway	23
Co. C	1st Lt. Edward Outlaw	8
Co. D	2nd Lt. Lewis Elias	16
Co. E	Cpt. William Kerr	3
Co. F	Sgt. Nathanial Mardre	7
Co. G	1st Sgt. Jones Watson	7
Co. H	Sgt. Stephen Blankenship	5
Co. I	Sgt. William Ramseur	5
Co. K	Cpt. James Young	11
Total		93

*For a complete listing of July 14, 1863, casualties, see Appendix A, Falling Waters Casualties.

The remnants of Pettigrew's brigade were the last to cross the pontoon bridge, with Maj. John Jones and a portion of his 26th North Carolina bringing up the rear. As the men hustled across the 800-foot-long expanse, Army of North Virginia engineers began hacking at the ropes fastening the boats to the Maryland side of the bridge. With the ropes severed, the pontoon bridge swung away from the eastern shore, cutting off the Union pursuit. Major Jones wrote, "We crossed the pontoon about 12 noon, just as the bridge was being cut loose."[113] First Lieutenant Edward Outlaw (Co. C) added, "As the brigade crossed ... the pontoon bridge was cut loose, and for the first time for many days the command drew a free breath."[114]

The Gettysburg campaign was now concluded for the soldiers on the Virginia side of the Potomac. Unfortunately for the Confederates who had not reached the pontoon bridge in time, they were all scooped up by the Federals and marched off to prisoner of war camps. A writer noted "[the] stragglers left on the Maryland side by this premature cutting loose of the bridge ... fell into the enemy's hands."[115] The Bethel Regiment's riflemen were gathered together and the roll called. Captain Frank Bird determined the 11th North Carolina had lost over 90 soldiers.[116] The next morning, Maj. John Jones put the battered Carolina brigade into the division's line of march, and the Southerners trekked to Bunker Hill, Virginia.[117]

Chapter 10

Bristoe Station, October 14, 1863

Captain Frank Bird's regiment was shattered. The battered riflemen stumbled around, going through the motions, stunned by the past two weeks' violence. Just fourteen days ago the regiment had been robust and the ranks filled with over 650 Carolinians. This morning only a shell remained. The Bethel formation's morning roll call ended quickly, as just over 200 men answered when their names were called.[1] Rations were distributed and supplies brought in, but nothing could be done to return over 400 missing brothers and neighbors. No one could have conceived of the war's ferocity; the regiment's part in the fighting at Gettysburg had lasted no more than ninety minutes, and the scramble at Falling Waters had taken barely two hours, and yet only one man out of three remained. The Carolinians now understood what fire, steel, and lead did to human courage. Second Lieutenant Lemuel Hoyle (Co. I), writing from his hospital bed as he recovered from his wounds, told his mother, "We have ... had to pass through the ordeal of fire and blood."[2]

11th North Carolina Muster[3]
July 15, 1863

Unit	Commander	Strength
F & S	Cpt. Frank Bird	2
Co. A	3rd Lt. William Taylor	29
Co. B	—	14
Co. C	1st Lt. Edward Outlaw	20
Co. D	2nd Lt. Lewis Elias	24
Co. E	Cpt. William Kerr	14
Co. F	Sgt. Thomas Small	22
Co. G	Cpt. John Freeland	26
Co. H	Sgt. Stephen Blankenship	16
Co. I	Sgt. Walter Ramseur	20
Co. K	Cpt. James Young	31
Total		218

Two days later, Cpt. Bird received the sad news that his friend Brig. Gen. James J. Pettigrew had died. Pettigrew, mortally wounded in the rearguard fight, had been transported across the pontoon bridge and taken to Bunker Hill. The injured general was housed in the John Boyd home, but the damage to his body was too severe, and he died on July 17, 1863. General Robert E. Lee remarked, "The Army has lost a brave soldier and the Confederacy an accomplished officer."[4]

On July 20, 1863, Lt. Col. William Martin returned to the regiment, having recuperated from his illness.[5] Captain Frank Bird eagerly turned command back to the unit's sole surviving field-grade officer. William Martin, though aware of the Bethel Regiment's casualties, was stunned by the weary, skeletal formation which paraded before him. The appalled lieutenant colonel and exhausted senior captain met to commence rebuilding their unit, only to be disappointed when informed Martin was now the senior brigade officer. He was forced to assume brigade leadership and Frank Bird again ran the regiment. Lieutenant Colonel Martin's first order to the brigade was to prepare to march—they were leaving Bunker Hill.

The Tar Heels hiked away from their camp, heading south toward Winchester. They crossed the Shenandoah River on July 22, and trekked through the Blue Ridge Mountains the next day. Two days later, on July 25, 1863, the footsore soldiers pitched camp outside Culpepper, Virginia.[6] Major General Henry Heth informed Lt. Col. Martin and the other brigade commanders the division would remain at Culpepper for some time. Their campsite was close to the railroad line and supplies would be arriving to reequip the division. Three days later, Col. Thomas Singletary and the 44th NC arrived and were added to the Tar Heel brigade.[7] Colonel Singletary became the brigade's senior officer, and Lt. Col. Martin moved his headquarters back to the Eleventh.

Lieutenant Colonel William Martin immediately began to address some of the regiment's leadership needs. Second Lt. William Turner (Co. E) was promoted to 1st lt.; the regiment's commissary sergeant, William Dickerson (Co. K), was elevated to 2nd lt. and returned to his company; Sgt. James Whitaker (Co. G) was advanced to 2nd lt.; and Pvt. Robert Lowrie (Co. H), whose two brothers, both officers in Co. H, were now dead, was promoted to 1st lt.[8] However, William Martin could go no further. Even though every company lacked an officer or two—Company B had none—Martin was prevented from promoting anyone else to fill the empty slots. The Confederate and North Carolina regulations maintained the statute which required a regiment to keep every officer on the roll books, even if that man was incapacitated by wounds or illness or was in a Federal prisoner of war facility. William Martin wrote saying "many of the vacancies could not be filled, and this defective organization continued to mar the efficiency of the regiment to the end of the war."[9] Martin, knowing he could not upgrade a soldier to any leadership position in Company B because all four officers, though captured or wounded, still remained on the books, shifted the newly promoted 1st Lt. Robert Lowrie (Co. H) to command the unit.[10] When Martin received word 2nd Lt. William Rozzell (Co. E) had died of his wounds while in a Federal prison hospital in New York he promoted 1st Sgt. Paul Grier (Co. E) to fill that lieutenant's slot.[11]

William Martin had more problems to deal with than just a shortage of leadership; his Carolinians' morale remained dismaying, and they expressed their malaise by deserting. Many of the riflemen were shattered by Gettysburg's trauma and saw no point in serving in an army which allowed its soldiers to be slaughtered to little effect. Other Tar Heels clamored for their brigade to be returned to North Carolina, to help protect their state. One wrote his mother, "There is some ... talk ... of our brigade being ordered to North Carolina. I wish to gracious we could be."[12] Unfortunately for those who wanted to return to North Carolina, Gen. Lee refused to give up any of his veteran combat units. Thus, over two dozen soldiers vanished from the 11th NC in July, and this number increased in August.[13] Lieutenant Lemuel Hoyle (Co. I) noted they were "trying to reorganize and get things into 'shipshape' but the work [did] not progress very rapidly."[14]

On August 3, 1863, the brigade formed and began marching toward Orange Court House, some twenty-five miles to the south. They crossed the Rapidan River the next day and pitched camp near the courthouse on August 5, 1863. General Henry Heth instructed his brigade commanders to inform their regimental leaders this is where they would be stationed for the rest of the summer. The soldiers took this news to heart and rapidly labored to make their shelters as comfortable as they could.[15] From that point on, the riflemen's main concerns centered on thoughts of home and obtaining food. Sergeant Lewis Warlick (Co. B) wrote, "[I] would like to be at Pleasant Hill to eat peaches and watermelon."[16]

Poor morale continued to plague the Carolinians. Lieutenant Lemuel Hoyle (Co. I) scratched out a letter to his mother, writing, "This seems to be the dark day of our young nation."[17] Though the numbers of deserters had leveled off—probably because those who chose to leave had already done so—the totals of men absent without leave ate heavily into each company muster. However, in the next few weeks some of the men wounded at Gettysburg returned, having recovered from their injuries; still, each company remained drastically understrength. Martin sent energetic Tar Heels back to North Carolina with orders to recruit replacements and a small number of "fresh fish" were added to the regiment— twenty by the first of October 1863.[18] But for the most part, recruiting was very difficult; as one soldier recorded, "We ... have a hard time of it taking up [recruits] for they say there is a great many of them [deserters] around here."[19]

General Robert E. Lee was acutely aware of the desertions sapping his army's strength. Some of his generals had carried out executions of captured deserters in an attempt to discourage the soldiers from running away, but this did nothing to encourage men to return. Lee convinced President Jefferson Davis to issue a decree "offering a general pardon to deserters who would return to their commands." This pronouncement also included the following: "All soldiers who were under trial or were serving sentence."[20] Fortunately for Lt. Col. Martin and the 11th North Carolina, many of the summer's deserters did return, and the regiment's ranks began to grow. William Martin also was able to add another officer. The regiment's adjutant, Lt. Henderson Lucas, who had been badly wounded at Gettysburg, succumbed to his injuries, opening that position. Martin plucked his younger brother, Sgt. Edward Martin from the 28th NC, and promoted him to regimental adjutant.[21]

On September 7, 1863, Brig. Gen. William W. Kirkland was assigned as commander of the brigade.[22] William Kirkland was 30 years old, a native of Hillsboro, North Carolina, and had been the colonel of the 21st NC. The brigade's new commander was tough, had a quick temper, and never shied away from a fight. Kirkland had enrolled at West Point but was expelled in 1855. Then, since he believed in a military life, he finagled a second lieutenant's position in the U.S. Marine Corps. Kirkland served as a Marine until 1860, and when the Civil War began, he soon acquired the rank of colonel of the 21st NC. Colonel Kirkland led from the front and was badly wounded in the fight at Winchester. He eventually recovered and led his regiment at Gettysburg with enough brilliance that Gen. Lee promoted him to brigadier general.[23] The veterans of Pettigrew's brigade accepted their new leader.

One Tar Heel noted, "He comes to us with a good reputation and ... he will make a good officer. We will like him but not as much as we did the lamented Pettigrew."²⁴

11th North Carolina Muster²⁵
October 14, 1863

Unit	Commander	Strength
F & S	Lt. Col. William Martin	
	Cpt. Frank Bird	
	Adj. Edward Martin	3
Co. A	3rd Lt. William Taylor	52
Co. B	1st Lt. Robert Lowrie (Co. H)	34
Co. C	1st Lt. Edward Outlaw	32
Co. D	2nd Lt. Lewis Elias	31
Co. E	Cpt. William Kerr	27
Co. F	1st Lt. Stephen Roberts	41
Co. G	Cpt. John Freeland	49
Co. H	Cpt. William Grier	29
Co. I	2nd Lt. Lemuel Hoyle	43
Co. K	Cpt. James Young	37
Total		378

The Bethel Regiment's numbers were much healthier by the end of September, when muster roll returns reached 375. Rumors of an impending campaign floated through the regiment's company streets, and the veterans began storing their excess clothing and equipment. A Carolinian recorded, "In times like this, one blanket is as much as any man wants hung to him." The road-wise soldier continued: "I never intend to carry another knapsack on my back as long as I stay in the service."²⁶ On October 8, 1863, the North Carolinians received orders to draw three days' rations and prepare for movement. Lieutenant Colonel William Martin notified the men "any soldiers lacking shoes [were excused] from the upcoming mission." Martin said, "Lee did not expect men with torn or bleeding feet to be able to keep up."²⁷

Brigadier General William Kirkland led his brigade out of camp around midnight, on October 8, 1863, when "the line wheeled into column and stepped off at [the] quick step."²⁸ The Confederates reached Madison Court House by 9:00 the next morning and from there trekked around the western side of the Blue Ridge Mountains and on to Sperryville, Virginia. Their next couple days of marching lasted from sunup to sunset, and when they halted the weary Confederates "tumbled down and slept" along the trail."²⁹ The fall weather was cool and bracing, and the soldiers once again foraged as they hiked. On Octo-

Thirty-year-old Brig. Gen. William W. Kirkland replaced Pettigrew as commander of the brigade in September 1863 (NC Confederate Centennial Commission, 1963).

ber 13, 1863, the gray column passed through Warrenton, Virginia, which Lt. Col. Martin described as "a village without a fence and with more bare chimneys than houses."[30] The soldiers bivouacked that night as a cold drizzle chilled the air. Many of the men went foraging and located a stock of produce. One Confederate wrote, "Some of the men received in their ration white cabbage of a fineness they never had seen."[31]

A cold, light rain continued to dampen the Southerners' gray- and butternut-colored uniforms as they moved out onto the road at 5:30 a.m., on October 14, 1863.[32] The Confederates were buoyed by news that their past days' march had flanked the Yankees and the bluecoats were on the run. The Carolinians tramped away from their bivouac and soon, as Lt. Col. Martin noted, "resumed pursuit ... passing the enemy's camp-fires and debris of breakfast, evidently left in haste."[33] They reached Greenwich, Virginia, by 10:00 a.m., having followed a highway littered "with the articles retreating soldiers throw away, knapsacks, blankets, [and] guns even."[34] General Ambrose Hill put Maj. Gen. Henry Heth's division into the lead at Greenwich, and the aggressive officer pressed his men to hustle after the fleeing Federals. Henry Heth recorded, "From Greenwich we passed on by the most direct road to Bristoe Station, picking up a number of stragglers."[35] The Confederates hurried forward, excited by the Northerners' flight. One wrote, "The eyes of the Southerners lighted.... It was ... almost like boys chasing a hare."[36]

At 1:30 p.m., as William Kirkland's brigade topped a ridge, Lt. Gen. Ambrose Hill and his staff were nearby, studying the scene before them. General Hill could see Union soldiers on both sides of Broad Run, scrambling to cross the water at a ford. These troops were in complete disarray, a circumstance that excited the Confederate Third Corps commander. If his infantry could catch these disorganized soldiers, Hill believed he could destroy an entire Yank division.[37] Lieutenant General Ambrose Hill recorded, "They were evidently taken completely by surprise, and ... in the utmost confusion.... I determined that no time should be lost."[38] Hill commanded Henry Heth to attack immediately.

Major General Henry Heth wrote, "On reaching a cleared space, some two or three hundred yards in our front, the enemy was discovered about three-quarters of a mile [away].... General Hill directed me to ... attack the fugitives."[39] General Heth deployed Brig. Gen. Kirkland's formation to the left and Brig. Gen. John Cooke's North Carolina brigade to the right. He then designated Brig. Gen. Henry Walker's Virginians and Tennesseans to follow behind, in reserve. General Kirkland had 1,500 men, Walker 750, and Cooke 2,500. Brigadier General John Cooke's Tar Heels were the largest brigade in the division because his formation had been protecting North Carolina and had not suffered battle casualties. This also meant Cooke's men were the most inexperienced. Nevertheless, Cooke's riflemen were ready to prove to their Carolina brothers they could fight.[40]

Lieutenant Colonel William Martin's veterans formed on the brigade's far left flank. His Tar Heels prepared for the upcoming fight quietly and without wasted energy. One rifleman wrote, "First one then another would swing his gun to the front, examine the lock, see that the vent was open ... wipe off any moisture that was seen, loosen his cartridge box and see that [the rounds] were all safe and dry."[41] Ten minutes later, the men were ordered to move forward. A soldier noted, "Slowly and silently we executed the order taking care not to break a twig or speak a word as we went forward."[42] They moved into a thick stand of pine trees, closing the distance between Gen. Hill's aspirations and the unsuspecting Union troops.

The forest's denseness immediately slowed the Southerners and unraveled their battle line. Kirkland's right flank collided with Cooke's left, bunching the formations and jumbling the commands. The two generals were forced to halt their advance and re-form their brigades. Meanwhile, Ambrose Hill urgently demanded they advance rapidly. One officer remarked, "Hill's eyes were on the enemy near the fords ... instant action was imperative ... [and] not a moment was to be lost."[43] The halt took ten minutes; it was now almost 2:00 p.m., and Kirkland and Cooke were but a thousand yards away from striking a disorganized foe. Ambrose Hill pressured Henry Heth to move and did not give him time to place skirmishers in front of the battle line.[44]

Kirkland and Cooke's 4,000 Tar Heels pushed through the vegetation, covering 250 yards in the next fifteen minutes; and then musket fire erupted, surprising everyone. Brigadier General John Cooke's far right regiment, the 46th NC, was being hit in the flank by Union skirmishers. No one knew where these bluecoats had come from, but their numbers were strong enough to cause that Carolina regiment serious problems. John Cooke immediately ordered the 46th to wheel to the right and confront this threat, and then he sought out his boss. Henry Heth recorded, "About this time General Cooke in person reported to me that the enemy would take him in flank as he moved forward."[45] Heth, as surprised as everyone else that Yankees should be on their right, halted the two brigades, and sent an orderly back to Hill. General Ambrose Hill wrote, "I sent back to General Anderson to ... take two brigades to the position threatened, and protect the right flank of Heth."[46] He then told Henry Heth to attack the Yanks milling around the ford.

Obeying Heth's commands, William Kirkland sent his five regiments forward, and his brigade pushed through the pine thickets. But John Cooke was troubled. He had been ordered forward; however, if he did so, his far right regiment, which was now turned to the face the troublesome skirmishers, would be left behind. Also, he was waiting for Anderson's men to arrive to protect the 46th NC, and they were nowhere to be seen. Brigadier General John Cooke unhappily remarked, "I will advance, and if they flank me I will face my men about and cut my way out."[47]

The Federal skirmishers, veterans from two brigades of Brig. Gen. Alexander Webb's division, pummeled the 46th NC with stinging musketry. John Cooke did not like the Yanks' strength and realized he would not be able to slide past them without his entire line being enfiladed. Cooke ordered his other regiments to oblique to the right and wheel into a battle line facing these Federals. By 2:30 p.m., Cooke's regiments were facing south and pushing against the bluecoats. He notified William Kirkland, who immediately halted his Carolinians' advance. The Tar Heel general then gave commands to form his brigade on Cooke's right. Kirkland's five regiments obliqued right and wheeled into position. General Ambrose Hill's plans of ambushing the Yankees at the ford had now been destroyed by contact with unexpected enemy troops. Brigadier General Henry Walker wrote, "Kirkland's brigade ... got into the open field, and commenced gaining ground to the right, by a wheel."[48]

It took only fifteen minutes for the combined weight of 4,000 Carolinians to break the Federal skirmish line, and the Yanks scampered away. Cooke and Kirkland ordered their men to pursue the bluecoats, and the Tar Heels pushed through the vegetation, grinding southward. Then the Confederate infantry emerged from the pine woods, out onto a clearing. The riflemen could see the bluecoats fleeing toward a railroad embankment, a thousand yards away. A ridge behind the railroad tracks was studded by two batteries of Union artillery, ten guns in total. The Northern cannons immediately opened upon Cooke's men. The Confederates moved forward and were soon sheltered from the artillery fire by a crinkle in the terrain. They advanced in this shallow depression and closed the distance between them and the railroad tracks by over a quarter of a mile.

The Confederates moved to within 250 yards of the railroad embankment, exchanging sporadic fire with small detachments of Union infantry. Meanwhile, William Kirkland sent out a skirmish line and it advanced towards the railroad embankment. He then followed his skirmishers with his main battle line. Cooke repeated Kirkland's maneuver and the two brigades stepped forward to within 100 yards of the railroad tracks. Cooke's regiments were to the right of the Bristoe road, Kirkland's to the left. The Confederate battle line extended almost a half-mile from left to right, with Lt. Col. William Martin's 375 Tar Heels posted on the far left, almost up against the banks of Broad Run. A Union officer recalled, "A more inspiring scene could not be imagined ... [as] the enemy's line of battle boldly moving forward."[49]

Suddenly, to the horror of the Confederates, a wall of Federals arose from behind the railroad embankment and fired a massive volley. Federal minié bullets ripped into the shoulder-to-shoulder ranks, knocking down scores of Southerners. Lieutenant Colonel Martin wrote, "From their shelter behind the railroad embankment they poured in a deadly fusillade [and] ... swept the field."[50] Brigadier General John Cooke, who was mounted, was also hit, a bullet shattering his leg, and tumbled to the ground among the gray-clad bodies piling up around him. The Union ranks were packed. In some places the Yanks were stacked several men deep, with the rear soldiers loading for those in front. Their musketry slaughtered the exposed Confederates. One Southerner wrote "every one of their shots told."[51] Another cried, "The shooting was a roar as from the portals of Hell."[52]

The Confederates in Cooke's regiments, caught out in the open, could retreat or go forward. The inexperienced soldiers had taken too much harassment from their veteran Carolina brothers, so now they raced forward. Brigadier General William Kirkland urged his regiments to keep pace with Cooke's unplanned assault. His Carolinians maintained their line, advancing along Cooke's left. Then, William Kirkland went down, his arm shattered by a ball.[53] Corporal Jacob Bartlett (Co. K) noted, "As we swept down the slope the enemy opened fire."[54] The Federal infantry fire ripped into the Confederates. One Yank wrote, "They fell thick as sheaves, stricken by our rain of bullets."[55] Union artillery added to the butchery, the ten cannon gouging bloody holes in the Confederate lines. Cooke's assault was melting away as dozens of men dropped or were knocked down. General Hill noted, "[Cooke's and] Kirkland's lines were exposed to a very deliberate and destructive fire."[56] One Confederate, amid the slaughter, noted they "were mowed down like grain before a reaper." Another rifleman, recalling the confusion among the ranks, wrote, "Nearly every man of strong voice was bawling out something of which I could distinguish the following: 'Cease fire! Lie down! Don't shoot; you are shooting your own men. Fall back!'"[57]

With Gen. Kirkland being carried back, command of his brigade fell to Col. Singletary (44th NC). The brigade's three right-most regiments, the 44th, 26th, and 47th, were being shredded by a savage fire equaling what had happened before the stone wall at Gettysburg on July 3. They could not advance, their movement stopped by the weight of the Yanks' musketry. However, on their left, the 52nd NC and 11th NC faced a different situation. The Union battle line stretched toward the east, matching the Confederate formations, but their far-right, last Federal regiment, the 82nd NY, was 150 yards from Broad Run. The 11th NC and a couple companies of the 52nd NC found themselves advancing against this empty space. In effect, while all of Cooke's and most of Kirkland's men were being chopped to pieces, the Bethel boys and some of the 52nd NC marched forward without taking a single casualty.

Lieutenant Colonel William Martin's regiment lapped over the top of the railroad embankment at 3:00 p.m., his riflemen taking the position with almost no loss. Finding no one occupying this section of the railroad defenses, Martin ordered his companies to change front, and his veterans wheeled to their right. This sudden appearance of Confederates on the Yanks' flank caused an immediate reaction. The commander of the 82nd NY shifted some of his men to protect his right just as Martin's Carolinians fired a volley into them. William Martin wrote "the 11th ... succeeded in reaching the railroad and dislodging the enemy."[58] The 82nd NY shuddered and its far-right companies gave ground, but the regiment did not crumble. Instead, bolstered by some nearby reserves, the New Yorkers returned fire. Major Thomas Baird (82nd NY) recorded "the enemy ... were crossing the railroad on our right ... [and as] we opened fire to the right oblique ... their advance was soon checked."[59]

Cooke's and Kirkland's attack collapsed ten minutes later. The survivors turned and ran as the attack formation dissolved into a mass of fleeing soldiers, leaving behind most of their casualties, as well as scores of Confederates who had dropped to the ground to escape the torrents of lead. These men were now trapped; if they got up to run they were shot down. They huddled among the bodies of the dead and wounded, cornered by their decision to seek shelter. The shooting ended a few minutes later. John Cooke's brigade had suffered over 500 casualties in less than twenty-five minutes, and William Kirkland's three regiments nearly 300.[60]

But the 11th North Carolina and more than a hundred men from the 52nd NC were still posted on the railroad embankment. Lieutenant Colonel William Martin's riflemen continued to exchange fire with the 82nd NY, the two regiments about 200 yards apart. Though their musketry was heavy, neither side hurt their opponent. However, William Martin could see the disaster that had unfolded for the rest of Cooke's and Kirkland's regiments, and he realized his local success now placed his troops in jeopardy. Then, artillery rounds impacted into the rear of the Bethel formation, knocking the men of Company D down like bowling pins. Private Lucius Baker's (Co. D) left hip was mauled by shrapnel, Pvt. John Cook (Co. D) was seriously mangled, and Pvt. Perry Summers (Co. D) was badly injured.[61] Captain Frank Bird pointed to a Federal battery behind them, deployed on the other side of Broad Run. The two officers watched as the Yank gunners hustled to reload their cannon. The next barrage pulverized the men in Company I. Sergeant Walter Ramseur (Co. I) was tossed to the ground, shrapnel ripping through his back, Pvt. Michael Carpenter's

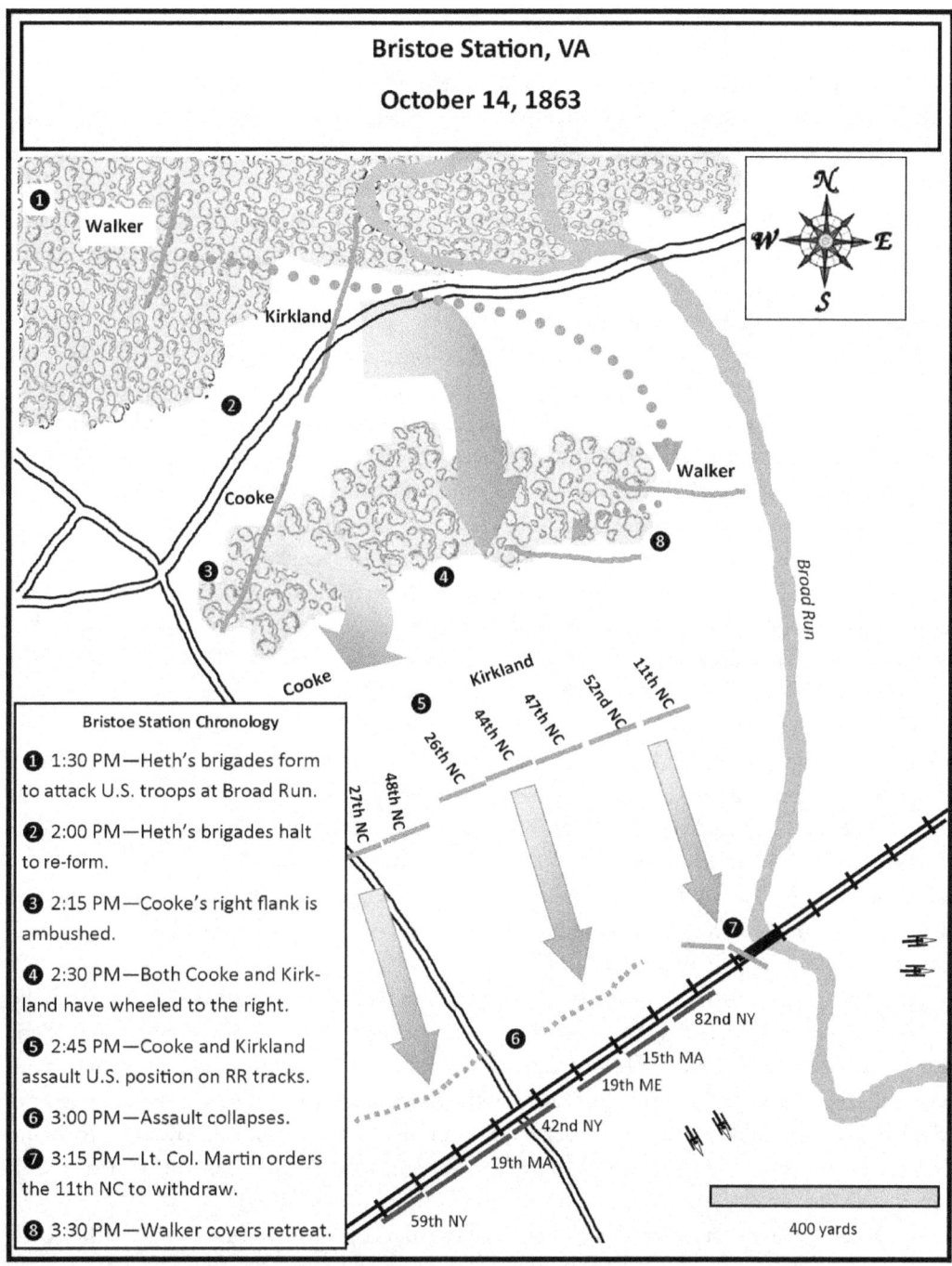

(Co. I) leg was shredded, and Pvt. Jacob Huss (Co. I) was killed.[62] William Martin quickly understood, Gen. Heth would later write, "the position was untenable."[63]

Meanwhile, squads of aggressive Yanks scrambled over the railroad tracks and out among the wounded and dead Confederates of Cooke's and Kirkland's regiments. They captured the 26th NC's battle flag and another (either the 52nd NC or the 47th NC), as well as officers and scores of unwounded soldiers. Then, Brig. Gen. Alexander Webb began organizing a counterattack against Martin's exposed regiment.

About this time, Brig. Gen. Henry Walker's Tennesseans emerged from the woods, not far from Broad Run. Henry Walker had not received word of the Carolinian brigades' wheel to the right; therefore his brigade had continued moving to the east. The Tennessee brigade reached the river unopposed, though Walker's men could hear the raging fight behind him, on his right. Then Gen. Walker shifted his regiments to the right and followed the riverbank, working his way back toward the sounds of the battle. His riflemen formed their ranks into a battle line as the last of the destroyed Carolina regiments fled into the woods. Henry Walker described the scene: "When I got into the open field I saw [Cooke and Kirkland] ... had been repulsed and [were] falling back in utter confusion." Walker continued: "A portion of Kirkland's brigade (two regiments) were ... on the left [by the railroad tracks]."[64] When Gen. Walker saw Union troops advancing beyond the railroad and moving towards Lt. Col. Martin's command he posted his Tennesseans to protect the broken brigades, but there was little he could do to assist Martin's Bethel Regiment.

The 11th North Carolina's companies were now taking infantry fire along their front and artillery fire from their rear. As Webb's countermoves sent units to strike the Bethel Regiment's left-flank companies, Lt. Col. William Martin envisioned his entire command being surrounded. He wrote, "After a painful suspense, [and] with both flanks exposed ... and [with] no reinforcements appearing ... [I] ordered a retreat."[65] The Carolinians fled towards the safety of Henry Walker's riflemen. The Union artillerymen across Broad Run shifted their fire to bombard the retreating Southerners, and Alexander Webb's bluecoats fired heavy volleys into their backs, making the withdrawal frightfully dangerous. Lieutenant Colonel William Martin was struck in the left arm, and then again in the head.[66] Lieutenant Edward Outlaw (Co. C) recorded, "Martin was twice shot down and severely wounded in this retreat."[67] Private John Shuffler's (Co. B) left ankle was shattered by a bullet, 2nd Lt. Paul Grier (Co. E) was killed, Pvt. Joseph Wingate (Co. F) was struck in the left arm, and Pvt. Noah Sigmore (Co. I) was killed.[68] Edward Outlaw (Co. C) wrote "the retreat ... was made under a galling fire from behind."[69]

Once the Carolinians swept past Walker's battle line and entered the safety of the trees, Cpt. Frank Bird called out to the company commanders to re-form the regiment. Senior NCO's took quick roll calls and Cpt. Bird was able to determine over fifty men were missing. He returned to the tree line and watched as Union troops swarmed over the tracks the 11th NC had held just moments before. He could also see a cluster of Bethel boys being led away as prisoners. Lieutenant Outlaw (Co. C) recorded, "A number of the men shrank from crossing the open field and were captured at the railroad."[70]

Other Confederate brigades assaulted the Federal positions, but for the 11th North Carolina and the rest of the Tar Heels in Kirkland's brigade, the fight was over. Once darkness silenced the guns, weary Carolinians slipped out onto the battlefield and retrieved wounded comrades. One Southerner wrote, "We groped out into the dark as far as we dared and brought out a number of poor, torn and limp fellows."[71] The war-weary Carolinians then huddled around campfires as rain began to fall. The survivors, though content to be alive, had little to be joyful about—more of their friends and relatives had been squandered by thoughtless commands. Fortunately, there was one moment of humor as a story floated among the riflemen: "During the retreat a man in Company K saw the carcass of a large cat that had gotten caught in the hail of bullets and joked, 'Now boys you can see the horrors of war; here is an old spotted cat shot to pieces.'"[73]

11th North Carolina Casualties[72]
October 14, 1863

Unit	Commander	Casualties*
F & S	Lt. Col. William Martin	1
Co. A	3rd Lt. William Taylor	3
Co. B	1st Lt. Robert Lowrie	5
Co. C	1st Lt. Edward Outlaw	5
Co. D	2nd Lt. Lewis Elias	7
Co. E	Cpt. William Kerr	3
Co. F	1st Lt. Stephen Roberts	11
Co. G	Cpt. John Freeland	5
Co. H	Cpt. William Grier	2
Co. I	2nd Lt. Lemuel Hoyle	11
Co. K	Cpt. James Young	4
Total		57

*For a complete listing of October 14, 1863, casualties, see Appendix A, Bristoe Station Casualties.

By the next morning, October 15, 1863, Maj. Gen. Henry Heth knew what he had lost; his casualty count totaled over 1,300: Cooke, 700; Kirkland, 602; and Walker, 11.[74] The Federal losses numbered just over 120 men.[75] General Heth, saddened by the needless slaughter of his men as well as the loss of John Cooke and William Kirkland, remarked, "We inflicted but little loss upon the enemy."[76] The survivors in the ranks were outraged. One officer penned they were "ill-judged [and] imprudently ordered" and condemned Gen. Hill for his poor leadership.[77] Another wrote, "I consider every man killed and wounded ... an unnecessary sacrifice, and ... am fully convinced that somebody, high in command, is greatly to be blamed, and if justice were done, would be cashiered."[78] Captain Frank Bird, again in command of the regiment and thankful it had been spared the horrendous casualties that destroyed their brother regiments, wrote, "Our regiment behaved very bravely."[79]

On October 15, 1863, Gen. Heth ordered a skirmish force to feel out the Union positions along the railroad embankment and reports quickly came back to him the Yankees had retreated during the night. Major General Heth sent his men forward and they crossed the open field and took the tracks. Medical teams collected the remaining wounded and ditches were dug to bury the dead, who now, as one person wrote, "were lying like lumps of clay on the sodden ground."[80] General Lee came by, surveyed the disaster and scolded Lt. Gen. Ambrose Hill. Then he quietly said, "Bury these poor men and let us say no more about it."[81]

Chapter 11

Winter 1863-1864

Captain Frank Bird led the 11th North Carolina away from the field dotted by Confederate burials and followed the other Carolina regiments. Again Col. Thomas Singletary (44th NC) was in charge of the brigade and he directed the sullen Confederates back to the Orange Court House area. The soldiers marched morosely; hundreds of men were missing from the brigade and for no purpose at all. Again the Carolinians felt they had been betrayed by their leadership. One rifleman scrawled a letter to his family: "It is a lonsom time ... now.... When I look around and see nun of our boys, and think what has becom of them, I cante helpe but cry."[1] Another soldier, shaken by the number of missing comrades, wrote, "When you and your friends have slept under one blanket, shared each other's daily bread; when you depended upon him and he on you; when together you have touched elbows and charged into the hell of deadly battle ... [and when] you are spared from death [or] wound, your first question will be: 'Is John safe?' If he is not there, you are filled with a horrible loss."[2]

The weary Tar Heels settled down just south of the courthouse and Col. Singletary met with his regimental leaders. He informed them Lt. Gen. Ambrose Hill wanted the brigade to establish winter quarter camps, and each commander was to organize their formations into compact, neat, settlements. Singletary's officers grumbled about their units' small sizes, courtesy of Hill's battlefield decisions, and suggested the North Carolina regiments return to the Old North State for the winter. The homesick men were all unhappy at being trapped in central Virginia.

Winter camps were laid out and the discouraged men faced their futures. They all wanted to go home, and they wrote their families long laments about their inability to acquire furloughs. A typical letter penned to loved ones read much like this rifleman's scribbled words: "Mother.... I will try to come home by Christmas ... but I will have to wait awhile.... I will come as soon as I can."[3] Sadly, very few soldiers were able to acquire furloughs; and once the men realized this, a number slipped out of camp and vanished. The Confederate high command immediately fought back as the desertion rate climbed, and soon the despondent soldiers were forced to attend executions. On November 1, 1863, a miserable Carolinian recorded, "The entire brigade marched at the slow time to the site and formed on three sides around the twelve-man firing squad." The Tar Heel continued: "The impact of the balls seemed to raise the man off his feet, and he fell backwards, and was dead almost

11. Winter 1863–1864 127

Executions of deserters increased during the winter of 1863-1864 (*Harper's Weekly*).

instantly."[4] Another added, "It was a most melancholy experience for all who saw it and one that none could desire to witness again."[5]

As winter deepened, the Tar Heels huddled around their campfires, struggling to stay warm and cook their meager rations. The Orange Court House area had been forced to endure the ravages of thousands of scavenging men for the second year in a row; there now was little left to sustain the men. Firewood was extremely scarce and thefts from woodpiles became a mounting challenge. By mid–November, soldiers were being court-martialed for this offense. One Southerner noted "firewood was so scarce that 18 men from the 44th North Carolina were put in the guard house for stealing fence rails."[6]

In late November 1863, Gen. Meade shifted his divisions, forcing Lee to respond. General Heth's division marched out of camp and toward Mine Run, where, as a soldier recalled, they "threw up temporary breastworks."[7] The Confederates were now quick to dig in the moment danger was close. The veteran riflemen no longer felt any desire to stand shoulder to shoulder out in the open and expose themselves to enemy bullets. Now, if there was time, the Southerners fashioned protective defenses. General Meade's bluecoats, themselves veterans with hard-earned knowledge of what it meant to attack across open ground against dug-in riflemen, also argued against making frontal assaults. The Federal soldiers could see what the Southerners had built, and one Yank officer wrote, "The Confederate breastworks ... were ... formidable." He continued: "A run of eight minutes would be required for our lines to close the distance between them and those of the enemy, during which our entire advancing lines would be subject to every description of fire."[8] So, through the cold days and nights of late November, the two sides faced each other, neither attacking. It became known as the "battle that never was."[9]

Major General Henry Heth wanted the Yankees to assault his position. He wrote, "I was hoping [they] would attack in order that I might square accounts with [them] for [their] treatment of me at Bristoe Station."[10] But Gen. George Meade refused to slaughter his men in fruitless assaults and the two forces stared at each other. The most notable event occurred on November 30, 1863, when a flock of turkeys flew over the Carolina brigade. A Tar Heel noted, "The pickets of both sides took potshots at [the birds]. One turkey was hit and fell dead in the no-man's-land between the lines.... No Confederate ventured forth to retrieve it, but a lone Unionist braved the open ground and crawled toward the prize. He was shot and killed."[11]

The temperatures plunged and one shivering soldier wrote, "Cold as Hell, clear as a bell, and blowing like damnation."[12] The Carolinians labored to stay warm as well as man their breastworks, until the Federals abandoned their works, ending the nearly bloodless campaign. When all trace of danger had passed, Col. Singletary led the brigade back to their winter camp, three and a half miles south of the courthouse. The miserable Tar Heels shuffled back to their camp, their numbers at 370.[13]

Captain Frank Bird's soldiers were now confident nothing else was going to happen. Resigned to the fact they were not going back to Carolina, there was nothing for them to do except upgrade their winter quarters. One Southerner described their efforts: "I selected three partners, and we at once went to work to build us a shack.... We began cutting poles and setting them up, and by day we had the structure ready for the roof and chimney; and by night the roof was on, a stick chimney built, and the cracks daubed to keep out the cold."[14] Captain Bird's companies contained small groups of Carolinians who had bonded closely together. One noted, "The company became a great family ... [and] every man in uniform was a comrade.... On a march usually two men tented together; in camp four could use their tent pieces to better advantage.... Men came together as tentmates by natural process of selection."[15]

Lieutenant Colonel William Martin returned to the regiment in early December 1863 and met with Cpt. Frank Bird; it was time to make some personnel changes. They had received the sad news Cpt. Mark Armfield (Co. B) had died of dysentery at the Johnson Island Prison.[16] Armfield's death opened his position and Lt. Col. Martin advanced Lt. Thomas Parks (Co. B) to captain. Martin also endorsed 1st Lt. Edward Outlaw (Co. C) for captain, promoted 2nd Lt. Lewis Elias (Co. D) to first lieutenant, and Sgt. William Todd (Co. C) to first lieutenant.[17] Mark Armfield's death also enabled Cpt. Frank Bird's promotion. Since Armfield had been the senior captain in the regiment, even though he was a prisoner of war he was next in line for advancement to field rank should he return. With the news of Armfield's death, Cpt. Bird became eligible for that rank. William Martin promoted Frank Bird to major.

Since the Bethel Regiment's soldiers knew they could not go home, they made the best of their situation. Private Andrew Rinck (Co. I) wrote his wife: "I would like to see you all again if I could but see no chance." He then gave instructions for running the farm, and requested, "I want you to send me a little bunch of each one of the children's hair."[18]

Another scribbled to his lady, "Tell little Hatton that he must be a good boy till I come home."[19]

The homesick soldiers sat around their fires and entertained themselves with stories of events which had transpired in the past months. One such experience that had occurred while on the march from Gettysburg impressed everyone. A Confederate recalled, "As our soldiers were marching along the road ... this old lady hailed [a Southerner] and asked him where he got his knapsack. The soldier told her that he took it from a dead Yankee.... On the side of the knapsack was the name of its former owner, regiment, and company in large letters. The old lady replied: 'That was my son.' The soldier stopped at once, took his own things out, and gave it to the lady."[20]

The Confederate supply system proved to be inadequate and by mid–January 1864 the Carolinians were forced to scramble for anything to eat. One officer wrote, "The progressive decline in the rations of the troops and in the forage of the animals brought to the camps a spectre of starvation."[21] Everyone suffered, from rifleman all the way up to field grade officer. Private Bellfield King (Co. G) remarked, "I reckon if they don't give the Soldiers more to eat there is a heap of them will [go] home."[22] Private Lambert Bristol (Co. B) wrote, "Nothing to eat, nothing to drink and out of soap."[23] And, the Bethel Regiment's quartermaster, Cpt. John Tate, recorded, "I am hungry all the time."[24]

With measly rations, insufficient winter clothing, and little likelihood of furloughs, the soldiers' morale remained dismal, and a general reluctance to follow orders began to build. Private Bristol (Co. B) confessed, "I am barefooted, I haven't had ... shoes since Gettysburg ... [and] if they don't give me a pair, I will resist doing duty, for I am not going to stand guard duty bare footed any longer."[25] Another admitted, "You don't know how selfish men become by soldiering.... Two years ago when one received a box from home he was expected to ask the whole company to come up and ... help themselves.... Now when a fellow ... has anything sent from home, the rest of the company don't expect to be asked to help themselves. Whoever he is messing with is all that expect[s] to share it with him."[26] And, Pvt. Andrew Rinck (Co. I) complained, "People are not to be trusted these days, for I had a shirt stole out of my knapsack."[27]

The regiment was forced to witness another execution, this one of a soldier from the 44th NC and one of their own. A horrified rifleman scrawled, "Again the condemned did not die at the first round but had to be killed at close range by the officer in charge of the firing squad."[28] Private Andrew Rinck (Co. I) cried, "I would like to be ... at home."[29]

In early February 1864, Lt. Col. William Martin received orders to march his regiment out of winter quarters and assume guard duties along the Rapidan River. The Carolinians bundled up as best they could and relieved the men of Cooke's brigade on the picket line. A Tar Heel recorded, "For forty days [we] held the line, alternately fishing and skating on the frozen river when off duty, until relieved by another brigade."[30] They returned to their winter huts on March 14, 1864, just in time to learn Brig. Gen. William Kirkland had recovered enough to resume brigade command.

In late February and early March 1864 several batches of exchanged soldiers arrived and were greeted with great elation. These were veterans captured at Gettysburg and Falling Waters, and their presence bulked up the shriveled company rosters. These returning

Carolinians who had survived the hardships of prison life at Ft. Delaware and Point Lookout, Maryland, were appalled by their comrades' condition. Sergeant Lewis Warlick (Co. B) remarked, "When I returned I found the old 'Bethel' looking quite different to what it did when I left." He continued, "New officers have taken the places of those who were killed and many strange faces are in the ranks who ... enlisted since I left."[31] Lieutenant Colonel Martin's aggressive recruitment drives had netted sixteen men in the last months of 1863, and another 67 joined or were conscripted in 1864's first months.[32] The Eleventh's ranks also were increased by transferring in individuals from other regiments. By March 1, 1864, the regiment's numbers stood at 440.[33]

The Bethel Regiment soldiers' morale improved as the dreary winter weather abated. The men enjoyed themselves playing cards, baseball, and sneaking alcohol into camp. The newly promoted 2nd Lt. Lewis Warlick (Co. B) wrote, "Our regiment is doing nothing, not called out but once a day and that to have dress parade."[34] Another Confederate wrote, "When not on drill [we] would play cards, drafts, make and fly kites, and occasionally make a raid at night."[35]

A massive snowstorm buried the Virginia landscape on March 22, 1864. An officer recorded, "It started falling ... late in the morning ... and did not stop for twenty-four hours. The average depth was twelve inches, but in places the snow drifted to four feet."[36] Since Brig. Gen. John Cooke's regiments were not far from Kirkland's brigade's campsites the Carolinians from the two brigades had rubbed shoulders all winter long and, as one Tar Heel noted, "a little friction had developed between the brigades." This Carolinian remarked, "The whole trouble start[ed] by making raids on each other in fun, which had grown into bad feelings."[37] Lieutenant Lemuel Hoyle (Co. I) was aware of these incursions and wrote, "[I] feared [there were] ... hard feelings between the two commands."[38] Generals William Kirkland and John Cooke decided this snowstorm gave them an opportunity to allow the men of the two brigades to compete against each other, so they challenged each other to a brigade-sized snowball fight.

A soldier in Kirkland's brigade described the action: "The brigades ... met in an large field, facing each other on opposite sides of a ravine.... At first the men contented themselves with using ordinary snowballs, and all was fun and frolic; but the battle had not progressed very far before we discovered that quite a number of Cooke's men had brought along their haversacks and filled them with snowballs dipped in water and pressed as hard as a ball of ice." The Carolinian continued: "As the contest waxed more animated, each side struggling for victory, the passions of

Seventeen-year-old Pvt. James Mitchell (Co. C) was captured at Bristoe Station, and then exchanged in early 1864 (Clark, 1901).

11. Winter 1863–1864 131

More than 6,000 Carolinians fought in the great snowball battle between Cooke's and Kirkland's brigades on March 23, 1864 (*Battles and Leaders of the Civil War*, 1887).

the combatants became aroused.... Hard substances, frequently stones, were used with telling effect, in a number of cases doing serious damage." He wrote more: "At one stage of the battle about twenty-five of Cooke's men made a charge to capture the colors of the 26th ... and were met ... by about an equal number of our men. The fight that followed was ... fought with fists, or anything we could get." Finally, "the combat ended only with the exhaustion of the men, each side agreeing that it should be considered a drawn battle."[39] Lieutenant Lewis Warlick (Co. B) remarked, "The engagement between ours and Cooke's brigades with snowballs ... was a great sight."[40]

Colonel Collett Leventhorpe's stay in Federal prisoner-of-war facilities ended when he was released in March 1864. Colonel Leventhorpe was not healthy; his wounds at Gettysburg continued to fester, and he realized he could not command the regiment. He resigned in late April 1864, "by reason of wounds received at Gettysburg."[41] William Martin was commissioned colonel and Frank Bird to lieutenant colonel on April 27, 1864.[42] The Bethel Regiment's next most-senior officer, Cpt. Albert Haynes (Co. I), languished in a prison cell at Johnson's Island, so the major's posting remained blocked. However, the regiment's most-senior captain in the ranks, the 27-year-old deputy sheriff from Charlotte, William Grier (Co. H), began to assume the duties as the junior wing commander. Captain Grier's company then went to 1st Lt. Robert Lowrie (Co. H).

One of Col. Martin's first orders was to begin extensive musket target practice. A Tar Heel noted, "They painted the outline of a man on a large plank and shot at it from a long distance to hone their firing discipline."[43] Colonel William Martin's riflemen may have improved their musketry, but little else had changed—the Confederate logistics system continued to be a depressing failure. Captain John Tate, the regimental quartermaster wrote, "I am now hauling forage from near the NC line—about 130 miles." John Tate also remarked, "Officers of every grade draw the same rations as the men."[44] Lieutenant Lewis Warlick (Co. B) recorded, "This morning we have nothing but corn bread for breakfast."[45]

As the weather warmed everyone began to get edgy about the upcoming season's campaign. One writer noted, "Winter gave way to spring and with the budding of the plants came the knowledge the Yankees would be on the advance again."[46] Lieutenant Lewis Warlick (Co. B) penned his family, "We are looking for marching orders every day as orders have been issued for all baggage ... to be sent to the rear." Warlick continued: "Lee is going to Culpepper ... to pounce on Grant's right flank ... and give him battle before he will be able to concentrate his troops."[47] Lieutenant Warlick knew the Union army was now being led by a new commander, and the Carolinian did not see this latest general as any different from the others selected by President Lincoln. Lieutenant Colonel Frank Bird predicted "General Lee would doubtless advance on Grant, the latest commander of the Federal Army of the Potomac."[48] There also were rumors that Lee might take his soldiers across the Potomac again. However, 2nd Lt. Lemuel Hoyle (Co. I), who had suffered three wounds at Gettysburg, counseled caution. Hoyle wrote, "It seems to me that the two disastrous campaigns, already made into the enemy's country, ought to be sufficient to teach our authorities the impolicy of invasion."[49]

On May 1, 1864, Col. William Martin reported to Brig. Gen. William Kirkland for an officer's meeting and announced his command totaled 478 officers and enlisted men.[50] His largest company, Lt. William Taylor's Company A, numbered 61, while the smallest unit, Cpt. Edward Outlaw's Company C, consisted of 29. William Martin's Carolinians were rested and in decent condition, though, as 2nd Lt. Lewis Warlick (Co. B) remarked, "The boys are ... badly clothed."[51]

The men accepted the fact they were again going to be facing danger, but they were ready. After all, they had stood beside their comrades for two years, and they were not going to shirk their duties now. An officer noticed this subtle difference and wrote, "Although the old, cheerful banter was audible, as the troops made ready ... the Army was worse equipped and not in as good spirits as it had been before Gettysburg. It was ready to fight [but] it sensed the most difficult of all its struggles."[52] The Carolina civilians-turned-soldiers understood the danger; they knew what bullets could do to human flesh. Private Andrew Rinck (Co. I) wrote his wife a long letter and ended it with "so I will close now.... I remain your affectionate husband until death."[53]

Chapter 12

The Wilderness and Spotsylvania, May 5–May 20, 1864

General Ulysses S. Grant moved his army on May 4, 1864, and Col. William Martin recorded, "The Federal army ... crossed the Rapidan ... with Richmond as Grant's avowed objective point." Martin also noted "Grant's ... intention [was] to fight General Lee between Culpepper and Richmond."[1] Colonel Martin had been so sure the Union forces were going to advance that "with the dawn of the 4th [he] ordered the men to prepare three days' rations."[2] Then, when Gen. Kirkland gave the directive for the brigade to prepare to march, Col. Martin was able to report, "In less than an hour ... all [were] gone, marching eastwardly."[3] Lieutenant General Ambrose Hill's Third Corps marched out of the Orange Court House area by noon, with Henry Heth's division leading the way.

Major General Henry Heth's division had four brigades; these units commanded by Brig. Gen. Joseph Davis, Brig. Gen. John Cooke, Brig. Gen. William Kirkland, and Brig. Gen. Henry Walker. William Kirkland's brigade consisted of the 11th NC (Col. William Martin), the 26th NC (Col. John Lane), the 44th NC (Col. Thomas Singletary), the 47th NC (Col. George Faribault), and the 52nd NC (Lt. Col. Benjamin Little). Kirkland's five Tar Heel regiments presented over 2,500 muskets on the line, a number similar to what Pettigrew's four regiments had taken into Gettysburg, except Kirkland's cohort of soldiers were much more battle-seasoned than those Pettigrew had taken into combat. Pettigrew's inexperienced troops went into battle, many feeling a distain for seeking shelter when the bullets started flying. Kirkland's Carolinians knew what they were facing, and they were prepared to do whatever was necessary to protect themselves.

Early the next morning, May 5, 1864, Col. William Martin's riflemen formed into a marching column. One Confederate noted "the heavy dew of a cool night, and the low-hanging fog disappeared under the rising sun ... [as] the day grew warm."[4] The Southerners trekked towards the east on the Orange Plank Road, entering into an area of thick vegetation the locals called the "Wilderness." Col. Martin's men gawked at the dense foliage and undergrowth and one later wrote, "It was a quiet, desolate place."[5] Another added, "It certainly is a wilderness; it is almost impossible for a man to walk, as the woods are thick with an underbrush growth and all kinds of shrubbery, old logs, grapevines, and goodness knows what."[6]

Major General Henry Heth's division led the march eastward, with Kirkland's brigade at the front. The column moved along quietly, covering ten miles quickly, the men intimidated by their surroundings. Then messengers raced by on horseback, spewing dust and rumors, but the experienced soldiers knew what was happening. A veteran noted, "The message that always made hearts beat faster was passed down the files: Federals were ahead."[8] The long line of riflemen halted and Gen. Heth ordered William Kirkland to send out his skirmishers. The 47th NC immediately deployed its skirmishers, reinforced by sharpshooters from each regiment. Then, the Carolina units formed into a battle line, screened by the skirmishers. Colonel William Martin's Bethel Regiment was posted on the brigade's extreme right, with the 47th on their left, then the 26th, and the 44th on the far left.[9] The 52nd NC moved in behind the brigade; however, when Col. Martin glanced back he noticed that regiment had vanished. A Tar Heel in the 52nd NC reported, "The 52nd Regiment was ordered to retrace its steps for the purpose of protecting our wagon train, which was reported to be threatened by the enemy's cavalry."[10]

11th North Carolina Muster[7]
May 5, 1864

Unit	Commander	Strength
F & S	Col. William Martin	
	Lt. Col. Frank Bird	5
Co. A	3rd Lt. William Taylor	71
Co. B	Cpt. Thomas Parks	47
Co. C	Cpt. Edward Outlaw	30
Co. D	1st Lt. Lewis Elias	47
Co. E	Cpt. William Kerr	36
Co. F	1st Lt. Stephen Roberts	37
Co. G	Cpt. John Freeland	49
Co. H	1st Lt. Robert Lowrie	43
Co. I	2nd Lt. Lemuel Hoyle	67
Co. K	Cpt. James Young	51
Total		483

At 9:00 a.m., the brigade's skirmishers inched forward and within moments the chatter of cavalry carbines shattered the morning air. The Carolinians scrambled for cover and returned fire. Colonel Martin made a note of their location; they were about two miles west of a settlement called Parker's Store. The Southern skirmishers outnumbered the Yanks, and using covering fire and leapfrog tactics, they pushed the troopers of the 5th NY cavalry backwards. This process was slow, as the Yank's dismounted horsemen were tough to see in the thick underbrush, and they were able to keep up a rapid fire with their breech-loading weapons. One of the Federal officers of the 5th NY cavalry wrote, "Our pickets ... disput[ed] every inch of the ground, only giving ground as they were pressed by the superior numbers of the enemy."[11] Henry Heth recorded, "I struck the enemy ... [with] only a strong skirmish line, and drove this force steadily before me."[12]

The Tar Heels pushed forward, dodging from tree to tree and forcing the New Yorkers to keep backpeddling. One Southerner wrote, "By mid-morning Kirkland's regiments had pushed the delaying cavalry force east of Parker's Store."[13] Another Confederate recorded, "We fought them very hard for three hours, they falling back all the time."[14] The 47th NC skirmishers and the selected sharpshooters from each of Kirkland's regiments downed many bluecoats, and the Yanks left behind a trail of casualties. A New Yorker wrote, "The 5th NY cavalry ... [was] driven in with severe loss, leaving many wounded on the field."[15]

At noon, Gen. Heth called a brief halt and directed John Cooke's brigade to pass through Kirkland's regiments. General Kirkland's tired skirmishers rejoined their formations. Cooke's brigade then pressed the Yank line for another hour, but by then Federal infantry skirmishers began to appear among the cavalry. Not long after this occurred, Northern infantry battle line replaced the skirmishers. The tempo of musketry increased. Cooke threw in more of his riflemen, and the Federals did the same. General Heth wrote, "My skirmish line was unable to drive the enemy's skirmishers any further ... [and] they halted."[16]

By now, Gen. Heth's two brigades had been in contact with Union troops for five hours and had driven the Northerners nearly three miles.[17] General Hill pressed Heth to attack and take the Brock Road–Orange Plank Road intersection. Henry Heth called his brigade commanders together and issued orders; he placed Cooke's men astride the road, Davis's brigade on his left, and the combined Walker/Archer formation to Cooke's right. Kirkland's regiments were ordered in reserve, behind Cooke.[18] General Heth wrote, "[My] division came up [and] line of battle was formed."[19]

Colonel Martin's companies hunkered down about two hundred yards behind Cooke's battle line. Martin checked with his unit commanders, making sure their men were prepared for battle. More ammunition was distributed, and water details raced back and forth to a nearby well, making sure everyone's canteens were filled. The afternoon had turned hot, and the dense vegetation stifled any air movement. The Carolinians tried to peer through the foliage in an attempt to find their enemy, but the undergrowth was too thick. A frustrated Confederate recorded, "[The vegetation] was a dense growth of small and large timber intermixed."[20] The minutes ticked away as Gen. Heth made his final preparations for his assault, but these finishing movements were hampered by the impenetrable shrubbery. Heth noted, "All was quiet for an hour or more."[21]

At 4:15 p.m., Union infantry arose from their positions among the trees and attacked Heth's three brigades. Federal commander Brig. Gen. George Getty sent forward his four brigades, supported by Brig. Gen. Gershom Mott's two brigades. Henry Heth remarked, "My line was assailed ... by a strong battle line."[22] The bluecoats pressed forward through the dense foliage and slammed into the Confederates. Heth noted, "My men were not behind breastworks; the enemy came within 90 yards of my line."[23] A Carolinian rifleman wrote, "The ground over which we were fighting was covered with dense undergrowth, and the enemy could scarcely be seen."[24] Bullets zipped through the trees, smacking into tree trunks, knocking small limbs to the ground and stripping so many leaves from branches that a green, leaf-litter rain fell upon the Tar Heels seeking shelter from the firing.

The three Confederate brigades shuddered and stumbled backwards. Henry Heth ordered William Kirkland to send in his four regiments and Col. Martin's Bethel boys inched forward, entering the maelstrom of fire. Federal lead immediately slammed into Carolina boys; Cpl. Emanuel Lewis's (Co. A) right hand was shattered by a ball, Pvt. James Wingate (Co. H) was struck in the thigh, and 2nd Lt. Lewis Warlick (Co. B) was hit in the right arm.[25] Other Tar Heels dropped among the trees, wounded or killed, as the men shifted forward, but added numbers bolstered Heth's three brigades and the Confederates were able to block the Yank's assault. Henry Heth recorded, "My entire line now opened a destructive fire ... [and] the enemy gave way."[26]

General Getty would not accept the fact his massive force had been stopped by a much smaller foe. He ordered another attack. This one also was beaten back as the stubborn Southerners refused to be pushed from their defensive positions amid the thick vegetation. One Confederate rifleman penned his family, "We lay down behind logs and trees to protect ourselves and fired back at them."[27] Getty's men made a third assault. Henry Heth recorded, "The enemy attacked me again, and met the same fate."[28] But more Bethel soldiers were hit. Sgt. John Lane (Co. D) was killed. Private George Patton (Co K) was struck in the left thigh, and he also suffered a shattered right ankle.[29] Pvt. Frederick "Wash" Dellinger (Co. I) received "a gunshot wound to the right breast."[30] A Tar Heel remarked it was "doubtful if any more violent and sanguinary contest occurred during the entire Civil War than just here."[31]

The riflemen were well within the kill zone, but because of the smothering vegetation, neither force was able to move forward or backward. Instead, the soldiers blasted away at each other, sometimes close enough that muzzle flashes singed their opponents' hair. A Confederate wrote "so severe was the rifle fire and the opposing armies so near each other that neither [could] advance on the other."[32] Another recorded, "Once in the din and flame and roar of the conflict, there is no time to think of consequences, no time for thought of the loved ones at home far away. The only consuming passion then is how to get at the enemy and punish him."[33] Thousands of riflemen blazed away, loading and firing as fast as each man was able. Dense smarms of lead flew through the air, destroying vegetation. One Confederate wrote, "I have never seen woods so completely riddled with bullets."[34] But the trees did not stop all of the bullets; more Tar Heels fell. Private Eugene Melton's (Co. D) right thigh was sliced open by a bullet, and Pvt. John Smith (Co. I) was hit in the leg.[35]

At 5:30 p.m., Gen. Heth's men received reinforcements, soldiers from Maj. Gen. Cadmus Wilcox's division, and Henry Heth decided to use this additional strength to force the Federals back. Henry Heth wrote, "As soon as Wilcox formed his line.... I thought the time had come for us to take a hand in the attack."[36] Heth issued commands to William Kirkland to attack, along with Wilcox's brigades, and Kirkland informed his regimental commanders. They advanced and Col. William Martin recalled, "In one of these charges ... we came upon MacRae's [Cooke's brigade] line lying down, and as we charged over him ... he sneered sardonically, 'Go ahead; you'll soon come back.'"[37] The moment Martin's riflemen stepped up from their hiding places Union bullets knocked many down. Private Phillip Dellinger's (Co. I) right leg was mangled beyond repair, Pvt. Joseph Richey (Co. I) was killed, and 1st Lt. Stephen Roberts (Co. F) took a bullet in his left leg.[38] Others fell as well; however, the bluecoats were forced to give ground of a couple hundred feet.

The Confederate push washed over a line of breastworks the Union troops had scratched into the terrain. Henry Heth wrote that his troops "succeeded in capturing a part of the enemy's breastworks."[39] The Tar Heels struggled forward, "advance[ing] ... with a yell."[40] Many were almost incoherent in their battle frenzy. One of these Bethel boys, 19-year-old Pvt. Woodston Garratt (Co. G), fought with demon-like fury. A Carolinian recorded, "Woodston was broken hearted at the death of his brother [at Gettysburg]. He could not recover from it [and] brooded over it, and became sullen and embittered.... It seemed the only object of his life was to revenge his brother's death." The writer continued: "He became reckless and was never so pleased as when in battle. In fact, he took a wild delight in it and ... wherever the fighting was the hottest; you could hear his voice over the din yelling, 'pour it to them boys.'"[41]

Colonel William Martin's riflemen pushed forward a few yards beyond the entrenchments but could advance no farther; the Yanks had been reinforced and would not budge. The two forces were barely more than a few yards apart, and the Tar Heels sought any type of shelter they could find. Private Zebedee Morris (Co. K) wrote, "[We] lay down behind a line of dead Union soldiers so thick that it provided cover from bullets."[42] Captain Edward Outlaw (Co. C) noted, "It was a novel experience and seem[ed] ghastly enough."[43]

A fresh Federal formation arose and charged the Carolinians. There was a brief, nearly hand-to-hand melee, during which time Sgt. James Rozzell (Co. E) was killed. Then Col. Martin's riflemen abandoned their position and in the confusion a few Tar Heels were cut off. One of these trapped men, 2nd Lt. Benjamin Boyd (Co. K), attempted to lead a platoon of men to safety. He directed them towards a gap in the Union troops' line, but Boyd's plan did not work, and soon he and four of his men were captured.[44] The rest of the Bethel Regiment's soldiers scurried back, passing over the top of MacRae's riflemen. Colonel William Martin remarked, "Sure enough ... [we] came back.... We struck, as [MacRae] had done ... and in vain we tried to dislodge ... the Federal line ... and [we] recoiled ... behind MacRae's line." Martin continued: "I fancy [he] smiled sardonically then."[45]

The Union commanders threw in more reinforcements and they shoved the Confederates back all along their line. The Southerners were exhausted and most of the riflemen had consumed their ammunition. General Heth recorded, "The enemy followed up their success and we were driven back [a] half mile."[46] The Federals pushed again, and Heth and Wilcox scrambled about, throwing in whatever reserves they could locate, trying to stave off this new wave of bluecoated soldiers.

Fortunately, darkness shrouded the battlefield and the weary soldiers stopped shooting at each other. Both sides' riflemen just lay down among the trees, hidden in the underbrush, barely fifty yards apart. They were so close to each other many of the wounded were left behind as it was too dangerous to retrieve them. The soldiers could hear their opponents' activities, especially the sounds of Yank soldiers scratching out entrenchments. The Confederates did not dig in. Their company commanders had been told they would receive orders to withdraw at any moment, and there was no use building defenses if they were going to be moving soon. The riflemen, though, were wary of the consequences of not scraping out some form of protection and wondered. As one Confederate noted, "[We] kept asking each other why [we] were not allowed to build breastworks."[47]

Generals Henry Heth and Cadmus Wilcox sought out their superior, Lt. Gen. Ambrose Hill, for permission to pull back their forces and reorganize their commands. The hectic day's fighting had forced Heth and Wilcox to employ whatever unit was closest, and these decisions resulted in scattered regiments and disorganized brigades. Therefore, neither officer had control over his own men. Hill told Heth and Wilcox that General Longstreet's

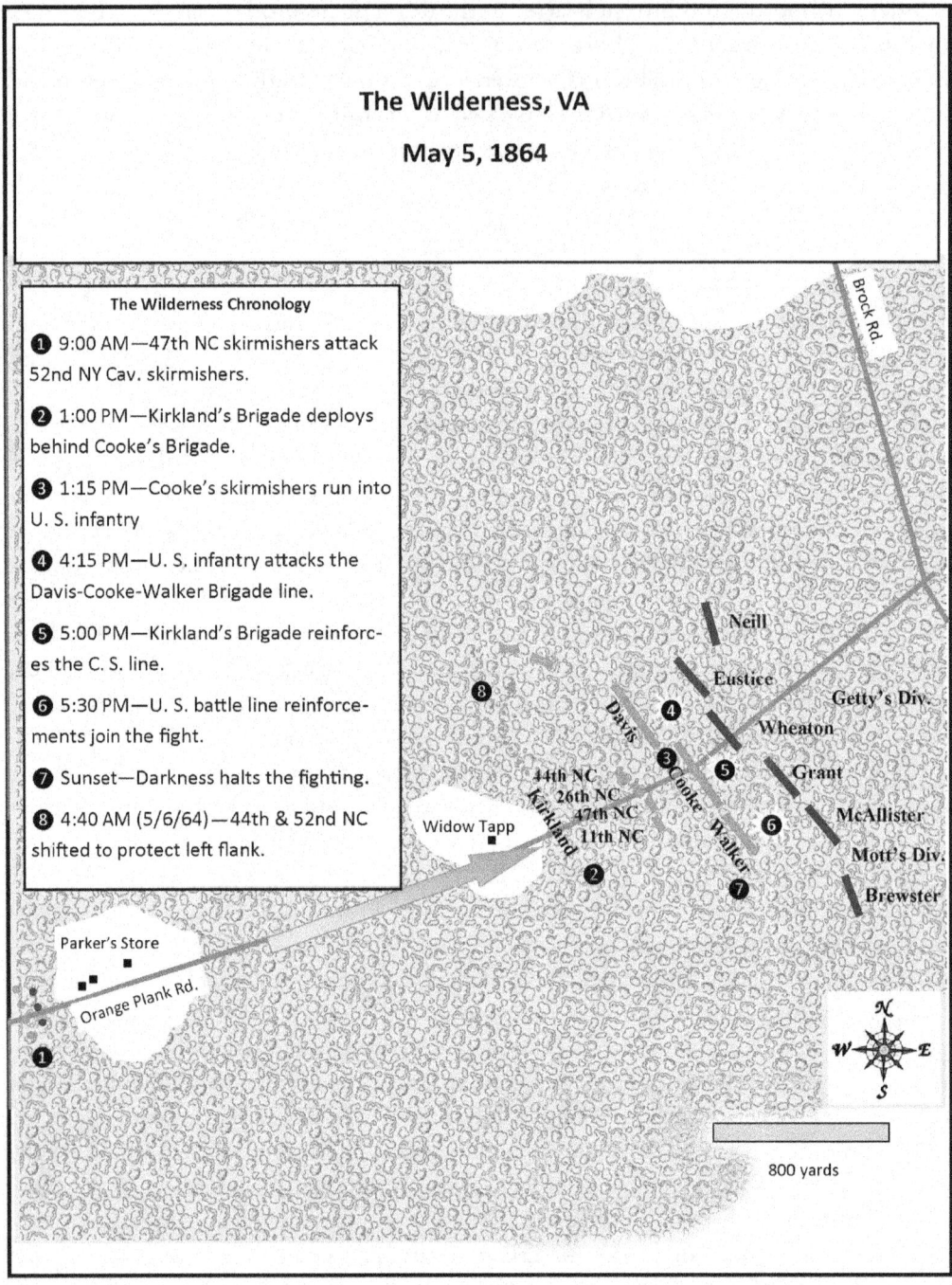

corps would be arriving in the next couple hours and there was no need to retreat. Henry Heth informed Hill, "A skirmish line could drive both my Division and Wilcox's, situated as we are now."[48] But Ambrose Hill was ill and in no mood to debate with his subordinates. Hill refused to change his mind and when Heth persisted, Gen. Hill shouted, "Damn it, Heth.... I don't want to hear any more about it; the men shall not be disturbed."[49] The disheartened Henry Heth returned to his brigade commanders and told them Longstreet was supposed to arrive during the night to relieve them; there would be no troop movements until then. Colonel William Martin informed his worn-out company commanders of this news. Captain Edward Outlaw (Co. C) recorded the men "were ordered to rest on their arms as night found them, without reformation of lines, as they were to be relieved at midnight by Longstreet's Corps."[50] Pickets were posted and soon most of the exhausted men were asleep. However, as one Confederate observed, "All through the night the enemy could be heard felling trees and fortifying in front of [their] position."[51]

Unfortunately, Longstreet's brigades did not reach the positions held by Heth and Wilcox. Just before dawn, on May 6, 1864, the two apprehensive division commanders found themselves in a perilous situation; their men were not in position to defend themselves. Taking matters in his own hands, Gen. Heth struggled to regain organizational control in the predawn moments. He ordered William Kirkland to find his regiments and shift them to the north of the Orange Plank Road. Kirkland located the 44th NC and 52nd NC and directed them several hundred yards north of the turnpike, but the rest of his regiments were so intermingled all he could do was tell his commanders to dig in as best as they could and prepare for the expected assault.[52] Colonel Martin noted, "When it was found that Longstreet had not come up, our men commenced to form line of battle."[53] The Tar Heels, as one recorded, "[began] to make crude breastworks of the materials in this dense forest of small gum, ash, Burchs [sic] and Briers."[54]

Just after sunrise, around 5:00 a.m., a cannon was fired and the Union infantry advanced.[55] The blue-coated horde surged toward the Confederates, instantly overrunning their pickets, and then slamming into the Southern battle line. One officer noted, "As most of Wilcox's men were slightly in advance of Heth's front, they first received the shock."[56] The Confederate line collapsed and the soldiers fled, running right into the troops behind them. Colonel William Martin's riflemen, who occupied a battlefront among the trees a few yards behind one of Wilcox's regiments, were frozen in place; they could not shoot at the oncoming Yanks. General Heth recorded, "It was impossible to fire a shot without firing into [our] own troops."[57]

The Northerners thundered towards the Tar Heels, shouting and firing as they advanced. Private Absalom Rudisill's (Co. D) right hand was destroyed by a bullet in these initial volleys.[58] A rifleman wrote, "We were in no position to resist such a charge."[59] The men of the Bethel Regiment jumped up from their hiding places and fled. Colonel William Martin remarked, "The unformed line was rolled up like a sheet of paper."[60] His soldiers scampered away, fleeing as fast as possible. The entire regiment got away, though a small number of men were left behind, including Pvt. Hance Jordan (Co. F), who was recorded as "missing," and Pvt. William Kincaid (Co. D), who was captured.[61] Not far away, the 47th NC held briefly and then pulled back, fighting to maintain a semblance of order. However, as one of the 47th's officers admitted, "the 47th initially retreated in good order but its ranks disintegrated as the regiment pulled itself through the brush."[62] And an officer in the 26th NC acknowledged, his "brigade came very near being stampeded."[63]

Union forces commanded by Brig. Gen. James Wadsworth moved against William Kirkland's regiments north of the turnpike; three Yank brigades advancing against the 44th

NC, the 52nd NC, and a scattering of other formations. The Northerners pushed forward, crashing their way through the dense underbrush, and struck the 44th and 52nd NC obliquely. An officer in the 52nd NC recorded, "The enemy having penetrated our lines ... opened fire upon the Fifty-second Regiment from the rear."[64] A veteran recalled, "It is the truly brave man at times who can turn and flee when he sees there is no longer virtue or honor in battling the unconquered enemy before him."[65] Another Confederate summarized the situation: "Scattered as they were, they soon were driven ... [and] they made for the rear at once."[66]

General Ambrose Hill's entire force fled in panic and gave away a thousand yards of yesterday's hard-earned ground in less than fifteen minutes. There was no way to control Wilcox's and Heth's rattled men as the surging Yanks pressed forward. All organization had broken down and the Confederates were incapable of mounting any form of defense. Another thousand yards of gain evaporated and an officer wrote, "The enemy ... turned on the Confederates and drove them back to the open field of the Tapp farm."[67] Major General Winfield Hancock recorded, "The Confederates were driven in confusion through the forest for about 1½ miles."[68]

Thirty-four-year-old Pvt. William Kincaid (Co. D) was captured on May 6, 1864 (Clark, 1901).

Then the first brigades of Lt. Gen. James Longstreet's corps hustled forward, approaching on the Orange Plank Road. They pushed aside the fleeing Confederates, shouting at them in disdain: "Do you belong to Lee's Army? ... You're worse than Bragg's men."[69] Longstreet's brigades formed into line of battle and slammed into the charging Federals. Henry Heth wrote in relief, "Longstreet now appeared, and forming rapidly, checked the Federal advance."[70] Longstreet's forces pushed the Northerners backwards and away from Heth's and Wilcox's shattered units.

William Kirkland's staff worked the rest of the day reorganizing his brigade. In the 11th North Carolina, Col. William Martin's officers and NCO's gathered together their companies and shouted out roll call. In time, Martin was able to determine their hurried flight had saved them from severe losses. General Kirkland then gave orders for his regiments to shift west and north of the Tapp farm and for the men to construct breastworks. Colonel Martin detailed pickets to deploy out in front of the 11th North Carolina and his Tar Heels immediately dug in. One wrote, "The boys collected all the rails and logs ... they could find and then with their bayonets, old tin cups, and their hands, in a short time had a fairly good fortification."[71] Though the Carolinians could hear the angry sounds of heavy battle east and south of them, the dense woods to their front did not contain Yankees. Captain Edward Outlaw (Co. C) wrote, "[We were] not hotly engaged the balance of this day."[72] Longstreet's men battled the Federals until darkness and by the time the sun had set, his Confederates were hunkering down in just about the same positions as Heth's and Wilcox's divisions had been before the Yank's early morning onslaught. That night, Gen. Heth noted "both armies threw up breastworks."[73]

Colonel William Martin's weary Tar Heels slept within the safety of their breastworks, protected by a thin screen of pickets posted out in front of their works. These tired men studied the underbrush before them, searching for any sign of approaching bluecoats. No Yanks appeared. Nevertheless, the night was filled with horror. The relentless day's fighting had set fire to the vegetation in many places, and now these blazes combined into terrifying firestorms that swept across portions of the battlefield. A Confederate wrote, "Dead trees in the woods were aflame like torches ... [and] the reflection of the fire gave the clouds a sickening yellow cast." The rifleman continued, scribbling in revulsion, "The nearer the men ventured to the fire, the louder were the frantic cries of the wounded who could not creep away as fast as the fire approached ... [and] hundred[s] of them soon suffocated or were burned to charred trunks of flesh."[74] Another Carolinian wrote, "The dead Yankees stunk so bad."[75]

The next morning, May 7, 1864, Col. Martin's men awoke to find themselves confronted by an unnerving silence. Occasionally a nervous picket would discharge his musket, but for the most part, no fighting could be heard. Colonel William Martin's adjutant, Lt. Edward Martin, completed the regiment's casualty report; the 11th North Carolina had lost almost 50 men.[76] Meanwhile, the Bethel boys had time to resupply their cartridge boxes, wolf down a chunk of hard cracker, and scribble notes to home. One Tar Heel wrote, "Pen cannot describe or words relate the many adventures which we have passed through."[78]

11th North Carolina Casualties[77]
May 5–6, 1864

Unit	Commander	Casualties*
F & S	Lt. Col. William Martin	0
Co. A	3rd Lt. William Taylor	5
Co. B	Cpt. Thomas Parks	1
Co. C	Cpt. Edward Outlaw	2
Co. D	1st Lt. Lewis Elias	8
Co. E	Cpt. William Kerr	2
Co. F	1st Lt. Stephen Roberts	4
Co. G	Cpt. John Freeland	0
Co. H	1st Lt. Robert Lowrie	8
Co. I	2nd Lt. Lemuel Hoyle	8
Co. K	Cpt. James Young	9
Total		47

*For a complete listing of the battle of the Wilderness casualties, see Appendix A, The Wilderness Casualties.

The past two days' fighting had been completely different from any the Carolinians had experienced before. Colonel Martin's veterans thought they understood battle, especially those who had survived the fiery caldron of Gettysburg. But what had occurred here in the Wilderness was unique and terrifying. Gettysburg's fight at McPherson's Woods had lasted just over half an hour, and Pickett's Charge even less than that. The actual time the Tar Heels had been in the killing zone at Falling Waters and at Bristoe Station also amounted to barely thirty or forty minutes. But on May 5, 1864, Col. Martin's riflemen had remained within that terrible, lethal space called the killing zone for over five hours. There wasn't any way the Carolina farm boys and shopkeepers could have been prepared for the trauma of such an extended stay in absolute danger.

Colonel Martin's soldiers' response to this lengthy time of terror had resulted in an attempt to escape the swarms of bullets filling the air with death, and the men hid behind anything they could locate—trees, underbrush, folds in the earth, and even piles of bodies. This was a distinctively different response to battle's dangers than their actions at Gettysburg, Falling Waters, and Bristoe Station, where the men had stood shoulder to shoulder. At McPherson's Woods, in thirty minutes of intense combat, 200 Carolinians fell; and in the final fifteen minutes of Pickett's Charge, 125 were shot down. But on May 5, 1864, five hours of horrendous fighting cost less than fifty soldiers, the trees and vegetation suffering the rest of the damage. The farm boys and store workers realized this difference; from now on each man needed no encouragement to dig in and construct shelter immediately upon the first hint of danger.[79]

The day went by quickly, with the men resting or improving their earthworks. The Southerners also wondered about the fate of their army. News of General James Longstreet's wounding hit them hard. Longstreet's men had saved their lives yesterday, and now that brilliant leader was fighting for his life. An officer wrote, "A minié ball had entered near [Longstreet's] throat and had crashed into the right shoulder ... [and] Hemorrhage was severe."[80]

Colonel Martin's riflemen remained within their fortifications until early afternoon on May 8, 1864, when William Kirkland called his regimental commanders together and told them to prepare their men to march. General Kirkland informed his officers Gen. Grant was not retreating like all of Lincoln's other generals had after a fight. Instead, he was shifting men towards the east and Lee was countering that unexpected move. Kirkland also notified the assemblage Gen. Ambrose Hill was too sick to continue in command, and Maj. Gen. Jubal Early had taken charge of their corps.[81] Then, Col. Martin recorded, "we started for Spotsylvania."[82] Henry Heth's division abandoned their earthworks and trekked five miles before bivouacking for the night in an open field.[83]

The next morning, May 9, 1864, the Tar Heels arose and quickly took to the road. They marched through the little settlement of Spotsylvania Court House and passed behind the Confederate brigades already posted. They continued east and southward until reaching the army's far right flank; there, they halted. Henry Heth reported, "My division ... held the extreme right of our army ... [and the] men were ordered to dig earthworks."[84] The men labored for the rest of the day beneath a broiling sun, sweating in the heat and unusually high humidity. By sunset their earthworks were secure and nearly impregnable.

The Carolinians were awakened before dawn on May 10, 1864, and ordered to march away from the security of their entrenchments. General Early hurried Heth's men to the west, right back towards where they had been yesterday afternoon. The day's heat became scorching, and the thick humidity punished the Tar Heels as they double-quicked towards their destination. One Carolinian wrote, "I don't think I ever saw a hotter day in all my life." The soldier continued: "We were almost worn out with fatigue from marching, or loss of sleep when we started from this place."[85] Colonel Martin, not mentioning the heat, remarked, "We [were] sent to ... the extreme Confederate left."[86] General Heth recorded his "division was ordered to take a circuitous route and drive the enemy from a position south of the Po River."[87] The Southerners covered nearly ten miles in less than three hours at a pace which distressed the men, causing many to fall out of the column, including Pvt. Augustus Lucas (Co. C), who was "lost on the march."[88] Another of these suffering soldiers confessed, "I was forced to drop from overheat, and the brigade left me. I never hated anything so bad in all my life."[89]

General Jubal Early instructed Henry Heth to form his division on a narrow lane paralleling Glady Run. Heth sent Brig. Gen. Joseph Davis's brigade to the left and William Kirkland's regiments to the right. The two brigades formed up, covering a front of nearly a thousand yards. Behind them, Cooke's and Walker's formations served as reserves. Colonel William Martin's 11th North Carolina came onto line as the brigade's far-right regiment. Skirmishers and sharpshooters deployed out in front of the two-brigade battle line, and then the Confederate riflemen awaited Gen. Early's command to advance. Some artillery was brought up and the gray gunners shelled the woods in front of the Tar Heels. This bombardment was slow and methodical, and Martin's riflemen were unable to determine if it did any good. They remembered the impressive artillery display by the Southern artillery at Gettysburg, as well as the knowledge it did almost no harm at all to the Union positions.

At 2:30 p.m., Gen. Early notified Henry Heth to attack. The Southerners moved forward, advancing towards the north. The riflemen splashed across Glady Run, mucked their way through a swampy lowland, and then entered the shell-damaged stand of trees and underbrush. William Kirkland's regiments pushed their way through the vegetation, emerged onto an open field and halted, a couple hundred yards away from a gravel stretch of highway, the Shady Grove Church Road.[90] Union infantry occupied a line of earthworks just south of the highway. Colonel Martin's riflemen glanced at each other and shook their heads. No one was interested in making a frontal assault across open ground against this position. Fortunately, orders flashed along the battle line: "Lie down, artillery [is] going to be brought up."

A Confederate battery thundered up behind the prone infantrymen and cannons unlimbered. The gun crews efficiently worked their pieces and soon explosive rounds began blasting the Federal works. Then orders were given to advance. The Southerners gave out a loud Rebel yell and raced forward. The bluecoats facing William Kirkland's Tar Heels were three New York regiments, two Pennsylvania formations, and a Delaware unit, combined in a brigade commanded by Col. John Brooke, some 1,500 soldiers.[91] John Brooke's men were fairly inexperienced, and the sight of William Kirkland's five regiments of howling Carolinians unnerved them. They immediately opened fire and a few Confederates fell, including Pvt. George Pool (Co. E), with a shattered right leg, and Cpl. James Harrelson (Co. I), also severely wounded.[92] The veteran Southerners all dropped to the ground and began shooting back at the Northerners.

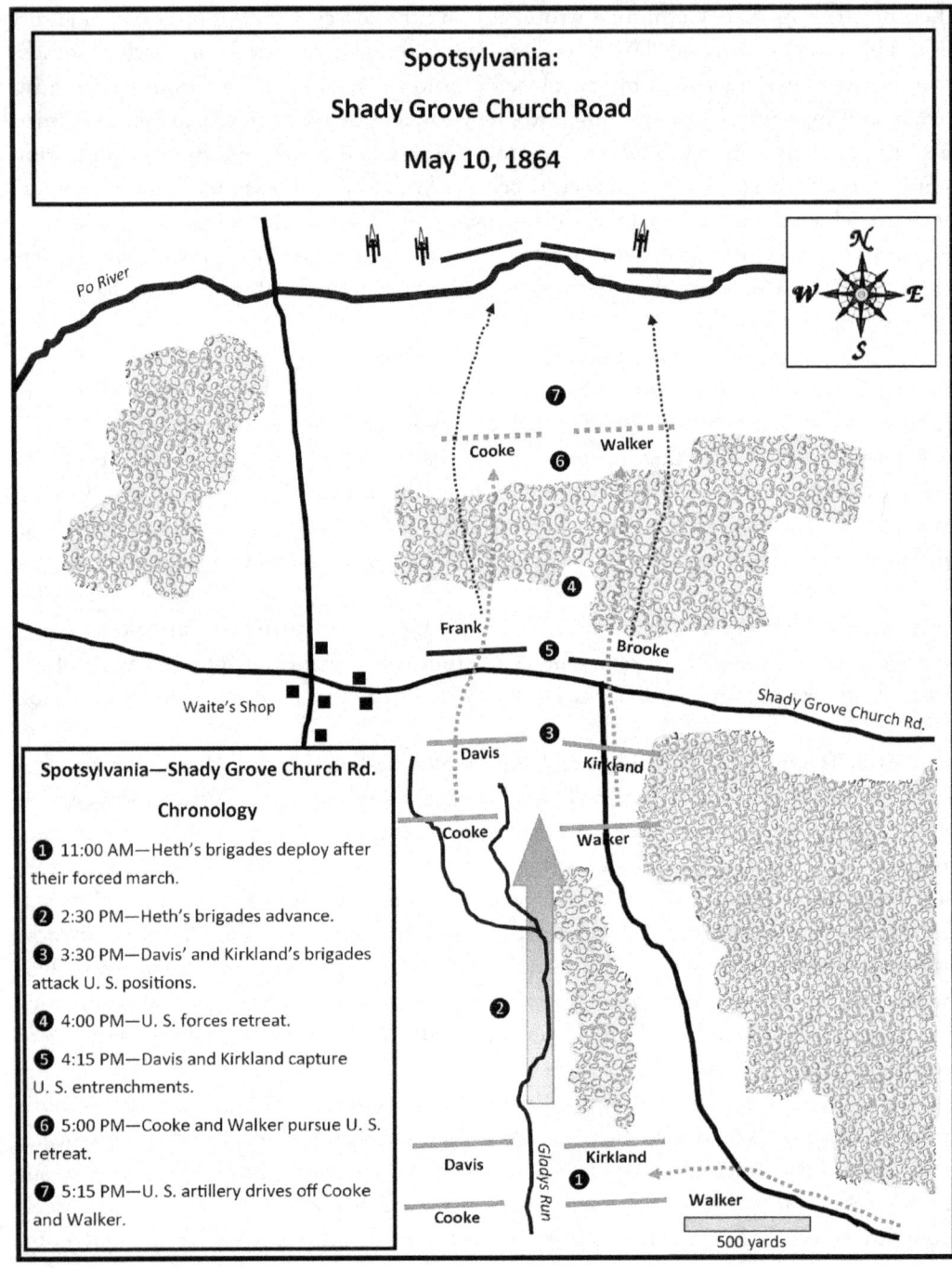

General William Kirkland shouted at his regimental commanders to get their men moving. Colonel Martin hollered at his boys, and he, along with his company officers, were able to get their soldiers up and again advancing. Moments later, a bullet grazed William Martin's body, wounding him slightly.[93] The Carolinians pressed closer, the riflemen loading and firing as they advanced. The Northerners continued shooting, and more of Col. Martin's men dropped. Private Levi Walker (Co. E) was killed, Sgt. John Clements (Co. G), struck in the hand, and Pvt. Ryan Haynes (Co. I) wounded.[94]

The bluecoats opposite John Davis's brigade broke, spilling out of the back of their earthworks and fleeing into the stand of woods behind them. The Yankees fighting Kirkland's Carolinians endured the Confederate fire a few minutes longer, injuring more Bethel men. Private John Hudspeth (Co. I) had a finger sliced away by a ball, and Sgt. William Brown (Co. A) was cruelly wounded.[95] Finally, though, the bluecoats' resolve collapsed and they abandoned their barricade, running for the safety of the near trees.[96] Colonel Martin's riflemen leaped into the deserted earthworks. Martin was able to write, "[We] attacked Barlow's Division ... and drove it back."[97]

Once the Confederates had gulped a swallow of water from their canteens and replenished their cartridge boxes, Gen. Kirkland gave the order to continue the advance. His regiments pushed towards the tree line, which soon vanished in clouds of smoke as the Federals unleashed massive volleys. More Tar Heels fell. First Sergeant John West (Co. K) was mortally wounded, Pvt. George Loudermilk (Co. B) was hit, and Pvt. Edmund Blackwood (Co. G) was also wounded.[98] The Confederate attack slowed and stalled as the Southerners halted to return fire.

The Union soldiers in front of Kirkland's battle line dissolved and the Northerners retreated. When their musketry lessened, the Carolinians advanced again. It only took the Confederates a couple minutes to reach the woods, but they did not venture into the stand of trees. Sparks from musket flashes had started several brush fires and these blazes combined to create an impenetrable wall of flames. Captain Edward Outlaw (Co. C) noted, "During this fight the woods in rear of the Federals took fire and they had to retreat ... through the burning forest."[99] Skirmishers were sent into the woods and they came back with word the Yankees were retreating across the Po River. The Carolinians were pulled back to the Union earthworks, and from there they watched in horror "as Federal dead and wounded were consumed by the fire."[100]

Colonel William Martin's company commanders called roll and he learned his regiment had suffered sixteen casualties.[101] Martin's riflemen marveled at the distance they had covered in their frontal assault and the amount of musketry the Union soldiers expended, and yet their own losses had been so low. One Tar Heel noted, "This was a battle in which the powder used far exceeded a commensurate loss of men."[102] General Heth, not concerned about the consumption of ammunition by the enemy, recorded, "My division ... steadily drove the enemy, until he succeeded in crossing to the north side of the Po."[103]

General Heth ordered his two reserve brigades to advance but a massed formation of Union artillery on the heights north of the Po River quickly discouraged thoughts of attacking. General Cooke's and Walker's brigades fell back to the positions held by Davis's and Kirkland's brigades by 5:00 p.m.[104] The troops all worked to improve their fortifications. An officer noted, "Digging dirt was ... less arduous ... than [attacking]."[105]

The next morning, May 11, 1864, the men were awakened and told to get out of their well-built entrenchments, with orders to march back to Spotsylvania. General Early led Heth's brigades by a more direct route than had been used the day before and by midmorning the Carolinians approached the breastworks they had prepared on the May 9, 1864. General

Kirkland ordered Col. William Martin and Col. Thomas Singletary (44th NC) to move their regiments into the breastworks at a point where the trenches extended outwards in a prominently exposed position the Tar Heels called "Heth's Salient."[106] One noted, "Our line ran for some distance until a ridge ... jutted out, forming a spur ... and so abrupt was the apex that traverses had to be constructed to protect our men from an enfilading fire."[107] The 52nd NC and 47th NC were given postings in the earthworks off to the Bethel Regiment's right. Meanwhile, William Kirkland ordered the 26th NC to leave the area and to guard a wagon train filled with forage. An officer in the 26th NC wrote, "Three farmers ... tendered General Lee two thousand bushels of corn ... [and] it was necessary to send a wagon train for it.... The Twenty-sixth was selected for this ... service."[108]

Colonel Martin sent out pickets in front of his regiment's position and told his company commanders to improve their portions of the earthworks. The Carolinians spent the rest of the day laboring in the dirt. The weather remained oppressively hot and humid, though by late afternoon massive columns of clouds were building above them. The regiment's farm boys, accustomed to reading the sky, predicted rain.

Precipitation began to fall a few hours after sunset, at first just lightly enough to dampen the uniforms of the men out on picket.[109] Later, the showers ended, but the water drained into the soldiers' trenches, depositing a couple inches of muddy liquid at the men's feet. Even later, because the air was still quite humid, a thick layer of ground fog blanketed the landscape. Just before sunrise, May 12, 1864, a massive explosion of musketry erupted from the Confederate positions a mile away, to the Bethel Regiment's left.[110] Colonel William Martin's riflemen rushed to their places within the salient, clutching their rifles, prepared to repel any Union attackers who approached or race to reinforce the units already involved in the fighting.

The sustained battle's roar in the trenches to Martin's regiment's left continued hour after hour; however, for his Tar Heels, nothing happened. His riflemen waited patiently behind their breastworks, though often casting glances over their shoulders in the direction of what had to be a horrendous conflict. One soldier wrote "there was a nameless something in the air which told every man that a crisis was at hand."[111] Another rifleman, trying to ignore the terror of thinking about entering that nearby maelstrom observed, "On our left, in the direction of the firing ... flocks of small birds and owls from the woods flew about in confusion."[112] The regiment did not move, but the rain returned, falling in torrents, pummeling the trench's clay walls and pooling at the riflemen's feet.

Suddenly, their pickets scampered into the lines, hollering the Yankees were attacking. One officer in Walker's brigade, just to the left of Martin's Carolinians, jumped up on top of the breastworks and shouted, "Get Ready boys, there are three lines of coffee coming!"[113] Moments later, a wall of Union troops emerged from the mist, three brigades commanded by Maj. Gen. Thomas Crittenden and two brigades led by Brig. Gen. Robert Potter. These Federals, all troops in Maj. Gen. Ambrose Burnside's IX Corps, attacked the salient, which Gen. Burnside described as "the enemy entrenchments ... in the form of a V."[114]

The Tar Heels opened fire upon the Yanks, downing the bluecoats with ease. Henry Heth recorded his "infantry poured a shower of lead into Burnside's troops."[115] A rifleman

12. The Wilderness and Spotsylvania, May 5–May 20, 1864   147

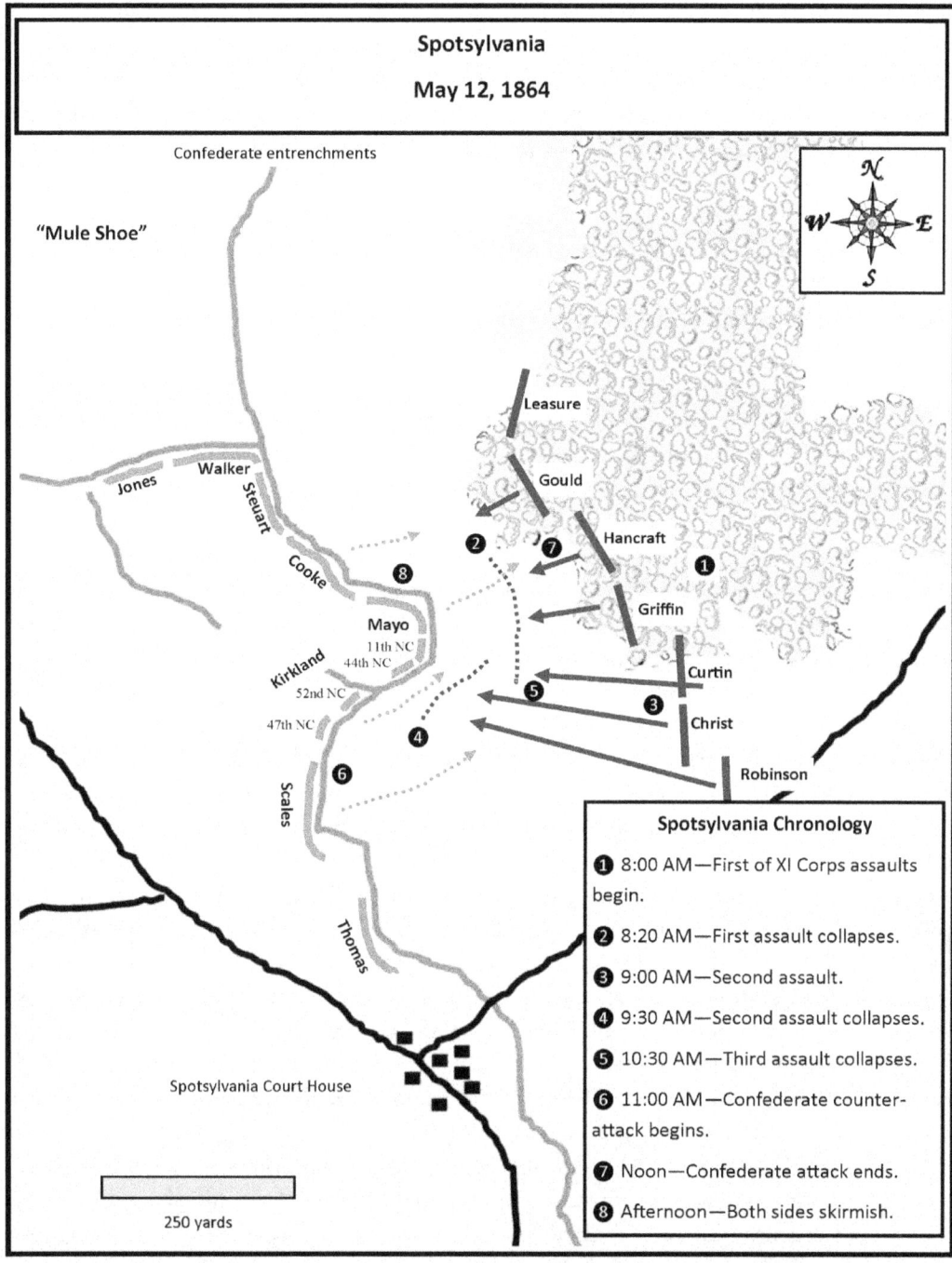

noted, "Undaunted, they advanced in the height of military discipline and received without wavering volley after volley, but at length our well-directed fire told on their ranks." He continued: "Their stout hearts were appalled, their efforts seemed fruitless, and they retreated."[116] General Burnside rallied his brigades and they advanced a second time. A Confederate remarked, "The enemy was repulsed with heavy loss."[117] Burnside then threw in his third division, two brigades led by Brig. Gen. Orlando Willcox, and they advanced, absorbed the Southerner's musketry, stood for a brief time, firing back, and finally retreated. Henry Heth wrote, "Burnside made three assaults ... each repulsed with great loss."[118] Colonel William Martin's riflemen, safely protected by their breastworks, suffered only a few casualties: Pvt. J.W. Crawley (Co. B), wounded in the neck, Pvt. Joseph Lenhardt (Co. I), wounded, and Pvt. Nathan Myers (Co. C), injured in the hand.[119] William Kirkland's 11th NC and 44th NC, along with the eight small regiments of Brig. Gen. Henry Walker's combined Virginia-Tennessee brigade, butchered Gen. Burnside's divisions. Lieutenant Colonel Frank Bird wrote, "The enemy made repeated charges on our works but were repulsed with [a] most terrific slaughter."[120] The Union commander would eventually report the loss of over 2,500 men.[121]

Once the Federals had retreated to the protection of a stand of pines, Gen. Robert E. Lee ordered a counterattack: "Move your men to the right and rear, and attack the left flank of the enemy."[122] William Kirkland and Henry Walker's men emerged from behind their defenses, swarmed across the body-strewn field, and slammed into the rear of the retreating bluecoats. The Yanks were shoved into a grove of pines, where, reinforced by some of Burnside's unbloodied brigades, the Northerners rallied and drove the Confederates back to their earthworks. During this free-for-all among the pines, 3rd Lt. Lucas Gash (Co. K) was seriously wounded, Pvt. Monroe Hovis (Co. A) shot through the left shoulder, Pvt. Allen Davis (Co. C) hit in the arm, and Pvt. Logan Warlick (Co. B) killed.[123]

The battle-weary Carolinians returned to their trenches and awaited the next Yankee assault, but Burnside had used up all his men. The last few hours of daylight were spent in sustained skirmishing, while Col. Martin's men were able to safely hide inside their fortifications. Now, their only enemy was the weather. The summer's deluge lasted all day long and the trenches became long ditches filled with mud-choked water. The men could not move about without having to struggle in the muck. One soaked and mud-splattered soldier complained, "The rain turned the trenches into mud pits."[124] A second soldier wrote, "You could hardly recognize any of us at present. Everyone looks as if he had passed through a hard spell of sickness, black and muddy as hogs."[125] And a third noted, "Both of my shoestrings broke and left my shoes sticking in the mud. I could not think of leaving my shoes, so I got down in [the mud] and pulled them out and carried them in my hand."[126] Lieutenant Lewis Warlick (Co. B) scribbled to his wife, "I haven't had any clean clothes since I left camp ... [as] the wagons are in the rear and we can not leave to go to where they are to get our clothes ... so you may suppose we are ... dirty."[127]

The Carolinians, exhausted by the day's events, slept as best they could in the mud and water that night. The next morning they returned to their posts along the earthworks' walls, bleary-eyed and filthy. Lt. Col. Frank Bird wrote, "We ... had the hardest and longest fighting of the war and it is still not over."[128] Another officer, taking note of his men, recorded, "This sanguinary contest had proceeded almost without abatement for three days, and having no opportunity to cook rations, the troops were well-nigh famished."[129] Another officer gazed upon his soldiers and wrote, "Now, after ten days of constant service, [my men were] ... hungry, weary, and unwashed—for I do not think a single soldier in my command who was fit for duty had time to take his shoes off or wash his face.[130] Colonel William Martin studied his mud-spattered men and shook his head in respect; these muck-covered Carolinians had been treated horribly by the weather and by their opponent, and yet the Tar Heels were ready to fight off the next Yankee assault.

11th North Carolina Casualties[131]
May 10–20, 1864

Unit	Commander	Casualties*
F & S	Lt. Col. William Martin	1
Co. A	3rd Lt. William Taylor	2
Co. B	Cpt. Thomas Parks	4
Co. C	Cpt. Edward Outlaw	4
Co. D	1st Lt. Lewis Elias	1
Co. E	Cpt. William Kerr	3
Co. F	1st Lt. S. Roberts	0
Co. G	Cpt. John Freeland	2
Co. H	1st Lt. Robert Lowrie	1
Co. I	2nd Lt. Lemuel Hoyle	6
Co. K	Cpt. James Young	3
Total		27

*For a complete listing of the battle of the Spotsylvania casualties, see Appendix A, Battle of Spotsylvania Casualties.

The next day, May 14, 1864, was another day of relative quiet, and a time in which the soldiers received news, both good and sad. The clouds blew away and the sun came, beginning the process of drying everything. That was the positive. The unhappy blow came with the news Gen. J.E.B. Stuart, the flamboyant Confederate commander who had so inspired the riflemen, had been killed. A soldier recorded, "It caused indescribable [distress] in the army."[132]

The Carolinians spent the next several days resting. The days were sunny and hot, and the men of both armies seemed to take time off from the war to tend to personal needs. Lieutenant Lewis Warlick (Co. B) recorded, "Today so far everything is quiet. The skirmishers don't even fire at each other, but seem to be quite friendly; meet[ing] each other and exchang[ing] papers."[133] This moment of peace allowed the soldiers to cavort about while they washed their uniforms and hung them out to dry. Rations were brought up, meals cooked and eaten, and letters written home. On May 17, 1864, many noted "the sunshine ... was unusually warm for the season."[134] The veterans guessed the situation would change. Now that the roads were again dry, the armies would be able to move their artillery and wagons.

On May 18, 1864, Union cannon shelled the Confederate lines, forcing the Southerners to take shelter in the their entrenchments. Lieutenant Lewis Warlick wrote, "We were under a terrific shelling." He, like the rest of the men in the Bethel Regiment, waited out the barrage. Warlick noted, it "lasted two hours with very little damage."[135] The battle-seasoned Tar Heels also speculated what the barrage meant; another attack was imminent. One wrote, "Our men are anxious for the Yankees to advance.... They are tired of waiting in mud-soaked trenches."[136]

However, to the Carolinians' surprise, they were wrong; the Yanks were not attacking. Instead, the shelling was a tactic to make them keep their heads down while the Union troops occupying the positions across from them withdrew. The Federals were on the move again, and to the Confederates' dismay, Gen. Grant was not retreating. No, the Union army was sliding to the east and south. Colonel William Martin remarked, "Grant gave [Spotsylvania] up and began his next flank movement."[137] Lt. Col. Frank Bird wrote, his words heavy with frustration, "Grant is very obstinate."[138]

Chapter 13

Summer 1864

The Bethel Regiment remained in its trenches until May 22, 1864, then orders came to move.[1] The Tar Heel brigade headed east and south, the last segment of Lee's army to respond to Grant's shifting tactics. The Carolinians were rested now, having spent many inactive days defending earthworks across from an absent foe. Brigadier General William Kirkland's brigade numbered about 1,500, with all of the men now battle-experienced veterans.[2] They all, whether old hands or new recruits, understood the perils of standing out in the open, and everyone carried some form of excavation tool.

Colonel William Martin's soldiers marched thirty miles before being directed to a stretch of high ground near the Virginia Central Railroad tracks.[3] The Southerners immediately began to dig rifle pits. They could tell by the extensive earthworks stretching as far as vision allowed that their position put them on the far left flank of the Confederate army. Presently, there were no Federal entrenchments in sight, but the Carolinians had learned from experience Gen. Grant quickly massed his blue divisions and they struck relentlessly. Around 4:00 p.m., heavy gunfire erupted in the distance, ahead of their fortifications, and within a few minutes couriers galloped up to William Kirkland, talking excitedly and pointing back towards the sounds of battle.

Brigadier General Kirkland ordered the brigade to form, and the five Tar Heel regiments hustled towards the fighting. They reached the area the locals called Jericho Mills as the sun set into a haze of gunsmoke after having rushed five miles. One soldier recorded, "Henry Heth put his brigades in line of battle behind Wilcox's to ... restore order to his crumbling flank."[4] But the fight had petered out; there was nothing for the men to do but try to cool down and tend to blisters and sore muscles. Then, once the landscape was completely dark, the Tar Heels were given the order to march back to the works they had built earlier in the day. The men may have been tired, but during the two hours it took to return to where they had started they filled the night sky with a chorus of complaints.

The next day, May 24, 1864, began quietly, though the farm boys-turned-veteran-soldiers could read the sky, and they knew a summer rainstorm approached. Colonel Martin's riflemen manned their portion of the earthworks and waited. The soldiers figured they would soon be wet and guessed Union soldiers would also make an appearance. Gunfire erupted off to their right. The Carolinians anticipated a call to respond and quietly prepared.

Fortunately, no word to move came, though the skies opened up and a deluge turned the ground into a muddy morass. Later, darkness stilled the sounds of combat and an evening breeze pushed the rain away.

At 1:00 p.m., on May 25, 1864, Brig. Gen. Kirkland formed up his Carolinians and marched them across the Little River, a rain-swollen stream of mud-choked water. Rumors swept through the drenched soldiers that Yankee formations had been sent to flank their left, and they were responding to this threat. The Tar Heel regiments slopped across this saturated ground for a mile before reaching a ridge jutting up above the marshy area. The soldiers quickly began to dig entrenchments. That evening 2nd Lt. Lewis Warlick (Co. B) wrote, "We have good earthworks here and I very much fear the enemy will not attack us."[5] Lieutenant Warlick, like most of his battle-experienced comrades, had seen the fields covered with dead bluecoats and guessed the Union army must have suffered greatly. Warlick remarked, "If the enemy continues to assault our lines we will weaken his ranks so after awhile we will be able to drive him across the river." He also noted their war had transformed and this change was ill-omened; Lt. Warlick wrote, "It is unlike any other fight, and Grant is unlike any other general."[6]

Eventually Confederate cavalry arrived and they took over the Tar Heels' position. The Tar Heels splashed their way back to their early-morning fortifications. Once back to their old position, they could see Federal earthworks had been built about 1,000 yards away. Colonel Martin sent out pickets in front of their works and this thin screen of vigilant soldiers eyed their blue-coated counterparts barely a quarter mile away. The Yank skirmishers did not do any shooting, and the Carolinians responding equally peaceably. The night went by quietly, as did the entire next day.

The Bethel riflemen awoke on May 27, 1864, to find the Federal earthworks abandoned. The Tar Heels gathered up their gear, knowing movement orders would soon follow. They left their works at 10:00 a.m. and hiked seventeen miles to Ashland Station before bivouacking, and then another ten more miles the next day.[7] These were not easy marches. As one writer recorded, "the Bethel troops ... slog[ged] through knee-deep mud."[8] On May 28, 1864, the brigade reached a position along Totopotomoy Creek, and "immediately commenced digging."[9] No new orders came for more marching, so the veterans improved their fortifications. A soldier noted, "It is a rule that, when the Rebels halt, the first day gives them a good rifle-pit; the second, the regular infantry parapet with artillery in position; and the third a parapet with an abatis in front and entrenched batteries behind." He added, "Sometimes they put this three days' work into the first twenty-four hours."[10] As darkness covered the landscape, Lt. Gen. Ambrose Hill reported, "I have a good line and would like to fight it."[11] The Federals, however, after a light probe on May 30, 1864, felt no inclination to attack.

At 10:00 p.m., on May 31, 1864, Col. William Martin marched the 11th North Carolina out of their secure position and the regiment moved three miles in the direction of Gaines' Mill.[12] The Southerners scratched out rifle pits in the dark and then slept. A frustrated rifleman complained, "I have been marching, fighting, and throwing up breastworks nearly all this month."[13] The next morning the Tar Heels abandoned their defenses and hiked to Gaines' Mill, where Gen. Kirkland deployed the brigade near the Mander house, a position

The 36th Wisconsin's assault was destroyed by the 11th NC and 47th NC on June 1, 1864, at Cold Harbor (Aubery, 1900).

with a good field of fire. The 47th NC was on the brigade's left, and the 26th NC covered its right. Col. Martin's regiment was tucked in beside the 47th NC.[14] The Carolinians instantly scrambled to dig rifle pits.

Union regiments moved towards the Tar Heels just as the riflemen had finished construction of their initial defenses. The hardened Southerners loaded their muskets and studied the approaching bluecoats, a couple regiments from Col. H. Boyd McKeen's brigade (Gibbon's Division). The Northerners had to cross nearly five hundred yards of open ground. Colonel William Martin and Lt. Col. Frank Bird moved along behind their riflemen, urging patience and calmness. One of the Federal formations, the inexperienced troopers of the 36th Wisconsin, surged forward, while the other two units, composed of battle-weary veterans from the 42nd NY and the 7th MI, lagged behind. Then, the 42nd NY and 7th MI halted, leaving the fresh soldiers of the 36th WI all by themselves. This formation, numbering 240 officers and men, hurried towards the Tar Heels.[15] A rifleman in the 46th NC recorded the Federals "desperately charged."[16]

Confederate artillery opened on the Wisconsin battalion when it was 200 yards away, and the Tar Heel riflemen unleashed their first volleys at fifty yards. One Carolinian remarked, "Our men were perfectly cool ... [and] our deadly fire ... was so steady and accurate."[17] Another wrote, "I could see the dust fog out of a man's clothing in two or three places at once when ... the ... balls would strike him at the same moment."[18] The Wisconsin formation melted away and the survivors fled. A Carolinian reported, "[I] could see the officers making frantic efforts to urge their men to move forward but they could not and they ran back into the woods."[19] Another Tar Heel noted "the enemy was completely broken and routed ... [and] a large number of them killed or wounded."[20] And another Southern admitted, "I must confess I felt sorry for them."[21] Lieutenant James Aubery of the 36th WI wrote, "Of the 240 men ... engaged in the charge, 140 were [lost] ... [and] this [was] a useless sacrifice of life."[22]

The Bethel Regiment's adjutant, Lt. Edward Martin, quickly took a muster count and informed his commander the 11th North Carolina had suffered extremely light casualties; three men from 2nd Lt. Lemuel Hoyle's Company I who had been out in front of the earthworks as pickets were wounded: Pvt. Michael Craft (arm), Pvt. Theodore Ramsour (leg badly mangled, requiring amputation), and Pvt. Robert Roseman (ankle). Inside the defenses, only two were hit: Pvt. William Wilkerson (Co. H), who had taken a bullet to his head, and Cpl. James Burden (Co. C), who was hit in the hip and left hand.[23]

11th North Carolina Muster[24]
June 1, 1864

Unit	Commander	Strength
F & S	Col. William Martin	
	Lt. Col. Frank Bird	3
Co. A	2nd Lt. William Taylor	57
Co. B	Cpt. Thomas Parks	42
Co. C	1st Lt. William Todd	32
Co. D	1st Lt. Lewis Elias	35
Co. E	Cpt. William Kerr	33
Co. F	2nd Lt. William Rea	31
Co. G	Cpt. John Freeland	52
Co. H	1st Lt. Robert Lowrie	41
Co. I	2nd Lt. Lemuel Hoyle	44
Co. K	Cpt. James Young	35
Total		405

The rest of the day went by quietly, though marred by sharpshooters firing at anyone who showed himself above the breastworks. The next morning the two sides continued to face each other until noon, when the Federals began to withdraw. Major General Jubal Early, still commanding Ambrose Hill's Third Corps, ordered Maj. Gen. Heth to attack the retreating Yanks. Henry Heth directed three brigades, those of Davis, Cooke, and Kirkland, to pursue. Their assault began at 3:00 p.m., with Cooke on the left, Davis on the right, and Kirkland in the center. William Kirkland's Tar Heels pushed into a thick stand of woods about the same time as a summer rainstorm soaked the landscape.[25]

Colonel William Martin now commanded 400 Carolinians. He was supported by Lt. Col. Frank Bird on the right wing and Cpt. William Grier at the left, and with four remaining captains. The rest of his company commanders were lieutenants. Martin's Tar Heels were in good spirits; yesterday's easy slaughter buoyed their morale. Their uniforms may have been shabby and their footwear suspect, but their weapons were well maintained and their cartridge boxes full. William Martin was extremely proud of his men, writing they could "get used to anything."[26]

Kirkland's Carolina regiments worked their way through the vegetation for two miles before emerging from the trees, now facing towards the south and less than one hundred

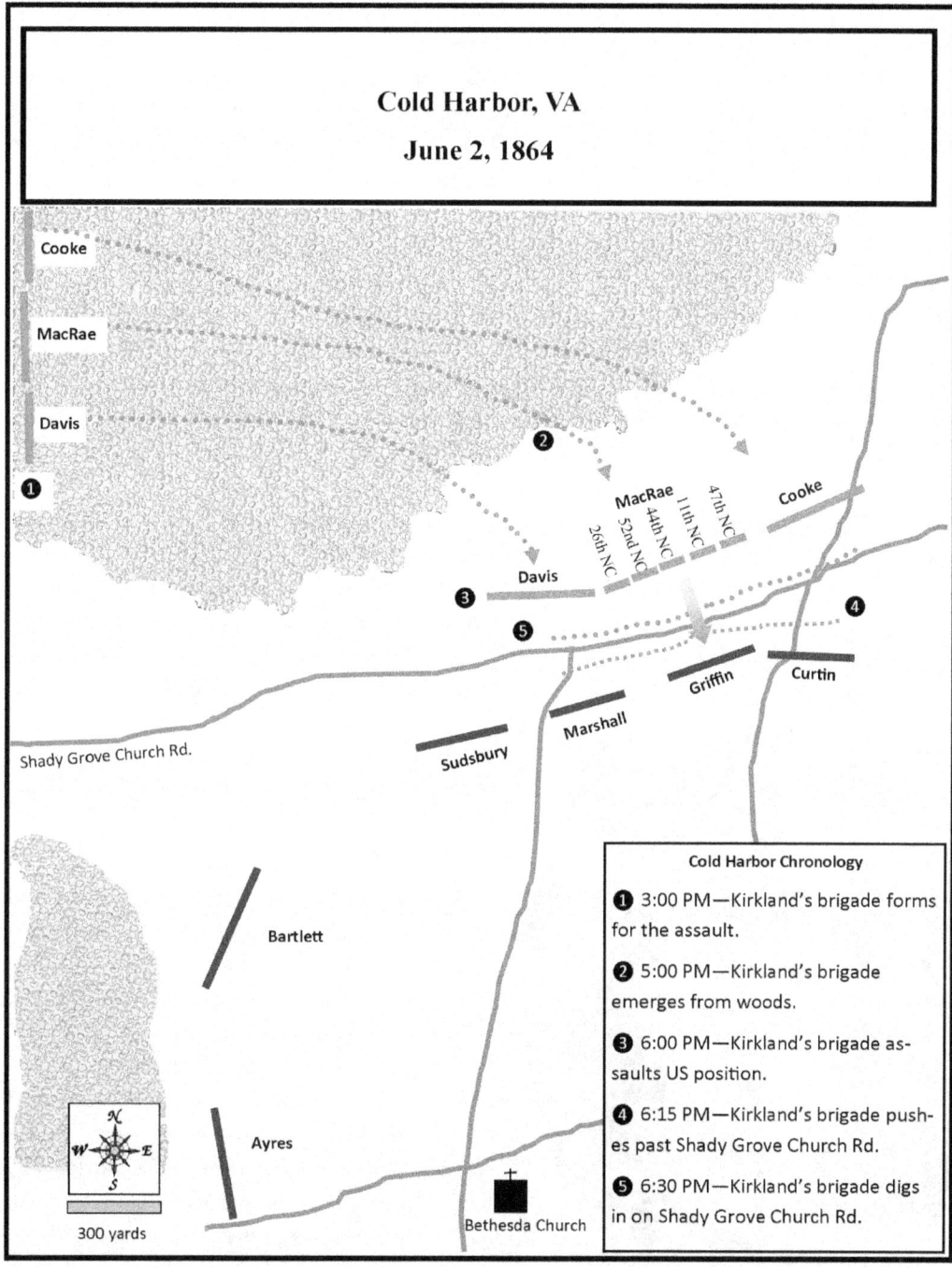

yards from the Shady Grove Church Road. General Kirkland halted his brigade as his skirmish line reached the road and began exchanging shots with Union pickets a couple hundred yards south of the road. Colonel Martin dressed his regiment as his veterans eyed a brigade of bluecoats a half mile away. The Carolinians knew what was coming: the command to attack. One wrote, "Each man looked into the eyes of his comrade with a long steady gaze, which was returned ... as tho' each said 'I'm with you old man.' Then a quiver ran thru the line as each man touched elbows and shoulders."[27]

The skirmishers were sent forward and they immediately kicked up a storm of Federal fire. One noted they "participated in a heavy skirmish with the enemy."[28] Then, when the skirmishers could drive the bluecoats no farther, Brig. Gen. Kirkland gave the order to advance. A Tar Heel recorded they "leapt ... and raised the rebel yell." He continued, saying, "Fury seized us ... [and] we rushed forward."[29] The Federal troops, New England soldiers from Col. Simon Griffin's brigade, opened fire. A Confederate rifleman wrote, "You could hear the swish of the shrapnel—the hum of the minie, [and] the plunge of grape."[30] Immediately, 1st Sgt. Thomas Davis (Co. G) fell, wounded.[31] Then, 3rd Lt. William Taylor (Co. A) was hit, followed by Pvt. Robert Hall (Co. H), who was struck in the left hand, and Pvt. Barry Henry (Co. H), who was injured by a bullet tearing through his forearm.[32] The Tar Heels' advance slowed as the Southern riflemen returned fire upon the Yanks. The two forces blasted away at each other as the Confederates closed to within one hundred yards of their foe.

Private William Harbison (Co. B) was struck in the right leg, the Minié bullet shattering the bone. His friends carried him to safety and Dr. John Wilson was forced to amputate his leg.[33] Corporal William Icehower (Co. A) was killed.[34] Finally, as the Carolinians pushed their way to within fifty yards of the Yanks' line, the bluecoat's resolve crumbled. A Tar Heel noted, "[We] charged the enemy out of their good breastworks."[35] The jubilant Southerners vaulted into the abandoned earthworks and quickly rifled through any discarded haversacks.

A harried brigade staff officer sought out Col. William Martin, informing him he was needed at an emergency brigade officers' meeting. Martin soon learned Brig. Gen. William Kirkland had "received a rifle ball through the thigh and [had been] taken from the field."[36] The brigade's senior regimental officer, 34-year-old Col. George Faribault (47th NC), assumed command. Faribault told his regimental leaders to tell their men to reinforce the works they had just captured. Colonel Martin hurried back to his Bethel boys and issued commands. A Carolinian recalled "the Tar Heels collected fence rails and dug to fortify their position."[37] They held this location for the rest of the day, driving off a number of lightly contested Union probes.

Thirty-four-year-old Lt. William Taylor (Co. A) was wounded at Cold Harbor, June 2, 1864 (Library of Congress).

But darkness did not halt the fighting. A

brief Federal artillery Union barrage was followed by a heavy screen of Federal skirmishers, who, because of the lack of visibility and the nearness of a stand of trees, were able to press within forty yards of the Southern position. A Tar Heel wrote, "They were in the woods, we on the edge of it with a small field between us."[38] The Carolinians could hear the Yanks coming and fired at their noise, and as one Tar Heel remarked, "We learned by sound rather than sight ... and kept them in check by shooting in the direction of their noise."[39] From then on, both sides shot at their opponents' muzzle flashes. One soldier wrote, "It was a blind fight." He also recorded, "The flow of bullets in both directions was terrific ... but in the dense woods neither side inflicted a lot of damage on the other."[40] The 11th North Carolina suffered one casualty, Pvt. Campbell King (Co. A) was wounded.[41] Eventually, the exhausted soldiers on both sides quit shooting and the night battle faded away. Sergeants sent out water details and the men gobbled some rations. Then Col. Faribault sent out orders for the brigade to pull back, as they were being replaced by Cooke's regiments. The weary men of the Bethel Regiment followed guides who took them back to their early morning's position not far from the Mander house.[42] One Tar Heel scribbled, "We silently stole away."[43]

11th North Carolina Casualties[44]
June 1–3, 1864

Unit	Commander	Casualties*
F & S	Lt. Col. William Martin	0
Co. A	3rd Lt. William Taylor	3
Co. B	Cpt. Thomas Parks	1
Co. C	1st Lt. William Todd	1
Co. D	1st Lt. Lewis Elias	4
Co. E	Cpt. William Kerr	0
Co. F	2nd Lt. William Rea	0
Co. G	Cpt. John Freeland	3
Co. H	1st Lt. Robert Lowrie	6
Co. I	2nd Lt. Lemuel Hoyle	4
Co. K	Cpt. James Young	1
Total		23

*For a complete listing of the battle of the Cold Harbor casualties, see Appendix A, Battle of Cold Harbor Casualties.

Colonel William Martin's tired men were not part of the defense against Grant's desperate assaults on June 3, 1864. Instead, his veterans improved their entrenchments, rested, and waited to be called to bolster any part of the line needing reinforcements. But the Confederate earthworks were impenetrable and the veteran riflemen's fire so lethal the Federal soldiers quickly gave up their useless assaults, regardless of their high commanders' desires to continue the attack. The grand charge lasted less than sixty minutes; however, in that terrible space of time over 7,000 Union soldiers were shot down. General Grant later wrote, "I have always regretted that the last assault at Cold Harbor was ever made."[45] That afternoon Col. Martin supplied a company of skirmishers and in the scrapping between pickets several Bethel men were wounded.

The next morning at 3:00 a.m., Col. Faribault led the brigade out of their position and they marched all day, heading south. They bivouacked miles from the battle lines and far from any form of danger. The men sprawled out and rested, completely free of any hazard. No orders came to move on June 5, 1864, and the Tar Heels, as one recorded, "for the first time since leaving Orange Court House ... rest[ed]."[46] The delighted Southerners napped, repaired clothing, and "greatly enjoyed this much needed repose."[47] Then, at 11:00 p.m., they fell into marching formation and trekked to a position near the right of the Confederate army, where they filed into a stretch of entrenchments.[48]

In midafternoon, on June 6, 1864, Gen. Heth pulled the brigade out of the line and sent them two miles farther to the right. He gave orders to Col. Faribault to tell his regimental leaders their men were to build deep entrenchments, "complete with bombproofs."[49] The Carolinians remained in this position, dodging sharpshooters and working on their fortifications for the next two days. Then, on June 9, 1864, the brigade left the front and marched to Bottom's Bridge, on the Chickahominy River, for, as one Tar Heel recorded, "picket duty" and to protect the York River railroad bridge.[50] This was an idyllic assignment; the Chickahominy River was over a half-mile wide, putting the Union pickets so far apart neither side felt any threat from the other. In fact, this distance between the two forces created a fellowship among the soldiers and they became rather affable. A Tar Heel wrote, "[We] are quite friendly with the Yankees.... We like our present position very well. If [only] we could stay here."[51] Life became so peaceful Lt. Lewis Warlick (Co. B) was able to inform his wife, "We [are] doing finely. [We] have good water, good shade, and plenty to eat.... I went out yesterday and caught a mess of fish ... [and] some of the boys found a bee tree."[52]

Just as everyone was settling into this comfortable routine Col. George Faribault instructed William Martin to prepare his men for movement. The brigade had received orders to march. That evening after dark on June 12, 1864, Col. Martin withdrew his pickets from their posts and lined the regiment up for their next march. The brigade left their cushy responsibilities and hiked to White Oak Swamp, where they camped near the Charles City Road. Colonel Martin's sergeants roused the men on June 14, 1864, and they went to work constructing breastworks. Then, once proper defenses had been erected, Col. Faribault assigned picket duties, making sure to alternate responsibilities among the five regiments. This gave all the soldiers extra time to rest. The men, when not on duty, had time to think about the war's progress, and to write home. Lieutenant Lewis Warlick (Co. B) penned to his wife that "the impression in camp is Grant is going to try [to reach] Richmond." Warlick added pensively, "I think we will have some hard fighting yet."[53]

On June 17, 1864, Grant's army shifted again, causing concern among the Tar Heels. Lieutenant Colonel Frank Bird wrote, "Grant has disappeared in our front once more and gone to the James River, obviously with the intention of crossing." Bird optimistically noted, "May he be as unsuccessful as on this side [of the river]."[54] The veteran soldiers prepared to move but no orders came from Gen. Henry Heth. A rifleman recorded simply, "on picket duty."[55]

At 3:00 a.m. on June 18, 1864, the Bethel Regiment was awakened and the sleepy men staggered out of camp, heading for a crossing of the James River. The brigade marched to the James and tramped across a pontoon bridge near Chafin's farm.[56] The long gray column hiked southward, one Carolinian noting they "marched for Petersburg ... a dusty and very fatiguing march."[57] Another soldier recalled "it was a very hot, fatiguing march and many of our men broke down." This rifleman continued: "As the column marches along, the further it gets the less it talks and laughs. Finally everything becomes silent except the irregular tottering step of the scattered ranks and an occasional cough produced by the stifling dust."[58] Another infantryman recorded, "The road [was] ankle deep with dust ... [which] was worse, if possible than the heat.... I could not see the length of a single company."[59] And a third wrote, "It was almost like going through a furnace ... [and] there was a lot of straggling."[60]

The Carolinians marched at a punishing pace beneath the sweltering sun, covering nearly fifteen miles by 3:00 p.m., before climbing onto railroad cars and riding the final handful of miles to Petersburg. The weary, dust-caked soldiers dismounted from their train and entered the city. Petersburg's citizens stared quietly at the bedraggled Confederates. One recorded, "So worn with travel and fighting, so dusty and ragged, their faces thin and drawn by privation that we scarcely knew them."[61] General Henry Heth led his brigades through Petersburg and halted a mile south of the city. A rifleman then noted the men "immediately began digging trenches, not even taking time to eat."[62]

On June 19, 1864, the Bethel Regiment occupied the western end of General Lee's army. Federal brigades inched close to the Southerners' entrenchments and sharpshooters began terrorizing anyone out in the open. Both sides were forced to dig only when it was dark. A rifleman wrote, "The breastworks were worked on each night until raised to a height above our heads, and we fired through portholes."[63] The Tar Heels hunkered down, adjusting themselves to a new form of warfare. One wrote, "[We] commenced the desultory and dreary work of duty in the trenches."[64] Snipers continued to plague the soldiers, and four days later, Pvt. Larking Livingston (Co. B) was struck in the left arm by a sharpshooter's bullet.[65]

On June 27, 1864, the brigade was assigned a new commander, Brig. Gen. William MacRae. The Tar Heels' new leader was also a Carolinian, from Wilmington. William MacRae was the seventh of nine sons of an immigrant from Scotland. His father had fought in the war of 1812 in a North Carolina militia unit, remained with the organization, and earned the rank of major general. William MacRae's father then became a successful merchant and had insisted his sons be well educated. The young MacRae finished his schooling and at age sixteen went to work in the machine shops of a Wilmington locomotive engineering company. He then studied civil engineering and joined an engineering firm with a couple of his brothers.[66]

William MacRae enlisted as a private when the war began but soon was elected captain of a company in the 15th North Carolina Infantry. He rose quickly, being promoted to lieutenant colonel in April 1862 and colonel of the 15th NC in February 1863. Because the 15th NC was in Cooke's brigade, Col. William Martin already knew MacRae and respected his thoughtful though aggressive military approach to leadership. MacRae was a small fellow, with, as one officer observed, "[a] voice ... like that of a woman."[67] But there was no one who doubted his combative presence. MacRae was the essence of a Scottish warrior, and "soon won the confidence and admiration of the brigade, both officers and men."[68] In addition, as Col. William Martin recorded, "he was a strict disciplinarian, [similar] to Pettigrew ... which Gen. Kirkland was not."[69]

Brigadier General William MacRae immediately went about the business of tightening discipline and improving brigade morale. He also organized a corps of full-time brigade sharpshooters, an idea slowly growing among the forward-thinking Confederate leaders. These brigade officers had discovered it was better to have a dedicated unit of skirmishers drawn from the best men out of each regiment rather than just sending out companies to perform that task. A small unit of motivated and highly skilled skirmishers was much more effective than larger, clumsier companies composed of proficient soldiers and not-so-good troops. William MacRae established this unit, consisting of eighty soldiers with fifteen personally selected men drawn from each of the five regiments, to be led by a captain, with a senior lieutenant as his executive officer. The riflemen were divided up into three 25-man platoons, each one led by a lieutenant. Gen. MacRae specified "no one could become a member unless he had specially distinguished himself by personal courage and coolness under fire."[70] These nominated sharpshooters were allowed to wear a "gold cross upon the left arm" and were given separate privileges.[71] MacRae chose Cpt. Thomas Lilly (26th NC) to lead the sharpshooter corps and 1st Lt. Duncan Waddell (Co. G) from the 11th NC as one of the lieutenants.[72] One of the Bethel Regiment's handpicked sharpshooters was Pvt. Woodston Garrett (Co. G).[73]

Twenty-nine-year-old Brig. Gen. William MacRae became brigade commander on June 27, 1864 (Library of Congress).

On July 8, 1864, Brig. Gen. William MacRae directed his regiments away from their entrenchments and marched them seven miles to a set of trenches near the Weldon Railroad tracks not far from Reams Station. Here, the Carolinians were immediately subjected to a heavy barrage of artillery fire. This was soon followed by a wave of Yank regiments surging across the space between the two sides. The Tar Heels slaughtered the attackers. Lieutenant Colonel Frank Bird wrote, "About 5 o'clock the enemy charged our lines on the left and center ... twice and were repulsed each time."[74] That evening, as the Tar Heels gazed out at the body-strewn no-man's land and listened to the moans, cries, and pleas from wounded Northerners, Lt. Lewis Warlick (Co. B) penned to his wife, "O cruel war, when shall we be relieved of its dreadful consequences?"[75] William MacRae returned his Tar Heels back to their portion of the earthworks and the veteran soldiers endured two weeks of trench warfare. A Tar Heel rifleman wrote, "On some parts of the line it is almost sertin [sic] death to show your head above the breastworks. Sharp shooting is continually kept up day and night." He continued: "Our works are strong."[76] General MacRae's new policies bolstered their determination and increased their morale, even while Col. William Martin's men were forced to withstand the dangers of trench life. A member of the 26th NC wrote,

"General MacRae ... changed the physical expression of the whole command in less than two weeks, giv[ing] the men infinite faith in him and themselves."[77] Another Carolinian added, "Our men are in fine spirits."[78]

On July 23, 1864, Cpt. William Kerr (Co. E) was shot by a sharpshooter, the bullet ripping through his left leg.[79] William Martin turned Company E over to 1st Lt. William Turner. Four days later, Gen. Heth ordered MacRae to pull his five regiments out of the works. The brigade slipped away at 2:00 p.m., heading northward. The Tar Heels crossed the James River on a pontoon bridge and trekked twenty miles before reaching the Confederate lines near Deep Bottom, just after dawn.[80] William MacRae posted his regiments and put out pickets while the footsore men wolfed down some corn bread and bacon. Then a thick screen of Union soldiers attacked. A Tar Heel remarked the "skirmish lines were heavily engaged for an hour or two."[81] When the Northerners' pressure increased, the Carolinian pickets were withdrawn and MacRae ordered all his riflemen to man the lines. One wrote, "We expected an attack upon our lines."[82] But the Union reconnaissance had been completed and the Yank officers determined the earthworks were held with strength; there would be no slaughter of brave Northerners. Two days later a sharpshooter's bullet drilled Pvt. Thomas Moore (Co. B) through the head. The 22-year-old farm boy from Morganton, North Carolina, died on July 30, 1864.[83]

Also on July 30, 1864, at 4:45 a.m., the war entered a new phase when Union forces detonated a huge stockpile of gunpowder in tunnels beneath the Confederate trenches. A massive crater 170 feet long, 120 feet wide, and thirty feet deep was gouged in the Southerners' lines, instantly killing over 275 Confederates. Then, Federal brigades commanded by Brig. Gen. James Ledlie rushed into the gaping hole, only to immediately stagger to a halt. One Yank recalled in horror "the enormous hole ... filled with dust, great blocks of clay, guns, broken carriages, projecting timbers, and men buried in various ways." He saw "some [Confederates buried] up to their necks, others to their waists, and some with only their feet and legs protruding from the earth."[84]

James Ledlie's brigades attempted to push through this enormous gap in the Confederate lines, but, as one wrote, "the whole scene of the explosion struck every one dumb with astonishment."[85] The attackers stumbled about long enough for nearby Southern formations to respond and counterattack from three sides. Major General Ambrose Burnside, in charge of the entire operation, then rushed in a division of black troops commanded by Brig. Gen. Edward Ferrero. Confederates commanded by Brig. Gen. William Mahone and Maj. Gen. Bushrod Johnson swarmed around the sides of the crater and fired into these confused bluecoats. Ferrero's soldiers met with the same fate, falling upon Ledlie's men.[86] By the time the Yanks had retreated from the crater they left behind over 500 dead and another 3,000 wounded or missing. Confederate casualties were less than half the Federals' losses and one senior Northern officer recorded, "It was the saddest affair I have witnessed in the war."[87]

That evening, Gen. Henry Heth sent Cooke's and MacRae's brigades to reinforce the crumpled Confederate line, and the Tar Heels "hustled through the night and reached the site of the explosion by daybreak."[88] Sergeant Jacob Bartlett (Co. K) wrote, "MacRae's brigade was placed ... near the crater."[89] William MacRae's regiments were located in the

Confederate defenses in the Crater (Johnson and Buel, 1887).

Confederate lines just south of the crater, placing the Bethel men only 150 yards from the Union fortifications.[90]

The soldiers from both sides seethed with anger. The Confederate soldiers were enraged by the atrociousness of the exploding mine, as well as the Federals' employment of black troops, and the Northern soldiers raged at their commanders' appalling leadership as well as the atrocities some Confederates committed upon the captured blacks. Sergeant Bartlett noted, "Every morning at three o'clock the artillery of both sides would open fire and keep it up until daylight." He continued: "at all times of the day the enemy was dropping bombs from their [mortars] into our trenches, and the boys who were not on duty in the ditch would scuttle into the broom proofs which were made by digging holes into the earth."[91] Lieutenant Lewis Warlick (Co. B) wrote, "The mine explosion of Grant's was a terrible affair."[92] On August 5, 1864, the Tar Heels were pulled out of the trenches and marched to the north, where they bivouacked a distance behind the lines, to, as one Carolinian recorded, "be placed in reserve."[93] A relieved Lt. Warlick (Co. B) wrote, "We are [now] lying in reserve a mile from the Yanks."[94]

Chapter 14

Late Summer 1864, August to Mid-September

Brigadier General William MacRae's Tar Heels slipped back into the trenches on August 9, 1864, and relieved William Cooke's men. Union sharpshooters immediately opened fire on the Carolinians, even before they were settled. A Tar Heel recorded, "Our line at this point [had] not exceeded 200 yards distance from the enemy's lines ... and the enemy kept up a constant firing both night and day."[1] In some places the two forces' entrenchments were barely one hundred yards apart. Colonel William Martin wrote the "lines ultimately came so close together that no pickets could be thrown out." Martin continued: "picket duty was performed by sharp-shooters in the trenches, who made it hazardous for any one on either side to expose any part of his person."[2]

MacRae regulated his soldiers' assignments, requiring "one-third of the men ... to be on duty in the trenches at all times, manning the fire steps by shifts."[3] The soldiers stationed at the firing steps faced both sniper fire and artillery bombardments, especially from with a new and frightening weapon—the mortar. Captain Edward Outlaw (Co. C) noted, "Mortar shelling was also added ... rendering bombproofs a necessity."[4] A rifleman scribbled to his family, "We [have] pens built and covered with logs and dirt to protect us from mortar fire ... [and] when the mortar fire begins we ... get in the pens for protection."[5]

Colonel Martin's riflemen wrestled with their privations and waited out the hours until William Cooke's brigade would return and replace them. A Confederate wrote, "We have to ly [sic] in our trenches day and night, rain or shine, hot or cold. [We] burrow in the ground the same as rats ... [and] when we hear a mortar shell coming, every man gets to his hole."[6] Besides the lethal danger of snipers and mortars, the men were tortured by insects. One rifleman grumbled they "had to contend with the hot sunshine and the bite of dog flies during the day and through the night, with mosquitoes ... [so] it was almost impossible to get any sleep."[7] In addition, even amid all these privations, the trenches had to be continually repaired and improved. A soldier recorded, "The work of entrenching could only be done at night. The fire of sharpshooters was incessant, and no man ... could stand erect and live an instant."[8] Another soldier, trying to make the best of this horrid experience, recalled "a hat put on a ramrod and raised a little would be perforated in a jiffy."[9] Sergeant Jacob Bartlett (Co. K) wrote, "Duty in the trenches became boring."[10] Fortunately, on August 13, 1864,

Cooke's brigade returned and MacRae's men were able to escape for a few days. A Tar Heel happily noted, "We ... were relieved, and camped temporarily in rear of our lines."[11]

11th North Carolina Muster[12]
August 14, 1864

Unit	Commander	Total
F & S	Col. William Martin	
	Lt. Col. Frank Bird	5
Co. A	2nd Lt. James Alexander (Co. E)	54
Co. B	Cpt. Thomas Parks	45
Co. C	1st Lt. James Rayner (F & S)	30
Co. D	2nd Lt. James McCorkle	42
Co. E	1st Lt. William Turner	26
Co. F	2nd Lt. James Saville (Co. H)	27
Co. G	Cpt. John Freeland	66
Co. H	1st Lt. Robert Lowrie	30
Co. I	2nd Lt. Lemuel Hoyle	40
Co. K	1st Lt. Lewis Warlick (Co. B)	21
Total		386

On August 14, 1864, Brig. Gen. William MacRae formed his brigade for inspection. His staff totaled the regimental returns and informed him the brigade mustered 1,587 men. The 11th NC had 386; the 26th NC, 294; the 44th NC, 338; the 47th NC, 356; and the 52nd NC, 212.[13] Colonel William Martin had been busy staffing each of his companies with officers. The past month's fighting and hardships cut into Martin's officer corps, as sickness and enemy bullets created continual turnover. Some of William Martin's companies lost all of their commissioned officers, requiring Martin to draw lieutenants from other companies that still had multiple officers. He placed these transferred lieutenants in charge of the units without officers. He also positioned his regimental adjutant, 1st Lt. James Rayner, as a company commander.

The Bethel Regiment followed MacRae's brigade back into the trenches at a spot where, as one rifleman noted, "[he] coulden look over the breste works with out beeing shot in the head."[14] Within hours, Pvt. John Cates (Co. G) was struck in the right shoulder by a sharpshooter.[15] The Tar Heels resumed their duties of manning the firing posts and fighting to stay alive. Meanwhile, General Grant's forces moved to cut the Weldon Railroad in the area around Globe Tavern. A Confederate noted, "On Thursday, 19th August, the enemy occupied the Weldon Railroad in heavy force."[16] Major General Henry Heth sent the two brigades he had in reserve, those of Davis and Walker, to confront the Yanks at the tracks.[17] A Southerner reported "the two brigades ... sent to drive them away ... failed."[18] General Heth then called for his Tar Heels. A Carolinian noted, "On the night of the 20th we were withdrawn from the trenches and moved to the south ... to attack the enemy."[19]

The Bethel Regiment followed a board-covered trench to a gully about a quarter-mile to the rear of their fortifications and then stumbled along a trail leading towards the Weldon Railroad tracks. Sergeant Jacob Bartlett (Co. K) recalled, "We were relieved ... and started on the march, to we knew not where, it being ... very dark." Bartlett also noted, "None of us had slept much in the [past] 14 nights and I went to sleep several times while on the march that night."[20] Furthermore, to add to the exhausted soldiers' misery as they lurched about in the dark, a heavy downpour turned their track into mush, leaving the men mud-splattered and drenched.

The Tar Heels halted near the Vaughn house before sunrise on August 21, 1864, and the weary riflemen sprawled about, napping while Col. Martin met with the other regimental officers and Gen. Heth. Martin's division commander explained the critical need to retake this rail line; the bluecoats had captured a section of the Weldon Railroad, a vital logistics connection supplying the Confederate army with food. If the Northerners were successful in holding and destroying this supply line it would be difficult to keep Gen. Lee's Army of Northern Virginia fed. Henry Heth then stated the obvious: they would have to make a frontal assault on the Yankees' entrenchments. Colonel Martin gazed in the direction of the Federal lines but could see nothing; a thick fog smothered all sound and all vision. General Henry Heth had assembled four brigades: William MacRae's, William Cooke's, Nathaniel Harris's brigade of Mississippians from Mahone's division, and William Kirkland's brigade from Hoke's division. Colonel Martin was pleased to speak with Brig. Gen. William Kirkland, who had recovered from his wounds and been assigned to a brigade composed of three regiments of North Carolinians. They parted, wishing each other good health.

Confederate artillery opened fire upon the Union fortifications at 7:30 a.m. as MacRae's Tar Heels deployed into a battle formation in a cornfield not far from the guns. The veteran infantrymen grimly awaited the command to move towards enemy muskets and cannon. Captain Edward Outlaw (Co. C) wrote, "We lay between our batteries (30 pieces) and theirs during the artillery duel and came in for some pretty severe shelling."[21] The artillery contest lasted for over an hour. However, by 9:00 a.m. both sides' gunners had exhausted their ammunition and the clash subsided. The fog had burnt off and it was now possible for the Confederates to see the ground they had to cover; they were 700 yards from the Union fortifications.

General MacRae sent his newly minted sharpshooter corps forward. These handpicked men advanced and came within range of the Yank pickets, and the two sides sparred. A Tar Heel recorded that the "sharpshooters ... after a pretty sharp skirmish ... drove the enemy's picket lines in."[22] Lieutenant Duncan Waddell (Co. G) led his platoon of sharpshooters against the bluecoats. He wrote, "[We] charged through the cornfield and drove the Yankee sharpshooters back into the woods and occupied their line of battle."[23] Then, it was time for William MacRae to send his infantrymen forward.

The Tar Heels pushed through the cornfield and woods, passing over two Union entrenchments the sharpshooters had cleared of skirmishers. Then the Carolina regiments emerged from the trees and the riflemen saw they were about 400 yards from the Northerners' fortifications. The Confederates surged forward, hollering. Federal artillery pummeled the Southern ranks. One Tar Heel noted, "Our brigade ... was exposed to a very terrific shelling ... while advancing."[24] William Martin's Bethel men began to fall. Private John Smith's (Co. I) leg was nearly ripped from his body, Pvt. Henry Kiser (Co. I) was killed, and 1st Sgt. Robert Bell (Co. I) was struck in the chest.[25] Pvt. Zebedee Morris (Co. K) "had his arm blown off by a cannon ball."[26] A rifleman remarked, "[We] would be killed every minute, for the ball[s] gist [*sic*] plowed the ground all a round."[27]

The Southern line staggered and slowed, but the resolute riflemen pressed forward, coming into musket range. The Union infantry opened fire. Minié bullets swept across the battlefield, and a Confederate noted, "The defenders raked the open ground so effectively that corn-stalks were cut off by the bullets."[28] Second Lieutenant William Rea (Co. F) was hit in the face, Pvt. John Long (Co. F) struck in the elbow, and Pvt. Thomas Benfield (Co. D) mortally wounded.[29] A Southerner recalled, "Each second brings a belching forth of death, and you hear the dull thud so often spoken of, as a bullet strikes the yielding body of a comrade—a sound like the striking of a base ball on a catcher's glove."[30] The Carolinians hesitated and began to fall back. One of the these Tar Heels wrote, "The enemy was ... found too strongly entrenched."[31]

William MacRae's riflemen retreated to the shelter of the trees and took cover in one of the abandoned Union breastworks. Federal artillery continued to pound the Tar Heels. Colonel William Martin realized a portion of his regiment remained vulnerable to the Union cannon and wanted those men moved immediately. He was not able to find the left wing commander, Cpt. William Grier (Co. H), so he grabbed Cpt. James Young (Co. K). Sergeant Jacob Bartlett (Co. K) wrote, "Captain Young was ordered to take command of the left wing of the regiment and move to the left in order not to be so much exposed to the artillery fire."[32] Once Cpt. Young shifted the unprotected Bethel men the Union gunners ceased firing. The assault ended and a Southerner recorded the "attempt ... to dislodge [the Federals] from this position—the effort failed."[33]

The Tar Heels remained hidden in the trees, waiting for darkness. Colonel William Martin wrote, "We lay low till night enabled us to withdraw under cover of darkness."[34] The attack, though short-lived, cost William MacRae's brigade almost fifty men, with seventeen of these casualties coming from Martin's 11th North Carolina.[35] That evening Maj. Gen. General Henry Heth recorded, "Another attack was made on the enemy but failed to accomplish anything."[36]

That night, as the 11th North Carolina fell back from their position in the captured Union rifle pits, they did so with such stealth at least one of their soldiers was left behind. Lieutenant Duncan Waddell (Co. G) recalled "Private Woodston Garrett (Co. G) was so tired out by the night's marching and then the day's fighting he fell asleep and did not awaken when the Bethel Regiment withdrew." Waddell continued: "He was still in the Union breastworks the next morning when Yank skirmishers retook the trench. The quick-thinking Garrett slipped into a Union uniform he stole from an abandoned knapsack and pretended to be a Yankee long enough to slip away and evade capture." Private Garrett took one of the skirmishers prisoner and forced him towards the Confederate positions. The two cautiously approached the Tar Heel pickets posted in a cornfield, and then "Garrett raised his hat in token of surrender when he reached MacRae's command and was allowed to come in."[37]

On the morning of August 24, 1864, a courier from Gen. MacRae reached Col. William Martin and informed him to prepare the regiment; the brigade would move out that afternoon. General Heth had informed William MacRae Federal forces were moving south and west of the established entrenchment lines and tearing up the Weldon Railroad tracks near Reams Station, ten miles south of their position. General Lee wanted a strike force to be assembled to deal with this Yankee incursion and MacRae's Brigade was included.[38] William Martin gathered his officers and warned them to prepare their companies.

The Bethel Regiment formed up with the brigade and marched from their Globe Tavern location at 4:00 p.m., heading west and south on Squirrel Road. Their column tramped southwards on Vaughn Road and near sunset reached a field near Armstrong Mill. Here, the Carolinians bivouacked beside a large cornfield, which the hungry men pillaged with enthusiasm. Private Ephraim Justice (Co. K) wrote, "We ate great quantities of some poor farmer's corn. Such is war, crushing and blighting all in its path."[39]

That evening Col. Martin and Lt. Col. Frank Bird walked among their veterans as the men gorged on roasted corn. The Tar Heels greeted their senior officers with respect and fondness. Martin and Bird pondered their regiment's condition. Its combat strength was barely 350 riflemen led by fewer than twenty remaining officers.[40] Tomorrow, mused Martin and Bird, their boys would again face mortal danger.

The regiment arose several hours before dawn, ate and fell into line. The Eleventh marched farther southward, following a dirt path to Gravel Run, where at noon the men were allowed to rest. The Tar Heels munched on leftover ears of corn and listened to the rumblings of cannon and musketry arising east of them. Rumors swept the gray formation; Wilcox's Division was attacking the Yankees at a place called Reams' Station. The veteran riflemen watched their officers' faces and knew it would not be long before they themselves rushed towards the sounds of battle.

General MacRae ordered his brigade onto a road leading directly toward the gunfire. His men trekked for two and a half hours before reaching a thick stand of pine. The brigade halted and MacRae gave the order for his Tar Heels to deploy into line of battle. Colonel Martin shifted his regiment into its brigade battle position, the Bethel formation manning the brigade's far left flank. The 26th NC rested to the 11th's right, followed by the other three units, the 44th NC, the 52nd NC, and the 47th NC.[41] General MacRae ordered the brigade's sharpshooters to deploy, and the formation's handpicked sharpshooters crept forward. Then, the brigade inched closer to the sounds of fighting.

Colonel Martin watched as Gen. Heth and Gen. Wilcox met with their brigade commanders; Lt. Gen. Ambrose Hill was sick again, so he had turned decision-making over to Heth and Wilcox.[42] They pointed animatedly towards the gunfire and hashed out each man's responsibilities. William Martin waited impatiently, taking stock of his Tar Heels, who also scrutinized their generals. Martin's soldiers were veterans. They were not eager to go into another battle, and most felt like Pvt. Andrew Rinck (Co. I), who scribbled to his family, "I don't like to charge the Yankees."[43] Regardless of their reservations, the colonel could tell by the looks on his Carolinians' faces they would follow orders and perform their allotted duty.

Not far from Col. Martin, the brigade's adjutant, Cpt. Louis Young, evaluated the 11th North Carolina's battle readiness and recorded optimistically, "As I looked into the eyes of the men ... it was easy to see that the [enemy] works would be taken."[44] The Bethel Regiment's colonel agreed with Cpt. Young about his men's morale; however, William Martin was not enthusiastic about an attack against fortified earthworks, though he was confident the Bethel boys would not fail to meet their obligations. Lieutenant Colonel Frank Bird was also proud of the regiment, but he was realistic about their chances. Bird had just written his sister: "The enemy [had] possession of the Weldon Railroad and I think will probably hold it. We had two or three pretty severe fights to dislodge them which proved unsuccessful. I was in the one of Sunday [August 21] but am not hurt."[45] Another Tar Heel standing in the ranks, Sgt. David McDonald (Co. E) wrote, "Open ground and enemy works, it made the men quiet."[46]

A few minutes later Gen. William MacRae called for his regimental commanders. Colonel Martin and Lt. Colonel Bird hurried to hear their regiment's assignment. General William MacRae, his Scots' blood stirred by what he had learned, efficiently gave orders. Gen. Heth wanted his brigades to attack the Union positions at the same time, "a hard blow, like with a clenched fist."[47] Cooke and Conner would move first, as their brigades had to work their way through a thick, wooded area. Once they cleared the woods, MacRae's boys were to advance, supported by McGowan's South Carolinians on their right.[48] MacRae, his face reddened by fury, informed his officers to instruct their men "while advancing ... every man must yell as though he were a division in himself, dash for the enemy's works, and not fire until there."[49]

Colonel Martin called his company officers together as Confederate artillery was pushed forward, seventeen guns commanded by Col. William Pegram. The weapons were unlimbered on the crest of a low hill 400 yards behind the Yanks' positions and moments later these guns opened up. Almost at the same time, the popping of the brigade's sharpshooters could be heard. Word came back to William Martin. Once his regiment cleared the trees there would be a cornfield, and then 800 yards of open ground to cover before reaching the enemy works.[50]

Pegram's artillerymen worked quickly, firing their guns so rapidly that a shell crashed into the Union fortifications nearly every second.[51] A Federal soldier, dismayed by Pegram's cannonade, wrote, "The artillery fire of the enemy was so rapid and the range so accurate ... [that] in some places men jumped on the outside of the earthworks for safety, preferring bullets to shells."[52] MacRae's eighty sharpshooters covered the Federal works with accurate musketry, forcing the bluecoats to keep their heads down and causing the Union artillery to shift some of their guns away from their counter-battery fire duties. The gunners of these redirected cannons shifted their ammunition to canister in an attempt to drive off the sharpshooters, but this proved to be nothing more than chasing after flies with a shotgun. The ultimate result was that the Yankee gunners consumed much of their canister supplies. Unfortunately, though, some of these artillery rounds did strike Tar Heel veterans; 1st Lt. Duncan Waddell (Co. G) was severely wounded, a piece of shot piercing his right lung.[53]

By 5:30 p.m., as Pegram's artillerymen slowed their frenetic pace, Gen. William MacRae impatiently waited for Cooke and Conner's brigades to emerge from the pine woods, but those formations were not to be seen. Word reached the irritated brigade commander that Cooke and Conner were delayed by the thick underbrush and their advance was far behind schedule. MacRae, knowing those few precious moments of safety following the conclusion of the artillery's bombardment were being wasted by Cooke and Conner, shouted, "I shall wait no longer for orders.... Give the order to advance at once."[54]

The 11th North Carolina Regiment surged forward, pushing its way out of the trees and into the cornfield. The Confederates moved without yelling as Gen. MacRae had been informed by his scouts and sharpshooters that Federals maintained a strong picket line not far from the edge of the cornfield. If the North Carolina boys could sneak up on these skirmishers, they might be able to bag the entire lot.[55]

Moving as quietly as a mob of 370 men can through a field of dried cornstalks, the Tar Heels emerged onto the open ground. The two right-flank regiments from William Cooke's brigade, the 46th NC and the 15th NC, had extracted themselves from the pine woods and had become detached from the rest of their brigade. Their commanders saw Col. Martin's troops sweep forward on their right, so they abandoned their entangled brigade-mates and joined up with the Bethel Regiment. There, barely fifty yards away, was the Union picket line. The surprised bluecoats arose in panic, shocked by the Tar Heels' sudden appearance. A soldier from the 11th New York wrote, "It was as if the woods were alive with Confederates, they seemed to spring up right out of the ground."[56] The Southerners raced forward, one later remarking, "[We] forgot [our] instructions and began yelling in ... eagerness to press home the assault."[57] Colonel William Martin noted, "No one fired. They absolutely dashed."[58] Another officer wrote, "The men threw themselves forward at the double-quick ... without firing a gun."[59]

The Union skirmishers scampered back towards the Federal earthworks, just yards ahead of MacRae's men. The main Yank battle line, manned by a hodgepodge of battered Union regiments (the 126th, 125th, 111th, 57th, 52nd, 39th, and 7th NY), waited in confusion. These formations had all been combined into a "Consolidated Brigade," now led by Major John Byron of the 88th New York. Some of the regiments were little more than disjointed collections of disheartened veterans and dispirited draftees. These New Yorkers watched in dismay as their brothers fled towards them, ruling out any possibility of shooting at the attacking Confederates. One troubled Yankee wrote, "With the [Rebels] right on [the skirmishers] heels, the main line had to withhold its fire until the skirmishers were clear."[60]

A few venturesome riflemen ignored the fleeing skirmishers and shot into the advancing Tar Heels, while others just fired their rifles without aiming. However, most just stood in confusion and watched. A Carolinian noted that "Hancock's men ... fired wildly above the mark."[61] Thus, their initial volleys proved to be limited and ineffective. Union artillerymen, though, working nine guns posted farther back opened up on the Confederates, and Northern steel struck Carolina flesh.[62] Lieutenant James Montgomery's (Co. A) leg was shattered, Pvt. John Warlick (Co. I) was hit in the left arm, and Pvt. John Morefield (Co. D) suffered a serious chest wound.[63] A Southerner recalled, "From almost the first step in the open field men began to fall, some wounded sadly, and some to rise no more, but there was no faltering."[64]

Colonel Martin and Lt. Col. Frank Bird shouted as they led their regiment forward. They hollered the Rebel yell and admonished their men to be brave and close upon the enemy. Their regiment's company commanders and file closers also urged their men forward, leading from the front. These veterans would not require their men to take on any risks they themselves would not accept. They all raced across the open field, closing the distance between them and the Yanks. More artillery struck the 11th North Carolina. Pvt. David Hubbard (Co. I) went down, his left leg shattered, and Pvt. John Alexander (Co. A) was killed.[65] Private Andrew Rinck (Co. I) was knocked down by the concussion from a shell.

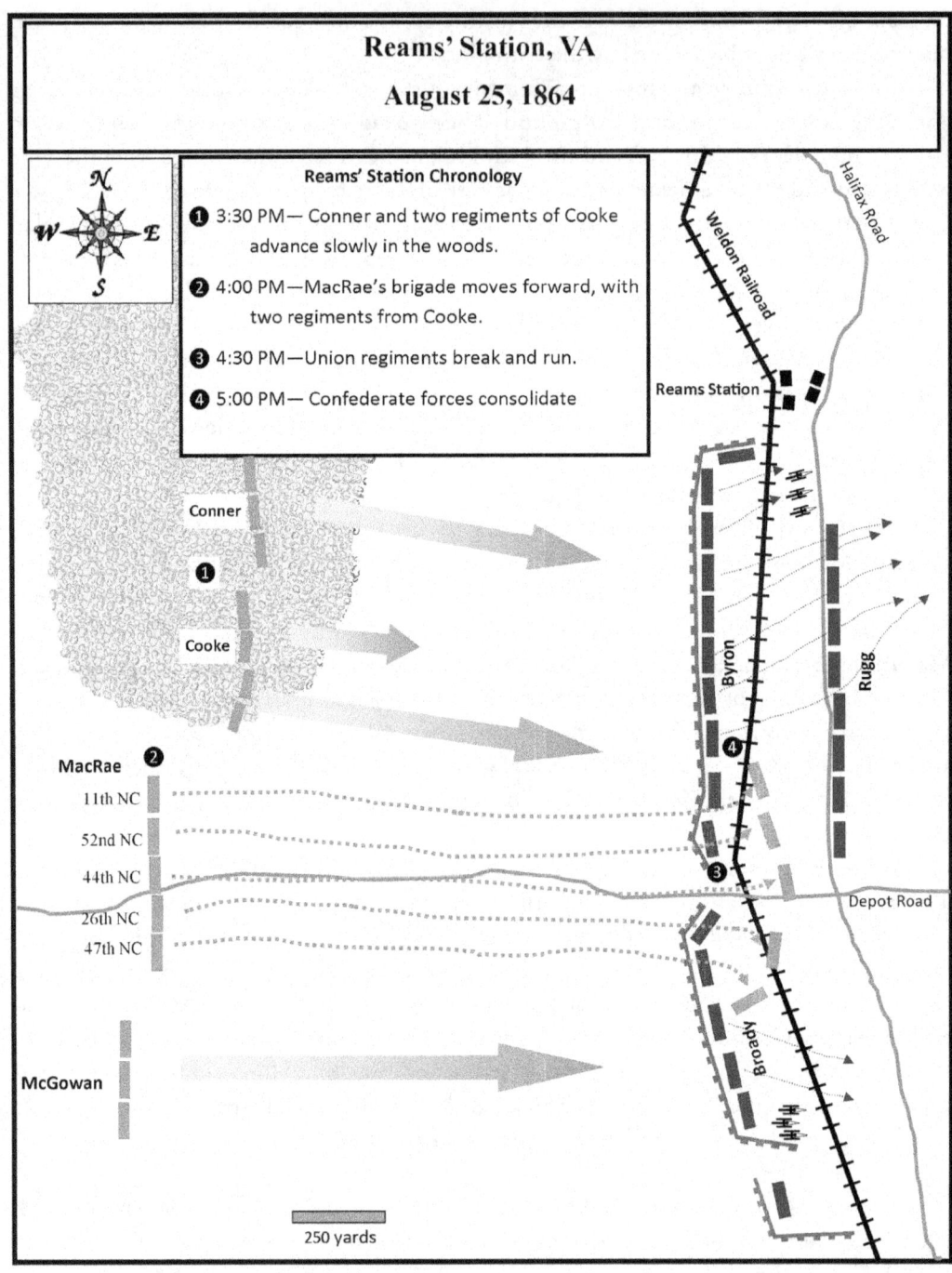

He recorded, "I was only bruised a little on my side." He also said, "A cannon ball ... cut off my cartridge box, [and] tore my knapsack all to pieces off my back."[66]

By now, the Tar Heel battle line was within fifty yards of the earthworks, and with most of the Union skirmishers safely within its protecting walls, the Yankees massed a volley. A New York officer wrote, "The Union line erupted in a wall of flame, temporarily halting the Confederate advance."⁶⁷ More Tar Heels fell, especially those out in front. First Sgt. Joseph Carter (Co. C) was killed, and Lt. Col. Frank Bird was "struck in the forehead by a bullet when he was about forty yards from the Federal breastworks."⁶⁸ Other North Carolinians were also hit, including Pvt. Robert Glenn (Co. I), who was wounded.⁶⁹

The North Carolinians paused momentarily as they worked through "the abatis protecting the enemy's lines ... interlaced with wire in places.⁷⁰ Then, they unleashed a volley into the Federal position and while reloading pushed forward. A Federal wrote, "Not to be denied, the rebels slowly struggled forward, cheering as they advanced."⁷¹ The discouraged New Yorkers fired back, though few with accuracy. Even so, at the distance of twenty yards their bullets found more Tar Heels, killing Pvt. James Hill (Co. E) and wounding Pvt. Miles Askew (Co. F). Private Joseph Humphreys (Co. H) also fell, and Cpt. James Young (Co. K) was struck in the side of his head.⁷² A Confederate noted, "It was fearful work."⁷³

Colonel William Martin led his Carolinians right to the edge of the earthworks and some of his men climbed atop the defenses and fired down into the bluecoats. A Tar Heel recalled, "The Federal infantry ... seemed to be dazed by the vehemence of [our] attack."⁷⁴ Suddenly, the Federal resolve crumbled and a dismayed New Yorker wrote, "The regiments ... panicked and broke to the rear."⁷⁵ Entire companies of bluecoats peeled away, fleeing to the east. Another Federal noted, "I ... saw a rebel color bearer [in the 11th NC] spring over our works and down into the cut almost at my feet."⁷⁶ And with that, the frightened Yank soldiers tossed their muskets to the ground and surrendered. One captured Northern officer remarked to a Tar Heel officer, "Lieutenant, your men fight well; that was a magnificent charge."⁷⁷

MacRae's other Carolina regiments surged over the Union breastworks and the Federal's resistance completely collapsed. One bluecoat later wrote, "With the 'Ki-yi' of the Johnnies steadily coming nearer ... a quick glance showed that nothing was left."⁷⁸ In some places, small groups of Yanks grappled with the flood of Southerners swarming around them; however, the Northerners who could run fled from their position, leaving everything behind. One Carolinian wrote, "The enemy were driven off in a hand-to-hand encounter in the works, in which in a few instances, clubbed rifles were used."⁷⁹ Federal flags were snatched out of shocked color guards' hands and swords ripped from officers' clutches. First Sergeant John Michaux (Co. B), Pvt. Robert Johnson (Co. D), and Pvt. Alvis Pendigrant (Co. G) each captured Federal flags.⁸⁰ Bluecoats surrendered by the hundreds. A Southerner wrote they "threw down their guns and commenced waving their hats."⁸¹ Excited Confederates gathered up these New Yorkers and hustled them out of the defenses. One Southern officer who saw the groups of captured bluecoats scurrying towards him remarked, "No guard was required to accompany the prisoners to the rear ... for they rushed along in crowds.... [I] thought the hurrying crowd of prisoners was a successful charge of the enemy."⁸²

While most of the Tar Heels were rounding up Union prisoners and pillaging their packs, the most aggressive soldiers climbed out of the entrenchments and chased after the fleeing Federals. First Lieutenant William Todd (Co. C) led a group of North Carolinians pressing eastward. Once out of the entrenchments, Todd's cluster of soldiers crossed the destroyed Weldon Railroad tracks and found themselves facing a second line of entrenchments, fifty yards away, manned by Union soldiers from Lt. Col. Horace Rugg's Brigade, a combined force composed of ten Northern regiments. This new line of riflemen fired into the Confederates. As 1st Lt. Todd turned to check on his comrades, he was struck in the right buttock. When Lt. Todd fell, the rest of the Tar Heels lost any notion of continuing the attack.[83] An officer in Rugg's brigade noted "the enemy [was] driven off."[84] The Carolinians scooped up their wounded officer and fell back to the captured trench.

Meanwhile, inside the captured Federal earthworks, Col. Martin's officers and sergeants struggled to get their men reorganized into a battle formation but the Carolinians were hard to control as they plundered Yankee haversacks. The Tar Heels, giddy with relief, rifled through their enemy's abandoned provisions. Their captured harvest was immense: nine artillery pieces, munitions, weapons, accouterments, and, most important, rations.[85] One excited Southerner wrote, "We also captured ... pistols, swords, saddles, guns, and an infinity of smaller plunder such as knapsacks, clothing ... blankets [and] pocket knives."[86] Not only had several thousand Union soldiers surrendered, an officer of the 36th Wisconsin noted, "[the Confederates] also took the whole party [of doctors] prisoners, [and] kept the Surgeons five days."[87]

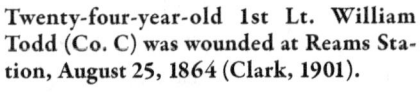

Twenty-four-year-old 1st Lt. William Todd (Co. C) was wounded at Reams Station, August 25, 1864 (Clark, 1901).

Darkness soon overtook the battlefield, leaving the Confederates in control of the first line of earthworks. But they had not only been able to take anything else; the Federals held the second line of works. The destroyed tracks of the Weldon Railroad lay twisted and snarled between the two lines. The jubilant Tar Heels gorged themselves on Yankee rations and congratulated each other on their victorious assault. Final tabulations of the Confederate victory were drawn. Heth's and Wilcox's brigades "captured nine pieces of artillery, twelve colors, 2,150 prisoners, and 3,100 stands of small arms."[88] General Lee, impressed by what had occurred, wrote about MacRae's and Cooke's men: "Their gallantry and conduct were never more deserving of admiration than in the engagement at Reams' Station."[89] General Heth proudly recorded, "This charge and its results, has proven to me that nothing is impossible to men determined to win."[90] Colonel William Martin, his heart closer to his men than was that of Heth or Lee, noted, "We carried their works handsomely ... [but] our loss was considerable, including Lieutenant-Colonel Bird."[91] Lieutenant Lemuel Hoyle (Co. I) added, "[Francis Bird] was a very gallant officer and much beloved by the men."[92]

That night, beneath the dim illumination of medical lanterns, surgeon James McCombs and his staff went to work on the Bethel Regiment's wounded. One of the surgeons wrote, "[You] should have seen our poor fellows Thursday night coming in wounded and bleeding and shivering with cold."[93] Doctor McCombs did what he could for Frank

Bird, but the officer's wounds to his forehead proved lethal and he died a few hours later. McComb had more work to do. Lt. James Montgomery's (Co. A) leg was so badly mutilated it had to be amputated, and Pvt. David Hubbard's (Co. I) left leg was removed.[94] Lieutenant Duncan Waddell's (Co. G) wound was stabilized but was so serious he would never rejoin the regiment. He finished the war as a recruiting officer in Charlotte.[95] The remaining injured Tar Heels were patched up and eventually all were able to return to the 11th North Carolina.

Later that night, the Federal forces withdrew, leaving the battlefield to the Confederates. The fight had been a dramatic Southern victory. The next morning the men in Col. Martin's regiment viewed the empty earthworks and briefly relaxed; the danger before them had evaporated. The soldiers recuperated, and as Pvt. John Warlick (Co. C) recovered from his injury, he wrote that Reams' Station was "the prettiest fight we were ever in."[96]

The triumphant Southerners' joys quickly dissipated when a cold rainstorm rumbled over the area, soaking the soldiers and reminding them nature always had the last word. The next day, Pvt. Andrew Rinck (Co. I) wrote, "We lay in their breastworks from morning until after dark in water about kneedeep."[97] That evening, word came to move and the Tar Heels "retreated back ... about one mile."[98] A Carolinian noted the troops "were placed in line, the right of our brigade resting on the Petersburg and Weldon Railroad." Another recorded, "We were called to attention, [and] stacked arms for the night. We cut bushes and forks and made a sort of arbor over us, [and] put leaves down and then spread our blankets."[99]

Brigadier General William MacRae took his Tar Heels back to their place in the Confederate fortifications and the Carolinians resumed their struggle to survive trench warfare. MacRae's brigade rotated in and out of the line with one of Heth's brigades. When Col. Martin's soldiers were relieved and resting, the men had time to write their families. Fall weather cooled the countryside and stilled some of the combatants' wrath, giving the homesick men quiet moments to think about home. One rifleman wrote home, his sentiments echoed by nearly all his comrades: "I feel very thankful for God's mercy and hope he will spare me." He continued, "We need rest and above all we want peace so we can go home to our loved ones."[100] Private Andrew Rinck (Co. I) penned his family, "I would like to know whether my little boy grows much or not."[101]

The news that Atlanta fell to Gen. Sherman's army reached the Bethel Regiment in early September. The season's horrific fighting, with all its painful casualties, the dreadfulness of trench life and the men's protracted time away from home combined to erode their morale. One despondent soldier wrote, "You don't know [how] I feel when so many of my fellow men have been slain and my life yet spared."[102] Another recorded, "[Our] morale waned ... [and] there [now] was no great battle any day, but a small battle to stay alive every day."[103] Lieutenant Lewis Warlick (Co. B) remarked, "You have no idea how bad I want to go home." He concluded his letter: "This cruel war it keeps me crazy all the time."[104]

This discontent that spread among the Carolinians swelled when Col. William Martin was forced to conduct a court-martial of one of his officers. Lieutenant Jones Watson (Co. G), a 41-year-old merchant from Chapel Hill, had been suffering from respiratory trouble for many months. Watson was not ill enough to merit a medical furlough, so he shuffled along, remaining with company throughout the summer. His condition worsened, and by the time the regiment reached Reams Station, Lt. Watson could not keep up. Finally, the ailing officer gave in and shambled away from his comrades, heading for the surgeons' tents. Unfortunately he chose to abandon his responsibilities as the 11th North Carolina advanced towards the Federal fortifications. When Lt. Watson reached the regimental medical station, surgeon James McCombs refused to believe he was ill and accused him of running from the fight. Doctor McCombs wrote up charges against Watson. The court met on September 5, 1864, and convicted him of "cowardice in the face of the enemy." Jones Watson was cashiered from the regiment.[105]

On September 16, 1864, the brigade was shifted farther west. One Tar Heel recorded, "We were moved to a point about a half mile south of the Boydton plank road, about three miles southwest of the city." The officer noted they "were employed in constructing rifle pits until the 20th ... [and] moved about one mile further south ... [and] engaged in constructing works of a more elaborate character."[106] This ceaseless entrenchment labor, followed by vacating those just-completed excavations only to reach another site and commence digging again, weighed heavily on the men's spirits. One rifleman objected, writing, "I can't stand camp life." He scribbled more, grumbling, "I do not know whether I will [ever] get a furlough."[107]

Chapter 15

Fall 1864, Jones Farm and Burgess Mill

On September 29, 1864, Brig. Gen. William MacRae reviewed his five regiments. MacRae's brigade totaled 1,231 men. His senior regimental commander was Col. William Martin; the past weeks' battles had stripped all his other regiments of their highest-ranking commanders. The 26th NC was led by Maj. James Adams; the 44th NC by Maj. Charles Stedman; the 47th NC by Maj. William Lankford; and the 52nd NC by Lt. William Carmichael.[1]

11th North Carolina Muster[2]
September 29, 1864

Unit	Commander	Total
F & S	Col. William Martin	
	Cpt. William Grier	3
Co. A	2nd Lt. William Taylor	50
Co. B	Cpt. Thomas Parks	43
Co. C	Cpt. Edward Outlaw	28
Co. D	1st Lt. Lewis Elias	39
Co. E	1st Lt. William Turner	25
Co. F	2nd Lt. Lewis Warlick (Co. B)	23
Co. G	Cpt. John Freeland	62
Co. H	1st Lt. Robert Lowrie	28
Co. I	2nd Lt. Lemuel Hoyle	33
Co. K	2nd Lt. James Whitaker (Co. G)	19
Total		353

The Bethel Regiment numbered just over 350, though fifteen of that number reported to Cpt. Thomas Lilly (26th NC) and the brigade sharpshooters. With Lt. Duncan Waddell wounded, the Bethel Regiment no longer had an officer available to lead one of the sharpshooter platoons; however, Brig. Gen. William MacRae promised Col. Martin he would be able to select a replacement officer to fill that slot. William Martin was impressed with 1st Lt. William Todd's performance and informed the young officer that once he recovered from his wound, he would assume that elite position.

Lieutenant Colonel Frank Bird's death left William Martin with no field-grade officers. The Bethel Regiment's two senior captains were prisoners of war, meaning Martin's highest ranking captains remaining with the unit could not be promoted. Captain William Grier

(Co. H) continued to serve as a wing commander, though now as the senior officer. The next-highest-ranking captain, John Freeland (Co. G), commanded the largest company in the regiment, with a third lieutenant as his second. Colonel Martin could not draw Freeland away from his 62-man company and leave the unit to be led by a junior lieutenant. William Martin was left with turning the left wing over to Lt. Edward Martin and the regimental ensign, Lt. James Rayner.[3]

Later that day, September 29, 1864, the brigade left its campsite and marched along the Boydton plank road, leaving behind half-finished fortifications. The veteran riflemen moved, knowing they were heading towards a location where the Yankees were trying to extend their lines farther to the west, beyond Globe Tavern. Confederate cavalry was supposed to have held the Federals at bay but the Union infantry rolled right over them. Now, it would be the Tar Heel riflemen who had to stop the Northerners' encroachment. One battle-weary Confederate remarked as he walked towards this next fight, "Oh, how I dread this."[4] That night the Tar Heels bivouacked near an area known as Jones Farm.

Morning came and the Confederates did not move. Everyone waited in suspense while reports filtered down to the riflemen: Union troops had attacked Southern positions farther south of Jones Farm. The Southerners rested until afternoon, when word arrived that Federals were approaching a stretch of partially built earthworks not far from the Duncan road. The bluecoats had captured Ft. Archer earlier in the day and moved northward along the Church Road, and now were attempting to breach the Confederate's final line of defenses. If the Yanks were able to take this stretch of works they would have broken the Confederate lines, a situation Gen. Robert E. Lee found intolerable. General Ambrose Hill had Wilcox's two brigades, South Carolinians under Brig. Gen. Samuel McGowan and Tar Heels commanded by Col. James Lane, and Henry Heth's men, James Archer's Tennesseans and William MacRae's Carolinians. They hustled towards the anticipated Union position. McGowan and Lane arrived on the scene first, with Archer and MacRae a few minutes later.

At 5:00 p.m., McGowan slammed into the right wing of the Union brigade led by Brig. Gen. Simon Griffin. Moments later, Lane smashed into Griffin's left-wing regiments. This was one of the few times when Confederates greatly unnumbered the Federals and the Southerners advanced with delight.[5] Griffin's regiments crumbled. Wilcox's troops pushed aggressively, shoving Griffin's men backwards with such ease the Union line gave away nearly a half-mile of ground within minutes. Meanwhile, Archer struggled to catch up with McGowan, and MacRae's Tar Heels hustled to support Lane.

General Lane's Carolinians shoved Griffin's left-wing regiments backwards another quarter-mile, ripping open a gap in the Northerners' front. Griffin's left flank was supposed to have been protected by Col. John Curtin's large, nine-regiment-strong brigade, but Curtin's 2,500 men were 500 yards behind and to the left of Griffin.[6] Colonel Curtin's men could only watch as Griffin's bluecoats panicked and fled, chased closely by two lines of shrieking Rebels. In the Confederate second line, William MacRae's brigade fragmented as his regiments raced to keep up with Lane's advance. MacRae's left wing, the 26th NC, 44th NC, and 47th NC, surged ahead of the 52nd NC and the 11th NC, who were slowed while passing through a stand of dense underbrush.[7]

Colonel Curtin's huge brigade was arrayed in two lines of battle, with the front formation consisting of four regiments. The brigade's right-flank regiment, the 36th MA, with its 500 soldiers, was posted in front of a fence in an open field; its men ordered to lie down. A grove of trees and thick underbrush prevented them from seeing the Tar Heels chasing Griffin's shattered regiments but they could hear the crackle of the musketry off to their right. A Bay State officer recorded, "Suddenly an aide came riding from the right ... and directed the major to throw forward the right of the regiment by a half wheel."[8] The Massachusetts troops then took to the ground again, wondering why they were not responding more to the ensuing conflict. One wrote, "It seemed a queer position to be in."[9]

As the 52nd NC attempted to catch up with Lane's brigade its right flank emerged from this stand of vegetation and encountered the Massachusetts fellows, who were positioned perfectly to pour a flanking fire into the Tar Heels. The Carolinian regiment's right-wing companies crumpled under the fire, throwing the entire regiment into disorder. Lieutenant William Carmichael, commanding the 52nd NC, attempted to rally his tangled companies but by now the Confederate riflemen could see Curtin's mass of Union troops stretching off to their right, and they realized they were greatly outnumbered. The regiment was on the verge of collapse.

Colonel William Martin sized up the situation and immediately gave the orders for his Tar Heels to "change front to the right."[10] The Bethel Regiment's companies maneuvered quickly, transforming from a front heading towards the south to a battle line facing the west. A Carolinian recorded, "At this critical moment of the battle [Martin], without asking or waiting for orders, changed the front of his great regiment to a right face and charged."[11] This was remarkably similar to the movement the regiment's right wing had performed at Gettysburg. William Martin's 350 veterans rushed forward, gathering up the men of the 52nd NC, and slammed into the 36th MA.

The 36th MA opened fire upon Martin's riflemen; a bullet struck Sgt. Samuel McElroy (Co. A) in the right side of his face, while a minié ball killed 1st Sgt. David McDonald (Co. E).[12] But by then the 11th North Carolina was extremely close to the New England troops, and Martin's riflemen unleashed a crisp volley. The Yanks panicked. One Massachusetts soldier noted "the regiment was subjected to a galling fire from ... our right."[13] Colonel Curtin countered this unexpected assault by shifting some of his other regiments, and a couple units were able to wheel to the right. Within a few minutes Curtin had three regiments able to square off with Martin's two.[14]

The two battle lines slugged it out. Private Henry Hill (Co A) received a wound in the left side of his head; Pvt. Alva Smith (Co. B) suffered a shattered right knee; and Pvt. Abraham Huffman (Co. D) was fatally struck.[15] However, as these and other Tar Heels fell, Col. Martin's left wing overlapped the Federal line and slipped behind them. A horrified Yank recorded, "A column of Confederates charged upon our right-rear."[16] Curtin's three regiments backpeddled, trying to escape being surrounded, and jammed up against other Union formations, unnerving many of these units' new recruits. One Federal officer noted, "Our recruits were full of fright, and some of them began firing recklessly ... this backfire [striking men in] the formation."[17] The entire Union position unraveled, with mobs of bluecoats drifting to the west, trying to escape the 11th and 52nd North Carolina musketry.

Fortunately, at this moment, two regiments of dismounted Confederate cavalry

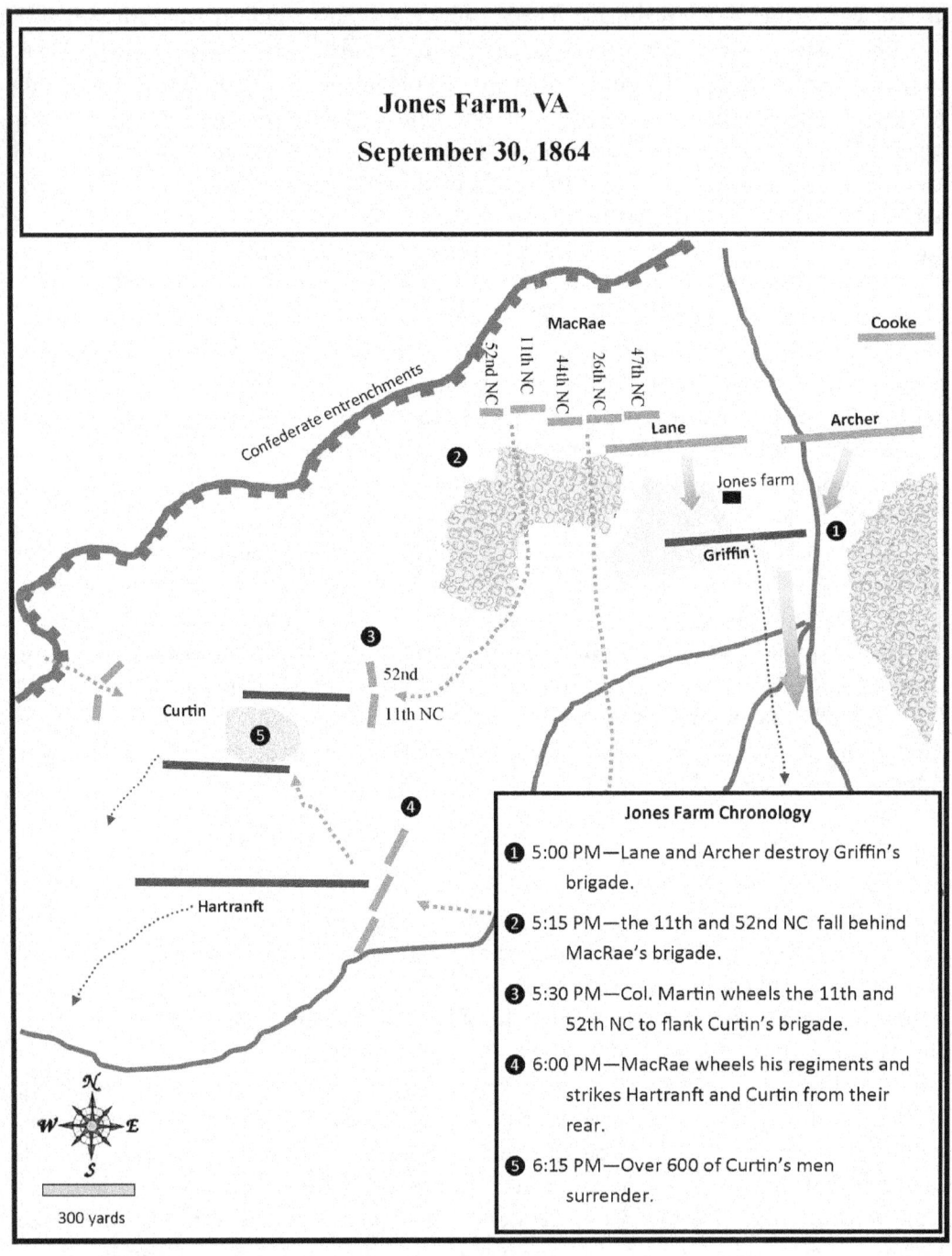

appeared from the west and opened fire upon Col. Curtin's rabble.[18] A Northerner wrote, "A line of the enemy's skirmishers now appeared ... on our left flank, and coolly picked off our men without opposition."[19] Another remarked, "It would have been impossible to devise a worse plight."[20] The mass of Union soldiers clumped together as the men sought shelter. But not all the Federals had given up; there were still some resolute companies fighting back. Second Lieutenant James Saville (Co. H) was hit in the left shoulder, Pvt. Thomas Holmes' (Co. A) left hip shattered, Pvt. William Blain (Co. D) mortally struck in the chest, and Pvt. William Flintoff's (Co. G) right side ripped open.[21]

By now, Brig. Gen. William MacRae was aware of what Martin's two regiments were doing. Since his brigade was not needed to help Lane, he turned his Tar Heels around and moved to join this fight. MacRae's three regiments crashed into the rear of Brig. Gen. John Hartranft's formation, which had been moving to assist Curtin, scattering these troops, and then the Carolinians surged forward, slamming into Curtin's mob, spewing his frightened men in all directions. One such fleeing Yank wrote, "Each man [did] his level best to preserve a life for future usefulness to his country."[22]

The Tar Heels closed in and rounded up the trapped Yankees. Captain Edward Outlaw (Co. C) recorded, "They [the Federals] were completely routed and [the 11th NC] captured 400 prisoners, more prisoners than we had men."[23] Ultimately, by the time darkness stopped martial activities, William MacRae's veterans had captured over 1,300 prisoners.[24] Major General Wade Hampton, whose dismounted horsemen had helped close the door on Curtin's men, wrote, "The whole affair was one of the handsomest I have ever seen."[25]

Later that evening the jubilant Bethel men returned to a position along the Confederate fortifications and scrounged for something to eat. The night crackled with scattered picket skirmishes, and occasional artillery duels. One such burst of Federal cannon fire detonated a handful of explosive rounds near the 11th North Carolina. A shocked Cpt. Edward Outlaw (Co. C) wrote, "Col. Martin was in the act ... of reforming the line, when he was struck by a shell which carried away a large slice of his left thigh."[26] Horrified Bethel men tenderly gathered up their commander and rushed him back to the 11th North Carolina's medical station. Surgeons John Wilson and James McCombs frantically stopped the bleeding but, as Cpt. Outlaw noted, "neither he nor the surgeons ... expected that [Martin] would recover."[27] A stunned Cpt. William Grier (Co. H) was now the regiment's leader. William Grier, the only original surviving captain from when the regiment was first formed, gathered up the men and marched them away from the day's battleground at 9:00 p.m.[28]

11th North Carolina Casualties[29]
September 30, 1864

Unit	Commander	Total
F & S	Col. William Martin	1
Co. A	2nd Lt. William Taylor	6
Co. B	Cpt. Thomas Parks	4
Co. C	Cpt. Edward Outlaw	1
Co. D	1st Lt. Lewis Elias	4
Co. E	1st Lt. William Turner	2
Co. F	2nd Lt. Lewis Warlick (Co. B)	0
Co. G	Cpt. John Freeland	1
Co. H	1st Lt. Robert Lowrie	4
Co. I	2nd Lt. Lemuel Hoyle	1
Co. K	2nd Lt. James Whitaker (Co. G)	1
Total		25

The Bethel Regiment had just participated in two brilliantly fought battles resulting in astonishing successes. The Tar Heels in the 11th North Carolina were content with their accomplishments; however this mood was shackled by the knowledge that more comrades were missing, as well as both of their talented and greatly respected field officers being gone; Lt. Col. Frank Bird had been killed at Reams Station on August 25, 1864, and now Col. William Martin labored for his life, badly wounded on September 30, 1864. These victories had come with a high price in Carolina blood.

Captain William Grier's sergeants had the regiment's tired riflemen up before sunrise and by 7:00 a.m. on October 1, 1864, the Bethel Regiment was formed in its brigade position to the west of the Squirrel Level Road, not far from the Davis house. Major General Henry Heth posted William MacRae's brigade in the front rank this day, with Archer's brigade positioned to their left. Davis's brigade was behind MacRae, and Cooke supported Archer. Henry Heth ordered MacRae to find out the strength of the Union position. MacRae send his sharpshooters forward and informed his regimental commanders to be ready to reinforce that skirmish unit.[30]

Captain Thomas Lilly (26th NC) deployed his handpicked veterans and they worked their way through a stand of trees and onto grass fields not far from the Chappell house. Here, they encountered a screen of Union skirmishers. The two forces dueled and Lilly's motivated and excellent marksmen drove the Yank skirmishers backwards. William MacRae moved his regiments forward, keeping pace with the sharpshooters' advance. By 9:00 a.m., Cpt. Lilly's force had forced the Union skirmishers to seek shelter within the Federal fortifications. General Heth inched forward and now, for the first time, was able to view the Northerner's defenses; one writer noted "it made him pause."[31]

Henry Heth did not want to attack the fortifications without knowing what type of Union strength hid within its protection; he had seen too many frontal assaults turn into meaningless slaughter. Heth sent a messenger to William MacRae, directing him to send forward a reconnaissance force. MacRae issued commands to his regimental commanders to cautiously probe the Union works. Captain William Grier carefully sent three companies forward; riflemen from D, F, and I, led by 1st Lt. Lewis Elias (Co. D).[32] Union volleys immediately swept across the open ground, killing Cpt. Sidney Cornwell (Co. I), and severely wounding Pvt. Roswald Bridges (Co. F) in the right thigh.[33]

Major James Adams (26th NC) and Maj. William Lankford (47th NC) both sent out small forces, but Maj. Charles Stedman (44th NC) and Lt. William Carmichael (52nd NC) misinterpreted their orders and advanced their entire regiments. Stedman's and Carmichael's Tar Heels, believing they were attacking mostly empty breastworks, and heady from their recent victories, surged forward, howling the Rebel yell. One writer recorded, "The overzealous troops ... thought they could rout any enemy they faced."[34] Brigadier General William MacRae raced his mount to catch up with his charging riflemen, shouting, "Go to half-step!" But "on they went at a double quick, charging the enemy with a yell."[35] The Federals waited for the two Carolina regiments to get quite close before opening fire. Stedman's and Carmichael's Tar Heels dropped by the dozens. Lieutenant Charles Stedman (44th NC) made the remark "his men were just mowed down."[36] The stunned Confederates immediately realized their folly and turned and retreated. Meanwhile, Lt. Elias's (Co. D) small battalion inched forward, and more Union minié bullets felled Bethel soldiers. Pvt. William Albright (Co. D) was struck in the head and Pvt. Daniel Upton (Co. D) hit in the left hand.[37] However, when Lt. Lewis Elias saw the 44th NC and 52nd NC fleeing, he ordered his skirmishers to withdraw. His riflemen hurried back to the 11th North Carolina's position, carrying their wounded with them.

William MacRae directed his brigade to fall back to the area around the Davis house, informing Gen. Heth the Union fortifications were well defended and any assaults against this position would result in unnecessary casualties and failure. Heth accepted MacRae's report and ordered his other brigades to hold steady. Heth wrote, "I concluded not to make a determined assault, which, if successful would have been with such heavy loss that no further attack could have been made."[38] Sadly, the morning's quick fight had resulted in ghastly casualties for the 44th NC. Their commander noted the regiment was "the worse cut up they have been the entire campaign."[39] MacRae posted a screen of skirmishers and his sullen riflemen waited out the day, morosely enduring a cold, winter rain drenching the landscape. The storm increased, dropping the temperatures, turning the ground to mush, and soaking the men. One miserable rifleman grumbled the night was "as disagreeable a time as I almost ever spent."[40]

Early the next morning, October 2, 1864, the wretched soldiers were formed in column and hustled at the double-quick several miles to the west, eventually ending up behind a stretch of earthworks along the Duncan Road, near the Hart house.[41] General Heth had received word another Union force was attempting to breach the Confederate lines and he ordered MacRae and Davis to repel this effort. Captain Grier's riflemen advanced, making sure their weapons were clean and ready to shoot. There were Yanks out in the open, racing towards them; and the Tar Heels opened fire. The bluecoats quickly realized the butternut-uniformed troops would reach the rifle pits before they did, so they scampered back, out of range. A Confederate officer recalled it was a "unique incident of two opposing forces running to reach the same point ... in this instance the very works we had recently built."[42]

The veteran Tar Heels stacked their muskets and began improving their breastworks. William MacRae realized how fortunate his Carolinians had been; if they had arrived fifteen minutes later the Yanks would have taken the works and been able to inflict serious damage to his brigade. MacRae encouraged his troops to fortify the earthworks; he was adamant about keeping them out of the Union forces' hands. Captain William Grier urged his men to work rapidly, and, as one historian noted, "the gray-coated soldiers worked like beavers to improve the fortifications."[43] William Grier could also see the Northern troops doing the exact thing, barely a half-mile away. Both sides were digging in. Captain Grier then posted Company A out in front of the regiment as pickets.[44]

At 3:00 p.m., a large brigade of Union troops commanded by Brig. Gen. Byron Pierce (II Corps) arose from a nearby gully. General Pierce recorded, "[My] line was formed in a ravine 200 yards from the enemy's works ... [and] it charged most gallantly to within a few rods of the works."[45] Lieutenant William Taylor's (Co. A) pickets fled towards their works, but before they could reach its safety, Sgt. Thomas Neily Co. A) was struck in the left thigh, Cpl. James Gribble (Co. A) was crippled by a musket ball shattering his left ankle, and Pvt. George Ewing (Co. A) suffered a wound to his left hip.[46] Once Lt. Taylor's men were inside the entrenchments the Bethel Regiment's riflemen poured fire onto the attackers, content to fight from within the safety of well-prepared fortifications. The Northerners fought back briefly, and in this exchange, Pvt. Emanuel Hennesse (Co. D) "was shot through the head ... [and] he lost part of his brain."[47] Lieutenant Lewis Warlick (Co. B) wrote, "Hennesse ... was alive the last I heard from him but he is sure to die."[48] Moments later the Union attack collapsed, and the Federals fell back, having lost over sixty men.[49]

The Northerners withdrew and began to dig in, creating a set of fortifications that included Pegram's farm and Peebles' farm. The Confederates did the same, improving their entrenchments along the Boydton plank road. Neither side's soldiers wanted to attack, and for the next week the battleground was quiet. The Tar Heels were especially strong in their resistance to going on the offensive; one of Gen. MacRae's staff officers noted, "For two months our Brigade has experienced constant and great hardships." He added, "They had done more than their share of the fighting."[50]

Brigadier General William MacRae called his regimental commanders together and admonished them to go to every effort to increase their unit's combat strength. Fortunately, successful political negotiations between Washington and Richmond had resulted in substantial numbers of prisoners of war being exchanged. The Bethel Regiment's veterans happily celebrated the return of over four dozen veterans who had been incarcerated at the prison compounds of Point Lookout, Maryland, Elmira, New York, and Fort Delaware, Delaware.[51] Captain William Grier's formation was also increased when the regiment's local recruiters were able to add another three dozen volunteers and conscripts.

Another way of augmenting the regiment's numbers was by the quick return of men who were recuperating from illnesses or battle wounds. Sometimes, though, the soldiers came back to their companies before they were completely recovered. Lieutenant Lemuel Hoyle (Co. I) remarked, "Some who have been wounded in battle and made permanently lame, come hobbling in on Sticks and c[anes]." Hoyle continued, wondering, "I do think it is perfectly outrageous, and the men who send them must have neither hearts nor consciences."[52] These unfit-for-duty Carolinians, who were trying to do anything they could to remain with their brothers in arms, placed unusual strains on their comrades. They wanted to be a part of the company but were not physically able, resulting in the healthy men having to perform the duties for both ill and well. One of these incapacitated veterans, Sgt. Samuel Black (Co. D), eagerly returned to his company, wanting to support his comrades; but his health had been badly damaged by his stay at the Point Lookout Prison and though his company-mates covered for him, Black's condition did not improve. Finally, Company D's commander, 1st Lt. Lewis Elias, was forced to send him to the hospital in Richmond. Sergeant Black would remain on medical leave until the end of the war.[53]

As the Bethel Regiment's numbers improved, the logistics supporting the Confederate soldiers declined. The loss of the Weldon Railroad, one of the main supply lines linking Richmond with North Carolina, had been severed by the Federals' late-summer offensives, meaning less materials and rations reached the Southern soldiers. The troops coped with this lack of resources by scrounging for clothing and equipment. Lieutenant Lewis Warlick (Co. B), who needed suspenders, wrote, "I could have gotten a pair on the battlefield ... but hated to take them off a dead man. I saw others at it but it looked like small business to rob the dead, so I declined taking anything from ... those who were dead." Lewis Warlick also noted "nearly all [the dead] were stripped of their pants."[54] Another Confederate did not have Warlick's reservations about taking from the dead. That soldier wrote, "I have a nice little Yankee axe, which is so light it can be carried in a knapsack.... All the Yankees have these little axes, and many of our men have supplied themselves with them, as they have with almost everything else the Yankees possess." This same Southerner also noted their growing rations adversity, writing, "[We] get nothing to eat now but bread and meat."[55]

On October 20, 1864, the Tar Heels were disappointed to hear their brothers in the Shenandoah Valley had been defeated at Cedar Creek. The unhappy soldiers digested the newspaper accounts and concluded the loss came because of poor leadership. Many called for Lt. Gen. Jubal Early's removal; one writing "a disappointed South tried and condemned 'Old Jube' and clamored for his head."[56] Another wrote, "We have a great many good fighters, but so few good generals."[57] They all concluded, regardless of whether or not Early would be removed, that "irreplaceable veterans were lost."[58]

Just as the Confederates were beginning to grow accustomed to the quietness of trench life on the far western portion of the Petersburg fortifications, Gen. Grant launched another offensive. On October 27, 1864, Union forces from the Second Corps flooded out of their works and shifted westward, aiming to capture the critical Boydton plank road and White Oak Road junction. These highways had become important travel lanes for Confederate wagon trains, and Federal control of this intersection would further hamper Southern logistics.[59] Grant's formations tramped westward, skirting the southern end of the Boydton plank road entrenchments, and quickly advancing towards the junction.

11th North Carolina Muster[60]
October 27, 1864

Unit	Commander	Total
F & S	Cpt. William Grier	
	Cpt. James Young	4
Co. A	2nd Lt. William Taylor	47
Co. B	Cpt. Thomas Parks	46
Co. C	Cpt. Edward Outlaw	27
Co. D	1st Lt. Lewis Elias	41
Co. E	1st Lt. William Turner	46
Co. F	Sgt. Nathanial Mardre	24
Co. G	Cpt. John Freeland	65
Co. H	1st Lt. Robert Lowrie	45
Co. I	2nd Lt. Lemuel Hoyle	43
Co. K	1st Lt. William Dickerson	33
Total		421

General Ambrose Hill learned of these movements and ordered Henry Heth to attack. Heth assembled his brigade commanders and issued commands. By 9:00 a.m., Heth had two infantry brigades rushing to the counterattack, William MacRae's Tar Heels and Virginians commanded by Brig. Gen. David Weisiger.[61] MacRae had about 1,100 soldiers, of which Cpt. Grier's 11th North Carolina had just over 400, with fifteen more going to the brigade sharpshooters, along with Lt. William Todd (Co. C), who was now assigned to that elite unit.[62]

The two brigades marched along a little-known, abandoned dirt road into a clump of dense vegetation, described by one rifleman "as an old blind wood road."[63] These Confederates, led by a local who knew his way through the woods, crossed the swampy waters of

Hatcher's Run near an old dam and crept forward, seeking the location of the Federal formations. Meanwhile, Union infantry scouts had detected this abandoned road and notified their commander, Brig. Gen. Byron Pierce, of its existence.

General Pierce shifted the 5th MI and 93rd NY to guard against a surprise attack originating from this road, and backed the infantry up with a battery of artillery.[64] The Michigan and New York regiments pushed into the thick brushwood and established a defensive line, though the riflemen and their officers could not see much because of the underbrush and had no field of fire. William MacRae's sharpshooters led the two-brigade advance and these veterans discovered the Yankees' presence and alerted MacRae. He reported this to Henry Heth, who remarked, "It was evident to me that our only chance of driving the enemy … was to attack him at once."[65]

Firing broke out between MacRae's sharpshooters and the Yank skirmish line at 4:00 p.m. While the sharpshooters occupied the Federal soldiers' attention, the two Confederate brigades quietly inched near. One Southern noted, "The thick woods protected us till we got in position and very soon we charged forward."[66] The Confederates struck Pierce's two regiments at 4:30 p.m., yelling loudly and smashing into the Union line before the bluecoats had time to react. They hit the Yanks at an angle, with MacRae's regiments banging into their right flank. The men of the 5th MI fought back fiercely, one recording "[they] exchanged 15 or 20 rounds with the enemy," wounding Pvt. Wilson Ruddick (Co. A) in the right leg, mortally injuring Pvt. George Keller (Co. B), and severely hurting Cpl. Luico Ferrell (Co. G).[67] Then, the Northerners were forced to give way.

Brigadier General Byron Pierce, who was with the rest of his brigade, heard the fighting in the woods but assumed it was nothing more than skirmishers feuding, so he did nothing. Moments later, fleeing bluecoats emerged from the woods, crashing into Pierce's other regiments. These retreating Yanks were soon followed by Virginians and Carolinians. The Confederate assault slammed into Pierce's men and crushed them. One Yank wrote, "It was impossible … to stop their impetuous charge, and the brigade was driven back in confusion."[68] The Federals, as one recorded, "fired a few rounds, but were overrun."[69] However, more Tar Heels fell; Privates Benjamin Whisenhunt (Co. D) and John Pendergrass (Co. G) were both wounded.[70]

Byron Pierce's brigade collapsed and the bluecoats ran away, heading west to the Boydton plank road, leaving behind two artillery pieces, which the Confederates captured. A Tar Heel noted "two men of Co. K, 11th North Carolina impulsively seized the remaining horses and hitched them up to the lone caisson and hauled it back across the run."[71] Scores of Union soldiers threw down their weapons and were rounded up by the exuberant Confederates, who immediately confiscated knapsacks and haversacks.[72]

William MacRae and David Weisiger regained control of their men and re-formed their regiments into a two-brigade-wide battlefront. They sent a line of skirmishers out in front and moved forward, heading toward the west, in pursuit of the last of the retreating men from Pierce's brigade. As they advanced, the Virginians of Weisiger's left-flank regiment began calling attention to what they could see. MacRae and Weisiger halted the battle line and checked on the commotion. The two generals were amazed; the open area south of them was covered by hundreds of wagons. The entire unprotected II Corps wagon train sat before them, maybe a mile away. This was an incredible discovery; there would be enough rations and ammunition to supply the Confederates for weeks! Both commanders swung their regiments around to the left and began moving towards this unbelievable treasure.[73]

But it wasn't quite that simple; the reason the wagon train was unguarded was because the Union corps commander, Maj. Gen. Winfield Hancock, had positioned his corps' brigades in a large, box-like formation, with his wagons sheltered in the center. MacRae and Weisiger had just punched through one side of the box and now were roving around in Hancock's corps' innards. Sergeant Jacob Bartlett (Co. K) remarked, "We had knocked a gap in the Yankee line."[74] Right now they may have been free to roam about, but Hancock's men were not going to permit this movement for long. As the Confederate battle line closed on the wagons, the reality of their situation became clear. As one wrote, they were "dangerously isolated and vulnerable."[75]

The northern edge of Hancock's box was manned by brigades approaching Hatcher's Run, near the bridge at the millpond. One of these brigades, commanded by Col. Robert McAllister, was in the perfect position to respond. Colonel McAllister about-faced his nine-regiment formation and sent them marching towards the Confederate's rear. McAllister noted, "There were large numbers of new recruits in the brigade. I deemed it best to about-face and move on the enemy with my rear rank in the front."[76] The terrain between McAllister's brigade and the Southerners was filled with small washes, thick hazel underbrush, and tall shrubs, forcing the Federals to move slowly in order to maintain their battle line. Observant Confederates quickly noticed this danger approaching and called out to their officers. Lieutenant Lewis Warlick (Co. B) recorded, "The first thing [we] knew, the enemy had formed a line of battle in [our] rear."[77] General William MacRae ordered his Tar Heels to turn around. MacRae's men were veterans; he gave the command, "Brigade, counter march by company," and the experienced soldiers in his fifty companies reformed efficiently, facing the approaching bluecoats in less than sixty seconds.[78] Now, the two Confederate brigades were standing in formation, side by side, one facing south, and the other to the north. The Carolinians opened fire on McAllister's men at a range of several hundred yards.

Colonel Robert McAllister's Massachusetts, New Jersey, and Pennsylvania troops returned fire and Tar Heels fell, including Pvt. James Abernathy (Co. I), who suffered a shattered left hand, and Pvt. John Cordell (Co. K), who was also wounded.[79] The Carolinians poured more lead into the Union ranks and McAllister's regiments stuttered to a halt, especially the units with large numbers of conscripts who were not ready for battle. Colonel Robert McAllister wrote, "We wavered and fell back."[80] A Southerner noted "McAllister's new recruits and draftees ... could not stand the punishment and broke."[81] The Yanks fell back several hundred yards. Then, once the rabble crossed over a ravine, McAllister's regimental officers regained control of their troops, and soon, a patched-together force again faced threatened the Confederates. MacRae and Weisiger now understood a serious danger lurked behind them.

Another Federal unit, this one from the west side of Hancock's box, moved towards the Southerners, ten regiments in the brigade commanded by Brig. Gen. Regis de Trobriand. His force had been facing to the west, guarding their portion of the perimeter against a thin screen of Confederate cavalry, but when he saw MacRae and Weisiger move towards

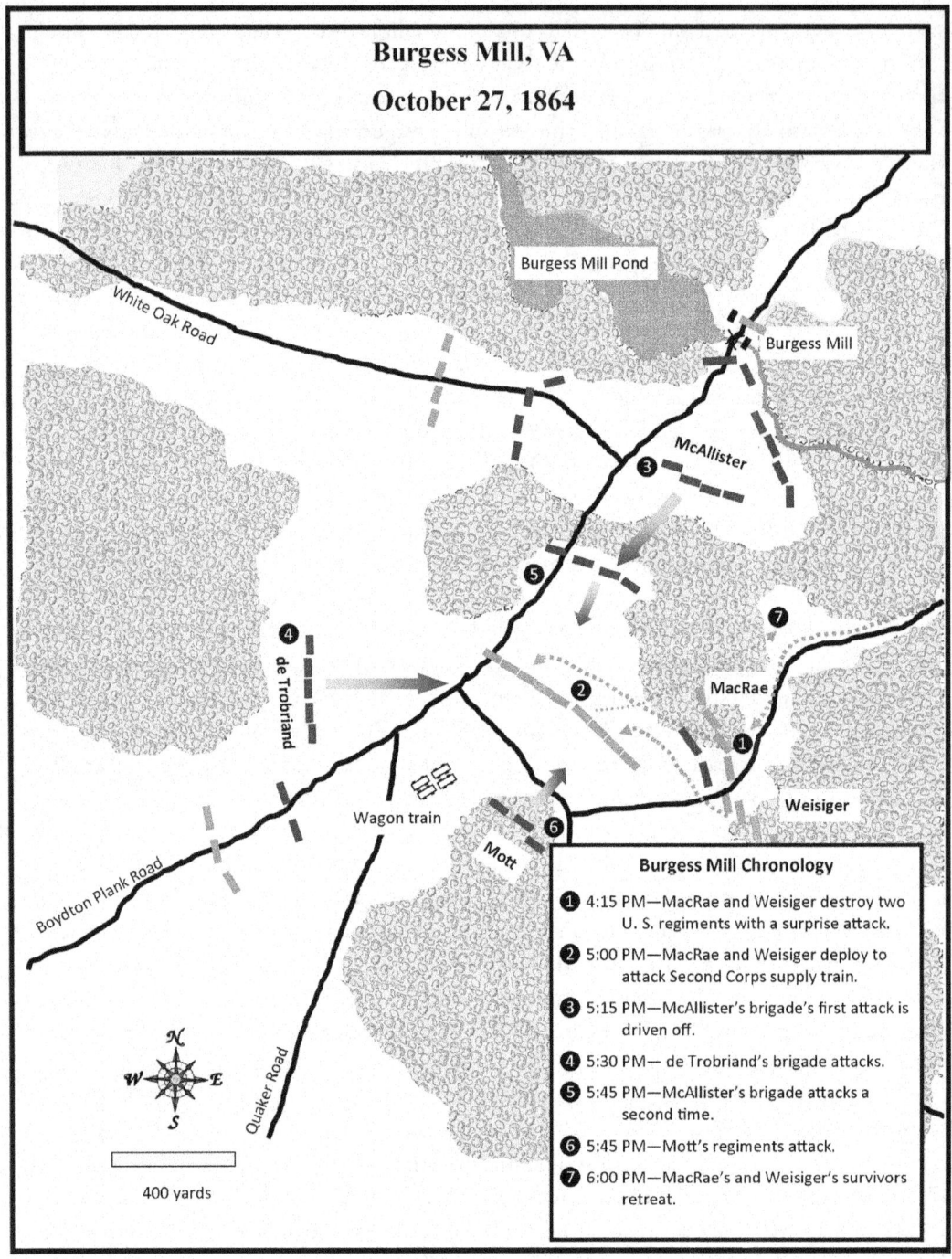

the wagon train, de Trobriand responded. He about-faced his regiments and sent them against the Confederates, advancing to the northeast. MacRae's Tar Heels, who were still facing to the north, did not see the bluecoat formation at first, but warning cries from the Virginians alerted the Carolinians to this new danger. A Tar Heel noted they had "no support on both our right and rear."[82] The Federals closed to within 200 yards and opened on the Confederates, their fire striking obliquely.[83] Private Robert Flow (Co. A) was wounded, as was Cpl. William Butler (Co. D). Private George Summeron (Co. H) was struck in the left leg and Pvt. Ezekiel Henderson (Co. K) was hit in the left thigh.[84]

General MacRae ordered the 44th NC to shift its front from covering the northern danger, to facing towards de Trobriand's threat. A Tar Heel in the 44th wrote, "MacRae formed a portion of his command obliquely to his main battle line."[85] The Confederate battle line was now facing north, south, and southwest, and the soldiers were beginning to believe they had entered a trap. One remarked, "No help came whilst ... men toiled, bled and died."[86] The Confederate riflemen in both brigades began searching for a route to safety. Some of Weisiger's Virginians on his far flank began to slip away from the brigade and scamper towards the safety of the trees to the east. Others saw these fellows race toward this shelter and started clamoring for the order to retreat. In the Bethel Regiment, as the Tar Heels saw the Yank peril closing in on them from so many directions, they turned to their commander, knowing Collett Leventhorpe and William Martin always knew the exact thing to do. But neither officer was present; Leventhorpe languished in a Federal prison and Martin was confined to a hospital bed. The regiment's senior officer, Cpt. William Grier, grew increasingly flustered by the complicated situation and struggled to give proper directives. The 11th North Carolina began to flounder.

As both Confederate brigades faltered, their shooting diminished, giving encouragement to de Trobriand's troops, as well as to Brig. Gen. McAllister, who ordered his battle line to attack. The Tar Heels saw McAllister's men advance again, and Sgt. Jacob Bartlett (Co. K) recorded, "The two ends were closing together ... [on] us."[87] More Confederates gave up thoughts of fighting and fled to the east. Lieutenant Lemuel Hoyle (Co. I) observed, "[Many] feared we would never get out—that we would all be either killed or captured."[88] McAllister noted, "We charged down the hill [and] the enemy became panic stricken."[89] Captain Grier called his company officers together for a hasty meeting. The situation had become critical. Lt. Hoyle (Co. I) wrote, "The regt's officers did not know what to do, some talked of surrendering, some of forming where we were and fighting to the last, others for cutting our way out."[90] The majority of the officers argued for retreat, though 1st Lt. William Turner (Co. E) disputed this decision and maintained his company would hold the ground as long as possible in order to cover the regiment's retreat. One Bethel soldier stated, "We did not falter; we faced about and cut our way out."[91] Another wrote "he contemplated surrendering rather than running, but he thought of home and what he would suffer and concluded to risk it."[92]

The two Confederate brigades dissolved into a mob of fleeing men. A soldier in the 47th NC recorded, "MacRae was on foot leading his command ... asking [his troops] to follow him out."[93] General de Trobriand bragged, "Up we went ... driving the enemy before us, and clearing the whole of the open field."[94] A small Union force came up from the south and attempted to cut off the Confederate route of retreat, but as, a member of the 44th NC noted, "[We] cut [our] way through a new line of battle which had partially formed."[95] Other soldiers were not as fortunate. One recorded, "Our men fell back into the woods from which they made this assault, many lost their way in the thick undergrowth, some being captured, others narrowly escaping capture."[96] Meanwhile, 1st Lt. William Turner

(Co. E) and the stalwarts in his company kept up a steady fire upon the advancing bluecoats. General de Trobriand admitted "a part of the Rebels promptly turned against us and the firing became very brisk."[97] Private Joseph Pennix (Co. E) was wounded, and Pvt. John Campbell (Co. E) suffered a shattered right arm.[98] Then, the bluecoats closed upon Turner's small command and the surrounded Tar Heels threw down their weapons. Some scrambled away and escaped. However, two dozen, including 1st Lt. William Turner, were captured.

The Tar Heels fled into the dense underbrush, chased closely by aggressive Northerners. The thick vegetation confused many of the men and some wandered about, lost. The bluecoats scooped up these disoriented riflemen, capturing dozens of Cpt. William Grier's troops, including Pvt. John Floyd (Co. C). A Confederate wrote, "The heavy loss of prisoners ... was due to the men losing their way in the dense woods."[99] Some of the Southerners found their way to a barn and hid there, only to be cut off and captured. A Yank officer noted "a number of rebels had taken refuge in a barn ... [and we] captured 200 and a flag."[100]

The retreat became a disaster for the Confederates. The Virginians, who were protected by the men of MacRae's brigade, reached the woods first and raced back across Hatcher's Run. There, safely protected by another butternut brigade, David Weisiger and his officers were able to re-form their regiments. When they took roll, Weisiger reported his formation had lost over 300. However, for William MacRae's Tar Heels, the situation was considerably more grave. His men had farther to run, and many were cut off by a determined Union pursuit. By the time the last of the Confederates were safely across Hatcher's Run, Lt. Lemuel Hoyle (Co. I) estimated the number of captured from the brigade at 500.[102] The day's fight had become a disaster. Later that evening, once the Bethel Regiment's company officers submitted their muster reports, Cpt. William Grier was able to record the 11th North Carolina's losses at 120.

That evening a cold winter rain soaked the discouraged Tar Heels. Captain Grier posted pickets to cover the bridge spanning Hatcher's Run but the Union soldiers did nothing to cause concern. In

Twenty-one-year-old Pvt. John Floyd (Co. C) was captured in the retreat at Burgess' Mill on October 27, 1864 (Clark, 1901).

11th North Carolina Casualties[101]
October 27, 1864

Unit	Commander	Casualties*
F & S	Cpt. William Grier	0
Co. A	2nd Lt. William Taylor	8
Co. B	Cpt. Thomas Parks	11
Co. C	Cpt. Edward Outlaw	5
Co. D	1st Lt. Lewis Elias	8
Co. E	1st Lt. William Turner	26
Co. F	Sgt. Nathaniel Mardre	6
Co. G	Cpt. John Freeland	17
Co. H	1st Lt. Robert Lowrie	19
Co. I	2nd Lt. Lemuel Hoyle	12
Co. K	1st Lt. William Dickerson	9
Total		121

*For a complete listing of the battle of the Burgess Mill casualties, see Appendix A, Battle of Burgess Mill Casualties.

fact, once the Northern commanders were able to assess their own casualties—they suffered 1,055—Gen. Hancock ordered his corps to withdraw.[103] The Confederates awoke the next morning to find the ground empty of Yanks. Brigadier General William MacRae called his regimental commanders together and took stock of his shattered brigade; he was dismayed. Lieutenant Lewis Warlick (Co. B) recorded, "we have [only] about five hundred arms-bearing men in the brigade."[104]

Chapter 16

Winter 1864-1865

The battered Bethel Regiment shuffled back toward their portion of the Petersburg defenses on October 29, 1864, the Tar Heels stunned by their losses. The fight at Burgess Mill had cost the regiment the most soldiers since the battle of Gettysburg. Captain William Grier, still the formation's senior officer, led his men into the trenches, knowing his leadership was in question. As a company commander he had sought field rank, but now that he had experienced that level's hardships and difficulties he was ready to return to his old position. But Confederate and North Carolina rank regulations were inflexible; a captain remained delegated as the leader of 300 men.

11th North Carolina Muster[1]
November 1, 1864

Unit	Commander	Total
F & S	Cpt. William Grier	
	Cpt. James Young	4
Co. A	2nd Lt. William Taylor	39
Co. B	2nd Lt. Lewis Warlick	35
Co. C	Cpt. Edward Outlaw	22
Co. D	1st Lt. Lewis Elias	33
Co. E	2nd Lt. James Alexander	20
Co. F	Sgt. Nathaniel Mardre	18
Co. G	Cpt. John Freeland	48
Co. H	1st Lt. Robert Lowrie	26
Co. I	2nd Lt. Lemuel Hoyle	32
Co. K	1st Sgt. Jacob Bartlett	25
Total		302

Brigadier General William MacRae gave orders to his five Tar Heel regiments to improve their fortifications, and the weary soldiers stacked their weapons and shouldered picks, axes, and shovels. The Federal lines were over a quarter of a mile away from MacRae's entrenchments, and at first neither side's soldiers bothered the others, enabling the Carolinians to work during the daylight hours. A Tar Heel rifleman noted "their line and ours are some 4 or 500 yards apart…. They keep still, not firing."[2]

The soldiers dug trenches three or four feet deep and six to eight feet wide, and piled the dirt on the "enemy" side, creating bulwarks sufficiently tall for people to safely walk within them. Timbers and sandbags were incorporated into the walls to keep the sides from collapsing, and small ledges were carved into the walls' sides as fire-steps, enabling guards or marksmen to man the parapets without putting themselves in danger. The Confederates then dug a scattered line of rifle pits in front of the trenches, with each pit usually large enough to protect two men. This line of rifle pits provided the entrenchments with an outer layer of defenses, preventing the Yanks from sneaking up on the trenches.[3] All in all, their defenses were virtually impregnable, provided they had enough riflemen.

By the time the fortifications were complete, Maj. Gen. Henry Heth's division controlled just over four miles of trench frontage.[4] General Heth maintained his headquarters at a farmstead called the Pickeral House, which was approximately 150 yards behind the rear of his soldiers' breastworks.[5] He assigned each one of his brigades a mile of trench and made the brigade commanders take charge of that section of the line. Brigadier General William MacRae's brigade was tasked with protecting about 6,000 feet of line, on Heth's far right, with William McComb's brigade on their left, and the Burgess Mill pond anchoring the right. MacRae assigned his five regiments varying lengths of distance, depending upon the size of the unit. The Bethel Regiment received just over 1,300 feet of trench line. Captain William Grier's ten companies each had 75 to 130 yards of distance to protect, depending upon muster strength; Cpt. John Freeland's Company G had the longest distance, while Sgt. Nathaniel Mardre's Company F maintained the smallest.

In early November 1864, General Robert E. Lee walked the length of his trenches, meeting with his veterans and examining the fortifications. A Tar Heel rifleman recalled "General Lee passed along the works on foot, inspecting the troops and breast-works."[6] Then, the Carolinians settled in, recuperating from the severity of the summer's battles and guarding against a possible Union attack. Though the lines were a quarter-mile apart, when new Yank regiments entered the Federal lines their marksmen lurked about, taking potshots at the Southerners, forcing the men posted out in the rifle pits to remain hidden during daylight hours, and preventing men from showing themselves above the fortifications' walls. In one instance, "[an officer] wanted to get a better look at the enemy works but heavy sniper fire prevented him from sticking his head over the parapet. Instead ... [he] held up a mirror and angled it so that he could view the enemy lines without exposing himself. In an instant, the mirror was shattered ... by a sniper's bullet, and the officer ... heard someone shout from the Federal trenches, 'set it up again Johnny.'"[7]

When Gen. Heth received word the Northerners were preparing for an assault he sent word to William MacRae that he needed a small force to go out into the space between the two lines and capture some bluecoats. Heth wanted the prisoners interrogated. On November 5, 1864, a company of Tar Heels was selected. One of the riflemen described the event: "[That] night [we] were ordered to ... charge the picket line ... the charge to be made at eleven o'clock.... [Our] captain had us all ready by ten o'clock and told us ... to stand square up to him and do our best." The Confederate continued: "We knew it was foolishness to attempt it ... but we were going to stand or fall with [the] captain." The veteran finished his story: "Our orders were countermanded much to our relief."[8] Eventually Heth's staff determined the intelligence was a rumor and no Union attack was made; thus the men in the two armies slipped into a peaceful coexistence. A Confederate wrote, "Fortunately for us, we found that an agreement had been reached into by the pickets not to fire unless it was necessary.... We make it up not to fire on each other until [we] get orders and then [we] would fire up in the air to [give] ... notice."[9] Another rifleman admitted, "The pickets soon began to fraternize.... When we weren't killing each other, we were the best of friends."[10]

General MacRae admonished his regimental commanders to strengthen their units. The Confederate government's expansion of the Conscription Law scooped in more men and some of these conscripts were fed into the Tar Heel units. The 11th North Carolina's company recruiters mustered in several dozen new men, with the largest number of recruits coming from the units based in Charlotte (Co. H and Co. E), and Chapel Hill (Co. G).[11] More men were added to the regiment's rolls as wounded and ill soldiers recovered, and when the last batches of exchanged prisoners returned. Lieutenant Lemuel Hoyle (Co. I) noted, "Recruits, conscripts, and absentees are coming in and before we are put into another battle, I hope our number will be very respectable again."[12] The Bethel formation, by December 1, 1864, had grown to 379.[13] A Carolinian optimistically recorded, "Numbers of conscripts are daily being sent forward ... to our army, and with but a few days drilling and the example of the old soldiers will be as good as any."[14] The new men got little drilling experience; instead, as 2nd Lt. Lewis Warlick (Co. B) wrote, "We have been busy the past week ... [as] there is a heavy detail every day working on the fort and other fatigue parties, besides a heavy picket line to keep up."[15]

As the winter temperatures dropped and cold, rain-filled storms rolled over Virginia, both the Union and Confederate forces along the far western end of the Petersburg trenches chose to limit their hostilities. As one soldier noted, "everything [was] quiet here now—only an occasional gun."[16] Captain William Grier went on a medical furlough and never returned, leaving the regiment to Cpt. James Young, a 28-year-old clerk from Asheville. One of Cpt. Young's first administrative duties was to observe court-martial proceedings; he also learned one of the 11th North Carolina's soldiers was to be executed for desertion. Private Joshua Starney (Co. D), a young farmer from Burke County who had been conscripted in September 1864, had spent most of his time dodging details and hiding from battles. He eventually was caught by provost guards, and on December 3, 1864, he was sentenced to death by firing squad. Captain James Young assigned 2nd Lt. Lemuel Hoyle (Co. I) to take charge of the execution.[17] One of the shooters, Pvt. John Warlick (Co. B), sadly recalled, "It was my duty to help shoot him. I aimed a bullet at his heart."[18] Lieutenant Lewis Warlick (Co. B) added, "Starney used to keep Shetland [ponies] ... [and] was shot for ... desertion." Lewis Warlick then wrote his wife, "I pray God I may be spared to see the end of this cruel war and return home to your side to live a peaceful and happy life."[19]

A week later the Bethel veterans received word their meat rations would be cut. The Confederate commissary department could no longer provide beef and pork at the levels of earlier in the fall. The Southern logistics system was collapsing, and with Grant's successful cutting of the Weldon and Petersburg Railroad, as well as hampering the Boydton plank road, supplies coming from North Carolina were growing scarce. One officer remarked "there [now was] an acute shortage of meat."[20] The hungry Carolinians, especially as Christmas neared, gazed off towards their distant homes and daydreamed. Lieutenant Lewis Warlick (Co. B) scribbled to his wife, "I wish we could get some nice things from home."[21]

The day before Christmas the weather turned cold and wet; one miserable soldier wrote "it rained all day, and the coldest kind of rain too."[22] Another added, "The weather has begun to get cold with a great deal of rain, which [makes] the trenches a very disagreeable place to stay in.[23] The next day, Christmas 1864, proved to be a melancholy day for all the Carolinians. One rifleman wrote his wife: "This is the third Christmas that I have been away from you ... and I wonder if I shall be spared to see another Christmas morning."[24] Another just blurted out, "It is the gloomiest Xmas that I ever saw."[25] And a third noted, "I had fondly hoped to spend this day at my beloved home, but have been disappointed. Would that I could but feel the hope that before another Christmas day comes, I and all the soldiers would be at our homes."[26]

Some of the Tar Heels received letters from their families and though these cherished notes were savored, they often filled the homesick men with despondency. One of these notes from a lonely wife caused a forlorn husband considerable despair. "We are all sad," she wrote. "I have nothing even to put in Sadie's stockings, which hangs so invitingly for Santa Claus.... [On Christmas] Sadie jumped out of bed very early ... to feel her stocking. She could not believe that there would ... be [nothing].... Finding nothing, she crept back into bed, pulled the cover over her face, and soon I heard her sobbing."[27] Another veteran was able to get a pass into Petersburg, but he returned to the trenches, downcast and introspective, and wrote his wife: "The people there are friendly, but they are too clean, too decent (is that the right word?) for me to feel comfortable around them." He then deliberated, "I wonder—when and if I return home—will I be able to fit in?"[28]

The Confederate high command let everyone know there would be a Christmas dinner brought out to the trenches for each soldier to enjoy. A rifleman described what they were to receive: "The people of Richmond and Petersburg [are] going to give the soldiers in the trenches a Christmas dinner with cabbage, beans, chicken, beef loaf, bread, and a lot of other good things." He added, "How glad we were when we heard that the [food was] in Petersburg."[29] However by early afternoon word reached the men this feast would be postponed until New Year's day.[30] The men shrugged their shoulders and accepted this news with resignation. A week later, on December 31, 1864, a Tar Heel recorded, "This day is the last of an eventful year in American History. It is the last page of an interesting book.... It is the closing of a scene of a bloody drama, to be followed, as it has been preceded, by other scenes of a sanguinary cast."[31]

The next morning, January 1, 1865, dawned cold and clear, and as the hungry Confederates formed for roll call, they buzzed with anticipation of the coming feast. Captain James Young had gone home on a medical furlough, so now the regiment was commanded by Cpt. William Kerr (Co. E), a 33-year-old coach maker from Charlotte. He still limped from the leg wound he had received on July 23, 1864, and some of his friends noted that he had a fondness for alcohol, but he was now the regiment's senior officer and the job was his, whether he was capable or not. The 11th North Carolina regiment's numbers had increased considerably during December, now totaling 442, and they all waited anxiously for the dinner's arrival.[32] Once the morning's parade was ended Cpt. Kerr posted a squad of volunteers to meet the expected meal and assist in its distribution to the troops. The men waited all day. One wrote, "Our mouths watered till January 1, 1865. On that day all who were able to, got up very early. The army was to do nothing. The ladies [of Richmond] were to do all ... [so] we waited.... We whiled away the tedious hours by telling stories and cracking jokes." Sadly, the meal did not arrive. The rifleman continued, "It was at 3:00 a.m. [January 2] when a comrade called and told me that a detail had just gone out to meet the precious wagon and bring in the feast. But O what a disappointment when the squad returned and issued to each man only one small sandwich made up of two tiny slices of bread and a thin piece of ham. A few men ventured to inquire, Is this all?" The citizens then explained, "It was all they could do; it was all they had.... And then every man ... indulged in a good cry."[33] Another soldier, even though he now realized just how bad things were for the civilians, remarked of the meal, "It hardly paid to throw the tobacco out of our mouths for what we got."[34]

The lack of food became the major problem, and the famished men stumbled about, carrying out their duties, but lacking much energy to maintain their trenches. One hungry soldier wrote, ""The daily ration seldom consisted of anything beyond a pint of corn meal and an ounce or two of bacon." He continued, "I was hungry ... so hungry that I thanked God that I had a backbone for my stomach to lean up against."[35] Lieutenant Lewis Warlick (Co. B) penned to his wife, "When I sit down to my meal of ... spoiled bacon and corn bread I think of the many good meals [we shared]... and wish I had some of them now."[36]

Ration shortages were not the only difficulty plaguing the troops; firewood no longer was available. A Tar Heel recorded, "We [have] no wood, only what little we could pick up here and there."[37] Another Carolinian added, "The men find it hard to find firewood.... They have to walk a long ways off and [have] no wagon to haul it in."[38] And another soldier griped, adding to their list of complaints, "This life in the trenches was awful—beyond description.... It [is] endurance without relief; sleeplessness without exhilaration; inactivity without rest; [and] constant apprehension requiring ceaseless watching." This soldier then noted what he hated most: "the unavoidable stench from the latrines."[39] He was joined by another, who summed up their situation: "Rumors and stories, about all we have to do is talk and shiver. We are bored and our morale is low."[40]

General Lee made another journey through the trenches, reviewing his afflicted soldiers, and inspecting the fortifications' condition. The winter rains had turned the entire landscape into a muddy quagmire, and water drained into the entrenchments, filling them with several inches of water. The soldiers were forced to wade through this muck every hour. A Confederate rifleman noted, "General Lee came through ... wading sometimes almost to his boot tops in the mud, but he never said a word about the mud. He knew we couldn't keep it out [of the trenches]."[41]

On January 27, 1865, Second Lt. Lewis Warlick (Co. B) wrote his wife: "Everything is quiet—no news afloat except camp rumors of every kind."[42] Another Tar Heel recorded, "Camp life ... was a hard one, and upon the whole a very sad one."[43] Another grumbled at his situation, and himself: "In rolling up my blankets I forgot to put my socks in and came off and left them. I never hated anything so bad in my life."[44] And another complained about picket duty, scribbling to his family, "Picket is very hard business. We have to go on the front line and remain 24 hours, then we are relieved on the front line, but without any comfortable place to rest or sleep."[45] Other Carolinians shrugged off these hardships. One such rifleman remarked, "Times is quiet here along the lines. I went down to Burgess mills with some boys [and went] skating on the ice. It was nice."[46]

By the end of January 1865 the effects of these adversities began to appear among the Tar Heel regiments; men began to desert. A rifleman observed, "Pa, I have no news to write you. Only the coldest weather you ever saw and [fire]wood a long ways off and ... scanty rations to feed the men on. There were seven of our men from the Brigade run off last night.... I expect that all will run off before long."[47] Escape from the lines dominated all the homesick soldiers' thoughts. Though the number of desertions remained low, all the men pleaded for legal getaways—furloughs—but this avenue of exodus was evaporating. Lieutenant Lewis Warlick (Co. B) informed his wife, "I went to Capt. Kerr Comdg. Regt. last Monday and asked him if he would forward a furlough for me, he replied, no, as Genl. MacRae had ordered him not to forward any more."[48]

January 1865's final days were also filled with rumors of a possible negotiated peace treaty. A rifleman noted, "The peace question is all the excitement in camp now.... I do hope peace will be made before spring."[49] On January 29, 1865, three Confederate peace commissioners crossed the lines, carrying white flags to meet with the Union officials, and made arrangements for a meeting at Hampton Roads on the steamboat *River Queen*. This news electrified the war-weary Southerners. One wrote, "Last night there came an order to the army from Senator Hunter of Virginia, one of the peace commissioners ... to see what terms that peace will come on." The Confederate soldier continued, "The sentence was this: all that is for Peace on honorable footing ... and if not, what kind of peace, if not honorable then we should fight until that kind should come.... The next question was this: Peace on any terms whether good or ... to give up to the Yankee Government?"[50]

On February 3, 1865, the excited soldiers watched the peace commission cross the lines. A Confederate rifleman recorded, "When the peace commission passed through the lines to meet President Lincoln in Hampton Roads, we fondly hoped ... that they would come to some terms to end the war."[51] The conference attendees were President Abraham Lincoln and his secretary of state, William Seward, and, for the Confederates, Vice President Alexander Stephens, Senator Robert Hunter, and Judge James Campbell. The Confederate delegation proposed an armistice and Lincoln refused. Then the Confederates suggested the independence of their nation and again Lincoln rejected their offer, and instead, demanded that reunion was the only option. After four hours of fruitless negotiations the meeting fell apart and the two sides separated."[52] A disappointed Confederate wrote "the conference accomplished nothing." He then noted "both sides knew that it would be a fight to the bitter end."[53]

The Bethel Regiment numbered 439 on February 1, 1865, with Cpt. James Young still in command.[54] As Cpt. Young reviewed the 11th North Carolina's companies he could easily see the pessimism which infected the ranks, especially as one soldier remarked, "The men are getting discouraged, and to tell the truth, they have cause to be."[55] Though the Bethel boys remained resolute in their support of each other, Cpt. Young detected a gloominess that worried him, one the other company commanders had also observed. They all agreed if something dramatic did not occur to change the situation the Eleventh would begin to suffer desertions. It was only a matter of time.

The USS *River Queen* was the site of the failed peace conference on February 3, 1865 (Library of Congress).

In late morning, on February 5, 1865, Cpt. James Young was ordered to pull his riflemen away from their posts and form the regiment to march, as the Yanks had again sent forces to their west in an attempt to sever the Duncan wagon road. General William MacRae was away from the brigade, so command of the five regiments fell to Lt. Col. James Adams of the 26th North Carolina. James Adams led the brigade through the trenches and southward, heading toward Armstrong's Mill, on Hatcher's Run, part of a three-brigade force Gen. Heth was sending to stop the Federals. The weather was bitter, with near-freezing temperatures numbing the riflemen's hands. One recorded, "It was sleeting and very cold."[56] General Henry Heth placed McComb's brigade on the left and Cooke's brigade to his right. Heth, knowing MacRae's troops were commanded by an inexperienced lieutenant colonel, kept the Tar Heels in reserve. As the Confederates moved into position Gen. William Cooke requested Lt. Col. Adams to release the brigade's sharpshooters to protect his right flank, and the temporary commander agreed.

McComb's Tennesseans and Cooke's Tar Heels pushed southward through ice-covered underbrush and winter-denuded trees, cautiously searching for the expected force of Yanks. McComb's skirmishers ran into bluecoats around 3:00 p.m.—men of Brig. Gen. Robert McAllister, the same men who had bedeviled the Tar Heels in October 1864 at Burgess Mills. Robert McAllister had done much to improve the fighting quality of his men since Burgess Mills; today, when his skirmisher encountered the Confederates, they immediately opened fire and forced the butternut troops to halt their advance.[57] Brigadier General William McComb brought his main battle line forward and they pushed into the Federals, shoving McAllister's thin line back to his main position. William Cooke advanced his Tar Heels and came up near McComb's right flank, though a distance of nearly a quarter-mile separated the two Southern formations. Lieutenant Colonel James Adams inched his Carolinians into a position between the two Confederate brigades, though safely posted in a stand of trees, several hundred yards behind Cooke and McComb.[58]

The Tennesseans pressed forward, out onto open ground, 600 yards from McAllister's four regiments of New Jersey and New York veterans, who were scratching out a line of rifle pits. One of the Union officers recalled "the well-known rebel yell rolled out on the evening breeze, and on rushed their massed columns."[59] McAllister also had two sections of artillery supporting his men. The cannoneers waited until the Tennesseans were 300 yards away and then unleashed their guns. One of the Yanks remarked, "Never did shells do more effective work."[60] General William MacRae's brigade adjutant, Cpt. Louis Young, recorded, "The effect of the first volley ... was to cause a stampede in the command of [McComb]."[61] The Tennesseans fled, retreating to the safety of the tree line.

Lieutenant Colonel Adams brought the Carolinians abreast with William Cooke's men and the two brigades pushed forward out of the trees. They were 800 yards away from McAllister's infantry, but within range of the Union artillery. The bluecoat gunners aimed their cannon at the Tar Heels. The first barrages pounded Cooke's men, and then the next struck among MacRae's troops. Several shells crashed among the Bethel Regiment's ranks, one striking in Company G and sending shrapnel tearing through 3rd Lt. William Whitted's thigh and wounding Pvt. John Gattis. Another round savaged Company H, wounding Pvt. John Pepper and nearly ripping Pvt. James Marshall's right leg from his body.[62] The 11th North Carolina line quivered and halted when another explosion killed Pvt. Gabriel Miller (Co. K) and wounded his cousin, Pvt. James Miller (Co. K). Adjutant Edward Martin went down with the next detonation, wounded by chunks of flesh-shredding metal, and Sgt. Nathaniel Mardre (Co. F) fell moments later, also injured by shrapnel.[63] This slaughter was pointless; after a few more Bethel men were injured, the Carolinians withdrew. A jubilant Union officer crowed, "The enemy were repulsed."[64]

The 26th North Carolina's lieutenant colonel led the sullen brigade back into the safety of the underbrush and the Southerners waited out the last hour of daylight. The falling sleet continued to coat everything with ice and the men struggled to build campfires. Captain James Young's companies turned in their evening roll calls and he learned the regiment had lost a dozen men, including Company F's leader, Sgt. Nathaniel Mardre.[65] The remaining NCO in that company was Sgt. Charles Davenport, who was quite unhappy to be informed he now commanded the unit.[66] Captain Young led the regiment back to their section of the Petersburg fortifications later the next day. The veterans trudged through the sleet and snow, knowing they had retreated from a fight, which was, as one rifleman recorded, "a demoralizing influence."[67]

The Union movements around Hatcher's Run resulted in the final cutting of the Duncan wagon road. Accompanied by the heavy rains which pounded the Virginia countryside and hampered railroad traffic on the Piedmont Railroad, the soldiers' rations were reduced even more. The Confederate army's food reserve diminished to just two days.[68] One famished Southern rifleman complained, "We are living on nothing but cornbread. We have had nothing else for four days."[69] Another grumbled, "Our rations [are] a little corn meal.... We get ... about enough for the day to make one good meal for a hungry man."[70] Meanwhile,

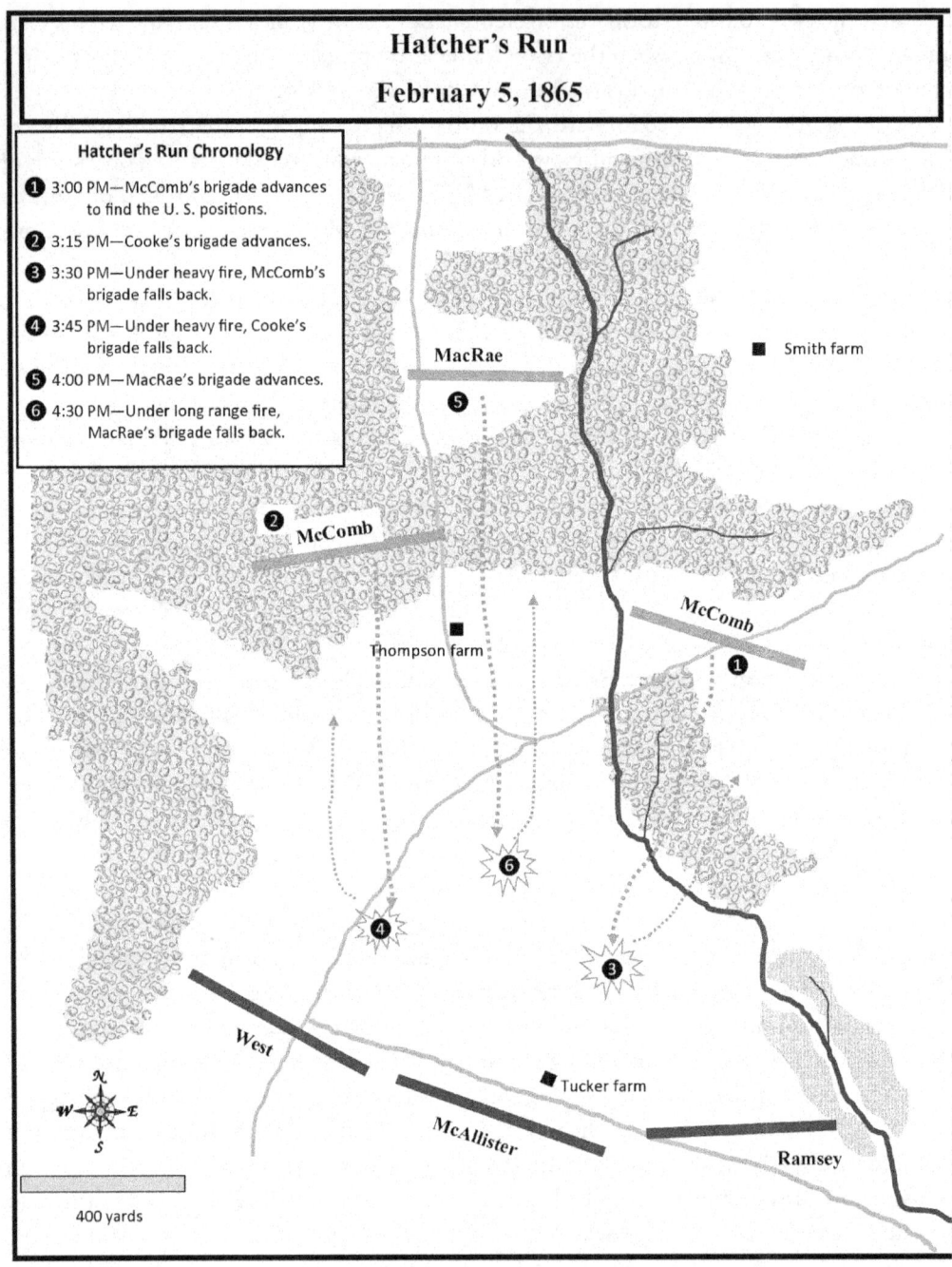

another noted, "We drill very little.... The truth is, the men [are] worn out in mind and body, and every effort [is] painfully irksome."[71] These soldiers, and multitudes more, aimed their wrath at the Confederate high command and murmured, "If they do not give us something else besides bread they will have to fight it out themselves."[72] Over a dozen Tar Heels slipped away during the nights, some crossing over to the Union positions while others just set out, heading for home.

16. Winter 1864–1865

Morale fell further. The starving and weary Confederates began to shirk duties or, at best, complete their work details slowly and without vigor. No one wanted to go out into no-man's-land and risk being shot, and everyone shuddered when they thought about the coming of good weather. Fresh Union soldiers were moved into the trenches opposite Heth's Tar Heels, and these bluecoats were much more aggressive. They began firing upon the Southerners, causing an exhausted Confederate to write, "The Yanks would take it into their heads that we were all asleep, I suppose, and wanted rousing, and [they would] open about a dozen guns ... keeping us fine fellows squeezed in the smallest possible space ... afraid to show our heads."[73] One war-drained rifleman scribbled to his family, "We have an indefinable dread, our nerves are subjected to a continual strain which we know cannot end till the war ends, or we are wiped out."[74]

On February 25, 1865, Cpt. William Kerr (Co. E) stood before a court-martial hearing and was forced to listen to one of his company sergeants, Andrew Hunter (Co. E), present evidence showing he had been drunk and absent without permission.[75] Captain Kerr was found guilty of these charges and dismissed from the regiment. Sgt. Hunter was so despondent about having been compelled to witness the charges that once the hearing ended he deserted.[76] The next day, more bad news descended upon the Tar Heels; they learned General Sherman's army was heading towards North Carolina. One dismayed rifleman wrote, "I sup-

The Petersburg trenches (*Harper's Weekly*, August 6, 1864).

posed that old Gen. Sherman is coming through South Carolina into North Carolina."[77] Then, more damaging hearsay battered the worn-out Confederates; rumors circulated that the politicians were considering arming the South's slaves and using them to reinforce the Army of Northern Virginia. The men took this news badly. One rifleman wrote, "I suppose that they are going to put ... negroes in the army. I think that will not do for the white soldiers. They say they won't stay here."[78]

On March 1, 1865, Col. William Martin returned to the 11th North Carolina, limping with a cane, as his thigh still had not completely healed.[79] He mustered his regiment and was distraught by the men's condition; the 11th North Carolina numbered 369.[80] Colonel Martin also noticed his discouraged soldiers were passing pieces of paper among the ranks and when he confiscated one of these notes he was horrified to see it was a Federal promise of good food and protected treatment to any Confederate who deserted to the Yanks. One of the Tar Heel riflemen recalled, "The enemy sent over circulars promising every man who would desert free transportation to any part of the North they wished to go, never to draft them in their armies, or they would give them work if they wished at good wages far in the rear."[81] Colonel Martin met with his company commanders and they informed him "the troops had not had any meat for five days ... [and] if the men [were] not fed they [would] not stay with the army."[82] Martin could do nothing to improve his soldiers' condition and even though he sympathized with their grievances he considered ways to protect his regiment's numbers. But his efforts were confounded by many soldiers who felt like one homesick Tar Heel who wrote, "I wish that I was out of this place. I would give all that I have to get out."[83]

Colonel William Martin advised his company commanders to select resolute veterans who could be trusted not to desert. These Tar Heel were to accompany each squad of pickets as a deterrent to those out on the picket line who were considering surrendering to the Federals. But even so, many of the 11th North Carolina's riflemen succumbed to the lure of promised food and good treatment; six men from Company G deserted on March 3, 1865, and a few days later, twelve more men disappeared from the ranks, followed by another handful vanishing the next week.[84] A rifleman, disheartened by these desertions, wrote, "What speaks worse for the spirit of the army, is that the men on the picket line fire off their guns into the air and will not try to shoot down those who are in the act of deserting to the enemy."[85] One of these deserters remarked he "explained to his captors that the usual number of men on the picket post was three, but it had recently been increased to four by adding a man who was known to be reliable. When asked how it was, then, that he had gotten away, the soldier replied, 'I was the reliable man.'"[86]

Nothing seemed to be going right for the Carolina soldiers; not only were they not receiving sufficient rations, but the men also no longer were getting paid. A highly frustrated rifleman groused, "[We] have suffered much inconvenience from not being paid regularly and promptly." He added, "It is a disgraceful shame that such injustice should be allowed."[87] The rumors of arming blacks and putting them into the defenses also continued to bombard the disgruntled soldiers. A perturbed enlisted man objected, writing, "I don't want to fight with negroes."[88]

As winter's icy grip softened, Col. Martin's war-weary, hungry, and discouraged Confederates watched as the regiment's numbers dwindled. The remaining stalwarts clung to each other in brotherhood, but as they gazed out upon the Federal entrenchments, they knew it would not be long before the Yanks would commence their spring offensive. One soldier noted, "I believe that this summer there will be one of the ... most severe campaigns ever witnessed upon earth."[89] Another recorded, "We all knew that when the campaign opened in the spring, General Lee would be compelled to surrender, and the men were badly discouraged, low spirited [and] they did not care to be killed for no purpose."[90]

Then, to everyone's surprise, on March 25, 1865, Gen. Lee launched an offensive, striking the Union position known as Fort Stedman. His Confederate forces crept across no-man's-land in the predawn darkness and crashed into the well-defended fortification, setting off a furious day-long fight that eventually spread out all along the trenches. Federal artillerymen opposite MacRae's brigade began shelling the Tar Heel's entrenchments, forcing the Carolinians to take cover in their bombproofs. At noon, a mass of bluecoats filed out of their works and assaulted the Confederate picket line. Second Lieutenant James Saville (Co. H), who commanded the 11th North Carolina's portion of the picket lines, shouted at his Tar Heels, who were hunkered down in their rifle pits, and they popped up, primed their muskets, and unleashed a volley into the advancing Yanks.

The Union troops, men from the 126th Ohio, suffered a number of casualties and then they scuttled back to safety. At 2:00 p.m., the Federals mounted a second assault, and this time the 126th OH was bolstered by the 6th MD and the 67th PA. They swept towards the Confederate's line of rifle pits, shouting. A Southern rifleman recorded, "On they came, shoulder to shoulder.... Again [our] fire broke from ... our rifle pits, extending to the right and left till the whole line, as far as rifles could reach ... crackling and sputtering." He continued, "But forward still swept the line of blue, heeding neither their dead nor their wounded ... then ... they have stopped! They stand still and fire, reload and fire. Our men, kneeling in the pits, take good aim.... It is but a minute before the enemy's line falters, appears about to break and flee."[91]

However, just before the bluecoats' assault collapsed, one courageous Yank changed the fight's momentum. Colonel Joseph Hill of the 6th MD, wrote, "Color-Sergt. Robert Spence, Company B, [advanced] ... being the first man in the works, and planted our starry banner thereon."[92] The Confederates watched this soldier, and one noted in awe, "Look, the color bearer runs forward alone with his flag. With a shout that rings again, the blue line follows in a swift charge through our deadliest fire. They reach the works and turning rapidly to the right and left, they sweep the line in both directions for a long distance."[93] Colonel Hill added, "[Spence] was wounded in the neck by a bullet from the enemy."[94] The bluecoats swarmed over the Southerners pinned down in their three- and four-man rifle pits. Some put up a fight. Pvt. Dudley Burch (Co. G) was wounded in the head, and Pvt. David Smith (Co. E) suffered a neck injury, but most just threw down their rifles and put up their hands.[95] Lieutenant James Saville (Co. H) and his second-in-command, Sgt. Charles Watt (Co. H), who led the 11th North Carolina's pickets, tried to rally their Bethel boys. However, both were soon overcome and captured.[96] The bluecoats took possession of a half-mile of Confederate rifle pits, and by the time the Yanks had rounded up all of Col. Martin's veterans, the 11th North Carolina had suffered over two dozen casualties.[97]

General Henry Heth examined the gap in the brigade's picket lines and immediately ordered a counterattack. He turned to Brig. Gen. Joseph Davis, but the general was not with his brigade. Joseph Davis was attending the funeral of President Jefferson Davis's son. Instead, Heth found Col. John Stone temporarily in charge of the brigade. Heth instructed Col. Stone to attack the Union troops occupying the Confederate picket line. Colonel John Stone called on his regiment, the 2nd MS, to make the charge.[98] He also requested the help of MacRae's brigade sharpshooters. William MacRae contributed half of his sharpshooters, and these forty men, led by 1st Lt. William Kyle (52nd NC) and 1st Lt. William Todd (Co. C), joined the attack.[99] This force, numbering fewer than 300 men, moved out into no-man's-land and spread out. They hit the thin Federal position and pushed some of the bluecoats backwards, but did not have the strength to recapture many of their old rifle pits and eventually were forced to fall back to the Confederate main line of fortifications.

The assault resulted in more casualties, including both North Carolina officers. First Lieutenant William Todd was wounded for the third time and would never return to the regiment. Lieutenant William Kyle's injury also took him out of the war. Brigade General MacRae then selected Cpt. John Thorpe (47th NC) as the sharpshooters' next leader. Captain John Thorpe was the soldier who, in 1861, had accompanied Pvt. Henry Wyatt (1st NC) in an attempt to burn a structure near their fortifications, during which Wyatt had been killed. MacRae wrote of Cpt. Thorpe: "He will do as much fighting and talk as little of it as any officer in our army."[100] That evening as darkness quieted the skirmishers it had become obvious to the Carolina riflemen that the Yankees had secured a vital position right in front of their works. The weary Tar Heels grimly stood at their posts, where they could hear the Union troops furiously digging less than 300 yards away. They all knew their demise was drawing near.

Chapter 17

The End: April 1865

On April 1, 1865, the men of the 11th North Carolina regiment occupied a section of the Confederate entrenchments, just west of the Burgess Mill pond. Colonel William Martin, though immobilized by his poorly healing thigh wound, led the formation assisted by Cpt. James Young and Ensign James Raynor. Martin's regiment only had nine other officers, and they were distributed among the various companies unevenly, resulting in several units' leaders being sergeants. The 11th North Carolina now numbered below 300, and there was little likelihood anymore replacements would bolster the regiment.[2] William Martin's riflemen were tired; more than half of them had been awake all night, ordered to remain at their firing positions in case of a surprise attack. These men had endured a long night, shivering from the cold rain drenching the landscape, and nervous from all the foreboding noises coming from the picket lines.[3]

11th North Carolina Muster[1]
April 1, 1865

Unit	Commander	Total
F & S	Col. William Martin	
	Cpt. James Young	4
Co. A	2nd Lt. William Taylor	37
Co. B	Cpt. Thomas Parks	43
Co. C	Cpt. Edward Outlaw	17
Co. D	1st Sgt. William Womack	24
Co. E	2nd Lt. James Alexander	23
Co. F	Sgt. William Benbury	16
Co. G	Cpt. John Freeland	34
Co. H	1st Lt. Robert Lowrie	36
Co. I	1st Sgt. John Ramseur	39
Co. K	1st Sgt. Jacob Bartlett	19
Total		292

Colonel Martin was worried. His riflemen no longer stood shoulder to shoulder; instead, each soldier manned a position with plenty of empty spaces between men. One Confederate officer noted, "The line was stretched to the breaking point. Eleven thousand men ... were occupying eleven miles of ... trenches."[4] The Carolinians grimly stared out at the Federal positions, knowing thousands of well-equipped, and well-fed Northerners waited for their commanders to put them on the offensive. Few of the Tar Heels believed this next fight was winnable.

The sounds of heavy fighting erupted off to the west that afternoon, forcing Martin's men to glance in that direction; they figured Gen. MacRae would soon get the call to rush his veterans to the sounds of those guns. No one was anxious to again have to face the Yankee hordes. The bluecoats' numbers seemed unlimited. No matter how many were shot down, there always were more to fill their ranks. Fortunately for Martin's drained riflemen, other brigades of Confederates moved towards the gunfire, those gaunt men hurrying past, rushing to reinforce their fighting brothers. The Bethel men sighed with relief as the sun set and the sounds of combat diminished; they had survived another day. Later, rumors swept through the fortifications, telling of a horrible Confederate defeat: Gen. Pickett's division had been destroyed at Five Forks.[5]

Once darkness settled in, Gen. William MacRae called his regimental officers together and explained the news about Pickett's men. He also informed them that, as one officer recalled, "East and Northeast of Burgess' mill, for a distance of ... two and a quarter miles.... Heth's ... trenches ... were, in effect, abandoned."[6] MacRae turned to his five regimental commanders and announced Gen. Heth had ordered him to send men to guard that gap. The Carolinian general looked at Col. William Martin and Lt. Col. Eric Erson of the 52nd NC. MacRae instructed them to take their regiments and occupy that space, and then he gazed at the hobbled Martin and told him 25-year-old Eric Erson was to take command of the two regiments. Martin's injury would prevent him from being mobile enough to lead both units.[7]

Lieutenant Colonel Erson guided his 280 soldiers and Martin's 290 out of their positions west of the Burgess Mill pond and into the empty trenches. Eric Erson recorded, "I was ordered ... to relieve a portion of McComb's brigade occupying from the right of McComb's winter quarters on the left, to the battery in front of McComb's winter quarters on the right."[8] He had less than 600 men to protect over two miles of fortifications, a sobering prospect. The Tar Heels filed into their postings, described by one Carolinian as being "next to a ravine that flowed into Arthur's Swamp, not far from the Jones's farm battlefield. [The 11th NC's] left rested at Mrs. Hart's house ... [with] The 28th NC ... positioned to [their] left."[9] Company commanders assigned squads to slip out into no-man's-land and protect the rifle pits of the Confederate picket line. One rifleman scribbled to his family, "I returned to the picket line (which by the way), was about as strong as the line at the breastworks."[10] Another wrote "there had been a big rain not long before, and the ground was partly flooded ... [and] it was a lucky man that didn't find himself stretched out in a shallow puddle of almost freezing water."[11] Most of the Carolinians shuddered at their prospects, and many acknowledged "there was no way they could hold back any type of Yankee assault."[12] Colonel William Martin limped along the length of his regiment's trench line, encouraging his troops and apprehensive. Later, he would write, "The works ... which would have been impregnable if defended by an adequate force ... in fact were occupied by a mere skirmish line ... [and] the men were placed five or six feet apart."[13]

The last hours of April 1 and the early moments of the second were filled with foreboding. One soldier noted "the night of April 1 was dark, damp, chilly, and gloomy."[14] Around 1:00 a.m. on April 2, 1865, nervous pickets off to the left of the William Martin's troops began shooting. Martin's Tar Heels could see nothing because of the darkness, but they could hear discomforting sounds which they suspected were Union soldiers. There was no return fire from the Northerners, though a Yankee did call out, pleading for the anxious Confederates to stop shooting, then hollering, "April Fools."[15] In time, the picket fire quieted down, but the Tar Heels listened, and although they said little, they seemed to feel the end was drawing near.[16] What they could not know was Gen. Meade had ordered a full-out assault on Heth's and Wilcox's thinly held fortifications. Forty-two regiments of Union soldiers had crept out of their trenches and slipped into no-man's-land. They then lay in massed formation, silently awaiting the signal to rush forward, ready to strike the seven thinly stretched Confederate regiments of Brig. Gen. James Lane's brigade, and Lt. Col. Eric Erson's North Carolinians—14,000 Northerners against no more than 2,800 Confederates.[17]

A single cannon fired, signaling the attack's commencement a few minutes after 4:30 a.m., just as the first hints of dawn began to lighten the landscape.[18] The Union soldiers leaped up from their muddy positions and surged forward. The point of their massive sledge hammer hit the 1,100 men of Lane's brigade just to the left of the 11th North Carolina. Lane's North Carolinians immediately opened fire, and one Yank wrote, "The Rebel works were marked by jets of flame from their rifles as they fired upon us."[19] Another bluecoat remarked, "Instantly a terrible fire of musketry and artillery was opened upon us."[20] However, within moments the butternut picket line was overrun, and the first wave of Yankees flooded over the breastworks and dropped into the Confederate trenches. One soldier recorded, "A hand to hand fight ensued within the main works in which many gallant officers and men fell killed and wounded."[21]

Lane's regiments were destroyed in less than thirty minutes, with a few survivors scattering to the north, or towards the west where William Martin's Tar Heels waited apprehensively. The Bethel boys were blinded by the darkness but keenly aware of the brutality occurring nearby. Among Lane's troops, the Carolinians in the 28th NC's left wing were scattered and many captured, while in the right wing was able to pull back, pretty much intact, with several companies of men retreating westward, through the trenches, seeking shelter among William Martin's Bethel men.[22]

Once the 28th NC's survivors passed through the 11th NC's riflemen and vanished, panic-stricken, into the predawn gloom, Col. Martin's veteran Tar Heels gripped their muskets and awaited their fate. They could hear a chaos of noise several hundred yards to the east, but there were no sounds of enemy soldiers approaching. Colonel Martin's veterans were not able to know the Union forces which had punctured Lane's brigade were now jumbled together in a muddled mass of confused soldiers. The same darkness which prohibited the Southerners from seeing the bluecoats also prevented the Northern officers from keeping control over their formations. One frustrated Yank officer remarked of this bedlam, "[My men] became bewildered in the darkness and lost their formation, some drifting off ... and we never heard of them afterwards."[23] However, as the approaching sunrise illuminated the battlefield, the Federal officers regained control of their units. A Union officer wrote, "After the main line of the enemy had been carried [my] regiment was reformed and wheeled to the left."[24]

As the eastern horizon brightened even more, the five regiments led by Col. William

Truex were wheeled to form a battle line facing west and straddling the trenches, and then the bluecoats began working their way forward, devouring any Confederates in their way. The commander of the 151st NY, Lt. Col. Charles Bogardes, recorded, "We wheeled to the left, passing down the line of works, driving everything before us."[25] William Martin's riflemen who occupied the 11th North Carolina's far left company could sense the approaching danger, but it was still too dark to see what was coming. One wrote, "Nearer and nearer it came—a storm of thunder and lightning by shells and a hail-storm of rifle bullets."[26] Sergeant Jacob Bartlett (Co. K) noted, "On our left they came with a tremendous yell, while in our front they were advancing without noise. We directed our fire toward the noise, it not being light enough to see those in front. My attention was so much attracted to the left the Yankees were coming over the breastworks, about four rods to my right, before I knew they were there."[27] Another remarked, "The entire line was enveloped in one living cloud of blue coats, whose muskets spurted fire and smoke and death."[28]

Colonel Truex's Yanks crashed into the thin edge of Bethel Regiment Tar Heels, crumbling the Confederates one veteran at a time. A Southern rifleman recalled, "The enemy came on in heavy columns shouting to us as they charged ... [and] they rushed over the low breast-works like an avalanche and ordered us to surrender, [calling out] 'Boys don't shoot, don't shoot, it will only be a needless waste of life and we will overpower you anyway.'"[29] The individual Carolinians, posted five to ten feet apart were forced to make instant, self-preservation decisions. One scribbled, "Every man decided for himself whether to fight, run, or surrender on the spot."[30] Private John Warlick (Co. I) recorded, "They were "as thick as black birds.... A Capt. who was in front of his men with sword drawn whacked me over the head twice; before I realized my situation his men were right at his heels with fixed bayonets, how easily they could have pinioned me to the wooden breast works, the old Capt. ordered me to get over the breast works and get to the rear; well I did too."[31]

A Federal rifleman recalled, "After going a little way into the.... Rebel works, where I saw a lad ... firing at our folks. Jamming on my bayonet I jumped to the works and ordered him to come out. He looked up and had the impudence, with a smile on his face, to say, 'I wish you would let me fire these five cartridges.' I think I swore some and told him I'd put the bayonet right through him unless he came out at once, and he came."[32] Like this Confederate, most of Martin's left-flank riflemen had little choice but to throw down their weapons and surrender; however, some fought back and were quickly shot down. Sergeant Jacob Miller (Co. I) was stabbed in the groin by a bayonet, and Pvt. Andrew Rinck (Co. I) was shot through the right shoulder and throat. He was then carried off and sent to a Federal hospital, where he died of his wounds two weeks later.[33] Others ran. Sgt. Jacob Bartlett (Co. K) wrote, "I looked around and saw that there was no one there except myself and the Yankees. I might not have known that they were there [but] they had been yelling and shooting at the boys who ran before I did. Well, I felt very light and was anxious to see how fast I could run, so I set out for a foot race and when I quit running, I looked back and could not see a Yankee any where."[34]

Those Tar Heels on Col. Martin's left who were able to escape retreated westward and congregated with their comrades in a Confederate artillery emplacement. This position was better fortified than the infantry entrenchments and was armed by six artillery pieces. As Truex's men neared, the Confederates fired a ragged volley, forcing the bluecoats back.³⁵ But Col. William Truex had five regiments to overwhelm the 11th North Carolina, and he quickly sent the 14th NJ to flank their position. The Federals rushed the battery from the north. The commander of the 14th NJ wrote, "The greater portion of my command went into the fort."³⁶ The fighting in the early morning gloom was brief and savage. Pvt. John Land (Co. B) was wounded and captured, Pvt. Jordan Landis (Co. B) shot through both thighs, and William Brogden (Co. C) wounded in the left hip and the eye.³⁷ Another Confederate recalled "he received a scalp wound, the muzzle of the gun being in such close proximity to his head as to blow powder into his face, nearly destroying his eyes and knocking him senseless." The rifleman added, "Of course, he was captured."³⁸ Scores of Carolinians surrendered, while others fled to the west. A Southerner wrote, "The [regiment] collapsed in short order from east to west."³⁹ A Northerner from the 14th NJ recorded, "The loss in the 14th regiment was comparatively small, as the fighting did not continue long."⁴⁰

Thirty-two-year-old Pvt. Andrew Rinck (Co. I) was mortally wounded on April 2, 1865 (Library of Congress).

Once Col. Martin's riflemen had been driven from the artillery battery the Yanks used the captured cannons against the Tar Heels. Colonel Martin noted this fact, writing, "The Federals swung around to the left and swept down the trenches, turning our own artillery against us."⁴¹ More Bethel men fell. Pvt. Joseph Pennix (Co. E) was injured in the left knee and Sgt. William Benbury (Co. F) severely hurt by wounds to the left thigh and right shoulder.⁴² By now, Col. Martin's regiment no longer was a fighting force, and dozens of war-weary Carolinians succumbed to the Federals' demands to ground their weapons and surrender. A Union officer recorded, "Soldiers of the 14th NJ entered the Confederate rifle pits defended by the 11th NC near an unpainted barn ... [and] within a few minutes, Truex's troops rounded up [many] Confederates ... [and] the prisoners were sent to the rear without guards."⁴³ William Martin ordered his survivors to withdraw and they scurried away from their trenches, streaming to the northwest. One wrote, "Our men ... in pitiful small numbers [were] in full retreat."⁴⁴ Another added, "Over fences, across fields, deep

Twenty-three-year-old Sgt. Joseph Earnhardt (Co. A) was captured in the trenches on April 2, 1865 (Clark, 1901).

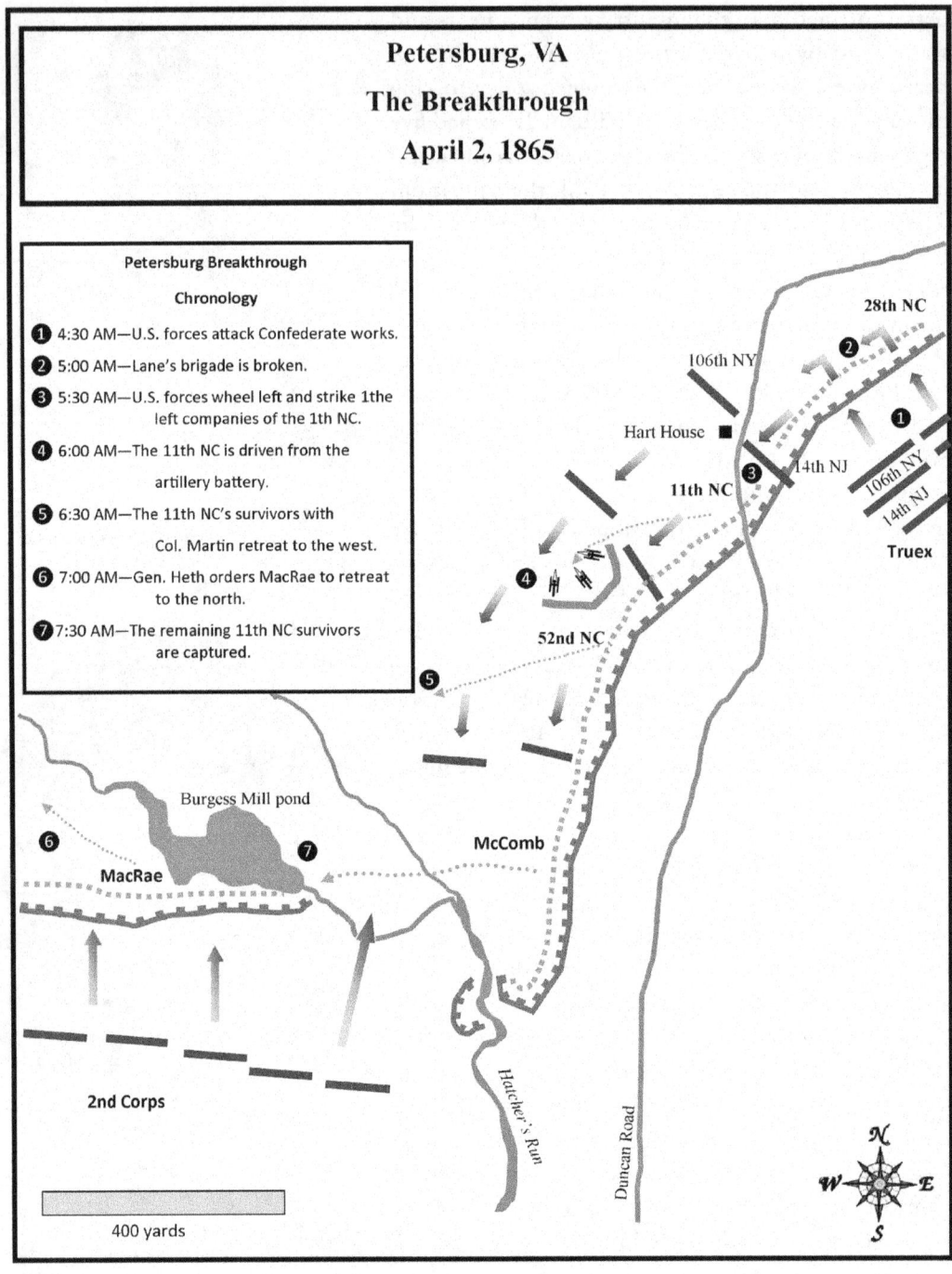

with soft ground from the rains, we made our way as best as we could. To lighten our loads, some of us discarded what we thought we could spare.... I emptied my little [haver]sack of corn meal."[45]

Not everyone was able to withdraw to the northwest; one cluster, including 2nd Lt. James Alexander (Co. E), 3rd Lt. Richard Alexander (Co. A), and Sgt. Maj. Robert Rhodes, drifted west, towards the 52nd NC. There was now enough light for Lt. Col. Eric Erson's Tar Heels to see what was happening, and their commander was in the process of wheeling his left wing to face the advancing bluecoats. Because of this shift, the small collection of Bethel men missed Erson's troops and continued along the trenches, moving west towards where the rest of MacRae's regiments manned the line, beyond the Burgess Mill pond.

By 5:00 a.m., the fighting subsided. Lane's brigade was shattered and gone, and the 11th and 52nd North Carolina regiments had been pushed out of the entrenchments. One Union officer crowed, "[We were] exuberant; in little more than a quarter of an hour [we] had destroyed two entire Confederate brigades and captured almost two miles of trench."[46] The bluecoats scampered about, apprehending gray-uniformed soldiers, cheering the capture of Southern artillery pieces, and securing Confederate battle flags. A Yank noted they "were wild with delight at their success in this grand assault."[47]

It was now light enough for Maj. Gen. Henry Heth to study the disaster occurring in the brigades east of him. He realized his remaining forces were now cut off from the rest of the Confederate army, and he could see Union troops maneuvering to flank his men. There was no longer any reason to maintain a grip on the western section of trenches. Heth ordered his troops to withdraw, and the brigades of McGowan, Scales, and MacRae began filing out of the earthworks and marching northwards on the Clairborne Road.

Around 8:00 a.m., Union forces advanced into Heth's freshly abandoned trenches and came up behind remnants of McComb's Tennesseans, as well as survivors from Lane's brigade and a few men from the 11th and 52nd North Carolina. This collection of butternut soldiers found themselves trapped between bluecoats advancing towards them from the east, while others were arriving from the south and west and the deep waters of the Burgess Mill pond. The Federals closed in on the Southerners. One officer noted, "Portions of Lane's, MacRae's, McComb's, and Nelson's brigades were pinned on the north bank of Hatcher's Run.... A few of the men made their escape by swimming the stream ... [but] the [rest were] entirely surrounded and all the members surrendered."[48] Nine members of the Bethel Regiment were captured by the Yanks, adding to the total of 11th North Carolina soldiers who had been lost in these early morning hours of April 2, 1865. A total of 185 men from Col. Martin's regiment were now prisoners.[49]

Colonel William Martin led a shrunken and very demoralized formation away from the teeming masses of bluecoats frolicking in the Confederate trenches. A messenger arrived, informing Martin to direct his troops to a rendezvous point at Sutherland Station, several miles to the north; Gen. Heth was re-forming his division there. William Martin was not sure how many riflemen he retained. Cpt. James Young (Co. K) had made a quick count, but his totals were shocking—the 11th North Carolina numbered 79 riflemen and officers and thirteen noncombatants.[50]

Major General Henry Heth assigned the brigades to his defensive position as they arrived. He posted McGowan's men to cover the Confederate left, then slotted MacRae's men in the middle, with Scales' troops on their right, and, finally, Cooke's Tar Heels protecting the far right. A butternut officer wrote, "This line ran ... on the edge of a highway ... almost parallel with the South Side Railroad. The right of the Confederate line rested by a large house on the west of the road by which we came ... [and] we were on the summit of a perfectly smooth open ridge, which commanded the slope towards our enemy for six or eight hundred yards."[51] A soldier in the 52nd NC recalled, "We ... selected a position on the brow of a slight hill in an open field and rapidly fortified our line, as well as we could, with bayonets used to break the earth, and such other means as were at command."[52]

At 11:00 a.m., Heth turned to William Cooke's fully intact brigade for skirmishers, and an officer noted, "Cooke deployed a heavy line of skirmishers to cover [their] weak front." This Southerner also recorded, "MacRae sent out his remaining sharpshooters and detailed more men from the line to make a total of 100 skirmishers."[53] General Heth, with his preparations completed, waited the Union formations' next move. He had almost 4,000 men, though a number of riflemen from McComb's and Lane's brigades had lost their weapons in their hurried retreat. A quick report from William McComb let Heth know the Tennessee brigade, which now totaled 400 troops, had muskets for only half its numbers.[54] Lane's surviving officers reported similar problems.

Moments later, Heth was jolted by a message from Gen. Robert E. Lee; Lt. Gen. Ambrose P. Hill was dead and Lee was ordering Heth to return to the Petersburg lines to assume command of the Third Corps. The courier told Henry Heth that A.P. Hill had been killed while trying to reach his battered formations. Hill encountered a small group of Yank soldiers and had been shot at close range. Later, a report would detail Hill's wounds: "The [bullet] struck the uplifted left hand of Hill, took off the thumb in the gauntlet and entered his heart."[55] Henry Heth turned the Sutherland Station defensive line over to Brig. Gen. John Cooke and hustled away to meet with Lee.

It did not take the Union forces long to discover the Southerners' position and a division of bluecoats moved to confront them. This force of Northerners came from the II Corps, men commanded by Brig. Gen. Nelson Miles. They had been part of the fight at Five Forks on April 1, 1865, and had marched through the night to reach where they now stood, a mile south of Cooke and his four shrunken brigades. Though Miles' veterans were tired from their all-night trek, Gen. Miles pushed them aggressively. His first strike came at noon when he sent Col. Henry Madill's brigade forward in an attempt to test the Southerners' resolve. A Confederate rifleman remarked, "[We] rolled a perfect sheet of lead across the open interval, striking down scores of the enemy, opening great gaps in their line."[56] Another rifleman, this one in the 52nd NC, added, "The enemy's advance was met with a well-delivered and telling volley from our rifles."[57] Colonel Madill fell, badly wounded, and after a few brief but punishing minutes, his New Yorkers turned and ran, having suffered over one hundred casualties.[58]

General Miles placed Col. Clinton MacDougal in charge of Madill's men and ordered the new brigade commander to restore order among the New Yorkers. Miles then maneuvered his brigades for a second assault. At 12:30 p.m., Miles' next attack began, when he sent forward MacDougal's re-formed troops and Col. Robert Nugent's brigade. These men went forward sullenly, with one Yank noting, "All were impressed by the uselessness of the charge."[59] The Confederates waited until the bluecoats got within range and then, as one rifleman recorded, "We opened upon them at three or four hundred yards and tore fearful rents in their line, covering the ground with dead and dying, and set forth, above all the roar of artillery and musketry, ringing peals of cheers."[60] The Union regiments staggered

17. The End: April 1865

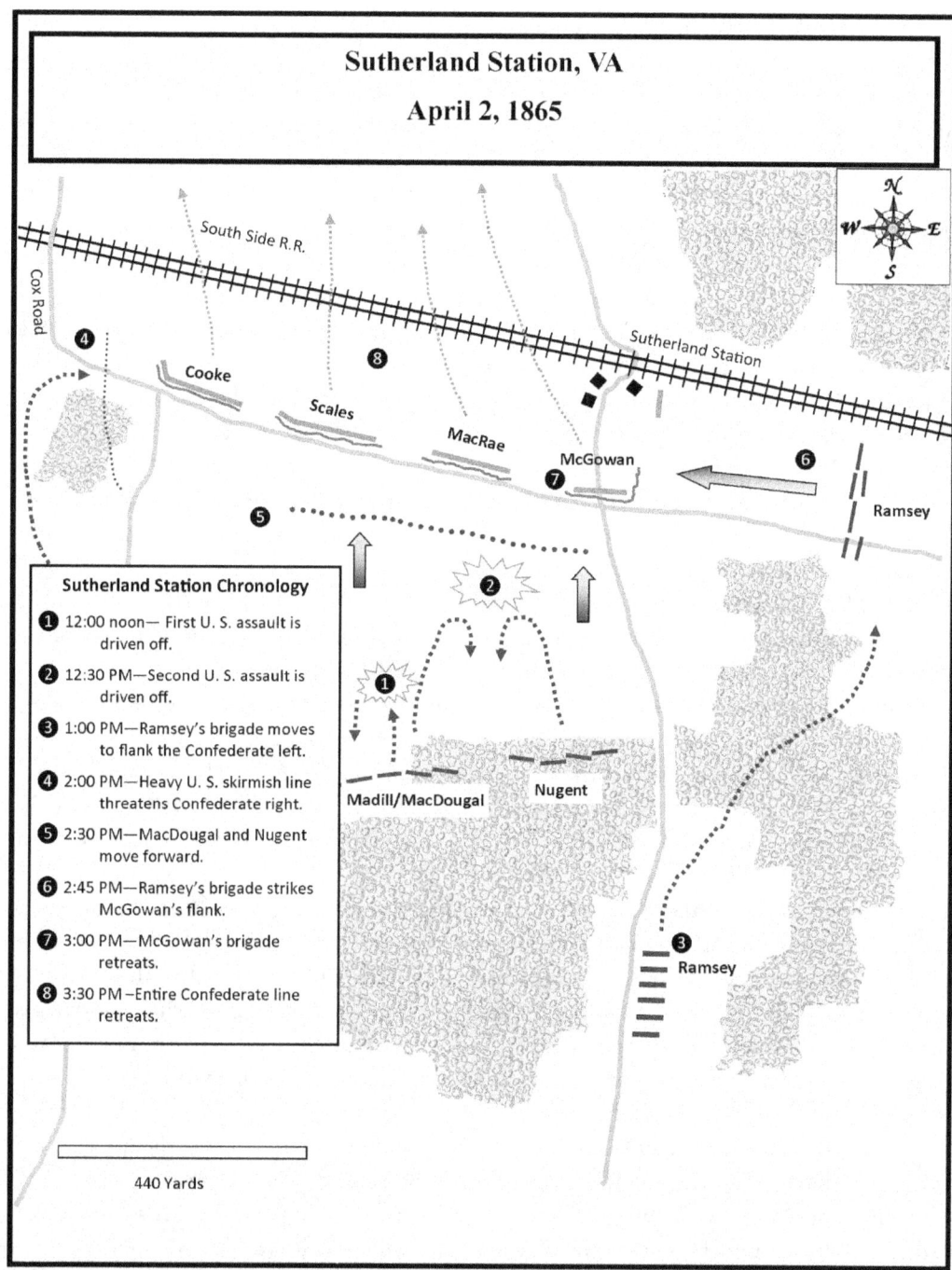

and then halted, with scores of soldiers being killed and wounded. A Tar Heel remarked, "Again they retreated with great loss."[61]

General Miles refused to be beaten by Cooke's men. After all, Nelson Miles' four brigades numbered over 8,000 troops; he had more than twice as many rifles as what faced him. However, Miles had also learned his men could not successfully defeat these Confederates by overrunning them with frontal assaults; he had to come up with a different plan. Just after 2:00 p.m., the Northern officer sent forward a thick screen of skirmishers to his left, overlapping Cooke's brigade and threatening to come around behind the Confederates' unprotected right flank. Brigadier General John Cooke tried to shift a few companies to bolster this flank, which held all the reserves he had available. Meanwhile, Nelson Miles sent his fourth brigade, this one led by Col. John Ramsey, around to the right with the intent of striking the Confederate left flank. Ramsey's regiments, their movements screened by a ridge, hustled along a shallow ravine, through some woods and then massed for the attack about 500 yards away from the gray formation's exposed left flank.

The third assault on the Sutherland Station defenses began around 2:30 p.m., when Ramsey's troops emerged from behind their hiding places and surged towards the Confederate line. Nelson Miles also sent MacDougal's and Nugent's brigades forward; suddenly the Northerners were hitting the Confederate line from the east and the south, and threatening from the west. One shocked Southerner noted, "In overwhelming force the blue columns of the enemy were discovered advancing from all directions."[62] McGowan's South Carolinians panicked and many fell back, leaving their more stalwart brothers unsupported to watch as the Yankee mass approached. One wrote, "It was ... too late to maneuver ... [so] we lay still and awaited the awful final."[63]

The Confederate line shivered. A butternut soldier recalled, "The impetuosity of the Federals was absolutely irresistible.... Some [men] were for resisting to the last, some advised immediate flight, [and] some gave up the cause and counseled unconditional surrender."[64] The Yanks raced forward, encouraged by the Confederates' hesitant resistance. A Northerner bragged, "[We] were like a pack of wolves turned loose."[65] A Tar Heel wrote "the fight was severe."[66] Federal lead thudded among Col. Martin's veterans. Pvt. John Butler (Co. D) suffered a ball through his right thigh, and Pvt. James Smith's (Co. F) foot was shattered by a minié bullet.[67] Then the Union riflemen were deep within the killing zone and the Confederates, as one recalled, exhibited "panic, despair, and confusion."[68] The Southerners' resolve collapsed, causing one elated Northerner to write, "We attacked his left ... with complete success, sweeping down inside the breastworks."[69] Brigadier General William MacRae recorded, "When McGowan ... gave way in confusion, I ordered up my sharpshooters to the support of his left, but they arrived too late to effect anything. In a few minutes Scales' brigade on my right gave way, leaving me alone to confront the enemy with 280 men.... At length [I] gave the order to fall back."[70]

MacRae's Tar Heels abandoned their position, the men scurrying north and west. But the Carolinians still had fight left in them; they turned and fired several well-placed volleys into the Yanks, convincing the bluecoats not to follow. The shaken Carolinians fled, scattering as they ran. One gray-uniformed soldier would later scribble, "The Confederacy was considered 'gone up' and every man felt it his duty, as well as his privilege, to save himself."[71] Another recalled, "We fled to the cover of woods and distance, and sought the unfriendly banks of the Appomattox."[72] Unfortunately, not all of Col. Martin's veterans got away; five were captured.[73]

When the fleeing Carolinians reached the Appomattox River they realized they could not cross the water without a boat. And regrettably, since MacRae's veterans had stopped to fire upon their pursuers several times, other Confederates had gotten to the river first and stolen all the boats. Frustratingly, the Tar Heels could see these emptied crafts sitting on the opposite bank, floating uselessly. Colonel Martin, seeing no way across the Appomattox, turned towards the west and led his small band of followers in that direction. His men made their way several miles before noticing the Yankees were not pursuing them. One wrote, "So we wandered—strung along the river bank for miles, straggling through brush and brier ... pressing forward to ... points undetermined in our minds."[74] Later that evening, Sgt. Jacob Bartlett (Co. K) noted, "[He] stopped ... at a house along the road and asked for food, as he had not eaten all day. A house servant offered him a piece of hoe cake and a slice of ham, which he ate on the run."[75] Then, once darkness settled over the countryside, Col. William Martin's band of veterans found a secluded area and the exhausted men spread out on the ground and slept. Martin gazed at the wreck that remained of his regiment; the events of this past day had destroyed the 11th North Carolina Infantry.

The next morning, April 3, 1865, the Bethel men scrounged for rations but could find very little to eat. Then they fell into marching order, completely out of habit, and followed their colonel westward, along the southern banks of the Appomattox River. Meanwhile, back in the Petersburg trenches, over two dozen of Col. Martin's 11th North Carolinians who had been separated from the regiment and had been able to hide or elude the Union troops for another twenty-four hours were caught and sent to the prison pens created for all the Confederates captured during the breakthrough.[76]

Strangely, for William Martin's survivors, for all of April 3, 1865, there were no Union troops to bother them. Martin's troopers relished the freedom of being away from the dangers and hideous smells of the Petersburg trenches. But they also knew their army had been badly defeated. One stunned soldier recorded, "There was little military bearing in the column straggling west ... [and] when a soldier became weary, he fell out, ate his scanty rations—if indeed he had any—rested, rose and resumed the march when his inclination dictated."[78] Finally, later that afternoon, the Tar Heels found a way to cross the Appomattox and were able to join the rest of the shattered Confederate army drifting west.[79]

11th North Carolina Casualties[77]
April 2–3, 1865

Unit	Commander	Total
F & S	Col. William Martin	2
Co. A	2nd Lt. William Taylor	30
Co. B	Cpt. Thomas Parks	34
Co. C	Cpt. Edward Outlaw	11
Co. D	1st Sgt. William Womack	16
Co. E	2nd Lt. James Alexander	15
Co. F	Sgt. William Benbury	15
Co. G	Cpt. John Freeland	29
Co. H	1st Lt. Robert Lowrie	27
Co. I	1st Sgt. John Ramseur	27
Co. K	1st Sgt. Jacob Bartlett	12
	Non Combatants	7
Total		223

For a complete listing of the casualties from the fighting on April 2, 1865, see Appendix A, Appomattox Campaign Casualties.

On April 4, 1865, the Confederates arose from their bivouac near sunrise and fell into a loose column. An officer wrote, "Most of them were hungry, but not all of those who marched on empty stomachs were without hope. The hungrier they were, the brighter seemed the prospect of the rations ... they were [told were] at Amelia Court House, their objective for the day."[80] Colonel William Martin limped along with his shriveled force, continually prompting his remaining leaders to keep track of their comrades and not lose any as the column shuffled westward.

General William MacRae's Confederates reached Amelia Court House around 4:00 p.m., only to learn there were no rations waiting for them.[81] A Southerner noted, "At last the van approached the village of Amelia Court House. The columns were halted on the road.... There was much stir among commissaries and quartermasters. Hours passed. No rations were issued."[82] A rifleman in the 52nd NC wrote, "We rested here ... sending out foraging parties for supplies, which resulted in—nothing."[83] Then, sounds of musketry were heard from the south, and MacRae's Carolinians and William McComb's Tennesseans were sent to reinforce the Confederate position. An officer remarked, "They were ordered to form a battle line outside town. The veterans quickly threw up light breastworks and then they waited for the Yanks to attack. The Union cavalry did not have infantry support, so they withdrew."[84] Not long afterwards, darkness descended upon the famished Confederates and they bedded down in the open fields near Amelia Court House, though one rifleman noted, "An indescribable sadness weighed upon us."[85]

The men awoke the next morning, many having now gone at least forty-eight hours without food. An officer recorded, "A gray 5th of April and a slow spring drizzle added to the misery of the thousands who slept in the fields and the woods."[86] General Lee called his senior officers together and, much to Maj. Gen. Henry Heth's dismay, disbanded the Third Corps, which Heth had been leading, and assigned his men to Lt. Gen. James Longstreet's First Corps.[87] Then Lee gave orders for the army to march toward Burkeville, letting everyone know he believed they would encounter one of the provision trains which had been ordered. The army moved out at 1:00 p.m., with Ewell's Second Corps in advance, followed by Longstreet's men, with the divisions of Heth and Wilcox following Fields, Mahone, and Pickett.[88]

Later that afternoon Union cavalry raced ahead of Lee's army and struck some of Ewell's brigades. Colonel Martin's Tar Heels could hear the heavy skirmishing occurring at the head of the column. One rifleman noted, "The procession halted and the men fell to the roadside, footsore and famished."[89] Another reported, "We could see smoke west of us, which was said to be caused by the burning of Confederate wagons by the enemy ... [and] we remained stationary until just before dark."[90] General Lee then decided his forces needed to march through the night to get back ahead of the Yankees. A Confederate recorded they "made a night march around the dug-in Union army at Jetersville, and head[ed] to Farmville where [Lee] was informed that 80,000 rations would be waiting for him."[91]

The starving soldiers were ordered to march. A rifleman remarked, "Once the sun went down strict orders came for an absolutely silent march.... We soon came into sight of the bivouac fires of the enemy ... [and] we went by a wide detour around them."[92] The weary Southerners quietly stumbled past the unsuspecting Federals, moving slowly during the dark hours. One Confederate recorded, "The troops ... dragged themselves to Deatonsville [from Jetersville, 5 1/2 miles] ...through a night that grew black as the hours passed ... [and] the men groped their way alongside an endless stream of [empty ration] wagons. " This soldier continued: "Drowsiness and nervousness were worse than were hunger and exhaustion ... [and] men staggered as if they were drunk." He finished his writing, noting, "Every few minutes, half-dead veterans would leave the column and lie down in despair."[93] Sadly, even though the troops marched all night long, they covered only seven miles, not enough to escape the Union army's grasp.

The next day, April 6, 1865, the Confederates continued to shuffle in a northwest direction, with Longstreet's men now leading the way. However, the night's march had strung out the column for miles, enabling empty spaces to appear between the various divisions. William MacRae's fatigued men followed in line and crossed over Sayler's Creek, heading for Rice's Station on the Southside Railroad. Union cavalry struck the head of the column, forcing the long line of riflemen to halt. Bluecoated horsemen then swept down, along the ranks, skirmishing with small groups of butternut soldiers thrown out to protect the Confederate flanks. A Carolinian wrote, "Longstreet put MacRae's men in the second line ... and our skirmish line was felt."[94] In this brief exchange of infantry muskets and cavalry carbines, Pvt. Gaston Stoeks (Co. C) was wounded in the left shoulder.[95] Then, the bluecoats backed off and a rifleman recalled "most of us snatched some of the repose so necessary to us and so long denied."[96]

The rest of Lee's army did not fare as well. Ewell's Corps became separated from Longstreet's column and ran into a strong Federal force near Sayler's Creek. By the time the fighting had ended, 7,000 battle-weary Confederates surrendered, demolishing most of Ewell's entire corps. General Lee, upon hearing the news of Ewell's defeat, wrote "that half of our Army is destroyed."[97] Lee called his remaining senior officers together, and as a freezing rain turned to snow flurries he gave the order for another night march.

The worn-out and starving Confederates stumbled through another night of movement. The roads turned to mush, hampering the soldiers' progress, and miring the mud-encrusted wheels of wagons and caissons. Colonel Martin's men were detailed to help the wagons stuck in the mud, a task completely exhausting the riflemen.[98] By daybreak, the mud-caked and dog-tired Bethel men were incapable of helping another stalled vehicle. All that the 11th North Carolina soldiers wanted to do was lie down and sleep. But they were ordered to continue their march to Farmville, where, surprisingly, there was some food. An excited Tar Heel exclaimed, "Passing through Farmville on the 7th our men snatched some rations from a government commissary store."[99]

On April 7, 1865, Longstreet formed his divisions into a defensive line three miles north of Farmville. Here, William MacRae's tired riflemen dug entrenchments near the Cumberland church as he posted skirmishers. Then the rest of the sleep-deprived men slumped behind their breastworks and dozed. They could not go much farther. Colonel Martin took a head count and determined his small band of comrades had decreased by eight, as exhausted and sick riflemen had dropped by the roadside, unable to march another step.[100] William Martin met with his remaining captains, Thomas Parks (Co. B), Edward Outlaw (Co. C), John Freeland (Co. G), and James Young (Co. K), and they discussed their prospects. Lee's army was finished; it was just a matter of a few days before the Federals captured or killed them all. William Martin wrote, "On the night of the 7th, in a consultation of the officers of the Eleventh Regiment, Captain Outlaw, of Company C, was advised to take charge of the flag and see that it was not lost. It was removed from the staff."[101] Edward Outlaw, a young teacher from Windsor, North Carolina, had been given charge of the regiment's colors because of his fierce and resolute reputation. Captain Outlaw insisted upon carrying a rifle, something few officers did, and he was a crack shot, often doing quite well at regimental target-shooting competitions against the best sharpshooters in the unit. As one rifleman noted, Edward Outlaw "had a blood thirsty streak.... He once confronted a Union soldier face to face when he realized that he was out of percussion caps. He bluffed the enemy soldier and demanded that the northerner hand over his ammunition pouch. Outlaw took out a cap, loaded his rifle, then shot the unsuspecting soldier."[102]

That evening, once the sun set, General Lee put his army into motion again, sending his exhausted legions out onto their third straight night march. A completely worn-out rifleman later wrote, "We toiled on wearily, and almost hopelessly."[103] Their new destination was the Appomattox train station, where, as one soldier hoped, "supply trains awaited them."[104] Another exhausted Confederate added, "I would go to sleep for a second only, to start up the next second to save myself, a most agonizing feeling and not restful."[105]

Twenty-three-year-old Cpt. Edward Outlaw (Co. C) was given the responsibility of hiding the regimental flag on April 7, 1865. The flag would never be unfurled again (Clark, 1901).

General Lee's half-awake soldiers shuffled forward all night long, and by late afternoon on April 8, 1865, they had traveled to within four miles of Appomattox Court House. Lee's hope of escaping the Union cavalry's clutches by night marches had not worked; instead, bluecoated cavalry squadrons commanded by Maj. Gen. George Custer had already reached the Appomattox train station and captured the Confederate supply train. General Lee's vanguard moved forward to Appomattox and brushed up against the Northerners while Longstreet's brigades were centered near the New Hope Church, three miles to the northeast. Since Union troops continued to close in on Longstreet's rear formations, he ordered all his units to dig in. A Tar Heel wrote, "MacRae's men ... had taken a position in the rear of Longstreet's command, now the rear of Lee's army."[106] Colonel William Martin positioned his seventy riflemen and officers and wrote, "[We] formed in a triangle ... the rear angle resting on the road ... the men six feet apart."[107] Martin then sent out a thin screen of pickets, who soon found themselves under fire from aggressive Yank skirmishers. Before the Tar Heels could retreat to the safety of their breastworks, Pvt. William Warlick (Co. B) was killed by a bullet.[108] He would be the last Bethel Regiment soldier to be killed in combat, ending a long line of dead commenced by Pvt. Henry Wyatt nearly four years earlier.

The next morning, April 9, 1865, Col. Martin's officers took roll. The 11th North Carolina regiment consisted of 64 officers and men and 14 noncombatants.[109] William Martin studied his men as they slumped against their fortifications' earthen walls; they were, as one rifleman noted, "haggard, [and their] steps slow and unsteady." He added, "A horrible calm brooded over us."[110] Then, MacRae received orders to hurry his men to support the expected fight near Appomattox Court House, and his war-weary survivors "moved up to near the court house ... expecting a battle. They filed to the right of the stage road."[111] Another wrote, "We moved towards Appomattox. The way was rugged and beset with stragglers ... so that we made slow progress."[112]

Earlier in the day Maj. Gen. John Gordon's ragged brigades had attempted to push the bluecoats out of the way and create an exit route for Lee's troops. An officer recorded, "Gordon assembled his men at the edge of the village ... [and] at dawn the Confederate battle line moved forward and encountered elements of Crooke's cavalry. These were easily pushed back but then, along a far ridge, Union infantry were seen forming in battle line.... Gordon's men realized that their escape route was sealed off so they began to fall back to the village."[114] Now, Gordon's riflemen were going to attempt a second assault, only this time reinforced by Heth's survivors.

11th North Carolina Muster[113]
April 9, 1865

Unit	Commander	Total
F & S	Col. William J. Martin	1
Co. A	2nd Lt. William Taylor	6
Co. B	Cpt. Thomas Parks	7
Co. C	Cpt. Edward Outlaw	2
Co. D	1st Sgt. William Womack	7
Co. E	1st Sgt. John McDonald	8
Co. F	Pvt. Jesse Bogue	1
Co. G	Cpt. John Freeland	5
Co. H	1st Lt. Robert Lowrie	9
Co. I	Cpl. John Aderholdt	12
Co. K	Cpt. James Young	6
Total		64

General MacRae ordered his five small regiments forward, a force of riflemen numbering barely 300 hungry and exhausted Carolinians. These veterans pressed forward, their gaunt faces grim with determination. One noted, "We bore rapidly towards the south of town towards the firing ... [and] when we reached the base of the ridge on whose crest the skirmishing was heard we were expecting to be thrown into the battle."[115] Then, as a Tar Heel in the 47th NC described it, "MacRae commanded, 'Halt.'"[116] Another soldier added, "The brigade was faced about and ordered back in the direction it had come. The firing ceased."[117] This strange action was followed by another, described by the 47th NC Tar Heel: "[MacRae] dismounted and lay down, and we too, began to lay down."[118]

Colonel William Martin studied his brigade commander as the general reclined, eyes closed and refusing to speak with anyone. Most of Martin's Tar Heels, though they were as puzzled as their colonel, rested or napped. A Confederate rifleman recalled "everyone wanted to know what was going on ... [and] officers stood about, talking solemnly."[119] Soon, messengers galloped back and forth, officers with white flags appeared, and, most important for the veteran infantrymen, the shooting stopped. Rumors immediately swept through the Confederates like a hurricane; soldiers had seen General Lee riding out to meet with the Yankees.

A little after 3:30 p.m. a rider approached Brig. Gen. William MacRae and, bowing his head the messenger murmured, "The war is over, General Lee had surrendered the army."[120] The Tar Heels clustered together, shocked, crushed, numb, saying little, some sobbing, while others just stood rigidly. One Confederate moaned, "My God, that I should have lived to see this! ... I did not think I should live till this day."[121] Colonel Martin ordered his sergeants to take charge of the regiment and keep the men together. He then called to his captains. William Martin wrote, "When General Lee rode to the front through the lines to meet General Grant ... the officers present with the regiment at once retired to a secluded thicket, and raking up a pile of twigs and leaves, committed the flag to the flames. Before burning it, Captains Edward Outlaw and James M. Young tore out pieces of each color."[122] The 11th North Carolina's battle flag no longer existed, and when the officers returned to the regiment's small band of survivors, every veteran agreed their colors would never be surrendered to the Northerners. Captain Outlaw (Co. C) recorded, "Sincere tears have often been shed around funeral pyres, but never more bitter and sorrowful tears bedewed any ashes than were shed over their flag."[123] James Young and Edward Outlaw each took home tiny patches of the formation's cherished banner and many years later both men would be buried with those beloved cloth fragments.

The Army of Northern Virginia was no longer a fighting force; now it was a vast mob of extremely hungry and armed men. Generals Lee and Grant quickly agreed that Federal rations would be supplied to the famished Southerners. As one officer recorded, "During the late afternoon, commissary wagons entered the Confederate camps from the Union lines. Nothing except bread was issued to some commands that evening ... but whatever the food, it was devoured ravenously and gratefully."[124] That evening, even though the war was over, guards were posted, but these pickets looked out over the darkened landscape, thinking not about lurking dangers but rather how to get home.

On April 10, 1865, dawn lightened the peaceful countryside, accompanied by a cold drizzle. A Confederate wrote, "[This day] brought rain, more food, and the refreshment that came from the first long, untroubled night of sleep that some of the troops had been allowed since April 3.... For the men, there was nothing to do except to hope for more rations, to plan the journey home and to wait for the issuance of paroles." He then added, "When we learned that we should be paroled, and go to our homes unmolested, the relief was unbounded."[125]

Two days later, on April 12, 1865, the Confederates formally stacked their rifles and turned their expectations to peace. One Southern described the ceremony: "The morning ... was chilly and gray but without the rain that had fallen almost continuously since the surrender.... The men stepped forward four paces across the road and stacked arms. Off came the cartridge boxes. In a moment these were hanging from the muskets.... Silence held…. We did not even look into each other's faces. They turned; they came back into the road, they marched ahead past the Court House. It was over."[126] For Colonel William Martin's 11th North Carolina, 74 veterans marched forward, stacked their weapons, suspended the banner-less flagstaff between the rifle stacks, and then, without a word, walked away.[127]

The next day, April 13, 1865, each Tar Heel began his plan for getting home. One wrote, "Every man looked out for himself."[128] Another recalled "when paroled we filled our haversacks with cheese and crackers and turned our faces [toward] home."[129] The trek back to North Carolina commenced that afternoon. One Tar Heel later wrote, "The same constancy and devotion to their country which had sustained them amid battle and strife unparalleled, nerved them to face courageously this dark time of defeat and disappoint-

Twenty-three-year-old Cpl. James Alexander (Co. A) marched in the surrender ceremony on April 12, 1865 (Library of Congress).

ment and to do their best to retrieve the widespread ruin of their beloved South."[130] It must also be remembered these resolute and courageous Carolinians were young men. Their passion and energy would be needed to rebuild the South. However, on this day, the youthful ex-soldiers thought about home and the girls they had been missing for the past four years. One such beau scribbled to his girl, "You must prepare for a jolly time when I come home…. I am anticipating a nice time with you!"[131] The war was over, the boys were going home.

11th North Carolina Infantry Casualties

1st North Carolina—Bethel Church, VA, June 10, 1861
7 = 1 Killed, 6 Wounded

Unit	Rank	Name	Remarks
F & S	1st Lt.	Ratchford, J. W.	Wounded: "Contusion in forehead."
Co. A	Pvt.	Rodgers, Council	Severely wounded: Discharged, 7/11/1861.
Co. A	Pvt.	Williams, Charles	Severely wounded: Returned to ranks after short stay in hospital.
Co. A	Pvt.	Wyatt, Henry	Mortally wounded: Died 5 hours later in Yorktown.
Co. D	Pvt.	Patterson, Samuel	Slightly wounded: Returned to ranks immediately.
Co. G	Pvt.	Poteat, Peter	Slightly wounded: Returned to ranks immediately.
Co. K	Pvt.	White, William	Wounded; Returned to ranks soon after.

11th North Carolina—Deaths Due to Sickness
161 Deaths

Date	Name	Unit	Rank	Cause of Death
3/6/62	Walker, J. H.	Co. E	Pvt.	Died of disease at Raleigh, NC
3/16/62	Green, Samuel	Co. F	Pvt.	Died of meningitis at Raleigh, NC
3/23/62	Stewart, Thaddeus C.	Co. C	Pvt.	Died of brain fever at Raleigh, NC
3/26/62	Castellaw, James C.	Co. C	Pvt.	Died of disease at Raleigh, NC
4/6/62	Pearson, Forest	Co. G	Pvt.	Died of disease at Raleigh, NC
4/8/62	Patton, George	Co. B	Pvt.	Died of typhoid fever at Raleigh, NC
4/9/62	Patton, John	Co. B	Pvt.	Died of typhoid fever at Raleigh, NC
4/13/62	Elliott, Charles W.	Co. F	Pvt.	Died of disease at Raleigh, NC
4/14/62	Whisenhunt, Alexander	Co. D	Pvt.	Died of pneumonia at Raleigh, NC
4/15/62	Lloyd, John W.	Co. G	Pvt.	Died of meningitis & fever at Raleigh, NC
4/18/62	Blakely, Monroe	Co. A	Pvt.	Died of disease at Raleigh, NC
4/18/62	Whisenhunt, Stanhope	Co. D	Pvt.	Died of disease at Raleigh, NC
4/20/62	Creasemon, Joseph	Co. A	Pvt.	Died of disease at Raleigh, NC
4/20/62	Jenkins, Doctrine	Co. C	Pvt.	Died of pneumonia & measles at Raleigh, NC
4/20/62	Williams, John A.	Co. B	Pvt.	Died of pneumonia at Raleigh, NC
4/22/62	Copeland, William D.	Co. C	Pvt.	Died of disease at Raleigh, NC
4/22/62	Whisenhunt, James	Co. D	Pvt.	Died of disease at Raleigh, NC
4/24/62	Askew, Enos	Co. F	Pvt.	Died of disease at home in Hertford Co., NC
4/26/62	Jernigan, Samuel	Co. C	Pvt.	Died of disease at Raleigh, NC

Date	Name	Unit	Rank	Cause of Death
5/1/62	Haynes, R. Workman	Co. I	Pvt.	Died of measles at Raleigh, NC
5/2/62	Morris, Archibald G	Co. K	Pvt.	Died of pneumonia & typhoid fever at Raleigh, NC
5/5/62	Earnhart, William	Co. D	Pvt.	Died of bronchitis at Raleigh, NC
5/5/62	Myers, Thomas L.	Co. C.	Pvt.	Died of disease at Raleigh, NC
5/13/62	Dail, Joshua	Co. F	Pvt.	Died of measles at Raleigh, NC
5/18/62	Griffin, George	Co. E	Pvt.	Died of disease at Wilmington, NC
5/21/62	Casper, Justin	Co. C	Pvt.	Died of disease at Raleigh, NC
6/8/62	Causby, John N.	Co. D	Cpl.	Died of disease at Wilmington, NC
6/11/62	Keller, David	Co. B	Pvt.	Died of diarrhea & measles at Wilmington, NC
6/13/62	Harbison, Tolbert	Co. B	Pvt.	Died of disease at Wilmington, NC
6/16/62	Moore, Levi	Co. F	Pvt.	Died of disease at Wilmington, NC
6/18/62	Morgan, John	Co. B	Pvt.	Died of disease at Wilmington, NC
6/25/62	Puett, John W.	Co. B	Pvt.	Died of disease at Wilmington, NC
6/27/62	Clark, Benjamin A.	Co. D	Mus.	Died of typhoid fever at Wilmington, NC
7/2/62	Allran, John P.	Co. I	Pvt.	Died of disease at Wilmington, NC
7/3/62	Watts, James I.	Co. I	Pvt.	Died of typhoid fever at Wilmington, NC
7/6/62	Robinson, Henry D.	Co. F	Pvt.	Died of typhoid fever at Wilmington, NC
7/9/62	Powell, Kemp W.	Co. D	Pvt.	Died of remittent fever at Wilmington, NC
7/11/62	Lowrie, Patrick	F & S	QMstr.	Died of disease at Wilmington, NC
7/12/62	Cole, George	Co. G	Pvt.	Died of typhoid fever at Wilmington, NC
7/12/62	Kerr, Rufus D.	Co. H	Pvt.	Died of typhoid fever at Wilmington, NC
7/12/62	Nichols, John S.	Co. E	CPT.	Died of disease on train from Wilmington, NC
7/15/62	Etters, James H.	Co. H	Pvt.	Died of disease at home in Mecklenburg Co., NC
7/16/62	Burgess, Henry T.	Co. G	Pvt.	Died of disease at home in Orange Co., NC
7/17/62	Carpenter, Albert	Co. I	Pvt.	Died of typhoid fever at Wilmington, NC
7/19/62	Pearson, Edward	Co. G	Pvt.	Died of fever at Wilmington, NC
7/21/62	Hathcock, Carney	Co. G	Pvt.	Died of typhoid fever at Wilmington, NC
7/21/62	Short, William W.	Co. B	Pvt.	Died of febris remittent at Wilmington, NC
7/25/62	Mizell, John N.	Co. C	Pvt.	Died of typhoid fever at Wilmington, NC
7/29/62	Beach, James C.	Co. D	Pvt.	Died of disease at Wilmington, NC
7/29/62	Davis, Alfred	Co. C	Pvt.	Died of disease at Wilmington, NC
7/30/62	Hood, James C.	Co. D	Pvt.	Died of disease at Wilmington, NC
7/30/62	McQuay, Seaborn	Co. E	Pvt.	Died of disease at Wilmington, NC
7/31/62	Hudspeth, Lewis	Co. A	Pvt.	Died of pneumonia at Wilmington, NC
8/6/62	McLure, James D.	Co. E	Pvt.	Died of continued fever at Wilmington, NC
8/7/62	Powell, William H.	Co. F	Pvt.	Died of typhoid fever at Wilmington, NC
8/8/62	Byrum, James	Co. A	Pvt.	Died of typhoid fever at Wilmington, NC
8/9/62	Boyce, Charles B.	Co. H	2nd Lt.	Died of disease at home in Mecklenburg Co., NC
8/10/62	Hartline, George H.	Co. E	Pvt.	Died of disease at Wilmington, NC
8/10/62	Hoggard, William	Co. C	Pvt.	Died of gonorrhea at Wilmington, NC
8/12/62	Havner, Michael	Co. I	Pvt.	Died of disease at Wilmington, NC
8/20/62	Brown, John A.	Co. I	Pvt.	Died of fever at Wilmington, NC
8/20/62	White, Riddick	Co. C	Pvt.	Died of continued fever at Wilmington, NC
8/21/62	Havner, Daniel	Co. I	Pvt.	Died of fever at home at Lincolnton, NC
8/22/62	Means, John S.	Co. E	Cpl.	Died of fever at Wilmington, NC
8/23/62	Gregory, Lemuel D.	Co. C	Pvt.	Died of typhoid fever at Wilmington, NC
9/1/62	Greer, Z. B.	Co. H	Pvt.	Died of typhoid fever at Wilmington, NC
9/1/62	Wood, John H.	Co. I	Pvt.	Died of typhoid fever at Wilmington, NC
9/16/62	Jennings, James R.	Co. G	CPT.	Died of yellow fever on train from Wilmington
9/24/62	Smith, Thomas	Co. K	Pvt.	Died of typhoid fever at Wilmington, NC
10/20/62	Clark, W. A.	Co. H	Pvt.	Died of disease at home in Charlotte, NC
10/20/62	Davis, Edward	Co. C	Pvt.	Died of ulcers at Weldon, NC
10/21/62	Welch, William B.	Co. F	Pvt.	Died of erysipelas at Petersburg, VA
10/23/62	Gilbert, J. Frank	Co. I	Pvt.	Died of yellow fever at Wilmington, NC
10/24/62	Harris, Abel F.	Co. K	Sgt.	Died of continued fever at Petersburg, VA

Date	Name	Unit	Rank	Cause of Death
10/29/62	Hudson, John W.	Co. F	Pvt.	Died of pneumonia at Franklin, VA
11/15/62	Ashley, Lee T.	Co. H	Pvt.	Died of disease at home in Mecklenburg Co., NC
11/21/62	Taylor, William H.	Co. C	Pvt.	Died of pneumonia at Franklin, VA
11/21/62	Young, James H.	Co. H	Pvt.	Died of disease at Richmond, VA
11/26/62	Ballard, Thomas J.	Co. I	Pvt.	Died of disease at Goldsboro, NC
12/15/62	Shrum, J. Frank	Co. I	Pvt.	Died of pneumonia at Petersburg, VA
12/16/62	Smith, John B.	Co. K	Pvt.	Died of pneumonia at Richmond, VA
12/20/62	Baker, Joseph	Co. K	Pvt.	Died of fever at home in Buncombe Co., NC
1/10/63	Boyles, Frank J.	Co. I	Pvt.	Died of pneumonia at Raleigh, NC
1/18/63	Hoggard, William M.	Co. C	Sgt.	Died of "erysipelas" at Weldon, NC
1/19/63	Goodwin, Eli	Co. F	Pvt.	Died of disease at Weldon, NC
1/23/63	Ratchford, Ezekiel C.	Co. A	Pvt.	Died of erysipelas at Weldon, NC
1/24/63	Ross, Robert A.	Co. H	Pvt.	Died of pneumonia at home at Charlotte, NC
1/27/63	Cates, William B.	Co. G	Pvt.	Died of disease at Raleigh, NC
1/28/63	Cates, William	Co. G	Pvt.	Died of typhoid fever at Raleigh, NC
2/10/63	Bazemore, William J.	Co. C	Pvt.	Died of disease at Weldon, NC
2/24/63	Adams, Baird	Co. K	Pvt.	Died of erysipelas at Weldon, VA
4/3/63	Boyce, Kenny	Co. F	Pvt.	Died of typhoid fever at Raleigh, NC
5/10/63	Christenbery, Caleb E.	Co. H	Pvt.	Died of pleuritic at Goldsboro, NC
5/20/63	Turner, Richard	Co. G	Pvt.	Died of disease at Richmond, VA
6/6/63	Whisenhunt, Wilburn	Co. D	Pvt.	Died of anemia at Raleigh, NC
6/26/63	Abernathy, Ezekial	Co. H	Pvt.	Died of disease at home in Mecklenburg Co., NC
6/27/63	Backus, Thomas	Co. F	Pvt.	Died of meningitis at Danville, VA
6/30/63	Nisbet, John G.	Co. E	Pvt.	Died of disease at home in Lancaster Co., SC
7/15/63	Etters, James H.	Co. H	Pvt.	Died of disease at home in Charlotte, NC
7/18/63	Anthony, Philip B.	Co. B	Pvt.	Died of typhoid fever at Harrisonburg, VA
8/1/63	Crouch, Peyton	Co. B	Pvt.	Died of pneumonia at Staunton, VA
8/2/63	Carothers, John D.	Co. H	Pvt.	Died of disease at Mt. Jackson, VA
8/10/63	Lane, Samuel	Co. D	Pvt.	Died of disease near Madison Court House, VA
9/17/63	Gilbert, Marcus	Co. I	Pvt.	Died of typhoid fever at Gordonsville, VA
9/23/63	Cryst, Henry J.	Co. I	Pvt.	Died of disease at home in Gaston Co. NC
9/23/63	Williams, Joseph	Co. D	Pvt.	Died of disease at home in Morganton, NC
10/14/63	Poteet, Samuel	Co. D	Pvt.	Died of disease at home in Morganton, NC
10/20/63	David, Edward	Co. C	Pvt.	Died of ulcers at Weldon, NC
11/29/63	Petty, John W.	Co. G	Pvt.	Died of meningitis at Richmond, VA
12/16/63	Pruett, Ransom	Co. D	Pvt.	Died of disease at Orange Court House, VA
12/26/63	Taylor, George W.	Co. D	Pvt.	Died of pneumonia & typhoid at Richmond, VA
12/28/63	Warlick, Portland	Co. B	2nd Lt.	Died of typhoid pneumonia at Richmond, VA
1/7/64	Cullifer, Simon	Co. C	Pvt.	Died of small pox in Windsor, NC
1/19/64	Nance, William W.	Co. I	Pvt.	Died of chronic diarrhea at Gordonsville, VA
1/20/64	Madden, James P.	Co. H	Pvt.	Died of chronic diarrhea at Charlottesville, VA
1/20/64	Burns, Elisha P.	Co. K	Pvt.	Died of pneumonia at Charlottesville, VA
1/24/64	Adams, James H.	Co. C	Cpl.	Died of "variola" in Lynchburg, VA
1/29/64	Howard, Anderson Z.	Co. K	Pvt.	Died of typhoid fever at Charlottesville, VA
2/8/64	Gattis, James K.	Co. G	Pvt.	Died of disease at Chapel Hill, NC
2/10/64	Harget, Aley	Co. H	Pvt.	Died of disease at Mecklenburg Co., NC
2/14/64	Lambert, Jonathan M.	Co. E	Pvt.	Died of disease at Richmond, VA
2/20/64	Price, J. A.	Co. H	Pvt.	Died of disease at Richmond, VA
2/25/64	Goodrum, Charles	Co. A	Pvt.	Died of disease at Lynchburg, VA
5/22/64	Justice, Samuel	Co. B	Pvt.	Died of chronic diarrhea at Richmond, VA
3/1/64	Singleton, Marcus D.	Co. B	Pvt.	Died of disease at home in Morganton, NC
5/8/64	Melton, William	Co. D	Pvt.	Died of pneumonia at Lynchburg, VA
5/16/64	Burns, Henry F.	Co. H	Pvt.	Died of disease at Lynchburg, VA
5/25/64	Allran, Jacob	Co. I	Pvt.	Died of pneumonia at Lynchburg, VA

Date	Name	Unit	Rank	Cause of Death
6/7/64	Welch, William G.	Co. F	Pvt.	Died of acute dysentery at Richmond, VA
6/10/64	Carothers, James	Co. H	Pvt.	Died of disease at Richmond, VA
6/24/64	Finger, Henry F.	Co. H	Pvt.	Died of typhoid fever at Richmond, VA
6/29/64	Reinhardt, Charles	Co. I	Pvt.	Died of "pleuritis" at Liberty, VA
7/6/64	Johnson, David	Co. B	Pvt.	Died of typhoid fever at Richmond, VA
7/14/64	Butler, Thomas P.	Co. D	Pvt.	Died of disease at Richmond, VA
7/24/64	Copeland, Timothy	Co. F	Pvt.	Died of disease at home in Chowan Co., NC
8/25/64	Hunter, Thomas H.	Co. A	Pvt.	Died of disease at Richmond, VA
8/27/64	Parris, William E.	Co. F	Pvt.	Died of "acute colitis" at Greensboro, NC
9/5/64	Phillips, Elijah	Co. B	Pvt.	Died of disease at Richmond, VA
9/10/64	Perry, Timothy	Co. F	Pvt.	Died of debilitas at Richmond, VA
10/4/64	Pendergrass, James M.	Co. G	Pvt.	Died of typhoid fever at Richmond, VA
10/7/64	Speagle, Aaron	Co. I	Pvt.	Died of typhoid fever at Richmond, VA
10/10/64	Whitaker, Thomas J.	Co. G	Pvt.	Died of chronic diarrhea at Richmond, VA
10/14/64	Williams, Forrest	Co. G	Pvt.	Died of disease at home Chatham Co., NC
10/14/64	Wacaster, Abraham	Co. I	Pvt.	Died of disease at home in Lincoln Co. NC
10/26/64	Hargroves, Richard	Co. C	Pvt.	Died of "anasarca" at Richmond, VA
10/28/64	Kyles, William	Co. E	Pvt.	Died of chronic diarrhea at Danville, VA
10/29/64	Ferree, Thomas C.	Co. B	Pvt.	Died of chronic diarrhea at Richmond, VA
10/31/64	Bynum, Benjamin S.	Co. I	Pvt.	Died of chronic diarrhea at Richmond, VA
12/14/64	Wacaster, Abraham	Co. I	Pvt.	Died of disease at home Iredell Co., NC
12/20/64	Kelly, Alfred B.	Co. K	Pvt.	Died of pneumonia at Salisbury, NC
12/25/64	Williams, Baird	Co. D	Pvt.	Died of disease at Richmond, VA
12/30/64	Reap, Thomas	Co. I	Pvt.	Died of chronic diarrhea at home in NC
1/2/65	Abernathy, William A	Co. I	Pvt.	Died of disease at home in Lincoln, Co. NC
1/19/65	Chester, Milton E.	Co. A	Pvt.	Died of disease at Richmond, VA
1/26/65	Lawson, Hudson	Co. E	Pvt.	Died of chronic diarrhea at Richmond, VA
2/1/65	Martin, William E.	Co. I	Pvt.	Died of hepatitis in Charlotte, NC
2/2/65	Craig, John W.	Co. G	Pvt.	Died of disease at home in Hillsboro, NC
2/19/65	Branch, Green A.	Co. B	Pvt.	Died of disease
2/23/65	Potts, John W.	Co. G	Pvt.	Died of "apoplexy" at Richmond, VA
3/13/65	Clark, James	Co. D	Pvt.	Died of chronic diarrhea
3/14/65	Mason, Elias	Co. K	Pvt.	Died of heart disease at Richmond, VA

Died of Disease as a Prisoner of War
72 Deaths

Date	Name	Unit	Rank	Cause of Death
8/5/63	Campbell, A. Lorenzo	Co. I	Pvt.	Died of pneumonia in Washington, DC
8/8/63	Strutt, Pinkney S.	Co. I	Pvt.	Died of "pyaemia" at David's Island, NY
8/25/63	Johnson, Robert	Co. I	Pvt.	Died of chronic diarrhea at Washington, DC
9/10/63	Wakefield, S. D.	Co. B	Pvt.	Died of chronic diarrhea at Ft. Delaware, DE
9/14/63	Norwood, David J.	Co. G	Pvt.	Died of "infection of lungs" at Ft. Delaware, DE
9/16/63	Carlton, Robert W.	Co. B	Cpl.	Died of chronic diarrhea at Point Lookout, MD
10/6/63	Floyd, Henry	Co. F	Pvt.	Died of disease at Ft. Delaware, DE
11/6/63	Garrett, Stephen	Co. F	Pvt.	Died of chronic diarrhea at Point Lookout, MD
11/26/63	Sigmore, Elijah	Co. I	Pvt.	Died of disease at Ft. Delaware, DE
11/27/63	Giles, William W.	Co. D	Pvt.	Died of chronic diarrhea at Point Lookout, MD
11/28/63	Watkins, Miniard	Co. K	Pvt.	Died of chronic diarrhea at Point Lookout, MD
12/3/63	Armfield, Mark	Co. B	Cpt.	Died of disease at Johnson's Island, OH
12/10/63	Morris, Cornelius	Co. K	Pvt.	Died of chronic diarrhea at Point Lookout, MD
12/21/63	Keller, John J.	Co. B	Pvt.	Died of disease at Point Lookout, MD
12/29/63	Wingate, James	Co. E	Pvt.	Died of chronic diarrhea at Point Lookout, MD
12/30/63	Ostwalt, Francis H.	Co. E	Pvt.	Died of small pox at Point Lookout, MD

Date	Name	Unit	Rank	Cause of Death
1/1/64	Bartlett, James P.	Co. K	Pvt.	Died of disease at Point Lookout, MD
1/6/64	Goodwin, Benjamin F.	Co. F	Pvt.	Died of disease at Point Lookout, MD
1/28/64	Stone, Alexander	Co. E	Pvt.	Died of chronic diarrhea at Point Lookout, MD
2/2/64	McGinn, Robert F.	Co. A	Pvt.	Died of disease at Point Lookout, MD
2/2/64	Morris, Monroe	Co. K	Pvt.	Died of disease at Point Lookout, MD
2/9/64	Henderson, Thomas	Co. A	Pvt.	Died of disease at Point Lookout, MD
2/10/64	Gregory, John T.	Co. C	Pvt.	Died of small pox at Point Lookout, MD
2/15/64	McGinnis, Sidney A.	Co. A	Pvt.	Died of disease at Point Lookout, MD
2/15/64	Creecy, James E.	Co. F	Cpl.	Died of disease at Point Lookout, MD
3/10/64	Causby, David A.	Co. B	Pvt.	Died of chronic diarrhea Point Lookout, MD
3/19/64	Carpenter, David	Co. I	Pvt.	Died of disease at Point Lookout, MD
4/15/64	Edwards, James M.	Co. H	Pvt.	Died of chronic diarrhea at Point Lookout, MD
5/8/64	Hovis, B. Monroe	Co. I	Pvt.	Died of disease at Point Lookout, MD
7/23/64	Puckett, Elias	Co. B	Pvt.	Died of typhoid fever at Ft. Delaware, DE
7/26/64	Williams, John A.	Co. D	Pvt.	Died of disease at Castle Prison, VA (CSA)
8/12/64	Bingham, Robert W.	Co. D	Pvt.	Died of chronic diarrhea at Point Lookout, MD
9/3/64	Allen, Ruffin	Co. G	Pvt.	Died of disease at Point Lookout, MD
9/16/64	Mace, Abraham	Co. D	Pvt.	Died of typhoid pneumonia at Elmira, NY
9/24/64	Reeves, Edward	Co. G	Pvt.	Died of chronic diarrhea at Elmira, NY
10/7/64	Shull, Anthony	Co. I	Pvt.	Died of chronic diarrhea at Elmira, NY
10/15/64	Lane, William	Co. F	Pvt.	Died of chronic diarrhea at Point Lookout, MD
10/27/64	Fair, Henry	Co. D	Pvt.	Died of chronic diarrhea at Point Lookout, MD
10/30/64	Bolick, B. Sidney	Co. I	Pvt.	Died of disease at Point Lookout, MD
11/10/64	Jolly, William	Co. G	Pvt.	Died of disease at Point Lookout, MD
11/12/64	Jackson, Joseph	Co. C	Pvt.	Died of hospital gangrene at Elmira, NY
11/20/64	Kyles, James	Co. K	Pvt.	Died of chronic diarrhea at Elmira, NY
11/23/64	Narron, John G.	Co. E	Pvt.	Died of strangulated hernia at Point Lookout
12/1/64	Smith, Thomas J.	Co. H	Pvt.	Died of disease at Point Lookout, MD
12/18/64	Edwards, Marshall	Co. E	Pvt.	Died of acute dysentery at Point Lookout, MD
1/2/65	Beal, Charles	Co. E	Pvt.	Died of peritonitis at Point Lookout, MD
1/2/65	Harris, Thomas	Co. F	Cpl.	Died of hepatitis at Point Lookout, MD
1/8/65	Atkin, Thomas S.	Co. K	Sgt.	Died of chronic diarrhea at Point Lookout, MD
1/12/65	Loftin, Martin	Co. E	Pvt.	Died of typhoid fever at Point Lookout, MD
1/25/65	Speagle, Calvin	Co. I	Pvt.	Died of chronic diarrhea at Point Lookout, MD
1/31/65	Deggerheart, John V.	Co. K	Pvt.	Died of acute dysentery at Point Lookout, MD
3/3/65	Burns, John J.	Co. K	Pvt.	Died of "inflammation of brain" at Ft. Delaware
3/4/65	Culberson, John W.	Co. E	Pvt.	Died of chronic diarrhea at Point Lookout, MD
3/5/65	Thatch, Stephen	Co. C	Pvt.	Died of chronic diarrhea at Point Lookout, MD
3/7/65	Jamison, James W.	Co. E	Pvt.	Died of inflammation of lungs at Point Lookout
3/9/65	Beal, John	Co. E	Pvt.	Died of catarrh at Point Lookout, MD
3/10/65	Bass, Burton	Co. E	Pvt.	Died of chronic diarrhea at Point Lookout, MD
3/18/65	Ward, William C.	Co. C	Pvt.	Died of pneumonia at Point Lookout, MD
3/19/65	Hartgrove, Richard D.	Co. E	Pvt.	Died of pneumonia at Point Lookout, MD
3/26/65	Garrison, Alfred	Co. E	Pvt.	Died of erysipelas at Point Lookout, MD
3/29/65	Strain, James A.	Co. G	Pvt.	Died of chronic diarrhea at Point Lookout, MD
4/21/65	Watts, John	Co. B	Pvt.	Died of inflammation of lungs at Point Lookout
4/24/65	Couch, William H.	Co. G	Cpl.	Died of chronic diarrhea at Point Lookout, MD
4/26/65	Kincaid, William W.	Co. D	Pvt.	Died of anemia at Ft. Delaware, DE
4/28/65	Henderson, Ezekiel	Co. K	Pvt.	Died of chronic diarrhea at Point Lookout, MD
4/29/65	Boyd, Jesse A.	Co. H	Pvt.	Died of pneumonia at Point Lookout, MD
4/29/65	Boyd, John J.	Co. H	Pvt.	Died of pneumonia at Point Lookout, MD
5/3/65	Kincaid, Robert	Co. B	Pvt.	Died of chronic diarrhea at Washington, DC
5/8/65	Chisenhall, Samuel	Co. G	Pvt.	Died of pneumonia at Point Lookout, MD
5/23/65	Scott, Rayford S.	Co. H	Pvt.	Died of "erysipelas" at Point Lookout, MD
6/2/65	Turner, William S.	Co. E	1st Lt.	Died of inflammation of lungs at Ft. Delaware
6/23/65	McMillon, Pleasant	Co. D	Pvt.	Died of pneumonia at Point Lookout, MD

White Hall, NC—December 16, 1862
34 = 7 Killed, 27 Wounded

Unit	Rank	Name	Remarks
Co. A	Pvt.	Brigman, Columbus	Wounded
Co. A	Pvt.	Query, Samuel	Wounded (lower extremities)
Co. B	1st Sgt	Bristol, Elam	Killed (head)
Co. B	Pvt.	Carroll, John	Wounded
Co. B	Pvt.	Duckworth, Walter	Killed (head)
Co. B	Pvt.	Loven, George	Wounded
Co. B	Pvt.	Morrison, A. H.	Wounded
Co. B	Pvt.	Shuffler, Harvey	Wounded
Co. B	Pvt.	Shuffler, William	Wounded
Co. C	Pvt.	Bazemore, Henry	Wounded
Co. C	Pvt.	Bazemore, William H.	Wounded (left hand)
Co. C	Pvt.	Corprew, Jonathan	Wounded
Co. D	Pvt.	Causby, George	Wounded
Co. D	Pvt.	Melton, William	Wounded
Co. D	Pvt.	Walls, M. Lafayette	Wounded
Co. E	2nd Lt.	Means, William	Killed
Co. E	Pvt.	Bird, William	Wounded
Co. E	Pvt.	Hartgrove, Richard	Wounded
Co. E	Pvt.	Hartgrove, William	Wounded
Co. E	Pvt.	Hartline, Paul	Wounded
Co. E	Pvt.	Jameson, Thomas	Wounded
Co. E	Pvt.	Walker, Benjamin	Killed
Co. F	Pvt.	Roundtree, Noah	Killed
Co. H	Sgt.	Clark, Patrick	Wounded
Co. H	Pvt.	Thrower, Jefferson	Wounded
Co. I	Pvt.	Craft, Michael	Wounded (shoulder)
Co. I	Pvt.	Dellinger, John	Killed
Co. I	Pvt.	Gault, James	Killed
Co. I	Pvt.	Hoover, David	Wounded
Co. I	Pvt.	Shull, Anthony	Wounded (slightly)
Co. K	Pvt.	Burns, John	Wounded
Co. K	Pvt.	Gudger, John	Wounded
Co. K	Pvt.	Morris, Charles	Wounded (head & left arm)
Co. K	Pvt.	Morris, Cornelius	Wounded

Gettysburg, PA—July 1, 1863
201 = 37 Killed, 164 Wounded

Unit	Rank	Name	Remarks
F & S	Col.	Leventhorpe, Collet	Wounded (left arm & hip), 7/1/63 at Gettysburg. Captured, 7/5/63 near Greencastle, PA.
F & S	Maj.	Ross, Egbert A.	Killed, 7/1/63 at Gettysburg.
F & S	Adj.	Lucas, Henderson	Wounded, 7/1/63 at Gettysburg. Died of wounds, 7/25/63 at Martinsburg, WV.
Co. A	2nd Lt.	Hand, Robert H.	Wounded (back), 7/1/63 at Gettysburg. Captured, 7/5/63 at Greencastle, PA.
Co. A	1st Sgt.	Alexander, Richard	Wounded (left shoulder), 7/1/63 at Gettysburg.
Co. A	Sgt.	Brown, William J.	Wounded, 7/1/63 and captured, 7/5/63 at Gettysburg field hospital.
Co. A	Cpl.	Icehower, William	Wounded, 7/1/63 and captured, 7/5/63 at Gettysburg field hospital.

Unit	Rank	Name	Remarks
Co. A	Pvt.	Alexander, Marshall	Wounded (right shoulder), 7/1/63 at Gettysburg.
Co. A	Pvt.	Allen, Hamilton W.	Wounded (right arm), 7/1/63 and captured, 7/5/63 at Greencastle, PA.
Co. A	Pvt.	Barnett, John L.	Wounded, 7/1/63 at Gettysburg. Died of wounds, 7/5/63 in field hospital.
Co. A	Pvt.	Darnell, Jackson J.	Wounded, 7/1/63 at Gettysburg.
Co. A	Pvt.	Earnhart, J. H.	Killed, 7/1/63 at Gettysburg.
Co. A	Pvt.	Elliott, William A.	Killed, 7/1/63 at Gettysburg.
Co. A	Pvt.	Galloway, James S.	Wounded (breast), 7/1/63 at Gettysburg. Died of wounds, 7/21/63 in hospital at Richmond.
Co. A	Pvt.	Goodrum, William J.	Wounded (abdomen), 7/1/63 and captured. Died of wounds, 7/18/63 in hospital at Chester, PA
Co. A	Pvt.	Hill, Milton	Wounded, 7/1/63 and captured, 7/5/63 at Gettysburg field hospital.
Co. A	Pvt.	Hunter, David P.	Wounded, 7/1/63 and captured, 7/5/63 at Gettysburg field hospital.
Co. A	Pvt.	Hutchison, James H.	Wounded, 7/1/63 at Gettysburg. Died from wounds, 7/5/63 at Gettysburg
Co. A	Pvt.	Jenkins, David	Wounded (right thigh), 7/1/63 and captured, 7/5/63 at Gettysburg field hospital.
Co. A	Pvt.	Johnson, Thomas N.	Wounded, 7/1/63 and captured, 7/5/63 at Gettysburg field hospital.
Co. A	Pvt.	McConnell, John F.	Wounded, 7/1/63 and captured at Gettysburg. Died of wounds (date not recorded) in field hospital at Gettysburg.
Co. A	Pvt.	McConnell, John H.	Wounded, 7/1/63 and captured at Gettysburg.
Co. A	Pvt.	Neal, George A.	Wounded (left arm amputated), 7/1/63 and captured at Gettysburg.
Co. A	Pvt.	Powell, Daniel	Killed, 7/1/63 at Gettysburg
Co. A	Pvt.	Prim, Thomas	Wounded, 7/1/63 at Gettysburg. Died of wounds (place and date unknown).
Co. A	Pvt.	Roberts, Peyton	Wounded (right foot), 7/1/63 and captured, 7/5/63 at Gettysburg field hospital.
Co. A	Pvt.	Stowe, James M.	Wounded (left thigh), 7/1/63 at Gettysburg and captured, 7/5/63 at Gettysburg field hospital.
Co. B	3rd Lt.	Dorsey, Elisha W.	Wounded (right leg amputated), 7/1/63 and captured, 7/5/63 at Gettysburg field hospital.
Co. B	Sgt.	Duval, John M.	Wounded (thigh), 7/1/63 at Gettysburg. Captured, 7/5/63 at Williamsport, MD. Died of wounds, 8/63 at Hagerstown, PA
Co. B	Sgt.	McGimsey, Walker	Wounded (knee), 7/1/63 at Gettysburg
Co. B	Sgt.	Michaux, John P.	Wounded (slightly), 7/1/63 and captured, 7/14/63 at Falling Waters, MD
Co. B	Sgt.	Warlick, John L.	Wounded (thigh), 7/1/63 and captured, 7/5/63 at Gettysburg field hospital.
Co. B	Cpl.	Carlton, Robert W.	Wounded, 7/1/63 and captured, 7/5/63 at Gettysburg field hospital.
Co. B	Pvt.	Andrews, George W.	Wounded (left leg), 7/1/63 and captured, 7/5/63 at Gettysburg field hospital.
Co. B	Pvt.	Anthony, Philip B.	Wounded (leg), 7/1/63 at Gettysburg. Died of wounds, 7/18/63 at Harrisonburg, VA
Co. B	Pvt.	Branch, Martin	Wounded (left knee), 7/1/63 and captured, 7/5/63 at Gettysburg field hospital.
Co. B	Pvt.	Bristol, Lambert A.	Wounded (slightly), 7/1/63 at Gettysburg
Co. B	Pvt.	Cannon, James	Wounded (slightly), 7/1/63 at Gettysburg
Co. B	Pvt.	Carswell, Rankin R.	Wounded (shoulder), 7/1/63 and captured, 7/3/63 at Gettysburg field hospital.

Unit	Rank	Name	Remarks
Co. B	Pvt.	Cook, John	Wounded (leg), 7/1/63 and captured, 7/5/63 at Gettysburg field hospital.
Co. B	Pvt.	Davis, Barry L.	Wounded, 7/1/63 at Gettysburg. Captured, 7/14/63 at Falling Waters, MD
Co. B	Pvt.	Day, Samuel M.	Wounded, 7/1/63 and captured, 7/5/63 at Gettysburg field hospital.
Co. B	Pvt.	Duckworth, William	Killed, 7/1/63 at Gettysburg
Co. B	Pvt.	Fincannon, John	Wounded (head), 7/1/63 at Gettysburg
Co. B	Pvt.	Keller, John J.	Wounded (hip), 7/1/63 and captured, 7/5/63 at Gettysburg field hospital.
Co. B	Pvt.	Landis, William T.	Wounded (left leg), 7/1/63
Co. B	Pvt.	Livingston, Jordan	Wounded (severely), 7/1/63 and captured, 7/5/63 at Gettysburg field hospital.
Co. B	Pvt.	Moore, Thomas B.	Wounded (shoulder), 7/1/63 and captured, 7/5/63 at Gettysburg field hospital.
Co. B	Pvt.	Morgan, Andrew A.	Wounded (right arm), 7/1/63 and captured, 7/5/63 at Gettysburg field hospital.
Co. B	Pvt.	Morrison, A. H.	Killed, 7/1/63 at Gettysburg
Co. B	Pvt.	Parks, James P.	Wounded (shoulder), 7/1/63 at Gettysburg. Captured, 7/14/63 at Falling Waters, MD
Co. B	Pvt.	Patton, William S.	Wounded (slightly, head), 7/1/63 at Gettysburg
Co. B	Pvt.	Pearson, Michael	Wounded (thigh), 7/1/63 at Gettysburg
Co. B	Pvt.	Shuffler, John	Wounded (slightly, shoulder), 7/1/63 at Gettysburg
Co. B	Pvt.	Singleton, Lucius	Wounded (left arm), 7/1/63 at Gettysburg
Co. B	Pvt.	Smith, Henry	Wounded (leg), 7/1/63; captured, 7/14/63 at Falling Waters, MD
Co. B	Pvt.	Smith, William A.	Wounded, 7/1/63 and captured, 7/5/63 at Gettysburg field hospital.
Co. B	Pvt.	Wakefield, Sidney	Wounded, 7/1/63 and captured, 7/5/63 at Gettysburg field hospital.
Co. B	Pvt.	Warlick, A. P.	Wounded (head, slightly), 7/1/63 at Gettysburg
Co. B	Pvt.	Williams, Joseph B.	Wounded (left foot), 7/1/63 at Gettysburg
Co. C	1st Lt.	Cooper, Thomas W.	Killed, 7/1/63 at Gettysburg
Co. C	2nd Lt.	Rhodes, Edward A.	Killed ("by bullet to his head"), 7/1/63 at Gettysburg
Co. C	1st Sgt.	Craige, Clingman	Wounded, 7/1/63 at Gettysburg, 7/15/63 at Williamsport, MD. Died of wounds, 9/15/63
Co. C	Sgt.	Parker, William G.	Wounded, 7/1/63 at Gettysburg. Died of wounds, 7/17/63 at Winchester, VA
Co. C	Sgt.	Rayner, James T.	Wounded (left leg), 7/1/63 and captured, 7/5/63 at Gettysburg field hospital.
Co. C	Cpl.	Powell, William W.	Wounded, 7/1/63 and captured, 7/5/63 at Gettysburg field hospital.
Co. C	Pvt.	Carter, Benjamin	Killed, 7/1/63 at Gettysburg
Co. C	Pvt.	Casper, Joseph W.	Killed, 7/1/63 at Gettysburg
Co. C	Pvt.	Corprew, Jonathan	Wounded, 7/1/63 at Gettysburg
Co. C	Pvt.	Gregory, William L.	Wounded, ("foot shot off"), 7/1/63 at Gettysburg. Captured, 7/15/63 at Williamsport, MD. Died of wounds.
Co. C	Pvt.	Mitchell, Jeremiah	Killed, 7/1/63 at Gettysburg
Co. C	Pvt.	Peele, Thomas H.	Killed, 7/1/63 at Gettysburg
Co. C	Pvt.	Pierce, James H.	Killed, 7/1/63 at Gettysburg
Co. C	Pvt.	Pritchard, Andrew J.	Wounded (right arm, right knee, right thigh, & right hip), 7/1/63 at Gettysburg
Co. C	Pvt.	Rice, Napoleon B.	Wounded, 7/1/63 at Gettysburg. Died of wounds, 7/17/63 at Winchester, VA
Co. C	Pvt.	Stone, David G.	Killed, 7/1/63 at Gettysburg
Co. C	Pvt.	Williams, James H.	Wounded (slightly), 7/1/63 at Gettysburg. Wounded and captured, 7/3/63 at Gettysburg. Died of wounds.

Unit	Rank	Name	Remarks
Co. D	Sgt.	Black, Samuel J.	Wounded (forehead), 7/1/63 at Gettysburg. Captured, 7/14/63 at Falling Waters, MD
Co. D	Cpl.	Winters, Moulton	Killed, 7/1/63 at Gettysburg
Co. D	Pvt.	Causby (Cosby), William	Wounded, 7/1/63 at Gettysburg
Co. D	Pvt.	Chrisenbery, Thomas	Killed, 7/1/63 at Gettysburg
Co. D	Pvt.	Giles, Sidney L.	Wounded (right leg), 7/1/63 at Gettysburg
Co. D	Pvt.	Kincaid, James W.	Killed, 7/1/63 at Gettysburg
Co. D	Pvt.	Largent, John P.	Wounded, 7/1/63 and captured, 7/5/63 at Gettysburg field hospital
Co. D	Pvt.	Miller, Jackson	Wounded (right thigh), 7/1/63 and captured, 7/5/63 at Gettysburg field hospital
Co. D	Pvt.	Pearson, John	Wounded, 7/1/63 at Gettysburg
Co. D	Pvt.	Saulman, John M.	Wounded (right ankle), 7/1/63 at Gettysburg
Co. D	Pvt.	Settlemire, David	Wounded (stomach), 7/1/63 at Gettysburg
Co. D	Pvt.	Wadkins, John B.	Wounded (left leg & right ankle), 7/1/63
Co. D	Pvt.	Walls, M. Lafayette	Killed, 7/1/63 at Gettysburg
Co. D	Pvt.	Williams, Elijah H.	Wounded, 7/1/63 at Gettysburg. Captured, 7/5/63 at Gettysburg field hospital
Co. D	Pvt.	Williams, William H.	Wounded, 7/1/63 at Gettysburg. Captured, 7/6/63 at Greencastle, PA.
Co. D	Pvt.	Wood, William	Wounded, 7/1/63 and captured, 7/5/63 at Gettysburg field hospital. In hospital, David's Island, NY. Died of wounds, 9/5/63
Co. E	1st Lt.	Clanton, John B.	Wounded, 7/1/63 and captured, 7/5/63 at Gettysburg field hospital. Died of wounds, 7/28/63 at Gettysburg
Co. E	2nd Lt.	Rozzell, William F.	Wounded, 7/1/63 and captured, 7/5/63 at Gettysburg field hospital. Died of wounds, 7/10/63 at Gettysburg
Co. E	1st Sgt.	McDonald, David	Wounded, 7/1/63 at Gettysburg
Co. E	Sgt.	Goodman, John E.	Killed, 7/1/63 at Gettysburg
Co. E	Cpl.	Cathey, William C.	Wounded (left arm amputated), 7/1/63 and captured, 7/5/63 at Gettysburg field hospital
Co. E	Cpl.	Hartgrove, William	Wounded (left thigh), 7/1/63 at Gettysburg
Co. E	Cpl.	Puckett, Julius J.	Wounded (right leg), 7/1/63 at Gettysburg
Co. E	Pvt.	Bass, James A.	Wounded (left arm), 7/1/63 at Gettysburg
Co. E	Pvt.	Bird, William L.	Wounded (right leg), 7/1/63 and captured, 7/5/63 at Gettysburg field hospital
Co. E	Pvt.	Brimer, John	Wounded (leg), 7/1/63 at Gettysburg
Co. E	Pvt.	Christy, James F.	Wounded (right leg), 7/1/63 at Gettysburg. Died of wounds, 9/4/63 "at home."
Co. E	Pvt.	Clark, James A.	Killed, 7/1/63 at Gettysburg
Co. E	Pvt.	Dixon, William W.	Wounded, 7/1/63 at Gettysburg. Died of wounds, 7/2/63.
Co. E	Pvt.	Hartgrove, Richard	Wounded (thigh), 7/1/63 at Gettysburg
Co. E	Pvt.	Hartline, David L.	Wounded (right foot), 7/1/63
Co. E	Pvt.	Helms, Ezekiel T.	Killed, 7/1/63 at Gettysburg
Co. E	Pvt.	Hill, James W.	Wounded (leg), 7/1/63 and captured, 7/5/63 at Gettysburg field hospital
Co. E	Pvt.	Lewis, Lindsay	Wounded (right foot), 7/1/63 at Gettysburg
Co. E	Pvt.	McQuay, William H.	Wounded, 7/1/63 at Gettysburg. Died of wounds, 7/7/63 in U.S. field hospital at Gettysburg
Co. E	Pvt.	Neal, George A.	Wounded (left arm amputated), 7/1/63 and captured, 7/5/63 at Gettysburg field hospital
Co. E	Pvt.	Puckett, William C.	Wounded (left thigh), 7/1/63 at Gettysburg
Co. E	Pvt.	Richey, William F.	Wounded, 7/1/63 and captured, 7/5/63 at Gettysburg field hospital. Died of wounds, 7/9/63
Co. E	Pvt.	Rievs, William R.	Wounded, 7/1/63 at Gettysburg

Unit	Rank	Name	Remarks
Co. E	Pvt.	Walker, Levi L.	Wounded, 7/1/63 and captured, 7/5/63 at Gettysburg field hospital
Co. E	Pvt.	Wingate, James	Wounded, 7/1/63 and captured, 7/5/63 at Gettysburg field hospital
Co. E	Pvt.	Wingate, Thomas	Wounded, 7/1/63 at Gettysburg
Co. E	Pvt.	Yaunts, Reubin C.	Killed, 7/1/63 at Gettysburg
Co. F	1st Lt.	Roberts, Stephen W.	Wounded (shoulder), 7/1/63 at Gettysburg
Co. F	Ord. Sgt.	McDowell, George B.	Wounded (hip & foot), 7/1/63 at Gettysburg
Co. F	Pvt.	Askew, Miles	Wounded (head), 7/1/63 and captured, 7/5/63 at Gettysburg field hospital
Co. F	Pvt.	Bates, Frederick W.	Wounded, 7/1/63 and captured, 7/5/63 at Gettysburg field hospital
Co. F	Pvt.	Conner, James R.	Wounded (thigh), 7/1/63 and captured, 7/5/63 at Gettysburg field hospital
Co. F	Pvt.	Jordan, Nathan C.	Wounded, 7/1/63 at Gettysburg, 7/5/63 at Gettysburg field hospital. Died of wounds, 7/5/63
Co. F	Pvt.	Parrish, William E.	Wounded (left thigh), 7/1/63 at Gettysburg
Co. F	Pvt.	Proctor, John R.	Wounded, 7/1/63 and captured, 7/5/63 at Gettysburg field hospital. Died of wounds, 7/10/63.
Co. F	Pvt.	White, James B.	Wounded (right arm), 7/1/63
Co. G	1st Lt.	McDade, John H.	Killed, 7/1/63 at Gettysburg
Co. G	2nd Lt.	Tenney, Nathaniel	Killed, 7/1/63 at Gettysburg
Co. G	2nd Lt.	Williams, James W.	Killed, 7/1/63 at Gettysburg
Co. G	Sgt.	Davis, Thomas	Wounded (right ankle), 7/1/63 and captured, 7/5/63 at Gettysburg field hospital
Co. G	Cpl.	Snipes, Jeter J.	Wounded (left lung), 7/1/63 and captured 7/5/63 at Gettysburg. Died of wounds, 7/19/63
Co. G	Pvt.	Blackwood, Philo	Wounded, 7/1/63 at Gettysburg
Co. G	Pvt.	Davis, Fendall	Wounded (right hip), 7/1/63 at Gettysburg
Co. G	Pvt.	Durham, William S.	Wounded, 7/1/63 at Gettysburg. Died of wounds, 7/3/63
Co. G	Pvt.	Edwards, Cornelius	Wounded, 7/1/63 at Gettysburg. Died of wounds, 7/6/63 at Williamsport, MD
Co. G	Pvt.	Ivey, William G.	Wounded, 7/1/63 and captured, 7/5/63 at Gettysburg field hospital. Died of wounds, 8/8/63
Co. G	Pvt.	King, Baxter	Wounded (hip), 7/1/63 at Gettysburg
Co. G	Pvt.	Lloyd, Thadeus	Wounded, 7/1/63 at Gettysburg
Co. G	Pvt.	Mincey, John	Wounded (left foot), 7/1/63 at Gettysburg
Co. G	Pvt.	Pendergrass, Charles H.	Wounded (right shoulder), 7/1/63 at Gettysburg
Co. G	Pvt.	Pendergrass, William	Killed, 7/1/63 at Gettysburg
Co. G	Pvt.	Sparrow, Van B.	Wounded, 7/1/63 at Gettysburg
Co. G	Pvt.	Strain, Thomas	Wounded (left shoulder), 7/1/63 at Gettysburg
Co. G	Pvt.	Suit, Brantly	Wounded, 7/1/63 at Gettysburg
Co. G	Pvt.	Tripp, Jerry	Wounded (breast & left shoulder), 7/1/63 at Gettysburg
Co. G	Pvt.	Williams, Samuel	Wounded, 7/1/63 at Gettysburg
Co. H	1st Lt.	Lowrie, James B.	Killed, 7/1/63 at Gettysburg
Co. H	2nd Lt.	Knox, John H.	Wounded (left wrist), 7/1/63 at Gettysburg
Co. H	Sgt.	Clark, Patrick M.	Wounded, 7/1/63 at Gettysburg
Co. H	Sgt.	Saville, Robert D.	Wounded, 7/1/63 at Gettysburg
Co. H	Pvt.	Campbell, Thomas	Killed, 7/1/63 at Gettysburg
Co. H	Pvt.	Coffey, Benjamin M.	Wounded (left leg amputated & blinded in right eye), 7/1/63 at Gettysburg. Captured, 7/30/63 at Winchester, VA
Co. H	Pvt.	Ingle, Peter	Wounded, 7/1/63 at Gettysburg
Co. H	Pvt.	Key, Abel	Wounded, 7/1/63 at Gettysburg
Co. H	Pvt.	Porter, Robert C.	Wounded (right thigh), 7/1/63 and captured, 7/5/63 at Gettysburg field hospital. "Acted very gallantly."

Unit	Rank	Name	Remarks
Co. I	Pvt.	Abernathy, James	Wounded (left hand), 7/1/63 at Gettysburg
Co. I	Pvt.	Allran, Jacob	Wounded, 7/1/63 at Gettysburg
Co. I	Pvt.	Avery, Absalon	Wounded, 7/1/63 at Gettysburg
Co. I	Pvt.	Blackburn, A. Lafayette	Wounded, 7/1/63 and captured, 7/5/63 at Gettysburg field hospital
Co. I	Pvt.	Boyles, John	Wounded, 7/1/63 and captured, 7/5/63 at Gettysburg field hospital. Died of wounds in hospital, 8/10/63 at Chambersburg, PA
Co. I	Pvt.	Carpenter, David	Wounded, 7/1/63 and captured, 7/5/63 at Gettysburg field hospital
Co. I	Pvt.	Carpenter, Henry	Wounded (left hip), 7/1/63 and captured, 7/5/63 at Gettysburg field hospital. In hospital in Baltimore, MD. Died of wounds, 7/31/63.
Co. I	Pvt.	Carpenter, Jacob J.	Wounded, 7/1/63 and captured, 7/5/63 at Gettysburg field hospital. Died of wounds, 7/21/63
Co. I	Pvt.	Carpenter, William	Wounded, 7/1/63 and captured, 7/5/63 at Gettysburg field hospital
Co. I	Pvt.	Cody, Absalom G.	Killed, 7/1/63 at Gettysburg
Co. I	Pvt.	Davis, Samuel	Wounded, 7/1/63 at Gettysburg
Co. I	Pvt.	Dellinger, Frederick	Wounded, 71/63, and captured, 7/5/63 at Gettysburg field hospital
Co. I	Pvt.	Dellinger, Phillip	Wounded, 7/1/63 and captured, 7/5/63 at Gettysburg field hospital
Co. I	Pvt.	Glenn, David M.	Wounded, 7/1/63 at Gettysburg
Co. I	Pvt.	Havner, Hosea	Wounded, 7/1/63 at Gettysburg
Co. I	Pvt.	Havner, Jacob L.	Wounded (left arm amputated), 7/1/63 at captured, 7/5/63 at Gettysburg field hospital
Co. I	Pvt.	Havner, John	Killed, 7/1/63 at Gettysburg
Co. I	Pvt.	Hauser, Henry	Wounded, 7/1/63 and captured, 7/5/63 at Gettysburg field hospital
Co. I	Pvt.	Haynes, Daniel H.	Killed, 7/1/63 at Gettysburg
Co. I	Pvt.	Hoover, David M.	Killed, 7/1/63 at Gettysburg
Co. I	Pvt.	Hubbart, David	Wounded, 7/1/63 at Gettysburg
Co. I	Pvt.	Keever, George P.	Wounded, 7/1/63 and captured, 7/5/63 at Gettysburg field hospital. Died of wounds, 7/7/63 at Gettysburg
Co. I	Pvt.	Kiser, Hiram A.	Wounded (face), 7/1/63 at Gettysburg
Co. I	Pvt.	Lenhardt, Joseph M.	Wounded, 7/1/63 at Gettysburg
Co. I	Pvt.	Pool, Albert J.	Wounded, 7/1/63 at Gettysburg
Co. I	Pvt.	Ramsey, R. Nelson	Killed, 7/1/63 at Gettysburg
Co. I	Pvt.	Reinhardt, Robert	Wounded (left arm), 7/1/63 at Gettysburg
Co. I	Pvt.	Richey, Joseph C.	Wounded, 7/1/63 at Gettysburg
Co. I	Pvt.	Seagler, Alfred A.	Killed, 7/1/63 at Gettysburg
Co. I	Pvt.	Shuford, Noah P.	Wounded (left leg), 7/1/63 at Gettysburg
Co. I	Pvt.	Sigmore, Elijah	Wounded, 7/1/63 and captured, 7/5/63 at Gettysburg field hospital. POW—Ft. Delaware Prison, DE. Died of disease, 11/26/63
Co. I	Pvt.	Smith, David D.	Wounded, 7/1/63 and captured, 7/5/63 at Gettysburg field hospital. Died of wounds (and "typhoid fever"), 7/20/62 at Chambersburg, PA or Baltimore, MD
Co. I	Pvt.	Speagle, Aaron	Wounded, 7/1/63 at Gettysburg
Co. I	Pvt.	Speagle, L. Monroe	Killed, 7/1/63 at Gettysburg
Co. I	Pvt.	Speagle, William P.	Wounded (right shoulder), 7/1/63 at Gettysburg
Co. I	Pvt.	Strutt, Pinkney S.	Wounded, 7/1/63 and captured, 7/5/63 at Gettysburg field hospital. Died of wounds ("pyaemia"), 8/18/63 at David's Island, NY
Co. I	Pvt.	Tallant, Aaron	Wounded, 7/1/63 at Gettysburg

Unit	Rank	Name	Remarks
Co. I	Pvt.	Wacaster, Adolphus	Wounded, 7/1/63 and captured, 7/5/63 at Gettysburg field hospital
Co. K	3rd Lt.	Young, Samuel M.	Wounded, 7/1/63 and captured, 7/5/63 at Gettysburg field hospital. Died of wounds, 7/7/63
Co. K	1st Sgt.	Triplett, James H.	Killed, 7/1/63 at Gettysburg
Co. K	1st Sgt.	West, William Riley	Wounded (head), 7/1/63 at Gettysburg
Co. K	Sgt.	Anderson, William	Killed, 7/1/63 at Gettysburg
Co. K	Sgt.	Patton, John M.	Wounded, 7/1/63 and captured, 7/5/63 at Gettysburg field hospital
Co. K	Cpl.	Gash, Lucius W.	Wounded (foot), 7/1/63 at Gettysburg
Co. K	Pvt.	Burnett, Thomas W.	Wounded (left arm), 7/1/63 at Gettysburg
Co. K	Pvt.	Creasman, Joseph	Killed, 7/1/63 at Gettysburg
Co. K	Pvt.	Darnold, James C.	Wounded, 7/1/63 and captured, 7/5/63 at Gettysburg field hospital. Died of wounds, 7/29/63
Co. K	Pvt.	McReed, William	Wounded, 7/1/63 at Gettysburg. Died of wounds, 7/15/63
Co. K	Pvt.	Morris, Zebidee W.	Killed, 7/1/63 at Gettysburg

Gettysburg, PA—July 3, 1863
156 = 16 Killed, 67 Wounded,
40 Wounded & Captured, 33 Captured

Unit	Rank	Name	Remarks
F & S	Cpt.	Armfield, Mark D.	Wounded, 7/3/63 and captured, 7/3/63 at Gettysburg
F & S	Sgt. Maj.	McCorkle, James G.	Wounded and captured, 7/3/63
Co. A	Cpt.	Hand, William L.	Captured, 7/3/63 at Gettysburg
Co. A	Sgt.	McElroy, Samuel J.	Wounded, 7/3/63 and captured at Gettysburg
Co. A	Sgt.	Neily, Thomas W	Wounded, 7/3/63 at Gettysburg
Co. A	Pvt.	Alexander, Miles A.	Wounded, 7/3/63 and captured at Gettysburg
Co. A	Pvt.	Alexander, Milton M.	Wounded, 7/3/63 and captured at Gettysburg
Co. A	Pvt.	Alexander, Robert C.	Captured, 7/3/63 at Gettysburg
Co. A	Pvt.	Allen, Cyrus A.	Wounded (arm), 7/3/63 and captured at Gettysburg.
Co. A	Pvt.	Auten, P. S.	Wounded, 7/3/63 and captured at Gettysburg. Died of wounds, 8/1/63 in Gettysburg field hospital.
Co. A	Pvt.	Bigham, James W.	Wounded (arm), 7/3/63 at Gettysburg
Co. A	Pvt.	Bigham, John R.	Wounded (thigh & right buttock), 7/3/63 at captured at Gettysburg
Co. A	Pvt.	Brigman, Columbus	Wounded, 7/3/63 at Gettysburg
Co. A	Pvt.	Dulin, Daniel	Wounded (left hip), 7/3/63 and captured at Gettysburg
Co. A	Pvt.	Earnhardt, William	Captured, 7/3/63 at Gettysburg
Co. A	Pvt.	Earnhart, Joseph M.	Wounded (right side), 7/3/63 at Gettysburg
Co. A	Pvt.	Ewing, George R.	Wounded, 7/3/63 and captured, 7/5/63 at Gettysburg field hospital.
Co. A	Pvt.	Ewing, William E.	Wounded, 7/3/63 and captured, 7/5/63 at Gettysburg field hospital.
Co. A	Pvt.	Garrison, J. S.	Killed, 7/3/63 at Gettysburg
Co. A	Pvt.	Glenn, David P.	Wounded (right arm amputated), 7/3/63 at Gettysburg
Co. A	Pvt.	Glover, Joshua	Wounded, 7/3/63 and captured at Gettysburg
Co. A	Pvt.	Hand, Andrew J.	Captured, 7/3/63 at Gettysburg
Co. A	Pvt.	Harris, Nathan O.	Wounded (right shoulder), 7/3/63, "shell wound," at Gettysburg
Co. A	Pvt.	Herring, G. T.	Wounded, 7/3/63 at Gettysburg
Co. A	Pvt.	Hobbs, Ferdinand	Wounded, 7/3/63 at Gettysburg

Unit	Rank	Name	Remarks
Co. A	Pvt.	McGinnis, Sidney A.	Captured, 7/3/63 at Gettysburg
Co. A	Pvt.	McWhirter, John	Wounded, 7/3/63 and captured at Gettysburg
Co. A	Pvt.	Montgomery, James	Wounded, 7/3/63 and captured at Gettysburg
Co. A	Pvt.	Newell, Alexander H.	Wounded ("contusion of the left shoulder"), 7/3/63 at Gettysburg
Co. A	Pvt.	Norment, Isaac	Wounded, 7/3/63 at Gettysburg
Co. A	Pvt.	Paysour, Caleb	Wounded, 7/3/63 and captured at Gettysburg
Co. A	Pvt.	Simpson, Robert F.	Wounded, 7/3/63 at Gettysburg and captured, 7/5/63 at Gettysburg field hospital.
Co. A	Pvt.	Smith, John S.	Wounded (head), 7/3/63 at Gettysburg. Died of wounds, 7/15/63 at Gettysburg
Co. A	Pvt.	Wallace, W. A.	Wounded, 7/3/63 at Gettysburg. Captured, 7/14/63 at Falling Waters, MD
Co. A	Pvt.	Wingate, Angus	Killed, 7/3/63 at Gettysburg
Co. A	Pvt.	Wright, Taylor	Wounded (back), 7/3/63 and captured at Gettysburg
Co. B	1st Lt.	Parks, Thomas R.	Wounded, 7/3/3/63 and captured, 7/14/63 at Falling Waters, MD
Co. B	2nd Lt.	Warlick, Portland A.	Wounded (left arm), 7/3/63 at Gettysburg. Died of wounds, 12/7/63 in Richmond.
Co. B	Cpl.	Hennessee, Robert J.	Captured, 7/3/63 at Gettysburg
Co. B	Cpl.	Parks, H. H.	Missing, 7/3/63 at Gettysburg. "supposed killed"
Co. B	Pvt.	Branch, Anthony C.	Wounded, 7/3/63 and captured, 7/5/63 at Gettysburg field hospital.
Co. B	Pvt.	Dorsey, Thomas A.	Wounded and captured, 7/3/63 at Gettysburg.
Co. B	Pvt.	Duckworth, Jonathan	Wounded, 7/3/63 and captured, 7/5/63 at Gettysburg field hospital.
Co. B	Pvt.	Landis, Jordan N.	Wounded, 7/3/63 and captured at Gettysburg
Co. B	Pvt.	Puckett, Elias W.	Wounded, 7/3/63 and captured at Gettysburg
Co. B	Pvt.	Stacy, George L.	Captured, 7/3/63 at Gettysburg
Co. B	Pvt.	Teem, John P.	Captured, 7/3/63 at Gettysburg
Co. B	Pvt.	Walker, Elisha F.	Wounded (shoulder & right side), 7/3/63 at Gettysburg
Co. C	Cpl.	Carter, Joseph B.	Killed, 7/3/63 at Gettysburg
Co. C	Pvt.	Floyd, James R.	Wounded, 7/3/63 and captured at Gettysburg
Co. C	Pvt.	Gregory, John T.	Captured, 7/3/63 at Gettysburg
Co. C	Pvt.	Holder, Thomas	Wounded and captured, 7/3/63 at Gettysburg. Died of wounds.
Co. C	Pvt.	Williams, James H.	Wounded and captured, 7/3/63 at Gettysburg. Died of wounds.
Co. D	1st Lt.	Kincaid, William J.	Wounded, 7/3/63 and captured, 7/5/63 at Gettysburg field hospital
Co. D	3rd Lt.	Kincaid, George W.	Killed, 7/3/63 at Gettysburg
Co. D	Cpl.	Clay, Joseph M.	Wounded ("lost an eye"), 7/3/63 and captured at Gettysburg
Co. D	Cpl.	Mace, William H.	Wounded, 7/3/63 at Gettysburg
Co. D	Cpl.	Simpson, John E.	Captured, 7/3/63 at Gettysburg
Co. D	Pvt.	Clark, Mitchell	Wounded, 7/3/63 and captured, 7/5/63 at Gettysburg field hospital
Co. D	Pvt.	Giles, William W.	Captured, 7/3/63 at Gettysburg, captured, 7/6/63 at Greencastle, PA
Co. D	Pvt.	Hennessee, Patrick	Captured, 7/3/63 at Gettysburg
Co. D	Pvt.	McKesson, James C.	Wounded and captured, 7/3/63 at Gettysburg
Co. D	Pvt.	Melton, Eugene A.	Captured, 7/3/63 at Gettysburg
Co. D	Pvt.	Sudderth, Elam M.	Killed, 7/3/63 at Gettysburg
Co. D	Pvt.	Summers, Perry	Wounded (breast), 7/3/63 at Gettysburg
Co. D	Pvt.	Tate, Hugh	Wounded (right thigh) and captured, 7/3/63 at Gettysburg. Right leg amputated. Died of wounds, 8/25/63 after a second amputation,
Co. D	Pvt.	Taylor, Charles	Wounded, 7/3/63 at Gettysburg. Captured, 7/14/63 at Falling Waters, MD

Unit	Rank	Name	Remarks
Co. D	Pvt.	Todd, R. L.	Wounded, 7/3/63 and captured at Gettysburg. Died of wounds, 7/26/63
Co. E	Pvt.	Bradley, John L.	Captured, 7/3/63 at Gettysburg
Co. E	Pvt.	Finger, John	Wounded (neck), 7/3/63, at Gettysburg
Co. E	Pvt.	Jameson, Thomas J.	Wounded, 7/3/63 at Gettysburg
Co. E	Pvt.	Martin, William	Wounded, 7/3/63 at Gettysburg
Co. E	Pvt.	McLure, Cyrus A.	Wounded, 7/3/63. Captured, 7/14/63 at Falling Waters, MD
Co. E	Pvt.	McQuay, James	Killed, 7/3/63 at Gettysburg
Co. E	Pvt.	Ostwalt, Francis	Captured, 7/3/63 at Gettysburg
Co. E	Pvt.	Williamson, Edward	Captured, 7/3/63 at Gettysburg
Co. F	Cpt.	Small, Edward A.	Captured, 7/3/63 at Gettysburg
Co. F	2nd Lt.	Rea, William D.	Wounded (left hip & right foot), 7/3/63 at Gettysburg
Co. F	3rd Lt.	Hoskins, Blake B.	Wounded, 7/3/63 and captured at Gettysburg. Died of wounds, 7/9/63 at Gettysburg
Co. F	Cpl.	Benbury, William E.	Wounded (arm), 7/3/63 at Gettysburg
Co. F	Cpl.	Briscoe, Robert	Wounded (leg), 7/3/63 and captured at Gettysburg. Died of wounds, 8/10/63.
Co. F	Pvt.	Byrum, A. J.	Wounded (left leg), 7/3/63. Died of wounds, 3/2/64
Co. F	Pvt.	Byrum, Isaac	Wounded (left leg amputated), 7/3/65 at Gettysburg. Captured, 7/5/63 at Gettysburg field hospital.
Co. F	Pvt.	Davidson, Louis	Wounded, 7/3/63 and captured at Gettysburg. Died of wounds, 7/27/63
Co. F	Pvt.	Floyd, Henry	Captured, 7/3/63 at Gettysburg
Co. F	Pvt.	Harris, Thomas C.	Wounded (left side), 7/3/63 and captured at Gettysburg
Co. F	Pvt.	Haskett, Thomas T.	Wounded (left leg), 7/3/63 and captured at Gettysburg
Co. F	Pvt.	Jones, Theophilus	Wounded, 7/3/63 and captured at Gettysburg
Co. F	Pvt.	Lane, Caleb	Captured, 7/3/63 at Gettysburg
Co. F	Pvt.	Lane, William	Captured, 7/3/63 at Gettysburg
Co. F	Pvt.	Long, Joseph S.	Wounded (left thigh & arm), 7/3/63 and captured at Gettysburg
Co. F	Pvt.	Smith, Charlton	Captured, 7/3/63 at Gettysburg
Co. F	Pvt.	Smith, William J.	Killed, 7/3/63 at Gettysburg
Co. F	Pvt.	Sutton, S. S.	Wounded (left arm), 7/3/63 at Gettysburg
Co. F	Pvt.	Taylor, Joseph W.	Captured, 7/3/63 at Gettysburg
Co. F	Pvt.	Thatch, Henry C.	Captured, 7/3/63 at Gettysburg
Co. F	Pvt.	Troutman, Joseph W.	Captured, 7/3/63 at Gettysburg
Co. F	Pvt.	Ward, Anderson S.	Wounded (ear), 7/3/63 at Gettysburg
Co. F	Pvt.	Whedbee, George W.	Wounded, 7/3/63 and captured at Gettysburg
Co. F	Pvt.	White, Isaac N.	Wounded, 7/3/63 and captured at Gettysburg
Co. F	Pvt.	White, James	Wounded, 7/3/63 and captured at Gettysburg. Died of wounds, 7/16/63.
Co. G	Cpl.	Norwood, David J.	Captured, 7/3/63 at Gettysburg
Co. G	Pvt.	Andrew, Wesley	Wounded, 7/3/65 and captured, 7/5/63 at Gettysburg field hospital. Died of wounds, 7/10/63
Co. G	Pvt.	Clements, John R.	Wounded (contusion of right hip), 7/3/63 at Gettysburg
Co. G	Pvt.	Daniel, Algernon	Wounded (both hips), 7/3/63 and captured, 7/5/63 at Gettysburg field hospital
Co. G	Pvt.	Flintoff, William D.	Wounded, 7/3/63 at Gettysburg
Co. G	Pvt.	Garrett, Esau	Wounded (lung), 7/3/63 and captured at Gettysburg. Died of wounds, 7/11/63 at Hagerstown, MD
Co. G	Pvt.	Pendergrass, John L.	Captured, 7/3/63 at Gettysburg
Co. G	Pvt.	Suggs, William	Captured, 7/3/63 at Gettysburg
Co. G	Pvt.	Thrift, William	Captured, 7/3/63 at Gettysburg
Co. G	Pvt.	Waddell, Duncan C.	Wounded, 7/3/63 and captured, 7/5/63 at Gettysburg field hospital. Appointed 1st Lt. 7/30/63 "for gallant conduct on the field at Gettysburg."

Unit	Rank	Name	Remarks
Co. H	2nd Lt.	Saville, James M.	Wounded, 7/3/63 at Gettysburg
Co. H	1st Sgt.	Harris, Frank C.	Wounded (left arm amputated), 7/3/63 and captured, 7/5/63 at Gettysburg field hospital.
Co. H	Pvt.	Hamel, Alexander R.	Wounded and captured, 7/3/63 at Gettysburg. Died of wounds, 8/28/63
Co. H	Pvt.	Morrison, William T.	Captured, 7/3/63 at Gettysburg
Co. H	Pvt.	Snider, John A.	Killed, 7/3/63 at Gettysburg
Co. I	Cpt.	Haynes, Albert S.	Wounded, 7/3/63 and captured, 7/5/63 at Gettysburg field hospital
Co. I	1st Lt.	Coon, David A.	Wounded (right foot & both eyes), 7/3/63 and captured at Gettysburg
Co. I	2nd Lt.	Hoyle, Lemuel J.	Wounded, 7/3/63 at Gettysburg
Co. I	3rd Lt.	Ramsour, Oliver A.	Wounded and captured, 7/3/63 at Gettysburg
Co. I	1st Sgt.	Bell, Robert M.	Wounded (severely), 7/3/63 at Gettysburg
Co. I	Sgt.	Haynes, Andrew R.	Killed, 7/3/63 at Gettysburg
Co. I	Sgt.	Jetton, William H.	Killed, 7/3/63 at Gettysburg
Co. I	Cpl.	Cathey, Robert A.	Killed, 7/3/63 at Gettysburg
Co. I	Cpl.	Hovis, Laban L.	Wounded (jaw), 7/3/63 and captured, 7/5/63 at Gettysburg field hospital
Co. I	Pvt.	Abernathy, William	Wounded and captured, 7/3/63 at Gettysburg
Co. I	Pvt.	Bisaner, Jacob H.	Wounded (left side), 7/3/63 and captured, 7/5/63 at Gettysburg field hospital
Co. I	Pvt.	Bolick, B. Sidney	Wounded and captured, 7/3/63 at Gettysburg
Co. I	Pvt.	Cornwell, Sidney	Wounded, 7/3/63 at Gettysburg
Co. I	Pvt.	Dellinger, P. Frank	Killed, 7/3/63 at Gettysburg
Co. I	Pvt.	Finger, Robert P.	Killed, 7/3/63 at Gettysburg
Co. I	Pvt.	Glasscock, Stanhope A.	Wounded, 7/3/65 and captured, 7/5/63 at Gettysburg field hospital. Died of wounds in field hospital, 7/19/63 at Gettysburg
Co. I	Pvt.	Havner, Adolphus J.	Killed, 7/3/63 at Gettysburg
Co. I	Pvt.	Havner, George H.	Wounded (left arm), 7/3/63 at Gettysburg
Co. I	Pvt.	Haun, Christy S.	Wounded, 7/3/63 at Gettysburg
Co. I	Pvt.	Haynes, John F.	Wounded, 7/3/63 and captured, 7/5/63 at Greencastle, PA
Co. I	Pvt.	Hoover, Daniel R.	Wounded, 7/3/63 at Gettysburg
Co. I	Pvt.	Hovis, B. Monroe	Captured, 7/3/63 at Gettysburg
Co. I	Pvt.	Johnson, Leonidas	Wounded (jaw), 7/3/63 at Gettysburg
Co. I	Pvt.	Lenhardt, Cameron L.	Wounded (left shoulder), 7/3/63 at Gettysburg. Died of wounds, 7/30/63.
Co. I	Pvt.	Lenhardt, Jacob M.	Killed, 7/3/63 at Gettysburg
Co. I	Pvt.	Oaks, John	Wounded (head), 7/3/63 and captured, 7/5/63 at Greencastle, PA
Co. I	Pvt.	Stroup, Daniel S.	Wounded and captured, 7/3/63 at Gettysburg
Co. I	Pvt.	Warlick, John C.	Wounded (right leg and left breast), 7/3/63 at Gettysburg
Co. I	Pvt.	Wood, Perry	Wounded (left hand), 7/3/63 at Gettysburg
Co. I	Pvt.	Wyont, David	Wounded, 7/3/63 at Gettysburg
Co. K	Pvt.	Bell, James A.	Wounded, 7/3/63 and captured, 7/5/63 at Gettysburg field hospital. Died of wounds, 7/10/63
Co. K	Pvt.	Burns, John J.	Captured, 7/3/63 at Gettysburg
Co. K	Pvt.	Cordell, David L.	Wounded (leg), 7/3/63 at Gettysburg
Co. K	Pvt.	Harris, Thomas L.	Captured, 7/3/63 at Gettysburg
Co. K	Pvt.	Henderson, Ezekiel	Wounded, 7/3/63 and captured, 7/5/63 at Gettysburg field hospital
Co. K	Pvt.	Morris, Monroe	Captured, 7/3/63 at Gettysburg
Co. K	Pvt.	Neighbour, Ferdinand	Captured, 7/3/63 at Gettysburg
Co. K	Pvt.	Pittman, John N.	Wounded (shoulder), 7/3/63 at Gettysburg
Co. K	Pvt.	Smith, Alfred B.	Wounded (face & neck), 7/3/63 and captured, 7/5/63 at Gettysburg field hospital
Co. K	Pvt.	Stroup, William J.	Killed, 7/3/63 at Gettysburg

Gettysburg, PA—July 5–10, 1863
81 Captured

Unit	Rank	Name	Remarks
Co. A	Sgt.	Brown, William J.	Wounded, 7/1/63 and captured, 7/5/63 at Gettysburg field hospital
Co. A	Cpl.	Icehower, William	Wounded, 7/1/63 and captured, 7/5/63 at Gettysburg field hospital
Co. A	Pvt.	Auten, P. S.	Wounded, 7/3/63 and captured at Gettysburg. Died of wounds, 8/1/63 in Gettysburg field hospital.
Co. A	Pvt.	Barnett, John L.	Wounded, 7/1/63 at Gettysburg. Died of wounds, 7/5/63 in field hospital.
Co. A	Pvt.	Ewing, George R.	Wounded, 7/3/63 and captured, 7/5/63 at Gettysburg field hospital.
Co. A	Pvt.	Ewing, William E.	Wounded, 7/3/63 and captured, 7/5/63 at Gettysburg field hospital.
Co. B	Cpt.	Armfield, Mark D.	Wounded, 7/3/63 and captured, 7/3/63 at Gettysburg
Co. B	3rd Lt.	Dorsey, Elisha W.	Wounded (right leg amputated), 7/1/63 and captured, 7/5/63 at Gettysburg field hospital.
Co. B	Sgt.	Duval, John M.	Wounded (thigh), 7/1/63 at Gettysburg. Captured, 7/5/63 at Williamsport, MD. Died of wounds, 8/63 at Hagerstown, PA
Co. B	Sgt.	Warlick, John L.	Wounded (thigh), 7/1/63 and captured, 7/5/63 at Gettysburg field hospital.
Co. B	Cpl.	Carlton, Robert W.	Wounded, 7/1/63 and captured, 7/5/63 at Gettysburg field hospital.
Co. B	Pvt.	Andrews, George W.	Wounded (left leg), 7/1/63 and captured, 7/5/63 at Gettysburg field hospital.
Co. B	Pvt.	Branch, Anthony	Wounded, 7/3/63 and captured, 7/5/63 at Gettysburg field hospital.
Co. B	Pvt.	Branch, Martin	Wounded (left knee), 7/1/63 and captured, 7/5/63 at Gettysburg field hospital.
Co. B	Pvt.	Carswell, Rankin R.	Wounded (shoulder), 7/1/63 and captured, 7/3/63 at Gettysburg field hospital.
Co. B	Pvt.	Cook, John	Wounded (leg), 7/1/63 and captured, 7/5/63 at Gettysburg field hospital.
Co. B	Pvt.	Day, Samuel M.	Wounded, 7/1/63 and captured, 7/5/63 at Gettysburg field hospital.
Co. B	Pvt.	Duckworth, Jonathan N.	Wounded, 7/3/63 and captured, 7/5/63 at Gettysburg field hospital.
Co. B	Pvt.	Keller, John J.	Wounded (hip), 7/1/63 and captured, 7/5/63 at Gettysburg field hospital.
Co. B	Pvt.	Livingston, Jordan	Wounded (severely), 7/1/63 and captured, 7/5/63 at Gettysburg field hospital.
Co. B	Pvt.	Moore, Thomas B.	Wounded (shoulder), 7/1/63 and captured, 7/5/63 at Gettysburg field hospital.
Co. B	Pvt.	Morgan, Andrew A.	Wounded (right arm), 7/1/63 and captured, 7/5/63 at Gettysburg field hospital.
Co. B	Pvt.	Smith, William A.	Wounded, 7/1/63 and captured, 7/5/63 at Gettysburg field hospital.
Co. B	Pvt.	Wakefield, Sidney	Wounded, 7/1/63 and captured, 7/5/63 at Gettysburg field hospital.
Co. C	Sgt.	Rayner, James T.	Wounded (left leg), 7/1/63 and captured, 7/5/63 at Gettysburg field hospital.
Co. C	Cpl.	Powell, William	Wounded, 7/1/63 and captured, 7/5/63 at Gettysburg field hospital.

Unit	Rank	Name	Remarks
Co. D	1st Lt.	Kincaid, William J.	Wounded, 7/3/63 and captured, 7/5/63 at Gettysburg field hospital
Co. D	Pvt.	Clark, Mitchell	Wounded, 7/3/63 and captured, 7/5/63 at Gettysburg field hospital
Co. D	Pvt.	Clarke, Mitchell	Wounded, 7/3/63 and captured, 7/5/63 at Gettysburg field hospital
Co. D	Pvt.	Largent, John P.	Wounded, 7/1/63 and captured, 7/5/63 at Gettysburg field hospital
Co. D	Pvt.	Miller, Jackson	Wounded (right thigh), 7/1/63 and captured, 7/5/63 at Gettysburg field hospital
Co. D	Pvt.	Tate, Hugh	Wounded (right thigh) and captured, 7/3/63 at Gettysburg. Right leg amputated. Died of wounds, 8/25/63 after a second amputation,
Co. D	Pvt.	Williams, Elijah H.	Wounded, 7/1/63 at Gettysburg. Captured, 7/5/63 at Gettysburg field hospital
Co. D	Pvt.	Wood, William	Wounded, 7/1/63 and captured, 7/5/63 at Gettysburg field hospital. In hospital, David's Island, NY. Died of wounds, 9/5/63
Co. E	1st Lt.	Clanton, John B.	Wounded, 7/1/63 and captured, 7/5/63 at Gettysburg field hospital. Died of wounds, 7/28/63 at Gettysburg
Co. E	2nd Lt.	Rozzell, William F.	Wounded, 7/1/63 and captured, 7/5/63 at Gettysburg field hospital. Died of wounds, 7/10/63 at Gettysburg
Co. E	Cpl.	Cathey, William C.	Wounded (left arm amputated), 7/1/63 and captured, 7/5/63 at Gettysburg field hospital
Co. E	Pvt.	Bird, William L.	Wounded (right leg), 7/1/63 and captured, 7/5/63 at Gettysburg field hospital
Co. E	Pvt.	Hill, James W.	Wounded (leg), 7/1/63 and captured, 7/5/63 at Gettysburg field hospital
Co. E	Pvt.	McQuay, William H.	Wounded, 7/1/63 at Gettysburg. Died of wounds, 7/7/63 in U.S. field hospital at Gettysburg
Co. E	Pvt.	Neal, George A.	Wounded (left arm amputated), 7/1/63 and captured, 7/5/63 at Gettysburg field hospital
Co. E	Pvt.	Richey, William F.	Wounded, 7/1/63 and captured, 7/5/63 at Gettysburg field hospital. Died of wounds, 7/9/63
Co. E	Pvt.	Walker, Levi L.	Wounded, 7/1/63 and captured, 7/5/63 at Gettysburg field hospital
Co. E	Pvt.	Wingate, James	Wounded, 7/1/63 and captured, 7/5/63 at Gettysburg field hospital
Co. F	Pvt.	Askew, Miles	Wounded (head), 7/1/63 and captured, 7/5/63 at Gettysburg field hospital
Co. F	Pvt.	Bates, Frederick	Wounded, 7/1/63 and captured, 7/5/63 at Gettysburg field hospital
Co. F	Pvt.	Byrum, Isaac	Wounded (left leg amputated), 7/3/65 at Gettysburg. Captured, 7/5/63 at Gettysburg field hospital.
Co. F	Pvt.	Conner, James R.	Wounded (thigh), 7/1/63 and captured, 7/5/63 at Gettysburg field hospital
Co. F	Pvt.	Jordan, Nathan C.	Wounded, 7/1/63 at Gettysburg, 7/5/63 at Gettysburg field hospital. Died of wounds, 7/5/63
Co. F	Pvt.	Proctor, John R.	Wounded, 7/1/63 and captured, 7/5/63 at Gettysburg field hospital. Died of wounds, 7/10/63.
Co. G	Sgt.	Davis, Thomas	Wounded (right ankle), 7/1/63 and captured, 7/5/63 at Gettysburg field hospital
Co. G	Pvt.	Andrew, Wesley	Wounded, 7/3/65 and captured, 7/5/63 at Gettysburg field hospital. Died of wounds, 7/10/63
Co. G	Pvt.	Daniel, Algernon	Wounded (both hips), 7/3/63 and captured, 7/5/63 at Gettysburg field hospital

Unit	Rank	Name	Remarks
Co. G	Pvt.	Ivey, William G.	Wounded, 7/3/65 and captured, 7/5/63 at Gettysburg field hospital. Died of wounds, 8/8/63
Co. G	Pvt.	Waddell, Duncan	Wounded, 7/3/63 and captured, 7/5/63 at Gettysburg field hospital.
Co. H	1st Sgt.	Harris, Frank C.	Wounded (left arm amputated), 7/3/63 and captured, 7/5/63 at Gettysburg field hospital.
Co. H	Pvt.	Porter, Robert C.	Wounded (right thigh), 7/1/63 and captured, 7/5/63 at Gettysburg field hospital.
Co. H	Pvt.	Sloop, Alexander	Captured, 7/5/63 at Gettysburg
Co. I	Cpt.	Haynes, Albert S.	Wounded, 7/3/63 and captured, 7/5/63 at Gettysburg field hospital
Co. I	Cpl.	Hovis, Laban L.	Wounded (jaw), 7/3/63 and captured, 7/5/63 at Gettysburg field hospital
Co. I	Pvt.	Bisaner, Jacob H.	Wounded (left side), 7/3/63 and captured, 7/5/63 at Gettysburg field hospital
Co. I	Pvt.	Blackburn, A. Lafayette	Wounded, 7/1/63 and captured, 7/5/63 at Gettysburg field hospital
Co. I	Pvt.	Boyles. John	Wounded, 7/1/63 and captured, 7/5/63 at Gettysburg field hospital. Died of wounds in hospital, 8/10/63 at Chambersburg, PA
Co. I	Pvt.	Carpenter, Henry	Wounded (left hip), 7/1/63 and captured, 7/5/63 at Gettysburg field hospital. In hospital in Baltimore, MD. Died of wounds, 7/31/63.
Co. I	Pvt.	Carpenter, Jacob J.	Wounded, 7/1/63 and captured, 7/5/63 at Gettysburg field hospital. Died of wounds, 7/21/63
Co. I	Pvt.	Carpenter, William	Wounded, 7/1/63 and captured, 7/5/63 at Gettysburg field hospital
Co. I	Pvt.	Dellinger, Frederick W.	Wounded, 71/63, and captured, 7/5/63 at Gettysburg field hospital
Co. I	Pvt.	Dellinger, Phillip	Wounded, 7/1/63 and captured, 7/5/63 at Gettysburg field hospital
Co. I	Pvt.	Glasscock, Stanhope A.	Wounded, 7/3/65 and captured, 7/5/63 at Gettysburg field hospital. Died of wounds in field hospital, 7/19/63 at Gettysburg
Co. I	Pvt.	Havner, Jacob L.	Wounded (left arm amputated), 7/1/63 at captured, 7/5/63 at Gettysburg field hospital
Co. I	Pvt.	Hauser, Henry	Wounded, 7/1/63 and captured, 7/5/63 at Gettysburg field hospital
Co. I	Pvt.	Keever, George P.	Wounded, 7/1/63 and captured, 7/5/63 at Gettysburg field hospital. Died of wounds, 7/7/63 at Gettysburg
Co. I	Pvt.	Sigmore, Elijah	Wounded, 7/1/63 and captured, 7/5/63 at Gettysburg field hospital. POW—Ft. Delaware Prison, DE. Died of disease, 11/26/63
Co. I	Pvt.	Smith, David D.	Wounded, 7/1/63 and captured, 7/5/63 at Gettysburg field hospital. Died of wounds (and "typhoid fever"), 7/20/62 at Chambersburg, PA or Baltimore, MD
Co. I	Pvt.	Strutt, Pinkney S.	Wounded, 7/1/63 and captured, 7/5/63 at Gettysburg field hospital. Died of wounds ("pyaemia"), 8/18/63 at David's Island, NY
Co. I	Pvt.	Wacaster, Adolphus	Wounded, 7/1/63 and captured, 7/5/63 at Gettysburg field hospital
Co. K	3rd Lt.	Young, Samuel M.	Wounded, 7/1/63 and captured, 7/5/63 at Gettysburg field hospital. Died of wounds, 7/7/63
Co. K	Sgt.	Patton, John M.	Wounded, 7/1/63 and captured, 7/5/63 at Gettysburg field hospital
Co. K	Pvt.	Bell, James A.	Wounded, 7/3/63 and captured, 7/5/63 at Gettysburg field hospital. Died of wounds, 7/10/63

Unit	Rank	Name	Remarks
Co. K	Pvt.	Darnold, James C.	Wounded, 7/1/63 and captured, 7/5/63 at Gettysburg field hospital. Died of wounds, 7/29/63
Co. K	Pvt.	Henderson, Ezekiel	Wounded, 7/3/63 and captured, 7/5/63 at Gettysburg field hospital
Co. K	Pvt.	Smith, Alfred B.	Wounded (face & neck), 7/3/63 and captured, 7/5/63 at Gettysburg field hospital

Greencastle, PA—July 5–6, 1863
12 Captured

Unit	Rank	Name	Remarks
F & S	Col.	Leventhorpe, Collet	Wounded (left arm & hip), 7/1/63 at Gettysburg. Captured, 7/5/63 near Greencastle, PA.
Co. A	2nd Lt.	Hand, Robert H.	Wounded (back), 7/1/63 at Gettysburg. Captured, 7/5/63 at Greencastle, PA.
Co. A	Pvt.	Allen, Hamilton	Wounded (right arm), 7/1/63 and captured, 7/5/63 at Greencastle, PA
Co. D	Pvt.	Causby (Cosby), George	Captured, 7/6/63 at Greencastle, PA
Co. D	Pvt.	Giles, William W.	Captured, 7/3/63 at Gettysburg, captured, 7/6/63 at Greencastle, PA
Co. D	Pvt.	Williams, William H.	Wounded, 7/1/63 at Gettysburg. Captured, 7/6/63 at Greencastle, PA.
Co. H	Pvt.	Russell, John C.	Captured, 7/5/63 at Greencastle, PA
Co. I	Pvt.	Clark, James M.	Captured, 7/5/63 at Greencastle, PA
Co. I	Pvt.	Haynes, John F.	Wounded, 7/3/63 and captured, 7/5/63 at Greencastle, PA
Co. I	Pvt.	Oaks, John	Wounded (head), 7/3/63 and captured, 7/5/63 at Greencastle, PA
Co. I	Mus.	Cline, William A.	TDY—Musician. Captured, 7/5/63 at Greencastle, PA
Co. I	Mus.	Coon, Adolphus S.	TDY—Musician. Captured, 7/5/63 at Greencastle, PA

Falling Waters, MD—July 14, 1863
93 = 1 Killed, 6 Wounded,
1 Wounded & Captured, 85 Captured

Unit	Rank	Name	Remarks
Co. A	Sgt.	Sims, James M.	Captured, 7/14/63 at Falling Waters, MD
Co. A	Cpl.	Ruddick, Theo C.	Captured, 7/14/63 at Falling Waters, MD
Co. A	Pvt.	Blakeley, James J.	Captured, 7/14/63 at Falling Waters, MD
Co. A	Pvt.	Earnhart, S. O.	Captured, 7/14/63 at Falling Waters, MD
Co. A	Pvt.	Groves, Robert A.	Captured, 7/14/63 at Falling Waters, MD
Co. A	Pvt.	Henderson, Thomas M.	Captured, 7/14/63 at Falling Waters, MD
Co. A	Pvt.	Jenkins, Jacob	Captured, 7/14/63 at Falling Waters, MD
Co. A	Pvt.	McGinn, Robert F.	Captured, 7/14/63 at Falling Waters, MD
Co. B	1st Lt.	Parks, Thomas	Captured, 7/14/63 at Falling Waters, MD
Co. B	Cpl.	Galloway, H. H.	Captured, 7/14/63 at Falling Waters, MD
Co. B	Pvt.	Andrews, James	Captured, 7/14/63 at Falling Waters, MD
Co. B	Pvt.	Bowman, Jacob	Captured, 7/14/63 at Falling Waters, MD
Co. B	Pvt.	Brewer, William	Captured, 7/14/63 at Falling Waters, MD
Co. B	Pvt.	Causby, David A.	Captured, 7/14/63 at Falling Waters, MD
Co. B	Pvt.	Clark, John M.	Captured, 7/14/63 at Falling Waters, MD
Co. B	Pvt.	Courtney, James	Captured, 7/14/63 at Falling Waters, MD
Co. B	Pvt.	Crawley, J. W.	Captured, 7/14/63 at Falling Waters, MD

Unit	Rank	Name	Remarks
Co. B	Pvt.	Griffin, David	Captured, 7/14/63 at Falling Waters, MD
Co. B	Pvt.	Griffin, James	Captured, 7/14/63 at Falling Waters, MD
Co. B	Pvt.	Harris, Lewis B.	Captured, 7/14/63 at Falling Waters, MD
Co. B	Pvt.	Morgan, Perry W.	Captured, 7/14/63 at Falling Waters, MD
Co. B	Pvt.	Parks, James	Captured, 7/14/63 at Falling Waters, MD
Co. B	Pvt.	Pearson, Thomas	Wounded (slightly), 7/14/63 at Falling Waters, MD
Co. B	Pvt.	Perry, Alfred	Captured, 7/14/63 at Falling Waters, MD
Co. B	Pvt.	Shuffler, Harvey	Killed, 7/7/63 at Williamsport, MD
Co. B	Pvt.	Shuffler, Sidney	Captured, 7/14/63 at Falling Waters, MD
Co. B	Pvt.	Shuffler, William	Captured, 7/14/63 at Falling Waters, MD
Co. B	Pvt.	Singleton, Silas S.	Captured, 7/14/63 at Falling Waters, MD
Co. B	Pvt.	Smith, Alva	Captured, 7/14/63 at Falling Waters, MD
Co. B	Pvt.	Smith, Henry	Captured, 7/14/63 at Falling Waters, MD
Co. B	Pvt.	Smith, James C.	Captured, 7/14/63 at Falling Waters, MD
Co. C	Sgt.	Todd, William H.	Wounded (left thigh), 7/14/63 at Falling Waters, MD
Co. C	Cpl.	Adams, James H.	Wounded (left hand), 7/14/63 at Falling Waters, MD
Co. C	Pvt.	Byrum, Reuben L.	Captured, 7/14/63 at Falling Waters, MD
Co. C	Pvt.	Casper, James H.	Captured, 7/14/63 at Falling Waters, MD
Co. C	Pvt.	Jackson, Joseph	Captured, 7/14/63 at Falling Waters, MD
Co. C	Pvt.	King, Joseph	Captured, 7/14/63 at Falling Waters, MD
Co. C	Pvt.	Parker, John H.	Captured, 7/14/63 at Falling Waters, MD
Co. C	Pvt.	Skiles, Robert	Captured, 7/14/63 at Falling Waters, MD
Co. D	1st Sgt.	Brittain, O. Joseph	Captured, 7/14/63 at Falling Waters, MD
Co. D	Sgt.	Black, Samuel J.	Captured, 7/14/63 at Falling Waters, MD
Co. D	Pvt.	Benfield, Thomas W.	Wounded (thigh), 7/14/63 at Falling Waters, MD
Co. D	Pvt.	Blue, David	Captured, 7/14/63 at Falling Waters, MD
Co. D	Pvt.	Brittain, Julius T.	Captured, 7/14/63 at Falling Waters, MD
Co. D	Pvt.	Cook, John D.	Wounded (left cheek), 7/14/63 at Falling Waters, MD
Co. D	Pvt.	Fair, Hezekiah	Captured, 7/14/63 at Falling Waters, MD
Co. D	Pvt.	Huffman, Abraham	Captured, 7/14/63 at Falling Waters, MD
Co. D	Pvt.	Johnson, John, W.	Captured, 7/14/63 at Falling Waters, MD
Co. D	Pvt.	Mace, Abraham	Captured, 7/14/63 at Falling Waters, MD
Co. D	Pvt.	Miller, Marshall (Mack)	Captured, 7/14/63 at Falling Waters, MD
Co. D	Pvt.	Poteet, John	Captured, 7/14/63 at Falling Waters, MD
Co. D	Pvt.	Taylor, Charles	Captured, 7/14/63 at Falling Waters, MD
Co. D	Pvt.	Whisenhunt, Benjamin R.	Captured, 7/14/63 at Falling Waters, MD
Co. D	Pvt.	Williams, Moulton	Captured, 7/14/63 at Falling Waters, MD
Co. D	Pvt.	Williams, William M.	Wounded, 7/14/63 at Falling Waters, MD
Co. E	Pvt.	Jameson, Jones W.	Captured, 7/14/63 at Falling Waters, MD
Co. E	Pvt.	McCorkle, Hugh P.	Captured, 7/14/63 at Falling Waters, MD
Co. E	Pvt.	McLure, Cyrus A.	Captured, 7/14/63 at Falling Waters, MD
Co. F	Sgt.	Mardre, Nathaniel	Captured, 7/14/63 at Falling Waters, MD
Co. F	Cpl.	Creecy, James E.	Captured, 7/14/63 at Falling Waters, MD
Co. F	Pvt.	Bagley, Thomas C.	Captured, 7/14/63 at Falling Waters, MD
Co. F	Pvt.	Bateman, Timothy C.	Captured, 7/14/63 at Falling Waters, MD
Co. F	Pvt.	Forehand, Adam	Captured, 7/14/63 at Falling Waters, MD
Co. F	Pvt.	Goodwin, Benjamin F.	Captured, 7/14/63 at Falling Waters, MD
Co. F	Pvt.	White, Robert	Captured, 7/14/63 at Falling Waters, MD
Co. G	Pvt.	Cheek, John A.	Captured, 7/14/63 at Falling Waters, MD
Co. G	Pvt.	Daniel, Robert	Captured, 7/14/63 at Falling Waters, MD
Co. G	Pvt.	Jolly, William	Captured, 7/14/63 at Falling Waters, MD
Co. G	Pvt.	King, Rufus	Captured, 7/14/63 at Falling Waters, MD
Co. G	Pvt.	Reeves, Edward	Captured, 7/14/63 at Falling Waters, MD
Co. G	Pvt.	Sparrow, William T.	Captured, 7/14/63 at Falling Waters, MD
Co. G	Pvt.	Whitaker, Thomas J.	Captured, 7/14/63 at Falling Waters, MD
Co. H	Sgt.	Caldwell, John S.	Captured, 7/14/63 at Falling Waters, MD

Unit	Rank	Name	Remarks
Co. H	Pvt.	Cooper, James M.	Captured, 7/14/63 at Falling Waters, MD
Co. H	Pvt.	Knox, William H.	Captured, 7/14/63 at Falling Waters, MD
Co. H	Pvt.	Mincey, Wiley	Captured, 7/14/63 at Falling Waters, MD
Co. H	Pvt.	Smith, Thomas J.	Captured, 7/14/63 at Falling Waters, MD
Co. I	Pvt.	Boyles, Joseph	Wounded (left arm) and captured, 7/14/63 at Falling Waters, MD
Co. I	Pvt.	Huss, John	Captured, 7/14/63 at Falling Waters, MD
Co. I	Pvt.	Jetton, Taylor B.	Captured, 7/14/63 at Falling Waters, MD
Co. I	Pvt.	Rinck, Daniel	Captured, 7/14/63 at Falling Waters, MD
Co. I	Pvt.	Shull, Anthony	Captured, 7/14/63 at Falling Waters, MD
Co. K	Pvt.	Bartlett, James P.	Captured, 7/6/63 at Williamsport, MD
Co. K	Pvt.	Cordell, James M.	Captured, 7/6/63 at Williamsport, MD
Co. K	Pvt.	Goodson, Thomas	Captured, 7/14/63 at Falling Waters, MD
Co. K	Pvt.	Hall, John P.	Captured, 7/14/63 at Falling Waters, MD
Co. K	Pvt.	Kyles, James	Captured, 7/14/63 at Falling Waters, MD
Co. K	Pvt.	Morris, Charles	Captured, 7/14/63 at Falling Waters, MD
Co. K	Pvt.	Morris, Cornelius	Captured, 7/14/63 at Falling Waters, MD
Co. K	Pvt.	Poor, William H.	Captured, 7/14/63 at Falling Waters, MD
Co. K	Pvt.	Powers, James R.	Captured, 7/14/63 at Falling Waters, MD
Co. K	Pvt.	Roberts, Martin P.	Captured, 7/14/63 at Falling Waters, MD
Co. K	Pvt.	Watkins, Uriah Preston	Captured, 7/14/63 at Falling Waters, MD

Bristoe Station, VA—October 14, 1863
57 = 3 Killed, 11 Wounded, 1 Wounded & Captured, 42 Captured

Unit	Rank	Name	Remarks
F & S	Lt. Col.	Martin, William	Wounded (left arm and head) at Bristoe Station, VA
Co. A	Pvt.	Cochrane, John F.	Captured, 10/14/63 at Bristoe Station, VA
Co. A	Pvt.	King, Campbell	Captured, 10/14/63 at Bristoe Station, VA
Co. A	Pvt.	Orr, N. C.	Captured, 10/14/63 at Bristoe Station, VA
Co. B	Pvt.	Cook, Thomas	Captured, 10/14/63 at Bristoe Station, VA
Co. B	Pvt.	Livingston, Larkin	Captured, 10/14/63 at Bristoe Station, VA
Co. B	Pvt.	Mull, Henry	Captured, 10/14/63 at Bristoe Station, VA
Co. B	Pvt.	Patton, William S.	Captured, 10/14/63 at Bristoe Station, VA
Co. B	Pvt.	Shuffler, John	Wounded (foot), 10/14/63 at Bristoe Station, VA
Co. C	Pvt.	Butler, Levin E.	Captured, 10/14/63 at Bristoe Station, VA
Co. C	Pvt.	Evans, Aaron J.	Captured, 10/14/63 at Bristoe Station, VA
Co. C	Pvt.	Mitchell, James E.	Captured, 10/14/63 at Bristoe Station, VA
Co. C	Pvt.	Rawls, James R.	Captured, 10/14/63 at Bristoe Station, VA
Co. C	Pvt.	Stone, John	Captured, 10/14/63 at Bristoe Station, VA
Co. D	Pvt.	Baker, Lucius	Wounded (left hip), 10/14/63 at Bristoe Station, VA
Co. D	Pvt.	Bingham, Robert W.	Captured, 10/14/63 at Bristoe Station, VA
Co. D	Pvt.	Clark, Benjamin	Captured, 10/14/63 at Bristoe Station, VA
Co. D	Pvt.	Cook, John D.	Wounded, 10/14/63 at Bristoe Station, VA. Died of wounds, 2/1/64 in Richmond hospital, VA
Co. D	Pvt.	Mace, William H.	Captured, 10/14/63 at Bristoe Station, VA
Co. D	Pvt.	Powell, William P.	Captured, 10/14/63 at Bristoe Station, VA
Co. D	Pvt.	Summers, Perry	Wounded, 10/14/63 at Bristoe Station, VA. Died of wounds, 10/15/63
Co. E	2nd Lt.	Grier, Paul B.	Killed, 10/14/63 at Bristoe Station, VA
Co. E	Pvt.	Belk, William A.	Captured, 10/14/63 at Bristoe Station, VA
Co. E	Pvt.	Finger, John	Wounded and captured, 10/14/63 at Bristoe Station, VA
Co. F	Pvt.	Bratton, William J.	Captured, 10/14/63 at Bristoe Station, VA

Unit	Rank	Name	Remarks
Co. F	Pvt.	Briggs, James	Captured, 10/14/62 at Bristoe Station, VA
Co. F	Pvt.	Creecy, Henry L.	Captured, 10/14/63 at Bristoe Station, VA
Co. F	Pvt.	Farmer, Joseph J.	Captured, 10/14/63 at Bristoe Station, VA
Co. F	Pvt.	Garrett, Stephen	Captured, 10/14/63 at Bristoe Station, VA
Co. F	Pvt.	Potter, John	Captured, 10/14/63 at Bristoe Station, VA
Co. F	Pvt.	Potter, Samuel	Captured, 10/14/63 at Bristoe Station, VA
Co. F	Pvt.	Stearns, David M.	Captured, 10/14/63 at Bristoe Station, VA
Co. F	Pvt.	Sutton, S. S.	Captured, 10/14/63 at Bristoe Station, VA
Co. F	Pvt.	Swain, James W.	Wounded (left ankle), 10/14/63 at Bristoe Station, VA
Co. F	Pvt.	Wingate, Joseph W.	Wounded (left arm), 10/14/63 at Bristoe Station, VA
Co. G	Pvt.	Allen, Ruffin	Captured, 10/14/63 at Bristoe Station, VA
Co. G	Pvt.	Davis, Henry A.	Captured, 10/14/63 at Bristoe Station, VA
Co. G	Pvt.	Pendergrass, George	Captured, 10/14/63 at Bristoe Station, VA
Co. G	Pvt.	Petty, Henry	Captured, 10/14/63 at Bristoe Station, VA
Co. G	Pvt.	Sparrow, Van B.	Captured, 10/14/63 at Bristoe Station, VA
Co. H	Pvt.	Smith, James W.	Missing in action, 10/14/63 at Bristoe Station, VA
Co. H	Pvt.	Thrower, Jeff T.	Captured, 10/14/63 at Bristoe Station, VA
Co. I	Sgt.	Ramseur, Walter G.	Wounded (back), 10/14/63 at Bristoe Station, VA "struck by a cannon ball" Died of wounds, 10/27/63 in hospital, Richmond, VA
Co. I	Pvt.	Carpenter, Michael	Wounded (leg), 10/23/63 at Bristoe Station, VA
Co. I	Pvt.	Hubbart, Charles	Captured, 10/14/63 at Bristoe Station, VA
Co. I	Pvt.	Huss, Jacob	Killed, 10/14/63 at Bristoe Station, VA
Co. I	Pvt.	Kiser, John A.	Wounded, 10/14/63 at Bristoe Station, VA. In hospital, Richmond. Died of wounds, 12/14/63
Co. I	Pvt.	Lenhardt, Joseph M.	Wounded, 10/14/63 at Bristoe Station, VA
Co. I	Pvt.	Mullin, Alfred E.	Captured, 10/14/63 at Bristoe Station, VA
Co. I	Pvt.	Ramsour, John M.	Captured, 10/17/63 at Bristoe Station, VA
Co. I	Pvt.	Sigmore, Noah	Killed, 10/14/63 at Bristoe Station, VA
Co. I	Pvt.	Weaver, Phillip C.	Wounded, 10/14/63 at Bristoe Station, VA
Co. I	Pvt.	Yoder, David	Captured, 10/14/63 at Bristoe Station, VA.
Co. K	Cpl.	Davidson, John M.	Captured, 10/14/63 at Bristoe Station, VA
Co. K	Pvt.	Justice, Foster	Captured, 10/14/63 at Bristoe Station, VA
Co. K	Pvt.	Trantham, John	Captured, 10/14/63 at Bristoe Station, VA
Co. K	Pvt.	Trantham, Joseph	Captured, 10/14/63 at Bristoe Station, VA

The Wilderness, VA—May 5-8, 1864
47 = 4 Killed, 33 Wounded, 1 Wounded & Captured, 6 Captured, 3 Missing

Unit	Rank	Name	Remarks
Co. A	Cpl.	Lewis Emanuel	Wounded (left hand), 5/5/64 at the Wilderness
Co. A	Pvt.	Howard, Thomas M.	Wounded, 5/5/64 at the Wilderness
Co. A	Pvt.	Kennedy, William	Wounded, 5/5/64 at the Wilderness
Co. A	Pvt.	Monteith, Moses O.	Wounded and captured, 5/5/64 at the Wilderness
Co. A	Pvt.	Pettus, John W.	Wounded, 5/5/64 at the Wilderness
Co. B	2nd Lt.	Warlick, Lewis	Wounded (right arm, slightly), 5/5/64 at the Wilderness
Co. C	Pvt.	Hargroves, Richard	Missing, 5/5/64 at the Wilderness
Co. C	Pvt.	Longee, Augustus H.	Captured, 5/5/64 at the Wilderness
Co. D	Sgt.	Lane, John E.	Killed, 5/5/64 at the Wilderness
Co. D	Pvt.	Kincaid, William W.	Captured, 5/6/64 at the Wilderness
Co. D	Pvt.	Melton, Eugene A.	Wounded (right thigh), 5/5/64 at the Wilderness
Co. D	Pvt.	Miller, Jackson	Wounded, 5/5/64 at the Wilderness

Unit	Rank	Name	Remarks
Co. D	Pvt.	Mosteller, Isaiah	Wounded, 5/5/64 at the Wilderness
Co. D	Pvt.	Ross, Stephen A.	Wounded, 5/5/64 at the Wilderness. Died of wounds, 8/7/64 in Richmond hospital
Co. D	Pvt.	Rudisill, Absalom	Wounded (right hand), 5/6/64 in the Wilderness
Co. D	Pvt.	Spain, H. D.	Wounded, 5/5/64 at the Wilderness
Co. E	Sgt.	Rozzell, James T.	Killed, 5/5/64 at the Wilderness
Co. E	Cpl.	Hartgrove, William W.	Wounded, 5/5/64 at the Wilderness
Co. F	1st Lt.	Roberts, Stephen W.	Wounded (left leg), 5/5/64 at the Wilderness
Co. F	Sgt.	Mardre, Nathaniel	Wounded, 5/5/64 at the Wilderness
Co. F	Pvt.	Jordan, Hance	Missing, 5/6/64 at the Wilderness
Co. F	Pvt.	Miller, James	Wounded, 5/5/64 at the Wilderness
Co. H	2nd Lt.	Knox, John H.	Wounded, 5/5/64 at the Wilderness. Died of wounds, 5/29/64 in hospital at Staunton, VA
Co. H	Sgt.	McMillan, James E.	Wounded, 5/5/64 at the Wilderness. Died of wounds, 6/25/64 in hospital at Lynchburg
Co. H	Cpl.	Thrower, Alex	Wounded, 5/5/64 at the Wilderness
Co. H	Pvt.	Alexander, John A.	Wounded, 5/5/64 at the Wilderness. Died of wounds, 6/2/64 at Staunton VA hospital
Co. H	Pvt.	Hudspeth, George	Wounded, 5/5/64 in the Wilderness
Co. H	Pvt.	Smith, James W.	Wounded, 5/5/64 at the Wilderness
Co. H	Pvt.	Stanford, James L.	Wounded, 5/5/64 at the Wilderness
Co. H	Pvt.	Wingate, R. James	Wounded (thigh), 5/5/64 at the Wilderness
Co. I	Pvt.	Cody, James	Wounded, 5/5/64 at the Wilderness
Co. I	Pvt.	Dellinger, Frederick W.	Wounded (right breast), 5/5/64 at the Wilderness
Co. I	Pvt.	Dellinger, Phillip	Wounded (right leg amputated), 5/5/64 at the Wilderness
Co. I	Pvt.	Glenn, David M.	Wounded, 5/5/64 at the Wilderness
Co. I	Pvt.	Richey, Joseph C.	Killed, 5/5/64 at the Wilderness
Co. I	Pvt.	Sherrill, William A.	Wounded, 5/5/64 at the Wilderness
Co. I	Pvt.	Smith, John J.	Wounded (leg), 5/5/64 at the Wilderness. Leg amputated, 8/64 in Petersburg, VA
Co. I	Pvt.	Wacaster, Adolphus	Captured, 5/5/64 at the Wilderness
Co. K	2nd Lt.	Boyd, Benjamin F	Captured, 5/5/64 at the Wilderness.
Co. K	Cpl.	Pickens, George A.	Wounded, 5/5/64 at the Wilderness.
Co. K	Cpl.	Bird, George W.	Wounded, 5/5/64 at the Wilderness. Died of wounds, 5/16/64
Co. K	Pvt.	Bartlett, John H.	Missing, 5/5/64 at the Wilderness.
Co. K	Pvt.	Brittain, William T.	Captured, 5/5/64 at the Wilderness
Co. K	Pvt.	Crow, Joseph W.	Wounded, 5/5/64 at the Wilderness
Co. K	Pvt.	Patton, George A.	Wounded (left thigh and right ankle), 5/5/64 at the Wilderness.
Co. K	Pvt.	Smith, William E.	Wounded, 5/5/64 at the Wilderness
Co. K	Pvt.	Watkins, Jesse M.	Captured, 5/8/64 at Wilderness

Spotsylvania, VA—May 10–22, 1864
27 = 2 Killed, 22 Wounded, 2 Captured, 1 Missing

Unit	Rank	Name	Remarks
F & S	Col.	Martin, William	Wounded (slightly), 5/10/64 at Spotsylvania
Co. A	Sgt.	Brown, William J.	Wounded, 5/10/64 at Spotsylvania
Co. A	Pvt.	Hovis, Monroe	Wounded (left shoulder), 5/12/64 at Spotsylvania
Co. B	Pvt.	Crawley, J. W.	Wounded (neck), 5/12/64 at Spotsylvania
Co. B	Pvt.	Loudermilk, George	Wounded, 5/10/64 at Spotsylvania
Co. B	Pvt.	Warlick, D. Logan	Killed, 5/12/64 at Spotsylvania

Unit	Rank	Name	Remarks
Co. B	Pvt.	Williams, Robert G.	Wounded, 5/10/64 at Spotsylvania
Co. C	Pvt.	Brogden, William G.	Wounded, 5/10/64 at Spotsylvania
Co. C	Pvt.	Davis, Allen	Wounded (arm), 5/12/64 at Spotsylvania
Co. C	Pvt.	Lucas, Augustus G.	"Lost on the march," 5/10/64 at Spotsylvania
Co. C	Pvt.	Myers, Nathan	Wounded (hand), 5/12/64 at Spotsylvania
Co. D	Pvt.	Hicks, Rufus	Captured, 5/24/64 at Spotsylvania
Co. E	Pvt.	Hartline, David L.	Wounded, 5/10/64 at Spotsylvania
Co. E	Pvt.	Pool, George S.	Wounded (right leg), 5/10/64 at Spotsylvania
Co. E	Pvt.	Walker, Levi L.	Killed, 5/10/64 at Spotsylvania
Co. G	Sgt.	Clements, John R.	Wounded (hand), 5/10/64 at Spotsylvania
Co. G	Pvt.	Blackwood, Edmond	Wounded, 5/10/64 at Spotsylvania
Co. H	Pvt.	Carothers, James A.	Wounded, 5/10/64 at Spotsylvania
Co. I	Cpl.	Harrelson, James F.	Wounded, 5/10/64 at the Spotsylvania
Co. I	Pvt.	Havner, Julius A.	Wounded, 5/10/64 at Spotsylvania
Co. I	Pvt.	Haynes, Ryann W.	Wounded, 5/10/64 at Spotsylvania
Co. I	Pvt.	Hudspeth, John T.	Wounded (finger), 5/10/64, at Spotsylvania
Co. I	Pvt.	Lenhardt, Joseph M.	Wounded, 5/12/64 at Spotsylvania
Co. I	Pvt.	Pool, Albert J.	Captured, 5/22/64 at Spotsylvania
Co. K	3rd Lt.	Gash, Lucius W	Wounded, 5/12/64 at Spotsylvania. Died of wounds, 5/14/64
Co. K	1st Sgt.	West, John Preston, Sr.	Wounded, 5/10/64 at Spotsylvania. Died of wounds, 5/11/64 at Spotsylvania
Co. K	Pvt.	Bell, George H.	Wounded, 5/10/64 at Spotsylvania.

Cold Harbor, VA—June 1–12, 1864
23 = 1 Killed, 21 Wounded, 1 Captured

June 1, 1864

Unit	Rank	Name	Remarks
Co. C	Cpl.	Burden, James M.	Wounded (hip & left hand), 6/1/64 Cold Harbor
Co. D	Pvt.	Hawkins, William P.	Wounded (left leg), 6/1/64 at Cold Harbor
Co. G	Pvt.	Clements, William G.	Wounded (finger), 6/1/64 at Cold Harbor
Co. D	Pvt.	Kinney, Alexander D.	Captured, 6/1/64 at Cold Harbor
Co. G	Pvt.	Smith, John	Wounded, 6/1/64 at Cold Harbor
Co. H	Pvt.	Taggert, John C.	Wounded (right breast), 6/1/64 at Cold Harbor
Co. H	Pvt.	Wilkerson, William H.	Wounded (head), 6/1/64 at Cold Harbor
Co. I	Pvt.	Craft, Michael J.	Wounded (arm), 6/1/64 at Cold Harbor
Co. I	Pvt.	Ramsour, Theodore J.	Wounded (leg amputated), 6/1/64 at Cold Harbor
Co. I	Pvt.	Roseman, Robert M.	Wounded (ankle), 6/1/64 at Cold Harbor
Co. K	Pvt.	McClure, Ottway B.	Wounded, 6/1/64 at Cold Harbor

June 2, 1864

Unit	Rank	Name	Remarks
Co. A	3rd Lt.	Taylor, William B.	Wounded, 6/2/64, Cold Harbor
Co. A	Cpl.	Icehower, William S.	Killed, 6/2/64 at Cold Harbor.
Co. B	Pvt.	Harbison, William T.	Wounded (right leg amputated), 6/2/64 at Cold Harbor
Co. G	1st Sgt.	Davis, Thomas	Wounded, 6/2/64 at Cold Harbor
Co. H	Pvt.	Hall, N. C.	Wounded, 6/2/64 at Cold Harbor
Co. H	Pvt.	Hall, Robert B.	Wounded (left hand), 6/2/24 at Cold Harbor
Co. H	Pvt.	Henry, Berry G.	Wounded (forearm), 6/2/64 at Cold Harbor
Co. H	Pvt.	Henry, Tyrell B.	Wounded, 6/2/64 at Cold Harbor

June 3–12, 1864

Unit	Rank	Name	Remarks
Co. A	Pvt.	King, Campbell	Wounded, 6/3/64 at Cold Harbor
Co. I	Pvt.	Hauser, Henry	Wounded, 6/6/64 at Cold Harbor.

Unit	Rank	Name	Remarks
Co. B	Cpl.	Warlick, A. Pink	Wounded, 6/12/64 near White Oak Swamp. Died of wounds, 6/30/64
Co. D	Pvt.	Johnson, Daniel L.	Wounded (hand), 6/12/64 at White Oak Swamp

Virginia—Summer 1864
22 = 4 Killed, 17 Wounded, 1 Captured

Late June–mid August 1864

Unit	Rank	Name	Remarks
Co. B	Pvt.	Livingston, Larkin	Wounded (left arm), 6/23/64 near Weldon Rd.
Co. E	Cpt.	Kerr, William	Wounded (left leg), 7/23/64 at Petersburg
Co. B	Pvt.	Moore, Thomas B.	Killed, 7/30/64 at New Market
Co. G	Pvt.	Cates, John W.	Wounded (right shoulder), 8/15/64 in Petersburg trenches

Weldon Road, VA: August 21–22, 1864

Unit	Rank	Name	Remarks
Co. A	Cpl.	Alexander, James N.	Wounded, 8/21/64 at Weldon Rd. Deserted, 9/30/64
Co. B	Pvt.	Cannon, James	Wounded, 8/21/64 at Weldon Rd., VA
Co. B	Pvt.	Pearson, Thomas	Wounded, 8/21/64 at Weldon Rd, VA
Co. D	Pvt.	Benfield, Thomas W.	Wounded, 8/21/64 at Weldon Rd, VA. Died of wounds, 9/19/64 in hospital in Richmond
Co. D	Pvt.	Causby, William	Wounded, 8/21/64 at Weldon Rd, VA
Co. A	Pvt.	Taylor, J. Q.	Died of self-inflicted wounds, 10/24/64
Co. F	2nd Lt.	Rea, William D.	Wounded (face), 8/21/64 at Weldon Rd, VA
Co. F	Sgt.	Small, Thomas M.	Wounded, 8/21/64 at Weldon Rd, VA
Co. F	Pvt.	Long, John	Wounded (elbow), 8/21/64 at Weldon Rd, VA
Co. F	Pvt.	Troutman, Joseph W.	Wounded, 8/22/64 at Weldon Rd, VA
Co. G	Pvt.	Campbell, Robert	Captured, 8/21/64 at Weldon Rd, VA
Co. H	Cpl.	Thrower, Alex	Wounded, 8/21/64 at Weldon Rd, VA
Co. I	1st Sgt.	Bell, Robert M.	Wounded (chest), 8/21/64 at Weldon Rd, VA. Died of wounds, 8/31/64
Co. I	Pvt.	Kiser, Henry	Killed, 8/21/64 at Weldon Rd, VA
Co. I	Pvt.	Smith, John J.	Wounded (leg amputated), 8/21/64 at Weldon Rd, VA
Co. K	Pvt.	Morris, Zebidee W.	Wounded (right arm), 8/21/64 at Weldon Rd, VA
Co. D	Pvt.	Morefield, John	Killed, 8/25/64 at Weldon Rd, VA

Reams' Station, VA—August 25–26, 1864
18 = 3 Killed, 14 Wounded, 1 Captured

Unit	Rank	Name	Remarks
F & S	Col.	Martin, William	Wounded (slightly, "grazed by a ball"), 8/25/64 at Reams' Station, VA
F & S	Lt. Col.	Bird, Francis "Frank"	Wounded, 8/25/64 at Reams' Station, VA. Died of wounds, 8/26/64
Co. A	3rd Lt.	Montgomery, James H.	Wounded (leg amputated), 8/25/64 at Reams' Station, VA. Died of wounds, 9/9/64
Co. A	Pvt.	Alexander, John G.	Killed, 8/25/64 at Reams' Station, VA
Co. C	1st Lt.	Todd, William H.	Wounded (right buttock), 8/25/64 at Reams' Station, VA
Co. C	1st Sgt.	Carter, Joseph B.	Killed, 8/25/64 at Reams' Station, VA
Co. D	Pvt.	Morefield, John	Mortally wounded, 8/25/64 at Reams' Station, VA. Died of wounds later that day.

Unit	Rank	Name	Remarks
Co. E	Pvt.	Hill, James W.	Killed, 8/25/64 at Reams' Station, VA
Co. F	Pvt.	Askew, Miles	Wounded, 8/25/64 at Reams' Station, VA
Co. G	1st Lt.	Waddell, Duncan C.	Wounded (right lung), 8/25/64 at Reams' Station, VA
Co. G	Pvt.	Whitaker, Thomas J.	Wounded, 8/25/64 at Reams' Station, VA
Co. H	Pvt.	Humphreys, Joseph L.	Wounded, 8/25/64 at Reams' Station, VA
Co. I	Pvt.	Glenn, Robert J.	Wounded, 8/25/64 at Reams' Station, VA
Co. I	Pvt.	Hubbart, David	Wounded (left leg amputated), 8/25/64 at Reams' Station, VA
Co. I	Pvt.	Rinck, Andrew	Wounded (slightly, "by a cannon ball"), 8/25/64 at Reams' Station, VA
Co. I	Pvt.	Seagle, Andrew	Captured, 8/22/64 at Reams' Station, VA
Co. I	Pvt.	Warlick, John C.	Wounded (left arm), 8/21/64 at Reams' Station, VA
Co. K	Cpt.	Young, James	Wounded (head), 8/25/64 at Reams Station, VA

Jones Farm, VA—September 30–October 2, 1864
38 = 3 Killed, 33 Wounded, 1 Captured

Jones' Farm, VA: September 30, 1864

Unit	Rank	Name	Remarks
F & S	Col.	Martin, William J.	Wounded (left thigh), 9/30/64 at Jones' Farm
Co. A	Sgt.	McElroy, Samuel J.	Wounded (right side of face), 9/30/64 at Jones' Farm
Co. A	Pvt.	Hill, Henry H.	Wounded (left side of head), 9/30/64 at Jones Farm
Co. A	Pvt.	Holmes, Thomas L.	Wounded (left hip), 9/30/64 at Jones Farm. Died of wounds, 10/25/64 in hospital in Richmond
Co. A	Pvt.	Stowe, Jacob C.	Wounded, 9/30/64 at Jones' Farm
Co. A	Pvt.	Whiters, B. A.	Wounded, 9/30/64 at Jones' Farm
Co. A	Pvt.	Wright, Taylor	Wounded, 9/30/64 at Jones Farm
Co. B	Pvt.	Shelton, James	Wounded, 9/30/64 at Jones Farm
Co. B	Pvt.	Smith, Alva	Wounded (right knee), 9/30/64 at Jones' Farm
Co. B	Pvt.	Teem, William C.	Wounded, 9/30/64 at Jones' Farm
Co. C	Cpl.	Butler, William H.	Wounded, 9/30/64 at Jones Farm
Co. D	Pvt.	Benfield, Martin	Wounded, 9/30/64 at Jones Farm
Co. D	Pvt.	Blain, William M.	Wounded, 9/30/64 at Jones' Farm. Died of wounds, 10/3/64 at hospital in Petersburg
Co. D	Pvt.	Huffman, Abraham	Killed, 9/30/64 at Jones' Farm
Co. D	Pvt.	Miller, Marshall (Mack)	Wounded, 9/30/64 at Jones' Farm. Died of wounds, 10/8/64 in hospital in Richmond
Co. E	1st Sgt.	McDonald, David W.	Killed, 9/30/64 at Jones' Farm
Co. E	Pvt.	Linebarger, Marshall	Captured, 9/30/64 at Jones' Farm
Co. G	Pvt.	Flintoff, William D.	Wounded (right side), 9/30/64 at Jones' Farm. Died of wounds, 11/9/64
Co. H	2nd Lt.	Saville, James M.	Wounded (left shoulder), 9/30/64 at Jones' Farm
Co. H	Pvt.	Hinnant, Henry	Wounded (right hand), 9/30/64 at Jones' Farm
Co. H	Pvt.	Knox, William H.	Wounded, 9/30/64 at Jones' Farm
Co. H	Pvt.	Thrower, Jeff T.	Wounded, 9/30/64 at Jones' Farm
Co. I	Pvt.	Blackburn, A. Lafayette	Wounded, 9/30/64 at Jones' Farm. Died of wounds, 10/30/64 in Richmond hospital
Co. K	Cpt.	Young, James M.	Wounded (head), 9/30/64 at Jones' Farm
Co. K	Pvt.	Smith, Richard	Wounded, 9/30/64 at Jones' Farm

Squirrel Level Road, VA: October 1, 1864

Unit	Rank	Name	Remarks
Co. D	Pvt.	Albright, William S.	Wounded (head), 10/1/64 at Squirrel Level Road. Died of wounds, 10/4/64 at hospital in Richmond
Co. D	Pvt.	Upton, Dan H.	Wounded (left hand), 10/1/64 at Squirrel Level Road

Unit	Rank	Name	Remarks
Co. F	Pvt.	Bridges, Roswald D.	Wounded (right thigh), 10/1/64 at Squirrel Level Road
Co. F	Pvt.	Parrish, Stephen	Wounded, 10/1/64 at Squirrel Level Road
Co. F	Pvt.	Taylor, Joseph	Wounded, 10/1/64 at Squirrel Level Road
Co. I	Pvt.	Cornwell, Sidney	Killed, 10/1/64 at Squirrel Level Road

DUNCAN/HARMON ROAD, VA: OCTOBER 2, 1864

Unit	Rank	Name	Remarks
Co. A	Sgt.	Neily, Thomas W	Wounded (left thigh), 10/2/64 at Duncan Rd.
Co. A	Cpl.	Gribble, James R.	Wounded (left ankle), 10/2/64 at Duncan Rd.
Co. A	Pvt.	Ewing, George R.	Wounded (left hip), 10/2/64 at Duncan Rd.
Co. B	Pvt.	Smith, Henry	Wounded (eye), 10/2/64 at Duncan Rd.
Co. C	Pvt.	Parker, Thomas H.	Wounded (left hand), 10/2/64 at Duncan Rd.
Co. D	Cpl.	Hennesse, Emmanuel	Wounded (forehead), 10/2/64 at Duncan Rd.

Burgess' Mill, VA—October 27, 1864
121 = 18 Wounded, 2 Wounded & Captured, 101 Captured

Unit	Rank	Name	Remarks
Co. A	Pvt.	Alexander, Marshall R.	Wounded, 10/27/64 at Burgess' Mill, VA.
Co. A	Pvt.	Flow, R. H.	Wounded, 10/27/64 at Burgess' Mill, VA.
Co. A	Pvt.	Hand, Andrew J.	Captured, 10/27/64 at Burgess' Mill, VA.
Co. A	Pvt.	Orr, James F.	Captured, 10/27/64 at Burgess' Mill, VA.
Co. A	Pvt.	Ruddick, Burl M.	Wounded, 10/27/64 at Burgess' Mill, VA.
Co. A	Pvt.	Ruddick, B. Wilson	Wounded (right leg), 10/27/64 at Burgess' Mill, VA.
Co. A	Pvt.	Ruddick, Theo C.	Captured, 10/27/64 at Burgess' Mill, VA.
Co. A	Pvt.	Taylor, Houston S.	Captured, 10/27/64 at Burgess' Mill, VA.
Co. B	3rd Lt.	Walker, Elisha F.	Captured, 10/27/64 at Burgess' Mill, VA.
Co. B	Cpl.	Crawley, J. W.	Captured, 10/27/74 at Burgess' Mill, VA.
Co. B	Pvt.	Gilbert, Johnson	Wounded (right foot), 10/27/64 Burgess' Mill, VA.
Co. B	Pvt.	Griffin, William	Captured, 10/27/64 at Burgess' Mill, VA.
Co. B	Pvt.	Harris, Lewis B.	Wounded, 10/27/64 at Burgess' Mill, VA.
Co. B	Pvt.	Keller, George	Wounded, 10/27/62 at Burgess' Mill, VA. Died of wounds, 10/28/62
Co. B	Pvt.	Mincey, Kinchen	Captured, 10/27/64 at Burgess' Mill, VA.
Co. B	Pvt.	Short, Daniel	Captured, 10/27/64 at Burgess' Mill, VA.
Co. B	Pvt.	Shuffler, Sidney	Captured, 10/27/64 at Burgess' Mill, VA.
Co. B	Pvt.	Swink, Archibald	Captured, 10/27/64 at Burgess' Mill, VA.
Co. B	Pvt.	Walker, J. R.	Captured, 10/27/64 at Burgess' Mill, VA.
Co. B	Pvt.	Williams, Joseph B.	Captured, 10/27/64 at Burgess' Mill, VA.
Co. C	2nd Lt.	Winston, Patrick H.	Captured, 10/14/64 at Burgess' Mill, VA.
Co. C	1st Sgt.	Floyd, John G.	Captured, 10/14/64 at Burgess' Mill, VA.
Co. C	Pvt.	Davis, John	Captured, 10/27/64 at Burgess' Mill, VA.
Co. C	Pvt.	Harmon, James F.	Captured, 10/27/64 at Burgess' Mill, VA.
Co. C	Pvt.	Ward, William C.	Captured, 10/27/64 at Burgess' Mill, VA.
Co. D	2nd Lt.	McCorkle, James G.	Captured, 10/27/64 at Burgess' Mill, VA.
Co. D	Cpl.	Butler, William H.	Wounded, 10/27/64 at Burgess' Mill, VA.
Co. D	Pvt.	Abee, Andrew J.	Captured, 10/27/74 at Burgess' Mill, VA.
Co. D	Pvt.	Fair, Henry	Captured, 10/227/64 at Burgess' Mill, VA.
Co. D	Pvt.	Johnson, Robert N.	Captured, 10/27/64 at Burgess' Mill, VA.
Co. D	Pvt.	Martin, Joseph	Captured, 10/27/64 at Burgess' Mill, VA.
Co. D	Pvt.	Rudisill, Absalom	Captured, 10/27/64 at Burgess' Mill, VA.
Co. D	Pvt.	Whisenhunt, R. Benjamin	Wounded, 10/27/64 at Burgess' Mill, VA.
Co. E	1st Lt.	Turner, William S.	Captured, 10/27/64 at Burgess' Mill, VA.
Co. E	Sgt.	Puckett, Julius J.	Captured, 10/27/64 at Burgess' Mill, VA.

Unit	Rank	Name	Remarks
Co. E	Sgt.	Wilson, Robert L.	Captured, 10/27/64 at Burgess' Mill, VA.
Co. E	Cpl.	Jameson, James W.	Captured, 10/27/64 at Burgess' Mill, VA.
Co. E	Cpl.	Walker, James H.	Captured, 10/27/64 at Burgess' Mill, VA.
Co. E	Pvt.	Bass, Burton	Captured, 10/27/64 at Burgess' Mill, VA.
Co. E	Pvt.	Beal, Charles	Captured, 10/27/64 at Burgess' Mill, VA.
Co. E	Pvt.	Beal, John	Captured, 10/27/64 at Burgess' Mill, VA.
Co. E	Pvt.	Beatty, John W.	Captured, 10/27/64 at Burgess' Mill, VA.
Co. E	Pvt.	Campbell, John W.	Wounded (right arm), 10/27/64 at Burgess' Mill, VA.
Co. E	Pvt.	Culberson, John W.	Captured, 10/27/64 at Burgess' Mill, VA.
Co. E	Pvt.	Edwards, Marshall	Captured, 10/27/64 at Burgess' Mill, VA.
Co. E	Pvt.	Garrison, Alfred	Captured, 10/27/64 at Burgess' Mill, VA.
Co. E	Pvt.	Hartgrove, Richard D. S.	Captured, 10/27/64 at Burgess' Mill, VA.
Co. E	Pvt.	Jameson, Jones W.	Captured, 10/27/64 at Burgess' Mill, VA.
Co. E	Pvt.	Johnston, J. W.	Captured, 10/27/64 at Burgess' Mill, VA.
Co. E	Pvt.	Kyles, Fielding	Captured, 10/27/64 at Burgess' Mill, VA.
Co. E	Pvt.	Loftin, Martin	Captured, 10/27/64 at Burgess' Mill, VA.
Co. E	Pvt.	McLure, Cyrus A.	Captured, 10/27/64 at Burgess' Mill, VA.
Co. E	Pvt.	Means, John	Captured, 10/27/64 at Burgess' Mill, VA.
Co. E	Pvt.	Narron, John G.	Captured, 10/27/64 at Burgess' Mill, VA.
Co. E	Pvt.	Pennix, Joseph W.	Wounded, 10/27/64 at Burgess' Mill, VA.
Co. E	Pvt.	Rhyne, David	Captured, 10/27/64 at Burgess' Mill, VA.
Co. E	Pvt.	Reid, James C.	Captured, 10/27/64 at Burgess' Mill, VA.
Co. E	Pvt.	Wingate, Thomas	Captured, 10/27/64 at Burgess' Mill, VA.
Co. E	Pvt.	York, George W.	Captured, 10/27/64 at Burgess' Mill, VA.
Co. F	Cpl.	Harris, Thomas C.	Captured, 10/27/64 at Burgess' Mill, VA.
Co. F	Pvt.	Briggs, Andrew	Captured, 10/27/64 at Burgess' Mill, VA.
Co. F	Pvt.	Briggs, James	Captured, 10/27/64 at Burgess' Mill, VA.
Co. F	Pvt.	Forehand, Adam	Captured, 10/27/64 at Burgess' Mill, VA.
Co. F	Pvt.	Pierce, Job	Captured, 10/27/64 at Burgess' Mill, VA.
Co. F	Pvt.	Sutton, S. S.	Wounded, 10/27/64 at Burgess' Mill, VA.
Co. G	Cpl.	Couch, William H.	Captured, 10/27/64 at Burgess' Mill, VA.
Co. G	Cpl.	Ferrell, Luico	Wounded, 10/27/64 at Burgess' Mill, VA. Died of wounds, 11/27/64
Co. G	Cpl.	Lewter, Charles M.	Captured, 10/27/64 at Burgess' Mill, VA.
Co. G	Pvt.	Cheek, Thomas F.	Captured, 10/27/64 at Burgess' Mill, VA.
Co. G	Pvt.	Clements, James H.	Captured, 10/27/64 at Burgess' Mill, VA.
Co. G	Pvt.	Davis, Duncan	Captured, 10/27/64 at Burgess' Mill, VA.
Co. G	Pvt.	Garrett, Woodston	Captured, 10/27/64 at Burgess' Mill, VA.
Co. G	Pvt.	King, William D.	Captured, 10/27/64 at Burgess' Mill, VA.
Co. G	Pvt.	Lloyd, William	Captured, 10/27/64 at Burgess' Mill, VA.
Co. G	Pvt.	Neville, John	Captured, 10/27/64 at Burgess' Mill, VA.
Co. G	Pvt.	Pendergrass, Charles H.	Captured, 10/27/64 at Burgess' Mill, VA.
Co. G	Pvt.	Pendergrass, John L.	Wounded, 10/27/64 at Burgess' Mill, VA.
Co. G	Pvt.	Potts, John W.	Captured, 10/27/64 at Burgess' Mill, VA.
Co. G	Pvt.	Rodgers, William H.	Captured, 10/27/64 at Burgess' Mill, VA.
Co. G	Pvt.	Strain, James A.	Captured, 10/27/64 at Burgess' Mill, VA.
Co. G	Pvt.	Strain, Thomas	Captured, 10/27/64 at Burgess' Mill, VA.
Co. G	Pvt.	Thrift, Pinkney	Captured, 10/27/64 at Burgess' Mill, VA.
Co. H	1st Sgt.	Blankenship, Stephen P.	Captured, 10/27/64 at Burgess' Mill, VA.
Co. H	Sgt.	Hanna, John N.	Captured, 10/27/64 at Burgess' Mill, VA.
Co. H	Pvt.	Ashley, William	Captured, 10/27/64 at Burgess' Mill, VA.
Co. H	Pvt.	Bryant, Sidney A.	Captured, 10/27/64 at Burgess' Mill, VA.
Co. H	Pvt.	Carpenter, William B.	Captured, 10/27/64 at Burgess' Mill, VA.
Co. H	Pvt.	Deggerhart, Jacob L.	Captured, 10/27/64 at Burgess' Mill, VA.
Co. H	Pvt.	Edwards, James M.	Captured, 10/27/64 at Burgess' Mill, VA.
Co. H	Pvt.	Ellis, Daniel	Captured, 10/27/64 at Burgess' Mill, VA.

Unit	Rank	Name	Remarks
Co. H	Pvt.	Harmon, Levi	Captured, 10/27/64 at Burgess' Mill, VA.
Co. H	Pvt.	Hayes, Jesse B.	Captured, 10/27/64 at Burgess' Mill, VA.
Co. H	Pvt.	Henry, Tyrell B.	Wounded, 10/27/64 at Burgess' Mill, VA.
Co. H	Pvt.	Hoover, Samuel L.	Captured, 10/27/64 at Burgess' Mill, VA.
Co. H	Pvt.	Ingle, Peter	Captured, 10/27/64 at Burgess' Mill, VA.
Co. H	Pvt.	McQuaige, James W.	Captured, 10/27/64 at Burgess' Mill, VA.
Co. H	Pvt.	Smith, James W.	Captured, 10/27/64 at Burgess' Mill, VA.
Co. H	Pvt.	Squires, John A.	Captured, 10/27/64 at Burgess' Mill, VA.
Co. H	Pvt.	Summeron, George	Wounded (left leg) and captured, 10/27/64 at Burgess' Mill, VA.
Co. H	Pvt.	Waller, Phoenix L.	Wounded, 10/27/64 at Burgess' Mill, VA.
Co. H	Pvt.	Warren, Thomas M.	Captured, 10/27/64 at Burgess' Mill, VA.
Co. I	Pvt.	Abernathy, James B.	Wounded (left hand), 10/27/64 at Burgess' Mill, VA.
Co. I	Pvt.	Avery, Absalon	Captured, 10/27/64 at Burgess' Mill, VA.
Co. I	Pvt.	Boyles, Joseph	Captured, 10/27/64 at Burgess' Mill, VA.
Co. I	Pvt.	Carpenter, Henry S.	Captured, 10/27/64 at Burgess' Mill, VA.
Co. I	Pvt.	Carpenter, William F.	Captured, 10/27/64 at Burgess' Mill, VA.
Co. I	Pvt.	Gault, Albert R.	Captured, 10/27/64 at Burgess' Mill, VA.
Co. I	Pvt.	Kincaid, Cephas G.	Captured, 10/27/64 at Burgess' Mill, VA.
Co. I	Pvt.	Mooney, McCameron	Captured, 10/27/64 at Burgess' Mill, VA.
Co. I	Pvt.	Speagle, Cain	Captured, 10/27/64 at Burgess' Mill, VA. POW—Point Lookout Prison, MD. Died of disease (chronic diarrhea), 1/25/65
Co. I	Pvt.	Weaver, Phillip C.	Captured, 10/27/64 at Burgess' Mill, VA.
Co. I	Pvt.	Wood, Perry	Captured, 10/27/64 at Burgess' Mill, VA. POW—Point Lookout Prison, MD. Died of disease, 5/19/65
Co. I	Pvt.	Wyant, David	Captured, 10/27/64 at Burgess' Mill, VA.
Co. K	1st Lt.	Dickerson, William T.	Captured, 10/27/64 at Burgess' Mill, VA.
Co. K	Sgt.	Atkins, Thomas S.	Captured, 10/27/64 at Burgess' Mill, VA.
Co. K	Cpl.	Burgin, Benjamin J.	Captured, 10/27/64 at Burgess' Mill, VA.
Co. K	Pvt.	Cordell, John H.	Wounded, 10/27/64 at Burgess' Mill, VA.
Co. K	Pvt.	Creasman, Abraham Sr.	Captured, 10/27/64 at Burgess' Mill, VA.
Co. K	Pvt.	Deggertheart, John V.	Captured, 10/27/64 at Burgess' Mill, VA.
Co. K	Pvt.	Henderson, Ezekiel	Wounded (left thigh) and captured, 10/27/64 at Burgess' Mill, VA.
Co. K	Pvt.	McKee, William H.	Captured, 10/27/64 at Burgess' Mill, VA.
Co. K	Pvt.	Miller, Joseph A.	Captured, 10/27/64 at Burgess' Mill, VA.

Hatcher's Run, VA—February 5, 1865
12 = 1 Killed, 8 Wounded, 3 Captured

Unit	Rank	Name	Remarks
F & S	Adj.	Martin, Edward	Wounded, February 5, 1865
Co. E	Pvt.	Rievs, John	Captured, February 5, 1865
Co. F	Sgt.	Mardre, John	Wounded, February 5, 1865
Co. G	3rd Lt.	Whitted, William	Wounded (thigh), February 5, 1865
Co. G	Pvt.	Chisenhall, Samuel	Captured, February 5, 1865
Co. G	Pvt.	Gattis, John	Wounded, February 5, 1865
Co. H	Pvt.	Marshall, James	Wounded (left leg amputated), February 5, 1865
Co. H	Pvt.	Pepper, John	Wounded, February 5, 1865
Co. I	Pvt.	Aderholdt, John	Wounded (arm), February 5, 1865
Co. I	Pvt.	Sherrill, William	Captured, February 5, 1865
Co. K	Pvt.	Miller, Gabriel	Killed, February 5, 1865
Co. K	Pvt.	Miller, James	Wounded, February 5, 1865

Jones Farm—Arthur's Swamp VA—March 25, 1865
27 = 2 Wounded, 1 Wounded & Captured, 24 Captured

Unit	Rank	Name	Remarks
Co. A	Pvt.	Alexander, Marshall R.	Captured, 3/25/65 in Petersburg picket line
Co. A	Pvt.	Fisher, James W.	Captured, 3/25/65 in Petersburg picket line
Co. A	Pvt.	Harris, Nathan O.	Captured, 3/25/65 in Petersburg picket line
Co. A	Pvt.	Monteith, Henry L. D.	Captured, 3/25/65 in Petersburg picket line
Co. A	Pvt.	Paysour, Caleb	Captured, 3/25/65 in Petersburg picket line
Co. B	Pvt.	Shelton, James	Captured, 3/25/65 in Petersburg picket line
Co. B	Pvt.	Williams, Robert G.	Captured, 3/25/65 in Petersburg picket line
Co. C	1st Lt.	Todd, William	Wounded, 3/25/65 in Petersburg picket line
Co. D	Pvt.	Griffin, Edmund	Captured, 3/25/65 in Petersburg picket line.
Co. D	Pvt.	Miller, Jackson	Captured, 3/25/65 in Petersburg picket line
Co. D	Pvt.	Mosteller, Isaiah	Captured, 3/25/65 in Petersburg picket line
Co. D	Pvt.	Pearson, Robert G.	Captured, 3/25/65 in Petersburg picket line
Co. D	Pvt.	Williams, Moulton	Captured, 3/25/65 in Petersburg picket line
Co. E	Pvt.	Adams, Hannibal A.	Captured, 3/25/65 in Petersburg picket line
Co. E	Pvt.	Bradshaw, John F.	Captured, 3/25/65 in Petersburg picket line
Co. E	Pvt.	Kyles, John	Captured, 3/25/65 in Petersburg picket line
Co. E	Pvt.	Smith, David J.	Wounded (neck), 3/25/65 in Petersburg picket line
Co. F	Pvt.	Simpson, Frederick	Captured, 3/25/65 in Petersburg picket line
Co. F	Pvt.	Ward, Aaron	Captured, 3/25/65 in Petersburg picket line
Co. G	Pvt.	Burch, Dudley Y.	Wounded (head) and captured, 3/25/65 in Petersburg picket line
Co. G	Pvt.	King, Baxter	Captured, 3/25/65 in Petersburg picket line
Co. H	2nd Lt.	Saville, James M.	Captured, 3/25/65 in Petersburg picket line
Co. H	Sgt.	Watt, Charles B.	Captured, 3/25/65 in Petersburg picket line
Co. H	Pvt.	Carpenter, Joseph C.	Captured, 3/25/65 in Petersburg picket line
Co. H	Pvt.	Knox, William H.	Captured, 3/25/65 in Petersburg picket line
Co. I	Pvt.	Havner, Julius A.	Captured, 3/25/65 in Petersburg picket line
Co. K	Pvt.	Spake, Christopher	Captured, 3/25/65 in Petersburg picket line

The Breakthrough of the Petersburg Trenches, VA—April 2, 1865
203 = 4 Wounded, 7 Wounded & Captured, 192 Captured

Unit	Rank	Name	Remarks
F & S	Sgt. Maj.	Rhodes, Robert H.	Captured, 4/2/65 at Hatcher's Run
Co. A	3rd Lt.	Alexander, Richard B.	Captured, 4/2/65 at Hatcher's Run
Co. A	Sgt.	Earnhart, Joseph M.	Captured, 4/2/65 in Petersburg trenches
Co. A	Sgt.	Gribble, James R.	Captured, 4/2/65 in Petersburg trenches
Co. A	Cpl.	Cochrane, John F.	Captured, 4/2/65 in Petersburg trenches
Co. A	Cpl.	Duckworth, Henry D.	Captured, 4/2/65 in Petersburg trenches
Co. A	Cpl.	Hill, Henry H.	Captured, 4/2/65 in Petersburg trenches
Co. A	Pvt.	Alexander, Webster S.	Captured, 4/2/65 in Petersburg trenches
Co. A	Pvt.	Allen, Cyrus A.	Captured, 4/2/65 in Petersburg trenches
Co. A	Pvt.	Black, Ezekiel	Captured, 4/2/65 in Petersburg trenches
Co. A	Pvt.	Black, Thomas J.	Captured, 4/2/65 near South Side RR
Co. A	Pvt.	Groves, Robert A.	Captured, 4/2/65 in Petersburg trenches
Co. A	Pvt.	Harris, Warren C.	Captured, 4/2/65 in Petersburg trenches
Co. A	Pvt.	Hobbs, Ferdinand	Captured, 4/2/65 in Petersburg trenches
Co. A	Pvt.	Howard, Thomas M.	Captured, 4/2/65 in Petersburg trenches
Co. A	Pvt.	Hunter, David P.	Captured, 4/2/65 in Petersburg trenches
Co. A	Pvt.	Kerns, John D.	Wounded and captured, 4/2/65 in Petersburg trenches

Unit	Rank	Name	Remarks
Co. A	Pvt.	Kerns, Thomas J.	Captured, 4/2/65 in Petersburg trenches
Co. A	Pvt.	King, Campbell	Captured, 4/2/65 in Petersburg trenches
Co. A	Pvt.	Knipper, Thomas	Captured, 4/2/65 in Petersburg trenches
Co. A	Pvt.	McConnell, John H.	Captured, 4/2/65 in Petersburg trenches
Co. A	Pvt.	Pettis, Stephen J.	Captured, 4/2/65 in Petersburg trenches
Co. A	Pvt.	Pettus, John W.	Captured, 4/2/65 in Petersburg trenches
Co. A	Pvt.	Query, Robert L.	Captured, 4/2/65 in Petersburg trenches
Co. A	Pvt.	Taylor, Robert C.	Captured, 4/2/65 in Petersburg trenches
Co. A	Pvt.	Thomasson, J. B.	Captured, 4/2/65 in Petersburg trenches
Co. A	Pvt.	Wallace, W. A.	Captured, 4/2/65 in Petersburg trenches
Co. A	Pvt.	Wingate, Murchison	Captured, 4/2/65 in Petersburg trenches
Co. B	Sgt.	Galloway, H. H.	Captured, 4/2/65 in Petersburg trenches
Co. B	Cpl.	Parks, James P.	Captured, 4/2/65 in Petersburg trenches
Co. B	Pvt.	Andrews, James	Captured, 4/2/65 in Petersburg trenches
Co. B	Pvt.	Bowman, Samuel	Captured, 4/2/65 in Petersburg trenches
Co. B	Pvt.	Branch, Martin	Captured, 4/2/65 in Petersburg trenches
Co. B	Pvt.	Branch, Reuben	Captured, 4/2/65 in Petersburg trenches
Co. B	Pvt.	Butler, John	Captured, 4/2/65 in Petersburg trenches
Co. B	Pvt.	Chester, John M.	Captured, 4/2/65 in Petersburg trenches
Co. B	Pvt.	Coleman, C. A.	Captured, 4/2/65 in Petersburg trenches
Co. B	Pvt.	Cook, John	Captured, 4/2/65 in Petersburg trenches
Co. B	Pvt.	Cooper, William E.	Captured, 4/2/65 in Petersburg trenches
Co. B	Pvt.	Crouch, Eliphus	Captured, 4/2/65 in Petersburg trenches
Co. B	Pvt.	Davis, Barry L.	Captured, 4/2/65 in Petersburg trenches
Co. B	Pvt.	Harris, Louis B.	Captured, 4/2/65 in Petersburg trenches
Co. B	Pvt.	Kincaid, William	Captured, 4/2/65 in Petersburg trenches
Co. B	Pvt.	Kinston, M.	Wounded, 4/2/65 in Petersburg trenches, and captured
Co. B	Pvt.	Land, John	Wounded, 4/2/65 and captured, 4/3/65 at Richmond
Co. B	Pvt.	Landis, Jordan N.	Wounded (both thighs), 4/2/65 in Petersburg trenches. Captured, 4/7/65 in Farmville.
Co. B	Pvt.	Loudermilk, George	Captured, 4/2/65 in Petersburg trenches
Co. B	Pvt.	Moses, S. Alfred	Captured, 4/2/65 in Petersburg trenches
Co. B	Pvt.	Parks, Austin L.	Captured, 4/2/65 in Petersburg trenches
Co. B	Pvt.	Patton, William S.	Captured, 4/2/65 in Petersburg trenches
Co. B	Pvt.	Pearson, Thomas	Captured, 4/2/65 in Petersburg trenches.
Co. B	Pvt.	Pendley, Adolphus	Captured, 4/2/65 in Petersburg trenches
Co. B	Pvt.	Shuffler, John	Captured, 4/2/65 in Petersburg trenches
Co. B	Pvt.	Shuffler, William	Captured, 4/2/65 in Petersburg trenches
Co. B	Pvt.	Singleton, Rufus W.	Captured, 4/2/65 at Hatcher's Run
Co. B	Pvt.	Smith, Anderson	Captured, 4/2/65 in Petersburg trenches
Co. B	Pvt.	Smith, Elijah C.	Captured, 4/2/65 at Hatcher's Run
Co. B	Pvt.	Smith, Henry	Captured, 4/2/65 in Petersburg trenches
Co. B	Pvt.	Teem, William C.	Captured, 4/2/65 in Petersburg trenches
Co. B	Pvt.	Walker, Joseph	Captured, 4/2/65 in Petersburg trenches
Co. B	Pvt.	Watts, John	Captured, 4/2/65 at Hatcher's Run
Co. C	Sgt.	Powell, William W.	Captured, 4/2/65 in Petersburg trenches
Co. C	Cpl.	Harrell, George B.	Captured, 4/2/65 in Petersburg trenches
Co. C	Pvt.	Bazemore, Henry	Captured, 4/2/65 in Petersburg trenches
Co. C	Pvt.	Brogden, William G.	Wounded (left hip & eye), 4/2/65 and captured in Petersburg trenches. Died of wounds, 6/2/65
Co. C	Pvt.	Byrum, Jesse B.	Captured, 4/2/65 in Petersburg trenches
Co. C	Pvt.	Byrum, Reuben L.	Captured, 4/2/65 in Petersburg trenches
Co. C	Pvt.	Mitchell, James E.	Captured, 4/2/65 at "the Southerland Station RR"
Co. C	Pvt.	Powers, Jesse A.	Captured, 4/2/65 in Petersburg trenches
Co. C	Pvt.	Smith, David H.	Captured, 4/2/65 at Hatcher's Run
Co. C	Pvt.	Williams, Oliver M.	Captured, 4/2/65 in Petersburg trenches

Unit	Rank	Name	Remarks
Co. D	Sgt.	Jordan, Noah W.	Captured, 4/2/65 in Petersburg trenches
Co. D	Pvt.	Butler, John M.	Wounded (right thigh), 4/2/65 at Sutherland Station
Co. D	Pvt.	Causby, George	Captured, 4/2/65 in Petersburg trenches
Co. D	Pvt.	Hawkins, William P.	Captured, 4/2/65 in Petersburg trenches
Co. D	Pvt.	Hennessee, Patrick W.	Captured, 4/2/65 in Petersburg trenches
Co. D	Pvt.	Lawmon, William L.	Captured, 4/2/65 in Petersburg trenches
Co. D	Pvt.	McMillon, Pleasant	Captured, 4/2/65 in Petersburg trenches
Co. D	Pvt.	Mitchell, John	Captured, 4/2/65 in Petersburg trenches
Co. D	Pvt.	Mosteller, John	Captured, 4/2/65 in Petersburg trenches
Co. D	Pvt.	Pearson, John	Captured, 4/2/65 in Petersburg trenches
Co. D	Pvt.	Powell, Joseph H.	Captured, 4/2/65 in Petersburg trenches
Co. D	Pvt.	Powell, William P.	Captured, 4/2/65 in Petersburg trenches
Co. D	Pvt.	Simpson, Thomas A.	Captured, 4/2/65 in Petersburg trenches
Co. D	Pvt.	Whisenhunt, Benjamin	Captured, 4/2/65 in Petersburg trenches
Co. D	Pvt.	Williams, John	Captured, 4/2/65 in Petersburg trenches
Co. E	2nd Lt.	Alexander, James F.	Captured, 4/2/65 at Hatcher's Run
Co. E	Cpl.	Hollingsworth, John B.	Captured, 4/2/65 in Petersburg trenches
Co. E	Cpl.	Jameson, Thomas J.	Captured, 4/2/65 in Petersburg trenches
Co. E	Pvt.	Auton, Samuel W.	Captured, 4/2/65 in Petersburg trenches
Co. E	Pvt.	Baker, William M.	Captured, 4/2/65 in Petersburg trenches
Co. E	Pvt.	Bird, William L.	Captured, 4/2/65 in Petersburg trenches
Co. E	Pvt.	Edwards, Shepherd	Captured, 4/2/65 in Petersburg trenches
Co. E	Pvt.	Hartline, Andrew	Captured, 4/2/65 in Petersburg trenches
Co. E	Pvt.	Hartline, Paul	Captured, 4/2/65 in Petersburg trenches
Co. E	Pvt.	Lambert, William T.	Captured, 4/2/65 in Petersburg trenches
Co. E	Pvt.	McCorkle, Hugh P.	Captured, 4/2/65 in Petersburg trenches
Co. E	Pvt.	Pennix, Joseph W.	Wounded (left knee) and captured, 4/2/65 in Petersburg trenches
Co. E	Pvt.	Reid, James C.	Captured, 4/2/65 at Sutherland Station
Co. E	Pvt.	Walker, John H.	Captured, 4/2/65 in Petersburg trenches
Co. F	Sgt.	Benbury, William E.	Wounded (left thigh & right shoulder), 4/2/65 and captured in Petersburg trenches
Co. F	Cpl.	Jordan, Robert S.	Captured, 4/2/65 in Petersburg trenches
Co. F	Cpl.	White, Isaac N.	Captured, 4/2/65 in Petersburg trenches
Co. F	Pvt.	Askew, Bryant	Captured, 4/2/65 in Petersburg trenches
Co. F	Pvt.	Bridges, Roswald D.	Captured, 4/2/65 in Petersburg trenches
Co. F	Pvt.	Dail, Joseph	Captured, 4/2/65 in Petersburg trenches
Co. F	Pvt.	Lassiter, George W.	Captured, 4/2/65 in Petersburg trenches
Co. F	Pvt.	Munds, Thomas	Captured, 4/2/65 in Petersburg trenches
Co. F	Pvt.	Smith, James J.	Wounded, (foot), 4/2/65 at Sutherland Station
Co. F	Pvt.	White, James B.	Captured, 4/2/65 in Petersburg trenches
Co. G	2nd Lt.	Whitaker, James R.	Captured, 4/2/65 at Hatcher's Run
Co. G	1st Sgt.	Davis, Thomas	Captured, 4/2/65 in Petersburg trenches
Co. G	Sgt.	Cheek, Nathaniel J.	Captured, 4/2/65 in Petersburg trenches
Co. G	Sgt.	Cheek, Virgil C.	Captured, 4/2/65 in Petersburg trenches
Co. G	Sgt.	Smith, John	Captured, 4/2/65 in Petersburg trenches
Co. G	Cpl.	Smith, Carney	Captured, 4/2/65 in Petersburg trenches
Co. G	Pvt.	Averett, David T.	Captured, 4/2/65 in Petersburg trenches
Co. G	Pvt.	Boon, James H.	Captured, 4/2/65 in Petersburg trenches
Co. G	Pvt.	Brockwell, A. John	Captured, 4/2/65 in Petersburg trenches
Co. G	Pvt.	Burgess, Washington	Captured, 4/2/65 in Petersburg trenches
Co. G	Pvt.	Chisenhall, Samuel	Captured, 4/2/65 in Petersburg trenches
Co. G	Pvt.	Clements, William G.	Captured, 4/2/65 in Petersburg trenches
Co. G	Pvt.	Davis, Henry A.	Captured, 4/2/65 in Petersburg trenches
Co. G	Pvt.	Gattis, James B.	Captured, 4/2/65 in Petersburg trenches
Co. G	Pvt.	Hester, John W.	Captured, 4/2/65 in Petersburg trenches

Unit	Rank	Name	Remarks
Co. G	Pvt.	Hunter, Anderson	Captured, 4/2/64 in Petersburg trenches
Co. G	Pvt.	King, Bellfield	Captured, 4/2/65 in Petersburg trenches
Co. G	Pvt.	King, James	Captured, 4/2/65 in Petersburg trenches
Co. G	Pvt.	King, John	Captured, 4/2/65 in Petersburg trenches
Co. G	Pvt.	King, William D.	Captured, 4/2/65 in Petersburg trenches
Co. G	Pvt.	Mincey, John	Captured, 4/2/65 in Petersburg trenches
Co. G	Pvt.	Pendergrass, Alvis	Captured, 4/2/65 in Petersburg trenches
Co. G	Pvt.	Petty, Henry	Captured, 4/2/65 in Petersburg trenches
Co. G	Pvt.	Riggsbee, Hawkins	Captured, 4/2/65 in Petersburg trenches
Co. G	Pvt.	Sledge, William P.	Captured, 4/2/65 in Petersburg trenches
Co. G	Pvt.	Tripp, William	Captured, 4/2/65 in Petersburg trenches
Co. G	Pvt.	Walters, Sidney	Captured, 4/2/65 in Petersburg trenches
Co. G	Pvt.	Williams, Johnson	Captured, 4/2/65 in Petersburg trenches
Co. G	Pvt.	Williams, Norris	Captured, 4/2/65 in Petersburg trenches
Co. H	Sgt.	Caldwell, John S.	Captured, 4/2/65 in Petersburg trenches
Co. H	Sgt.	Neely, John W	Captured, 4/2/65 in Petersburg trenches
Co. H	Cpl.	Humphreys, Thomas L.	Captured, 4/2/65 in Petersburg trenches
Co. H	Cpl.	Kilpatrick, William F.	Captured, 4/2/65 in Petersburg trenches
Co. H	Pvt.	Belk, William	Captured, 4/2/65 in Petersburg trenches
Co. H	Pvt.	Boyd, Jesse A.	Captured, 4/2/65 in Petersburg trenches
Co. H	Pvt.	Boyd, John J.	Captured, 4/2/65 in Petersburg trenches
Co. H	Pvt.	Boyd, David	Captured, 4/2/65 in Petersburg trenches
Co. H	Pvt.	Brower, Alfred M.	Captured, 4/2/65 in Petersburg trenches
Co. H	Pvt.	Carothers, James A.	Captured, 4/2/65 in Petersburg trenches
Co. H	Pvt.	Clark, Patrick M.	Captured, 4/2/65 in Petersburg trenches
Co. H	Pvt.	Cobb, Calvin R.	Captured, 4/2/65 in Petersburg trenches
Co. H	Pvt.	Cox, Eli	Captured, 4/2/65 in Petersburg trenches.
Co. H	Pvt.	Duckworth John A.	Captured, 4/2/65 in Petersburg trenches
Co. H	Pvt.	Earnhart, George	Captured, 4/2/65 in Petersburg trenches
Co. H	Pvt.	Fite, William J.	Captured, 4/2/65 in Petersburg trenches
Co. H	Pvt.	Hoffman, Miles	Captured, 4/2/65 in Petersburg trenches
Co. H	Pvt.	Hovis, Moses	Captured, 4/2/65 in Petersburg trenches
Co. H	Pvt.	Hudspeth, George	Captured, 4/2/65 in Petersburg trenches
Co. H	Pvt.	Mincey, Wiley	Captured, 4/2/65 in Petersburg trenches
Co. H	Pvt.	Newman, Elias	Captured, 4/2/65 in Petersburg trenches
Co. H	Pvt.	Rhine, Arthur M.	Captured, 4/2/65 in Petersburg trenches
Co. H	Pvt.	Rochelle, Thomas B.	Captured, 4/2/65 in Petersburg trenches
Co. H	Pvt.	Snead, Franklin	Captured, 4/2/65 in Petersburg trenches
Co. H	Pvt.	Stanford, James L.	Captured, 4/2/65 in Petersburg trenches
Co. H	Pvt.	Summy, John B.	Captured, 4/2/65 in Petersburg trenches
Co. H	Pvt.	Taggert, John C.	Captured, 4/2/65 in Petersburg trenches
Co. I	1st Sgt.	Ramsour, John F.	Captured, 4/2/65 in Petersburg trenches
Co. I	Sgt.	Miller, Jacob A.	Wounded (groin), 4/2/65 at Sutherland Station
Co. I	Sgt.	Rhodes, Jacob B.	Captured, 4/2/65 in Petersburg trenches
Co. I	Cpl.	Hovis, Laban L.	Captured, 4/2/65 in Petersburg trenches
Co. I	Pvt.	Clanton, William L.	Captured, 4/2/65 in Petersburg trenches
Co. I	Pvt.	Culbert, Daniel	Captured, 4/2/65 at Hatcher's Run
Co. I	Pvt.	Glenn, David M.	Captured, 4/2/65 at Southerland Station
Co. I	Pvt.	Hallman, Abel	Captured, 4/2/65 in Petersburg trenches
Co. I	Pvt.	Haynes, Ryann W.	Captured, 4/2/65 in Petersburg trenches
Co. I	Pvt.	Hill, William L.	Captured, 4/2/65 in Petersburg trenches
Co. I	Pvt.	Hubbard, Daniel	Captured, 4/2/65 in Petersburg trenches
Co. I	Pvt.	Huss, John	Captured, 4/2/65 in Petersburg trenches
Co. I	Pvt.	Jetton, Taylor B.	Captured, 4/2/65 in Petersburg trenches
Co. I	Pvt.	Johnson, Harvey M.	Captured, 4/2/65 in Petersburg trenches
Co. I	Pvt.	Oaks, John	Captured, 4/2/65 in Petersburg trenches

Unit	Rank	Name	Remarks
Co. I	Pvt.	Quickel, Levi H.	Captured, 4/2/65 in Petersburg trenches
Co. I	Pvt.	Rinck, Andrew	Wounded (right shoulder and throat), 4/2/65 and captured in Petersburg trenches. Died of wounds, 4/13/65 at Ft. Monroe, VA
Co. I	Pvt.	Shuford, Sidney	Captured, 4/2/65 in Petersburg trenches
Co. I	Pvt.	Stroup, Daniel S.	Captured, 4/2/65 in Petersburg trenches
Co. I	Pvt.	Summerow, Peter J.	Captured, 4/2/65 in Petersburg trenches
Co. I	Pvt.	Warlick, John C.	Captured, 4/2/65 in Petersburg trenches
Co. I	Pvt.	Wilson, Harrison S.	Captured, 4/2/65 in Petersburg trenches
Co. K	Sgt.	Pickens, George A.	Captured, 4/2/65 in Petersburg trenches
Co. K	Cpl.	Lindsay, Andrew J.	Captured, 4/2/65 in Petersburg trenches
Co. K	Pvt.	Bird, Thomas J.	Captured, 4/2/65 in Petersburg trenches.
Co. K	Pvt.	Clayton, William L.	Captured, 4/2/65 in Petersburg trenches.
Co. K	Pvt.	Cordell, John H.	Captured, 4/2/65 in Petersburg trenches.
Co. K	Pvt.	McClure, Ottway B.	Captured, 4/2/65 in Petersburg trenches
Co. K	Pvt.	Patton, George A.	Captured, 4/2/65 in Petersburg trenches
Co. K	Pvt.	Patton, James L.	Captured, 4/2/65 in Petersburg trenches
Co. K	Pvt.	Shope, Thomas J.	Captured, 4/2/65 in Petersburg trenches
Co. K	Pvt.	Stepp, Joseph M.	Captured, 4/2/65 in Petersburg trenches
Co. K	Pvt.	Stroup, S. F.	Captured, 4/2/65 in Petersburg trenches

Non Combatants

Unit	Rank	Name	Remarks
Co. A	Pvt.	Paysour, S. Peter	TDY—Captured, 4/2/65 in Petersburg trenches
Co. A	Musician	Wingate, Charles	TDY—Band (F & S): Captured, 4/2/65 in Petersburg trenches
Co. B	Pvt.	Sudderth, Robert W.	TDY—Brigade HQ: Captured, 4/2/65 in Petersburg trenches
Co. C	Musician	Todd, Elisha	TDY—Chief Musician in Regt. Band. Captured, 4/2/65 in Petersburg trenches

Petersburg Trenches—April 3, 1865
20 Captured

Unit	Rank	Name	Remarks
Co. A	Pvt.	Black, James M.	Captured, 4/3/65 in Petersburg trenches
Co. A	Pvt.	Norment, Isaac	Captured, 4/3/65 in Petersburg trenches
Co. A	Pvt.	Orr, James F.	Captured, 4/3/65 in Petersburg trenches
Co. B	Cpl.	Singleton, Lucius	Captured, 4/3/65 in Petersburg trenches
Co. C	Sgt.	Todd, Lewis	Captured, 4/3/65 in Petersburg trenches
Co. D	Pvt.	Saulman, James W.	Captured, 4/3/65 in Petersburg trenches
Co. E	Pvt.	Walker, Landsey L.	Captured, 4/3/65 in Petersburg trenches
Co. F	Pvt.	Askew, Joshua	Captured, 4/3/65 in Petersburg trenches
Co. F	Pvt.	Leary, William H.	Captured, 4/3/65 in Petersburg trenches
Co. F	Pvt.	Miller, James	Captured, 4/3/65 in Petersburg trenches
Co. F	Pvt.	Saunders, William F.	Captured, 4/3/65 in Petersburg trenches
Co. F	Pvt.	Ward, Anderson S.	Captured, 4/3/65 in Petersburg trenches
Co. I	Sgt.	Bisaner, Jacob H.	Captured, 4/3/65 in Petersburg trenches
Co. I	Pvt.	Carpenter, Michael	Captured, 4/3/65 in Petersburg trenches
Co. I	Pvt.	Glenn, Robert J.	Captured, 4/3/65 in Petersburg trenches
Co. I	Pvt.	Parker, Asa	Captured, 4/3/65 in Petersburg trenches
Co. K	Pvt.	Bird, Wilson R.	Captured, 4/3/65 in Petersburg trenches

Non Combatant

Unit	Rank	Name	Remarks
F & S	Qtr. Mstr.	Sims, James M.	Captured, 4/3/65 in Petersburg trenches
F & S	Ensign	Rayner, James T.	Captured, 4/3/65 on the Appomattox River.
Co. D	Musician	Hicks, Joseph	TDY—Regt. Band. Captured, 4/3/65 in Petersburg trenches

Retreat to Appomattox, VA—April 4–8, 1865
10 = 1 Killed, 1 Wounded, 8 Captured

Unit	Rank	Name	Remarks
Co. A	Pvt.	Orman, J. E.	Captured, 4/6–8/65 on road to Appomattox
Co. B	Pvt.	Landis, Jordan N.	Captured, 4/7/65 in Farmville.
Co. B	Pvt.	Warlick, William J.	Killed, 4/8/65 near Appomattox Court House
Co. C	Cpl.	Burden, James M.	Captured, 4/6/65 at Burkeville, VA
Co. C	Pvt.	Myers, Nathan	Captured, 4/6/65 at Harper's Farm, VA
Co. C	Pvt.	Parker, Thomas H.	Captured, 4/6/65 at Amelia Court House, VA
Co. C	Pvt.	Stokes, Gaston	Wounded (left shoulder), 4/6/65 at Farmville
Co. D	Pvt.	Giles, Alexander	Captured, 4/5/65 at Amelia Court House
Co. K	Pvt.	Crow, Joseph W.	Captured, 4/6/65 at Farmville

Non Combatant

Unit	Rank	Name	Remarks
Co. I	Sgt.	Motz, George	TDY: Regt. Commissary Sgt. Captured, 4/6/65 at Farmville, VA

11th North Carolina Appomattox
Surrender Roster April 9, 1865
78 Surrendered

Unit	Rank	Name	Enlistment Date	Remarks
F & S	Col.	Martin, William J.	4/28/62	Surrendered, 4/9/65 at Appomattox Court House
Co. A	2nd Lt.	Taylor, William B.	2/1/62	Surrendered, 4/9/65 at Appomattox Court House
Co. A	1st Sgt.	Neily, Thomas W	2/1/62	Surrendered, 4/9/65 at Appomattox Court House
Co. A	Cpl.	Alexander, James	2/1/62	Surrendered, 4/9/65 at Appomattox Court House
Co. A	Cpl.	Bigham, James W.	7/7/62	Surrendered, 4/9/65 at Appomattox Court House
Co. A	Pvt.	Hovis, Monroe	2/1/62	Surrendered, 4/9/65 at Appomattox Court House
Co. A	Pvt.	Pettus, H. M.	5/5/62	Surrendered, 4/9/65 at Appomattox Court House
Co. B	Cpt.	Parks, Thomas R.	2/15/62	Surrendered, 4/9/65 at Appomattox Court House
Co. B	Sgt.	Hennessa, Robert J.	2/1/62	Surrendered, 4/9/65 at Appomattox Court House
Co. B	Sgt.	McGimsey, Walker	12/21/62	Surrendered, 4/9/65 at Appomattox Court House
Co. B	Pvt.	Elliott, Hiram C.	2/26/63	Surrendered, 4/9/65 at Appomattox Court House
Co. B	Pvt.	Kincaid, Robert	8/1/64	Surrendered, 4/9/65 at Appomattox Court House
Co. B	Pvt.	Livingston, Larkin	2/1/62	Surrendered, 4/9/65 at Appomattox Court House
Co. B	Pvt.	Singleton, James V.	2/1/62	Surrendered, 4/9/65 at Appomattox Court House
Co. C	Cpt.	Outlaw, Edward R.	1/22/62	Surrendered, 4/9/65 at Appomattox Court House
Co. C	Pvt.	Davis, Allen	1/23/62	Surrendered, 4/9/65 at Appomattox Court House
Co. D	1st Sgt.	Womack, William	2/10/62	Surrendered, 4/9/65 at Appomattox Court House
Co. D	Sgt.	Butler, William H.	2/26/62	Surrendered, 4/9/65 at Appomattox Court House
Co. D	Pvt.	Brittain, Samuel	2/14/62	Surrendered, 4/9/65 at Appomattox Court House
Co. D	Pvt.	Butler, John M.	2/15/62	Surrendered, 4/9/65 at Appomattox Court House
Co. D	Pvt.	Causby, William	3/12/62	Surrendered, 4/9/65 at Appomattox Court House
Co. D	Pvt.	Clark, Mitchell	3/17/62	Surrendered, 4/9/65 at Appomattox Court House
Co. D	Pvt.	Clay, James	12/1/64	Surrendered, 4/9/65 at Appomattox Court House
Co. E	1st Sgt.	McDonald, John H.	3/12/62	Surrendered, 4/9/65 at Appomattox Court House
Co. E	Sgt.	Hartgrove, William	3/10/62	Surrendered, 4/9/65 at Appomattox Court House
Co. E	Pvt.	Hartline, Adam	10/27/64	Surrendered, 4/9/65 at Appomattox Court House
Co. E	Pvt.	Holton, Harrison	3/16/64	Surrendered, 4/9/65 at Appomattox Court House
Co. E	Pvt.	McLellan, William	5/5/62	Surrendered, 4/9/65 at Appomattox Court House
Co. E	Pvt.	Pennix, John A.	9/15/64	Surrendered, 4/9/65 at Appomattox Court House
Co. E	Pvt.	Puckett, William C.	3/10/62	Surrendered, 4/9/65 at Appomattox Court House

Unit	Rank	Name	Enlistment Date	Remarks
Co. E	Pvt.	Sprinkle, J. I.	12/1/64	Surrendered, 4/9/65 at Appomattox Court House
Co. F	Pvt.	Bogue, Jesse	2/15/62	Surrendered, 4/9/65 at Appomattox Court House
Co. G	Cpt.	Freeland, John F.	2/6/62	Surrendered, 4/9/65 at Appomattox Court House
Co. G	Sgt.	Harwood, Wesley J.	2/26/62	Surrendered, 4/9/65 at Appomattox Court House
Co. G	Pvt.	Fowler, Washington	9/6/62	Surrendered, 4/9/65 at Appomattox Court House
Co. G	Pvt.	McDade, Henry L.	2/26/62	Surrendered, 4/9/65 at Appomattox Court House
Co. G	Pvt.	Mangum, William	8/28/64	Surrendered, 4/9/65 at Appomattox Court House
Co. H	1st Lt.	Lowrie, Robert B.	6/13/62	Surrendered, 4/9/65 at Appomattox Court House
Co. H	Sgt.	Smith, John T.	3/12/62	Surrendered, 4/9/65 at Appomattox Court House
Co. H	Pvt.	Andrews, E. M.	12/2/64	Surrendered, 4/9/65 at Appomattox Court House
Co. H	Pvt.	Blair, Stephen W.	3/14/62	Surrendered, 4/9/65 at Appomattox Court House
Co. H	Pvt.	Holland, Robert	9/8/64	Surrendered, 4/9/65 at Appomattox Court House
Co. H	Pvt.	Humphreys, Joseph	3/14/62	Surrendered, 4/9/65 at Appomattox Court House
Co. H	Pvt.	Keener, Peter	9/17/64	Surrendered, 4/9/65 at Appomattox Court House
Co. H	Pvt.	Sanders, Jacob	9/3/64	Surrendered, 4/9/65 at Appomattox Court House
Co. H	Pvt.	Wilson, W. H	12/1/64	Surrendered, 4/9/65 at Appomattox Court House
Co. I	Cpl.	Aderholdt, John A.	5/8/62	Surrendered, 4/9/65 at Appomattox Court House
Co. I	Pvt.	Cody, James	3/9/62	Surrendered, 4/9/65 at Appomattox Court House
Co. I	Pvt.	Cody, John	2/8/64	Surrendered, 4/9/65 at Appomattox Court House
Co. I	Pvt.	Cox, Henry V.	3/25/62	Surrendered, 4/9/65 at Appomattox Court House
Co. I	Pvt.	Evans, John	2/13/64	Surrendered, 4/9/65 at Appomattox Court House
Co. I	Pvt.	Gault, Albert R.	8/15/64	Surrendered, 4/9/65 at Appomattox Court House
Co. I	Pvt.	Haynes, David A.	3/15/62	Surrendered, 4/9/65 at Appomattox Court House
Co. I	Pvt.	Hudspeth, John T.	3/15/62	Surrendered, 4/9/65 at Appomattox Court House
Co. I	Pvt.	Lenhardt, Joseph M.	3/11/62	Surrendered, 4/9/65 at Appomattox Court House
Co. I	Pvt.	McCoy, William H.	5/23/62	Surrendered, 4/9/65 at Appomattox Court House
Co. I	Pvt.	Mullin, Alfred E.	11/13/62	Surrendered, 4/9/65 at Appomattox Court House
Co. I	Pvt.	Wise, Zenas	3/15/62	Surrendered, 4/9/65 at Appomattox Court House
Co. K	Cpt.	Young, James M.	3/1/62	Surrendered, 4/9/65 at Appomattox Court House
Co. K	1st Sgt.	Bartlett, Jacob S.	3/1/62	Surrendered, 4/9/65 at Appomattox Court House
Co. K	Pvt.	Creasman, Abraham	4/27/63	Surrendered, 4/9/65 at Appomattox Court House
Co. K	Pvt.	Dickerson, J. R.	11/1/64	Surrendered, 4/9/65 at Appomattox Court House
Co. K	Pvt.	Hall, John P.	3/1/62	Surrendered, 4/9/65 at Appomattox Court House
Co. K	Pvt.	Luther, Washington	11/1/64	Surrendered, 4/9/65 at Appomattox Court House

Non-Combatant

Unit	Rank	Name	Enlistment Date	Remarks
F & S	Asst. Surgeon	McCombs, James	4/5/62	Surrendered, 4/9/65 at Appomattox Court House
F & S	Ord. Sgt.	Mardre, William	1/23/62	Surrendered, 4/9/65 at Appomattox Court House
F & S	Hosp. Stwd	Wilson, William	4/1/63	Surrendered, 4/9/65 at Appomattox Court House
Co. A	Pvt.	Herring, G. T.	2/1/62	TDY—Surrendered, 4/9/65 at Appomattox Court House
Co. A	Pvt.	Hunter, Madison	2/1/62	TDY—Division Pioneer: Surrendered, 4/9/65 at Appomattox Court House
Co. A	Pvt.	Kennedy, William	2/1/62	TDY—Medical; Surrendered, 4/9/65 at Appomattox Court House
Co. A	Pvt.	Monteith, R. J.	2/1/62	TDY—Surrendered, 4/9/65 at Appomattox Court House
Co. B	Pvt.	Phillips, C. S.	2/1/62	TDY—Ambulance driver. Surrendered, 4/9/65 at Appomattox Court House
Co. C	Pvt.	Blackstone, William R.	1/23/62	TDY—Nurse at Division infirmary. Surrendered, 4/9/65 at Appomattox Court House
Co. D	Pvt.	Wadkins, John B.	3/10/62	TDY: Teamster. Surrendered, 4/9/65 at Appomattox Court House

Unit	Rank	Name	Enlistment Date	Remarks
Co. E	Pvt.	Hartline, David L.	2/28/62	TDY—Teamster. Surrendered, 4/9/65 at Appomattox Court House
Co. G	Musician	Davis, James T.	2/26/62	TDY—Regt. Band. Surrendered, 4/9/65 at Appomattox Court House
Co. I	Musician	Cline, William	9/8/62	TDY: Band. Surrendered, 4/9/65 at Appomattox Court House
Co. I	Musician	Coon, Adolphus	3/14/62	TDY: Band. Surrendered, 4/9/65 at Appomattox Court House

11th North Carolina Infantry Roster

Boldface type indicates soldiers who died in the Civil War.

Field and Staff

Rank	Name	DOB	Residence	Occupation	Remarks
Col.	Leventhorpe, Collett	1815	Rutherforton, Rutherford Co	Physician	Wounded (left arm & hip), 7/3/63. Captured, 7/5/63 near Greencastle, PA. POW—Point Lookout Prison, MD. Exchanged, 3/10/64. Resigned, 4/27/64 "by reason of wounds received at Gettysburg."
Lt. Col.	Martin, William Joseph	1830	Chapel Hill, Orange Co.	Professor	Wounded, (head and left arm), 10/14/63 at Bristoe Station, VA. Col.—4/27/64. Wounded (left thigh), 9/30/64 at Jones Farm, VA. Surrendered, 4/9/65 at Appomattox Court House.
Maj.	Eliason, William Adlai	1831	Upperville, Fauquier Co. VA	Soldier	Transferred, 5/62, to Lt. Col. 49th Regt. NC Troops.
Adj.	**Lucas, Henderson C**	**1840**	**Yanceyville, Caswell Co.**	**Dentist**	**Commissioned, Regt. Adjutant, 7/11/62. Wounded, 7/1/63 at Gettysburg. Died of wounds, 7/25/63 at Martinsburg, WV.**
QMstr Cpt.	Tate, John M.	1835	W. Charlotte, Mecklenburg Co.	Dry good dealer	Promoted, Cpt.—7/10/62, Regt. Quartermaster, Regt. F & S. Transferred, 7/8/64 to Wilcox's Division as Cpt. Division Quartermaster.
Cmsry	Summey, John S. E.	1820	Asheville, Buncombe Co.	Clerk	Cpt.—Commissioned, 8/7/62 as Regt. Assistant Quartermaster. 5/63; Transferred to all "unspecified post at Asheville, NC" when the position was abolished.
Surg.	Wilson, John Jr.	1834	Charlotte, Mecklenburg Co.	Physician	Surgeon—Appointed, 6/30/62. Ordered to Raleigh, 11/28/64 to serves "as Surgeon of the military prison hospital at Salisbury."
Asst. Surg.	McCombs, James Parks	1836	Taylorsville, Alexandria Co.	Physician	Appointed Assistant Surgeon, 4/5/62. Captured, 7/5/63 at Gettysburg. Exchanged, 11/21/63. Surrendered, 4/9/65 at Appomattox Court House.
Chap.	Ridley, J. S.	1833	Webster, Jackson Co.	Minister	Appointed, 4/30/62.

Rank	Name	DOB	Residence	Occupation	Remarks
Sgt. Maj.	McCorkle, James G.	1839	W. Charlotte, Mecklenburg Co.	Clerk	Sgt. Maj.—Promoted, 4/62. Transferred to F&S. Captured, 7/3/63 at Gettysburg. Exchanged, 7/31/63. 2nd Lt.—Promoted, 11/26/63, transferred to Co. D.

Additional Officers

Rank	Name	DOB	Residence	Occupation	Remarks
Lt. Col.	Bird, Francis "Frank," W.	1830	Windsor, Bertie Co.	Lawyer	Promoted, 4/27/64. Wounded, 8/25/64 at Reams' Station. Died of wounds, 8/26/64
Cmsry Sgt.	Dickerson, William T.	1822	Asheville, Buncombe Co.	Farmer	Appointed, 8/9/62. 2nd Lt.—7/30/63, returned to Co. K.
Qmstr Sgt.	Finger, Sidney M.	1838	Lincolnton, Lincoln Co.	Farm labor	Promoted, 7/62. Transferred, 6/16/63. "Appointed Assistant Quartermaster (Cpt.) of the Eight Congressional District of North Carolina."
Surg.	Fugua, William M.	—	Yanceyville, Caswell Co.	Physician	Appointed, 11/29/64.
Cmsry Sgt.	Lowrie, James B.	1838	W. Charlotte, Mecklenburg Co.	Farm labor	Assigned, 5/8/62. Returned to Co. H, 8/16/62.
Asst. QMstr	Lowrie, Patrick Johnson	1832	W. Charlotte, Mecklenburg Co.	Farmer	Transferred, 7/11/62. Died of Yellow Fever, 7/12/62 at Wilmington, NC.
Ord. Sgt.	Madre, William B.	1831	Windsor, Bertie Co.	Mechanic	Promoted, 10/1/63. Surrendered, 4/9/65 at Appomattox Court House.
Adj.	Martin, Edward A.	1841	Orange Co.	—	Promoted, 9/3/63, Regt. Adjutant. Wounded, 2/5/65 at Hatcher's Run.
Ord. Sgt.	Motz, George	1840	Lincolnton, Lincoln Co.	Farm labor	Promoted, 11/3/62. Reduced to Sgt. (Co. I), 9/63.
Lt. Col.	Owens, William A.	1833	W. Charlotte, Mecklenburg Co.	Lawyer	Promoted to Lt. Col., 3/31/62. Transferred, 5/6/62 to the 53rd Regt. NC Inf.
Ensgn	Rayner, James T.	1844	Colerain, Bertie Co.	Clerk	Promoted, 8/16/64. Captured, 4/3/65 on the Appomattox River.
Sgt. Maj.	Rhodes, Robert H.	—	Windsor, Bertie Co.	—	Promoted, 10/64. Captured, 4/2/65 at Petersburg.
Maj.	Ross, Egbert A.	1842	W. Charlotte, Mecklenburg Co.	Student	Appointed, 5/6/62 Killed, 7/1/63 at Gettysburg
QMstr Sgt.	Sims, James Monroe	1839	W. Charlotte, Mecklenburg Co.	Clerk	Promoted, 11/1/63. Captured, 4/3/65 in Petersburg trenches.
Chap.	Smith, Aristides S.	1810	Norfolk, Norfolk Co. VA	Minister	Appointed, 11/17/62. Resigned, 1/20/64, "by reason of his age and rheumatism."
QMstr Cpt.	Tate, John M.	1835	W. Charlotte, Mecklenburg Co.	Dry Goods Dealer	Promoted, 7/10/62, Regt. Quartermaster. Transferred, 7/8/64 to Wilcox's Division as Cpt. Division Quartermaster
Hosp. Stwrd.	Wilson, William M.	1843	W. Charlotte, Mecklenburg Co.	Clerk	Promoted, 6/64. Paroled, 4/9/65 at Appomattox Court House.

Company A
Mecklenburg County

Rank	Name	DOB	Residence	Occupation	Remarks
Cpt.	Ross, Egbert A.	1842	W. Charlotte, Mecklenburg Co.	Military Student	Maj.—5/6/62. Transferred to F & S. Killed, 7/1/63 at Gettysburg.

Rank	Name	DOB	Residence	Occupation	Remarks
1st Lt.	Hand, Wm. Lee	1842	Charlotte, Mecklenburg Co.	—	Cpt.—5/6/62. Captured, 7/3/63 at Gettysburg.
2nd Lt.	Alexander, Charles W.	1836	W. Charlotte, Mecklenburg. Co.	Carpenter	1st Lt.—5/6/62. Retired, 7/15/63 to the Invalid Corps by reason of "extensive exotosis of upper and internal portion of left femur."
2nd Lt.	Hand, Robert H.	1840	Charlotte, Mecklenburg Co.	—	Wounded (back), 7/1/63 at Gettysburg. Captured, 7/5/63 at Greencastle, PA.
1st Sgt.	McCorkle, James G.	1839	W. Charlotte, Mecklenburg Co.	Clerk	Sgt. Maj.—4/62. Transferred to F & S.
Sgt.	McElroy, Samuel J.	1841	W. Charlotte, Mecklenburg Co.	Farm labor	Wounded, 7/1/63 and captured at Gettysburg. Wounded (right side of face), 9/30/64 at Globe Tavern. Missing, 3/1/65.
Sgt.	Sims, James M.	1835	W. Charlotte, Mecklenburg Co.	Carpenter	Captured, 7/14/63 at Falling Waters. QM Sgt.—11/1/63 and transferred to F & S.
Sgt.	Taylor, William B.	1840	W. Charlotte, Mecklenburg Co.	Machinist	3rd Lt.—6/2/62. Wounded, 6/2/64, at Cold Harbor. 2nd Lt.—8/64. Surrendered, 4/9/65 at Appomattox Court House.
Cpl.	Gribble, James R.	1840	E. Charlotte, Mecklenburg Co.	Student	Wounded (left ankle), 10/2/64 at Jones Farm. Sgt.—1/65. Captured, 4/2/65 at Petersburg.
Cpl.	**Icehower, William S.**	**1843**	**Charlotte, Mecklenburg Co.**	**Farm labor**	**Wounded, 7/1/63 and captured at Gettysburg. Killed, 6/2/64 at Cold Harbor.**
Cpl.	Neely, Thomas W.	1844	W. Charlotte, Mecklenburg Co.	Farm labor	Sgt.—6/2/63. Wounded, 7/3/63 at Gettysburg. Wounded (left thigh), 10/2/64 at Pegram's Farm. 1st Sgt.—11/30/64. Surrendered, 4/9/65 at Appomattox Court House.
Cpl.	Ruddock, Theo C.	1836	W. Charlotte, Mecklenburg Co.	Farm labor	Captured, 7/14/63 at Falling Waters, MD. Pvt.—9/64. Captured, 10/27/64 at Burgess' Mill.
Pvt.	Alexander, James N.	1842	W. Charlotte, Mecklenburg Co.	Miller's Asst.	Cpl.—7/64. Wounded, 8/64 in Petersburg trenches. Surrendered, 4/9/65 at Appomattox Court House.
Pvt.	**Alexander, John**	**1842**	**W. Charlotte, Mecklenburg Co.**	**Farm labor**	**Killed, 8/25/64 at Reams' Station.**
Pvt.	Alexander, Miles A.	1836	W. Charlotte, Mecklenburg Co.	Farm labor	Wounded, 7/3/63 and captured at Gettysburg.
Pvt.	Alexander, Marshall R.	1837	W. Charlotte, Mecklenburg Co.	Farm labor	Wounded (right shoulder), 7/1/63 at Gettysburg. Wounded, 10/27/64 at Burgess' Mill. Captured, 3/25/65 at Petersburg trenches.
Pvt.	Alexander, Milton M.	1834	E. Charlotte, Mecklenburg Co.	Salesman	Wounded, 7/3/63 and captured at Gettysburg.
Pvt.	Alexander, Richard B.	1840	W. Charlotte, Mecklenburg Co.	Day laborer	Sgt.—5/30/62. Wounded (left shoulder), 7/1/63 at Gettysburg. 3rd Lt.—10/11/64. Captured, 4/2/65 at Hatcher's Run.
Pvt.	Alexander, Robert C.	1844	E. Charlotte, Mecklenburg Co.	Carpenter's Asst.	Captured, 7/3/63 at Gettysburg.
Pvt.	Barnett, Elam L.	1839	W. Charlotte, Mecklenburg Co.	Farm labor	Discharged (disability), 1/63.
Pvt.	Barnett, James F.	1843	W. Charlotte, Mecklenburg Co.	Farm labor	Transferred to Co. C, 37th NC Inf. 1/1/64.

Rank	Name	DOB	Residence	Occupation	Remarks
Pvt.	Barnett, John L.	1843	W. Charlotte, Mecklenburg Co.	Farm labor	Wounded, 7/1/63 at Gettysburg. Died of wounds, 7/5/63.
Pvt.	Bigham, John R.	1843	W. Charlotte, Mecklenburg Co.	Farm labor	Wounded (right thigh & buttock), 7/3/63 at Gettysburg. Died of wounds, 8/28/64.
Pvt.	Black, James M.	1832	W. Charlotte, Mecklenburg Co.	Farmer	Captured, 4/3/65 in Petersburg trenches.
Pvt.	Black, Thomas J.	1844	W. Charlotte, Mecklenburg Co.	Farm labor	Captured, 4/2/65 at Southside RR.
Pvt.	Blakely, Monroe	1842	Mecklenburg Co.	—	Died of disease, 4/18/62.
Pvt.	Brigman, Columbus C.	1831	W. Charlotte, Mecklenburg Co.	Day Laborer	Wounded, 12/16/62 at White Hall. Wounded, 7/3/63 at Gettysburg. Died of wounds, 12/3/63.
Pvt.	Brown, William J.	1843	W. Charlotte, Mecklenburg Co.	Farm labor	Cpl.—6/2/62. Sgt.—6/15/63. Wounded, 7/1/63 and captured at Gettysburg. Wounded, 5/10/64 at Spotsylvania.
Pvt.	Byram, James	1815	W. Charlotte, Mecklenburg Co.	Farmer	Died of disease (typhoid fever), 8/8/62.
Pvt.	Chester, Milton E.	1839	Mecklenburg Co.	—	Died of disease, 1/19/65, at Richmond, VA.
Pvt.	Cochrane, John F.	1836	Olin, Iredell Co.	Farmer	Captured, 10/14/63 at Bristoe Station. Cpl.—3/65. Captured, 4/2/65 at Petersburg.
Pvt.	Creasemon, Joseph	1845	Sulphur Springs, Buncombe Co.	Farm labor	Died of disease, 4/20/62.
Pvt.	Deaton, James C.	1833	W. Charlotte, Mecklenburg Co.	Day laborer	Discharged (disability), 11/13/62.
Pvt.	Duckworth, Henry D.	1846	W. Charlotte, Mecklenburg Co.	Day laborer	Cpl.—1/65. Captured, 4/2/65 at Petersburg.
Pvt.	Dulin, Daniel	1841	E. Charlotte, Mecklenburg Co.	Farm labor	Wounded (left hip) and captured, 7/3/63 at Gettysburg.
Pvt.	Earnhart, J. H.	1840	Mecklenburg Co.	—	Killed, 7/1/63 at Gettysburg.
Pvt.	Earnhart, Joseph M.	1842	—	—	Wounded (right side), 7/3/63. Cpl.—1/64. Sgt.—9/64. Captured, 4/2/65 at Petersburg.
Pvt.	Ewing, George R.	1842	W. Charlotte, Mecklenburg Co.	Farm labor	Wounded, 7/1/63 and captured at Gettysburg. Wounded (left leg, left hip), 10/24/64. Missing, 4/1/65.
Pvt.	Farthing, Paul	1821	Beaver Dam, Watauga Co.	Farmer	Transferred to 37th NC Inf.
Pvt.	Fisher, James W.	1840	Mecklenburg Co.	—	Captured, 3/25/65 in Petersburg trenches.
Pvt.	Flow, Robert H.	1841	W. Charlotte, Mecklenburg Co.	Farm labor	Captured, 10/27/64 at Burgess' Mill.
Pvt.	Ford, William C.	1832	W. Charlotte, Mecklenburg Co.	Day laborer	Missing, 3/1/65.
Pvt.	Frazier, Isaac S.	1842	Paw Creek, Mecklenburg Co.	Farm labor	Wounded (left shoulder), 11/18/62 at Franklin, VA.
Pvt.	Galloway, James S.	1837	W. Charlotte, Mecklenburg Co.	Brick maker	Wounded (breast), 7/1/63 at Gettysburg. Died of wounds, 7/21/63.
Pvt.	Gibson, James A.	1838	W. Charlotte, Mecklenburg Co.	Farm labor	Transferred to Regt. band, 10/64.

Rank	Name	DOB	Residence	Occupation	Remarks
Pvt.	Glenn, David P.	1841	W. Charlotte, Mecklenburg Co.	Farm labor	Wounded (right arm amputated), 7/3/63 at Gettysburg.
Pvt.	Glenn, Franklin C.	1835	W. Charlotte, Mecklenburg Co.	Farmer	Missing, 3/1/65.
Pvt.	Gray, Walter W.	1842	E. Charlotte, Mecklenburg Co.	Asst. Carpenter	Missing, 3/1/65.
Pvt.	Groves, Robert A.	1840	Pleasant Ridge, Mecklenburg Co.	Shoe maker	Captured, 7/14/63 at Falling Waters, MD. Captured, 4/2/65 at Petersburg.
Pvt.	Hand, Andrew J.	1828	Charlotte, Mecklenburg Co.	—	Captured, 7/3/63 at Gettysburg. Captured, 10/27/64 at Burgess' Mill.
Pvt.	Henderson, Isaac S.	1842	W. Charlotte, Mecklenburg Co.	Farm labor	Missing, 3/1/65.
Pvt.	**Henderson, Thomas M.**	**1840**	**W. Charlotte, Mecklenburg Co.**	**Farm labor**	**Captured, 7/14/63 at Falling Waters, MD. Point Lookout Prison, MD. Died of disease, 2/9/64.**
Pvt.	Herring, George T.	—	Mecklenburg Co.	—	Wounded, 7/3/63 at Gettysburg. Surrendered, 4/9/65 at Appomattox Court House.
Pvt.	Hill, Henry H.	1841	W. Charlotte, Mecklenburg Co.	Cabinet maker	Wounded (left side of head), 9/30/64 at Jones Farm. Cpl.—2/65. Captured, 4/2/65 at Petersburg.
Pvt.	Hill, Milton	1832	W. Charlotte, Mecklenburg Co.	Cabinet maker	Captured, 7/3/63 at Gettysburg. Captured, 4/3/65 in hospital in Richmond.
Pvt.	**Holmes, Thomas L.**	**1839**	**W. Charlotte, Mecklenburg Co.**	**Farm labor**	**Wounded (left hip), 9/30/64 at Jones Farm. Died of wounds, 10/25/64 in Richmond hospital.**
Pvt.	Hovis, B. Monroe	1839	Dallas, Gaston Co.	Farm labor	Wounded (left shoulder), 5/12/64 at Spotsylvania. Surrendered, 4/9/65 at Appomattox Court House.
Pvt.	**Hudspeth, Lewis**	**1840**	**Mecklenburg Co.**	**Farm labor**	**Died of disease (pneumonia), 7/31/62 at Wilmington, NC.**
Pvt.	Hunter, David P.	1842	Mecklenburg Co.	Farm labor	Wounded, 7/1/63 and captured at Gettysburg. Captured, 4/2/65 at Petersburg.
Pvt.	Hunter, Madison	1844	W. Charlotte, Mecklenburg Co.	Farm labor	TDY—Pioneer most of the war. Surrendered, 4/9/65 at Appomattox Court House.
Pvt.	**Hunter, Thomas H.**	**1844**	**W. Charlotte, Mecklenburg Co.**	**Farm labor**	**Died of disease, 8/25/64 at Richmond, VA.**
Pvt.	**Hutchison, James H.**	**1838**	**W. Charlotte, Mecklenburg Co.**	**Farm labor**	**Wounded, 7/1/63 at Gettysburg. Died from wounds, 7/5/63.**
Pvt.	Jenkins, David	1842	Dallas, Gaston Co.	Farm labor	Wounded (right thigh), 7/1/63 and captured at Gettysburg.
Pvt.	Johnson, Thomas N.	—	Mecklenburg Co.	—	Wounded, 7/3/63 and captured at Gettysburg.
Pvt.	Johnston, Alfred	1842	E. Charlotte, Mecklenburg Co.	Farm labor	Discharged (disability—"phthisis pulmonalis"), 9/2/63.
Pvt.	Kennedy, William	1841	Statesville, Iredell Co.	Farm labor	Wounded, 5/5/64 at the Wilderness. Surrendered, 4/9/65 at Appomattox Court House.
Pvt.	Kerns, John D.	1836	W. Charlotte, Mecklenburg Co.	Farmer	Wounded, 4/2/65 and captured, 4/2/65 at Petersburg.

Rank	Name	DOB	Residence	Occupation	Remarks
Pvt.	Kerns, Thomas J.	1836	W. Charlotte, Mecklenburg Co.	Farm labor	Captured, 4/2/65 at Petersburg.
Pvt.	Knipper, Thomas	1836	Mecklenburg Co.	—	Captured, 4/2/65 at Petersburg.
Pvt.	Lewis, Emanuel	1843	South Point, Gaston Co.	Farm labor	Cpl.—6/15/63. Wounded (left hand), 5/5/64 at the Wilderness. Sgt.—12/64. Retired because of wounds, 2/65.
Pvt.	**McConnell, John F.**	**1844**	**W. Charlotte, Mecklenburg Co.**	**Farm labor**	**Wounded, 7/1/63 and captured at Gettysburg. Died of wounds (date not recorded) in field hospital at Gettysburg.**
Pvt.	McConnell, John H.	1843	W. Charlotte, Mecklenburg Co.	Asst. Carpenter	Wounded, 7/1/63 and captured at Gettysburg. Captured, 4/2/65 at Petersburg.
Pvt.	McConnell, Thomas Y.	1844	W. Charlotte, Mecklenburg Co.	Farm labor	Missing, 3/1/65.
Pvt.	McWhirter, John	1842	Mecklenburg Co.	Farm labor	Wounded, 7/3/63 and captured at Gettysburg.
Pvt.	Monteith, Henry L.	1842	W. Charlotte, Mecklenburg Co.	Farm labor	Captured, 3/25/65 in Petersburg trenches.
Pvt.	Monteith, Robert J.	1838	W. Charlotte, Mecklenburg Co.	Overseer	Surrendered, 4/9/65 at Appomattox Court House.
Pvt.	**Montgomery, James H.**	**1836**	**W. Charlotte, Mecklenburg Co.**	**Farmer**	**Wounded, 7/3/63 and captured at Gettysburg. 3rd Lt.—8/64. Wounded (leg amputated), 8/25/64 at Reams' Station. Died of wounds, 9/9/64.**
Pvt.	Neal, George A.	1844	Paw Creek, Mecklenburg Co.	Farm labor	Wounded (left arm amputated), 7/1/63 and captured at Gettysburg. Furloughed because of wounds, 10/7/64.
Pvt.	**Newell, Alexander H.**	**1841**	**W. Charlotte, Mecklenburg Co.**	**Farm labor**	**Wounded (contusion of the left shoulder), 7/3/63 at Gettysburg. Died of disease, 8/27/64.**
Pvt.	Norment, Isaac	1837	W. Charlotte, Mecklenburg Co.	—	Wounded, 7/1/63 at Gettysburg. Captured, 4/3/65 in Petersburg trenches.
Pvt.	Norment, John	1839	W. Charlotte, Mecklenburg Co.	—	Missing, 3/1/65.
Pvt.	Orman, J. E.	1845	Mecklenburg Co.	Farm labor	Captured, 4/6–8/65 on road to Appomattox.
Pvt.	Orr, James F.	1825	W. Charlotte, Mecklenburg Co.	Farmer	Captured, 10/27/64 at Burgess' Mill, VA. Captured, 4/3/65 near Petersburg.
Pvt.	Orr, N. C.	1840	E. Charlotte, Mecklenburg Co.	Merchant	Captured, 10/14/63 at Bristoe Station, VA.
Pvt.	**Powell, Daniel**	**1835**	**Gaston Co.**	**—**	**Killed, 7/1/63 at Gettysburg.**
Pvt.	Query, Robert L.	1840	W. Charlotte, Mecklenburg Co.	Farm labor	Captured, 4/2/65 at Petersburg.
Pvt.	Query, Samuel F.	1839	W. Charlotte, Mecklenburg Co.	Farm labor	Wounded ("lower left extremities"), 12/16/62 at White Hall, NC.
Pvt.	**Ratchford, Ezekiel C.**	**1835**	**Erasmus, Gaston Co.**	**Farmer**	**Died of disease ("erysipelas"), 1/23/63 at Weldon, NC.**
Pvt.	Roberts, Peyton	1841	E. Charlotte, Mecklenburg Co.	Farm labor	Wounded (right foot), 7/3/63 and captured at Gettysburg. Discharged (wounds), 2/17/65.
Pvt.	Ross, Robert A.	1821	W. Charlotte, Mecklenburg Co.	Farmer	Transferred to Co. H, 7/11/62.

Rank	Name	DOB	Residence	Occupation	Remarks
Pvt.	Ruddick, Burl M.	1844	W. Charlotte, Mecklenburg Co.	Farm labor	Wounded, 10/27/64 at Burgess' Mill. Missing, 3/1/65.
Pvt.	Ruddick, B. William	1846	W. Charlotte, Mecklenburg Co.	Farm labor	Wounded (right leg), 10/27/64 at Burgess' Mill.
Pvt.	Simpson, Robert F.	1830	Clear Creek, Mecklenburg Co.	Farmer	Wounded, 7/3/63 at Gettysburg and captured, 7/5/63 at Greencastle, PA.
Pvt.	Stowe, Jacob C.	1840	Woodlawn, Gaston Co.	Asst. Blacksmith	Wounded, 9/30/64 at Jones Farm, VA. Died wounds, 11/2/64 in Richmond hospital.
Pvt.	Stowe, James M.	1837	W. Charlotte, Mecklenburg Co.	Day laborer	Wounded (left thigh), 7/1/63 at Gettysburg and captured, 7/5/63 at Greencastle, PA.
Pvt.	Taylor, Harvey S.	1844	E. Charlotte, Mecklenburg Co.	Farm labor	Captured, 10/27/64 at Burgess' Mill.
Pvt.	Taylor, Robert C.	1842	E. Charlotte, Mecklenburg Co.	Farm labor	Captured, 4/2/65 at Petersburg.
Pvt.	Thompson, J. B.	1832	Mecklenburg Co.	—	Discharged (disability), 5/30/62.
Pvt.	Wallace, William A.	1843	E. Charlotte, Mecklenburg Co.	Farm labor	Wounded, 7/3/63 at Gettysburg. Captured, 7/14/63 at Falling Waters, MD. Captured, 4/2/65 at Petersburg.
Pvt.	Whithers, B. A.	1836	Mecklenburg Co.	—	Wounded, 9/30/64 at Jones Farm.
Pvt.	Williams, Spain H.	1833	Seagles, Lincoln Co.	Farmer	Missing, 3/1/65.
Pvt.	**Wingate, Angus**	**1839**	**Lincolnton, Lincoln Co.**	**Carriage maker**	**Killed, 7/3/63 at Gettysburg.**
Pvt.	Wingate, Charles C.	1837	Lincolnton, Lincoln Co.	Farm labor	Promoted to musician, 9/64, transferred to F & S.
Pvt.	Wingate, Murchison	1840	Lincolnton, Lincoln Co.	Farm labor	Captured, 4/2/65 at Petersburg.

1862 Recruits

Rank	Name	DOB	Residence	Occupation	Remarks
Pvt.	Allen, Hamilton W.	1837	E. Charlotte, Mecklenburg Co.	Farm labor	Enlisted, 5/3/62. Wounded (right arm), 7/1/63 and captured, 75/63 at Greencastle, PA. Transferred, 2/10/65 to Veteran Reserve Corps.
Pvt.	Allen, Jacob C.	1830	E. Charlotte, Mecklenburg Co.	Farm labor	Enlisted, 5/3/62. Discharged (disability) 7/62.
Pvt.	**Auten, P. S.**	**1836**	**Mecklenburg Co.**	**—**	**Enlisted, 7/7/62. Wounded, 7/3/63 and captured at Gettysburg. Died of wounds, 8/1/63 in Gettysburg field hospital.**
Pvt.	Bigham, James W.	1835	Mecklenburg Co.	—	Enlisted, 7/7/62. Wounded (arm), 7/3/63 at Gettysburg. Cpl.—12/63. Surrendered, 4/9/65. at Appomattox Court House.
Pvt.	**Bigham, John H.**	**1843**	**W. Charlotte, Mecklenburg Co.**	**Farm labor**	**Enlisted, 12/27/62. Died of disease (pneumonia), 11/19/63.**
Pvt.	**Campbell, William H.**	**1840**	**E. Charlotte, Mecklenburg Co.**	**Farm labor**	**Enlisted, 5/3/62. Died of disease, 7/24/62.**
Pvt.	**Elliott, William A.**	**1841**	**W. Charlotte, Mecklenburg Co.**	**Farm labor**	**Enlisted, 7/7/62. Killed, 7/1/63 at Gettysburg.**
Pvt.	Elms, John P.	1836	W. Charlotte, Mecklenburg Co.	Clerk	Enlisted, 5/15/62. 1st Sgt.—6/2/62. Transferred, 6/16/63 to 37th NC Inf.

Rank	Name	DOB	Residence	Occupation	Remarks
Pvt.	Ewing, William E.	1837	Mecklenburg Co.	—	Enlisted, 7/7/62. Wounded, 7/3/63 and captured at Gettysburg. Missing, 4/1/65.
Pvt.	**Garrison, J. S.**	**1844**	**W. Charlotte, Mecklenburg Co.**	**Farm labor**	**Enlisted, 12/29/62. Killed, 7/3/63 at Gettysburg.**
Pvt.	Harris, Nathaniel O.	1839	Olin, Iredell Co.	Farm labor	Enlisted, 5/3/62. Wounded (right shoulder), 7/3/63, "shell wound," at Gettysburg. Captured, 3/25/65 in Petersburg trenches.
Pvt.	Harris, Warren C. C.	1836	W. Charlotte, Mecklenburg Co.	Farm labor	Enlisted, 5/3/62. Captured, 4/2/65 at Petersburg.
Pvt.	Hill, Miles	1828	W. Charlotte, Mecklenburg Co.	Cabinet maker	Enlisted, 7/7/62. Captured, 4/3/65 in hospital at Richmond.
Pvt.	Hobbs, Ferdinand	1845	W. Charlotte, Mecklenburg Co.	Farm labor	Enlisted, 5/15/62. Wounded, 7/3/63 at Gettysburg. Captured, 4/2/65 at Petersburg.
Pvt.	Howard, Thomas M.	1836	Mountain Island, Gaston Co.	Factory hand	Enlisted, 5/15/62. Wounded, 5/5/64 at the Wilderness. Captured, 4/2/65 at Petersburg.
Pvt.	Jenkins, Jacob	1842	Woodlawn, Gaston Co.	Farm labor	Enlisted, 7/7/62. Captured, 7/14/63 at Falling Waters, MD. Missing, 3/1/65.
Pvt.	King, Campbell	1837	Long Creek, Mecklenburg Co.	Butcher	Enlisted, 5/3/62. Captured, 10/14/63 at Bristoe Station. Wounded, 6/3/64 at Cold Harbor. Captured, 4/2/65 at Petersburg.
Pvt.	King, John A.	1838	W. Charlotte, Mecklenburg Co.	Day laborer	Enlisted, 5/3/62. Missing, 3/1/65.
Pvt.	Kinney, Benjamin	1822	W. Charlotte, Mecklenburg Co.	Farmer	Enlisted, 12/29/62. Missing, 3/1/65.
Pvt.	**McGinn, Robert F.**	**1829**	**W. Charlotte, Mecklenburg Co.**	**Farmer**	**Enlisted, 5/15/62. Captured, 7/14/63 at Falling Waters, MD. Died of disease, 2/2/64 as POW at Point Lookout, MD.**
Pvt.	Monteith, Moses O.	1834	W. Charlotte, Mecklenburg Co.	Farm labor	Enlisted, 7/7/62. Wounded, 5/5/64 at the Wilderness.
Pvt.	Pettus, H. M.	1839	Gaston Co.	—	Enlisted, 5/15/62. Surrendered, 4/9/65 at Appomattox Court House.
Pvt.	Raborn, M. D.	1844	Mecklenburg Co.	Farm labor	Enlisted, 5/2/62. Missing, 3/1/65.
Pvt.	West, Jack L.	1833	Stanley Cr. Gaston Co.	Farmer	Enlisted, 5/15/62. Discharged ("by reason of lung disease"), 5/28/63.

1863 Recruits

Rank	Name	DOB	Residence	Occupation	Remarks
Pvt.	Allen, Cyrus A.	1844	Charlotte, Mecklenburg Co.	Farm labor	Enlisted, 3/1/63. Wounded, 7/3/63 and captured at Gettysburg. Captured, 4/2/65 at Petersburg.
Pvt.	Blakely, James J.	1840	W. Charlotte, Mecklenburg Co.	Farm labor	Enlisted, 3/1/63. Captured, 7/14/63 at Falling Waters.
Pvt.	**Darnell, Jackson J.**	**1830**	**W. Charlotte, Mecklenburg Co.**	**Day labor**	**Enlisted, 3/1/63. Wounded, 7/1/63 at Gettysburg. Wounded, 5/6/64 at the Wilderness. Died of wounds, 9/23/64.**
Pvt.	**Earnhardt, William C.**	**1828**	**Mecklenburg Co.**	**—**	**Enlisted, 4/1/63. Died of disease (chronic diarrhea), 8/23/63.**
Pvt.	**Earnhart, S. O.**	**1823**	**Mecklenburg Co.**	**—**	**Enlisted, 4/1/63. Captured, 7/14/63 at Falling Waters. Died of disease (chronic diarrhea), 4/15/64.**

Rank	Name	DOB	Residence	Occupation	Remarks
Pvt.	Glover, Joshua	1829	W. Charlotte, Mecklenburg Co.	Farmer	Enlisted, 3/1/63: Wounded, 7/3/63 and captured at Gettysburg: Missing, 3/1/65.
Pvt.	**Goodrum, William J.**	1845	W. Charlotte, Mecklenburg Co.	Farm labor	**Enlisted, 3/1/63 Wounded (abdomen), 7/1/63 and captured at Gettysburg. Died of wounds, 7/18/63 in Chester, PA.**
Pvt.	McGinnis, Sidney A.	1836	E. Charlotte, Mecklenburg Co.	Farm labor	Enlisted, 3/1/63. Captured, 7/3/63 at Gettysburg. Died of disease, 2/15/64 as POW at Point Lookout, MD.
Pvt.	McWhirter, James	1845	Mecklenburg Co.	Farm labor	Enlisted, 10/3/63. Died of disease ("febris cont. com."), 1/31/64 at Gordonsville, VA.
Pvt.	Peysour, Caleb	1830	Gaston Co.	—	Enlisted, 3/1/63. Wounded, 7/1/63, captured at Gettysburg. Captured, 3/25/65 at Petersburg.
Pvt.	**Prim, Thomas**	1845	W. Charlotte, Mecklenburg Co.	Farm labor	**Enlisted, 3/1/63. Wounded, 7/1/63 at Gettysburg. Died of wounds (place and date unknown).**
Pvt.	Simpson, John W.	1845	W. Charlotte, Mecklenburg Co.	Farm labor	Enlisted, 3/1/63. Reported absent due to sickness much of the war.
Pvt.	**Smith, John S.**	1827	W. Charlotte, Mecklenburg Co.	Day labor	**Enlisted, 3/1/63. Wounded (head), 7/3/63 at Gettysburg. Died of wounds, 7/15/63 at Gettysburg.**
Pvt.	Wilson, William M.	1845	W. Charlotte, Mecklenburg Co.	Farm labor	Enlisted, 4/1/63. Captured, 7/4/63 at Chambersburg, PA. Hospital Stwrd: 6/64 and transferred to F & S.
Pvt.	Wright, Taylor	1845	Stowesville, Gaston Co.	Farm labor	Enlisted, 3/1/63. Wounded (back), 7/3/63 and captured at Gettysburg. Wounded, 9/30/64 at Jones Farm. Missing, 3/1/65.

1864 Recruits

Rank	Name	DOB	Residence	Occupation	Remarks
Pvt.	Alexander, Webster S.	1846	W. Charlotte, Mecklenburg Co.	Farm labor	Enlisted, 2/3/64. Captured, 4/2/65 at Petersburg.
Pvt.	Black, Ezekiel	1820	W. Charlotte, Mecklenburg Co.	Farmer	Enlisted, 10/29/64. Captured, 4/2/65.
Pvt.	Duckworth, James A.	1825	Morganton, Burke Co.	Farmer	Enlisted, 4/22/64. Missing, 3/1/65.
Pvt.	**Goodrum, Charles H.**	1845	W. Charlotte, Mecklenburg Co.	Farm labor	**Enlisted, 2/25/64. Died of disease, 7/16/64 at Lynchburg, VA.**
Pvt.	Herron, James M.	1828	W. Charlotte, Mecklenburg Co.	Farmer	Enlisted, 11/12/64 at Camp Holmes. Missing, 3/1/65.
Pvt.	Hunter, Andrew J.	1832	W. Charlotte, Mecklenburg Co.	Farm labor	Enlisted, 6/11/64. Transferred, 10/15/64 to Co. E.
Pvt.	McCall, Jacob A.	1846	W. Charlotte, Mecklenburg Co.	Asst. Carpenter	Enlisted, 2/29/64. Missing, 3/1/65.
Pvt.	Pettis, Stephen J.	—	Mecklenburg Co.	—	Enlisted, 12/64. Captured, 4/2/65 at Petersburg.
Pvt.	Pettus, John W.	—	Gaston Co.	—	Transferred, 1/64 from Co. C, 37th Regt. NC Inf. Wounded, 5/5/64 at the Wilderness. Captured, 4/2/65 at Petersburg.
Pvt.	Peysour, S. Peter	—	Gaston Co.	—	Enlisted, 11/27/64. Captured, 4/2/65 at Petersburg.

Rank	Name	DOB	Residence	Occupation	Remarks
Pvt.	Taylor, J. Q.	—	Mecklenburg Co.	—	Enlisted, 1/27/64. Died of self-inflicted wounds, 10/24/64.
Pvt.	Thomasson, James B.	1833	Tally Hollow, Granville Co.	Farmer	Enlisted, 10/29/64. Captured, 4/2/65 at Petersburg.

Company B
Burke, Wilkes, and Caldwell Counties

Rank	Name	DOB	Residence	Occupation	Remarks
Cpt.	Armfield, Mark D.	1807	Morganton, Burke Co.	Railroad agent	Captured, 7/3/63 at Gettysburg. Died of disease ("general debility"), 12/3/63 as a POW at Johnson's Island, OH.
1st Lt.	Parks, Thomas R.	1820	Upper Creek, Burke Co.	Overseer	Wounded, (shoulder), 7/3/63 at Gettysburg. Captured, 7/14/63 at Falling Waters, MD. Cpt.—12/3/63. Surrendered at Appomattox Court House, 4/9/65.
2nd Lt.	Warlick, Portland A.	1829	Morganton, Burke Co.	Farmer	Wounded (left arm), 7/3/63 at Gettysburg. Died in hospital in Richmond ("typhoid pneumonia"), 12/28/63.
3rd Lt.	Dorsey, Elisha W.	1836	Morganton, Burke Co.	Merchant	Wounded (right leg amputated), 7/1/63 and captured at Gettysburg. Captured in Richmond hospital, 4/3/65.
1st Sgt.	Bristol, Elam B.	1842	Morganton, Burke Co.	Student	Killed, 12/16/62 at White Hall, NC.
Sgt.	Duval, John M.	1844	Morganton, Burke Co.	Student	Wounded (thigh), 7/1/63 at Gettysburg. Captured, 7/5/63 at Williamsport, MD. Died of wounds, 8/63 at Hagerstown, PA.
Sgt.	Erwin, George P.	1841	Morganton, Burke Co.	Student	1st Sgt.-12/20/62. Transferred, 5/63 to 60th Regt. NC Troops.
Sgt.	Michaux, John P.	1842	Morganton, Burke Co.	Farm labor	Captured, 7/14/63 at Falling Waters, MD. 1st Sgt.—2/15/64, Missing, 3/1/65.
Cpl.	Carlton, Robert W.	1829	Morganton, Burke Co.	Farm labor	Wounded, 7/1/63 and captured at Gettysburg. Died of disease ("chronic diarrhea"), 9/16/63 as POW at Point Lookout, MD.
Cpl.	Galloway, H. H.	1817	W. Charlotte, Mecklenburg Co.	Farmer	Captured, 7/14/63 at Falling Waters, MD. Sgt.-5/64. Captured, 4/2/65 at Petersburg.
Cpl.	Hennessa, Robert J.	1841	Morganton, Burke Co.	Farm labor	Captured, 7/3/63 at Gettysburg. Sgt.—2/15/64. Surrendered, 4/9/65 at Appomattox Court House.
Cpl.	Moore, Thomas B.	1841	Morganton, Burke Co.	Farm labor	Pvt.—7/62. Wounded, 7/1/63 and captured at Gettysburg. Killed, 7/30/64 at New Market.
Music	Carroll, John	1825	Morganton, Burke Co.	Farmer	Pvt.—9/62. Wounded, 12/16/62 at White Hall, NC.
Pvt.	Andrews, George W.	1834	Wilkes Co.	—	Wounded (left leg), 7/1/63 and captured at. Gettysburg
Pvt.	Andrews, James	1844	Wilkes Co.	—	Captured, 7/14/63 at Falling Waters, MD. Captured, 4/2/65 at Petersburg.
Pvt.	Andrews, William	1835	Wilkes Co.	—	Missing, 3/1/65

Rank	Name	DOB	Residence	Occupation	Remarks
Pvt.	Anthony, Joseph J.	1830	Morganton, Burke Co.	Farmer	Hospitalized, 7/6/62 at Wilmington, NC with gunshot wound. Died of disease ("febris typhoides") at Richmond hospital, 6/13/63.
Pvt.	Anthony, Philip B.	1832	Morganton, Burke Co.	Farmer	Wounded, 7/1/63 at Gettysburg. Died of wounds ("febris typhoides"), 7/18/63 at Harrisonburg, VA.
Pvt.	Baker, Martin	—	Morganton, Burke Co.	Farmer	Transferred to "another company in Caldwell Co."
Pvt.	Bowman, Jacob	1832	Copenhagen, Caldwell Co.	Farmer	Captured, 7/14/63 at Falling Waters, MD. Deserted, 5/2/64
Pvt.	Branch, Anderson C.	1842	Morganton, Burke Co.	Farm labor	Wounded and captured, 7/3/63 at Gettysburg.
Pvt.	Branch, Martin	1841	Morganton, Burke Co.	Farm labor	Wounded (left knee), 7/1/63 and captured at Gettysburg. Captured, 4/2/65 at Petersburg.
Pvt.	Branch, Reuben	1844	Upper Creek, Burke Co.	Farm labor	Captured, 4/2/65 at Petersburg.
Pvt.	Bristol, Lambert A.	1846	Morganton, Burke Co.	Student	Discharged, 4/1/64.
Pvt.	Cannon, James	1840	Lenoir, Caldwell Co.	Farm labor	Wounded, 8/21/64 at Weldon Rd., VA.
Pvt.	Causby, David A.	1824	Morganton, Burke Co.	Farm labor	Captured, 7/14/63 at Falling Waters, MD. Died of disease ("chronic diarrhea"), 3/10/64 as POW at Point Lookout, MD.
Pvt.	Clark, John M.	1837	Morganton, Burke Co.	Farm labor	Captured, 7/14/63 at Falling Waters, MD.
Pvt.	Clark, B. B.	1841	Burke Co.	Farm labor	AWOL, 11/64.
Pvt.	Cook, Thomas	1840	Morganton, Burke Co.	Farm labor	Captured, 10/14/63 at Bristoe Station, VA.
Pvt.	Courtney, James	1825	Copenhagen, Caldwell Co.	Farmer	Captured, 7/14/63 at Falling Waters, MD. Discharged, 2/3/65.
Pvt.	Crawley, J. W.	1841	Morganton, Burke Co.	Farm labor	Captured, 7/14/63 at Falling Waters, MD. Wounded (neck), 5/11/64 at Spotsylvania. Cpl.—8/29/64. Captured, 10/27/74 at Burgess' Mill.
Pvt.	Crouch, Eliphus	1840	Lower Creek, Burke Co.	Farm labor	Captured, 4/2/65 at Petersburg.
Pvt.	Crouch, Peyton	1837	Morganton, Burke Co.	Farm labor	Died of disease (pneumonia), 8/1/63 at Staunton, VA.
Pvt.	Crump, Elijah H.	1838	Lenoir, Caldwell Co.	Farmer	"He joined another company in Caldwell Co," 8/62.
Pvt.	Dale, David	1832	Silver Creek, Burke Co.	Farmer	Discharged (disability), 6/23/62.
Pvt.	Davis, Barry L.	1843	Black Mountain, McDowell Co.	Farm labor	Wounded, 7/1/63 at Gettysburg. Captured, 7/14/63 at Falling Waters, MD. Captured, 4/2/65 at Petersburg.
Pvt.	Day, Samuel M.	1824	Lenoir, Caldwell Co.	Farmer	Wounded, 7/1/63. Captured, 7/5/63 at Gettysburg.

Rank	Name	DOB	Residence	Occupation	Remarks
Pvt.	Dorsey, Thomas A.	1843	Morganton, Burke Co.	Farm labor	Wounded, 7/3/63 and captured, 7/5/63 at Gettysburg. Cpl.-2/15/64. Transferred, 12/7/64 to 3rd Regt. NC Cav.
Pvt.	Duckworth, Jonathan N.	1846	Morganton, Burke Co.	Farm labor	Wounded, 7/3/63 and captured, 7/5/63 at Gettysburg. Discharged, 2/3/65. "By reason of 'the expiration of his enlistment.'"
Pvt.	**Duckworth, Walter**	**1832**	**Morganton, Burke Co.**	**Farmer**	**Killed, 12/16/62 at White Hall, NC.**
Pvt.	Ernest, Hamilton	1839	Burke Co.	Farm labor	Discharged, 8/19/62. "Frequent paraxems of nervous depression."
Pvt.	**Ferree, Thomas C.**	**1838**	**Morganton, Burke Co.**	**Farm labor**	**Sgt.-9/1/63. Died of disease ("diarrhoea chronic"), 10/29/64 at Richmond, VA.**
Pvt.	**Fincannon, John**	**1832**	**Morganton, Burke Co.**	**Farmer**	**Wounded, 7/1/63 at Gettysburg. Died of disease, 8/18/64 in Petersburg.**
Pvt.	Fox, William J.	1828	Morganton, Burke Co.	Farmer	Transferred, 12/7/64 to 3rd Regt. NC Cav.
Pvt.	Gilbert, Johnson Franklin	1832	Morganton, Burke Co.	Stair maker	Wounded (right foot), 10/27/64 at Burgess' Mill.
Pvt.	Griffin, David	1832	Burke Co.	—	Captured, 7/14/63 at Falling Waters, MD.
Pvt.	Griffin, James	1834	Burke Co.	—	Captured, 7/14/63 at Falling Waters, MD.
Pvt.	Griffin, William	1836	Morganton, Burke Co.	Farmer	Captured, 10/27/64 at Burgess' Mill.
Pvt.	**Harbison, Tolbert**	**1842**	**Morganton, Burke Co.**	**Farm labor**	**Died of disease, 6/13/62 at Wilmington, NC.**
Pvt.	Harbison, William T.	1844	Morganton, Burke Co.	Farm labor	Wounded (right leg amputated), 6/2/64 at Cold Harbor.
Pvt.	Harris, Lewis B.	1844	Morganton, Burke Co.	Farm labor	Captured, 7/14/63 at Falling Waters, MD. Wounded, 10/27/64 at Burgess' Mill. Captured, 4/2/65 at Petersburg.
Pvt.	Hawks, Reuben	1820	Morganton, Burke Co.	Farmer	Discharged, 4/24/64 by reason of "chronic rheumatism."
Pvt.	**Justice, Samuel**	**1817**	**Smith's Bridge, Macon Co.**	**Farmer**	**Died of disease ("diarrhoea chronic"), 5/22/64 at Richmond hospital.**
Pvt.	**Keller, David**	**1839**	**King's Creek, Caldwell Co.**	**Farmer**	**Died of disease ("typhoid fever"), 6/11/62 at Wilmington, NC.**
Pvt.	**Keller, George**	**1829**	**King's Creek, Caldwell Co.**	**Farmer**	**Wounded, 10/27/64 at Burgess' Mill. Died of wounds, 10/28/64.**
Pvt.	Landis, Jordan N.	1827	McDowell Co.	Farmer	Wounded, 7/3/63 and captured at Gettysburg. Wounded (both thighs), 4/2/65 at Petersburg. Captured, 4/7/65 in Farmville.
Pvt.	Landis, William T.	1838	Dyartsville, McDowell Co.	Farm labor	Wounded (left leg), 7/1/63.
Pvt.	Lane, Thomas H.	1841	Burke Co.	Farm labor	Discharged, disability ("chronic contraction of the finger & thumb on the right hand with complete loss of power"), 9/22/62.
Pvt.	Livingston, Jordan	1841	Warrior Cr., Wilkes Co.	Farm labor	Wounded, 7/1/63 at Gettysburg. Captured, 7/5/63 at Gettysburg field hospital. Captured, 4/3/65 in hospital at Richmond.

Rank	Name	DOB	Residence	Occupation	Remarks
Pvt.	Livingston, Larkin	1844	Warrior Cr., Wilkes Co.	Farm labor	Captured, 10/14/63 at Bristoe Station, VA. Wounded (left arm), 6/23/64 near Weldon Rd. Surrendered, 4/9/65 at Appomattox Court House.
Pvt.	London, James W.	1838	Cleveland Co.	Farm labor	Sgt.—11/1/64. Wounded (left arm amputated), 2/6/65 near Burgess' Mill, Petersburg trenches.
Pvt.	Loudermilk, George	1826	Morganton, Burke Co.	Farmer	Wounded, 5/10/64 at Spotsylvania. Captured, 4/2/65 at Petersburg.
Pvt.	Mace, William H.	1838	Greensboro, Guilford Co.	Farm labor	Transferred to Co. D, 4/18/62.
Pvt.	McCall, William W.	1821	Copenhagen, Caldwell Co.	Farmer	Discharged (disabilities—"chronic debility & emaciation proceeding from hepatic disease of long standing"), 3/8/64.
Pvt.	Moody, David E.	1817	Morganton, Burke Co.	Farmer	Discharged, 4/10/63 ("by reason of old age, general debility, and rheumatism").
Pvt.	Moore, Joseph A.	1841	McDowell Co.	Farm labor	Transferred, 12/7/64 to Co. F, 3rd Regt. NC Cav.
Pvt.	Morgan, Andrew A.	1840	Morganton, Burke Co.	Farm labor	Wounded (right arm), 7/3/63 and captured at Gettysburg. Discharged (due to wounds), 4/1/64.
Pvt.	**Morgan, John**	**1845**	**Burke Co.**	**Farm labor**	**Died of disease, 6/18/62 at Wilmington, NC.**
Pvt.	Morgan, Perry W.	1834	Morganton, Burke Co.	Farmer	Captured, 7/14/63 at Falling Waters, MD.
Pvt.	**Morrison, A. H.**	**1835**	**Morganton, Burke Co.**	**Farm labor**	**Wounded, 12/16/62 at White Hall, NC. Killed, 7/1/63 at Gettysburg.**
Pvt.	Moses, S. Alfred	1834	Burke Co.	—	Captured, 4/2/65 at Petersburg.
Pvt.	Mull, Henry	1842	Morganton, Burke Co.	Farm labor	Captured, 10/14/63 at Bristoe Station, VA.
Pvt.	Parks, H. H.	1840	Morganton, Burke Co.	Farm labor	Cpl.—11/62. Missing, 7/3/63 at Gettysburg. "Supposed killed."
Pvt.	**Patton, George**	**1847**	**Burke Co.**	**Farm labor**	**Died of disease (typhoid fever), 4/8/62 at Camp Mangum, Raleigh, NC.**
Pvt.	**Patton, John**	**1844**	**Morganton, Burke Co.**	**Farm labor**	**Died of disease (typhoid fever), 4/9/62 at Camp Mangum, Raleigh, NC.**
Pvt.	Patton, William S.	1844	Morganton, Burke Co.	Farm labor	Captured, 10/14/63 at Bristoe Station, VA. Captured, 4/2/65 at Petersburg.
Pvt.	Pearson, Michael	1817	Morganton, Burke Co.	Farmer	Wounded, 7/1/63 at Gettysburg. Discharged, 2/3/65.
Pvt.	Pearson, Thomas	1834	Morganton, Burke Co.	Brick maker	Wounded, 7/14/63 at Falling Waters. Wounded, 8/21/64 at Weldon Rd. Captured, 4/2/65 at Petersburg.
Pvt.	Perry, Alfred	1827	Burke Co.	—	Captured, 7/14/63 at Falling Waters, MD. Missing, 3/1/65.
Pvt.	Phillips, C. S.	1846	Burke Co.	Farm labor	Surrendered, 4/9/65 at Appomattox Court House.
Pvt.	**Phillips, Elijah**	**1820**	**Morganton, Burke Co.**	**Farmer**	**Died of disease, 9/5/64 at hospital in Richmond.**

Rank	Name	DOB	Residence	Occupation	Remarks
Pvt.	Puckett, Elias W.	1842	Morganton, Burke Co.	Farm labor	Wounded 7/3/63, and captured, 7/5/63 at Gettysburg. Died of disease (typhoid fever), 7/23/64 as POW at Ft. Delaware, DE.
Pvt.	Puett, John W.	1845	Morganton, Burke Co.	Blacksmith asst.	Died of disease, 6/25/62 in Wilmington, NC.
Pvt.	Short, William W.	1827	Morganton, Burke Co.	Farmer	Died of disease ("febris remittent"), 7/21/62 at Wilmington, NC.
Pvt.	Shuffler, Harvey	1840	Morganton, Burke Co.	Farm labor	Wounded, 12/16/62 at White Hall, NC. Killed, 7/7/63 at Williamsport, MD.
Pvt.	Shuffler, John	1832	Morganton, Burke Co.	Farmer	Wounded (foot), 10/14/63 at Bristoe Station, VA. Captured, 4/2/65 at Petersburg.
Pvt.	Shuffler, Sidney	1844	Morganton, Burke Co.	Farm labor	Captured, 7/14/63 at Falling Waters, MD. Captured, 10/27/64 at Burgess' Mill.
Pvt.	Shuffler, William	1835	Morganton, Burke Co.	Farmer	Wounded, 12/16/62 at White Hall, NC. Captured, 7/14/63 at Falling Waters, MD. Captured, 4/2/65 at Petersburg.
Pvt.	Sims, Samuel	1832	Burke Co.	—	"Court-martialed and sentenced to five years at hard labor," 3/10/64
Pvt.	Singleton, J. Vincent	1835	Morganton, Burke Co.	Farmer	Surrendered, 4/9/65 at Appomattox Court House.
Pvt.	Singleton, Lucius	1845	Morganton, Burke Co.	Farm labor	Wounded (left arm), 7/1/63 at Gettysburg. Cpl.—2/15/64. Captured, 4/3/65 in Petersburg trenches.
Pvt.	Singleton, Marcus D.	1842	Morganton, Burke Co.	Farm labor	Died, 3/1/64 at home in Morganton, NC.
Pvt.	Singleton, Silas S.	1840	Morganton, Burke Co.	Farm labor	Captured, 7/14/63 at Falling Waters, MD. Paroled, 5/15/65 at Lynchburg.
Pvt.	Smith, Alva	1844	Morganton, Burke Co.	Farm labor	Captured, 7/14/63 at Falling Waters, MD. Wounded (right knee), 9/30/64 at Jones Farm. Retired, 12/22/64 to the Invalid Corps.
Pvt.	Smith, Anderson	1837	Morganton, Burke Co.	Farm labor	Missing "on the march," 5/63. Returned to the company and court-martialed, 6/22/64. Captured, 4/2/65 at Petersburg.
Pvt.	Smith, James C.	1837	Morganton, Burke Co.	Farmer	Captured, 7/14/63 at Falling Waters, MD. Cpl.—7/26/64. Missing, 3/1/65.
Pvt.	Smith, Thomas	1836	Morganton, Burke Co.	Farm labor	Deserted, 6/22/63 near Culpepper, VA.
Pvt.	Smith, William A.	1829	Morganton, Burke Co.	Farmer	Wounded, 7/1/63 and captured, 7/5/63 at Gettysburg. Died of wounds, 10/1/63 at hospital at David's Island, NY.
Pvt.	Stacy, George L.	1844	Morganton, Burke Co.	Farm labor	Captured, 7/3/63 at Gettysburg.
Pvt.	Teem, John P.	1844	Morganton, Burke Co.	Farm labor	Captured, 7/3/63 at Gettysburg.
Pvt.	Wakefield, S. D.	1845	Morganton, Burke Co.	Student	Wounded and captured, 7/3/63 at Gettysburg. Died of wounds and chronic diarrhea, 9/10/63 as POW at Ft. Delaware, DE.

Rank	Name	DOB	Residence	Occupation	Remarks
Pvt.	Walker, Elisha F.	1834	Morganton, Burke Co.	Farmer & Teacher	Wounded (shoulder & right side), 7/3/63 at Gettysburg. 3rd Lt.—2/15/64. Wounded (leg), 5/5/64 at the Wilderness. Captured, 10/27/64 at Burgess' Mill.
Pvt.	**Warlick, A. Pinkney**	**1843**	**Morganton, Burke Co.**	**Farm labor**	**Wounded, 7/1/63 at Gettysburg. Cpl.—11/1/63. Wounded, 6/12/64 near White Oak Swamp, VA. Died, 6/30/64 of wounds and "chronic diarrhea."**
Pvt.	Warlick, John Lewis	1834	Morganton, Burke Co.	Farm overseer	Cpl.—Promoted, 8/19/62. Sgt.—12/22/62. Wounded, 7/1/63 and captured, 7/5/63 at Gettysburg. 1st Sgt.—12/63. 2nd Lt.—2/15/64. Captured, 4/11/65 at Farmville, VA.
Pvt.	**Williams, John A.**	**1836**	**Morganton, Burke Co.**	**Farmer**	**Died of disease (pneumonia), 4/20/62 at hospital in Raleigh.**
Pvt.	Williams, Joseph B.	1842	Morganton, Burke Co.	Farm labor	Wounded (left foot), 7/1/63 at Gettysburg. Captured, 10/27/64 at Burgess' Mill.
Pvt.	Williams, Robert G.	1843	Morganton, Burke Co.	Farm labor	Wounded, 5/10/64 at Spotsylvania. Captured, 3/27/65 in Petersburg trenches.

1862 Recruits

Rank	Name	DOB	Residence	Occupation	Remarks
Pvt.	Cook, John	1842	Morganton, Burke Co.	Farm labor	Enlisted, 5/5/62. Wounded, 7/1/63 and captured, 7/3/63 at Gettysburg field hospital. Captured, 4/2/65 at Petersburg.
Pvt.	**Duckworth, William**	**1828**	**Morganton, Burke Co.**	**Farmer**	**Enlisted, 12/15/62. Killed, 7/1/63 at Gettysburg.**
Pvt.	Loven, George A.	1838	Childersville, Yancey Co.	Farmer	Enlisted, 11/10/62. Wounded, 12/16/62 at White Hall, NC.
Sgt.	McGimsey, Walker W.	1834	Linville, Burke Co.	Farmer	Enlisted, 12/21/62. Wounded, 7/1/63 at Gettysburg. Surrendered, 4/9/65 at Appomattox Court House.
Pvt.	Parks, James P.	1844	Morganton, Burke Co.	Farm labor	Enlisted, 11/10/62. Captured, 7/14/63 at Falling Waters, MD. Cpl.—10/64. Captured, 4/2/65 at Petersburg.

1863 Recruits

Rank	Name	DOB	Residence	Occupation	Remarks
Pvt.	Brewer, William	1829	McDowell Co.	Farmer	Enlisted, 2/9/63. Captured, 7/14/63 at Falling Waters, MD.
Pvt.	Butler, John	1831	Golden Valley, Rutherford Co.	Farmer	Enlisted, 11/16/63. Captured, 4/2/65 at Petersburg.
Pvt.	Carswell, Nathan	1835	Morganton, Burke Co.	Farm labor	Enlisted, 2/11/63. Deserted, 8/5/63.
Pvt.	Carswell, Rankin R.	1837	Morganton, Burke Co.	Farm labor	Enlisted, 2/11/63. Wounded, 7/1/63 and captured at Gettysburg. 3/64, reported AWOL; "in the woods as a deserter."
Pvt.	Carswell, Thomas H.	1836	Morganton, Burke Co.	Farm labor	Enlisted, 2/11/63. Deserted, 3/29/65.
Pvt.	Chapman, William	1837	Morganton, Burke Co.	Farm labor	Enlisted, 2/11/63. Deserted, 6/22/63
Pvt.	**Cook, David**	**1835**	**Morganton, Burke Co.**	**Farmer**	**Enlisted, 3/5/63. Died of disease ("typhoid pneumonia"), 2/6/64 in Richmond.**

Rank	Name	DOB	Residence	Occupation	Remarks
Pvt.	Elliott, Hiram C.	1824	Greensboro, Guilford Co.	Farmer	Enlisted, 2/26/63. Surrendered, 4/9/65 at Appomattox Court House.
Pvt.	Johnson, John	1837	Morganton, Burke Co.	Farmer	Enlisted, 3/5/63. Deserted, 4/29/63.
Pvt.	Johnson, Solomon	1833	Burke Co.	—	Enlisted, 3/5/63. Deserted, 4/29/63
Pvt.	**Keller, John J.**	**1846**	**King's Creek, Caldwell Co.**	**Farm labor**	**Enlisted, 2/11/63. Wounded, 7/1/63 and captured, 7/5/63 at Gettysburg. Died of disease, 12/21/63 as POW at Point Lookout, MD.**
Pvt.	Mincey, Kinchen	1825	Franklin, Macon Co.	Farmer	Enlisted, 2/11/63. Captured, 10/27/64 at Burgess' Mill.
Pvt.	Short, Daniel	—	—	—	Enlisted, 11/16/63. Captured, 10/27/64 at Burgess' Mill.
Pvt.	Smith, Alexander	1835	Morganton, Burke Co.	Farm labor	Enlisted, 3/5/63. Deserted, 6/22/63 at Culpeper, VA.
Pvt.	Smith, Henry	1845	Morganton, Burke Co.	Farm labor	Enlisted, 2/13/63. Captured, 7/14/63 at Falling Waters, MD. Wounded (eye), 10/2/64 at Jones' Farm. Captured, 4/2/65 at Petersburg.
Pvt.	Swink, Archibald	1839	Morganton, Burke Co.	Farm labor	Enlisted, 2/13/63. Captured, 10/27/64 at Burgess' Mill.
Pvt.	Teem, William C.	1839	Upper Cr., Burke Co.	Farm labor	Enlisted, 8/31/63. Wounded, 9/30/64 at Jones' Farm. Captured, 4/2/65 at Petersburg.
Pvt.	Walker, James R.	1845	Broad R., Rutherford Co.	Day laborer	Enlisted, 10/1/63. Captured, 10/27/64 at Burgess' Mill.
Pvt.	Walker, Joseph	1825	Morganton, Burke Co.	Farmer	Enlisted, 2/28/63. Captured, 4/2/65 at Petersburg.
Pvt.	**Warlick, David L.**	**1824**	**Morganton, Burke Co.**	**Farmer**	**Enlisted, 11/1/63. Killed, 5/12/64 at Spotsylvania.**
Pvt.	Watts, Hosea	1831	Morganton, Burke Co.	Farmer	Enlisted, 3/5/63. Deserted, 4/29/63.
Pvt.	York, William	1822	Morganton, Burke Co.	Farmer	Enlisted, 3/5/63. Deserted, 4/29/63.

1864 Recruits

Rank	Name	DOB	Residence	Occupation	Remarks
Pvt.	Bowman, Samuel	1844	Catawba View, Caldwell Co.	Farm labor	Transferred, 12/5/64 from Co. F, 3rd NC Cav. Captured, 4/2/65 at Petersburg.
Pvt.	Chester, John. M.	1845	Lenoir, Caldwell Co.	Farm labor	Enlisted, 5/23/64 at Camp Vance, NC. Captured, 4/2/65 at Petersburg.
Pvt.	Clauntz, Jones	—	—	—	Enlisted, 10/24/64. Captured in hospital in Richmond, 4/3/65.
Pvt.	Coffey, John C.	1846	Collettsville, Caldwell Co.	Farm labor	Enlisted, 5/23/64. Missing, 3/1/65.
Pvt.	Cooper, William E.	1845	Morganton, Burke Co.	Farm labor	Transferred, 12/5/64 from the 3rd Regt. NC Cav. Captured, 4/2/65 at Petersburg.
Pvt.	Eaton, James H.	1844	Lincolnton, Lincoln Co.	Day laborer	Transferred, 12/5/64 from Co. G, 1st Regt. NC Cav. Missing, 3/1/65.
Pvt.	Garrison, Lorenzo D.	1836	Morganton, Burke Co.	Day laborer	Enlisted, 10/23/64. Deserted, 3/29/65.

Rank	Name	DOB	Residence	Occupation	Remarks
Pvt.	Johnson, David	—	Burke Co.	—	Enlisted, 1/25/64. Died of disease (typhoid fever), 7/6/64 in Richmond hospital.
Pvt.	Kincaid, Robert	1819	Collettsville, Caldwell Co.	Farmer	Enlisted, 8/1/64. Surrendered, 4/9/65 at Appomattox Court House. Died of disease (chronic diarrhea), 5/3/65 at hospital in Washington, D.C.
Pvt.	Kincaid, William	1845	Morganton, Burke Co.	Farm labor	Enlisted, 11/2/64. Captured, 4/2/65 at Petersburg.
Pvt.	Kinston, M.	—	—	—	Enlisted, 12/64(?). Wounded, 4/2/65 at Petersburg, and captured. POW—Point Lookout, MD. Died of wounds, 4/23/65.
Pvt.	Land, John	1846	Warrior Creek, Wilkes Co.	Farm labor	Enlisted, 11/15/64. Wounded, 4/2/65 at Petersburg. Captured, 4/3/65 in Richmond hospital. Died in hospital at Richmond, 7/9/65.
Pvt.	Ledford, William	1845	Ft. Hembree, Cherokee Co.	Farm labor	Enlisted, 1/25/64. Missing, 3/1/65.
Pvt.	Parks, Austin L.	1842	Morganton, Burke Co.	Farm labor	Transferred, 2/9/64 from Co. F, 3rd Regt. NC Cav. Captured, 4/2/65 at Petersburg.
Pvt.	Pendley, Adolphus	1826	Morganton, Burke Co.	Farm labor	Enlisted, 10/23/64. Captured, 4/2/65 at Petersburg.
Pvt.	Shelton, James	1843	Mt. Airy, Surry Co.	Farm labor	Enlisted, 1/24/64. Wounded, 9/30/64 at Jones Farm. Captured, 3/25/65 in Petersburg trenches.
Pvt.	Singleton, Rufus W.	1845	Morganton, Burke Co.	Farm labor	Enlisted, 10/5/64. Captured, 4/2/65 at Hatcher's Run.
Pvt.	Sudderth, Robert W.	1844	Morganton, Burke Co.	Farm labor	Transferred, 12/5/64 from Co. F, 3rd Regt. NC Cav. Captured, 4/2/65 at Petersburg.
Pvt.	Warlick, William J.	1845	Morganton, Burke Co.	Farm labor	Enlisted, 4/15/64. Killed, 4/8/65 near Appomattox Court House.
Pvt.	Watts, John	1815	Morganton, Burke Co.	Farmer	Enlisted, 11/20/64. Captured, 4/2/65 at Hatcher's Run. Died of disease ("inf. of the lungs"), 4/21/65 at Point Lookout, Md.
Pvt.	Williams, Martin	1847	Morganton, Burke Co.	Farm labor	Enlisted, 10/5/64. Missing, 1/65.

1865 Recruits

Rank	Name	DOB	Residence	Occupation	Remarks
Pvt.	Branch, Green A.	—	Burke Co.	—	Enlisted, 1/65. Died of disease, 2/19/65.
Pvt.	Coleman, Columbus A.	1850	Morganton, Burke Co.	Farm labor	Enlisted, 1/7/65. Captured, 4/2/65 at Petersburg.
Pvt.	Smith, Elam C.	1848	Morganton, Burke Co.	Farm labor	Enlisted, 1/7/65. Captured, 4/2/65 at Hatcher's Run.

Company C
Bertie County

Rank	Name	DOB	Residence	Occupation	Remarks
Cpt.	Bird, Francis "Frank," W.	1830	Windsor, Bertie Co.	Lawyer	Maj.—12/3/63, transferred to F & S. Killed, 8/25/64 at Reams' Station.

Rank	Name	DOB	Residence	Occupation	Remarks
1st Lt.	Cooper, Thomas W.	1841	Windsor, Bertie Co.	Estate overseer	Killed, 7/1/63 at Gettysburg.
2nd Lt.	Outlaw, Edward R.	1842	Windsor, Bertie Co.	Teacher	1st Lt.—1/22/63. Cpt.—1/64. Surrendered, 4/9/65 at Appomattox Court House.
2nd Lt.	Rhodes, Edward A.	1842	Windsor, Bertie Co.	—	Killed ("by bullet to his head"), 7/3/63 at Gettysburg.
1st Sgt.	Craig, Clingman	1841	Windsor, Bertie Co.	Student at Brown University	Wounded, 7/1/63, captured, 7/14/63 at Hagerstown, MD. 2nd Lt.—, 7/30/62. Died of wounds, 9/15/63.
Sgt.	Gilliam, Francis	1840	Plymouth, Washington Co.	Student	Promoted to Assistant Surgeon, 11/62, CS Medical Corps.
Sgt.	Hoggard, William M.	1820	Windsor, Bertie Co.	Farmer	Died of disease ("erysipelas"), 1/18/63 at Weldon, NC.
Sgt.	Rayner, James T.	1834	Murfreesboro, Hertford Co.	Overseer	Wounded (left leg), 7/1/63 and captured, 7/4/63 at Gettysburg. Regt. Ensign (1st Lt.)—8/16/64. Transferred to Regt. F & S.
Sgt.	Thompson, David	1832	Mount Olive, Duplin Co. NC	Farmer	Deserted, 1/19/63.
Cpl.	Adams, James H.	1840	Windsor, Bertie Co.	Asst. Carpenter	Wounded (left hand), 7/14/63 at Falling Waters, MD. Sgt.—11/1/63. Died of disease ("variola"), 1/24/64 at hospital in Lynchburg, VA.
Cpl.	Britton, Daniel W.	1844	Colerain, Bertie Co.	Farm labor	Sgt.—1/63. Transferred, 3/18/64 to Co. G, 32nd Regt. NC Inf.
Cpl.	Carter, Joseph B.	1840	Windsor, Bertie Co.	—	Sgt.—9/1/63. 1st Sgt.—2/15/64. Killed, 8/25/64 at Reams' Station.
Cpl.	Todd, William H.	1840	Windsor, Bertie Co.	Farm labor	Sgt.—12/29/62. Wounded (left thigh), 7/14/63 at Falling Waters, MD. 1st Lt.—1/64. Wounded (right buttock), 8/25/64 at Reams' Station. Missing, 3/1/65.
Pvt.	Baker, Gilbert	1844	Windsor, Bertie Co.	Farm labor	Discharged (chronic rheumatism), 8/17/62.
Pvt.	Bazemore, Armstead L.	1842	Windsor, Bertie Co.	Farm labor	Sgt.—10/1/64. Missing, 3/1/65.
Pvt.	Bazemore, Henry	1838	Windsor, Bertie Co.	Physician's Asst.	Wounded, 12/16/62 at White Hall, NC. Captured, 4/2/65 at Petersburg.
Pvt.	Bazemore, William H.	1835	Windsor, Bertie Co.	Farmer	Wounded (left hand), 12/16/62 at White Hall, NC. Deserted, 3/6/65.
Pvt.	Bazemore, William J.	1835	Windsor, Bertie Co.	Farm labor	Died of disease, 2/10/63 at hospital in Weldon, NC.
Pvt.	Blackstone, William R.	1826	Pittsboro, Chatham Co.	Farmer	Surrendered, 4/9/65 at Appomattox Court House.
Pvt.	Burden, James M.	1825	Windsor, Bertie Co.	Miller	Wounded (hip & left hand), 7/1/64 Cold Harbor. Cpl.—11/15/64. Captured, 4/6/65 at Burkeville, VA.
Pvt.	Butler, John	1833	Windsor, Bertie Co.	Farmer	Deserted, 1/23/63.
Pvt.	Butler, Levin E.	1842	Windsor, Bertie Co.	Farm labor	Captured, 10/14/63 at Bristoe Station, VA. Missing, 3/1/65.

Rank	Name	DOB	Residence	Occupation	Remarks
Pvt.	Butler, Thaddeus W.	1834	Windsor, Bertie Co.	Farmer	Deserted, 8/26/63.
Pvt.	Butler, William H.	1839	Colerain, Bertie Co.	Asst. Carpenter	Musician—8/19/62. Cpl.—2/15/64. Wounded, 9/30/64 at Jones' Farm. Missing, 3/1/65.
Pvt.	Byrum, Jesse B.	1836	Mill Landing, Bertie Co.	Farm labor	Captured, 7/14/63 at Falling Waters, MD. Captured, 4/2/65 at Petersburg.
Pvt.	Byrum, Reuben L.	1841	Mill Landing, Bertie Co.	Farm labor	Captured, 7/14/63 at Falling Waters, MD. Captured, 4/2/65 at Petersburg.
Pvt.	Cale, Thomas F.	1844	Windsor, Bertie Co.	Farm labor	Deserted, 10/20/64.
Pvt.	Cale, William H.	1843	Windsor, Bertie Co.	Farm labor	Deserted, 9/1/62.
Pvt.	Casper, James H.	1841	Windsor, Bertie Co.	Farm labor	Captured, 7/14/63 at Falling Waters, MD.
Pvt.	**Casper, Joseph W.**	1840	**Windsor, Bertie Co.**	Farm labor	Killed, 7/3/63 at Gettysburg.
Pvt.	**Casper, Justin**	1844	**Windsor, Bertie Co.**	Farm labor	Died of disease, 5/21/62 at hospital in Raleigh.
Pvt.	Casper, William J.	1836	Windsor, Bertie Co.	Farm labor	Deserted, 10/24/64.
Pvt.	**Castellaw, James C.**	1826	**Windsor, Bertie Co.**	Farmer	**Died of disease, 3/26/62 at Camp Mangum, Raleigh, NC.**
Pvt.	**Copeland, William D.**	1821	Roxobel, Bertie Co.	Farm labor	Died of disease, 4/22/62 at hospital in Raleigh, NC.
Pvt.	Corprew, Jonathan	1842	Windsor, Bertie Co.	Coach maker	Wounded, 12/16/62 at White Hall, NC. Wounded, 7/1/63 at Gettysburg. Deserted, 10/24/63.
Pvt.	Cullifer, John C.	1840	Windsor, Bertie Co.	Farm labor	Deserted, 1/10/64.
Pvt.	Cullifer, William T.	1842	Windsor, Bertie Co.	Farm labor	Deserted, 12/31/62.
Pvt.	**Davis, Alfred**	1839	**Windsor, Bertie Co.**	Farm labor	**Died of disease, 7/29/62 at Wilmington, NC.**
Pvt.	Davis, Allen	1834	Windsor, Bertie Co.	Farm labor	Wounded (arm), 5/12/64 at Spotsylvania. Surrendered, 4/9/65 at Appomattox Court House.
Pvt.	Davis, Augustus	1840	Windsor, Bertie Co.	Farm labor	Accidentally wounded, 7/62. Wounded, 8/29/62. Deserted, 11/7/64.
Pvt.	**Davis, Edward**	1839	**Windsor, Bertie Co.**	Farm labor	**Died of disease (ulcers), 10/20/63 at hospital at Weldon, NC.**
Pvt.	Evans, Aaron J.	1841	Windsor, Bertie Co.	Clerk's Asst.	Captured, 10/14/63 at Bristoe Station, VA.
Pvt.	Floyd, James R.	1844	Windsor, Bertie Co.	Farm labor	Wounded, 7/3/63 and captured at Gettysburg. Cpl.—3/64. Sgt.—10/1/64. Missing, 3/1/65.
Pvt.	Floyd, John G.	1842	Windsor, Bertie Co.	Overseer	Cpl.—12/29/62. Sgt.—2/15/64. 1st Sgt.—10/1/64. Captured, 10/14/64 at Burgess' Mill.

Rank	Name	DOB	Residence	Occupation	Remarks
Pvt.	Freeman, Jacob W.	1829	Colerain, Bertie Co.	Farm labor	AWOL, 8/19/63. Killed, 6/26/64 in Bertie Co.
Pvt.	Gilliam, John H.	1808	Windsor, Bertie Co.	Blacksmith	Discharged (disability—"by reason of his age and a general failure of health"), 4/9/64.
Pvt.	Gregory, John T.	1842	Mary Hill, Bertie Co.	Farm labor	Captured, 7/3/63 at Gettysburg. Died of disease (smallpox), 2/10/64 as POW at Point Lookout, MD.
Pvt.	Gregory, Lemuel D.	1843	Mary Hill, Bertie Co.	Farm labor	Died of disease (febris typhoid), 8/23/62 at Wilmington, NC.
Pvt.	Gregory, William L.	1837	Mary Hill, Bertie Co.	Farmer	Wounded ("foot shot off"), 7/1/63 at Gettysburg. Captured, 7/15/63 at Williamsport, MD. Died of wounds (no date).
Pvt.	Harrell, George B.	1840	Colerain, Bertie Co	Overseer	Cpl.—10/1/64. Captured, 4/2/65 at Petersburg.
Pvt.	Hoggard, William	1834	Windsor, Bertie Co.	Farm labor	Died of disease ("gonorrhea"), 8/10/62 in Wilmington, NC.
Pvt.	Holder, Thomas	1844	Windsor, Bertie Co.	Farm labor	Wounded and captured, 7/3/63 at Gettysburg. Died of wounds (no date recorded).
Pvt.	Hughes, Henry	1812	Snake Bite, Bertie Co.	Farmer	Deserted, 9/30/62 ("from the guard house at Camp Davis").
Pvt.	Jackson, Joseph	1833	Windsor, Bertie Co.	Coach maker	Captured, 7/14/63 at Falling Waters, MD. Died of disease ("hospital gangrene"), 11/12/64 as POW at Elmira, NY.
Pvt.	Jenkins, Doctrine	1839	Bertie Co.	—	Died of disease (pneumonia & rubeola), 4/20/62 at hospital in Raleigh, NC.
Pvt.	Jernigan, Samuel	1841	Windsor, Bertie Co.	Farm labor	Died of disease, 4/26/62 at Camp Mangum, Raleigh, NC.
Pvt.	King, Joseph	1843	Windsor, Bertie Co.	Farm labor	Captured, 7/14/63 at Falling Waters.
Pvt.	Kuter, James L.	1838	Bertie Co.	—	Deserted, 12/31/62.
Pvt.	Leggett, William	1841	Windsor, Bertie Co.	Farm labor	Deserted, 3/6/65.
Pvt.	Mardre, William B.	1831	Windsor, Bertie Co.	Mechanic	Ord. Sgt.—10/1/63 and transferred to F & S.
Pvt.	Mitchell, James E.	1845	Windsor, Bertie Co.	Farm labor	Captured, 10/14/63 at Bristoe Station. Captured, 4/2/65 on "the South Side RR," at Sutherland Station.
Pvt.	Mitchell, Jeremiah P.	1843	Windsor, Bertie Co.	Clerk	Killed, 7/1/63 at Gettysburg.
Pvt.	Mizell, John N.	1845	Windsor, Bertie Co.	Mechanic's asst.	Died of disease ("febris typhoid"), 7/25/62 at Wilmington, NC.
Pvt.	Morris, William D.	1819	Roxobel, Bertie Co.	Farmer	Missing, 4/1/63.
Pvt.	Myers, Nathan	1838	Snake Bite, Bertie Co.	Farm labor	Wounded (hand), 5/18/64 at Spotsylvania. Captured, 4/6/65 at Harper's Farm, VA.
Pvt.	Myers, Thomas L.	1835	Snake Bite, Bertie Co.	Farm labor	Died of disease, 5/5/62 at Camp Mangum, Raleigh, NC.
Pvt.	Owens, Richard A.	1841	Columbus, Polk Co.	Farm labor	Cpl.—10/1/63. Deserted, 2/17/64 at Plymouth, VA

Rank	Name	DOB	Residence	Occupation	Remarks
Pvt.	Parker, John H.	1841	Woodville, Bertie Co.	Farm labor	Captured, 7/14/63 at Falling Waters. Joined U.S. forces, 2/25/64.
Pvt.	Parker, Thomas H.	1838	Woodville, Bertie Co.	Farm labor	Wounded (left hand), 10/2/64 at Jones' Farm. Captured, 4/6/65 at Amelia Court House, VA.
Pvt.	**Parker, William G.**	**1820**	**Windsor, Bertie Co.**	**Farmer**	**Sgt.—1/63. Wounded, 7/1/63 at Gettysburg. Died of wounds, 7/17/63 at Winchester, VA.**
Pvt.	**Peele, Thomas H.**	**1842**	**Windsor, Bertie Co.**	**Farm labor**	**Killed, 7/3/63 at Gettysburg.**
Pvt.	Phelps, Thomas	1820	Colerain, Bertie Co.	Farmer	Discharged (disability—"He was in the early part of his life a very intemperate man, which has caused him to decline very rapidly in his old age ... [He is] afflicted constantly with rheumatism."), 4/24/64.
Pvt.	Phelps, William J.	1846	Colerain, Bertie Co.	Farm labor	Discharged (disability), 4/22/62 at Camp Mangum, Raleigh, NC.
Pvt.	**Pierce, James H.**	**1840**	**Mary Hill, Bertie Co.**	**Farm labor**	**Killed, 7/1/63 at Gettysburg.**
Pvt.	Powell, William W.	1841	Bertie Co.	Farm labor	Cpl.—1/63. Wounded, 7/1/63 and captured, 7/5/63 at Gettysburg. Sgt.—2/27/64. Captured, 4/2/65 at Petersburg.
Pvt.	Pritchard, Andrew J.	1843	Windsor, Bertie Co.	Farm labor	Wounded (right arm, right knee, right thigh, & right hip), 7/1/63 at Gettysburg. Captured, 4/3/65 in hospital in Richmond.
Pvt.	Pritchard, James W.	1847	Windsor, Bertie Co.	Farm labor	Missing, 3/1/65.
Pvt.	Pritchard, Joseph J.	1842	Windsor, Bertie Co.	Mechanic's asst.	Deserted, 1/28/64.
Pvt.	Rawls, James R.	1839	Murfreesboro, Hertford Co.	Farm labor	Captured, 10/14/63 at Bristoe Station. Cpl.—10/1/64. Deserted, 10/11/64.
Pvt.	Rice, Napoleon B.	1842	Windsor, Bertie Co.	Farm labor	Wounded, 7/1/63 at Gettysburg. Died of wounds, 7/17/63 at Winchester, VA.
Pvt.	Skiles, Robert M.	1830	Windsor, Bertie Co.	Farmer	Captured, 7/14/63 at Falling Waters, MD. Deserted, 2/12/65.
Pvt.	Stewart, Thaddeus C.	1844	Windsor, Bertie Co.	Tailor	Died ("brain fever"), 3/23/62 at Raleigh, NC.
Pvt.	**Stone, David G.**	**1841**	**Windsor, Bertie Co.**	**Farm labor**	**Killed, 7/1/63 at Gettysburg.**
Pvt.	Taylor, William H.	1837	Colerain, Bertie Co.	Farm labor	Died of disease (pneumonia), 11/21/62 at Franklin Depot, VA.
Pvt.	Thatch, Stephen	1836	Edenton, Chowan Co.	Farm labor	Captured, 1/27/64 at Plymouth, NC. Died of disease, (chronic diarrhea), 3/5/65 as POW at Point Lookout, MD.
Pvt.	Todd, Augustus	1831	Windsor, Bertie Co.	Day laborer	Deserted, 1/19/63.
Pvt.	Todd, Elisha	1842	Windsor, Bertie Co.	Farm labor	Appointed, Chief Musician, 3/64. Transferred to Regt. band.

Rank	Name	DOB	Residence	Occupation	Remarks
Pvt.	Trumbull, John D.	1840	Bertie Co.	—	Deserted, 11/14/62.
Pvt.	Ward, Warren J.	1846	Windsor, Bertie Co.	Farm labor	Missing, 1/15/63.
Pvt.	Ward, Whitmel T.	1822	Windsor, Bertie Co.	Farmer	Discharged (disability—"rejected by surgeon"), 9/1/62.
Pvt.	Ward, William T.	1841	Windsor, Bertie Co.	Student	1st Sgt.—9/1/63. Deserted, 1/5/64 in Bertie Co.
Pvt.	White, Riddick	1844	Windsor, Bertie Co.	Farm labor	Died of disease ("continued fever"), 8/20/62 in Wilmington, NC.
Pvt.	Williams, James H.	1844	Windsor, Bertie Co.	Farm labor	Wounded, 7/1/63, captured, 7/5/63 at Gettysburg. Died of wounds (no date recorded).
Pvt.	Williams, William	1840	Windsor, Bertie Co.	Farmer	Deserted, 1/15/63.

1862 Recruits

Rank	Name	DOB	Residence	Occupation	Remarks
Pvt.	Brogden, William G.	1845	Roxobel, Bertie Co.	Farm labor	Enlisted, 5/7/62. Wounded, 5/11/64 at Spotsylvania. Wounded (left hip & eye), 4/2/65 and captured at Petersburg. Hospitalized at Old Capitol Prison, Washington, D.C. Died of wounds, 6/2/65.
Pvt.	Carter, Benjamin	1840	Windsor, Bertie Co.	Overseer	Enlisted, 5/7/62. Killed, 7/3/63 at Gettysburg.
Pvt.	Casper, George M.	1826	Windsor, Bertie Co.	Farmer	Enlisted, 5/15/62. Deserted, 10/24/64.
Pvt.	Cooper, Asa	1821	Windsor, Bertie Co.	Mechanic	Enlisted, 5/15/62. Missing, 3/1/65.
Pvt.	Cullifer, Simon	1814	Windsor, Bertie Co.	Farmer	Enlisted, 5/7/62. Died of disease (smallpox or "erysipelas"), 1/7/64 at Windsor, NC.
Pvt.	Davis, John	1829	Windsor, Bertie Co.	Tenant farmer	Enlisted, 5/17/62. Captured, 10/27/64 at Burgess' Mill.
Pvt.	Skiles, Henry	1833	Windsor, Bertie Co.	Shingle cutter	Enlisted, 5/17/62. Deserted, 10/24/64.
Pvt.	Skiles, James W.	1832	Windsor, Bertie Co.	Farmer	Enlisted, 5/17/62 in New Hanover Co. Deserted, 1/15/63.
Pvt.	Smithwick, Alfred	1837	Windsor, Bertie Co.	Teacher	Enlisted, 5/17/62. Discharged (disability), 5/29/62.
Pvt.	Stone, John	1846	Windsor, Bertie Co.	Farm labor	Enlisted, 5/7/62. Captured, 10/14/63 at Bristoe Station.
Pvt.	Thomas, Joseph T.	1835	Windsor, Bertie Co.	Farmer	Enlisted, 5/3/62. Discharged (disability—"by reason of heart disease"), 8/17/62.
Pvt.	Todd, Lewis	1829	Windsor, Bertie Co.	Overseer	Enlisted, 5/3/62. Cpl.—10/63. Sgt.—3/64. Captured, 4/3/65 at Amelia Court House.

1863 Recruits

Rank	Name	DOB	Residence	Occupation	Remarks
Pvt.	Harmon, James F.	1845	Windsor, Bertie Co.	Farm labor	Enlisted, 11/23/63. Captured, 10/27/64 at Burgess' Mill.
Pvt.	Todd, Nehemiah J.	1846	Windsor, Bertie Co.	Farm labor	Enlisted, 11/24/63. Musician—3/64. Transferred, 10/64 to Regt. Band.

1864 Recruits

Rank	Name	DOB	Residence	Occupation	Remarks
Pvt.	Casper, Thomas	1839	Windsor, Bertie Co.	Day laborer	Transferred, 3/18/64 from Co. G, 32nd NC Inf. Deserted, 10/24/64.
Pvt.	Garner, Elias	—	Mecklenburg Co.	—	Enlisted, 4/26/64 at Wake Co. NC. Deserted, 7/1/64.
Pvt.	Hargroves, Israel	1823	Pittsboro, Chatham Co.	Farm labor	Enlisted, 5/5/64 at Wake Co. Discharged (disability—"He is at times perfectly insane. He preaches when under these fits, both night and day, to imaginary audiences."), 3/9/65.
Pvt.	**Hargroves, Richard**	**1824**	**Pittsboro, Chatham Co.**	**Farm labor**	**Enlisted, 4/24/64. Missing, 5/5/64 at the Wilderness. Died ("anasarca"), 10/26/64 at hospital in Richmond.**
Pvt.	Hawks, James W.	1843	Merry Mountain, Warren Co.	Farm labor	Transferred, 12/6/64 from Co. E, 1st Regt. NC Cav. Captured, 3/29/65 at Dinwiddie Court House, VA.
Pvt.	Jones, Wiley	1846	Davidson Co.	Farm labor	Enlisted, 4/26/64 at Wake Co. NC. Deserted, 10/24/64.
Pvt.	Longee, Augustus H.	1822	Raleigh, Wake Co.	Printer	Enlisted, 4/16/64 at Wake Co. NC. Captured, 5/5/64 at the Wilderness.
Pvt.	Lucas, Augustus G.	1832	Washington, Beaufort Co.	Farm labor	Enlisted, 4/26/64 at Wake Co. NC. "Lost on the march," 5/10/64 at Spotsylvania.
Pvt.	Powell, William A.	1845	Morrisville, Wake Co.	Farm labor	Enlisted, 9/17/64 at Wake Co. NC. Missing, 3/1/65.
Pvt.	Powers, Jesse A.	1832	Yadkinville, Yadkin Co.	Farm labor	Enlisted, 4/28/64. Captured, 4/2/65 at Petersburg.
Pvt.	Rhodes, Robert H.	—	—	—	Transferred, 2/9/64 from Co. A, 5th Regt. NC Cav. Sgt. Maj.—10/64 and transferred to F & S.
Pvt.	Smith, David H.	1847	Dallas, Gaston Co.	Farm labor	Enlisted, 12/64. Captured, 4/2/65 at Hatcher's Run.
Pvt.	Stokes, Gaston	1847	Morrisville, Wake Co.	Farm labor	Enlisted, 9/17/64 in Wake Co. Wounded (left shoulder), 4/6/65 at Farmville.
Pvt.	**Ward, William C.**	**1845**	**Windsor, Bertie Co.**	**Farm labor**	**Enlisted, 2/15/64. Captured, 10/27/64 at Burgess' Mill. Died of disease (pneumonia), 3/18/65 as POW at Point Lookout, MD.**
Pvt.	Williams, Oliver M.	1845	Chapel Hill, Orange Co.	Farm labor	Enlisted, 9/17/64 in Wake Co. Captured, 4/2/65 at Petersburg.
Pvt.	Williamson, Henry C.	—	—	—	Enlisted, 4/26/64 at Wake Co. Deserted, 7/1/64.
2nd Lt.	Winston, Patrick H.	1820	Windsor, Bertie Co.	Lawyer	Transferred, 2/27/64 from 32nd NC Inf. and promoted to 2nd Lt. Captured, 10/27/64 at Burgess' Mill.
Pvt.	Wright, John	—	—	—	Enlisted, 4/26/64 at Wake Co. Deserted, 9/20/64.

Company D
Burke County

Rank	Name	DOB	Residence	Occupation	Remarks
Cpt.	Brown, Calvin S.	1828	Morganton, Burke Co.	Hotel keeper	Discharged (disability—"by reason of sun-stroke"), 1/7/64.
1st Lt.	Kincaid, William J.	1840	Morganton, Burke Co.	Clerk	Wounded (left knee), 7/3/63 and captured, 7/5/63 at Gettysburg. Cpt.—1/7/64 while a POW at Johnson's Island, OH.
2nd Lt.	Tate, John M.	1835	Charlotte, Mecklenburg Co.	Dry Goods Dealer	1st Lt.—Promoted, 4/22/62, to Assistant Quartermaster. Transferred to Regt. F & S.
1st Sgt.	Elias, Lewis	1845	Statesville, Iredell Co.	Merchant clerk	2nd Lt.—4/22/62. 1st Lt.—1/7/64. Missing, 3/1/65.
Sgt.	Black, Samuel J.	1818	Morganton, Burke Co.	Overseer	Captured, 7/14/63 at Falling Waters, MD.
Sgt.	Brittain, O. Joseph	1816	Morganton, Burke Co.	Sheriff	1st Sgt.—4/22/62. Captured, 7/14/63 at Falling Waters, MD. Transferred, 12/8/64 to Co. F, 3rd Regt. NC Cav.
Sgt.	Hennessee, Patrick W.	1833	Morganton, Burke Co.	Farm manager	Pvt.—4/15/63. Captured, 7/3/63 at Gettysburg. Captured, 4/2/65 at Petersburg.
Sgt.	Kincaid, George W.	1836	Morganton, Burke Co.	Farm labor	3rd Lt.—5/24/62. Killed, 7/3/63 at Gettysburg.
Cpl.	Causby (Cosby), John N.	1840	Morganton, Burke Co.	Farm labor	Died of disease, 6/8/62 in hospital in Wilmington, NC.
Cpl.	Lane, John E.	1839	Morganton, Burke Co.	Farm labor	Sgt.—5/24/62. Killed, 5/5/64 at the Wilderness.
Cpl.	Tate, Hugh	1829	Morganton, Burke Co.	Farmer	Sgt.—4/22/62. Pvt.—10/20/62. Wounded (right thigh) and captured, 7/3/63 at Gettysburg. Right leg amputated. Died of wounds, 8/25/63 after a second amputation.
Cpl.	Winters, Moulton	1840	Morganton, Burke Co.	Farm labor	Killed, 7/1/63 at Gettysburg.
Music	Clark, Benjamin A.	1826	Morganton, Burke Co.	Farmer	Died of disease (typhoid fever), 6/27/62 at hospital in Wilmington, NC.
Pvt.	Baker, Lucius	1840	Morganton, Burke Co.	Farm labor	Wounded (left hip), 10/14/63 at Bristoe Station.
Pvt.	Beach, James C.	1846	Morganton, Burke Co.	Farm labor	Died of disease, 7/29/62 at hospital in Wilmington, NC.
Pvt.	Benfield, Thomas W.	1837	Morganton, Burke Co.	Farm labor	Wounded (thigh), 7/14/63 at Falling Waters, MD. Wounded, 8/21/64 at Weldon Rd. Died of wounds, 9/19/64 in hospital in Richmond.
Pvt.	Bingham, Robert W.	1837	Wilkerson, Wilkes Co.	Farm labor	Captured, 10/14/63 at Bristoe Station. Died of disease (diarrhea), 8/12/64 as POW at Point Lookout, MD.
Pvt.	Blain, William M.	1828	Fairmont, Marion Co. VA	Printer	Wounded, 9/30/64 at Jones' Farm. Died of wounds, 10/3/64 at hospital in Petersburg.
Pvt.	Blue, David	1839	Burke Co.	Farm labor	Captured, 7/14/63 at Falling Waters, MD. Missing, 3/1/65.

Rank	Name	DOB	Residence	Occupation	Remarks
Pvt.	Brittain, Julius T.	1846	Morganton, Burke Co.	Farm labor	Captured, 7/14/63 at Falling Waters, MD. Transferred, 12/8/64 to Co. F, 3rd Regt. NC Cav.
Pvt.	Brittain, Samuel	1841	Morganton, Burke Co.	Farm labor	Surrendered, 4/9/65 at Appomattox Court House.
Pvt.	Butler, John M.	1845	Marion, McDowell Co.	Farm labor	Wounded (right thigh), 4/2/65 at Sutherland Station. Surrendered, 4/9/65 at Appomattox Court House.
Pvt.	Causby (Cosby), George	1844	Morganton, Burke Co.	Farm labor	Wounded, 12/16/62 at White Hall, NC. Captured, 7/6/63 at Greencastle, PA. Captured, 4/2/65 at Petersburg.
Pvt.	Causby (Cosby), William	1846	Morganton, Burke Co.	Farm labor	Wounded, 7/1/63 at Gettysburg. Wounded, 8/21/64 at Weldon Rd. Surrendered, 4/9/65 at Appomattox Court House.
Pvt.	Clark, Benjamin	1825	Burke Co.	Farmer	Captured, 10/14/63 at Bristoe Station. Captured, 4/3/65 in hospital in Richmond.
Pvt.	Clark, Michael	1837	Sandy Mush, Buncombe Co.	Tenant Farmer	Wounded, 7/3/63 and captured, 7/5/63 at Gettysburg. Surrendered, 4/9/65 at Appomattox Court House.
Pvt.	Clay, Joseph M.	1840	Morganton, Burke Co.	Farm labor	Cpl.—5/24/62. Sgt.—4/15/63. Wounded ("lost an eye"), 7/3/63 and captured at Gettysburg. Missing, 3/1/65.
Pvt.	Cody, W. A.	1834	Monroeton, Rockingham Co.	Slave handler	Deserted, 4/24/62.
Pvt.	**Earnhart, William**	**1815**	**Morganton, Burke Co.**	**Farmer**	**Died of disease (bronchitis), 5/5/62.**
Pvt.	Giles, Sidney L.	1827	Morganton, Burke Co.	Farm labor	Wounded (right leg), 7/1/63 at Gettysburg.
Pvt.	Good, George	1825	Morganton, Burke Co.	Farmer	Missing, 3/1/65.
Pvt.	Hennessee, Emanuel A.	1832	Morganton, Burke Co.	Farm labor	Cpl.—9/1/63. Wounded (forehead), 10/2/64 at Weldon Rd.
Pvt.	Henson, Adam	1840	Broad River, Rutherford Co.	Farm labor	Deserted, 8/3/63.
Pvt.	Hern, W. Ranson	1816	Morganton, Burke Co.	Tailor	Discharged, 2/22/65 "by reason of expiration of term of service, and because he was over [the] conscript age."
Pvt.	Hicks, Joseph S.	1830	Morganton, Burke Co.	Day laborer	Musician—Promoted, 10/64 to regt. band.
Pvt.	**Hood, James C.**	**1843**	**Morganton, Burke Co.**	**Farm labor**	**Died of disease, 7/30/62 at Wilmington, NC.**
Pvt.	Johnson, Daniel L.	1843	Morganton, Burke Co.	Farm labor	Wounded (hand), 6/12/64 at White Oak Swamp. Deserted, 3/21/65.
Pvt.	Johnson, John W.	1834	Morganton, Burke Co.	Farm labor	Captured, 7/14/63 at Falling Waters, MD.
Pvt.	Johnson, Robert N.	1842	Morganton, Burke Co.	Farm labor	Captured, 10/27/64 at Burgess' Mill.
Pvt.	Jordan, Noah W.	1837	Murfreesboro, Hertford Co.	Overseer	Cpl.—10/20/62. Sgt.—11/10/64. Captured, 4/2/65 at Petersburg.

Rank	Name	DOB	Residence	Occupation	Remarks
Pvt.	Keith, John C.	1843	Burke Co.	—	Wounded ("accidental discharge of his gun"), 11/62. Died of wounds, 1/14/63 in hospital at Goldsboro, NC.
Pvt.	Kincaid, James W.	1833	Morganton, Burke Co.	Farm labor	Killed, 7/1/63 at Gettysburg.
Pvt.	Kincaid, William W.	1830	Morganton, Burke Co.	Farmer	Deserted, 7/16/63 at Winchester, VA. Captured, 5/6/64 at Spotsylvania. Died of disease ("anemia or debility"), 4/26/65 as POW at Ft. Delaware, DE.
Pvt.	Lane, Samuel	1812	Morganton, Burke Co.	Farmer	Deserted, 8/2/63. Died, 8/10/63 near Madison Court House, VA.
Pvt.	Melton, Eugene A.	1846	Morganton, Burke Co.	Day laborer	Captured, 7/3/63 at Gettysburg. Wounded (right thigh), 5/5/64 at the Wilderness. Captured, 10/3/64 "while on picket duty."
Pvt.	Melton, William	1838	Oak Springs, Rutherford Co.	Day Labor	Wounded, 12/16/62 at Whitehall. Died of pneumonia, 5/8/64 at Lynchburg.
Pvt.	Miller, Jackson	1840	Morganton, Burke Co.	Farm labor	Wounded (right thigh), 7/1/63 and captured, 7/5/63 at Gettysburg. Captured, 3/25/65 in Petersburg trenches.
Pvt.	Miller, Marshall (Mack)	1834	Morganton, Burke Co.	Farm labor	Captured, 7/14/63 at Falling Waters, MD. Wounded, 9/30/64 at Jones' Farm. Died of wounds, 10/8/64 in hospital in Richmond.
Pvt.	Pearson, John	1837	Morganton, Burke Co.	Farm labor	Wounded, 7/1/63 at Gettysburg. Captured, 4/2/65 at Petersburg.
Pvt.	Poteet, Samuel	1839	Morganton, Burke Co.	Farm labor	Died (cause not reported), 10/14/63, "at home."
Pvt.	Powell, Kemp (Camp) W.	1837	Morganton, Burke Co.	Farmer	Died of disease (remittent fever), 7/9/62 at Wilmington, NC.
Pvt.	Powell, Moses	1847	Morganton, Burke Co.	Farm labor	Missing, 3/1/65.
Pvt.	Powell, William P.	1848	Morganton, Burke Co.	Farm labor	Captured, 10/14/63 at Bristoe Station. Captured, 4/2/65 at Petersburg.
Pvt.	Saulman, James W.	1835	Morganton, Burke Co.	Farm labor	Captured, 4/3/65 at Petersburg.
Pvt.	Simpson, John E.	1839	Morganton, Burke Co.	Farm labor	Cpl.—6/8/62. Captured, 7/3/63 at Gettysburg.
Pvt.	Sudderth, Elam M.	1825	Morganton, Burke Co.	Estate overseer	Killed, 7/3/63 at Gettysburg.
Pvt.	Summers, Perry	1841	Morganton, Burke Co.	Farm labor	Wounded (breast), 7/3/63 at Gettysburg. Wounded, 10/14/63 at Bristoe Station. Died of wounds, 10/15/63.
Pvt.	Taylor, Charles	1834	Morganton, Burke Co.	Farm labor	Wounded, 7/3/63 at Gettysburg. Captured, 7/14/63 at Falling Waters, MD. Died (cause not reported), 12/1/63, "at home."
Pvt.	Taylor, George W.	1815	Morganton, Burke Co.	Farm labor	Deserted, 8/2/63. Died of disease (pneumonia & typhoid), 12/26/63, in Richmond.
Pvt.	Taylor, Joel	1846	Morganton, Burke Co.	Farm labor	Discharged (disability—"phthisis"), 7/4/62.

Rank	Name	DOB	Residence	Occupation	Remarks
Pvt.	Todd, R. L.	1844	Burke Co.	Farm labor	Wounded, 7/3/63 and captured at Gettysburg. Died of wounds, 7/26/63.
Pvt.	Wadkins, John B.	1836	Morganton, Burke Co.	Farm labor	Wounded (left leg & right ankle), 7/1/63. Surrendered, 4/9/65 at Appomattox Court House.
Pvt.	Walls, M. Lafayette	1820	Morganton, Burke Co.	Farm labor	Wounded, 12/16/62 at White Hall, NC. Killed, 7/1/63 at Gettysburg.
Pvt.	Whisenhunt, Alexander	1832	Morganton, Burke Co.	Farm labor	Died of disease (pneumonia), 4/14/62 at Raleigh, NC.
Pvt.	Whisenhunt, Benjamin	1832	Morganton, Burke Co.	Farm labor	Captured, 7/14/63 at Falling Waters, MD. Captured, 4/2/65 at Petersburg.
Pvt.	Whisenhunt, James	1843	Morganton, Burke Co.	Farm labor	Died of disease, 4/22/62 at Camp Mangum, Raleigh, NC.
Pvt.	Whisenhunt, Stanhope	1832	Globe, Caldwell Co.	Farmer	Died of disease, 4/18/62 at Camp Mangum, Raleigh, NC.
Pvt.	Whisenhunt, Wilburn	1840	Morganton, Burke Co.	Farm labor	Died of disease (anemia), 6/6/63 at hospital in Raleigh, NC.
Pvt.	Williams, Elijah H.	1836	Morganton, Burke Co.	Farm labor	Wounded, 7/1/63 at Gettysburg. Captured, 7/5/63 at Gettysburg, PA. Missing, 3/1/65.
Pvt.	Williams, John A.	1827	Morganton, Burke Co.	Farm labor	Deserted, 11/13/63. Apprehended, court-martialed, and confined at Richmond, "with ball and chain." Date not reported. Died (cause not reported), 7/26/64 at Castle Prison, Richmond.
Pvt.	Williams, J. L.	1835	Morganton, Burke Co.	Farm labor	Discharged (sickness—"inability and bronchitis following measles with a tendency to dropsy."), 7/4/62.
Pvt.	Williams, John	1834	Morganton, Burke Co.	Farm labor	Captured, 4/2/65 at Petersburg.
Pvt.	Williams, Joseph	1837	Morganton, Burke Co.	Farm labor	Died (cause not reported), 9/23/63, "at home."
Pvt.	Williams, Molton	1842	Morganton, Burke Co.	Farm labor	Captured, 7/14/63 at Falling Waters, MD. Captured, 3/25/65 in Petersburg trenches.
Pvt.	Williams, William H.	1838	Morganton, Burke Co.	Farm labor	Wounded, 7/1/63 at Gettysburg. Captured, 7/6/63 at Greencastle. Missing, 3/1/65.
Pvt.	Williams, William M.	1842	Morganton, Burke Co.	Farm labor	Wounded, 7/14/63 at Falling Waters, MD. Missing, 3/1/65.
Pvt.	Womack, William T.	1832	Yanceyville, Caswell Co.	Farm labor	Cpl.—4/11/62. Sgt.—10/20/62. 1st Sgt.—12/8/64. Surrendered, 4/9/65 at Appomattox Court House.
Pvt.	Wood, William	1844	Burke Co.	—	Wounded, 7/1/63 and captured, 7/5/63 at Gettysburg. Died of wounds, 9/5/63 in hospital at David's Island, NY.

1862 Recruits

Rank	Name	DOB	Residence	Occupation	Remarks
Pvt.	Fair, Henry	1843	Morganton, Burke Co.	Farm labor	Enlisted, 5/1/62. Captured, 10/27/64 at Burgess' Mill. Died of disease (chronic diarrhea & scurvy), 4/18/65 as POW at Point Lookout, MD.

Rank	Name	DOB	Residence	Occupation	Remarks
Pvt.	Fair, Hezekiah	1838	Morganton, Burke Co.	Farmer	Enlisted, 5/1/62. Captured, 7/14/63 at Falling Waters, MD.
Pvt.	Giles, Alexander	1840	Morganton, Burke Co.	Farm labor	Enlisted, 5/1/62. Captured, 4/5/65 at Amelia Court House.
Pvt.	**Giles, William W.**	**1833**	**Morganton, Burke Co.**	**Farm labor**	**Enlisted, 5/1/62. Wounded, 7/3/63, and captured, 7/6/63 at Greencastle. Died of disease (chronic diarrhea), 11/27/63 as POW at Point Lookout, MD.**
Pvt.	Hicks, Rufus	1839	Morganton, Burke Co.	Day labor	Enlisted, 9/14/62. Captured, 2/24/64 at North Anna River, VA.
Pvt.	Largent, John P.	1841	Morganton, Burke Co.	Farm labor	Enlisted, 5/1/62. Wounded, 7/1/63 and captured, 7/5/63 at Gettysburg. Cpl.—12/8/64. Deserted, 3/21/65.
Pvt.	**Loudon, Thomas**	**1836**	**Burke Co.**	**—**	**Enlisted, 5/1/62. Died of disease ("continued fever"), 7/11/62 at Wilmington, NC.**
Pvt.	McKesson, James C.	1833	Morganton, Burke Co.	Farm labor	Enlisted, 5/1/62. Wounded and captured, 7/3/63 at Gettysburg. Missing, 3/1/65.

1863 Recruits

Rank	Name	DOB	Residence	Occupation	Remarks
Pvt.	Butler, Erwin	1833	Burke Co.	Farmer	Enlisted, 2/28/63. Deserted, 6/18/63.
Pvt.	Butler, William H.	1815	Marion, McDowell Co.	Day laborer	Enlisted, 2/26/63. Cpl.—9/1/63. Wounded, 10/27/64 at Burgess' Mill. Sgt.—12/8/64. Surrendered, 4/9/65 at Appomattox Court House.
Pvt.	**Chrisenbery, Thomas C.**	**1833**	**Morganton, Burke Co.**	**Farmer**	**Enlisted, 1/31/63. Killed, 7/1/63 at Gettysburg.**
Pvt.	Cook, John D.	1841	Morganton, Burke Co.	Farm labor	Enlisted, 2/15/63. Wounded (left cheek), 7/14/63 at Falling Waters, MD. Wounded, 10/14/63 at Bristoe Station, VA. Died of wounds, 2/1/64 in Richmond hospital.
Pvt.	Huffman, Abraham (Abe)	1825	Morganton, Burke Co.	Farmer	Enlisted, 2/28/63. Captured, 7/14/63 at Falling Waters, MD. Killed, 9/30/64 at Jones' Farm.
Pvt.	Mace, Abraham	1845	Morganton, Burke Co.	Farm labor	Enlisted, 2/28/63. Captured, 7/14/63 at Falling Waters, MD. Died of disease ("typhoid pneumonia"), 9/16/64 as POW at Elmira, NY.
2nd Lt.	McCorkle, James G.	1839	Charlotte, Mecklenburg Co.	Clerk	Promoted and transferred to Co. D, 11/26/63. Captured, 10/27/64 at Burgess' Mill.
Pvt.	Mitchell, Jackson	1835	Morganton, Burke Co.	Farm labor	Enlisted, 1/1/63. Deserted, 6/18/63.
Pvt.	Mitchell, John	1833	Morganton, Burke Co.	Railroad day labor	Enlisted, 1/1/63. Deserted, 6/17/63. Returned, 8/30/63. Captured, 4/2/65 at Petersburg.
Pvt.	Mosteller, Isaiah	1825	Burke Co.	—	Enlisted, 2/26/63. Wounded, 5/5/64 at the Wilderness. Captured, 3/25/65 in Petersburg trenches.
Pvt.	Pearson, Robert G.	1821	Morganton, Burke Co.	Farmer	Enlisted, 1/1/63. Captured, 3/25/65 in Petersburg trenches.

Rank	Name	DOB	Residence	Occupation	Remarks
Pvt.	Poteet, John	1826	Morganton, Burke Co.	Farmer	Enlisted, 1/1/63. Captured, 7/14/63 at Falling Waters, MD. Transferred, 12/8/64 to Co. F, 3rd Regt. NC Cav.
Pvt.	**Pruett, Ransom**	**1825**	**Morganton, Burke Co.**	**Farm labor**	**Enlisted, 2/28/63. Died (cause not reported) in camp, 12/16/63, at Orange Court House, VA.**
Pvt.	Ramsey, Jonas	1843	Morganton, Burke Co.	Farm labor	Enlisted, 2/14/63. Deserted, 6/17/63.
Pvt.	Saulman, John M.	1845	Morganton, Burke Co.	Farm labor	Enlisted, 2/10/63. Wounded (right ankle), 7/1/63 at Gettysburg.
Pvt.	Settlemire, David	1825	Morganton, Burke Co.	Farmer	Enlisted, 2/28/63. Wounded (stomach), 7/1/63 at Gettysburg.
Pvt.	Williams, Marcus	1832	Morganton, Burke Co.	Farm labor	Enlisted, 2/25/63. Discharged (disability—"anemia and ascites"), 9/14/63.

1864 Recruits

Rank	Name	DOB	Residence	Occupation	Remarks
Pvt.	Abee, Andrew J.	1825	Morganton, Burke Co.	Farmer	Enlisted, 9/10/64. Captured, 10/27/74 at Burgess' Mill.
Pvt.	**Albright, William S.**	**1828**	**Moffit Springs, Randolph Co.**	**Farmer**	**Enlisted, 6/27/64. Wounded (head), 10/1/64 at Jones' Farm. Died of wounds, 10/4/64 at hospital in Richmond.**
Pvt.	Benfield, Martin	1820	Morganton, Burke Co.	Farmer	Enlisted, 2/23/64. Wounded, 9/30/64 at Jones Farm.
Pvt.	Black, Clinton M.	1822	Morganton, Burke Co.	Farm labor	Enlisted, 11/18/64. Missing, 3/1/65.
Pvt.	**Butler, Thomas P.**	**1846**	**Asheville, Buncombe Co.**	**Farm labor**	**Enlisted, 2/16/64. Died, 7/14/64 in hospital in Richmond.**
Pvt.	**Clark, James C.**	**1846**	**Lenoir, Caldwell Co.**	**Farm labor**	**Enlisted, 6/10/64. Died of disease (chronic diarrhea), 3/13/65.**
Pvt.	Clay, James H.	1843	Morganton, Burke Co.	Farm labor	Transferred, 12/64 from Co. F, 3rd Regt. NC Cav. Surrendered, 4/9/65 at Appomattox Court House.
Pvt.	Donaldson, Stanhope L.	1827	Mount Mourn, Iredell Co.	Farmer	Enlisted, 6/14/64. Cpl.—12/8/64. Missing, 3/1/65.
Pvt.	Griffin, Edmund (Alfred)	1839	Hazeldell, Caldwell Co.	Farm labor	Enlisted, 12/64. Captured, 3/25/65 in Petersburg trenches.
Pvt.	Hawkins, William P.	1842	Morganton, Burke Co.	Farm labor	Enlisted, 3/22/64. Wounded (left leg), 6/1/64 at Cold Harbor. Captured, 4/2/65 at Petersburg.
Pvt.	Jenkins, Hiram	1841	Dobson, Surry Co.	Farm labor	Enlisted, 7/9/64. Missing, 3/1/65.
Pvt.	Kinney, Alexander D.	1839	Jacksonhill, Davidson Co.	Farm labor	Enlisted, 12/64. Captured, 5/30/64 at Cold Harbor.
Pvt.	Lawmon, William L.	—	Burke Co.	—	Enlisted, 9/6/64. Captured, 4/2/65 at Petersburg.
Pvt.	Martin, Joseph	1845	Morganton, Burke Co.	Farm labor	Enlisted, 9/6/64. Captured, 10/27/64 at Burgess' Mill.

Rank	Name	DOB	Residence	Occupation	Remarks
Pvt.	McMillon, Pleasant	—	—	—	Enlisted, 7/9/64. Captured, 4/2/65 at Petersburg. Died of disease (pneumonia), 6/23/65 as POW at Point Lookout, MD.
Pvt.	Morefield, John	1824	Morganton, Burke Co.	Stage Driver	Enlisted, 3/25/64. Mortally wounded, 8/25/64 at Reams' Station. Died of wounds later that day.
Pvt.	Mosteller, John	—	Burke Co.	—	Enlisted, 11/11/64. Captured, 4/2/65 at Petersburg.
Pvt.	Poindexter, Denson F.	1837	Marsh, Surry Co.	Farmer	Enlisted, 7/9/64 in Surry Co. Discharged ("deformity of the spine"), 10/8/64.
Pvt.	Powell, Joseph H.	1845	Morganton, Burke Co.	Farm labor	Enlisted, 2/16/64. Captured, 4/2/65 at Petersburg.
Pvt.	Ross, Stephen A.	1847	Morganton, Burke Co.	Farm labor	Enlisted, 1/18/64. Wounded, 5/5/64 at the Wilderness. Died of wounds, 8/7/64 in Richmond hospital.
Pvt.	Rudisill, Absalom	—	White Pine, Gaston Co.	—	Enlisted, 3/3/64. Wounded (right hand), 5/6/64 in the Wilderness. Captured, 10/27/64 at Burgess' Mill.
Pvt.	Simpson, Thomas A.	1843	Morganton, Burke Co.	Farm labor	Enlisted, 2/23/64. Captured, 4/2/65 at Petersburg.
Pvt.	Spain, H. D.	1838	Kingston, Lenoir Co.	Mason	Transferred, 4/2/64 from Co. H. Wounded, 5/5/64 at the Wilderness.
Pvt.	Starney, Joshua	—	Burke Co.	—	Enlisted, 9/15/64. Deserted. Recaptured and "shot for desertion," 12/4/64.
Pvt.	Upton, Dan H.	1822	Mud Lick, Chatham Co.	Farmer	Enlisted, 9/15/64. Wounded (left hand), 10/1/64 at Jones' Farm.
Pvt.	Williams, Baird	1836	Morganton, Burke Co.	Farmer	Enlisted, 2/23/64. Died (cause not reported), 12/25/64 at Richmond.
Pvt.	Williams, W. A.	—	Burke Co.	—	Enlisted, 3/12/64. Captured, 4/3/65 in Richmond hospital.

Company E
Mecklenburg and Iredell Counties

Rank	Name	DOB	Residence	Occupation	Remarks
Cpt.	Nichols, John S.	1832	Columbia, Richland Co. SC	Merchant	Died of disease, 7/12/62 at Wilmington NC.
1st Lt.	Kerr, William J.	1831	W. Charlotte, Mecklenburg Co.	Coach maker	Cpt.—7/11/62. Wounded (left leg), 7/23/64 near Petersburg. Resigned, 3/16/65 ("while under charges of drunkenness and AWOL").
2nd Lt.	Clanton, John B.	1831	W. Charlotte, Mecklenburg Co.	Farmer	1st Lt.—7/11/62. Wounded, 7/1/63 and captured at Gettysburg. Died of wounds, 7/28/63 at Gettysburg.
3rd Lt.	Means, William N. S.	1837	Mount Pleasant, Cabarrus Co.	Farm labor	2nd Lt.—7/12/62. Killed, 12/16/62 at White Hall, NC.
1st Sgt.	Rozzell, William F.	1840	W. Charlotte, Mecklenburg Co.	Merchant	3rd Lt.—7/12/62. 2nd Lt.—1/22/63. Wounded, 7/1/63 and captured at Gettysburg. Died of wounds, 7/15/63 at Gettysburg.

Rank	Name	DOB	Residence	Occupation	Remarks
Sgt.	Alexander, James F.	1834	Charlotte, Mecklenburg Co.	Tailor	Pvt.—12/14/62. 2nd Lt.—12/14/63. Captured, 4/2/65 at Hatcher's Run.
Sgt.	McDonald, David W.	1841	W. Charlotte, Mecklenburg Co.	Farm labor	1st Sgt.—6/12/62. Wounded, 7/1/63 at Gettysburg. Killed, 9/30/64 at Jones' Farm, VA.
Sgt.	Turner, William S.	1840	Morrisville, Wake Co.	Farm labor	2nd Lt.—1/22/63. 1st Lt.—7/23/63. Captured, 10/27/64 at Burgess' Mill. Died of disease ("inf. of lungs"), 6/2/65 as POW at Ft. Delaware, DE.
Cpl.	Goodman, John E.	1829	Statesville, Iredell Co.	Farmer	Sgt.—7/12/62. Killed, 7/1/63 at Gettysburg.
Cpl.	McDonald, John H.	1835	Jackson Springs, Moore Co.	Farm labor	Sgt.—7/64. 1st Sgt.—10/1/64. Surrendered, 4/9/65 at Appomattox Court House.
Cpl.	Means, John S.	1840	W. Charlotte, Mecklenburg Co.	Farm labor	Died of disease ("fever"), 8/22/62 at Wilmington, NC.
Cpl.	Wilson, Robert L.	1836	W. Charlotte, Mecklenburg Co.	Farm labor	Sgt.—1/22/63. Captured, 10/27/64 at Burgess' Mill.
Pvt.	Abernathy, Enoch R.	1806	Charlotte, Mecklenburg Co.	Farmer	Discharged, 11/10/64 ("infirmity of age & chronic orchitis").
Pvt.	Alexander, Peter	1803	W. Charlotte, Mecklenburg Co.	Day laborer	Discharged, 12/16/63 (disability due to chronic rheumatism).
Pvt.	Auten, Samuel W.	1837	Farm Creek, Mecklenburg Co.	Farm labor	Captured, 4/2/65 at Petersburg.
Pvt.	Baker, Joel M.	1845	W. Charlotte, Mecklenburg Co.	Day laborer	Missing, 3/1/65.
Pvt.	**Bass, Burton**	**1839**	**Black Creek, Wilson Co.**	**Farmer**	**Captured, 10/27/64 at Burgess' Mill. Died of disease (chronic diarrhea), 3/10/65 as POW at Point Lookout, MD.**
Pvt.	Bass, James A.	1835	School Dist. 67, Iredell Co.	Day laborer	Wounded (left arm), 7/1/63 at Gettysburg. Discharged due to wounds ("exostosis of left tibia"), 11/10/64.
Pvt.	Beatty, John W.	1819	Mecklenburg Co.	Farmer	Captured; 10/27/64 at Burgess' Mills.
Pvt.	Belk, William A.	1843	Mecklenburg Co.	Farm labor	Captured, 10/14/63 at Bristoe Station, VA.
Pvt.	Bird, William L.	1839	W. Charlotte, Mecklenburg Co.	Day laborer	Wounded, 12/16/62 at White Hall, NC. Wounded (right leg), 7/1/63 and captured, 7/5/63 at Gettysburg. Captured, 4/2/65 at Petersburg.
Pvt.	Bradley, John L.	1840	Coddle Creek, Iredell Co.	Farm labor	Captured, 7/3/63 at Gettysburg.
Pvt.	Brimer, John	1836	Stowesville, Gaston Co.	Day laborer	Wounded (leg), 7/1/63 at Gettysburg.

Rank	Name	DOB	Residence	Occupation	Remarks
Pvt.	Cathey, William C.	1836	W. Charlotte, Mecklenburg Co.	Farm labor	Cpl.—1/22/63. Wounded (left arm amputated), 7/1/63 and captured at Gettysburg. Retired to the Invalid Corps, 12/15/64.
Pvt.	Christy, James F.	1842	Statesville, Iredell Co.	Day laborer	Wounded (right leg), 7/1/63 at Gettysburg. Died of wounds, 9/4/63 "at home."
Pvt.	Dixon, William W.	1820	W. Charlotte, Mecklenburg Co.	Farmer	Wounded, 7/1/63 at Gettysburg. Died of wounds, 7/2/63.
Pvt.	Eller, Alexander	1820	Statesville, Iredell Co.	Day laborer	Discharged, 7/16/64 (disability—"oedema of the lower extremities & [he] is generally unfit for active field service.")
Pvt.	Eller, Samuel W.	1845	Statesville, Iredell Co.	Farm labor	Deserted, 9/14/63 at Rapidan, VA.
Pvt.	Finger, John	1836	Mecklenburg Co.	—	Wounded (neck), 7/3/63, at Gettysburg. Wounded and captured, 10/14/63 at Bristoe Station.
Pvt.	Grier, Thomas H.	1840	W. Charlotte, Mecklenburg Co.	Farm labor	Discharged (disability), 8/2/62.
Pvt.	Griffin, George	1844	Walkersville, Union Co.	Day laborer	Died of disease, 5/18/62 at Wilmington, NC.
Pvt.	Hartgrove, Richard D.	1844	W. Charlotte, Mecklenburg Co.	Farm labor	Wounded, 12/16/62 at White Hall, NC. Wounded (thigh), 7/3/63 at Gettysburg. Captured, 10/27/64 at Burgess' Mill. Died of disease (pneumonia), 3/19/65 as POW at Point Lookout, MD.
Pvt.	Hartgrove, William W.	1839	W. Charlotte, Mecklenburg Co.	Farm labor	Wounded, 12/16/62 at White Hall, NC. Cpl.—1/22/63. Wounded (left thigh), 7/3/63 at Gettysburg. Wounded, 5/5/64 at the Wilderness. Sgt.—10/65. Surrendered, 4/9/65 at Appomattox Court House.
Pvt.	Hartline, David L.	1838	Statesville, Iredell Co.	Farm labor	Wounded (right foot), 7/3/63. Wounded, 5/10/64 at Spotsylvania. Surrendered, 4/9/65 at Appomattox Court House.
Pvt.	Hartline, George H.	1835	Statesville, Iredell Co.	Farm labor	Died of disease, 8/10/62 at Wilmington.
Pvt.	Hartline, Paul	1825	Statesville, Iredell Co.	Farmer	Wounded, 12/16/62 at White Hall, NC. Captured, 4/2/65 at Petersburg.
Pvt.	Hill, James W.	1827	W. Charlotte, Mecklenburg Co.	Farmer	Wounded (leg), 7/1/63 and captured at Gettysburg. Killed at Reams' Station, 8/26/64.
Pvt.	Hipp, Stephen	1815	W. Charlotte, Mecklenburg Co.	Day laborer	Discharged (disability), 8/2/62.
Pvt.	Hollingsworth, John B.	1839	Mecklenburg Co.	—	Cpl.—10/64. Captured, 4/2/65 at Petersburg.
Pvt.	Jamison, Thomas J.	1827	W. Charlotte, Mecklenburg Co.	Carpenter	Wounded, 12/16/62 at White Hall, NC. Wounded, 7/3/63 at Gettysburg. Cpl.—12/18/64. Captured, 4/2/65 at Petersburg.

Rank	Name	DOB	Residence	Occupation	Remarks
Pvt.	King, Arguile	1806	W. Charlotte, Mecklenburg Co.	Farmer	Discharged (disability—"chronic rheumatism & the natural infirmity of age"), 4/1/64.
Pvt.	Kyles, Fielding	1820	Iredell Co.	—	Captured, 10/27/64 at Burgess' Mill.
Pvt.	**Kyles, William**	**1824**	**Iredell Co.**	—	**Died of disease (chronic diarrhea), 10/28/64 at Danville, VA**
Pvt.	**Lambert, Jonathan M.**	**1842**	**Goldston, Chatham Co.**	**Farm labor**	**Died of disease, 2/14/64 in Richmond VA.**
Pvt.	Lewis, Lindsay	1839	Greensboro, Guilford Co.	Day laborer	Wounded (right foot), 7/1/63 at Gettysburg. Missing, 3/1/65.
Pvt.	McCarmick, John	1825	Lumberton, Robeson Co.	Farmer	Sgt.—9/3/62. Pvt.—9/64. Deserted, 3/13/65.
Pvt.	Martin, William	1842	Erasmus, Gaston Co.	Farm labor	Wounded, 7/3/63 at Gettysburg. Deserted, 3/8/65.
Pvt.	McCorkle, Hugh P.	1827	W. Charlotte, Mecklenburg Co.	Millwright	Captured, 7/14/63 at Falling Waters, MD. Captured, 4/2/65 at Petersburg.
Pvt.	McLure, Cyrus A.	1834	W. Charlotte, Mecklenburg Co.	Farm labor	Wounded (left index finger amputated), 7/3/63 and captured, 7/14/63 at Falling Waters. Captured, 10/27/64 at Burgess' Mill.
Pvt.	**McLure, James D.**	**1837**	**W. Charlotte, Mecklenburg Co.**	**Farm labor**	**Died of disease ("continued fever"), 8/6/62 at Wilmington, NC.**
Pvt.	McQuay, James	1827	W. Charlotte, Mecklenburg Co.	Carpenter	Killed, 7/3/63 at Gettysburg.
Pvt.	**McQuay, Seaborn**	**1834**	**W. Charlotte, Mecklenburg Co.**	**Farm labor**	**Died of typhoid fever, 7/30/62 at Wilmington, NC.**
Pvt.	**McQuay, Wm. Henry**	**1842**	**W. Charlotte, Mecklenburg Co.**	**Blacksmith**	**Wounded, 7/1/63 at Gettysburg. Died of wounds, 7/7/63 in U.S. field hospital at Gettysburg.**
Pvt.	Miller, John E.	1831	Pisgah, Alexander Co.	Farmer	Deserted, 10/8/62.
Pvt.	Mitschka (Mitcha), John	1822	Mecklenburg Co.	—	Captured, 7/5/63 at Gettysburg.
Pvt.	Murdoch, William D.	1840	Asheboro, Randolph Co.	Farm labor	Wounded (right foot), 5/5/64 at the Wilderness. Deserted, 9/64.
Pvt.	**Nisbet, John G.**	**1816**	**Jacksonham, Lancaster Co. SC**	**Farmer**	**Died of disease, 6/30/63 ("at home").**
Pvt.	**Ostwalt, Francis Henry**	**1824**	**Statesville, Iredell Co.**	**Farmer**	**Captured, 7/3/63 at Gettysburg. Died of disease (smallpox) 12/30/63 as POW at Point Lookout, MD.**
Pvt.	Pool, George S.	1829	Morganton, Burke Co.	Teamster	Wounded (right leg), 5/10/64 at Spotsylvania. Hospitalized by "gunshot wound of the lower right extremities," 3/17/65 in Charlotte, NC.

Rank	Name	DOB	Residence	Occupation	Remarks
Pvt.	Puckett, Julius J.	1838	W. Charlotte, Mecklenburg Co.	Day laborer	Cpl.—8/62. Wounded (right leg), 7/1/63 at Gettysburg. Sgt.—10/64. Captured, 10/27/64 at Burgess' Mill.
Pvt.	Puckett, William C.	1840	W. Charlotte, Mecklenburg Co.	Farm labor	Wounded (left thigh), 7/1/63 at Gettysburg. Surrendered, 4/9/65 at Appomattox Court House.
Pvt.	Sherrill, Wilburn A.	1830	Sherrill's Ford, Catawba Co.	Farmer	Discharged (disability), 10/25/62.
Pvt.	Smith, David J.	1839	W. Charlotte, Mecklenburg Co.	Farm labor	Wounded (neck), 3/27/65 in Petersburg trenches.
Pvt.	Stinson, John B.	1823	W. Charlotte, Mecklenburg Co.	Farmer	Discharged, 6/20/62.
Pvt.	Stone, Alexander	1832	W. Charlotte, Mecklenburg Co.	Day laborer	Captured, 7/7/63 at Williamsport, MD. Died of disease (acute diarrhea), 1/28/64 as POW at Point Lookout, MD.
Pvt.	Walker, Benjamin H.	1827	Mecklenburg Co.	—	Killed, 12/16/62 at White Hall, NC.
Pvt.	Walker, John H.	1846	W. Charlotte, Mecklenburg Co.	Farm labor	Captured, 4/2/65 at Petersburg.
Pvt.	Walker, J. H.	—	Mecklenburg Co.	—	Died of disease, 3/6/62 at Camp Magnum, Raleigh NC.
Pvt.	Walker, Levi L.	1830	W. Charlotte, Mecklenburg Co.	Farm labor	Wounded, 7/1/63 and captured, 7/5/63 at Gettysburg. Killed, 5/10/64 at Spotsylvania Court House.
Pvt.	Williamson, Edward Y.	1845	E. Charlotte, Mecklenburg Co.	Farm labor	Captured, 7/3/63 at Gettysburg. Died of disease ("cerebretis"), 8/20/63 as POW at Ft. Delaware, DE.
Pvt.	Wingate, James	1826	Mecklenburg Co.	—	Wounded, 7/1/63 and captured at Gettysburg. Died of disease ("scorbutis &diarrhea"), 12/29/63 as POW at Point Lookout, MD.
Pvt.	Wingate, Thomas	1834	Mountain Shoals, Catawba Co.	Farmer	Wounded, 7/3/63 at Gettysburg. Captured, 10/27/64 at Burgess' Mill.
Pvt.	Yaunts, Reubin C.	1834	Mecklenburg Co.	—	Court—martialed, 6/21/62. "Confined at guard tent to wear ball and chain for six months." Killed, 7/1/63 at Gettysburg.

1862 Recruits

Rank	Name	DOB	Residence	Occupation	Remarks
Pvt.	Kistler, Paul H.	1842	Lincolnton, Lincoln Co.	Farm labor	Enlisted, 5/9/62 at Camp Holmes. Discharged, 5/23/63 ("being a minor").
Pvt.	McLellan, William	1839	Concord, Cabarrus Co.	Farm labor	Enlisted, 5/5/62. Captured, 7/5/63 at Gettysburg. Surrendered, 4/9/65 at Appomattox Court House.
Pvt.	Walker, James H.	1829	W. Charlotte, Mecklenburg Co.	Farmer	Enlisted, 5/9/62 at Mecklenburg Co. Cpl.—9/30/64. Captured, 10/27/64 at Burgess' Mill.

1863 Recruits

Rank	Name	DOB	Residence	Occupation	Remarks
Pvt.	Clark, James A.	1825	W. Charlotte, Mecklenburg Co.	Farmer	Enlisted, 4/1/63. Killed, 7/1/63 at Gettysburg.
Pvt.	Erwin, Joseph J.	1845	Davidson, Iredell Co.	Farm labor	Enlisted, 12/25/63 at Orange Court House, VA. Discharged, 4/21/64 (disability—"general debility with abdominal dropsy & disease of hip.")
2nd Lt.	Grier, Paul B.	1839	W. Charlotte, Mecklenburg Co.	Farm labor	Appointed and commissioned, 8/29/63. Killed, 10/14/63 at Bristoe Station, VA.
Pvt.	Helms, Ezekiel T.	1839	W. Charlotte, Mecklenburg Co.	Farm labor	Enlisted, 3/12/63. Killed, 7/1/63 at Gettysburg.
Pvt.	Jamison, James W.	1837	W. Charlotte, Mecklenburg Co.	—	Enlisted, 3/7/63 at Mecklenburg Co. Cpl.—9/64. Captured, 10/27/64 at Burgess' Mill. Died of disease (inflammation of lungs), 3/7/65 as POW at Point Lookout, MD.
Pvt.	Jamison, Jones W.	1843	W. Charlotte, Mecklenburg Co.	Farm labor	Enlisted, 2/28/63 at Mecklenburg Co. Captured, 7/14/63 at Falling Waters MD. Captured, 10/27/64 at Burgess' Mill.
Pvt.	Neal, George A.	1847	Yanceyville, Caswell Co.	Farm labor	Enlisted, 2/1/63. Wounded (left arm amputated), 7/1/63 and captured at Gettysburg. Discharged (wounds) 2/17/64.
Pvt.	Richey, William F.	1833	Statesville, Iredell Co.	Day laborer	Enlisted, 4/19/63. Wounded, 7/1/63 and captured at Gettysburg. Died of wounds, 7/9/63.

1864 Recruits

Rank	Name	DOB	Residence	Occupation	Remarks
Pvt.	Adams, Hannibal A.	1842	Anderson Store, Caswell Co.	Farm worker	Transferred, 12/1/64 from Co. C, 3rd Regt. NC Cav. Captured, 3/25/65 at Petersburg.
Pvt.	Ashley, Moses	—	Mecklenburg Co.	—	Enlisted, 10/1/64 at Camp Holmes. Missing, 3/1/65.
Pvt.	Baker, Aaron W.	1846	W. Charlotte, Mecklenburg Co.	Day laborer	Enlisted, 4/19/64. Missing, 3/1/65.
Pvt.	Baker, William M.	1828	Summerville, Harnett Co.	Day laborer	Transferred, 11/64 from Co. C, 3rd Regt. NC Cav. Captured 4/2/65 at Petersburg.
Pvt.	Ballard, Benjamin H.	1825	Catawba Springs, Lincoln Co.	Day laborer	Enlisted—10/1/64 at Camp Holmes. Deserted, 3/13/65.
Pvt.	Beal, Charles	1846	Mountain Creek, Catawba Co.	Farm labor	Enlisted, 10/1/64 at Camp Holmes. Captured, 10/27/64 at Burgess' Mills. Died of disease (peritonitis), 1/2/65 as POW at Point Lookout, MD.
Pvt.	Beal, John	1844	Mountain Creek, Catawba Co.	Farm labor	Enlisted, 10/1/64. Captured, 10/27/64 at Burgess' Mills. Died of disease (catarrh), 3/9/65 as POW at Point Lookout, MD.
Pvt.	Bradshaw, John F.	1846	Lincoln Co.	Farm labor	Enlisted, 10/1/64 at Camp Holmes. Captured, 3/25/65 in Petersburg trenches.

Rank	Name	DOB	Residence	Occupation	Remarks
Pvt.	Campbell, John W.	—	Union, Lincoln Co.	—	Enlisted, 10/1/64 at Camp Holmes. Wounded (right arm) 10/27/64 at Burgess' Mill.
Pvt.	Campbell, Milton	1833	Union, Lincoln Co.	Farmer	Enlisted, 10/23/64 at Camp Holmes. Discharged, 11/19/64 ("want of physical vigor & development").
Pvt.	Clemmens, Robert R.	—	—	—	Enlisted, 9/15/64 at Camp Holmes. Hospitalized, 4/1/65 at Farmville, VA.
Pvt.	**Culberson, John W.**	—	—	—	**Enlisted, 10/1/64 at Camp Holmes. Captured, 10/27/64 at Burgess' Mill. Died of disease (chronic diarrhea), 3/4/65 at Point Lookout, MD.**
Pvt.	Denton, John	—	Lenoir Co.	—	Transferred from Co. C, 3rd NC Cavalry, 11/30/64. Missing, 3/1/65.
Pvt.	**Edwards, Marshall**	1846	**Burnsville, Anson Co.**	**Farm labor**	**Enlisted, 9/15/64 at Camp Holmes. Captured, 10/27/64 at Burgess' Mill. Died of disease (acute dysentery), 12/18/64 as POW at Point Lookout, MD.**
Pvt.	Edwards, Shepherd	1827	Burnsville, Anson Co.	Farmer	Enlisted, 9/15/64 at Camp Holmes. Captured, 4/2/65 at Petersburg.
Pvt.	Ellwood, John J.	—	Mecklenburg Co.	—	Enlisted, 2/19/64. Deserted, 3/22/64.
Pvt.	**Garrison, Alfred**	**1838**	**Spring Hill, Lincoln Co.**	**Farm labor**	**Enlisted, 10/1/64 at Camp Holmes. Captured, 10/27/64 at Burgess' Mill. Died of disease ("erysipelas"), 3/26/65 as POW at Point Lookout, MD.**
Pvt.	Harris, Charles C.	—	Mecklenburg Co.	—	Listed on rolls, 11/64. Captured, 4/2/65 at Petersburg.
Pvt.	Hartline, Adam	1846	Statesville, Iredell Co.	Farm labor	Enlisted, 10/27/64 at Camp Holmes. Surrendered, 4/9/65 at Appomattox Court House.
Pvt.	Hartline, Andrew	1844	Statesville, Iredell Co.	Farm labor	Enlisted, 10/27/64 at Camp Holmes. Captured, 4/2/65 at Petersburg.
Pvt.	Holdsclaw, Robert H.	—	Sherril's Ford, Catawba Co.	Farm labor	Transferred, 11/64 from Co. K, 5th Regt. NC Inf. Missing, 3/1/65.
Pvt.	Holton, Harrison	1841	W. Charlotte, Mecklenburg Co.	Printer	Enlisted, 3/16/64. Surrendered, 4/9/65 at Appomattox Court House.
Sgt.	Hunter, Andrew J.	1828	W. Charlotte, Mecklenburg Co.	Farm labor	Transferred, 10/15/64 from Co. A. Promoted, 10/15/64. Missing, 3/1/65.
Pvt.	Kyles, John	—	Iredell Co.	—	Enlisted, 10/27/64 at Camp Holmes. Captured, 3/25/65 at Petersburg.
Pvt.	Lambert, William T.	1845	Iredell Co.	Farm labor	Enlisted, 10/27/64 at Camp Holmes. Captured, 4/2/65 at Petersburg.
Pvt.	**Lawson, Hudson**	—	—	—	**Enlisted, 9/15/64 at Camp Holmes, Raleigh. Died of disease (diarrhea), 1/26/65 at Richmond.**
Pvt.	Ledwell, David	1838	W. Charlotte, Mecklenburg Co.	Day laborer	Enlisted, 9/1/64 at Camp Holmes, Raleigh. Missing, 3/1/65.

Rank	Name	DOB	Residence	Occupation	Remarks
Pvt.	Linebarger, Manassas	1832	Wood Lawn, Gaston Co.	Farmer	Enlisted, 9/1/64 at Camp Holmes. Captured, 9/30/64 at Jones' Farm.
Pvt.	**Loftin, Martin**	**1840**	**Jackson Hill, Davidson Co.**	**Farm labor**	**Enlisted, 9/1/64 at Camp Holmes. Captured, 10/27/64 at Burgess' Mill. Died of disease (typhoid fever), 2/12/65 as POW at Point Lookout, MD.**
Pvt.	Maddox, George W.	1842	Pittsboro, Chatham Co.	Farm labor	Enlisted, 9/1/64 at Camp Holmes. Missing, 3/1/65.
Pvt.	Matheson, John	1837	New Sterling, Iredell Co.	Shoe maker	Reported on the rolls, 9/15/64. Deserted, 3/9/65.
Pvt.	Means, John	1837	Mount Pleasant, Cabarrus Co.	Farm labor	Enlisted, 4/24/64. Captured, 10/27/64 at Burgess' Mills.
Pvt.	Monday, Osborne M.	1838	Sherrill's Ford, Catawba Co.	Farm labor	Transferred, 11/64 from Co. K, 5th Regt. NC Inf. Deserted, 3/9/65 at Petersburg trenches.
Pvt.	**Narron, John G.**	**1846**	**St. Charles, Johnston Co.**	**Farm labor**	**Enlisted, 9/15/64 at Camp Holmes. Captured, 10/27/64 at Burgess' Mill. Died of disease (strangulated inguinal hernia), 11/23/64 as POW at Point Lookout, MD.**
Pvt.	Null, John S.	1846	Catawba Station, Catawba Co.	Farm labor	Transferred, 11/64 from Co. K, 5th Regt. NC Inf. Deserted, 3/9/65 at Petersburg trenches.
Pvt.	Pennix, John A.	1825	Greensboro, Guilford Co.	Farmer	Enlisted—9/15/64 at Camp Holmes. Surrendered, 4/9/65 at Appomattox Court House.
Pvt.	Pennix, Joseph W.	1845	Greensboro, Guilford Co.	Farm labor	Enlisted, 9/15/64 at Camp Holmes. Captured, 10/27/64 at Burgess' Mill. Wounded (left knee), 4/2/65 at Petersburg.
Pvt.	Reid, James C.	1835	W. Charlotte, Mecklenburg Co.	Farmer	Enlisted, 2/19/64. Wounded and Captured, 10/27/64 at Burgess' Mill. Captured, 4/2/65 at Petersburg trenches ("Cox Road").
Pvt.	Rhyne, David	1845	Mountain Island, Gaston Co.	Farm labor	Enlisted, 9/1/64 at Camp Holmes. Captured, 10/27/64 at Burgess' Mill.
Pvt.	Rievs, William R.	1836	Mecklenburg Co.	—	Wounded, 7/3/63 at Gettysburg. Captured, 2/5/65 at Petersburg trenches.
Pvt.	**Rozzell, James T.**	**1843**	**W. Charlotte, Mecklenburg Co.**	**Farm labor**	**Cpl.—7/12/62. Sgt.—1/22/63. Killed, 5/5/64 at the Wilderness.**
Pvt.	Sprinkle, J. I.	1836	W. Charlotte, Mecklenburg Co.	Conductor	Enlisted, 12/64. Surrendered, 4/9/65 at Appomattox Court House.
Pvt.	Turner, John W.	1818	Marley's Mill, Randolph Co.	Farmer	Enlisted, 9/15/64 at Camp Holmes. Missing, 3/15/65.
Pvt.	Walker, Landsey L.	1825	Newtonville, Caswell Co.	Blacksmith	Enlisted, 9/15/64 at Camp Holmes. Captured, 4/3/65 near Petersburg trenches.
Pvt.	Wilson, John R.	1825	Burnsville, Yancey Co.	Farmer	Enlisted, 4/9/64. Missing, 3/1/65.
Pvt.	York, George W.	1835	Albemarle, Stanly Co.	Farm labor	Enlisted, 9/1/64 at Camp Holmes. Captured, 10/27/64 at Burgess' Mill.

Company F
Chowan, Hertford, and Perquimans Counties

Rank	Name	DOB	Residence	Occupation	Remarks
Cpt.	Small, Edward A.	1835	Edenton, Chowan Co.	Merchant	Captured, 7/3/63 at Gettysburg.
1st Lt.	Knapp, Theodore J.	1833	Hertford, Chowan Co.	Baptist minister	Chaplain—Appointed, 10/62. Resigned, 10/16/62 "by reason of poor health."
2nd Lt.	Roberts, Stephen W.	1833	Edenton, Chowan Co.	Manager	1st Lt.—9/25/62. Wounded (shoulder), 7/1/63 at Gettysburg. Wounded (left leg), 5/5/64 at the Wilderness. Missing, 3/7/65.
3rd Lt.	**Hoskins, Blake B.**	**1843**	**Tarboro, Edgecombe Co.**	**Clerk**	**Wounded, 7/1/63 and captured at Gettysburg. Died of wounds, 7/9/63 at Gettysburg.**
Ord. Sgt.	McDowell, George B.	1830	Hertford, Chowan Co.	Dry goods merchant	Wounded (hip & foot), 7/1/63 at Gettysburg. 1st Sgt.—1/64. Transferred, 7/64 to the 47th NC Infantry.
Sgt.	Davenport, Charles G.	1831	Edenton, Chowan Co.	Farmer	1st Sgt.—12/8/64. Missing, 3/1/65.
Sgt.	Mardre, Nathaniel	1843	Hertford, Perquimans Co.	Farm labor	Captured, 7/14/63 at Falling Waters, MD. Wounded, 5/5/64 at the Wilderness. Wounded, 2/65 in Petersburg trenches.
Sgt.	Rea, William D.	1841	Edenton, Chowan Co.	Farm labor	2nd Lt.—11/25/62. Wounded (left hip & right foot), 7/3/63 at Gettysburg. Wounded (face), 8/21/64 near Petersburg. Retired, 2/1/65 "by reason of disability."
Sgt.	Small, Thomas M.	1838	Chowan Co.	Carpenter	Wounded, 8/21/64 in Petersburg trenches.
Sgt.	Troutman, Joseph W.	1834	Perquimans Co.	—	Pvt.—4/18/62. Captured, 7/3/63 at Gettysburg. Wounded, 8/22/64 in Petersburg trenches.
Cpl.	**Briscoe, Robert**	**1820**	**Murfreesboro, Hertford Co.**	**Overseer**	**Wounded (leg), 7/3/63 and captured at Gettysburg. Hospitalized at Chester, PA. Died of wounds, 8/10/63 ("of exhaustion following gunshot wound").**
Cpl.	**Creecy, James E.**	**1839**	**Hertford, Perquimans Co.**	**Day laborer**	**Captured, 7/14/63 at Falling Waters, MD. Died of disease, 2/15/64 as POW at Point Lookout, MD.**
Cpl.	Leary, William H.	1841	Hertford, Chowan Co.	Farm labor	Pvt.—6/15/64. Captured, 4/3/65 in Petersburg trenches.
Pvt.	Ashley, Benbury	1815	Edenton, Chowan Co.	Farm labor	Discharged, 4/3/63 "by reason of disability."
Pvt.	Askew, Bryant	1846	Murfreesboro, Hertford Co.	Farm labor	Captured, 4/2/65 at Petersburg.
Pvt.	**Askew, Enos**	**1837**	**Murfreesboro, Hertford Co.**	**Farm labor**	**Died of disease, 4/24/62 in Hertford Co. NC.**
Pvt.	Askew, Joshua	1837	Murfreesboro, Hertford Co.	Farmer	Captured, 4/3/65 in Petersburg trenches.
Pvt.	Askew, Miles	1846	Edenton, Chowan Co.	Seamstress' asst.	Wounded (head), 7/1/63 and captured, 7/5/63 at Gettysburg. Wounded, 8/25/64 at Reams' Station, VA.

Rank	Name	DOB	Residence	Occupation	Remarks
Pvt.	Backus, Thomas	1814	Harrellsville, Chowan Co.	Farmer	Died of disease ("meningitis" or "brain disease"), 6/27/63 at Danville, VA.
Pvt.	Bailey, Richard	1835	Yeopim, Perquimans Co.	Tailor	Transferred, 4/1/64 to C.S. Navy.
Pvt.	Bateman, Timothy C.	1844	Edenton, Chowan Co.	Farm labor	Captured, 7/14/63 at Falling Waters, MD.
Pvt.	Bates, Frederick W.	1829	Yeopim, Perquimans Co.	Engineer	Cpl.—4/1/62. Pvt.—11/62. Wounded, 7/1/63 and captured at Gettysburg.
Pvt.	Benbury, William E.	1842	Edenton, Chowan Co.	Farm labor	Cpl.—11/62. Wounded (arm), 7/3/63 at Gettysburg. Sgt.—12/7/64. Wounded (left thigh & right shoulder), 4/2/65 and captured at Petersburg.
Pvt.	Bogue, Jesse	1830	Sutton's Creek, Perquimans Co.	Farmer	Wounded (right arm), 1/30/64. Surrendered, 4/9/65 at Appomattox Court House.
Pvt.	Boyce, Kenny	1844	Edenton, Chowan Co.	Farm labor	Died of disease (typhoid fever), 4/3/62 at Raleigh, NC.
Pvt.	Bratten, William J.	1829	Hertford, Perquimans Co.	Farm labor	Captured, 10/14/63 at Bristoe Station, VA.
Pvt.	Bridges, Roswald D.	1830	Cleveland Co.	Farmer	Wounded (right thigh), 10/1/64 near Jones' Farm, VA. Captured, 4/2/65 at Petersburg.
Pvt.	Briggs, Andrew	1844	Edenton, Chowan Co.	Farm labor	Captured, 10/27/64 at Burgess' Mill.
Pvt.	Briggs, James	1843	Edenton, Chowan Co.	Farm labor	Captured, 10/27/64 at Burgess' Mill.
Pvt.	Byrum, A. J.	1841	Chowan Co.	Farm labor	Wounded (left leg), 7/3/63 at Gettysburg. Died of wounds, 3/27/64.
Pvt.	Byrum, George F.	1843	Merry Hill, Bertie Co.	Farm labor	Deserted, 10/62 at Franklin, NC.
Pvt.	Byrum, Isaac	1840	Edenton, Chowan Co.	Farm labor	Wounded (left leg amputated), 7/3/65 at Gettysburg. Captured, 7/5/63. Retired to Invalid Corps, 6/2/64.
Pvt.	Conner, James R.	1841	Windsor, Bertie Co.	Farm labor	Wounded (thigh), 7/1/63 and captured at Gettysburg. Deserted, 11/63.
Pvt.	Copeland, Timothy	1821	Edenton, Chowan Co.	Farmer	Died of disease, 7/24/64 at Chowan Co. NC.
Pvt.	Creecy, Henry L.	1842	Hertford, Perquimans Co.	Day labor	Captured, 10/14/63 at Bristoe Station, VA.
Pvt.	Dail, Joshua	1840	Up River, Perquimans Co.	Farm labor	Died of disease (measles) 5/13/62 at Camp Holmes, VA.
Pvt.	Davidson, Lewis	1824	Murfreesboro, Hertford Co.	Day labor	Wounded, 7/3/63 and captured at Gettysburg. Died of wounds, 7/27/63 at David's Island, NY.
Pvt.	Deans, William D.	1843	Edenton, Chowan Co.	Farm labor	Discharged (disability—"unfit for duty"), 10/3/62.
Pvt.	Elliott, Charles W.	1841	Edenton, Chowan Co.	Farm labor	Died of disease, 4/13/62 at Camp Mangum, NC.
Pvt.	Farmer, Joseph J.	1840	Hertford Co.	Farm labor	Captured, 10/14/63 at Bristoe Station, VA.
Pvt.	Fleetwood, Joseph	1829	Hertford, Perquimans Co.	Farmer	Discharged (disability), 5/1/62.

Rank	Name	DOB	Residence	Occupation	Remarks
Pvt.	Floyd, Henry	1831	Hertford Co.	—	Captured, 7/3/63 at Gettysburg. Died of disease, 10/6/63 as POW at Ft. Delaware, DE.
Pvt.	Forehand, Adam	1840	Edenton, Chowan Co.	Farm labor	Captured, 7/14/63 at Falling Waters, MD. Captured, 10/27/64 at Burgess' Mill.
Pvt.	Garrett, Stephen	1813	Hertford, Chowan Co.	Farmer	Captured, 10/14/63 at Bristoe Station, VA. Died of disease (chronic diarrhea), 11/6/63 as POW at Point Lookout, MD.
Pvt.	Gatling, William J.	1829	Murfreesboro, Hertford Co.	Physician	Discharged (disability), 8/4/62.
Pvt.	Goodwin, Amariah	1836	Ballahack, Perquimans Co.	Carpenter	Deserted, 7/19/64 from Petersburg.
Pvt.	Goodwin, Benjamin F.	1840	Hertford, Chowan Co.	Farm labor	Captured, 7/14/63 at Falling Waters, MD. Died of disease, 1/6/64 as POW at Point Lookout, MD.
Pvt.	Goodwin, Eli	1840	Hertford, Chowan Co.	Farm labor	Died of disease, 1/19/63.
Pvt.	Green, Samuel	1838	Hertford Co.	—	Died of disease (meningitis), 3/16/62 in hospital in Raleigh, NC.
Pvt.	Griffin, Joshua	1843	Williamston, Martin Co.	Farm labor	Deserted, 2/23/65 in Petersburg trenches.
Pvt.	Harris, Thomas C.	1833	Edenton, Perquimans Co.	Farmer	Wounded (left side), 7/3/63 and captured at Gettysburg. Cpl.—1/64. Captured, 10/27/64 at Burgess' Mill. Died of disease (hepatitis), 1/2/65 as POW at Point Lookout, MD.
Pvt.	Haskett, Thomas T.	1839	Bethel, Perquimans Co.	Farm labor	Wounded (left leg), 7/3/63 and captured at Gettysburg. Retired to the Invalid Corps, 4/1/64 "by reason of wounds received at Gettysburg."
Pvt.	Hedricks, Thomas	1808	Hertford, Perquimans Co.	Farm labor	Transferred to the C.S. Navy, 4/1/64.
Pvt.	Hendrix, Nathan	1842	Woodville, Perquimans Co.	Farm labor	AWOL, 10/29/63.
Pvt.	Hudson, John W.	1823	Edenton, Chowan Co.	Farmer	Died of disease (pneumonia), 10/29/62 at Franklin, VA.
Pvt.	Jones, Theophilus	1818	Bethel, Perquimans Co.	Farmer	Wounded, 7/3/63 and captured at Gettysburg.
Pvt.	Jordan, Hance	1837	Edenton, Chowan Co.	Farm labor	Missing, 5/6/64 at the Wilderness.
Pvt.	Jordan, Nathan C.	1834	Edenton, Chowan Co.	Farm labor	Wounded, 7/1/63 at Gettysburg. Died of wounds, 7/5/63.
Pvt.	Jordan, Robert S.	1838	Hertford, Perquimans Co.	Farm labor	Cpl.—12/7/64. Captured, 4/2/65 at Petersburg.
Pvt.	Lane, Caleb	1834	Ballahack, Perquimans Co.	Farm labor	Captured, 7/3/63 at Gettysburg.
Pvt.	Lane, William	1840	Ballahack, Perquimans Co.	Farm labor	Captured, 7/3/63 at Gettysburg. Died of disease (acute diarrhea), 10/15/64 as POW at Point Lookout, MD.

Rank	Name	DOB	Residence	Occupation	Remarks
Pvt.	Lassiter, George W.	1842	Edenton, Chowan Co.	Farm labor	Captured, 4/2/65 at Petersburg.
Pvt.	Leary, Quinton L.	1844	Edenton, Chowan Co.	Farm labor	Discharged (disability), 8/16/62.
Pvt.	Long, John	1834	Hertford, Perquimans Co.	Farmer	Wounded (elbow), 8/21/64 in Petersburg trenches. Retired to the Invalid Corps, 2/21/65.
Pvt.	Long, Joseph S.	1844	Hertford, Perquimans Co.	Farm labor	Wounded (left thigh & arm), 7/3/63 and captured at Gettysburg. Cpl.—6/15/64. Missing, 3/1/65.
Pvt.	Long, Richard	1831	Hertford, Perquimans Co.	Farm labor	Discharged (disability), 8/13/62.
Pvt.	Mansfield, Calvin	1835	Ballahack, Perquimans Co.	Farm labor	"In confinement," 11/62. Captured, 7/14/63 at Falling Waters, MD. Reported "AWOL"—"never rejoined the company," 6/9/64.
Pvt.	Miller, James	1844	Edenton, Chowan Co.	Farm labor	Wounded, 5/5/64 at the Wilderness. Captured, 4/3/65 in Petersburg trenches.
Pvt.	Modlin, Elisha	1841	Edenton, Chowan Co.	Farm labor	Missing, 3/1/65.
Pvt.	**Moore, Levi**	1844	**Neuse River, Johnston Co.**	**Farm labor**	**Died of disease, 6/16/62 at Wilmington, NC.**
Pvt.	Munds, Thomas	1838	Edenton, Chowan Co.	Farm labor	Injured (gunshot wound), 1/12/64. Hospitalized at Charlottesville, VA. Captured, 4/2/65 at Petersburg.
Pvt.	Nixon, Thomas W.	1838	Washington Co.	Farm labor	Deserted, 11/26/62 at Smithville, NC.
Pvt.	Nowell, Jacob	1833	Ahoskie, Hertford Co.	Farmer	Captured, 7/28/63 at Hazel Run, VA.
Pvt.	Parrish, Stephen	1829	Neuse River, Johnston Co.	Farmer	Wounded, 10/1/64 near Jones' Farm, VA.
Pvt.	**Parrish, William E.**	1841	Chowan Co.	Farm labor	**Wounded (left thigh), 7/1/63 at Gettysburg. Died of disease ("collitis acute"), 8/27/64 at Greensboro, NC.**
Pvt.	**Perry, Timothy**	1836	Edenton, Chowan Co.	Farm labor	**Died of disease ("debilitas"), 9/10/64 at Richmond.**
Pvt.	Pierce, Job	1839	Hertford Co.	Farm labor	Captured, 10/27/64 at Burgess' Mill.
Pvt.	Pierce, Richard	1844	Hertford Co.	Farm labor	Transferred, 9/13/62 to 31st NC Inf.
Pvt.	Potter, John	1831	Goose Creek, Beaufort Co.	Farmer	"In confinement," 11/62. Captured, 10/14/63 at Bristoe Station.
Pvt.	Potter, Samuel	1841	Hertford, Perquimans Co.	Farm labor	Captured, 10/14/63 at Bristoe Station. Missing, 4/1/65.
Pvt.	**Powell, William H.**	1842	**Tranter's Creek, Beaufort Co.**	**Farm labor**	**Died of disease (febris typhoid), 8/7/62 at Wilmington, NC.**
Pvt.	**Proctor, John R.**	1844	**Tarboro, Edgecombe Co.**	**Day labor**	**Wounded, 7/1/63 and captured, 7/5/63 at Gettysburg. Died of wounds, 8/63 at Hagerstown, MD.**
Pvt.	**Robinson, Henry D.**	1844	Hertford Co.	Farm labor	**Died of disease (typhoid fever), 7/6/62 at Wilmington, NC.**

Rank	Name	DOB	Residence	Occupation	Remarks
Pvt.	Robinson, John	1814	Hertford Co.	Farmer	Discharged (disability), 7/20/62.
Pvt.	**Roundtree, Noah**	**1831**	**Mintonsville, Gates Co.**	**Farmer**	**Killed, 12/16/62 at White Hall, NC.**
Pvt.	Saunders, George R.	1844	Perquimans Co.	Farm labor	Listed as "deserter," 1/64.
Pvt.	Saunders, William F.	1844	Hertford Co.	Farm labor	Captured, 4/3/65 in Petersburg trenches.
Pvt.	Simpson, Frederick	1843	Edenton, Chowan Co.	Farm labor	Captured, 3/25/65 in Petersburg trenches.
Pvt.	Smith, Charlton	1830	Ballahack, Perquimans Co.	Farmer	Captured, 7/3/63 at Gettysburg.
Pvt.	Smith, James J.	1841	Hertford, Perquimans Co.	Farm labor	Wounded (foot), 4/2/65 at Sutherland Station. Paroled, 4/12/65 at Farmville, VA.
Pvt.	**Smith, William J.**	**1835**	**Edenton, Chowan Co.**	**Day labor**	**Killed, 7/3/63 at Gettysburg.**
Pvt.	Stearns, David M.	1843	Edenton, Chowan Co.	Day labor	Captured, 10/14/63 at Bristoe Station, VA.
Pvt.	Stearns, James W.	1828	Edenton, Chowan Co.	Day labor	Deserted, 7/19/64 at Petersburg.
Pvt.	Stearns, John	1836	Edenton, Chowan Co.	Day Labor	Deserted, 10/62 at Franklin, NC.
Pvt.	Sutton, Seth S.	1837	Edenton, Chowan Co.	Farm manager	Wounded (left arm), 7/3/63 at Gettysburg. Captured, 10/14/63 at Bristoe Station. Wounded, 10/27/64 at Burgess' Mill.
Pvt.	Swain, James W.	1815	Hertford, Perquimans Co.	Farmer	Wounded (left ankle), 10/14/63 at Bristoe Station. Discharged, 4/21/64 "by reason of wounds received at Bristoe Station."
Pvt.	Taylor, Joseph W.	1845	Hertford Co.	Farm labor	Captured, 7/3/63 at Gettysburg. Wounded, 10/1/64 near Jones' Farm, VA.
Pvt.	Thatch, Henry C.	1836	Edenton, Chowan Co.	Farm manager	Captured, 7/3/63 at Gettysburg.
Pvt.	Ward, Aaron	1827	Edenton, Chowan Co.	Farmer	Captured, 3/25/65 in Petersburg trenches.
Pvt.	Ward, Anderson S.	1843	Edenton, Chowan Co.	Farm labor	Captured, 4/3/65 in Petersburg trenches.
Pvt.	**Welch, William B.**	**1841**	**Hertford, Perquimans Co.**	**Farm labor**	**Died of disease ("erysipelas"), 10/21/62 in Petersburg, VA.**
Pvt.	**Welch, William G.**	**1812**	**Hertford, Perquimans Co.**	**Horse doctor**	**Died of disease ("dysentery acute"), 6/7/64 in Richmond.**
Pvt.	Whedbee, George W.	1843	New Hope, Perquimans Co.	Farm labor	Wounded, 7/3/63 and captured at Gettysburg. Deserted, 7/19/64 at Petersburg.
Pvt.	White, Isaac N.	1843	Hertford, Perquimans Co.	Farm labor	Wounded, 7/3/63 and captured at Gettysburg. Cpl.—1/64. Captured, 4/2/65 at Petersburg.
Pvt.	**White, James**	**1840**	**Hertford, Perquimans Co.**	**Farm labor**	**Wounded, 7/3/63 and captured at Gettysburg. In hospital, Baltimore, MD. Died of wounds, 7/16/63.**
Pvt.	White, James B.	1834	Mackey's Ferry, Washington Co.	Day laborer	Wounded (right arm), 7/1/63. Captured, 4/2/65 at Petersburg.

Rank	Name	DOB	Residence	Occupation	Remarks
Pvt.	White, Robert	1844	Statesville, Iredell Co.	Farm labor	Captured, 7/14/63 at Falling Waters, MD.
Pvt.	Williams, James	1844	Hertford, Perquimans Co.	Farm labor	Listed as "deserter," 5/63.
Pvt.	Wingate, Joseph W.	1842	Hertford, Perquimans Co.	Farm labor	Wounded (left arm), 10/14/63 at Bristoe Station, VA. Retired, 4/8/64 due to wounds.

1863 Recruits

Rank	Name	DOB	Residence	Occupation	Remarks
Pvt.	Bagley, Thomas C.	1845	Gatesville, Gates Co.	Farm labor	Transferred from Co. I, 17th NC Regt. Inf.), 1/19/63. Captured, 7/14/63 at Falling Waters, MD.

1864 Recruits

Rank	Name	DOB	Residence	Occupation	Remarks
Pvt.	Dail, Joseph	1847	Hertford, Perquimans Co.	Farm labor	Enlisted, 1/25/64 at Orange Court House, VA. Captured, 4/2/65 at Petersburg.

Company G
Orange and Chatham Counties

Rank	Name	DOB	Residence	Occupation	Remarks
Cpt.	**Jennings, James R.**	**1829**	**Chapel Hill, Orange Co.**	**Restaurant owner**	**Died of disease (yellow fever), 9/16/62 at Wilmington, NC.**
1st Lt.	Freeland, John F.	1840	Chapel Hill, Orange Co.	Clerk	Cpt.—9/16/62. Surrendered, 4/9/65 at Appomattox Court House.
2nd Lt.	**McDade, John H.**	**1832**	**Chapel Hill, Orange Co.**	**UNC Professor**	**1st Lt.—9/16/62. Killed, 7/1/63 at Gettysburg.**
2nd Lt.	Norwood, Thomas F.	1841	Hillsboro, Orange Co.	Lawyer's Asst.	Resigned (sickness—"very feeble health"), 8/7/62.
1st Sgt.	**Tenney, Nathaniel B.**	**1836**	**Chapel Hill, Orange Co.**	**Druggist**	**2nd Lt.—9/17/62. Killed, 7/1/63 at Gettysburg.**
Sgt.	Davis, Thomas	1838	Chapel Hill, Orange Co.	Carpenter	Wounded (right ankle), 7/1/63 and captured at Gettysburg. 1st Sgt.—1/64. Wounded, 6/2/64 at Cold Harbor. Captured, 4/2/65 at Petersburg.
Sgt.	McDade, Henry L.	1838	Orange Co.	Farm labor	Captured, 7/23/63 at Martinsburg, WV. Pvt.—10/11/64. Surrendered, 4/9/65 at Appomattox Court House.
Sgt.	Watson, Jones M.	1813	Chapel Hill, Orange Co.	Merchant	1st Sgt.—10/62. 3rd Lt.—7/30/63. Cashiered, 9/5/64 (reason not reported).
Sgt.	Whitted, Wm. Graham	1840	Chapel Hill, Orange Co.	Blacksmith	Captured, 7/14/63 at Falling Waters, MD. 3rd Lt.—10/11/64. Wounded (thigh), 2/5/64 at Hatcher's Run.
Cpl.	**Durham, William S.**	**1842**	**Warrenton, Warren Co.**	**Farm worker**	**Pvt.—6/63. Wounded, 7/1/63 at Gettysburg. Died of wounds, 7/3/63.**
Cpl.	Harwood, Wesley J.	1832	Chapel Hill, Orange Co.	Overseer	Sgt.—10/11/64. Surrendered, 4/9/65 at Appomattox Court House.
Cpl.	Whitaker, James R.	1838	Orange Co.	Farm labor	Sgt.—9/17/62. 2nd Lt.—7/30/63. Captured, 4/2/65 at Hatcher's Run.
Pvt.	Blackwood, Philo	1843	Chapel Hill, Orange Co.	Farm labor	Wounded, 7/1/63 at Gettysburg. Missing, 3/1/65.

Rank	Name	DOB	Residence	Occupation	Remarks
Pvt.	Blackwood, Robert	1832	Chapel Hill, Orange Co.	Farmer	5/1/62; No further records.
Pvt.	Brockwell, Anderson	1810	Chapel Hill, Orange Co.	Farmer	Discharged ("by reason of injuries of the spine and pelvic viscera received in a railroad accident"), 9/16/63.
Pvt.	Burch, Dudley Y.	1835	Orange Co.	Farmer	Wounded (head) and captured, 3/25/65 in Petersburg trenches.
Pvt.	**Burgess, Henry T.**	**1843**	**Orange Co.**	**Farm labor**	**Died of measles, 7/16/62 "at home."**
Pvt.	Burgess, Washington	1838	Orange Co.	Farm labor	Captured, 4/2/65 at Petersburg.
Pvt.	Campbell, Robert	1843	Orange Co.	Tailor	Captured, 8/21/64 at Weldon Rd.
Pvt.	Canady, Gideon	1814	So. Chapel Hill, Orange Co.	Farm labor	Discharged ("by reason of chronic lameness caused probably by rheumatism"), 9/12/63.
Pvt.	Cates, John W.	1843	Chapel Hill, Orange Co.	Carpenter's Asst.	Wounded (right shoulder), 8/17/64 in Petersburg trenches. Deserted, 3/20/65.
Pvt.	Cates, Stephen P.	1836	Chapel Hill, Orange Co.	Farmer	4/1/62: No further records.
Pvt.	**Cates, William**	**1834**	**Rock Springs, Orange Co.**	**Blacksmith**	**Died of disease ("febris typhoides"), 1/28/63 in hospital in Raleigh.**
Pvt.	**Cates, William B.**	**1835**	**Chapel Hill, Orange Co.**	**Farmer**	**Died of disease, 1/27/63 at Raleigh, NC.**
Pvt.	Cheek, John A.	1832	University Station, Orange Co.	Carpenter	Captured, 7/14/63 at Falling Waters.. Deserted, 3/7/65
Pvt.	Cheek, Nathaniel J.	1836	Chapel Hill, Orange Co.	Carpenter	Cpl.—12/63. Sgt.—10/11/64. Captured, 4/2/65 at Petersburg.
Pvt.	**Chisenhall, Samuel**	**1842**	**Durhamsville, Orange Co.**	**Farm labor**	**Captured, 4/2/65 at Petersburg. Confined at Point Lookout, MD. Died of disease (pneumonia), 5/8/65.**
Pvt.	Clements, James H.	1842	Chapel Hill, Orange Co.	Clerk	Captured, 10/27/64 at Burgess' Mill.
Pvt.	Clements, John R.	1837	Chapel Hill, Orange Co.	Salesman	Wounded (contusion of right hip), 7/3/63 at Gettysburg. Sgt.—8/63. Wounded (hand), 5/10/64 at Spotsylvania. Deserted, 3/2/65.
Pvt.	Clements, William G.	1844	Morrisville, Wake Co.	Farm labor	Wounded (finger), 6/1/64 at Cold Harbor. Captured, 4/2/65 at Petersburg.
Pvt.	**Cole, George**	**1845**	**Chapel Hill, Orange Co.**	**Day labor**	**Died of disease ("febris typhoides"), 7/12/62 at Wilmington, NC.**
Pvt.	Daniel, Algernon	1844	Chapel Hill, Orange Co.	Farm labor	Wounded (both hips), 7/3/63 and captured, 7/5/63 at Gettysburg. Retired due to wounds, 2/17/65.
Pvt.	Daniel, Alvis	1835	Chapel Hill, Orange Co.	Cabinet maker	Discharged ("chronic diarrhea with debility"), 6/22/62.
Pvt.	Daniel, Robert	1838	Chapel Hill, Orange Co.	Farm labor	Captured, 7/14/63 at Falling Waters, MD. Furloughed, 3/6/65 from hospital at Richmond.

Rank	Name	DOB	Residence	Occupation	Remarks
Pvt.	Davis, Benjamin	1812	Rockford, Surry Co.	Blacksmith	Paroled at Raleigh, 4/22/65.
Pvt.	Davis, Demarcus	1835	Newlin, Alamance Co.	Farmer	Discharged (disabilities), 3/15/64.
Pvt.	Davis, Fendall	1845	Chapel Hill, Orange Co.	Farm labor	Wounded (right hip), 7/1/63 at Gettysburg. Deserted, 3/3/65.
Pvt.	Davis, Henry A.	1844	Chapel Hill, Orange Co.	Boot maker's Asst.	Captured, 10/14/63 at Bristoe Station. Captured, 4/2/65 at Petersburg.
Pvt.	Davis, James T.	1844	Chapel Hill, Orange Co.	Boot maker's Asst.	Musician—Promoted, 9/64 and transferred to Regt. Band.
Pvt.	Davis, Marcus	1836	Chapel Hill, Orange Co.	Farm tool salesman	Discharged ("by reason of paralysis"), 3/15/64.
Pvt.	Douglass, Ashley "Ash"	1814	Chapel Hill, Orange Co.	Farmer	Discharged (disability—"injury of the left lower maxillary bone"), 9/2/62.
Pvt.	**Edwards, Cornelius**	1837	**Chapel Hill, Orange Co.**	Cooper	Wounded, 7/1/63 at Gettysburg. Died of wounds, 7/6/63 at Williamsport, MD.
Pvt.	**Flintoff, William D.**	1845	**Chapel Hill, Orange Co.**	Day labor	Wounded, 7/3/63 at Gettysburg. Wounded (right side), 9/30/64 at Jones' Farm. Died of wounds, 11/9/64.
Pvt.	Franklin, William R.	1824	Chapel Hill, Orange Co.	Carpenter	Missing, 3/1/65.
Pvt.	**Garrett, Esau**	1845	**Rock Springs, Orange Co.**	Farm labor	Wounded (lung), 7/3/63 and captured at Gettysburg. Died of wounds, 7/11/63 at Hagerstown, MD.
Pvt.	Garrett, Woodston	1844	Chapel Hill, Orange Co.	Farm labor	Captured, 10/27/64 at Burgess' Mill.
Pvt.	**Hathcock, Carney**	1842	**Chapel Hill, Orange Co.**	Farm labor	Died of disease ("febris typhoides"), 7/21/62 at Wilmington, NC.
Pvt.	Hathcock, Franklin	1839	Chapel Hill, Orange Co.	Farm labor	Deserted, 7/21/63 at Orange Court House, VA.
Pvt.	Hester, John W.	1841	Chapel Hill, Orange Co.	Farm labor	Captured, 4/2/65 at Petersburg.
Pvt.	Huskey, William	1840	Chapel Hill, Orange Co.	Teamster	Deserted, 10/20/64.
Pvt.	Ivey, Edward	1811	Chapel Hill, Orange Co.	Farmer	Hospitalized by accidental shooting, 4/11/64. Retired to Invalid Corps, 4/20/64 in Richmond.
Pvt.	Ivey, Thomas	1822	Chapel Hill, Orange Co.	Farmer	Discharged (disability), 5/9/62.
Pvt.	**Ivey, William G.**	1840	Chapel Hill, Orange Co.	Boot maker	Wounded, 7/3/65 and captured, 7/5/63 at Gettysburg. Died of wounds, 8/8/63 as POW at David's Island, NY.
Pvt.	Jolly, William	1839	Goldston, Chatham Co.	Day labor	Captured, 7/14/63 at Falling Waters, MD. Died of disease, 11/10/64 at Point Lookout, MD.
Pvt.	King, Baxter	1843	Chapel Hill, Orange Co.	Farm labor	Wounded (hip), 7/1/63 at Gettysburg. Captured, 3/25/65 in Petersburg trenches.
Pvt.	King, John	1825	Chapel Hill, Orange Co.	Brick maker	Captured, 4/2/65 at Petersburg.

Rank	Name	DOB	Residence	Occupation	Remarks
Pvt.	King, Rufus	1842	Orange Co.	Farm labor	Captured, 7/14/63 at Falling Waters, MD. Deserted, 3/20/65.
Pvt.	**Lloyd, John W.**	**1844**	**Chatham Co.**	**Farm labor**	**Died of disease ("intermittent fever and meningitis"), 4/15/62 at hospital in Raleigh.**
Pvt.	Lloyd, Thadeus	1839	Chapel Hill, Orange Co.	Farm labor	Wounded, 7/1/63 at Gettysburg. Deserted, 3/22/65.
Pvt.	Marcon, Henderson	1827	Orange Co.	Farmer	Deserted, 10/10/63.
Pvt.	Mincey, John	1841	Chapel Hill, Orange Co.	Farm labor	Wounded (left foot), 7/1/63 at Gettysburg. Captured, 4/2/65 at Petersburg.
Pvt.	Neville, John S.	1842	Chapel Hill, Orange Co.	Farm labor	Discharged, 7/21/62.
Pvt.	Norwood, David J.	1842	Chatham Co.	Farm labor	Cpl.—10/62. Captured, 7/3/63 at Gettysburg. Died of disease ("infection of lungs"), 9/14/63 as POW at Ft. Delaware, DE.
Pvt.	Pearson, Edward	1842	Pittsboro, Chatham Co.	Farm labor	Died of disease (fever), 7/19/62 at Wilmington, NC.
Pvt.	Pearson, Forrest	1844	Pittsboro, Chatham Co.	Farm labor	Died of disease, 4/6/62 at Camp Mangum near Raleigh.
Pvt.	Pearson, Henry C.	1817	Pittsboro, Chatham Co.	Farmer	Deserted, 3/14/65.
Pvt.	Pendergrass, Alvis	1840	Chapel Hill, Orange Co.	Farm labor	Captured, 4/2/65 at Petersburg.
Pvt.	Pendergrass, George	1842	Chapel Hill, Orange Co.	Farm labor	Captured, 10/14/63 at Bristoe Station.
Pvt.	Pendergrass, James A.	1835	Chapel Hill, Orange Co.	Farm labor	Missing, 3/1/65.
Pvt.	Pendergrass, John L.	1833	Chapel Hill, Orange Co.	Farm labor	Captured, 7/3/63 at Gettysburg. Wounded, 10/27/64 at Burgess' Mill.
Pvt.	Pendergrass, Thompson	1815	Chapel Hill, Orange Co.	Farmer	Discharged (reason not reported), 7/19/62.
Pvt.	Pendergrass, William	1836	Chapel Hill, Orange Co.	Farm labor	Killed, 7/1/63 at Gettysburg.
Pvt.	Petty, Henry	1843	Mud Lick, Chatham Co.	Farm labor	Captured, 10/14/63 at Bristoe Station. Captured, 4/2/65 at Petersburg.
Pvt.	**Petty, John W.**	**1835**	**Mud Lick, Chatham Co.**	**Farm labor**	**Died of disease (meningitis), 11/29/63 in hospital in Richmond.**
Pvt.	Reeves, Edward	1828	Cypress Creek, Bladen Co.	Farm labor	Captured, 7/14/63 at Falling Waters, MD. Died of disease (chronic diarrhea), 9/24/64 as POW at Elmira, NY.
Pvt.	Sartain, Zera	1840	Orange Co.	Farm labor	Discharged (reason not reported), 5/9/62 at Camp Mangum, Raleigh.
Pvt.	Smith, Carney	1844	Belvoir, Chatham Co.	Day laborer	Cpl.—3/65. Captured, 4/2/65 at Petersburg.
Pvt.	Sparrow, George W.	1842	East Chatham Co.	Farm labor	Deserted, 3/14/65.
Pvt.	Sparrow, Houston	1840	Chapel Hill, Orange Co.	Farm labor	Deserted, 3/3/65.

Rank	Name	DOB	Residence	Occupation	Remarks
Pvt.	Sparrow, Van B.	1835	Chapel Hill, Orange Co.	Carpenter	Wounded, 7/1/63 at Gettysburg. Captured, 10/14/63 at Bristoe Station. Missing, 3/1/65.
Pvt.	Sparrow, William T.	1835	Chapel Hill, Orange Co.	Farm labor	Captured, 7/14/63 at Falling Waters, MD. Deserted, 3/14/65.
Pvt.	**Strain, James A.**	**1840**	**Chapel Hill, Orange Co.**	**Farm labor**	**Captured, 10/27/64 at Burgess' Mill. Died of disease (chronic diarrhea), 3/29/65 as POW at Point Lookout, MD.**
Pvt.	Suit, Brantley	1840	Chapel Hill, Orange Co.	Farm labor	Wounded, 7/1/63 at Gettysburg. Deserted, 2/1/65.
Pvt.	Thompson, James J.	1837	Rock Springs, Orange Co.	Farm labor	Missing, 3/1/65.
Pvt.	Thrift, Pinkney "Peter"	1834	Gulf, Chatham Co.	Farm labor	Captured, 10/27/64 at Burgess' Mill.
Pvt.	Thrift, William	1840	Goldston, Chatham Co.	Farm labor	Captured, 7/3/63 at Gettysburg.
Pvt.	Tilly, William A.	1831	Orange Co.	Farmer	Sgt.—8/63. Wounded (right leg), 11/27/63 at Mine Run. Retired to invalid corps, 9/17/64.
Pvt.	Tripp, Jerry	1842	Pittsboro, Chatham Co.	Farm labor	Wounded (breast & left shoulder), 7/1/63 at Gettysburg. Deserted, 3/14/65.
Pvt.	Vann, Lemuel D.	1842	Chapel Hill, Orange Co.	Farm labor	Deserted, 7/21/63. Deserted, 3/3/65.
Pvt.	**Whitaker, Thomas J.**	**1844**	**Chapel Hill, Orange Co.**	**Farm labor**	**Captured, 7/14/63 at Falling Waters, MD. Wounded, 8/25/64 at Reams' Station. Died of disease (diarrhea), 10/10/64 in hospital in Richmond.**
Pvt.	**Williams, Forrest**	**1840**	**Chatham Co.**	**Farm labor**	**Died of disease, 10/14/64, at home.**
Pvt.	Williams, James W.	1839	White Cross, Orange Co.	Farm labor	Regt. Ord. Sgt.—5/1/62. Transferred to F & S.
Pvt.	Williams, Norris	1842	Chatham Co.	Farm labor	Captured, 4/2/65 at Petersburg.
Pvt.	Williams, Samuel	1844	Chatham Co.	Farm labor	Wounded, 7/1/63 at Gettysburg. Retired to Invalid Corps, 8/16/64.

1862 Recruits

Rank	Name	DOB	Residence	Occupation	Remarks
Pvt.	Couch, William H.	1834	Chapel Hill, Orange Co.	Cabinet maker	Enlisted, 7/15/62. Cpl.—6/64. Captured, 10/27/64 at Burgess' Mill. Died of disease (chronic diarrhea), 4/24/65 as POW at Point Lookout, MD.
Pvt.	Craig, John W.	—	Hillsboro, Orange Co.	Farm labor	Enlisted, 7/15/62. Died of disease, 2/20/65.
Pvt.	Ferrell, Luico	1839	Chapel Hill, Orange Co.	Carpenter	Enlisted, 7/15/62. Cpl.—10/11/64. Wounded, 10/27/64 at Burgess' Mill. Died of wounds, 11/27/64.
Pvt.	Fowler, Washington "Wash"	1835	Chapel Hill, Orange Co.	Teamster	Enlisted, 9/6/62. Surrendered, 4/9/65 at Appomattox Court House.
Pvt.	**Gattis, James K.**	**1810**	**Chapel Hill, Orange Co.**	**Carpenter**	**Enlisted, 5/3/62. Died of disease, 2/8/64 in Chapel Hill.**
Pvt.	King, Bellfield	1845	Gulf, Chatham Co.	Farm labor	Enlisted, 5/3/62. Captured, 4/2/65 at Petersburg.

Rank	Name	DOB	Residence	Occupation	Remarks
Pvt.	King, Whitfield	1845	Gulf, Chatham Co.	Farm labor	Enlisted, 5/3/62. Died of disease (measles), 6/10/62 at Camp Davis, near Wilmington, NC.
Pvt.	Lewter (Luter), Charles M.	1842	Chapel Hill, Orange Co.	Farm labor	Enlisted, 7/15/62. Cpl.—10/11/64. Captured, 10/27/64 at Burgess' Mill.
Pvt.	Lloyd, William	—	Orange Co.	—	Enlisted, 7/15/62. Captured, 10/27/64 at Burgess' Mill.
Pvt.	Neville, John	1830	Chapel Hill, Orange Co.	Farmer	Enlisted, 8/29/62 at Camp Davis. Captured, 10/27/64 at Burgess' Mill.
Pvt.	Pendergrass, George W.	1829	Chapel Hill, Orange Co.	Day laborer	Enlisted, 5/9/62. Discharged (chronic rheumatism), 9/27/63.
Pvt.	Pendergrass, James M.	1827	Rock Springs, Orange Co.	Farmer	Enlisted, 8/29/62. Died of disease (febris typhoides), 10/4/64 at hospital in Richmond.
Pvt.	Pendergrass, William H.	1842	Chapel Hill, Orange Co.	Farm labor	Enlisted, 12/20/62. Missing, 3/1/65.
Pvt.	Snipes, Jeter J.	1842	White Cross, Orange Co.	Farm labor	Enlisted, 5/3/62. Wounded (left lung), 7/3/63 and captured at Gettysburg. Died of wounds, 7/19/63 at Chester, PA.
Pvt.	Suggs, William M.	1820	Raleigh, Wake Co.	Carpenter	Enlisted, 9/10/62. Captured, 7/3/63 at Gettysburg. Cpl.—4/64. Sgt.—10/11/64. Deserted, 3/3/65.

1863 Recruits

Rank	Name	DOB	Residence	Occupation	Remarks
Pvt.	Allen, Ruffin	1826	Chapel Hill, Orange Co.	Farm labor	Enlisted, 2/1/63. Captured, 10/14/63 at Bristoe Station. Died of disease, 9/3/64 as POW at Point Lookout, MD.
Pvt.	Andrews, Wesley	1834	Chapel Hill, Orange Co.	Farmer	Enlisted, 2/1/63. Wounded, 7/3/63 and captured, 7/5/63 at Gettysburg. Died of wounds, 7/10/63.
Pvt.	Brockwell, A. John	1836	Chapel Hill, Orange Co.	Farm labor	Enlisted, 2/1/63. Captured, 4/2/65 at Petersburg.
Pvt.	Cheek, Thomas F.	1836	Durhamsville, Orange Co.	Tailor	Enlisted, 9/28/63. Captured, 10/27/64 at Burgess' Mill.
Pvt.	Cheek, Virgil C.	1845	Chapel Hill, Orange Co.	Farm labor	Enlisted, 1/1/63. Cpl.—10/11/64. Sgt.—3/65. Captured, 4/2/65 at Petersburg.
Pvt.	Davis, Duncan	1831	University Station, Orange Co.	Farmer	Enlisted, 12/15/63. Captured, 10/27/64 at Burgess' Mill.
Pvt.	Gattis, James B.	1832	Chapel Hill, Orange Co.	Boarding house keeper	Enlisted, 10/23/63. Captured, 4/2/65 at Petersburg.
Pvt.	Hunter, Anderson	1841	Chapel Hill, Orange Co.	Farm labor	Enlisted, 2/1/63. Captured, 4/2/64 at Petersburg.
Pvt.	King, William H.	1842	White Cross, Orange Co.	Farm labor	Enlisted, 2/1/63. Captured, 6/14/64 near Petersburg. Reported AWOL, 1/65.
Pvt.	King, Willis	1824	Gulf, Chatham Co.	Farmer	Enlisted, 12/1/63. Missing, 3/1/65.
Pvt.	Mangum, William C.	1839	Berea, Granville Co.	Farm labor	Enlisted, 8/28/63. Surrendered, 4/9/65 at Appomattox Court House.

Rank	Name	DOB	Residence	Occupation	Remarks
Pvt.	Pendergrass, Charles H.	1846	Chapel Hill, Orange Co.	Farm labor	Enlisted, 2/1/63. Wounded (right shoulder), 7/1/63 at Gettysburg. Captured, 10/27/64 at Burgess' Mill.
Pvt.	**Potts, John W.**	—	**Chapel Hill, Orange Co.**	**Farm labor**	**Enlisted, 9/28/63. Captured, 10/27/64 at Burgess' Mill. Died of disease (apoplexy), 2/23/65 in Richmond hospital.**
Pvt.	Riggsbee, Hawkins	1829	Chapel Hill, Orange Co.	Farm labor	Enlisted, 2/1/63. Captured, 4/2/65 at Petersburg.
Pvt.	Smith, John	1838	Orange Co.	—	Enlisted, 2/1/63. Wounded, 6/10/64 at Cold Harbor. Cpl.—11/1/64. Sgt.—3/65. Captured, 4/2/65 at Petersburg.
Pvt.	Strain, Thomas	1837	Chapel Hill, Orange Co.	Teamster	Enlisted, 3/1/63. Wounded (left shoulder), 7/1/63 at Gettysburg. Captured, 10/27/64 at Burgess' Mill.
Pvt.	Tenney, William C.	1842	Chapel Hill, Orange Co.	Carpenter's Asst.	Enlisted, 2/1/63. Captured, 7/5/63 at Gettysburg, Carlisle, PA.
Pvt.	**Turner, Richard**	**1835**	**Orange Co.**	—	**Enlisted, 2/1/63. Died of disease, 5/20/63 in hospital in Richmond.**
Pvt.	Waddell, Duncan C.	1845	Durhamsville, Orange Co.	Student	Enlisted, 2/15/63. Wounded, 7/3/63 and captured, 7/5/63 at Gettysburg. Appointed 1st Lt. 7/30/63 "for gallant conduct on the field at Gettysburg." Wounded (right lung), 8/25/64 at Reams' Station.
Pvt.	Walters, George F.	1845	Orange Co.	Farm labor	Enlisted, 4/25/63. Missing, 3/1/65.

1864 Recruits

Rank	Name	DOB	Residence	Occupation	Remarks
Pvt.	Andrews, George	1831	Franklinton, Franklin Co.	Tenant farmer	Enlisted, 11/64. Missing, 3/1/65.
Pvt.	Averett, David T.	1818	Prospect Hill, Bladen Co.	Teacher	Transferred, 12/64 from Co. B, 1st Regt. NC Cav. Captured, 4/2/65 at Petersburg.
Pvt.	Barts, Allen	1844	Yanceyville, Caswell Co.	Mechanic's Asst.	Enlisted, 8/18/64. Accounted for through 4/10/65.
Pvt.	Bennett, Harold M.	1838	Crosses, Chatham Co.	Farm labor	Enlisted, 8/15/64. Missing, 3/1/65.
Pvt.	Blackwood, Edmond	1845	Chapel Hill, Orange Co.	Farm labor	Enlisted, 4/10/64 at Camp Hill. Wounded, 5/10/64 at Spotsylvania. Deserted, 3/3/65.
Pvt.	Booker, James C.	1841	Morrisville, Wake Co.	Farm labor	Enlisted, 8/15/64. Missing, 3/1/65.
Pvt.	Boon, James H.	1829	Chapel Hill, Orange Co.	Sawyer	Enlisted, 9/28/64. Captured, 4/2/65 at Petersburg.
Pvt.	Canady, Ruffin	1835	Chapel Hill, Orange Co.	Farm labor	Enlisted, 7/17/64. Missing, 3/1/65.
Pvt.	Cates, Thomas	1840	Orange Co.	Day laborer	Enlisted, 10/19/64. Deserted, 3/20/65.
Pvt.	Clements, George R.	1831	Plymouth, Washington Co.	Clerk	Enlisted, 3/20/64. Deserted, 3/20/65.
Pvt.	Crumpler, H. C.	1848	Honeycutt, Sampson Co.	Farm labor	Enlisted, 8/11/64. Transferred, 12/6/64 to Barringer's Cav.
Pvt.	Gattis, John T.	1844	Chapel Hill, Orange Co.	Farm labor	Enlisted, 4/11/64. Wounded, 2/9/65 at Hatcher's Run.

Rank	Name	DOB	Residence	Occupation	Remarks
Pvt.	Graves, C. J.	—	Wake Co.	—	Enlisted, 12/64? Deserted, 3/14/65.
Pvt.	Holloway, William H.	1834	Green Hills, Northampton Co.	Farmer	Enlisted, 8/13/64. Transferred, 2/1/65 to Co. E, 47th Regt. NC Inf.
Pvt.	King, James	1846	Morrisville, Wake Co.	Farm labor	Enlisted, 10/26/64. Captured, 4/2/65 at Petersburg.
Pvt.	King, William D.	1830	Raleigh, Wake Co.	Farm labor	Enlisted, 8/15/64. Captured, 4/2/65 at Petersburg.
Pvt.	Mann, Caswell S.	1842	Morrisville, Wake Co.	Farm labor	Transferred, 12/64 from Co. E, 5th Regt. NC Cav. Captured, 4/3/65 in Richmond hospital.
Pvt.	Merritt, James Y.	1845	Chapel Hill, Orange Co.	Farm labor	Enlisted, 4/2/64. Deserted, 3/14/65.
Pvt.	Nutt, Erasmus D.	1821	Chapel Hill, Orange Co.	Millwright	Enlisted, 10/19/64 at Wake Co. Deserted, 3/3/65.
Pvt.	Rodgers, William H.	1846	Chapel Hill, Orange Co.	Student	Enlisted, 8/18/64. Captured, 10/27/64 at Burgess' Mill.
Pvt.	Rollins, Thomas B.	1836	Morrisville, Wake Co.	Farm labor	Transferred, 8/13/64 from Co. G, 5th Regt. NC Cav. Transferred, 12/6/64 to Barringer's Cav.
Pvt.	Seagraves, Charles J.	—	—	—	Transferred, 12/64 from Co. E, 5th Regt. NC Cav. Captured, 4/3/65 in Richmond hospital.
Pvt.	Sledge, William P.	1813	Hillardston, Nash Co.	Farmer	Transferred, 12/64 from Co. G, 3rd Regt. NC Cav. Captured, 4/2/65 at Petersburg.
Pvt.	Sparrow, Helory	1831	Chapel Hill, Orange Co.	Carpenter	Enlisted, 10/19/64. Wounded (hip), 2/5/65 at Hatcher's Run. Deserted, 3/14/65.
Pvt.	Sparrow, Hutson	1826	Chapel Hill, Orange Co.	Farmer	Enlisted, 10/19/64. Wounded, 2/5/65 at Hatcher's Run.
Pvt.	Stephens, T. Gaston	1838	Morrisville, Wake Co.	Farm labor	Enlisted, 9/26/64 at Wake Co. Transferred, 12/6/64 to Co. I, 3rd Regt. NC Cav.
Pvt.	Tilly, John M.	—	Orange Co.	—	Enlisted, 8/15/64. Missing, 2/65.
Pvt.	Tripp, William	1844	Pittsboro, Chatham Co.	Farm labor	Enlisted, 10/28/64 in Wake Co. Captured, 4/2/65 at Petersburg.
Pvt.	Weathers, Richard	1843	Cape Fear, Chatham Co.	Farm labor	Enlisted, 9/26/64 in Wake Co. Transferred, 12/6/64 to Barringer's Cav.
Pvt.	Williams, Johnson	—	Chatham Co.	—	Enlisted, 10/28/64 in Wake Co. Captured, 4/2/65 at Petersburg.

1865 Recruits

Rank	Name	DOB	Residence	Occupation	Remarks
Pvt.	Mann, Williams S.	1840	Morrisville, Wake Co.	Farm labor	Transferred, 2/16/65 from Co. E, 5th Regt. NC Cav. Deserted, 3/14/65.
Pvt.	Walters, Sidney	—	Orange Co.	—	Enlisted, 2/22/65. Captured, 4/2/65 at Petersburg.

Company H
Mecklenburg County

Rank	Name	DOB	Residence	Occupation	Remarks
Cpt.	Grier, William L.	1836	W. Charlotte, Mecklenburg Co.	Deputy sheriff	Missing, 3/1/65.

Rank	Name	DOB	Residence	Occupation	Remarks
1st Lt.	Lowrie, Patrick J.	1832	Charlotte, Mecklenburg Co.	Farm labor	Cpt.—Transferred, 7/11/62, Assistant Quartermaster, Regt. F & S. Died of disease, 7/12/62 at Wilmington, NC.
2nd Lt.	Boyce, Charles B.	1837	Charlotte, Mecklenburg Co.	—	Died of typhoid fever, 8/9/62 "in Mecklenburg Co."
2nd Lt.	Lowrie, James B.	1838	Charlotte, Mecklenburg Co.	Farm labor	Assigned to Regt. as Commissary Sgt., 5/8/62. Returned to Co. H, 8/16/62. 1st Lt.—10/9/62. Killed, 7/1/63 at Gettysburg.
1st Sgt.	Saville, James M.	1840	W. Charlotte, Mecklenburg Co.	Farm labor	2nd Lt.—5/26/62. Wounded, 7/3/63 at Gettysburg. Wounded (left shoulder), 9/30/64 at Jones' Farm. Captured, 3/25/65 at Hatcher's Run.
Sgt.	Caldwell, J. Smiley	1835	W. Charlotte, Mecklenburg Co.	Teacher	Captured, 7/14/63 at Falling Waters, MD. Captured, 4/2/65 at Petersburg.
Sgt.	Clark, Patrick M.	1828	W. Charlotte, Mecklenburg Co.	Farmer	Wounded, 12/16/62 at White Hall, NC. Wounded, 7/1/63 at Gettysburg. Pvt.—11/64. Captured, 4/2/65 at Petersburg.
Sgt.	Knox, John H.	1839	W. Charlotte, Mecklenburg Co.	Farm labor	2nd Lt.—8/16/62. Wounded (left wrist), 7/1/63 at Gettysburg. Wounded, 5/5/64 at the Wilderness. Died of wounds, 5/29/64 in hospital at Staunton, VA.
Sgt.	Saville, Robert D.	1838	W. Charlotte, Mecklenburg Co.	Farm labor	Wounded, 7/1/63 at Gettysburg. Discharged (wounds), 12/15/63.
Cpl.	Bell, E. Charles	1829	E. Charlotte, Mecklenburg Co.	Farmer	Mustered in, 3/14/62. No further records.
Pvt.	Abernathy, Ezekial	1822	Charlotte, Mecklenburg Co.	Farmer	Died of disease, 6/26/63, "at home in Mecklenburg Co."
Pvt.	Ashley, Lee T.	1834	Mecklenburg Co.	—	Died of disease, 11/15/62 at Mecklenburg Co.
Pvt.	Ashley, William	1843	Mecklenburg Co.	Farm labor	Captured, 10/27/64 at Burgess' Mill.
Pvt.	Biggart, James	1803	E. Charlotte, Mecklenburg Co.	Stone mason	Absent on TDY most of time. Paroled, 5/65 in Charlotte.
Pvt.	Black, John B.	1828	E. Charlotte, Mecklenburg Co.	Farmer	Discharged, 8/4/62.
Pvt.	Blair, Stephen W.	1844	New Market, Randolph Co.	Farm labor	Surrendered, 4/9/65 at Appomattox Court House.
Pvt.	Boyce, Hugh	1832	E. Charlotte, Mecklenburg Co.	Farmer	Enlisted, 3/14/62. Discharged, 4/62.
Pvt.	Brown, James W.	1838	W. Charlotte, Mecklenburg Co.	Carpenter	Cpl.—5/1/62. Pvt.—9/1/62. Transferred, 9/4/64 to Co. B, 3rd Regt. NC Inf.

Rank	Name	DOB	Residence	Occupation	Remarks
Pvt.	Bryant, Sidney A.	1835	Paw Creek, Mecklenburg Co.	Farm labor	Captured, 10/27/64 at Burgess' Mill.
Pvt.	Burns, Robert	1841	Ft. Mill, York Co. SC	Farm labor	Transferred, 8/8/64 to Co. E, 17th SC Inf.
Pvt.	**Campbell, Thomas J.**	**1841**	**E. Charlotte, Mecklenburg Co.**	**Farm labor**	**Killed, 7/1/63 at Gettysburg.**
Pvt.	Carothers, James A.	1828	W. Charlotte, Mecklenburg Co.	Farmer	Wounded, 5/10/64 at Spotsylvania Court House. Captured, 4/2/65 at Petersburg.
Pvt.	**Clark, William A.**	**1843**	**W. Charlotte, Mecklenburg Co.**	**Farm labor**	**Died of disease, 10/20/62 in Charlotte.**
Pvt.	Cobb, Charles E.	1845	Mecklenburg Co.	Farm labor	Discharged (reason not reported), 10/30/62.
Pvt.	Coffey, Benjamin M.	1843	W. Charlotte, Mecklenburg Co.	Farm labor	Wounded (left leg amputated & blinded in right eye), 7/1/63 at Gettysburg. Captured, 7/30/63 at Winchester, VA.
Pvt.	Cooper, James M.	1829	W. Charlotte, Mecklenburg Co.	Farmer	Captured, 7/14/63 at Falling Waters, MD.
Pvt.	Deggerhart, L. D.	—	Mecklenburg Co.	—	Discharged (disability) 5/1/62.
Pvt.	Dixon, Hugh M.	1839	E. Charlotte, Mecklenburg Co.	Farmer	Died of disease, 1/6/63, "at home."
Pvt.	Drewey, Andres G.	1836	Mecklenburg Co.	—	Missing, 1/4/65.
Pvt.	**Etters, James H.**	**1815**	**W. Charlotte, Mecklenburg Co.**	**Day labor**	**Died of disease, 7/15/63, "at home."**
Pvt.	**Greer, Z. B.**	**1843**	**Mecklenburg Co.**	**—**	**Died of disease (typhoid fever), 9/1/62 at Wilmington.**
Pvt.	Harmon, Levi	1840	W. Charlotte, Mecklenburg Co.	Tailor	Captured, 10/27/64 at Burgess' Mill.
Pvt.	Harris, Francis C.	1838	Fort Mill, York Co. SC	Farmer	1st Sgt.—6/2/62. Wounded (left arm amputated), 7/3/63 and Captured, 7/5/63 at Gettysburg. Discharged because of wounds, 3/14/64.
Pvt.	Harris, James H	1826	Oakway, Pickens Co. SC	Farmer	Discharged, 1/8/65.
Pvt.	Harris, John C.	1829	Fort Mill, York Co. SC	Farmer	Cpl.—12/1/62. Pvt.—4/30/63. Transferred, 8/8/64 to Co. E, 17th SC Inf.
Pvt.	Harris, Robert H.	1835	Fort Mill, York Co. SC	Farmer	Discharged, 5/62.
Pvt.	Hayes, Jesse B.	1834	E. Charlotte, Mecklenburg Co.	Farm labor	Captured, 10/27/64 at Burgess' Mill.

Rank	Name	DOB	Residence	Occupation	Remarks
Pvt.	Hotchkiss, Seth A.	1842	Kingston, Lenoir Co.	Book keeper	Sgt.—8/15/62. Pvt.—3/28/63. Captured, 7/5/63 at Gettysburg.
Pvt.	Humphreys, Joseph L.	1826	—	—	Wounded, 8/25/64 at Reams' Station. Surrendered, 4/9/65 at Appomattox Court House.
Pvt.	Ingle, Peter	1824	Mountain Island, Gaston Co.	Factory labor	Wounded, 7/1/63 at Gettysburg. Captured, 10/27/64 at Burgess' Mill.
Pvt.	Kerr, David Rufus	1844	W. Charlotte, Mecklenburg Co.	Farm labor	Died of typhoid fever, 7/12/62 at Wilmington, NC.
Pvt.	Key, Abel	1825	Rock Cut, Iredell Co.	Farmer	Wounded, 7/1/63 at Gettysburg. Died of disease (unreported), 12/15/64.
Pvt.	Knox, William H.	1840	W. Charlotte, Mecklenburg Co.	Farm labor	Captured, 7/14/63 at Falling Waters, MD. Wounded, 9/30/64 at Jones Farm. Captured, 3/25/65 in Petersburg trenches.
Pvt.	Madden, James P.	1838	Mecklenburg Co.	—	Died of disease (chronic diarrhea), 1/20/64 at Charlottesville, VA.
Pvt.	McMillan, James E.	1825	Lumberton, Robeson Co.	Farmer	Cpl.—8/1/62. Sgt.—12/15/63. Wounded, 5/5/64 at the Wilderness. Died of wounds, 6/25/64 in hospital at Lynchburg.
Pvt.	Mincey, Wiley	1842	Mecklenburg Co.	—	Captured, 7/14/63 at Falling Waters, MD. Captured, 4/2/65 at Petersburg.
Pvt.	Neely, John W	1843	W. Charlotte, Mecklenburg Co.	Farm labor	Cpl.—8/8/64. Sgt.—12/64. Captured, 4/2/65 at Petersburg.
Pvt.	Newman, Elias	1837	Whiteville, Columbus Co.	Carpenter	Captured, 4/2/65 at Petersburg.
Pvt.	Russell, John C.	1842	W. Charlotte, Mecklenburg Co.	Farm labor	Captured, 7/3/63 at Greencastle, PA.
Pvt.	Sloop, Alexander	1815	Miranda, Iredell Co.	Farmer	Captured, 7/5/63 at Gettysburg, PA.
Pvt.	Smith, Albert J.	1841	W. Charlotte, Mecklenburg Co.	Farm labor	Discharged ("valvular disease of the heart"), 8/28/63.
Pvt.	Smith, James W.	1838	W. Charlotte, Mecklenburg Co.	Day labor	Missing in action, 10/14/63 at Bristoe Station. Wounded, 5/5/64 at the Wilderness. Captured, 10/27/64 at Burgess' Mill.
Pvt.	Smith, John T.	1838	Boydton, York Co. SC	Farmer	Cpl.—4/30/63. Sgt.—4/2/64. Surrendered, 4/9/65 at Appomattox Court House.
Pvt.	Smith, Thomas J.	1843	Coates Tavern, York Co. SC	Farm labor	Captured, 7/14/63 at Falling Waters, MD. Died of disease, 12/64 (?) as POW at Point Lookout, MD.
Pvt.	Thrower, Alex	1844	E. Charlotte, Mecklenburg Co.	Farm labor	Cpl.—4/30/63. Wounded, 5/5/64 at the Wilderness. Wounded, 8/21/64 at Weldon Rd.
Pvt.	Wilkerson, William H.	1842	Mecklenburg Co.	Farm labor	Wounded (head), 6/1/64 at Cold Harbor.
Pvt.	Wingate, R. James	1843	W. Charlotte, Mecklenburg Co.	Farm labor	Wounded (thigh), 5/5/64 at the Wilderness. "In arrest," 1/65.

Rank	Name	DOB	Residence	Occupation	Remarks
Pvt.	Young, James H.	1843	Mecklenburg Co.	—	Died of disease, 11/21/62 in Richmond hospital.

1862 Recruits

Rank	Name	DOB	Residence	Occupation	Remarks
Pvt.	Blankenship, J. N.	1837	Cane Creek, Rutherford Co.	Farmer	Enlisted, 5/1/62. Discharged, 6/15/62 at Camp David.
Pvt.	Blankenship, Stephen P.	1835	W. Charlotte, Mecklenburg Co.	Farmer	Cpl.—8/62. Sgt.—4/30/63. 1st Sgt.—4/2/64. Captured, 10/27/64 at Burgess' Mill.
Pvt.	Campbell, John C.	1836	Crains Creek, Moore Co.	Farm labor	Cpl.—8/5/62. Transferred to Co. E, 17th NC Inf. 8/8/64.
Pvt.	Christenbery, Caleb E.	1831	Mallard Creek, Mecklenburg Co.	Farmer	Enlisted, 5/1/62. Died of disease (pleuritis), 5/10/63 at Goldsboro, NC.
Pvt.	Cromwell, Elias M.	1821	Tarboro, Edgecombe Co.	Farmer	Enlisted, 6/1/62. Musician—8/64. Transferred to Regt. Band, 11/1/64.
Pvt.	Elms, James A.	1831	W. Charlotte, Mecklenburg Co.	Farmer	Enlisted, 6/20/62. Died of disease, 6/20/62, at Camp Davis at Wilmington, NC.
Pvt.	Greer, Edward	1845	Mecklenburg Co.	—	Enlisted, 5/1/62. Discharged, 11/62.
Pvt.	Hamel, Alexander R.	1829	W. Charlotte, Mecklenburg Co.	Tailor	Enlisted, 10/27/62 at Mecklenburg Co. Wounded and Captured, 7/3/63 at Gettysburg. Died of wounds, 8/28/63 as POW at David's Island, NY.
Pvt.	Hanna, John N.	1834	W. Charlotte, Mecklenburg Co.	Blacksmith	Enlisted, 5/1/62 at Mecklenburg Co. Cpl.—4/1/64. Sgt.—9/30/64. Captured, 10/27/64 at Burgess' Mill.
Pvt.	Harget, Aley "Alex"	1832	W. Charlotte, Mecklenburg Co.	Farmer	Enlisted, 5/1/62 at Mecklenburg Co. Died of disease, 2/10/64, at home.
Pvt.	Herron, John W.	1845	W. Charlotte, Mecklenburg Co.	Day labor	Enlisted, 5/1/62. Discharged, 8/4/62.
Pvt.	Hill, Cornelius H.	1840	Raleigh, Wake Co.	Student	Enlisted, 5/1/62. Cpl.—5/1/62. Discharged, 10/18/62.
Pvt.	Hoover, Samuel L.	1832	W. Charlotte, Mecklenburg Co.	Farmer	Enlisted, 5/1/62. Captured, 10/27/64 at Burgess' Mill.
Pvt.	Humphreys, Thomas L.	1832	Mecklenburg Co.	—	Enlisted, 5/1/62. Cpl.—3/1/65. Captured, 4/2/65 at Petersburg.
Pvt.	Lowrie, Robert B.	1832	Charlotte, Mecklenburg Co.	—	Transferred, 6/13/62 from Co. C, 10th Regt. NC Inf. 1st Lt.—7/30/63. Surrendered, 4/9/65 at Appomattox Court House.
Pvt.	McQuaige, James W.	1832	Mecklenburg Co.	—	Enlisted, 5/1/62. Captured, 10/27/64 at Burgess' Mill.
Pvt.	McQuaige, W. D.	—	Mecklenburg Co.	—	Enlisted, 5/1/62. Discharged, 1/63, "by Civil Authority."
Pvt.	Merritt, Samuel N.	1826	Chapel Hill, Orange Co.	Farmer	Enlisted, 5/1/62. Discharged, 8/12/62.

Rank	Name	DOB	Residence	Occupation	Remarks
Pvt.	Morrison, William T.	1837	W. Charlotte, Mecklenburg Co.	Day labor	Transferred, 11/1/62 from Co. F, 15th MS Inf. Captured, 7/3/63 at Gettysburg. Musician—transferred to Regt. Band, 10/64.
Pvt.	Reid, William M.	1832	W. Charlotte, Mecklenburg Co.	Day labor	Enlisted, 5/1/62 at Mecklenburg Co. Cpl.—8/8/64. Missing, 2/1/65.
Pvt.	**Ross, Robert A.**	**1821**	**W. Charlotte, Mecklenburg Co.**	**Farmer**	**Transferred from Co. A, 7/11/62. Died of disease (pneumonia), 1/24/63 at home.**
Pvt.	Thrower, Jeff T.	1842	E. Charlotte, Mecklenburg Co.	Farm labor	Enlisted, 5/1/62 at Mecklenburg Co. Wounded, 12/16/62 at White Hall, NC. Captured, 10/14/63 at Bristoe Station. Wounded, 9/30/64 at Jones' Farm.
Pvt.	Tredenick, Richard	1837	E. Charlotte, Mecklenburg Co.	Day labor	Enlisted, 5/1/62. AWOL, 7/62. No further records.

1863 Recruits

Rank	Name	DOB	Residence	Occupation	Remarks
Pvt.	**Alexander, John A.**	**1844**	**W. Charlotte, Mecklenburg Co.**	**Farm labor**	**Enlisted, 3/12/63 at Mecklenburg Co. Wounded, 5/5/64 at the Wilderness. Died of wounds, 6/2/64 at Staunton VA.**
Pvt.	Blankenship, Thomas G.	1816	Olin, Iredell Co.	Farmer	Enlisted, 10/1/63 at Camp Vance. Discharged, 9/22/64, "anasarca produced by cardiac obstruction and old unreduced dislocation of ankle."
Pvt.	**Carothers, John D.**	**1827**	**W. Charlotte, Mecklenburg Co.**	**Farmer**	**Enlisted, 4/4/63 at Mecklenburg Co. Died of disease, 8/2/63 at Mt. Jackson, VA.**
Pvt.	Deggerhart, Jacob L.	1844	Mecklenburg Co.	Farm labor	Enlisted, 11/21/63. Captured, 10/27/64 at Burgess' Mill, VA.
Pvt.	**Dollihite, W. H.**	**1828**	**Goldsboro, Wayne Co.**	**Farmer**	**Enlisted, 1/21/63. Died of disease (typhoid fever), 2/15/63, "at Goldsboro, NC."**
Pvt.	Hinnant, Henry	1839	Sandy Level, Johnston Co.	Farm labor	Enlisted, 7/23/63 at Camp Holmes. Wounded (right hand), 9/30/64 at Jones' Farm.
Pvt.	Johnson, John W.	1844	Montpelier, Richmond Co.	Farm labor	Enlisted, 12/15/63 at Camp Vance. Missing, 3/1/65.
Pvt.	Porter, Robert C.	1848	W. Charlotte, Mecklenburg Co.	Day laborer	Enlisted, 3/2/63. Wounded (right thigh), 7/1/63 and captured, 7/5/63 at Gettysburg. Deserted, 3/22/65.
Pvt.	Rice, John S.	1845	W. Charlotte, Mecklenburg Co.	Farm labor	Enlisted, 10/23/63 at Camp Vance. Missing, 3/1/65.
Pvt.	**Snider, Jeremiah A.**	**1832**	**Salem, Forsythe Co.**	**Farmer**	**Enlisted, 1/21/63. Killed, 7/3/63 at Gettysburg.**
Pvt.	Taggert, John C.	1820	W. Charlotte, Mecklenburg Co.	Carpenter	Enlisted, 10/1/63 at Camp Vance, NC. Wounded (right breast), 6/1/64 at Cold Harbor. Captured, 4/2/65 at Petersburg.
Pvt.	Watt, John Charles B.	1836	Fairfield, Fairfield Co. SC	Farmer	Transferred, 4/13/63 from Co. B, 4th Regt. SC Cav. Sgt.—3/65. Captured, 3/25/65 in Petersburg trenches.

1864 Recruits

Rank	Name	DOB	Residence	Occupation	Remarks
Pvt.	Andrews, E. M.	—	Mecklenburg Co.	—	Enlisted, 12/2/64 at Wake Co. NC. Surrendered, 4/9/65 at Appomattox Court House.
Pvt.	Ashley, William	1843	Mecklenburg Co.	Farm labor	Enlisted, 2/1/64 at Charlotte. Captured, 10/27/64 at Burgess' Mill.
Pvt.	Bailey, William	1827	W. Charlotte, Mecklenburg Co.	Farmer	Enlisted, 12/3/64 at Camp Stokes. Missing, 3/1/65.
Pvt.	Belk, William	1847	Mt. Ulla, Rowan Co.	Farm labor	Enlisted, 9/3/64 at Camp Holmes. Captured, 4/2/65 at Petersburg.
Pvt.	**Boyd, Jesse A.**	1842	W. Charlotte, Mecklenburg Co.	Farmer	**Transferred, 11/15/64 from Co. H, 18th SC Inf. Captured, 4/2/65 at Petersburg. Confined at Point Lookout, MD. Died of disease (pneumonia), 4/29/65.**
Pvt.	**Boyd, John J.**	1837	W. Charlotte, Mecklenburg Co.	Farmer	**12/64: First listed on rolls. Captured, 4/2/65 at Petersburg. Confined at Point Lookout, MD. Died of disease—"infection of lungs"), 4/29/65.**
Pvt.	Brower, Alfred M.	1821	Buffalo Ford, Randolph Co.	Farmer	Enlisted, 9/12/64 at Camp Holmes. Captured, 4/2/65 at Petersburg.
Pvt.	**Burns, Henry F.**	1847	Ft. Mill, York Co. SC	Farm labor	**Enlisted, 1/1/64. Died (disease—cause not reported), 5/16/64 at Lynchburg, VA.**
Pvt.	**Carothers, James**	1830	W. Charlotte, Mecklenburg Co.	Farmer	**Enlisted, 4/20/64 at Wake Co. NC. Died of disease, 6/10/64 in Richmond.**
Pvt.	Carpenter, Joseph C.	1821	White Pine, Gaston Co.	Farmer	Enlisted, 9/17/64 at Camp Holmes. Captured, 3/25/65 in Petersburg trenches.
Pvt.	Carpenter, William B.	1821	White Pine, Gaston Co.	Farmer	Enlisted, 9/17/64 at Camp Holmes. Captured, 10/27/64 at Burgess' Mill, VA.
Pvt.	Carter, R. J.	—	Mecklenburg Co.	—	Enlisted, 9/21/64 at Camp Holmes. Transferred, 12/8/64 to Barringer's Cav.
Pvt.	Cobb, Calvin R.	1844	Mountain Creek, Catawba Co.	Farm labor	Enlisted, 4/20/64. Captured, 4/2/65 at Petersburg.
Pvt.	Coleman, H. G.	—	—	—	Enlisted, 9/21/64 at Camp Holmes. Transferred, 12/8/64 to Barringer's Cav.
Pvt.	Cox, Eli	1828	Dallas, Gaston Co.	Farmer	Enlisted, 11/3/64 at Camp Stokes. Captured, 4/2/65 at Petersburg.
Pvt.	Duckworth, John A.	1822	W. Charlotte, Mecklenburg Co.	Day labor	Enlisted, 4/2/64 at Wake Co. Captured, 4/2/65 at Petersburg.
Pvt.	Earnhart, George	1832	Rockville, Rowan Co.	Day labor	Enlisted, 9/3/64 at Camp Holmes, Raleigh, NC. Captured, 4/2/65 at Petersburg.
Pvt.	**Edwards, James M.**	1840	E. Charlotte, Mecklenburg Co.	Farm labor	**Enlisted, 4/26/64 at Wake Co. Captured, 10/27/64 at Burgess' Mill. . Died of disease (diarrhea and scurvy), 4/15/65 as POW at Point Lookout, MD.**
Pvt.	Ellis, Daniel	1832	Rockfish, Cumberland Co.	Farmer	Enlisted, 9/10/64 at Camp Holmes. Captured, 10/27/64 at Burgess' Mill.

Rank	Name	DOB	Residence	Occupation	Remarks
Pvt.	Finger, Henry F.	1846	Lincolnton, Lincoln Co.	Farm labor	Enlisted, 4/5/64 at Wake Co. Died of disease (typhoid fever), 6/24/64 in Richmond, VA.
Pvt.	Fite, William J.	1829	Woodlawn, Gaston Co.	Miller	Enlisted, 11/3/64 at Camp Holmes. Captured, 4/2/65 at Petersburg.
Pvt.	Hall, N. C.	—	Roger's Store, Wake Co.	—	Enlisted, 4/20/64 at Wake Co. NC. Wounded, 6/2/64 at Cold Harbor.
Pvt.	Hall, Robert B.	1830	Roger's Store, Wake Co.	Farmer	Enlisted, 4/20/64 at Wake Co. Wounded (left hand), 6/2/24 at Cold Harbor. Deserted, 2/6/65.
Pvt.	Henderson, Wright	1824	Piney Green, Onslow Co.	Farmer	Transferred, 11/64 from Co. B, 3rd Regt. NC Cav. Deserted, 3/6/65.
Pvt.	Henry, Berry G.	1842	W. Charlotte, Mecklenburg Co.	Farm labor	Enlisted, 4/20/64 at Wake Co. Wounded (forearm), 6/2/64 at Cold Harbor. Retired due to wounds, 2/17/65.
Pvt.	Henry, Tyrell B.	1840	W. Charlotte, Mecklenburg Co.	Farm labor	Enlisted, 4/20/64 at Wake Co. Wounded, 6/2/64 at Cold Harbor. Wounded, 10/27/64 at Burgess' Mill. Captured, 4/3/65 in hospital in Richmond. "Escaped from hospital," 5/6/65.
Pvt.	Hoffman, Miles	1825	Dallas, Gaston Co.	Farmer	Enlisted, 9/10/64 at Camp Holmes. Captured, 4/2/65 at Petersburg.
Pvt.	Holland, Robert	1842	Dallas, Gaston Co.	Farm labor	Enlisted, 9/8/64 at Camp Holmes. Surrendered, 4/9/65 at Appomattox Court House.
Pvt.	Hovis, Moses	1842	Dallas, Gaston Co.	Farm labor	Enlisted, 4/5/64 in Wake Co. Captured, 4/2/65 at Petersburg.
Pvt.	Hudspeth, George	—	Liberty, Lincoln Co.	—	Enlisted, 5/4/64 at Wake Co. Wounded, 5/5/64 in the Wilderness. Captured, 4/2/65 at Petersburg.
Pvt.	Humphreys, David	1846	Mecklenburg Co.	Farm labor	Enlisted, 4/20/64 at Wake Co. Discharged (chronic rheumatism), 7/16/64.
Pvt.	Keener, Peter	1823	Lincolnton, Lincoln Co.	Farmer	Enlisted, 9/17/64 at Camp Holmes, Raleigh NC. Surrendered, 4/9/65 at Appomattox Court House.
Cpl.	Kilpatrick, William F.	1830	Johnston Mill, Pitt Co. NC	Carpenter	Transferred, 12/5/64 from Co. I, 1st Regt. NC Cav. Captured, 4/2/65 at Petersburg.
Pvt.	Marshall, James M.	1841	W. Charlotte, Mecklenburg Co.	—	Transferred, 11/30/64 from Co. B, 3rd Regt. NC Cav. Wounded (left leg amputated), 2/5/65 at Hatcher's Run.
Pvt.	Marshall, John	1825	W. Charlotte, Mecklenburg Co.	Farm labor	Transferred, 11/64 from Co. B, 3rd Regt. NC Cav. Deserted, 12/16/64.
Music	McConnell, James H.	1832	W. Charlotte, Mecklenburg Co.	Farmer	Transferred, 9/4/64 from Co. B, 3rd Regt. NC Inf. in exchange for Pvt. William Brown. Transferred to Regt. Band, 10/64.
Pvt.	Page, John D.	1846	W. Charlotte, Mecklenburg Co.	Farm labor	Enlisted, 9/8/64 at Camp Holmes. Transferred, 12/8/64 to Co. H, Barringer's Cav.
Pvt.	Parks, Thomas B.	1820	Mecklenburg Co.	Farmer	Enlisted, 9/8/64 at Camp Holmes. Transferred, 12/8/64 to Co. I, 2nd Regt. NC Cav.

Rank	Name	DOB	Residence	Occupation	Remarks
Pvt.	Pepper, John	1838	Danbury, Stokes Co.	Farm labor	Enlisted, 9/8/64. Wounded, 2/5/65 at Hatcher's Run.
Pvt.	**Price, J. A.**	**1845**	**Wittenberg, Alexander Co.**	**Farm labor**	**Enlisted, 9/8/64 at Camp Holmes. Died of disease, 2/20/64 in Richmond.**
Pvt.	Rhine, Arthur M.	1846	Hickory Tavern, Catawba Co.	Farm labor	Enlisted, 9/17/64 at Camp Holmes. Captured, 4/2/65 at Petersburg.
Pvt.	Rochelle, Thomas B.	—	So. Washington, New Hanover Co.	Farm labor	Transferred, 11/64 from Co. B, 3rd Regt. NC Cav. Captured, 4/2/65 at Petersburg.
Pvt.	Sanders, Jacob	1846	Jackson, Union Co.	Farm labor	Enlisted, 9/3/64 at Camp Holmes. Surrendered, 4/9/65 at Appomattox Court House.
Pvt.	**Scott, Rayford S.**	**1838**	**Catherine Lake, Onslow Co.**	**Farmer**	**Transferred, 11/64 from Co. B, 3rd Regt. NC Cav. Captured, 3/29/65 at Hatcher's Run. Died of disease ("erysipelas"), 5/23/65 as POW at Point Lookout, MD.**
Pvt.	Snead, Franklin	1845	Murphy, Cherokee Co.	Farm labor	Enlisted, 4/5/64 at Wake Co. Captured, 4/2/65 at Petersburg.
Pvt.	Spain, H. P.	1838	Kinston, Lenoir Co.	Mason	Enlisted, 2/10/64. Transferred to Company D, 4/2/64.
Pvt.	Squires, John A.	1846	E. Charlotte, Mecklenburg Co.	Farm labor	Enlisted, 9/3/64 at Camp Holmes. Captured, 10/27/64 at Burgess' Mill.
Pvt.	Stanford, James L.	1842	W. Charlotte, Mecklenburg Co.	Farm labor	Enlisted, 2/1/64. Wounded, 5/5/64 at the Wilderness. Captured, 4/2/65 at Petersburg.
Pvt.	Summeron, George	1818	Lincoln Co.	—	Enlisted, 9/17/64 at Camp Holmes. Wounded (left leg) and captured, 10/27/64 at Burgess' Mill.
Pvt.	Summy, John B.	1825	Hendersonville, Henderson Co.	Farmer	Enlisted, 9/17/64 at camp Holmes. Captured, 4/2/65 at Petersburg.
Pvt.	Turbefield, James	—	Newton, Catawba Co.	—	Enlisted, 11/3/64 at Camp Holmes. Deserted, 2/15/65.
Pvt.	Waller, Phoenix L.	1832	Pleasant Mtn., Pitt Co.	Overseer	Enlisted, 9/3/64 at Camp Holmes. Wounded, 10/27/64 at Burgess' Mill. Wounded, 2/28/65 in Petersburg trenches.
Pvt.	Warren, Thomas M.	1819	Raleigh, Wake Co.	Farmer	Enlisted, 9/10/64 at Camp Holmes. Captured, 10/27/64 at Burgess' Mill.
Pvt.	Waters, Allen "Alfred"	1835	Long Acre, Beaufort Co.	Farm labor	Transferred, 12/64 from Co. H, 3rd Regt. NC Cav. Missing, 3/1/65.
Pvt.	Wilkerson, James F.	—	—	—	Enlisted, 9/10/64 at Camp Holmes. Transferred, 12/8/64 to Barringer's Cav.
Pvt.	Wilkerson, John	—	Mecklenburg Co.	—	Enlisted, 5/1/64 in Mecklenburg Co. Deserted, 3/22/65.
Pvt.	Wilson, J. F.	—	—	—	Enlisted, 9/8/64 at Camp Holmes. Missing, 11/1/64.

1865 Recruits

Rank	Name	DOB	Residence	Occupation	Remarks
Pvt.	Boyd, David	1845	W. Charlotte, Mecklenburg Co.	Farm labor	1/65: First listed on rolls. Captured, 4/2/65 at Petersburg.

Rank	Name	DOB	Residence	Occupation	Remarks
Pvt.	Womble, J. M.	—	—	—	Enlisted, 9/10/64 at Camp Holmes. Deserted, 12/25/64.
Pvt.	Wooten, Bryant H.	1836	Holly Shelter, New Hanover Co.	Farmer	Transferred, 12/6/64 from Co. I, 1st Regt. NC Cav. Deserted, 12/18/64.

Company I
Lincoln and Gaston Counties

Rank	Name	DOB	Residence	Occupation	Remarks
Cpt.	Haynes, Albert S.	1838	Lincolnton, Lincoln Co.	Merchant	Wounded (chest & shoulder), 7/3/63 and captured, 7/5/63 at Gettysburg.
1st Lt.	Coon, David A.	1834	Lincolnton, Lincoln Co.	Music teacher	Wounded (right foot & both eyes), 7/3/63 and captured at Gettysburg.
2nd Lt.	Hoyle, Lemuel J.	1839	Bellwood, Cleveland Co.	Merchant	Wounded (3 times), 7/3/63 at Gettysburg. Missing, 3/1/65.
3rd Lt.	Ramseur, Oliver A.	1835	Cleveland Co.	Engineer	Wounded and captured, 7/3/63 at Gettysburg.
1st Sgt.	Bell, Robert M.	1824	Lincolnton, Lincoln Co.	Overseer	Wounded, 7/3/63 at Gettysburg. Wounded (chest), 8/21/64 at Petersburg. Died of wounds, 9/1/64 at hospital, Richmond.
Sgt.	Finger, Calvin D.	1835	Lincolnton, Lincoln Co.	Millwright	Missing, 3/1/65.
Sgt.	Haynes, Andrew R.	1839	Lincolnton, Lincoln Co.	—	Killed, 7/3/63 at Gettysburg.
Sgt.	Jetton, William H.	1840	Lincolnton, Lincoln Co.	Clerk in court	Killed, 7/3/63 at Gettysburg.
Sgt.	Ramseur, Walter G.	1835	Lincolnton, Lincoln Co.	Mechanic	Wounded (back), 10/14/63 at Bristoe Station. Died of wounds, 10/27/63 in hospital, Richmond. "Struck by a cannon ball."
Cpl.	Finger, Sidney M.	1838	Lincolnton, Lincoln Co.	Merchant	Qtr Mstr Sgt.—7/62 and transferred to regt. F & S.
Cpl.	Harrelson, James F.	1821	Craigeville, Gaston Co.	Farmer	Wounded, 5/10/64 at the Wilderness. Captured, 4/3/65 near Richmond, VA.
Cpl.	Hovis, Laban L.	1839	Spring Hill, Lincoln Co.	Farm labor	Wounded (jaw), 7/3/63 and captured at Gettysburg. Captured, 4/2/65 at Petersburg.
Pvt.	Abernathy, James A.	1844	Lincolnton, Lincoln Co.	Farm labor	Wounded (left hand), 7/1/63 at Gettysburg. Discharged (wounds), 12/15/63.
Pvt.	Abernathy, William A.	1834	Cottage Home, Lincoln Co.	Farm labor	Wounded and captured, 7/3/63 at Gettysburg. Died of disease, "at home," 1/2/65.
Pvt.	Allran, Jacob	1828	Mull Grove, Lincoln Co.	Day labor	Wounded, 7/1/63 at Gettysburg. Died of disease (pneumonia), 5/25/64 at Lynchburg, VA.
Pvt.	Allran, John P.	1834	Seagle's Store, Lincoln Co.	Potter	Died of disease, 7/2/62, at Wilmington, NC.
Pvt.	Ballard, Thomas J.	1839	Killian's Mill, Lincoln Co.	Farm labor	Died of disease, 12/26/62 in Goldsboro, NC.
Pvt.	Bell, Martin	1845	Dallas, Gaston Co.	Asst. Shoemaker	Transferred, 5/1/62 to Co. H, 49th Regt. NC Inf.

Rank	Name	DOB	Residence	Occupation	Remarks
Pvt.	Bisaner, Jacob H.	1844	Lincolnton, Lincoln Co.	Blacksmith Asst.	Wounded (left side), 7/3/63 and captured, 7/5/63 at Gettysburg. Sgt.—8/31/64. Captured, 4/3/65 at Petersburg.
Pvt.	Blackburn, A. Lafayette	1842	Rock Mill, Lincoln Co.	Farm labor	Wounded, 7/1/63 and captured at Gettysburg. Wounded, 9/30/64 at Jones' Farm, VA. Died of wounds, 10/30/64 in Richmond.
Pvt.	Bolick, B. Sidney	1842	Early Grove, Catawba Co.	Farm labor	Wounded and captured, 7/3/63 at Gettysburg. Died of disease, 10/30/63 as POW at Point Lookout, MD.
Pvt.	Boyles, Frank J.	1844	Lincolnton, Lincoln Co.	Farm labor	Died of disease (pneumonia), 1/10/63 at Raleigh, NC.
Pvt.	Boyles, William S.	1839	W. Charlotte, Mecklenburg Co.	Wagon maker	Deserted, 10/7/64.
Pvt.	Brown, John A.	1839	Craigeville, Gaston Co.	Railroad worker	Died of disease ("fever"), 8/20/62 at Wilmington, NC.
Pvt.	Carpenter, Albert	1844	Lincolnton, Lincoln Co.	Farm labor	Died of disease ("febris typhoides"), 7/17/62 in Wilmington, NC.
Pvt.	Carpenter, David	1841	Lincolnton, Lincoln Co.	Carpenter	Wounded, 7/1/63 and captured, 7/5/63 at Gettysburg. Died of disease, 3/19/64 as POW at Point Lookout, MD.
Pvt.	Carpenter, Henry S.	1839	Dallas, Gaston Co.	Farmer	Captured, 10/27/64 at Burgess' Mill.
Pvt.	Carpenter, Jacob J.	1838	Dallas, Gaston Co.	Farm labor	Wounded, 7/1/63 and captured at Gettysburg. Died of wounds, 7/21/63.
Pvt.	Carpenter, Joseph	1839	Dallas, Gaston Co.	Farm labor	Died of disease, 9/21/62 at Wilmington, NC.
Pvt.	Carpenter, Michael	1844	Seagles, Lincoln Co.	Farm labor	Wounded (leg), 10/23/63 at Bristoe Station. Captured, 3/25/64 near Petersburg.
Pvt.	Carpenter, William F.	1833	Seagles, Lincoln Co.	Carriage maker	Wounded, 7/1/63 and captured at Gettysburg. Captured, 10/27/64 at Burgess' Mill.
Pvt.	Cathey, Robert A.	1838	Lincoln Co.	Farm labor	Cpl.—5/1/62. Killed, 7/3/63 at Gettysburg.
Pvt.	Clark, James M.	1831	White Pine, Gaston Co.	Farmer	Captured, 7/5/63 at Greencastle, PA.
Pvt.	Cody, James	1843	Lincolnton, Lincoln Co.	Farm labor	Wounded, 5/5/64 at the Wilderness. Surrendered, 4/9/65 at Appomattox Court House.
Pvt.	Coon, Adolphus S.	1842	Lincolnton, Lincoln Co.	Farm labor	Music—9/62. Captured, 7/5/63 at Greencastle, PA. Transferred to regt. band, 3/65.
Pvt.	Cornwell, Sidney	1845	Lincolnton, Lincoln Co.	Asst. carriage maker	Wounded, 7/3/63 at Gettysburg. Killed, 10/1/64 at Jones' Farm.
Pvt.	Cox, Henry V.	1819	Seagles, Lincoln Co.	Farmer	Surrendered, 4/9/65 at Appomattox Court House.
Pvt.	Craft, Michael J.	1835	Craigeville, Gaston Co.	Farm labor	Wounded, 12/16/62 at White Hall, NC. Wounded (arm), 6/1/64 at Cold Harbor. Missing, 3/1/65.
Pvt.	Cryst, Henry J.	1832	Gaston Co.	—	Died, "at home," 9/23/63.

Rank	Name	DOB	Residence	Occupation	Remarks
Pvt.	Davis, Samuel	—	Lincoln Co.	—	Wounded, 7/1/63 at Gettysburg. Missing, 3/1/65.
Pvt.	Dellinger, Frederick Washington (Wash)	1844	Rock Mill, Lincoln Co.	Farm labor	Wounded, 7/1/63, and captured, 7/5/63 at Gettysburg, PA. Wounded (right breast), 5/5/64 at the Wilderness. Transferred, 2/1/65 to Co. E, 34th Regt. NC Inf.
Pvt.	Dellinger, John F.	1843	Rock Mill, Lincoln Co.	Farm labor	Killed, 12/16/62 at White Hall, NC.
Pvt.	Dellinger, Peter Frank	1843	Lincolnton, Lincoln Co.	Farm labor	Killed, 7/3/63 at Gettysburg. "Shot in stomach."
Pvt.	Dellinger, Phillip	1840	Rock Mill, Lincoln Co.	Farm labor	Wounded, 7/1/63 and captured, 7/5/63 at Gettysburg. Wounded (right leg amputated), 5/5/64 at the Wilderness. Retired to the Invalid Corps, 11/15/64.
Pvt.	Finger, Robert P.	1842	Lincolnton, Lincoln Co.	Farm labor	Killed, 7/3/63 at Gettysburg.
Pvt.	Gault, James	1845	Newton, Catawba Co.	Farm labor	Killed, 12/16/62 at White Hall, NC.
Pvt.	Gilbert, J. Frank	1829	Lincoln Co.	—	Died of disease (yellow fever), 10/23/62 at Wilmington, NC.
Pvt.	Glasscock, Spencer S.	1815	Craigeville, Gaston Co.	Overseer	Discharged, disabilities ("age & chronic rheumatism"), 10/23/62.
Pvt.	Glasscock, Stanhope A.	1839	Cleveland Co.	—	Wounded, 7/3/65 and captured, 7/5/63 at Gettysburg. Died of wounds in field hospital, 7/19/63 at Gettysburg.
Pvt.	Glenn, David M.	1846	Lincolnton, Lincoln Co.	Farm labor	Wounded, 7/1/63 at Gettysburg. Wounded, 5/5/64 at the Wilderness. Captured, 4/2/65 at Southerland Station.
Pvt.	Glenn, Robert J.	1843	Lincolnton, Lincoln Co.	Farm labor	Wounded, 8/25/64 at Reams' Station. Captured, 4/3/65 at Petersburg.
Pvt.	Hallman, Abel	1832	Lincolnton, Lincoln Co.	Farm labor	Captured, 4/2/65 at Petersburg.
Pvt.	Hallman, Andrew "Andy"	1830	Lincolnton, Lincoln Co.	House carpenter	Missing, 3/1/65.
Pvt.	Hallman, Michael	1839	Lincolnton, Lincoln Co.	Shoemaker	Discharged due to rheumatism, 1/27/63.
Pvt.	Harvey, Nelson	1818	Gaston Co.	—	Discharged (disability), 6/6/62.
Pvt.	Haun, Christian "Christy" S.	1844	Jacob's Fork, Catawba Co.	Farm labor	Wounded, 7/3/63 at Gettysburg. Missing, 3/1/65.
Pvt.	Hauser, Henry	1840	Lincolnton, Lincoln Co.	Farm labor	Wounded, 7/1/63 and captured, 7/5/63 at Gettysburg. Wounded, 6/6/64 at Cold Harbor.
Pvt.	Havner, Adolphus J.	1847	Lincolnton, Lincoln Co.	Farm labor	Killed, 7/3/63 at Gettysburg.
Pvt.	Havner, Daniel M.	1835	Lincolnton, Lincoln Co.	Farm labor	Died of disease ("fever"), 8/21/62 at home.
Pvt.	Havner, Hosea	1846	Lincolnton, Lincoln Co.	Farm labor	Wounded, 7/1/63 at Gettysburg. Captured, 4/3/65 at Richmond.

Rank	Name	DOB	Residence	Occupation	Remarks
Pvt.	Havner, Jacob L.	1833	Lincolnton, Lincoln Co.	Farmer	Wounded (left arm amputated), 7/1/63 at captured, 7/5/63 at Gettysburg. Discharged due to wounds, 3/14/64.
Pvt.	**Havner, John**	**1845**	**Lincolnton, Lincoln Co.**	**Farm labor**	**Killed, 7/1/63 at Gettysburg.**
Pvt.	Havner, Julius A.	1833	Lincolnton, Lincoln Co.	Farmer	Wounded, 5/10/64 at Spotsylvania. Captured, 3/25/65 in Petersburg trenches.
Pvt.	**Havner, Michael**	**1825**	**Lincolnton, Lincoln Co.**	**Farmer**	**Died of disease, 8/12/62 at Wilmington, NC.**
Pvt.	Haynes, Daniel A.	1815	Seagles' Store, Lincoln Co.	Farmer	Surrendered, 4/9/65 at Appomattox Court House.
Pvt.	**Haynes, Daniel H.**	**1845**	**Spring Forge, Lincoln Co.**	**Miller's Asst.**	**Killed, 7/1/63 at Gettysburg.**
Pvt.	Haynes, John F.	1833	Spring Forge, Lincoln Co.	Farmer	Wounded, 7/3/63 and captured, 7/6/63 at Greencastle, PA.
Pvt.	Haynes, R. Workman	1842	Lincoln Co.	Farm labor	Died of disease (measles), 5/1/62 at Camp Mangum, Raleigh, NC.
Pvt.	Hoover, David M.	1842	Lincolnton, Lincoln Co.	Farm labor	Wounded, 12/16/62 at White Hall, NC. Killed, 7/1/63 at Gettysburg.
Pvt.	**Hovis, B. Monroe**	**1836**	**Woodlawn, Gaston Co.**	**Farm labor**	**Captured, 7/3/63 at Gettysburg. Died of disease, 5/8/64 as POW at Point Lookout, MD.**
Pvt.	Hubbert, Charles	1836	Mull Grove, Catawba Co.	Day labor	Captured, 10/14/63 at Bristoe Station.
Pvt.	Hubbert, David	1828	Mull Grove, Catawba Co.	Day labor	Wounded, 7/1/63 at Gettysburg. Wounded (left leg amputated), 8/25/64 at Reams' Station.
Pvt.	Hubbert, Matthew	1798	Jacob's Fork, Catawba Co.	Day labor	Discharged (disability, "the natural infirmities of age"), 1/14/63.
Pvt.	Hudspeth, John T.	1831	Lincoln Co.	—	Wounded (finger), 6/10/64, at Cold Harbor. Surrendered, 4/9/65 at Appomattox Court House.
Pvt.	**Huss, Jacob**	**1839**	**Lincoln Co.**	**Farm labor**	**Killed, 10/14/63 at Bristoe Station.**
Pvt.	Huss, John	1842	Lincolnton, Lincoln Co.	Farm labor	Captured, 7/14/63 at Falling Waters, MD. Captured, 4/2/65 at Petersburg.
Pvt.	**Keever, George P.**	**1844**	**Lincolnton, Lincoln Co.**	**Farm labor**	**Wounded, 7/1/63 and captured, 7/5/63 at Gettysburg. Died of wounds, 7/7/63 at Gettysburg.**
Pvt.	Kiser, Hiram A.	1844	Dallas, Gaston Co.	Farm labor	Wounded (head), 7/1/63 at Gettysburg.
Pvt.	Kiser, Jacob	1838	Old Furnace, Gaston Co.	Farm labor	Deserted (AWOL), 7/22/63. Transferred to Barringer's Cav. Brigade, 12/7/64.
Pvt.	**Lenhardt, Cameron L.**	**1842**	**Lincolnton, Lincoln Co.**	**Farm labor**	**Wounded (left shoulder), 7/3/63. Died of wounds, 7/30/63.**
Pvt.	Lenhardt, Joseph M.	1826	Lincolnton, Lincoln Co.	Farmer	Wounded, 7/1/63 at Gettysburg. Wounded, 10/14/63 at Bristoe Station. Wounded, 5/11/64 at Spotsylvania. Surrendered, 4/9/65 at Appomattox Court House.

Rank	Name	DOB	Residence	Occupation	Remarks
Pvt.	Martin, William E.	1842	Erasmus, Gaston Co.	Farm labor	Music—9/62. Transferred to Regt. band, 10/64. Died of hepatitis, 2/1/65 in Charlotte, NC.
Pvt.	Mooney, McCameron	1844	Rock Mill, Lincoln Co.	Farm labor	Captured, 10/27/64 at Burgess' Mill.
Pvt.	Page, Lemuel	1813	Seagles' Store, Lincoln Co.	Farmer	Discharged (disability—"palsy and general debility and age"), 10/23/62.
Pvt.	Parker, Asa	1844	Cleveland Co.	Farm labor	Captured, 4/5/65 near Petersburg.
Pvt.	Pool, Albert J.	1842	Yorkville, York Co. SC	Farm labor	Wounded, 7/1/63 at Gettysburg. Captured, 5/22/64 at Spotsylvania, VA.
Pvt.	Ramseur, John F.	1842	Old Furnace, Gaston Co.	Asst. miller	Sgt.—11/1/63. 1st Sgt.—8/31/63. Captured, 4/2/65 at Petersburg.
Pvt.	Ramsour, Theodore J.	1832	Lincolnton, Lincoln Co.	Farm labor	Wounded (leg amputated), 6/1/64 at Cold Harbor. Retired to Invalid Corps, 12/1/64.
Pvt.	Ramsey, Robert N.	1843	Lincolnton, Lincoln Co.	Farm labor	Killed, 7/1/63 at Gettysburg.
Pvt.	Reap, Thomas	1841	Jacob's Fork, Catawba Co.	Farm labor	Died of disease (chronic diarrhea), 12/64 at home.
Pvt.	Richey, Joseph C.	1827	Lincoln Co.	—	Wounded, 7/1/63 at Gettysburg. Killed, 5/5/64 at the Wilderness.
Pvt.	Rinck, Daniel	1835	Hickory Tavern, Catawba Co.	Farm labor	Captured, 7/14/63 at Falling Waters, MD. Missing, 3/1/65.
Pvt.	Rinck, Noah	1820	Lincolnton, Lincoln Co.	Farmer	Discharged (disability—"paraplegia"), 3/18/64.
Pvt.	Seagle, Andrew	1830	Lincolnton, Lincoln Co.	Farmer	Captured, 8/22/64 at Reams' Station.
Pvt.	Seagler, Alfred A.	1818	Newton, Catawba Co.	Farmer	Killed, 7/1/63 at Gettysburg.
Pvt.	Sherrill, William A.	1841	Lincolnton, Lincoln Co.	Farm labor	Wounded, 5/5/64 at the Wilderness. Captured, 2/6/65 in Petersburg trenches.
Pvt.	Shrum, John F. "Frank"	1842	Dallas, Gaston Co.	Farm labor	Died of disease (pneumonia), 12/15/62 at Petersburg, VA.
Pvt.	Shull, Anthony	1834	Craigeville, Gaston Co.	Farmer	Wounded, 12/16/62 at White Hall, NC. Captured, 7/14/65 at Falling Waters, MD. Died of disease (chronic diarrhea), 10/7/64 as POW at Elmira, NY.
Pvt.	Speagle, William P.	1844	Jacob's Fork, Catawba Co.	Farm labor	Wounded (right shoulder), 7/1/63 at Gettysburg. Captured in hospital in Richmond, 4/3/65.
Pvt.	Stroup, Daniel S.	1843	Craigeville, Gaston Co.	Farm labor	Wounded and captured, 7/3/63 at Gettysburg. Captured, 4/2/65 at Petersburg.
Pvt.	Strutt, Pinkney S.	1843	Lincolnton, Lincoln Co.	Farm labor	Wounded, 7/1/63 and captured, 7/5/63 at Gettysburg. Died of wounds ("pyaemia"), 8/18/63 at David's Island, NY.
Pvt.	Sullivan, Coatsworth	1837	Lincolnton, Lincoln Co.	Farmer	Wounded (left leg), 3/30/65 in Petersburg trenches.
Pvt.	Totherow, George	1842	Lincoln Co.	—	Discharged (disability), 12/22/62.
Pvt.	Wacaster, Abraham	1811	Lincoln Co.	—	Died of disease, 12/14/64, "at home."

Rank	Name	DOB	Residence	Occupation	Remarks
Pvt.	Wacaster, Adolphus	1842	Lincoln Co.	—	Wounded, 7/1/63 and captured, 7/5/63 at Gettysburg. Captured, 5/5/64 at the Wilderness.
Pvt.	**Watts, James I.**	**1823**	**White Pine, Gaston Co.**	**Miller**	**Died of disease ("febris typhoid"), 7/3/62 at Wilmington, NC.**
Pvt.	Wise, Zenas	1838	Lincolnton, Lincoln Co.	Farm labor	Surrendered, 4/9/65 at Appomattox Court House.
Pvt.	**Wood, John H.**	**1837**	**Lincolnton, Lincoln Co.**	**Farm labor**	**Died of disease (typhoid fever), 9/2/62 at Wilmington, NC.**
Pvt.	Wood, Perry	1841	Lincolnton, Lincoln Co.	Farm labor	Wounded (left hand), 7/3/63 at Gettysburg. Captured, 10/27/64 at Burgess' Mill.

1862 Recruits

Rank	Name	DOB	Residence	Occupation	Remarks
Pvt.	Aderholdt, John A.	1839	Cherryville, Gaston Co.	Farm labor	Enlisted, 5/8/62. Cpl.—11/1/63. Wounded (arm), 2/65. Surrendered, 4/9/65 at Appomattox Court House.
Pvt.	Avery, Absalon	1829	Lincolnton, Lincoln Co.	Farm labor	Enlisted, 5/8/62. Wounded, 7/1/63 at Gettysburg. Captured, 10/27/64 at Burgess' Mill.
Pvt.	**Boyles, Alexander**	**1837**	**Seagle's Store, Lincoln Co.**	**Farm labor**	**Enlisted, 5/8/62. Died of disease, 12/10/62 at Goldsboro, NC.**
Pvt.	**Boyles. John**	**1840**	**Seagle's Store, Lincoln Co.**	**Farm labor**	**Enlisted, 5/8/62. Wounded, 7/1/63 and captured at Gettysburg. Died of wounds in hospital, 8/10/63 at Chambersburg, PA.**
Pvt.	Boyles, Joseph	1816	Lincolnton, Lincoln Co.	Farmer	Enlisted, 7/15/62. Wounded (left arm) and captured, 7/14/63 at Falling Waters, MD. Captured, 10/27/64 at Burgess' Mill.
Music	Cline, William A.	1832	Lincolnton, Lincoln Co.	Hatter	Enlisted, 9/8/62. Captured, 7/5/63 at Greencastle, PA. Transferred to Regt. band, 2/65.
Pvt.	Havner, George H.	1835	Lincolnton, Lincoln Co.	Farmer	Enlisted, 6/8/62. Accidental gunshot wound; in hospital, 7/6/62 in Wilmington, NC. Wounded (left arm), 7/3/63 at Gettysburg. Missing, 3/1/65.
Pvt.	Hoover, Daniel R.	1845	Killian's Mill, Lincoln Co.	Farm labor	Enlisted, 5/8/62. Wounded, 7/3/63 at Gettysburg. Retired ("disability from wounds") to the Invalid Corps, 12/15/64.
Pvt.	Jetton, Taylor B.	1847	Lincolnton, Lincoln Co.	Carpenter's Asst.	Enlisted, 7/10/62. Captured, 7/14/63 at Falling Waters, MD. Captured, 4/2/65 at Petersburg.
Pvt.	McCoy, William H.	1843	W. Charlotte, Mecklenburg Co.	Day laborer	Enlisted, 5/23/62. Surrendered, 4/9/65 at Appomattox Court House.
Pvt.	Miller, Jacob A.	1833	Lincolnton, Lincoln Co.	Farmer	Enlisted, 5/8/62. Sgt.—11/1/63. Wounded (groin), 4/2/65 near Burkeville Jct., VA.
Pvt.	Motz, Charles	1844	Lincoln Co.	Farm labor	Music—9/62. Captured, 7/5/63 at Greencastle, PA.
Pvt.	Motz, George	1841	Lincoln Co.	—	Enlisted, 5/13/62. Sgt.—1/3/62. Transferred to Regt. Field & Staff. Returned to Co. I, 9/64. Captured, 4/6/65 at Farmville, VA.
Pvt.	Mullin, Alfred E.	1837	Lincolnton, Lincoln Co.	Farmer	Enlisted, 11/13/62 at Camp Wilson, VA. Captured, 10/14/63 at Bristoe Station. Sur-

Rank	Name	DOB	Residence	Occupation	Remarks
					rendered, 4/9/65 at Appomattox Court House.
Pvt.	Rhodes, Jacob B.	1834	Lincolnton, Lincoln Co.	Millwright	Enlisted, 5/8/62. Sgt.—11/1/63. Captured, 4/2/65 at Petersburg.
Pvt.	Seagle, Monroe	1835	Lincoln Co.	—	Enlisted, 5/8/62. Music—9/62. Transferred to Regt. band, 9/64.
Pvt.	Shuford, Sidney	1828	Seagle's Store, Lincoln Co.	Blacksmith	Enlisted, 5/8/62. Captured, 4/2/65 at Petersburg.
Pvt.	Summerow, Peter J.	1844	Lincoln Co.	—	Enlisted, 5/8/62. Captured, 4/2/65 at Petersburg.
Pvt.	Warlick, John C.	1842	Lincolnton, Lincoln Co.	Farm labor	Enlisted, 5/8/62. Wounded (right leg and left breast), 7/3/63 at Gettysburg. Wounded (left arm), 8/21/64 at Reams' Station. Captured, 4/2/65 at Petersburg.
Pvt.	Weaver, Phillip C.	1829	Lincolnton, Lincoln Co.	Farmer	Enlisted, 12/20/62. Wounded, 10/14/63 at Bristoe Station. Captured, 10/27/64 at Burgess' Mill.

1863 Recruits

Rank	Name	DOB	Residence	Occupation	Remarks
Pvt.	Bynum, Benjamin S.	1820	Liberty Hill, Iredell Co.	Farmer	Enlisted, 10/17/63 at Camp Vance. Died of disease (chronic diarrhea), 10/31/64 at Richmond.
Pvt.	Campbell, A. Lorenzo	1845	Lincoln Co.	Farm labor	Enlisted, 5/13/63. Captured, 7/21/63 at Chester Gap, VA. Died of disease (pneumonia), 8/5/63 in Washington, D.C.
Pvt.	Carpenter, Henry	1823	Lincolnton, Lincoln Co.	Farmer	Enlisted, 3/26/63. Wounded (left hip), 7/1/63 and captured, 7/5/63 at Gettysburg. In hospital in Baltimore, MD. Died of wounds, 7/31/63.
Pvt.	Clanton, William L.	1824	Sweet Home, Iredell Co.	Farmer	Enlisted, 10/17/63 at Camp Vance, NC. Captured, 4/2/65 at Petersburg.
Pvt.	Cody, Absalom G.	1847	Lincolnton, Lincoln Co.	Farm labor	Enlisted, 3/23/63. Killed, 7/1/63 at Gettysburg.
Pvt.	Gilbert, Marcus	1825	Lincolnton, Lincoln Co.	Farmer	Enlisted, 3/3/63. Died of disease ("febris typhoides"), 9/17/63 in Gordonsville, VA.
Pvt.	Hubbert, Daniel	1828	Mull Grove, Catawba Co.	Day labor	Enlisted, 3/23/63. Captured, 4/2/65 at Petersburg.
Pvt.	Johnson, Leonidas (Lee)	1838	Lincoln Co.	Salesman	Enlisted, 1/2/63 at Halifax Co. NC. Wounded (jaw), 7/3/63 at Gettysburg. Missing, 3/1/65.
Pvt.	Johnson, Robert	1844	Mull Grove, Catawba Co.	Farm labor	Enlisted, 3/3/63. Captured, 7/21/63 at Chester Gap, VA. Died of disease (chronic diarrhea), 8/25/63 as POW at Old Capitol Prison, in Washington, D.C.
Pvt.	Kincaid, Cephas G.	1845	Morganton, Burke Co.	Farm labor	Enlisted, 7/3/63 at Lincoln Co. Captured, 10/27/64 at Burgess' Mill.
Pvt.	Lenhardt, Jacob M.	1833	Rock Mill, Lincoln Co.	Farmer	Enlisted, 3/9/63. Killed, 7/3/63 at Gettysburg.
Pvt.	Nance, William W.	1837	Vestel's Ford, Gaston Co.	Farm labor	Enlisted, 10/17/63 at Camp Vance, NC. Died of disease (chronic diarrhea), 1/19/64 at Gordonsville, VA.

Rank	Name	DOB	Residence	Occupation	Remarks
Pvt.	Oaks, John	1836	Lincoln Co.	—	Enlisted, 3/23/63. Wounded (head), 7/3/63 and captured, 7/5/63 at Greencastle. Captured, 4/2/65 at Petersburg.
Pvt.	Quickel, Levi H.	1845	Lincolnton, Lincoln Co.	Farm labor	Enlisted, 8/20/63. Captured, 4/2/65 at Petersburg.
Pvt.	Ramseur, John M.	1846	Lincolnton, Lincoln Co.	Farm labor	Enlisted, 8/20/63. Captured, 10/17/63 at Bristoe Station.
Pvt.	**Reinhardt, Charles**	**1844**	**Spring Forge, Lincoln Co.**	**Farm labor**	**Enlisted, 9/23/63. Died of disease ("pleuritis"), 6/29/64 at Liberty, VA.**
Pvt.	Reinhardt, Robert	1841	Spring Forge, Lincoln Co.	Farm labor	Enlisted, 1/1/63. Wounded (left arm), 7/1/63 at Gettysburg. Absent due to wounds ("necrosis of left arm"), 3/8/65.
Pvt.	Rinck, Andrew	1823	Hickory Tavern, Catawba Co.	Farmer	Enlisted, 10/17/63 at Camp Vance. Wounded (right shoulder and throat), 4/2/65 at Petersburg and captured. Died of wounds, 4/13/65 at Ft. Monroe, VA.
Pvt.	Shuford, Noah P.	1826	Seagle's Store, Lincoln Co.	Potter	Enlisted, 3/23/63. Wounded (left leg), 7/1/63 at Gettysburg.
Pvt.	**Sigmon, Noah**	**1828**	**Jacob's Fork, Catawba Co.**	**Farmer**	**Enlisted, 3/16/63. Killed, 10/14/63 at Bristoe Station.**
Pvt.	**Sigmore, Elijah**	**1825**	**Jacob's Fork, Catawba Co.**	**Farmer**	**Enlisted, 3/26/63. Wounded, 7/1/63 and captured, 7/5/63 at Gettysburg. Died of disease, 11/26/63 as POW at Ft. Delaware, DE.**
Pvt.	**Smith, David G.**	**1826**	**Lincolnton, Lincoln Co.**	**Day labor**	**Enlisted, 3/26/63. Wounded, 7/1/63 and captured, 7/5/63 at Gettysburg ("left sick at hospital"). Died of wounds (and "typhoid fever"), 7/20/62.**
Pvt.	Smith, John J.	1826	Seagle's Store, Lincoln Co.	Farmer	Enlisted, 3/26/63. Wounded (leg amputated), 6/1/64 at Cold Harbor. In Petersburg hospital.
Pvt.	**Speagle, Aaron**	**1824**	**Jacob's Fork, Catawba Co.**	**Farmer**	**Enlisted, 4/8/63. Wounded, 7/1/63 at Gettysburg. Died of disease ("febris typhoid"), 10/7/64 at Richmond.**
Pvt.	**Speagle, Logan "Monroe"**	**1846**	**Jacob's Fork, Catawba Co.**	**Farm labor**	**Enlisted, 3/3/63. Killed, 7/1/63 at Gettysburg.**
Pvt.	Tallant, Aaron	1830	Morganton, Burke Co.	Farmer	Enlisted, 4/8/63. Wounded, 7/1/63 at Gettysburg. Missing, 3/1/65.
Pvt.	Wyant, David	1847	Mull Grove, Catawba Co.	Farm labor	Enlisted, 3/23/63. Wounded, 7/3/63 at Gettysburg. Captured, 10/27/64 at Burgess' Mills.
Pvt.	Yoder, David	1844	Seagle's Store, Lincoln Co.	Farm labor	Enlisted, 3/3/63. Captured, 10/14/63 at Bristoe Station.

1864 Recruits

Rank	Name	DOB	Residence	Occupation	Remarks
Pvt.	Abernathy, James B.	1844	Lincolnton, Lincoln Co.	Farm labor	Enlisted, 10/19/64. Wounded (left hand), 10/27/64 at Burgess' Mill. Retired to the Invalid Corps, 12/15/64.
Pvt.	Cody, John	1846	Lincolnton, Lincoln Co.	Farm labor	Enlisted, 2/8/64. Shot while on leave, 9/14/64 in Charlotte. Surrendered, 4/9/65 at Appomattox Court House.

Rank	Name	DOB	Residence	Occupation	Remarks
Pvt.	Culbert, Daniel	—	Lincoln Co.	—	Enlisted, 12/64 (?). Captured, 4/2/65 at Hatcher's Run.
Pvt.	Evans, John	—	Lincoln Co.	—	Enlisted, 2/13/64. Surrendered, 4/9/65 at Appomattox Court House.
Pvt.	Gault, Albert R.	1846	Newton, Catawba Co.	Farm labor	Enlisted, 8/15/64. Captured, 10/27/64 at Burgess' Mill. Surrendered, 4/9/65 at Appomattox Court House.
Pvt.	Haynes, Ryann W.	1847	Craigeville, Gaston Co.	Farm labor	Enlisted, 2/19/64. Wounded, 5/10/64 at Spotsylvania. Captured, 4/2/65 at Petersburg.
Pvt.	Hill, William L.	1847	Seagles' Store, Lincoln Co.	Farm labor	Enlisted, 10/28/64 at Camp Holmes. Captured, 4/2/65 at Petersburg.
Pvt.	Johnson, Harvey M.	1846	Mull Grove, Catawba Co.	Farm labor	Enlisted, 8/15/64 at Lincoln Co. NC. Captured, 4/2/65 at Petersburg.
Pvt.	**Kiser, Henry**	1849	Dallas, Gaston Co.	Farm labor	**Enlisted, 2/19/64. Killed, 8/21/64 near Petersburg.**
Pvt.	Roseman, Robert M.	1846	Lincolnton, Lincoln Co.	Store clerk's asst.	Enlisted, 3/20/64. Wounded (ankle), 6/64 near Richmond.
Pvt.	**Speagle, Calvin**	1847	Jacob's Fork, Catawba Co.	Farm labor	**Enlisted, 8/19/64 at Camp Holmes. Captured, 10/27/64 at Burgess' Mill. Died of disease (chronic diarrhea), 1/25/65 as POW at Point Lookout, MD.**
Pvt.	Wilson, Harrison S.	1821	Lincolnton, Lincoln Co.	Farmer	Enlisted, 9/20/64. Captured, 4/2/65 at Petersburg.

Company K
Buncombe County

Rank	Name	DOB	Residence	Occupation	Remarks
Cpt.	Young, James M.	1836	Asheville, Buncombe Co.	Clerk	Wounded (head), 8/25/64 at Reams' Station. Surrender, 4/9/65 at Appomattox Court House.
1st Lt.	Coleman, Robert L.	1836	Buncombe Co.	Clerk	Transferred, 9/1/62 to 60th NC Inf.
2nd Lt.	**Burgin, John A**	1839	Asheville, Buncombe Co.	Clerk	**1st Lt.—11/1/62. Killed, 7/3/63 at Gettysburg.**
1st Sgt.	West, William R.	1823	Reem's Creek, Buncombe Co.	Carpenter	Wounded (head), 7/1/63 at Gettysburg. Retired to Invalid Corps, 4/11/64.
Sgt.	Dickerson, William T.	1824	Buncombe Co.	—	Com. Sgt.—Transferred to Regt. Field & Staff, 8/9/62. 2nd Lt. in Co. K—7/30/63. 1st Lt.—11/1/63. Captured, 10/27/64 at Burgess' Mill.
Sgt.	Harris, Abel F.	1834	Swannanoa, Buncombe Co.	Farm labor	Died, disease ("continued fever"), 10/24/62 in Petersburg, VA.
Sgt.	**Triplett, James H.**	1844	Asheville, Buncombe Co.	Blacksmith asst.	**1st Sgt.—9/1/62. Killed, 7/1/63 at Gettysburg.**
Sgt.	**West, John P. Sr.**	1823	Reem's Creek, Buncombe Co.	Carpenter	**1st Sgt.—4/11/64. Wounded, 5/10/64 at Spotsylvania. Died of wounds, 5/11/64.**
Cpl.	**Anderson, William W.**	1841	Bethania, Forsyth Co.	Tobacco labor	**Sgt.—11/10/62. Killed, 7/1/63 at Gettysburg.**

Rank	Name	DOB	Residence	Occupation	Remarks
Cpl.	McKee, William H.	1835	Swannanoa, Buncombe Co.	Mechanic	Pvt.—10/27/63. Captured, 10/27/64. POW—Point Lookout Prison, MD.
Cpl.	Patton, John M.	1844	Swannanoa, Buncombe Co.	Farm labor	Sgt.—11/10/62. Wounded, 7/1/63 and captured, 7/5/63 at Gettysburg. 2nd Lt.—3/12/64. Transferred, 7/31/64, to Co. G, 7th Regt. NC Cav.
Cpl.	Wells, Oliver	1845	Lincolnton, Lincoln Co.	Student	Wounded, 7/1/63 at Gettysburg. Captured, 10/14/63 at Bristoe Station.
Pvt.	Adams, Baird	1810	Webster, Jackson Co.	Farmer	Died of disease (erysipelas), 2/24/63 at Weldon, NC.
Pvt.	Allison, Thomas J.	1840	Swannanoa, Buncombe Co.	Farm labor	Deserted, 3/14/65.
Pvt.	Atkin, Thomas S.	1846	Asheville, Buncombe Co.	Editor's Asst.	Cpl.—9/1/63. Sgt.—9/30/64. Captured, 10/27/64, Burgess Mills. Died of disease (chronic diarrhea), 1/8/65 as POW at Point Lookout, MD.
Pvt.	Baker, Joseph	1845	Swannanoa, Buncombe Co.	Farm labor	Died of disease (fever), "at home," 12/20/62.
Pvt.	Ball, Jeremiah C.	1841	Reems Creek, Buncombe Co.	Farm labor	Deserted, 3/19/64.
Pvt.	Bartlett, Jacob S.	1843	Swannanoa, Buncombe Co.	Farm labor	Cpl.—11/10/62. Sgt.—1/64. 1st Sgt.—9/1/64. Surrendered, 4/9/65 at Appomattox Court House.
Pvt.	Bell, George H.	1846	Swannanoa, Buncombe Co.	Student	Wounded, 4/18/63 at Blount's Creek, NC. Wounded, 5/11/64 at Spotsylvania Court House.
Pvt.	Bird, George W.	1844	Swannanoa, Buncombe Co.	Farm labor	Cpl.—4/11/64. Wounded, 5/5/64 at the Wilderness. Died of wounds, 5/16/64 at Gordonsville, VA.
Pvt.	Black, Patrick	1805	Swannanoa, Buncombe Co.	Farm labor	Wounded, 4/9/63 at Blount's Creek, NC. Discharged, 10/17/64 "by reason of a want of physical vigor and endurance in consequence of his advanced years."
Pvt.	Brown, Thomas K.	1844	Swannanoa, Buncombe Co.	Farm labor	Cpl.—9/1/63. Sgt.—10/64. Missing, 3/1/65.
Pvt.	Burgin, Benjamin J.	1841	Swannanoa, Buncombe Co.	Farm labor	Cpl.—9/64. Captured, 10/27/64 at Burgess' Mill.
Pvt.	Burnett, Thomas W.	1845	Swannanoa, Buncombe Co.	Farm labor	Wounded (left arm), 7/1/63 at Gettysburg. Released to the Invalid Corps, 5/12/64.
Pvt.	Burnett, William A.	1837	Swannanoa, Buncombe Co.	—	Deserted, "to the enemy," 6/30/64.
Pvt.	Burns, Elisha P.	1842	Buncombe Co.	Farm labor	Died of disease (pneumonia), 1/20/64 at Charlottesville, VA.
Pvt.	Burns, John J.	1840	Buncombe Co.	Farm labor	Wounded, 12/16/62 at White Hall, NC. Captured, 7/3/63 at Gettysburg. Died of disease ("inflammation of brain"), 3/3/65 as POW at Ft. Delaware, DE.
Pvt.	Cordell, John H.	1831	Swannanoa, Buncombe Co.	Farmer	Wounded, 10/27/64 at Burgess' Mill. Captured, 4/2/65 at Petersburg.

Rank	Name	DOB	Residence	Occupation	Remarks
Pvt.	Cordell, Joseph	1835	Swannanoa, Buncombe Co.	Farmer	Deserted, 6/30/64.
Pvt.	Creasman, Abraham Jr.	1824	Swannanoa, Buncombe Co.	Farmer	Missing, 3/1/65.
Pvt.	Creasman, William L.	1839	Shufordville, Buncombe Co.	Farm labor	Deserted (AWOL), 7/26/63.
Pvt.	Crook, Jasper A.	1842	Swannanoa, Buncombe Co.	Cooper's Asst.	Cpl.—9/64. Missing, 3/1/65.
Pvt.	Crow, Joseph W.	1844	Swannanoa, Buncombe Co.	Farmer	Wounded (shoulder & neck), 6/2/64 at Cold Harbor. Captured, 4/11/65 at Farmville, VA.
Pvt.	Crow, Levi	1846	Pickey's Co. SC	Farm labor	Missing, 3/1/65.
Pvt.	Davidson, John M.	1844	Asheville, Buncombe Co.	Farm labor	Cpl.—11/10/62. Sgt.—9/64. Captured, 10/14/64 at Bristoe Station.
Pvt.	Deggertheart, John V.	1843	Mecklenburg Co.	—	Captured, 10/27/64 at Burgess' Mill, VA. Died of disease (acute dysentery), 1/31/65 as POW at Point Lookout, MD.
Pvt.	Gash, Lusious W. (Lucas)	1845	Swannanoa, Buncombe Co.	Farm labor	Cpl.—7/1/62. Wounded (foot), 7/1/63 at Gettysburg. Sgt.—11/1/63. 3rd Lt.—1/27/64. Wounded, 5/12/64 at Spotsylvania Court House. Died of wounds, 5/14/64.
Pvt.	Glendown, Joseph B.	1844	Swannanoa, Buncombe Co.	Farm labor	Killed, at High Point, NC ("by a railway car."), 1/3/64.
Pvt.	Goodson, John L.	1843	Swannanoa, Buncombe Co.	Farm labor	Musician—11/63. Pvt.—12/63. Musician, 9/64. Transferred to the regt. band. Pvt.—1/1/65. Deserted, 3/14/65.
Pvt.	Goodson, Thomas	1817	Swannanoa, Buncombe Co.	Farmer	Captured, 7/14/63 at Falling Waters, MD. Died, 11/1/64 (unknown causes).
Pvt.	Gudger, John P.	1826	Swannanoa, Buncombe Co.	Farm labor	Wounded, 12/16/62 at White Hall, NC. Died, 10/29/63 ("at home").
Pvt.	Hall, John P.	1839	Swannanoa, Buncombe Co.	Farm labor	Captured, 7/14/63 at Falling Waters, MD. Surrendered, 4/9/65 at Appomattox Court House.
Pvt.	Harris, Thomas L.	1836	Swannanoa, Buncombe Co.	Farmer	Captured, 7/3/63 at Gettysburg. Deserted, 3/9/65.
Pvt.	Howard, Anderson Z.	1835	Buncombe Co.	—	Died of disease (typhoid fever), 1/29/64 at Charlottesville, VA.
Pvt.	Justice, Foster	1841	Fairview, Buncombe Co.	Farm labor	Captured, 10/14/63 at Bristoe Station.
Pvt.	Kelly, Alfred B.	1840	McDowell Co.	Farm labor	Died of disease (pneumonia), 12/20/64 in Salisbury, NC.
Pvt.	Kelly, Patrick	1830	Old Fort, McDowell Co.	Day labor	Transferred to C.S. Navy, 4/1/64.
Pvt.	Morris, Archibald G.	1846	Raysville, Buncombe Co.	Farm labor	Died of disease ("pneumonia and typhoid fever"), 5/2/62 in Raleigh.
Pvt.	Morris, Charles	1828	Edneyville, Henderson Co.	Farmer	Wounded (head & left arm), 12/16/62 at White Hall, NC. Captured, 7/14/63 at Falling Waters, MD.
Pvt.	Morris, Cornelius	1829	Blue Ridge, Henderson Co.	Farmer	Wounded, 12/16/62 at White Hall, NC. Captured, 7/14/63 at Falling Waters, MD.

Rank	Name	DOB	Residence	Occupation	Remarks
					Died of disease ("diarrhea and catarrh"), 12/10/63 as POW at Point Lookout, MD.
Pvt.	Morrison, William V.	1844	Buncombe Co.	Farm labor	Killed, 7/1/63 at Gettysburg.
Pvt.	Patton, George A.	1843	Swannanoa, Buncombe Co.	Farm labor	Wounded (left thigh and right ankle), 5/5/64 in the Wilderness. Captured, 4/2/65 at Petersburg.
Pvt.	Patton, Robert C.	1828	Swannanoa, Buncombe Co.	Farmer	Discharged (disability), 6/3/62.
Pvt.	Pittman, John N.	1832	Buncombe Co.	Farmer	Wounded (shoulder), 7/3/63 at Gettysburg. Deserted, 6/30/64.
Pvt.	Poor, William H.	1842	Swannanoa, Buncombe Co.	Farm labor	Captured, 7/14/63 at Falling Waters, MD. Missing, 3/17/65.
Pvt.	Powers, James R.	1832	Buncombe Co.	Farmer	Captured, 7/14/63 at Falling Waters, MD.
Pvt.	Smith, Alfred B.	1839	Swannanoa, Buncombe Co.	Farm labor	Wounded (face and neck, 7/3/63) and captured, 7/5/63 at Gettysburg. Retired to Invalid Corps, 4/11/64.
Pvt.	Smith, John B.	1830	Erasmus, Gaston Co.	Farmer	Died of disease (pneumonia), 12/16/62 in Richmond.
Pvt.	Smith, Richard	1835	Asheville, Buncombe Co.	Brick maker	Wounded, 9/30/64 at Jones' Farm. Captured, 4/3/65 in Richmond hospital.
Pvt.	Smith, Thomas	1842	Swannanoa, Buncombe Co.	Farm labor	Died of disease ("febris typhoidus"), 9/24/62, at Wilson NC.
Pvt.	Stroup, William J.	1833	Chestnut Oak, Gaston Co.	Farmer	Killed, 7/3/63 at Gettysburg.
Pvt.	Suttles, John	1838	Fairview, Buncombe Co.	Farm labor	Deserted, 6/10/64.
Pvt.	Trantham, John	1845	Fairview, Buncombe Co.	Farm labor	Captured, 10/14/63 at Bristoe Station.
Pvt.	Trantham, Joseph	1846	Fairview, Buncombe Co.	Farm labor	Captured, 10/14/63 at Bristoe Station.
Pvt.	Watkins, Jesse M.	1830	Buncombe Co.	Farmer	Captured, 5/8/64 at Spotsylvania.
Pvt.	West, John P. Jr.	1845	Reem's Creek, Buncombe Co.	Carpenter Asst.	Cpl.—9/64. WIA (right leg amputated), 2/10/65 at Hatcher's Run. Died of wounds ("hemorrhage"), 4/27/65 in Richmond hospital.
Pvt.	Young, Samuel M.	1835	Swannanoa, Buncombe Co.	Trader	Sgt.—8/9/62. 3rd Lt.—11/10/62. Wounded, 7/1/63 and captured, 7/5/63 at Gettysburg. Died of wounds, 7/7/63 at field hospital.

1862 Recruits

Rank	Name	DOB	Residence	Occupation	Remarks
Pvt.	Darnold, James C.	1844	Swannanoa, Buncombe Co.	Farm labor	Enlisted, 8/19/62 at Hanover Co. VA. Wounded, 7/1/63 and captured, 7/5/63 at Gettysburg. Died of wounds, 7/29/63 as POW at hospital at David's Island, NY.
Pvt.	Miller, David U.	1839	Ramseytown, Yancey Co.	Farm labor	Enlisted, 9/17/62. Deserted, 3/18/65.
Pvt.	Morris, Monroe	1835	Buncombe Co.	—	Enlisted, 10/27/62 at Franklin, VA. Captured, 7/3/63 at Gettysburg. Died of dis-

Rank	Name	DOB	Residence	Occupation	Remarks
					ease, 2/2/64 as POW at Point Lookout, MD.
Pvt.	Pickens, George A.	1844	Flat Creek, Buncombe Co.	Farm labor	Enlisted, 12/20/62. Cpl.—4/11/64. Wounded, 5/5/64 at the Wilderness. Sgt.—1/1/65. Captured, 4/2/65 at Petersburg.
Pvt.	Watkins, Miniard E.	—	Buncombe Co.	—	Enlisted, 10/27/62 at Franklin, VA. Captured, 7/14/63 at Falling Waters, MD. Died of disease (diarrhea), 11/28/63 as POW at Point Lookout.
Pvt.	Watkins, Uriah P.	—	Buncombe Co.	—	Enlisted, 5/15/62. Captured, 7/14/63 at Falling Waters, MD. Deserted, 1/65.

1863 Recruits

Rank	Name	DOB	Residence	Occupation	Remarks
Pvt.	Bartlett, James P.	1823	Buncombe Co.	Farmer	Enlisted, 4/27/63. Captured, 7/6/63 at Williamsport, MD. Died of disease, 1/1/64 as POW at Point Lookout, MD.
Pvt.	Bartlett, John H.	1823	Buncombe Co.	Farmer	Enlisted, 4/27/63. Missing, 5/5/64 at the Wilderness.
Pvt.	Bell, James A.	1845	Swannanoa, Buncombe Co.	Blacksmith Asst.	Enlisted, 3/1/63. Wounded, 7/3/63 and captured, 7/5/63 at Gettysburg. Died of wounds, 7/10/63 in Gettysburg field hospital.
Pvt.	Bird, Wilson R.	1843	Black Mountain, McDowell Co.	Farm labor	Enlisted, 9/14/63. Captured, 4/3/65 at Petersburg.
3rd Lt.	Boyd, Benjamin F.	1838	W. Charlotte, Mecklenburg Co.	Clerk	2nd Lt. —11/1/63. Captured, 5/5/64 (?) in the Wilderness.
Pvt.	Brittain, William T.	1830	Morganton, Burke Co.	Farmer	Transferred, 11/24/63 from Co. G, 1st Regt. NC Cav.
Pvt.	Cordell, David L.	1835	Swannanoa, Buncombe Co.	Farmer	Enlisted, 3/1/63. Wounded (leg) and captured, 7/3/63 at Gettysburg. Deserted, 8/22/64.
Pvt.	Cordell, James M.	1844	Swannanoa, Buncombe Co.	Farm labor	Enlisted, 4/27/63. Captured, 7/6/63 at Williamsport, MD.
Pvt.	Creasman, Abraham Sr.	1805	Swannanoa, Buncombe Co.	Farmer	Enlisted, 4/27/63. Captured, 10/27/64 at Burgess' Mill. Surrendered, 4/9/65 at Appomattox Court House.
Pvt.	Creasman, Jacob	1813	Swannanoa, Buncombe Co.	Farmer	Enlisted, 9/14/63. Captured, sick in hospital, Petersburg, 4/3/65.
Pvt.	Creasman, Joseph	1844	Shufordville, Buncombe Co.	Farm labor	Enlisted, 4/27/63. Killed, 7/1/63 at Gettysburg.
Pvt.	Davis, F. M.	1827	Flint Rock, Catawba Co.	Day laborer	Enlisted, 9/14/63. Missing, 3/1/65.
Pvt.	Goodson, Henry	—	Buncombe Co.	—	Enlisted, 9/14/63. Missing, 3/1/65.
Pvt.	Henderson, Ezekiel	1830	Shufordville, Buncombe Co.	Carpenter	Enlisted, 3/27/63. Wounded, 7/3/63 and captured, 7/5/63 at Gettysburg. Wounded (left thigh) and captured, 10/27/64 at Burgess' Mill. Died of disease (chronic diarrhea), 4/28/65 as POW at Point Lookout, Md.
Rank	Name	DOB	Residence	Occupation	Remarks

Rank	Name	DOB	Residence	Occupation	Remarks
Pvt.	Justice, Ephraim	1830	Old Fort, McDowell Co.	Farmer	Enlisted, 10/9/63. Missing, 3/1/65.
Pvt.	Kyles, James	1833	Granite Hill, Iredell Co.	Farm labor	Enlisted, 4/27/63. Captured at Falling Waters, MD. Died of disease (chronic diarrhea), 11/20/64 as POW at Elmira, NY.
1st Sgt.	Martin, Edward A.	1840	—	—	Transferred and promoted, 8/18/63 from Co. G, 28th NC Inf. 1st Lt.—promoted to Regt. Adjutant, 9/3/63, transferred to F & S.
Pvt.	Mason, Elias	1833	McDowell Co.	—	Enlisted, 3/30/63. Died of disease ("organic disease of the heart producing ascites"), 3/14/65.
Pvt.	McReed, William	1845	Buncombe Co.	Farm labor	Enlisted, 4/27/63. Wounded, 7/1/63 at Gettysburg. Died of wounds, 7/15/63 in field hospital.
Pvt.	Miller, Gabriel P.	1825	Swannanoa, Buncombe Co.	Farmer	Enlisted, 3/20/63. Killed, 2/26/65 in Petersburg trenches.
Pvt.	Miller, William A.	1846	Swannanoa, Buncombe Co.	Farm labor	Enlisted, 11/1/63. Missing, 2/22/65.
Pvt.	Morris, Zebidee W.	1823	Raysville, Madison Co.	Farmer	Enlisted, 3/27/63. Wounded (left ankle), 8/12/63. Wounded (right arm), 8/21/64 at Petersburg.
Pvt.	Neighbour, Ferdinand	1844	Buncombe Co.	Farm labor	Enlisted, 4/27/63. Captured, 7/3/63 at Gettysburg. Deserted, 12/27/64.
Pvt.	Patton, James L.	1845	Swannanoa, Buncombe Co.	Farm labor	Enlisted, 3/1/63. Captured, 4/2/65 at Petersburg.
Pvt.	Roberts, Martin P.	1845	Asheville, Buncombe Co.	Student	Enlisted, 6/3/63. Captured, 7/14/63 at Falling Waters, MD.
Pvt.	Shroat, Alfred B. "Burl"	1842	Shufordville, Buncombe Co.	Farm labor	Enlisted, 9/14/63. Died of disease ("debilitas"), 4/28/64 in Richmond.
Pvt.	Smith, William E.	1828	Buncombe Co	Farmer	Enlisted, 3/1/63. Wounded, 5/5/64 at the Wilderness. Deserted, 3/14/65.

1864 Recruits

Rank	Name	DOB	Residence	Occupation	Remarks
Pvt.	Bird, Thomas J.	1823	Mills River, Henderson Co.	Coach maker	Enlisted, 11/3/64. Captured, 4/2/65 at Petersburg.
Pvt.	Clayton, William L.	1846	Fairview, Buncombe Co.	Farm labor	Enlisted, 4/9/64 at Camp Vance, NC. Captured, 4/2/65 at Petersburg.
Pvt.	Dickerson, J. R.	—	Buncombe Co.	—	Transferred, 11/64 from 1st Regt. NC Cav. Surrendered, 4/9/65 at Appomattox Court House.
Pvt.	Dishman, William	1846	New Hope, Iredell Co.	Farm labor	Enlisted, 11/15/64. Deserted, 3/13/65.
Pvt.	Everett, James H.	1839	Danielsville, Dickson Co.	Farm labor	Transferred, 12/31/64 from Co. B, 1st NC Cav. Deserted, 3/9/65.
Pvt.	Johnston, John F.	—	—	—	Enlisted, 4/4/64 at Camp Vance, NC. Wounded, 7/64 near Petersburg. Died from wounds ("gangrene"), 9/26/64 in Richmond.
Pvt.	Lindsay, Andrew J.	1833	Swannanoa, Buncombe Co.	Tinner's Asst.	Enlisted, 11/3/64. Cpl.—1/1/65. Captured, 4/2/65 at Petersburg.

Rank	Name	DOB	Residence	Occupation	Remarks
Pvt.	Luther, Washington	1832	Howling Creek, Buncombe Co.	House carpenter	Transferred from 1st Regt. NC Cav., 11/64. Surrendered, 4/9/65 at Appomattox Court House.
Pvt.	McClure, Ottway B.	—	Buncombe Co.	—	Enlisted, 3/1/64. Wounded, 6/1/64 at Cold Harbor. Captured, 4/2/65 at Petersburg.
Pvt.	**Miller, James M.**	**1841**	**Dick's Creek, Buncombe Co.**	**Farm labor**	**Enlisted, 4/4/64 at Camp Vance, NC. Wounded, 2/5/65 at Hatcher's Run. Died of wounds, 2/7/65.**
Pvt.	Miller, Joseph A.	1847	Swannanoa, Buncombe Co.	Farm labor	Enlisted, 3/1/64 in Buncombe Co. Captured, 10/27/64 at Burgess' Mill.
Pvt.	Patton, Calvin	1820	Swannanoa, Buncombe Co.	Farmer	Enlisted, 4/15/64. Discharged (disability—"paralysis affecting his right shoulder and arm ... dropsy in the legs"), 8/1/64.
Pvt.	Propst, L. H.	—	Newton, Catawba Co.	—	Enlisted, 10/28/64. Missing, 3/1/65.
Pvt.	Shope, Thomas J.	1847	Swannanoa, Buncombe Co.	Farm labor	Enlisted, 2/1/64. Captured, 4/2/65 at Petersburg.
Pvt.	Spake, Christopher "Christy"	1826	Craigeville, Gaston Co.	Farmer	Enlisted, 11/4/64. Captured, 3/25/65 in Petersburg trenches.
Pvt.	Stepp, Joseph M.	1825	Swannanoa, Buncombe Co.	Farmer	Enlisted, 11/3/64. Captured, 4/2/65 at Petersburg.

1865 Recruits

Rank	Name	DOB	Residence	Occupation	Remarks
Pvt.	Stroup, S. F.	1848	Webster, Jackson Co.	Farm labor	Enlisted, 1/1/65. Captured, 4/2/65 at Petersburg.

Chapter Notes

Chapter 1

1. Hale, Edward J., "The Bethel Regiment: The First North Carolina Volunteers," in *Histories of the Several Regiments and Battalions from North Carolina in the Great War, 1861–65*, ed. Walter Clark (Raleigh: E.M. Uzzell, 1901), vol. 1, pp. 89–90.
2. "The Flag of the Bethel Regiment," *Eastern Democrat*, 26 April 1861.
3. *Petersburg Express*, 20 May 1861. The *Express* article noted "three companies of the First Regiment of North Carolina Volunteers—the Fayetteville Independent Infantry, Captain Huske, p. the Fayetteville Light Infantry, Captain Starr ... and the Southern Stars, Captain Hoke ... arrived in this city by a special train from Raleigh at 7:30 o'clock on Saturday evening." The *Richmond Examiner*, 23 May 1861, recorded, "One Wednesday morning the rest of the regiment (of which the first installment reached this city on Sunday), amounting to seven hundred, reached this city by the southern road at one o'clock."
4. *Richmond Examiner*, 23 May 1861.
5. Warner, Ezra J., *Generals in Gray: Lives of the Confederate Commanders* (Baton Rouge: Louisiana State University Press, 1959), 136.
6. Hale, Edward J., *Histories of Several Regiments*, 78–9.
7. *Ibid.*, 79.
8. *Ibid.*, 109.
9. Leon, Louis, *Diary of a Tar Heel Confederate Soldier* (Charlotte: Stone, 1913), 1.
10. Parks, Thomas, letter, 12 May 1861. Parks' letters have been included in Lawing, Mike, and Carolyn Lawing, eds., *My Dearest Friend: The Civil War Correspondence of Cornelia McGrimsey and Lewis Warlick* (Durham: Carolina Academic Press, 2000).
11. Ross, Egbert, letter, 13 May 1861, University of North Carolina, Southern Historical Collection, Chapel Hill.
12. *Raleigh State Journal*, 8 May 1861.
13. Warlick letter, 12 May 1861. Warlick's letters have been included in Lawing, Mike, and Carolyn Lawing, eds., *My Dearest Friend: The Civil War Correspondence of Cornelia McGrimsey and Lewis Warlick* (Durham: Carolina Academic Press, 2000).
14. Warlick letter, 12 May 1861.
15. Ross, Egbert, letter, 13 May 1861.
16. Leon, Louis, 1.
17. Warlick letter, 29 May 1861.
18. *North Carolina Whig*, 7 May 1861.
19. Hoke, J. F., "Adjutant General's Orders," 19 May 1861, Adjutant General's Office, Raleigh.
20. Isely, R.W., "The Secession of North Carolina," *Confederate Veteran* 37 (1931), 450.
21. *New Bern Daily Progress*, 22 May 1861.
22. *Western Democrat*, 21 May 1861.
23. Titcomb, Bettie, letter, 21 May 1861, William J. Martin Collection, Davidson College Archives, Davidson, NC.
24. Wilson, Amanda, diary, 3 June 1861, in Venner, William T., ed., *Queen City Lady: The 1861 Journal of Amanda Wilson* (Cincinnati: Larrea Books, 1996).
25. Warlick letter, 23 May 1861.
26. *Petersburg Express*, 22 May 1861.
27. Warlick letter, 23 May 1861.
28. Sadler, Julius, *Compiled Service Records of Confederate Soldiers Who Served in Organizations from the State of North Carolina*, hereafter referred to as *CSRC*. Sadler's service record notes, "Killed, May 26 by Car[iage] ... Killed between Rich[mond] and West Point."
29. *Western Democrat*, 25 May 1861.
30. Leon, Louis, 2.
31. Warlick letter, 29 May 1861.
32. Chapman, Craig S., *More Terrible Than Victory: North Carolina's Bloody Bethel Regiment, 1861–1865* (Dulles, VA: Brassey's, 1998), 25.
33. Leon, Louis, 3.
34. Saunders, Joseph H., letter, 16 June 1861, Joseph H. Saunders Papers, Southern Historical Collection, Wilson Library, University of North Carolina at Chapel Hill.
35. Hill, Daniel H., *The War of the Rebellion: A Compilation of the Official Records of the Union and Confederate Armies* (Washington, D.C.: Government Printing Office, 1880–1901), Vol. 2, Report No. 8.
36. Saunders, Joseph H., letter, 16 June 1861, Southern Historical Collection, Wilson Library, University of North Carolina at Chapel Hill.
37. Butler, Benjamin F., 10 June 1861, *Official Records*, Vol. 2, No. 1.
38. Pierce, Ebenezer W., 12 June 1861, *Official Records*, Vol. 2, No. 2.
39. Townsend, Frederick, 12 June 1861, *Official Records*, Vol. 2, No. 3.
40. Buel, Clarence C., and Robert U. Johnson, *Battles and Leaders of the Civil War* (New York: Century, 1914), Vol. 2, 148.
41. Hill, Jr., Daniel H., *Confederate Military History* (Atlanta: Confederate, 1899), Vol. 5, pp. 13–4.

42. Bendix, John E., 12 June 1861, *Official Records*, Vol. 2, No. 4.
43. Townsend, Frederick, 12 June 1861, *Official Records*, Vol. 2, No. 3.
44. Bendix, John E., 12 June 1861, *Official Records*, Vol. 2, No. 4.
45. Townsend, Frederick, 12 June 1861, *Official Records*, Vol. 2, No. 3.
46. Warlick letter, 11 June 1861.
47. Hill, Daniel H., *Official Records*, Vol. 2, No. 8.
48. Hale, Edward J., *Histories of Several Regiments*, 90.
49. Freeman, Douglas S., *Lee's Lieutenants: Manassas to Malvern Hill* (New York: Scribner's, 1942), Vol. 1, p. 17.
50. *Daily Dispatch*, 11 June 1861.
51. "Dispatch," 18 October 1901, in *Southern Historical Society Papers* (Richmond), Vol. 29 (1901).
52. Pierce, Ebenezer W., 12 June 1861, *Official Records*, Vol. 2, No. 2.
53. "Dispatch," 18 October 1901, in *Southern Historical Society Papers* (Richmond), Vol. 29 (1901).
54. Hill, Daniel H., *Official Records*, Vol. 2, No. 8.
55. "Dispatch," 18 October 1901, in *Southern Historical Society Papers* (Richmond), Vol. 29 (1901).
56. Randolph, George W., *Official Records*, Vol. 2, No. 10.
57. Warlick letter, 11 June 1861.
58. Poteat, Peter, *CSRC*.
59. Hill, Daniel H., *Official Records*, Vol. 2, No. 8.
60. Randolph, George W., *Official Records*, Vol. 2, No. 10.
61. Montague, Edgar B., *Official Records*, Vol. 2, No. 11.
62. Kilpatrick, Judson, *Official Records*, Vol. 2, No. 5.
63. Stuart, William D., *Official Records*, Vol. 2, No. 9.
64. Kilpatrick, Judson, *Official Records*, Vol. 2, No. 5.
65. Dinkins, James, "The Battle of Big Bethel, VA," *Confederate Veteran* 26 (1918), 291.
66. Rogers, Council, and Williams, Charles, *CSRC*.
67. Kilpatrick, Judson, *Official Records*, Vol. 2, No. 5.
68. Leon, Louis, 3.
69. Townsend, Frederick, 12 June 1861, *Official Records*, Vol. 2, No. 3.
70. *Ibid.*
71. *Ibid.*
72. Ratchford, J.W., *CSRC*.
73. Buel, Clarence C., and Robert U. Johnson, *Battles and Leaders*, Vol. 2, 149.
74. Webb, Charles, letter, *Lamoille Newsdealer*, 21 June 1861.
75. Carr, Joseph, in *Battles and Leaders*, Vol. 2, pp. 149–50.
76. Carr, Joseph, in *Confederate Military History*, Vol. 5, p. 14.
77. Whitney, Dana, memoir, "Civil War Cache," Hartford, CT.
78. Webb, Charles, letter, *Lamoille Newsdealer*, 21 June 1861.
79. Benedict, George G., *Vermont in the Civil War* (Burlington: Free Press Association, 1888), Vol. 1, pp. 42–57.
80. Hale, Edward J., *Histories of Several Regiments*, 90–1.
81. Benedict, George G., *Vermont in the Civil War*, Vol. 1, pp. 42–57.
82. Butler, Benjamin F., *Official Records*, Vol. 2, No. 1.
83. White, William, *CSRC*.
84. Barney, Valentine G., letter, 11 June 1861.
85. Hill, Daniel H., *Official Records*, Vol. 2, No. 8.
86. Hale, Edward J., *Histories of Several Regiments*, 101.
87. Thorpe, John H., in Hale, Edward J., *Histories of Several Regiments*, 101.
88. Randolph, George W., *Official Records*, Vol. 2, No. 10.
89. *Weekly Raleigh Register*, 19 June 1861.
90. *Daily Dispatch*, 11 June 1861.
91. Magruder, John B., *Official Records*, Vol. 2, No. 7.
92. Leon, Louis, 3.
93. "Dispatch," 18 October 1901, in *Southern Historical Society Papers* (Richmond), Vol. 29 (1901).
94. Warlick letter, 11 June 1861.
95. Bridges, Hal, *Lee's Maverick General: Daniel Harvey Hill* (New York: McGraw-Hill, 1961), 29.
96. Warlick letter, 11 June 1861.
97. Ross, Egbert, in Chapman, Craig S., 35.
98. Huske, Benjamin, in Chapman, Craig, S., 35.
99. Leon, Louis, 4.
100. Hord, B.M., "The Battle of Big Bethel, VA," *Confederate Veteran* 26 (1918), 419.
101. Butler, Benjamin F., *Official Records*, Vol. 2, No. 1.
102. Freeman, Douglas S., Vol. 1, p. 18. Hale, Edward J., *Histories of Several Regiments*, 105.
103. State Convention, Resolution No. 6, 17 June 1861.
104. Hale, Edward J., *Histories of Several Regiments*, 130–1.

Chapter 2

1. Leon, Louis, 4.
2. Hill, Jr., Daniel H., *Confederate Military History*, Vol. 5, p. 15.
3. Warlick letter, 16 June 1861.
4. Freeman, Douglas, *Lee's Lieutenants*, Vol. 1, pp. 21–22.
5. "Memorial Address," *Southern Historical Society Papers*, Vol. 21 (1893), 117.
6. Warlick letter, 6 July 1861.
7. Chapman, Craig S., *More Terrible Than Victory*, 39.
8. Lloyd, Whitnel P., *CSRC*, 9 July 1861.
9. Warlick letter, 16 June 1861.
10. Chapman, Craig S., *More Terrible Than Victory*, 39.
11. Leon, Louis, 3.
12. Warlick letters, 23 June 1861, 3 August 1861.
13. Warlick letter, 31 August 1861.
14. Chapman, Craig S., *More Terrible Than Victory*, 41.
15. 1st NC Regimental returns, *CRSC*.
16. Warlick letter, 31 August 1861.
17. Hawkins, Rush, in Johnson and Buel, *Battles and Leaders of the Civil War*, Vol. 1, pp. 632–40.
18. Huske, Henry, letter, 1 September 1861.
19. Warlick letter, 31 August 1861.
20. Huske, Henry, letter, 1 September 1861.
21. Clark, Henry T., in Hill, *Confederate Military History*, Vol. 5, p. 22.
22. *Ibid.*
23. Hill, Jr., Daniel H., *Confederate Military History*, Vol. 5, p. 23.
24. Hawkins, Rush, in Johnson and Buel, *Battles and Leaders of the Civil War*, Vol. 1, p. 645.
25. Wilkes, John, letter, 2 September 1861.
26. Warlick letter, 15 September 1861.
27. Lane, James, and Hoke, Robert, *CSRC*.
28. Warlick letter, 31 August 1861.
29. Warlick letter, 7 October 1861.

30. Hale, Edward J. *Histories of Several Regiments*, 122.
31. Daniels, Dennis F., "History of the Polk Prison Property" (Raleigh: Research Branch, Division of Archives and History, North Carolina Department of Cultural Resources, 2001), 9–10.
32. Leon, Louis, 4–5.
33. Carpenter, Kinchen J., in Williams, Julie C., ed., *War Diary of Kinchen Jahu Carpenter, Company I, 50th North Carolina Regiment, War Between the States* (Rutherford, NC: Self-published, 1955), 5.
34. Day, William A., *A True History of Company I, 49th Regiment, North Carolina Troops: in the Great Civil War Between the North and the South* (Newton, NC: Enterprise Job Office, 1898), 10–11.
35. Wills, George W., "Spirit of the Age," *Raleigh Weekly*, 21 April 1862.
36. Carpenter, Kinchen J., in Williams, Julie C., ed., *War Diary of Kinchen Jahu Carpenter* (1955), 5–6.
37. Day, William A., *A True History of Company I, 49th Regiment*, 1898, 11.
38. Ibid., 11–12.
39. Daniels, Dennis F., "History of the Polk Prison Property," 2001, 13.
40. Fraley, Ashbel, "Purposes for Brigade Drill," in Watford, Christopher, ed., *The Civil War in North Carolina: Soldiers and Civilians' Letters and Diaries, 1861–1865* (Jefferson, NC: McFarland, 2003).
41. Hill, Jr., Daniel H., *Confederate Military History*, Vol. 5, p. 12.
42. 1st North Carolina Infantry, 11th North Carolina Infantry, *CSRC*.
43. Ibid.
44. *General Order Book, 1862–1863*, 31 March 1862.
45. Ibid.
46. Gilliam, Francis, *CSRC*.
47. Hubbard, Matthew, *CSRC*.
48. Powell, William, *CSRC*.
49. Burke (NC) County Historical Society. *The Heritage of Burke County*, 1981.
50. Mast, Greg, *State Troops and Volunteers: A Photographic Record of North Carolina's Soldiers* (Raleigh: North Carolina Department of Cultural Resources, Division of Archives and History, 1995), 114.
51. Bazemore, Henry, *CSRC*.
52. Burke County Historical Society, *The Heritage of Burke County* (1981), 462.
53. Mast, Greg, *State Troops and Volunteers: A Photographic Record* (1995), 269.
54. Warlick letter, 21 May 1862.
55. Ross, Egbert, *General Order Book*, 1 April 1862.
56. Ibid.
57. Owens, William A., *General Order Book*, 10 April 1862; Owens, William A., *CSRC*.
58. Hardy, Michael, *Civil War Charlotte*, 77.
59. Ibid., 27.
60. Lattimore, T. D., *History of the 34th North Carolina* (1901), Vol. 2, p. 582.
61. Ibid.
62. Hardy, Michael. *Civil War Charlotte*, 77.
63. Smith, Henry L., "Memorial," *Davidson Monthly*, April 1896.
64. Johnston, George, letter to William J. Martin, 30 August 1861.
65. Bryan, R., letter to William J. Martin, 30 July 1861.
66. Sterling, Edward, letter to William J. Martin, 14 August 1861.
67. Sterling, Richard, letter to William J. Martin, 12 August 1861.
68. Grechern, William, letter to William J. Martin, 12 August 1861.
69. Lane, James, *Charlotte Observer*, 17 February 1895.
70. Clark, Henry, *General Order Book*, 19 April 1862.
71. Leventhorpe, Louis Bryan, "Reminiscences: Brigadier General Collett Leventhorpe," Civil War Collection, Military Collection, State Archives of North Carolina, Raleigh, 1896.
72. Jones, Edmund, "Memorial Service Address," in Leventhorpe, Louis Bryan, "Reminiscences: Brigadier General Collett Leventhorpe," 1896.
73. Warner, Ezra J., *Generals in Gray*, 185.
74. Leventhorpe, Collett, *General Order Book*, 21 April 1862.
75. Yaunts, Reuben, *CSRC*.
76. Leventhorpe, Collett, *General Order Book*, 9 May 1862.
77. Leventhorpe, Collett, letter. In David M. Rubenstein Rare Book & Manuscript Library, Duke University. All Leventhorpe correspondence is from this institution.
78. Martin, John, *General Order Book*, 24 April 1862.
79. Leventhorpe, Collett, *General Order Book*, 8 May 1862.
80. Jones, Edmund, "Memorial Service Address," in Leventhorpe, Louis Bryan, "Reminiscences: Brigadier General Collett Leventhorpe," 1896.
81. Owens, William A., *CSRC*.
82. Leventhorpe, Collett, in personal collection.
83. Cooper, Thomas W., letter, 14 July 1862.
84. Castellaw, James C., *CSRC*.
85. *CSRC*, 11th North Carolina Infantry.
86. Whisenhunt, Alexander, Whisenhunt, James, Whisenhunt, Stanhope, *CSRC*.
87. Armfield, Mark D., letter 11 July 1862, *CSRC*.
88. Ibid.
89. *CSRC*, 11th North Carolina Infantry.
90. Lucas, H.C., *General Order Book*, 13 May 1862.

Chapter 3

1. Bird, Francis, letter, 16 June 1862. Francis Bird Collection, University of North Carolina, Southern Historical Collection, Chapel Hill, NC. All Bird correspondence is from this institution.
2. Warlick letter, 21 May 1862.
3. Lucas, H.C., *General Order Book*, 13 May 1862.
4. Burke, James C., *The Wilmington and Weldon Railroad in the Civil War* (Jefferson, NC: McFarland, 2012).
5. Bright, Leslie D., *The Blockade Runner* Modern Greece *and Her Cargo* (Raleigh: Underwater Archaeology Branch, North Carolina Department of Cultural Resources, 1977), 2–3.
6. Leventhorpe, Collett, letter, 17 May 1862, in Leventhorpe, Louis Bryan, "Reminiscences: Brigadier General Collett Leventhorpe," 1896.
7. Martin, William, and Outlaw, Edward, in Hale, Edward J., *Histories of Several Regiments*, 586.
8. Martin, William, and Outlaw, Edward, in Hale, Edward J., *Histories of Several Regiments*, 586.
9. Bird, Francis, letter, 26 May 1862, Southern Historical Collection, Wilson Library, University of North Carolina at Chapel Hill.
10. Martin, William, and Outlaw, Edward, in Hale, Edward J., *Histories of Several Regiments*, 586.
11. Chapman, Craig S., *More Terrible Than Victory*, 54.
12. Brown, John J., letter, 17 August 1862.

13. Tuther, Jr., T., comp., *Kelley's Wilmington Directory, Business Directory for 1860-61* (Wilmington: Geo. H. Kelley Bookseller and Stationer, 1860), 72.
14. Cain, William, letter, 18 October 1862. University of North Carolina, Southern Historical Collection, Chapel Hill, NC.
15. Wellman, Manly W., "Tar Heel Lover," *News and Observer*, 16 September 1861.
16. Hoggard, William, *CSRC*.
17. Gragg, Rod, *Covered with Glory: The 26th North Carolina Infantry at the Battle of Gettysburg* (New York: HarperCollins, 2000), 13.
18. Leventhorpe, Collett, *General Order Book*, 25 July 1862.
19. Brown, John J., letter, 17 August 1862.
20. Dellinger, Frederick W., letter, 6 May 1862.
21. Warlick letter, 3 June 1862.
22. Brown, John J., letter, 8 August 1862.
23. French, Samuel, *General Order Book*, 15 June 1862.
24. Warlick letter, 17 June 1862.
25. Bird, Francis, letter, 16 June 1862, Southern Historical Collection, Wilson Library, University of North Carolina at Chapel Hill.
26. Cain, William, letter, 18 October 1862.
27. Bird, Francis, letter, 16 June 1862, Southern Historical Collection, Wilson Library, University of North Carolina at Chapel Hill.
28. "Blockade of Wilmington," *Harper's Weekly*, 3 December 1864.
29. Hardy, Michael C., *North Carolina in the Civil War*, 31.
30. Bright, Leslie D., *The Blockade Runner Modern Greece and Her Cargo*, 6–7.
31. Hill, Daniel H., *General Order Book*, 5 August 1862.
32. Hill, Daniel H., *General Order Book*, 28 August 1862.
33. Bright, Leslie D., *The Blockade Runner Modern Greece and Her Cargo*, 10.
34. Ross, Egbert, letter, 5 July 1862.
35. Leventhorpe, Collett, *Wilmington Journal*, 10 July 1862.
36. Warlick letter, 24 June 1862.
37. Gragg, Rod, *Covered with Glory*, 15.
38. Warlick letter, 17 August 1862.
39. Causby, John, *CSRC*.
40. 11th NC Regiment, *CSRC*.
41. 11th NC Regiment, *CSRC*.
42. Cooke, R.J., "General Hospital No. 4" (unpublished paper, 2005).
43. Kerr, David, *CSRC*.
44. Grier, William, letter, 1 September 1862, *CSRC*.
45. *Western Democrat*, 16 September 1862; Means, John, *CSRC*.
46. *North Carolina Standard*, 1 October 1862.
47. Gilbert, J. Franklin, *CSRC*.
48. Kelley, James, "Form No. 22: Burial Costs," 13 August 1862, *CSRC*.
49. 11th NC Regiment, *CSRC*.
50. Chapman, Craig S., *More Terrible Than Victory*, 57.
51. Brown, John J., letter, 8 August 1862.
52. Chapman, Craig S., *More Terrible Than Victory*, 59.
53. Drane, Henry M., letter, 23 October 1862.
54. Clingman, Thomas, *General Order Book*, 13 September 1862.
55. Warlick letter, 16 September 1862.
56. Bristol, Elam, letter, 23 November 1862.
57. Leventhorpe, Collett, in Leventhorpe, Louis Bryan, "Reminiscences: Brigadier General Collett Leventhorpe," 1896.
58. *Journal Office*, 16 October 1862.
59. Chapman, Craig S., *More Terrible Than Victory*, 59.
60. Hardy, Michael C., *Civil War Charlotte: Last Capital of the Confederacy* (Charleston, SC: History Press, 2012), 32–4.
61. Hardy, Michael C., *Civil War Charlotte*, 33.
62. Warlick letter, 12 October 1862.
63. Bird, Francis, letter, 28 October 1862, Southern Historical Collection, Wilson Library, University of North Carolina at Chapel Hill.
64. Warlick letter, 12 October 1862.
65. Keith, John C., *CSRC*.
66. Leventhorpe, Collett, in Leventhorpe, Louis Bryan, "Reminiscences."
67. Warlick letter, 19 November 1862.
68. Peck, John J., *Official Records*, Vol. 18, p. 31.
69. Frazier, Isaac, *CSRC*.
70. Warlick letter, 19 November 1862.
71. *Ibid.*
72. *Ibid.*
73. Erwin, George P., letter, 24 November 1862.
74. Warlick letter, 23 November 1862.
75. Leventhorpe, Collett, letter, 4 December 1862.
76. *Ibid.*
77. Warlick letter, 23 November 1862.
78. Leventhorpe, Collett, letter, 4 December 1862.
79. Martin, William, and Outlaw, Edward, in Hale, Edward J., *Histories of Several Regiments*, 587.

Chapter 4

1. Martin, William, and Outlaw, Edward, in Hale, Edward J., *Histories of Several Regiments*, 587.
2. Wayne County, North Carolina, Federal Census, 1860.
3. Bright, Leslie S., Rowland, William H., and Bardon, James C., *The CSS Neuse: A Question of Iron and Time* (Raleigh: North Carolina Office of Archives and History, 1981).
4. 11th North Carolina, *CSRC*.
5. Warlick letter, 18 December 1862.
6. 11th North Carolina, *CSRC*.
7. Warlick letter, 20 September 1862.
8. Warlick, John C., "Battle of White Hall, N.C.," *Confederate Veteran* 12, p. 178.
9. Carbone, John, *The Civil War in Coastal North Carolina* (Raleigh: Office of Archives and History, North Carolina Department of Cultural Resources, 2001), 72.
10. Warlick, John C., *Confederate Veteran*, Vol. 12, p. 178.
11. Warlick letter, 18 December 1862.
12. Warlick, John C., *Confederate Veteran*, Vol. 12, p. 178.
13. Robertson, Beverly H., *Official Records*, Vol. 18, No. 16.
14. Kirwin, Thomas, *Memorial History of the Seventeenth Regiment Massachusetts Volunteer Infantry in the Civil War from 1861–1865* (Salem, MA: Salem Press, 1911), 155.
15. Evans, Nathan G., *Official Records*, Vol. 18, No. 35.
16. Buel, Clarence C., and Robert U. Johnson, *Battles and Leaders*, Vol. 1, pp. 640–45.

17. Robertson, Beverly H., *Official Records*, Vol. 18, No. 16.
18. "Kinston," *Confederate Veteran* 6, p. 207.
19. "Battle of Whitehall," *Harper's Weekly*, 10 January 1863.
20. Ledlie, James H., *Official Records*, Vol. 18, No. 4.
21. Jenney, Edwin S., *Official Records*, Vol. 18, No. 5.
22. Warlick, John C., *Confederate Veteran*, Vol. 12: 178.
23. Robertson, Beverly H., *Official Records*. Vol. 18, No. 16.
24. *Ibid*.
25. Benjamin Walker, Charles Morris, Jefferson Thrower, *CSRC*.
26. Martin, William, and Outlaw, Edward, in Hale, Edward J., *Histories of Several Regiments*, 587–88.
27. Warlick, John C., *Confederate Veteran* 12, p. 178.
28. Heckman, Charles, *Official Records*, Vol. 18, No. 23.
29. Zabriskie, Abram, *Official Records*, Vol. 18, No. 24.
30. Kirwin, Thomas, *Memorial History* (1911), 153.
31. Hill, Jr., Daniel H., *Confederate Military History*, 112.
32. Means, William, and Roundtree, Noah, *CSRC*.
33. Craft, Michael, Query, Samuel, William, Bazemore, *CSRC*.
34. Zabriskie, Abram, *Official Records*, Vol. 18, No. 24.
35. Warlick letter, 18 December 1862.
36. Robertson, Beverly H., *Official Records*, Vol. 18, No. 16.
37. Chambers, John G., *Official Records*, Vol. 18, No. 14.
38. Kirwin, Thomas, *Memorial History* (1911), 153.
39. Warlick letter, 30 December 1862.
40. Kirwin, Thomas, *Memorial History* (1911), 154–5.
41. Gault, James, and Duckworth, Walter, *CRSC*.
42. Warlick letter, 30 December 1862.
43. Kirwin, Thomas, *Memorial History*, 1911, 161.
44. Chambers, John G., *Official Records*, Vol. 18, No. 14.
45. "Return of Casualties in the Union Forces," *Official Records*, Vol. 18, No. 2.
46. Leggett, Robert, *Official Records*, Vol. 18, No. 19.
47. Gardner, James B., *Record of the Service of the Forty-fourth Massachusetts Volunteer Militia in North Carolina, August 1862 to May 1863* (Boston: Privately printed, 1887), 140.
48. Gardner, James B., *Record of the Service of the Forty-fourth Massachusetts*, 140.
49. Codman, Charles, R., *Official Records*, Vol. 18, No. 16.
50. Kirwin, Thomas, *Memorial History*, 1911, 154.
51. Warlick letter, 30 December 1862.
52. Warlick, John C., *Confederate Veteran* 12, p. 178.
53. Jenney, Edwin S., *Official Records*, Vol. 18, No. 5.
54. Ledlie, James H., *Official Records*, Vol. 18, No. 4.
55. Codman, Charles, R., *Official Records*, Vol. 18, No. 16.
56. *North Carolina Standard*, 24 December 1862.
57. Warlick letter, 18 December 1862.
58. Barrett, John G., *North Carolina as a Civil War Battleground, 1861–1865* (Raleigh: State Department of Archives and History, 1960), 52.
59. Robertson, Beverly H., *Official Records*, Vol. 18, No. 16.
60. Wellman, Manly W., "Tar Heel Lover," *News and Observer*, 24 December 1862.
61. Warlick letter, 30 December 1862.
62. Bristol, Lambert A., letter, 4 January 1863.
63. 11th North Carolina Infantry, *CSRC*.
64. "Return of Casualties in the Union Forces," *Official Records*, Vol. 18, No. 2.

Chapter 5

1. Bentley, Franklin, letter, 2 December 1862.
2. Rozzell, William, and Turner, William, *CSRC*.
3. Erwin, George P., *CSRC*.
4. Warlick letter, 22 December 1862.
5. Warlick letter, 30 December 1862.
6. *General Order Book*, 22 December 1862.
7. Leventhorpe, Collett, letter (n.d.) December 1862.
8. "The Late Gen. Pettigrew," *Raleigh Register*, 18 August 1863.
9. Bond, William R., *Pettigrew or Pickett? An Historical Essay* (Scotland Neck, NC: W.L.L. Hall, 1888), 5.
10. Bond, William R., *Pettigrew or Pickett? An Historical Essay*, 6.
11. Hess, Earl J., *Lee's Tar Heels: The Pettigrew-Kirkland-MacRae Brigade* (Chapel Hill: University of North Carolina Press, 2002), 35–7.
12. Chestnut, Mary B., *A Diary from Dixie* (New York: D. Appleton, 1905), 145.
13. *Ibid*.
14. Hess, Earl J., *Lee's Tar Heels*, 39.
15. Hill, Jr., Daniel H., *Confederate Military History*, 337.
16. Hess, Earl J., *Lee's Tar Heels*, 39–42.
17. Warlick letter, 22 December 1862.
18. Elliott, William A., 9 December 1862.
19. Warlick letter, 30 December 1862.
20. Dellinger, Peter F., letter, 7 December 1862.
21. Burgwyn, William, letter, 12 February 1863.
22. Warlick letter, 22 December 1862.
23. Burgwyn, William, letter, 12 February 1863.
24. Freeman, Douglas S., *Lee's Lieutenants*, Vol. 2, p. 431.
25. Heil, M.F., letter, (n.d.) April 1863.
26. Leon, Louis, letter, 4 February 1863.
27. Farmer, John F., letter, 29 January 1863.
28. Warlick letter, 22 December 1862.
29. Dellinger, Peter F., letter, 7 December 1862.
30. Dellinger, Peter F., letter, 27 January 1863.
31. Elliott, William A., letter, 13 December 1862.
32. Elliott, William A., letter, 27 January 1863.
33. Arrowood, James A., letter, 22 November 1862.
34. Warlick letter, 22 December 1862.
35. Dellinger, Peter F., 7 December 1862.
36. Warlick letter, 25 January 1863.
37. Elliott, William A., letter, 27 January 1863.
38. Dellinger, Peter F., letter, 27 January 1863.
39. Yancey, J., letter 8 February 1863.
40. Martin, Bunny, letter 10 September 1862.
41. Elliott, William A., letter, 23 January 1863.
42. McSween, Murdock J., letter 26 March 1863.
43. Dellinger, Frederick, letter, 25 January 1863.
44. Warlick letter, 25 January 1863.
45. Lawling, Mike, and Lawling, Carol, eds., *My Dearest Friend*, 130.
46. Warlick letter, 25 January 1863.
47. Leventhorpe, Collett, *General Order Book*, 1 January 1863.
48. Parker, William, letter, 4 January 1863.
49. Hoggard, William, *CSRC*.
50. 11th North Carolina Infantry, *CSRC*.
51. Carpenter, R.W., letter, 10 April 1863.
52. Hill, Jr., Daniel H., *Confederate Military History*, 121.
53. Leventhorpe, Collett, *General Order Book*, 24 February 1863.
54. Warlick letter, 25 January 1863.

55. *Ibid.*
56. *Ibid.*
57. Leventhorpe, Collett, letter, 14 January 1863.
58. Jones, Edmund, letter, 20 January 1863.
59. Elliott, William A., letter 23 January 1863.
60. Hoyle, Lemuel, letter, 9 January 1863.
61. Leventhorpe, Collett, letter, 20 January 1863.
62. *Ibid.*
63. Pettigrew, James J., *General Order Book*, 1 February 1863.
64. Warlick letter, 25 January 1863.
65. Leon, Luis, letter, 4 February 1863.
66. Smith, Henry L., "Memorial Number: Col. Wm. J. Martin, M.A., LL.D.," *Davidson Monthly*, April 1896.
67. Chapman, Craig S., *More Terrible Than Victory*, 71.
68. Parker, William, letter, 22 February 1863.
69. Elliott, William, letter (n.d.) February 1863.
70. *Ibid.*
71. Elliott, William, letter, 22 February 1863.
72. Parker, William, letter, 22 February 1863.
73. Leventhorpe, Collett, letter, 22 February 1863.
74. Leventhorpe, Collett, letter, 10 March 1863.
75. Hess, Earl J., *Lee's Tar Heels*, 90.
76. Hamilton, J.G. de Roulhac, ed., *The Papers of Randolph Abbott Shotwell*, vol. 1, p. 455.
77. *Ibid.*, 455–6.
78. Elliott, William, letter, 25 March 1863.
79. Hamilton, J.G. de Roulhac, ed., *The Papers of Randolph Abbott Shotwell*, vol. 1, p. 456.
80. Elliott, William, letter, 25 March 1863.
81. Hill, Henry, letter, 25 March 1863.
82. Hamilton, J.G. de Roulhac, ed., *The Papers of Randolph Abbott Shotwell*, vol. 1, p. 458.
83. *Ibid.*, 459.
84. Parker, William, letter, 24 March 1863.
85. Hamilton, J.G. de Roulhac, ed., *The Papers of Randolph Abbott Shotwell*, vol. 1, p. 459.
86. Burgwyn, Henry, Letter, 28 March 1863.
87. Murdock, John, letter, 30 March 1863.
88. "Piney Woods of North Carolina," *Harper's New Monthly Magazine*, May 1857, 750.
89. *Ibid.*
90. Foster, John G., *Official Records*, Vol. 18, No. 1.
91. Leventhorpe, Collett, letter, 2 April 1863.
92. Hess, Earl J., *Lee's Tar Heels*, 94.
93. Jarratt, Isaac A., letter, 6 April 1863.
94. Leventhorpe, Collett, letter, 3 April 1863.
95. Myers, Ambrose, letter, 8 April 1863.
96. Spinola, Francis B., *Official Records*, Vol. 18, No. 12.
97. Leventhorpe, Collett, letter, 3 April 1863.
98. Midgett, Ray, "The Siege of Washington, NC," *Pamlico's Past*, 7 April 2013.
99. Henry, Prince, *Official Records*, Vol. 18, No. 8.
100. Foster, John G., *Official Records*, Vol. 18, No. 1.
101. Elliott, William, letter, 8 April 1863.
102. Warlick letter, 20 April 1863.
103. Elliott, William, letter, 8 April 1863.
104. Foster, John G., *Official Records*, Vol. 18, No. 1.
105. Erwin, George, letter, 20 April 1863.
106. Spinola, Francis B., *Official Records*. Vol. 18, No. 12.
107. *Ibid.*
108. Leventhorpe, Collett, letter, 10 April 1863.
109. Spinola, Francis B., *Official Records*, Vol. 18, No. 12.
110. Spinola, Francis B., *Official Records*, Vol. 18, No. 12.
111. Martin, William J., and Outlaw, Edward, in Hale, Edward J., *Histories of Several Regiments*, 588.
112. Spinola, Francis B., *Official Records*, Vol. 18, No. 12.
113. Richmond, Silas, *Official Records*, Vol. 18, No. 9.
114. Black, Patrick, *CSRC*.
115. Spinola, Francis B., *Official Records*, Vol. 18, No. 12.
116. Leventhorpe, Collett, letter, 10 April 1863.
117. Erwin, George, letter, 20 April 1863.
118. Leventhorpe, Collett, letter, 10 April 1863.
119. Spinola, Francis B., *Official Records*, Vol. 18, No. 12.
120. Foster, John G., *Official Records*, Vol. 18, No. 1.
121. *Ibid.*
122. Warlick letter, 26 April 1863.
123. *Ibid.*
124. Pettigrew, James, General Order Book, 25 April 1863.
125. Warlick letter, 26 April 1863.
126. Warlick letter, 26 April 1863.
127. Parker, William, letter, 20 April 1863.
128. Warlick letter, 26 April 1863.
129. Elliott, William, letter, 27 April 1863.
130. Warlick letter, 26 April 1863.
131. Elliott, William, letter, 27 April 1863.
132. *Ibid.*
133. Elliott, William, letter, 30 April 1863.
134. *Ibid.*
135. Leventhorpe, Collett, letter, 28 May 1863.

Chapter 6

1. Black, Robert C., *The Railroads of the Confederacy* (Chapel Hill: University of North Carolina Press, 1952), 31.
2. *Ibid.*
3. Elliott, William, letter, 2 May 1863.
4. Burgwyn, Henry, letter, 11 May 1863.
5. Elliott, William, letter 2, May 1863.
6. Wright, James, letter, 2 May 1863.
7. McLure, Cyrus, letter, 2 May 1863.
8. Parker, William, letter, 4 May 1863.
9. Hess, Earl J., *Lee's Tar Heels*, 101.
10. Chapman, Craig S., *More Terrible Than Victory*, 83.
11. Bartlett, Jacob, "Recollections," Southern Historical Collection, Wilson Library, University of North Carolina at Chapel Hill.
12. Martin, William, and Outlaw, Edward, in Hale, Edward J., *Histories of Several Regiments*, 588.
13. Parker, William, letter, 6 May 1863.
14. Elliott, William, letter, 5 May 1863.
15. *Ibid.*
16. *Ibid.*
17. Warlick letter, 25 May 1863.
18. Bird, Francis, letter, 16 May 1863, Southern Historical Collection, Wilson Library, University of North Carolina at Chapel Hill.
19. Elliott, William, letter, 10 May 1863.
20. Pettigrew, James, *General Order Book*, 17 May 1863, 28 May 1863.
21. Elliott, William, letter, 10 May 1863, 19 May 1863.
22. Freeman, Douglas S., *Lee's Lieutenants*, Vol. 2, p. 710.
23. Venner, William T., *The 7th Tennessee Infantry in the Civil War* (Jefferson, NC: McFarland, 2013), 77.

24. Warner, Ezra J., *Generals in Gray*, 113.
25. Freeman, Douglas S., *Lee's Lieutenants*, Vol. 2, p. 507.
26. Warner, Ezra J., *Generals in Gray*, 134–5.
27. Leventhorpe, Collett, letter, 28 May 1863.
28. Burgwyn, Henry, diary, 9 June 1863.
29. Parker, William, letter, 11 June 1863.
30. Warlick letter, 25 May 1863.
31. Elliott, William, letter, 25 May 1863.
32. Warlick letter, 25 May 1863.
33. Leventhorpe, Collett, letter, 4 June 1863.
34. Venner, William T., *The 7th Tennessee Infantry in the Civil War*, 79.
35. Chapman, Craig S., *More Terrible Than Victory*, 87.
36. Parker, William, letter, 11 June 1863.
37. Warlick letter, 6 June 1863.
38. Dellinger, Peter, letter, 15 June 1863.
39. Warlick letter, 6 June 1863.
40. Parker, William, letter, 29 May 1863.
41. Elliott, William, letter, 25 May 1863.
42. Bush, Jacob A., "From 1861 to 1865 as I Remember," *Lenoir* (NC) *Topic*, 25 March 1922.
43. Bradshaw, James, letter, 18 June 1863.
44. Chapman, Craig S., *More Terrible Than Victory*, 87.
45. Davis, Archie K., *Boy Colonel of the Confederacy: The Life and Times of Henry King Burgwyn, Jr.* (Chapel Hill: University of North Carolina Press, 1985), 272.
46. Ibid.
47. Letter, 20 June 1863, Jessie L. Henry Collection, David M. Rubernstein Rare Book and Manuscript Library, Duke University, Durham, NC.
48. Leventhorpe, Collett, General Order Book, 20 June 1863.
49. Chapman, Craig S., *More Terrible Than Victory*, 88.
50. Lineback, Julius, letter, 19 June 1863.
51. Welch, Spencer, *A Confederate Surgeon's Letters to His Wife* (New York: Neale, 1911), 55.
52. Gragg, Rod, *Covered with Glory*, 57–8.
53. Taylor, William, letter, 22 June 1863.
54. 11th North Carolina Regiment, *CSRC*.
55. Gragg, Rod, *Covered with Glory*, 59.
56. Albright, Henry, letter, 23 June 1863, Mss.Coll#16, Civil War Collection, Series 1, Henry C. Albright, http://archives.greensborohistory.org/manuscripts/civil-war.
57. Lineback, Julius, Civil War Diary, 25 June 1863.
58. Gragg, Rod, *Covered with Glory*, 60.
59. Hess, Earl J., *Lee's Tar Heels*, 114.
60. Cowand, Joseph, letters, 28 June 1863.
61. *Salisbury* (NC) *Carolina Watchman*, 27 July 1863.
62. Gragg, Rod, *Covered with Glory*, 66.
63. Ibid., 67.
64. Hotchkins, Jedediah, *Make Me a Map of the Valley: The Civil War Journal of Stonewall Jackson's Topographer* (Dallas: Southern Methodist University Press, 1973), 155.
65. Welch, Spencer, *A Confederate Surgeon's Letters to His Wife*, 57.
66. *Carolina Watchman*, 5 August 1863.
67. Gragg, Rod, *Covered with Glory*, 65.
68. *Carolina Watchman*, 27 July 1863.
69. Strikeleather, J.A., "Recollections of the Late War," *Company Front*, October 1993.
70. Gragg, Rod, *Covered with Glory*, 64.
71. Underwood, George, *The 26th Regiment N.C. Troops: Pettigrew's Brigade, Heth's Division, Hill's Corps, A.N.V.* (Goldsboro, NC: Nash and Brothers, 1901), 40.
72. *Carolina Watchman*, 5 August 1863.
73. *Carolina Watchman*, 27 July 1863.
74. Simpson, Tally, letter, 28 June 1863.
75. Lineback, Julius, Civil War Diary, 27 June 1863.
76. *Carolina Watchman*, 27 July 1863.
77. Welch, Spencer, *A Confederate Surgeon's Letters to His Wife*, 60.
78. Ibid., 57.
79. Gragg, Rod, *Covered with Glory*, 77.
80. Chapman, Craig S., *More Terrible Than Victory*, 89.
81. 11th North Carolina Infantry, *CSRC*.
82. Welch, Spencer, *A Confederate Surgeon's Letters to His Wife*, 57.
83. Leventhorpe, Collett, letter, 14 May 1867.
84. 11th North Carolina Regiment, *CSRC*.
85. Gragg, Rod, *Covered with Glory*, 77.
86. Welch, Spencer, *A Confederate Surgeon's Letters to His Wife*, 61.
87. Ibid.
88. Ibid., 63.
89. 11th North Carolina Regiment, *CSRC*.
90. Heth, Henry, *Official Records*, Vol. 27, No. 549.
91. Hess, Earl J., *Lee's Tar Heels*, 115.
92. Ashe, S.A., "The First Day at Gettysburg," *Confederate Veteran* 38 (1932), p. 378.
93. Chapman, Craig S., *More Terrible Than Victory*, 91.
94. Young, Louis G., "Pettigrew's Brigade at Gettysburg," in Clark, Walter, *Histories of the Several Regiments and Battalions from North Carolina, in the Great War, 1861–1865* (Raleigh: E.M. Uzzell, 1901), Vol. 5, p. 115.
95. Young, Louis G., "Pettigrew's Brigade at Gettysburg," 115.
96. Hess, Earl J., *Lee's Tar Heels*, 116.
97. Young, Louis G., "Pettigrew's Brigade at Gettysburg," 116.
98. Hess, Earl J., *Lee's Tar Heels*, 115–6.
99. Young, Louis G., "Pettigrew's Brigade at Gettysburg," 116.
100. Morrison, James, ed., *The Memoirs of Henry Heth* (Westport, CT: Greenwood, 1974), 173.
101. Young, Louis G., "Pettigrew's Brigade at Gettysburg," 116.
102. Morrison, James, ed., *The Memoirs of Henry Heth*, 173.

Chapter 7

1. Elliott, Patrick, personal Web site communication, 19 December 2006.
2. *Western Democrat*, 29 December 1863.
3. 11th North Carolina Infantry, *CSRC*.
4. Jones, Edmund, in Leventhorpe, Collett papers, 11 May 1865.
5. Harris, Ferguson, "Gen. Jas. J. Archer," *Confederate Veteran* 3 (1895), 18.
6. Hess, Earl J., *Lee's Tar Heels*, 119.
7. Fulton, W.F., "The Fifth Alabama Battalion at Gettysburg, *Confederate Veteran* 31 (1925), 379.
8. Hess, Earl J., *Lee's Tar Heels*, 119.
9. Cutler, Lyander, *Official Records*, Vol. 27, No. 37.
10. Nolan, Alan T., *The Iron Brigade* (Ann Arbor, MI: Hardscrabble Books, 1983), 237.
11. Heth, Henry, *Official Records*, Vol. 27, No. 549.
12. Freeman, Douglas, *Lee's Lieutenants*, Vol. 3, p. 78.
13. Jones, John, *Official Records*, Vol. 27, No. 550.
14. Ibid.
15. Hess, Earl J., *Lee's Tar Heels*, 120.

16. Jones, John, *Official Records*, Vol. 27, No. 550.
17. Heth, Henry, *Official Records*, Vol. 27, No. 549.
18. Chapman, Craig S., *More Terrible Than Victory*, 93.
19. Nolan, Alan T., *The Iron Brigade*, 233.
20. Morrison, James, ed., *The Memoirs of Henry Heth*, 175.
21. Jones, John, *Official Records*, Vol. 27, No. 550.
22. Underwood, George, *The 26th Regiment N.C. Troops, Pettigrew's Brigade, Heth's Division*, 47.
23. Jones, Edmund, in Leventhorpe, Collett papers, 11 May 1865.
24. Underwood, George, *The 26th Regiment N.C. Troops: Pettigrew's Brigade, Heth's Division*, 48.
25. Jones, Edmund, in Leventhorpe, Collett papers, 11 May 1865.
26. Hess, Earl J., *Lee's Tar Heels*, 122.
27. Underwood, George, *The 26th Regiment N.C. Troops: Pettigrew's Brigade, Heth's Division*, 49.
28. *Ibid.*, 46.
29. Jones, Edmund, in Leventhorpe, Collett papers, 11 May 1865.
30. Joseph Casper and Andrew Pritchard, *CSRC*.
31. Jerry Tripp and Benjamin Coffey, *CSRC*.
32. Venner, William T., *The 19th Indiana Infantry at Gettysburg: Hoosiers' Courage* (Shippensburg, PA: Burd Street Press, 1998), 67.
33. Underwood, George, *The 26th Regiment N.C. Troops: Pettigrew's Brigade, Heth's Division*, 49.
34. *Ibid.*
35. Erwin, George, letter, 3 July 1863.
36. Haynes, Sidney, letter in *Charlotte Observer*, 23 September 1894.
37. McDade, John, Gregory, William, *CSRC*.
38. Welch, Spencer, *A Confederate Surgeon's Letters to His Wife*, 65.
39. Thomas, Gerald, "Experiences of Bertie County's Confederate Soldiers," Windsor, NC, no date.
40. Venner, William T., *The 19th Indiana Infantry at Gettysburg: Hoosiers' Courage*, 67.
41. Jones, John, *Official Records*, Vol. 27, No. 550.
42. Clanton, John. Goodman, John. Cathey, William, *CSRC*.
43. Underwood, George, *The 26th Regiment N.C. Troops: Pettigrew's Brigade, Heth's Division*, 49.
44. Helms, Ezekiel, *CSRC*.
45. Hess, Earl J., *Lee's Tar Heels*, 124.
46. *Carolina Watchman*, 27 July 1863.
47. Curtis, Orson B., *History of the Twenty-Fourth Michigan of the Iron Brigade* (Detroit: Winn and Hammond, 1891), 167.
48. Venner, William T., *The 19th Indiana Infantry at Gettysburg: Hoosiers' Courage*, 172.
49. Yaunts, Reubin, *CSRC*.
50. Venner, William T., *The 19th Indiana Infantry at Gettysburg: Hoosiers' Courage*, 68.
51. Belo, Alfred H., "The Battle of Gettysburg," *Confederate Veteran* 8 (1900), 165.
52. Harris, Frank. Powell, Daniel. Anthony, Philip, *CSRC*.
53. Jones, John, *Official Records*, Vol. 27, No. 550.
54. Chapman, Craig S., *More Terrible Than Victory*, 96.
55. Venner, William T., *The 19th Indiana Infantry at Gettysburg: Hoosiers' Courage*, 71.
56. Bird, Francis, letter, 17 July 1863, Southern Historical Collection, Wilson Library, University of North Carolina at Chapel Hill.
57. James Clark, John Cook, and Baxter King, *CSRC*.
58. Venner, William T., *The 19th Indiana Infantry at Gettysburg: Hoosiers' Courage*, 71.
59. Hess, Earl J., *Lee's Tar Heels*, 124.
60. Underwood, George, *The 26th Regiment N.C. Troops: Pettigrew's Brigade, Heth's Division*, 50.
61. Nathan Tenney, Clingman Craige, Walter McGrimsey, and Thomas Burnett, *CSRC*.
62. *Fayetteville Observer*, 17 September 1863.
63. *Fayetteville Observer*, 7 September 1863.
64. Venner, William T., *The 7th Tennessee Infantry in the Civil War*, 91.
65. Jeter Snipes, Thomas Peele, James Rayner, and Joseph Creaseman, *CSRC*.
66. Underwood, George, *The 26th Regiment N.C. Troops: Pettigrew's Brigade, Heth's Division*, 49.
67. Purifoy, John, "The Battle of Gettysburg, July 1, 1863," *Confederate Veteran* 31 (1925), 22.
68. Haynes, Albert S., *Charlotte Observer*, 23 September 1894.
69. Jones, Edmund, in Leventhorpe, Collett papers, 11 May 1865.
70. Rea, Daniel B. "Tribute to Major E.A. Ross," in Tompkins, D.A., *History of Mecklenburg County and the City of Charlotte* (Charlotte: Observer Printing House, 1903), 204.
71. Thomas, Gerald, "Experiences of Bertie County's Confederate Soldiers."
72. Lewis, Gil, personal communication, 25 March 2014.
73. James Christy and Lucius Gash, *CSRC*.
74. Taylor, William, letter, 29 July 1863.
75. Triplett, James, *CSRC*.
76. Venner, William T., *The 7th Tennessee Infantry in the Civil War*, 91.
77. Belo, Alfred H., "The Battle of Gettysburg," *Confederate Veteran* 8 (1900), 165.
78. Welch, Spencer, *A Confederate Surgeon's Letters to His Wife*, 65.
79. Stephen Roberts and George McDowell, *CSRC*.
80. Black, Michael, personal communication, 24 July 2014.
81. Morrison, James, ed., *The Memoirs of Henry Heth*, 175.
82. Freeman, Douglas, *Lee's Lieutenants*, Vol. 2, p. 711.
83. Venner, William T., *The 19th Indiana Infantry at Gettysburg: Hoosiers' Courage*, 64.
84. *Ibid.*, 66.
85. *Fayetteville Observer*, 17 September 1863.
86. Porter, Robert, *CRSC*.
87. Jones, John, *Official Records*, Vol. 27, No. 550.
88. *Carolina Watchman*, 27 July 1863.
89. Taylor, William, letter, 29 July 1863.
90. Porter, Robert, *CSRC*.
91. William Duckworth and Martin Branch, *CSRC*.
92. Venner, William T., *The 19th Indiana Infantry at Gettysburg: Hoosiers' Courage*, 92.
93. Hess, Earl J., *Lee's Tar Heels*, 126.
94. Jones, John, *Official Records*, Vol. 27, No. 550.
95. *Ibid.*
96. *Fayetteville Observer*, 17 September 1863.
97. James Lowrie and James Galloway, *CSRC*, p. Whiteside, Pam, personal communication, 1 August 2014.
98. Sidney Giles, William Goodrum, Daniel Powell, and William Cathey, *CSRC*.
99. Underwood, George, *The 26th Regiment N.C. Troops: Pettigrew's Brigade, Heth's Division*, 51.
100. Hand, William, *CSRC*.
101. Settlemire, David, *CSRC*.

102. Bird, Francis, letter, 17 July 1863, Southern Historical Collection, Wilson Library, University of North Carolina at Chapel Hill.
103. Belo, Alfred H., "The Battle of Gettysburg," *Confederate Veteran* 8 (1900), 165.
104. Taylor, William, letter, 29 July 1863.
105. Young, Louis, letter 10 February 1864.
106. Pettigrew, James, letter, 9 July 1863.
107. Young, Louis, letter, 10 February 1864.
108. Coddington, Edwin B., *The Gettysburg Campaign: A Study in Command* (New York: Touchstone, 1997), 294.
109. *North Carolina Standard*, 8 July 1863.
110. Purifoy, John, "The Battle of Gettysburg," July 1, 1863, *Confederate Veteran* 31 (1925), 22.
111. Jones, John, *Official Records*, Vol. 27, No. 550.
112. Venner, William T., *The 7th Tennessee Infantry in the Civil War*, 92.
113. Hess, Earl J., *Lee's Tar Heels*, 136.
114. Venner, William T., *The 7th Tennessee Infantry in the Civil War*, 92.
115. Hess, Earl J., *Lee's Tar Heels*, 136.
116. Young, Louis, "Pettigrew's Brigade at Gettysburg," in Clark, Walter, ed., *Histories of the Several Regiments and Battalions from North Carolina in the Great War, 1861–65*, p. 119.
117. Erwin, George, letter, 3 July 1863.
118. Welch, Spencer, *A Confederate Surgeon's Letters to His Wife*, 67.
119. Erwin, George, letter, 3 July 1863.
120. *Fayetteville Observer*, 7 September 1863.
121. Taylor, William, letter, 29 July 1863.
122. Hill, Daniel H., letter, 13 August 1863.
123. Hartline, David, personal communication, 25 March 2014.
124. Welch, Spencer, *A Confederate Surgeon's Letters to His Wife*, 67.
125. Venner, William T., *The 7th Tennessee Infantry in the Civil War*, 93.
126. 11th North Carolina Infantry, *CSRC*.

Chapter 8

1. 11th North Carolina Infantry, *CSRC*.
2. Hill, Ambrose P., *Official Records*, Vol. 27, No. 534.
3. 11th North Carolina Infantry, *CSRC*.
4. Haynes, Albert S., *CSRC*.
5. Gragg, Rod, *Covered with Glory*, 152.
6. Ernsberger, Don, *Also for Glory: The Pettigrew-Trimble Charge at Gettysburg, July 3, 1863* (Bloomington, IN: Xlibris, 2008), 124.
7. Young, Louis, "Pettigrew's Brigade at Gettysburg," 124–5.
8. Ernsberger, Don, *Also for Glory*, 127.
9. Young, Louis, letter, 10 February 1864.
10. Ernsberger, Don, *Also for Glory*, 142.
11. Crocker, James F., *Gettysburg: Pickett's Charge and Other War Address* (Portsmouth, VA: W.A. Fisk, 1915), 37.
12. *North Carolina Standard*, 29 July 1863.
13. Ernsberger, Don, *Also for Glory*, 129.
14. *Carolina Watchman*, 27 July 1863.
15. Chapman, Craig S., *More Terrible Than Victory*, 107.
16. *North Carolina Standard*, 29 July 1863.
17. Welch, Spencer, *A Confederate Surgeon's Letters to His Wife*, 68.
18. Redwood, Allen C., "A Boy in Gray," *Scribner's Monthly* 12, no. 5 (September 1881).
19. *Ibid*.
20. Stewart, George R., *Pickett's Charge: A Microhistory of the Final Attack at Gettysburg, July 3, 1863* (Boston: Houghton Mifflin, 1959), 150.
21. Crocker, James F., *Gettysburg: Pickett's Charge*, 38.
22. Fry, Birkett D., "Pickett's Charge at Gettysburg," *Southern Historical Society Papers* 7 (14 December 1879).
23. Gragg, Rod, *Covered with Glory*, 161.
24. Jones, John T., "Pettigrew's Brigade at Gettysburg," in Clark, Walter, ed., *Histories of the Several Regiments and Battalions from North Carolina in the Great War*, 133.
25. *Raleigh Observer*, 30 November 1877.
26. Haynes, Albert S., letter, 23 September 1894.
27. Moore, John W., *History of North Carolina* (Raleigh: Alfred Williams, 1880), vol. 2, p. 205.
28. Crocker, James F., *Gettysburg: Pickett's Charge*, 42.
29. Young, Louis, "Pettigrew's Brigade at Gettysburg," 126.
30. *Ibid.*, 127.
31. Priest, John M., *Into the Fight: Pickett's Charge at Gettysburg* (Shippensburg, PA: White Mane, 1998), 102, p. Smith, Skip, personal communication, 19 August 2014.
32. Nathan Harris, Alexander Newell, and John Smith, *CSRC*.
33. Young, Louis, "Pettigrew's Brigade at Gettysburg," 127.
34. Clements, John, *CSRC*.
35. *North Carolina Standard*, 29 July 1863.
36. *Chowan Herald*, "Chowan soldier's wooden leg now part of Civil War collection," 8 March 2000, p. Rea, William, *CSRC*.
37. Perry, Darren, personal communication, 8 August 2014.
38. *Confederate Veteran* 38 (1932), 264.
39. Hoyle, Lemuel, *CSRC*.
40. *Confederate Veteran* 31 (1923), 346.
41. Gragg, Rod, *Covered with Glory*, 173.
42. Young, Louis, "Pettigrew's Brigade at Gettysburg," 126.
43. *Confederate Veteran* 32 (1924), 226.
44. *Ibid*.
45. David Glenn and Patrick Warlick, *CSRC*.
46. John Finger, Francis Harris and William Smith, *CSRC*.
47. Gragg, Rod, *Covered with Glory*, 191.
48. Ernsberger, Don, *Also for Glory*, 205.
49. Haynes, Albert S., letter, 23 September 1894.
50. Page, Charles D., *History of the Fourteenth Regiment, Connecticut Vol. Infantry* (Meriden, CT: Horton, 1906), 152.
51. Outlaw, Edward, and Martin, William, in Hale, Edward J, ed., *Histories of Several Regiments*, 590.
52. McCorkle, James, *CSRC*.
53. *Confederate Veteran* 38 (1932), 264.
54. *Carolina Watchman*, "Hard to Kill," 6 September 1883.
55. Lee Johnson, and John Pittman, *CSRC*.
56. *Confederate Veteran* 32 (1924), 226.
57. Priest, John M., John M., *Into the Fight: Pickett's Charge at Gettysburg*, 107.
58. Ernsberger, Don, *Also for Glory*, 247.
59. *Confederate Veteran* 6 (1898), 68.
60. *North Carolina Standard*, 5 August 1863.
61. Thomas, Gerald, "Experiences of Bertie County's Confederate Soldiers."
62. Whisnant, Anthony, personal communication, 25 March 2014.
63. *Confederate Veteran* 6 (1898), 68.

64. Jones, John T., "Pettigrew's Brigade at Gettysburg," in Clark, Walter, ed., *Histories of the Several Regiments*, 133.
65. 11th North Carolina Infantry, *CSRC*.
66. Ernsberger, Don, *Also for Glory*, 174.
67. Joseph Long, Taylor Wright and George Kincaid, *CSRC*.
68. Little, Benjamin F., letter, 20 September 1877.
69. *Raleigh Observer*, 30 November 1877.
70. Haynes, Albert S., letter, 8 October 1877.
71. Haynes, Albert S., letter, 23 September 1894.
72. Haynes, Albert S., *CSRC*.
73. Hennessee, Nick, personal communication, 31 March 2014.
74. Hugh Tate, Angus Wingate, Joseph Carter and Danuiel Dulin, *CSRC*.
75. Oliver Ramsaur, Joseph Clay, Robert Briscoe and James McQuay, *CSRC*.
76. Gragg, Rod, *Covered with Glory*, 196.
77. Little, Benjamin F., letter, 20 September 1877.
78. *Confederate Veteran* 6 (1898), 68.
79. Morris, William, G., letter, 1 October 1877.
80. Venner, William T., *The Seventh Tennessee Infantry*, 109.
81. Martin, Hall, personal communication, 30 January 2014.
82. Suggs, William, *CSRC*.
83. Outlaw, Edward, and Martin, William, in Hale, Edward J, ed., *Histories of Several Regiments*, 590.
84. *Raleigh Observer*, 30 November 1877.
85. Ernsberger, Don, *Also for Glory*, 235.
86. Lassiter, Kelly, personal communication, 4 February 2014.
87. McAnear, Thomas, personal communication, 29 January 2014.
88. 11th North Carolina Infantry, *CSRC*.
89. Suggs, William, letter, 12 September 1868.
90. Ernsberger, Don, *Also for Glory*, 243.
91. Gragg, Rod, *Covered with Glory*, 205.
92. *Ibid*.
93. Ernsberger, Don, *Also for Glory*, 241.
94. *North Carolina Standard*, 22 July 1863.
95. *Confederate Veteran* 4 (1896), 114.
96. *North Carolina Standard*, 29 July 1863.
97. Young, Louis, "Pettigrew's Brigade at Gettysburg," 129.
98. Young, Louis, letter, 10 February 1864.
99. Outlaw, Edward, and Martin, William, in Hale, Edward J, ed., *Histories of Several Regiments*, 590.
100. John Freeland, John Watson, William Kerr and Lewis Elias, *CSRC*.
101. 11th North Carolina Infantry, *CSRC*.
102. Erwin, George, letter, 3 July 1863.
103. *North Carolina Standard*, 22 July 1863.
104. Hill, Ambrose P., *Official Records*, Vol. 27, No. 534.
105. Erwin, George, letter, 3 July 1863.
106. Hoyle, Lemuel, letter, 12 July 1863.
107. Haynes, Albert, letter, 8 October 1877.
108. Ernsberger, Don, *Also for Glory*, 241.
109. Hess, Earl J., *Lee's Tar Heels*, 154.

Chapter 9

1. 11th North Carolina Infantry, *CSRC*.
2. *Ibid*.
3. Young, Joseph J., *Official Records*, Vol. 27, No. 551.
4. *Weekly Standard*, 29 July 1863.
5. Pendergraft, Don, "Chowan Soldier's Wooden Leg," *Chowan* (NC) *Herald*, 8 March 2000.
6. Neville, Walter, no date.
7. Brown, Kent M., *Retreat from Gettysburg: Lee, Logistics, and the Pennsylvania Campaign* (Chapel Hill: University of North Carolina Press, 2005), 70.
8. Brown, Kent M., *Retreat from Gettysburg*, 57.
9. Alleman, Tillie Pierce, *At Gettysburg, p. or, What a Girl Saw and Heard of the Battle* (New York: W. Lake Borland, 1889), 44.
10. Brown, Kent M., *Retreat from Gettysburg*, 6.
11. 11th North Carolina Infantry, *CSRC*.
12. Leventhorpe, Collett, letter, n.d.
13. Brown, Kent M., *Retreat from Gettysburg*, 110.
14. *Greensboro Patriot*, 23 July 1863.
15. 11th North Carolina Infantry, *CSRC*.
16. Haynes, Albert S., letter, 23 September 1863.
17. Imboden, John, "The Confederate Retreat from Gettysburg," in Buel, Clarence C., and Robert U. Johnson, *Battles and Leaders of the Civil War* (New York: Century, 1914), 423.
18. Peake, Heather K., "General John D. Imboden and the Confederate Retreat from Gettysburg" (Huntingdon, TN: Civil War Interactive, no date), 1.
19. Leon, Luis, diary, 4 July 1863.
20. Gragg, Rod, *Covered with Glory*, 209.
21. Jones, John. *Official Records*, Vol. 27, No. 550.
22. *Carolina Watchman*, 6 September 1883.
23. Brown, Kent M., *Retreat from Gettysburg*, 127.
24. *Ibid*., 150.
25. Imboden, John, "The Confederate Retreat from Gettysburg," 423.
26. *Ibid*., 424.
27. Mills, George, "History of the 16th North Carolina," in Clark, ed. (1901), Vol. 2, p. 40.
28. 11th North Carolina Regiment, *CSRC*.
29. Leventhorpe, Collett, letter, n.d.
30. Brown, Kent M., *Retreat from Gettysburg*, 280.
31. *Ibid*., 148.
32. *Ibid*., 42.
33. Leon, Luis, diary, 5–6 July 1863.
34. Welch, Spencer, *A Confederate Surgeon's Letters to His Wife*, 69.
35. Brown, Kent M., *Retreat from Gettysburg*, 275.
36. Hess, Earl J., *Lee's Tar Heels*, 161.
37. Bird, Frances, letter 15 July 1863, Southern Historical Collection, Wilson Library, University of North Carolina at Chapel Hill.
38. Leon, Luis, diary, 8 July 1863.
39. Brown, Kent M., *Retreat from Gettysburg*, 312.
40. *Ibid*., 310.
41. Leon, Luis, diary, 10 July 1863.
42. Brown, Kent M., *Retreat from Gettysburg*, 312.
43. *Ibid*.
44. Leon, Luis, diary, 11 July 1863.
45. Leon, Luis, diary, 12 July 1863.
46. Hess, Earl J., *Lee's Tar Heels*, 162.
47. Jones, John, *Official Records*, Vol. 27, No. 550.
48. Leon, Luis, diary, 13 July 1863.
49. Welch, Spencer, *A Confederate Surgeon's Letters to His Wife*, 70.
50. Ernsberger, Don, *Also for Glory*, 276.
51. *Ibid*., 275.
52. Bond, William R., *Pickett or Pettigrew?: An Historical Essay* (Scotland Neck, NC: W.L.L. Hall, 1888), 8.
53. Heth, Henry, *Official Records*, Vol. 27, No. 549.
54. Leon, Luis, diary, 13 July 1863.
55. Brown, Kent M., *Retreat from Gettysburg*, 335.

56. Heth, Henry, *Official Records*, Vol. 27, No. 549.
57. Franks, George, "The Final Battle of the Gettysburg Campaign: Falling Waters," Maryland, 14 July 1863, *Strategy and Tactics*, 2007.
58. Heth, Henry, *Official Records*, Vol. 27, No. 549.
59. Jones, John. *Official Records*, Vol. 27, No. 550.
60. Franks, George F., *Battle of Falling Waters," 1863* (North Charleston, SC: Create Space, 2013), 55–6.
61. Ernsberger, Don, *Also for Glory*, 288.
62. Brown, Kent M., *Retreat from Gettysburg*, 337.
63. Jones, John. *Official Records*, Vol. 27, No. 550.
64. Heth, Henry, *Official Records*, Vol. 27, No. 549.
65. Brown, Kent M., *Retreat from Gettysburg*, 337.
66. *Confederate Veteran* 18 (1910), 462.
67. Kilpatrick, Hugh J., *Official Records*, Vol. 27, No. 359.
68. *Ibid.*
69. Heth, Henry, *Official Records*, Vol. 27, No. 549.
70. Franks, George F., *Battle of Falling Waters,"* 56.
71. Outlaw, Edward, and Martin, William, in Hale, Edward J, ed., *Histories of Several Regiments*, 591.
72. Fulton, W.F., "The Fifth Alabama Battalion at Gettysburg," *Confederate Veteran* 31 (1923), 379.
73. Brown, Kent M., *Retreat from Gettysburg*, 344.
74. Fulton, W.F., "The Fifth Alabama Battalion at Gettysburg," *Confederate Veteran* 31 (1923), 379.
75. Franks, George F., *Battle of Falling Waters*, 47.
76. Fulton, W.F., "The Fifth Alabama Battalion at Gettysburg," *Confederate Veteran* 31 (1923), 379.
77. McCall, John T., "7th Tennessee—Battle of Falling Waters," *Confederate Veteran* 6 (1898), 406.
78. Ernsberger, Don, *Also for Glory*, 291.
79. McCall, John T., "7th Tennessee—Battle of Falling Waters," *Confederate Veteran* 6 (1898), 406.
80. Brown, Kent M., *Retreat from Gettysburg*, 347.
81. Franks, George, "The Final Battle of the Gettysburg Campaign: Falling Waters," 57.
82. *Confederate Military History*, Vol. 5, p. 339.
83. Brown, Kent M., *Retreat from Gettysburg*, 347.
84. Outlaw, Edward, and Martin, William, in Hale, Edward J, ed., *Histories of Several Regiments*, 591.
85. Heth, Henry, *Official Records*, Vol. 27, No. 549.
86. Brown, Kent M., *Retreat from Gettysburg*, 347.
87. Bird, Frances, letter, 15 July 1763, Southern Historical Collection, Wilson Library, University of North Carolina at Chapel Hill.
88. Jones, John. *Official Records*, Vol. 27, No. 550.
89. Franks, George F., *Battle of Falling Waters*, 56–7.
90. Heth, Henry, *Official Records*, Vol. 27, No. 549.
91. Franks, George F., *Battle of Falling Waters*, 49.
92. Franks, George, "The Final Battle of the Gettysburg Campaign: Falling Waters," 58.
93. Heth, Henry, *Official Records*, Vol. 27, No. 549.
94. King, Joseph. Adams, James, *CSRC*.
95. Franks, George, "The Final Battle of the Gettysburg Campaign: Falling Waters," 58.
96. Heth, Henry, *Official Records*, Vol. 27, No. 549.
97. Jones, John. *Official Records*, Vol. 27, No. 550.
98. Venner, William T., *The Seventh Tennessee Infantry*, 116.
99. Thomas Pearson and John Cook, *CSRC*.
100. *Confederate Veteran* 18 (1910), 462.
101. Ernsberger, Don, *Also for Glory*, 298.
102. *Confederate Veteran* 18 (1910), 462.
103. *Ibid.*
104. Franks, George, "The Final Battle of the Gettysburg Campaign: Falling Waters," 66.
105. Ernsberger, Don, *Also for Glory*, 291–2.
106. Chapman, Craig S., *More Terrible Than Victory*, 119.
107. Todd, William. Boyles, Joseph, *CSRC*.
108. Hatch, Charles, *Official Records*, Vol. 27, No. 95.
109. Buford, John. *Official Records*, Vol. 27, No. 337.
110. Ernsberger, Don, *Also for Glory*, 299.
111. *Confederate Veteran* 18 (1910), 463.
112. 11th North Carolina Infantry, *CSRC*.
113. Jones, John, *Official Records*, Vol. 27, No. 550.
114. Outlaw, Edward, and Martin, William, in Hale, Edward J, ed., *Histories of Several Regiments*, 591.
115. Underwood, George, *The 26th Regiment N.C. Troops: Pettigrew's Brigade, Heth's Division*, 76.
116. 11th North Carolina Infantry, *CSRC*.
117. Jones, John. *Official Records*, Vol. 27, No. 550.

Chapter 10

1. 11th North Carolina Infantry, *CSRC*.
2. Hoyle, Lemuel, letter, 12 July 1863.
3. 11th North Carolina Infantry, *CSRC*.
4. Freeman, Douglas, *Lee's Lieutenants*, Vol. 3, p. 193.
5. Martin, William J., *CSRC*.
6. Hess, Earl J., *Lee's Tar Heels*, 168.
7. Chapman, Craig S., *More Terrible Than Victory*, 125.
8. William Turner, William Dickerson, James Whitaker and Robert Lowrie, *CSRC*.
9. Outlaw, Edward, and Martin, William, in Hale, Edward J, ed., *Histories of Several Regiments*, 590–1.
10. Lowrie, Robert, *CSRC*.
11. *Western Democrat*, 6 October 1863, p. Grier, Paul, *CSRC*.
12. Craig, Joel, and Baker, Sharlene, *As You May Never See Us Again: The Civil War Letters of George and Walter Battle, 4th North Carolina Infantry* (Wake Forest, NC: Scuppernong, 2004), 51.
13. 11th North Carolina Infantry, *CSRC*.
14. Hoyle, Lemuel, letter, 1 August 1863.
15. Hess, Earl J., *Lee's Tar Heels*, 177.
16. Warlick letter, 8 August 1863.
17. Hoyle, Lemuel, letter, 17 August 1863.
18. 11th North Carolina Infantry, *CSRC*.
19. Perkins, A.E., letter, 13 August 1863.
20. Freeman, Douglas, *Lee's Lieutenants*, vol. 3, p. 219.
21. Martin, Edward A., *CSRC*.
22. Outlaw, Edward, and Martin, William, in Hale, Edward J, ed., *Histories of Several Regiments*, 592.
23. *Confederate Military History*, vol. 5, p. 321–2.
24. Hess, Earl J., *Lee's Tar Heels*, 185.
25. 11th North Carolina Infantry, *CSRC*.
26. Craig, Joel, and Baker, Sharlene, *As You May Never See Us Again*, 52–3.
27. Chapman, Craig S., *More Terrible Than Victory*, 129.
28. *Ibid.*
29. *Ibid.*, 130.
30. Outlaw, Edward, and Martin, William, in Hale, Edward J, ed., *Histories of Several Regiments*, 592.
31. Freeman, Douglas, *Lee's Lieutenants*, Vol. 3, p. 240.
32. Heth, Henry, *Official Records*, Vol. 29, No. 104.
33. Outlaw, Edward, and Martin, William, in Hale, Edward J, ed., *Histories of Several Regiments*, 592.
34. Freeman, Douglas, *Lee's Lieutenants*, Vol. 3, p. 241.
35. Heth, Henry, *Official Records*, Vol. 29, No. 104.
36. Freeman, Douglas, *Lee's Lieutenants*, Vol. 3, p. 241.

37. *Ibid.*, 242.
38. Hill, Ambrose, *Official Records*, Vol. 29, No. 102.
39. Heth, Henry, *Official Records*, Vol. 29, No. 104.
40. Berkoff, Todd S., "Botched Battle at Bristoe," *Eastern Theater*, 5 September 2012.
41. Chapman, Craig S., *More Terrible Than Victory*, 131.
42. *Ibid.*, 132.
43. Freeman, Douglas, *Lee's Lieutenants*, Vol. 3, p. 242.
44. Henderson, William D., *The Road to Bristoe Station: Campaigning with Lee and Meade, August 1–October 20, 1863* (Lynchburg, VA: H.E. Howard, 1987), 172.
45. Heth, Henry, *Official Records*, Vol. 29, No. 104.
46. Hill, Ambrose, *Official Records*, Vol. 29, No. 102.
47. Henderson, William D., *The Road to Bristoe Station*, 176.
48. Walker, Henry, *Official Records*, Vol. 29, No. 105.
49. Berkoff, Todd S., "Botched Battle at Bristoe," *Eastern Theater*.
50. Outlaw, Edward, and Martin, William, in Hale, Edward J, ed., *Histories of Several Regiments*, 593.
51. *Confederate Military History*, Vol. 5, p. 165.
52. Chapman, Craig S., *More Terrible Than Victory*, 133.
53. Outlaw, Edward, and Martin, William, in Hale, Edward J, ed., *Histories of Several Regiments*, 593.
54. Bartlett, Jacob, "Recollections," Southern Historical Collection, Wilson Library, University of North Carolina at Chapel Hill.
55. Chapman, Craig S., *More Terrible Than Victory*, 136.
56. Hill, Ambrose, *Official Records*, Vol. 29, No. 102.
57. Berkoff, Todd S., "Botched Battle at Bristoe," *Eastern Theater*.
58. Outlaw, Edward, and Martin, William, in Hale, Edward J, ed., *Histories of Several Regiments*, 593.
59. Baird, Thomas, *Official Records*, Vol. 29, No. 38.
60. Heth, Henry, *Official Records*, Vol. 29, No. 104.
61. Baker, Lucius. Cook, John. Summers, Perry, *CSRC*.
62. Ramseur, Walter. Carpenter, Michael. Huss, Jacob, *CSRC*.
63. Heth, Henry, *Official Records*. Vol. 29, No. 104.
64. Walker, Henry, *Official Records*, Vol. 29, No. 105.
65. Outlaw, Edward, and Martin, William, in Hale, Edward J, ed., *Histories of Several Regiments*, 593.
66. Martin, William, *CSRC*.
67. Outlaw, Edward, and Martin, William, in Hale, Edward J, ed., *Histories of Several Regiments*, 593.
68. Shuffler, John. Grier, Paul. Wingate, Joseph. Sigmore, Noah, *CSRC*.
69. Outlaw, Edward, and Martin, William, in Hale, Edward J, ed., *Histories of Several Regiments*, 593.
70. Outlaw, Edward, and Martin, William, in Hale, Edward J, ed., *Histories of Several Regiments*, 593.
71. Chapman, Craig S., *More Terrible Than Victory*, 136.
72. 11th North Carolina Infantry, *CSRC*.
73. Hess, Earl J., *Lee's Tar Heels*, 191.
74. Heth, Henry, *Official Records*. Vol. 29, No. 104.
75. Berkoff, Todd S., "Botched Battle at Bristoe," *Eastern Theater*.
76. Morrison, James L., *The Memoirs of Henry Heth*, 180.
77. Hess, Earl J., *Lee's Tar Heels*, 193.
78. *Ibid.*
79. Bird, Frances, letter, 15 October 1863, Southern Historical Collection, Wilson Library, University of North Carolina at Chapel Hill.
80. Hess, Earl J., *Lee's Tar Heels*, 194.
81. Freeman, Douglas, *Lee's Lieutenants*, Vol. 3, p. 247.

Chapter 11

1. Hess, Earl J., *Lee's Tar Heels*, 195.
2. "Rambling Thoughts of the Civil War," *Confederate Veteran* 17 (1909), 227.
3. Capehart, Thomas, letter, 27 November 1863.
4. Hess, Earl J., *Lee's Tar Heels*, 195.
5. Curtis, O.B., *History of the 24th Michigan of the Iron Brigade*, 147.
6. Hess, Earl J., *Lee's Tar Heels*, 196.
7. Morrison, James L., *The Memoirs of Henry Heth*, 180.
8. Venner, William T., *The Seventh Tennessee Infantry*, 119.
9. Chapman, Craig S., *More Terrible Than Victory*, 138.
10. Morrison, James L., *The Memoirs of Henry Heth*, 180.
11. Hess, Earl J., *Lee's Tar Heels*, 198.
12. Chapman, Craig S., *More Terrible Than Victory*, 138.
13. 11th North Carolina Infantry, *CSRC*.
14. "A Battle of Snowballs," *Confederate Veteran* 26 (1918), 304.
15. "Rambling Thoughts of the Civil War," *Confederate Veteran* 17 (1909), 227.
16. Armfield, Mark, *CSRC*.
17. 11th North Carolina Infantry, *CSRC*.
18. Rinck, Andrew, letter, 4 January 1864.
19. Venner, William T., *The Seventh Tennessee Infantry*, 120.
20. *Confederate Veteran* 14 (1926), 90.
21. Freeman, Douglas, *Lee's Lieutenants*, Vol. 3, p. 317.
22. King, Bellfield, letter, 18 January 1864.
23. Bristol, Lambert, letter, January 1864.
24. Tate, John, letter, 10 April 1864.
25. Bristol, Lambert, letter, January 1864.
26. Craig, Joel, and Baker, Charlene, *As You May Never See Us Again*, 64.
27. Rinck, Andrew, Letter, 5 April 1864.
28. Hess, Earl J., *Lee's Tar Heels*, 202.
29. Rinck, Andrew, Letter, 5 April 1864.
30. Hess, Earl J., *Lee's Tar Heels*, 200.
31. Warlick letter, 22 March 1864.
32. 11th North Carolina Infantry, *CSRC*.
33. Ibid.
34. Warlick letter, 22 March 1864.
35. "A Battle of Snowballs," *Confederate Veteran* 26 (1918), 304.
36. Hess, Earl J., *Lee's Tar Heels*, 203.
37. "A Battle of Snowballs," *Confederate Veteran* 26 (1918), 304.
38. Hoyle, Lemuel, letter, 28 March 1864.
39. "A Battle of Snowballs," *Confederate Veteran* 26 (1918), 304.
40. Warlick letter, 29 March 1864.
41. Leventhorpe, Collett, *CSRC*.
42. William Martin and Francis Bird, *CSRC*.
43. Hess, Earl J., *Lee's Tar Heels*, 206.
44. Tate, John, letter, 10 April 1864.
45. Warlick letter, 11 April 1864.
46. Venner, William T., *The Seventh Tennessee Infantry*, 121.
47. Warlick letter, 11 April 1864.
48. Bird, Francis, letter, 18 April 1864, Southern Historical Collection, Wilson Library, University of North Carolina at Chapel Hill.
49. Hoyle, Lemuel, letter, 28 March 1864.
50. 11th North Carolina Infantry, *CSRC*.
51. Warlick letter, 11 April 1864.

52. Freeman, Douglas, *Lee's Lieutenants*, Vol. 3, pp. 345–6.
53. Rinck, Andrew, letter, 5 April 1864.

Chapter 12

1. Outlaw, Edward, and Martin, William, in Clark, Walter, ed., *Histories of Several Regiments*, 594.
2. Freeman, Douglas, *Lee's Lieutenants*, Vol. 3, p. 344.
3. Heth, Henry, "Official Report," 7 December 1864.
4. Freeman, Douglas, *Lee's Lieutenants*, Vol. 3, p. 349.
5. Casstevens, Frances H., *The 28th North Carolina Infantry: A Civil War History and Roster* (Jefferson, NC: McFarland, 2008), 120.
6. Leon, Louis, diary, 5 May 1864.
7. 11th North Carolina Infantry, *CSRC*.
8. Freeman, Douglas, *Lee's Lieutenants*, Vol. 3, p. 349.
9. Hess, Earl J., *Lee's Tar Heels*, 211.
10. Robinson, John H., "Fifty-Second Regiment," in Clark, Walter, ed., *Histories of Several Regiments*, Vol. 3, p. 244.
11. Krom, A.H., *New York Tribune*, 31 May 1864.
12. Morrison, James L., *The Memoirs of Henry Heth*, 182.
13. Chapman, Craig S., *More Terrible Than Victory*, 148.
14. Leon, Louis, diary, 5 May 1864.
15. "The Two Armies Face to Face," *New York Tribune*, 9 May 1864.
16. Morrison, James L., *The Memoirs of Henry Heth*, 182.
17. Krom, A.H., *New York Tribune*, 31 May 1864.
18. Hess, Earl J., *Lee's Tar Heels*, 209.
19. Morrison, James L., *The Memoirs of Henry Heth*, 182.
20. Hess, Earl J., *Lee's Tar Heels*, 209.
21. Morrison, James L., *The Memoirs of Henry Heth*, 182.
22. *Ibid.*, 182.
23. *Ibid.*, 182.
24. Robinson, John H., "Fifty-Second Regiment," in Clark, Walter, ed., *Histories of Several Regiments*, Vol. 3, p. 245.
25. Emanuel Lewis, R. James Wingate and J. Lewis Warlick, *CSCR*.
26. Morrison, James L., *The Memoirs of Henry Heth*, 183.
27. Day, William A., *The History of Company I* (Sherrill's Ford, NC: Catawba County, 1893), 23.
28. Morrison, James L., *The Memoirs of Henry Heth*, 183.
29. John Lane and George Patton, *CSRC*.
30. Whisnant, Anthony, personal communication, 25 March 2014.
31. Stedman, Charles, "Forty-Fourth Regiment," in Clark, Walter, ed., *Histories of Several Regiments*, Vol. 3, p. 27.
32. Thorp, John H., "Forty-Seventh Regiment," in Clark, Walter, ed., *Histories of Several Regiments*, Vol. 3, p. 94.
33. "Rambling Thoughts of the Civil War," *Confederate Veteran* 17 (1909), 228.
34. Welch, Spencer, *A Confederate Surgeon's Letters to His Wife*, 95.
35. Melton, Eugene. Smith, John, *CSRC*.
36. Morrison, James L., *The Memoirs of Henry Heth*, 183.
37. Outlaw, Edward, and Martin, William, in Clark, Walter, ed., *Histories of Several Regiments*, 594.
38. Phillip Dellinger, Joseph Richey and Stephen Roberts, *CSRC*.
39. Morrison, James L., *The Memoirs of Henry Heth*, 183.
40. Outlaw, Edward, and Martin, William, in Clark, Walter, ed., *Histories of Several Regiments*, 594.
41. Garratt, Woodston. North Carolina Department of Archives and History.
42. Morris, Zebedee, letter, 16 May 1864.
43. Outlaw, Edward, and Martin, William, in Clark, Walter, ed., *Histories of Several Regiments*, 594.
44. Boyd, Benjamin, *CSRC*.
45. Outlaw, Edward, and Martin, William, in Clark, Walter, ed., *Histories of Several Regiments*, 595.
46. Morrison, James L., *The Memoirs of Henry Heth*, 183.
47. McComb, William, journal, 5 May 1864.
48. Freeman, Douglas, *Lee's Lieutenants*, Vol. 3, p. 354.
49. Morrison, James L., *The Memoirs of Henry Heth*, 184.
50. Outlaw, Edward, and Martin, William, in Clark, Walter, ed., *Histories of Several Regiments*, 595.
51. McComb, William, journal, 5 May 1864.
52. Robinson, John H., "Fifty-Second Regiment," in Clark, Walter, ed., *Histories of Several Regiments*, Vol. 3, p. 245.
53. *Ibid.*, 595.
54. Hess, Earl J., *Lee's Tar Heels*, 214.
55. Morrison, James L., *The Memoirs of Henry Heth*, 185.
56. Freeman, Douglas, *Lee's Lieutenants*, Vol. 3, p. 355.
57. Morrison, James L., *The Memoirs of Henry Heth*, 185.
58. Rudisill, Absalom, *CSRC*.
59. McComb, William, journal, 6 May 1864.
60. Outlaw, Edward, and Martin, William, in Clark, Walter, ed., *Histories of Several Regiments*, 595.
61. Jordan, Hance. Kincaid, William, *CSRC*.
62. Hess, Earl J., *Lee's Tar Heels*, 214.
63. Underwood, George, "Twenty-Sixth Regiment," in Clark, Walter, ed., *Histories of Several Regiments*, Vol. 2, 382.
64. Robinson, John H., "Fifty-Second Regiment," in Clark, Walter, ed., *Histories of Several Regiments*, Vol. 3, p. 245.
65. "Rambling Thoughts of the Civil War," *Confederate Veteran* 17 (1909), 228.
66. Freeman, Douglas, *Lee's Lieutenants*, Vol. 3, p. 355.
67. *Ibid.*
68. Hancock, Winfield, *Official Records*, Vol. 36, No. 15, p. 321.
69. Freeman, Douglas, *Lee's Lieutenants*, Vol. 3, p. 358.
70. Morrison, James L., *The Memoirs of Henry Heth*, 185.
71. Venner, William T., *The Seventh Tennessee Infantry*, 127.
72. Outlaw, Edward, and Martin, William, in Clark, Walter, ed., *Histories of Several Regiments*, 595.
73. Morrison, James L., *The Memoirs of Henry Heth*, 185.
74. Freeman, Douglas, *Lee's Lieutenants*, Vol. 3, p. 372.
75. Casstevens, Frances H., *The 28th North Carolina Infantry*, 120.
76. 11th North Carolina Infantry, *CSRC*.
77. *Ibid.*
78. Craig, Joel, and Baker, Sharlene. *As You May Never See Us Again*, 74.

79. Keegan, John, *The Face of Battle* (New York: Penguin Books, 1976).
80. Freeman, Douglas, *Lee's Lieutenants*, Vol. 3, p. 365.
81. Hess, Earl J., *Lee's Tar Heels*, 217.
82. Outlaw, Edward, and Martin, William, in Clark, Walter, ed., *Histories of Several Regiments*, 595.
83. Hess, Earl J., *Lee's Tar Heels*, 217.
84. Morrison, James L., *The Memoirs of Henry Heth*, 185–6.
85. Craig, Joel, and Baker, Sharlene, *As You May Never See Us Again*, 74.
86. Outlaw, Edward, and Martin, William, in Clark, Walter, ed., *Histories of Several Regiments*, 596.
87. Morrison, James L., *The Memoirs of Henry Heth*, 187–8.
88. Lucas, Augustus, *CSRC*.
89. Craig, Joel, and Baker, Sharlene. *As You May Never See Us Again*, 75.
90. Hess, Earl J., *Lee's Tar Heels*, 219.
91. *Ibid.*
92. Pool, George. Harrelson, James, *CSRC*.
93. Chapman, Craig S., *More Terrible Than Victory*, 166.
94. Levi Walker, John Clements and Ryan Haynes, *CSRC*.
95. John Hudspeth and William Brown, *CSRC*.
96. Hess, Earl J., *Lee's Tar Heels*, 219–20.
97. Outlaw, Edward, and Martin, William, in Clark, Walter, ed., *Histories of Several Regiments*, 596.
98. John West, George Loudermilk and Edmund Blackwood, *CSRC*.
99. Outlaw, Edward, and Martin, William, in Clark, Walter, ed., *Histories of Several Regiments*, 596.
100. Hess, Earl J., *Lee's Tar Heels*, 221.
101. 11th North Carolina infantry, *CSRC*.
102. Thorp, John H., "Forty-Seventh Regiment," in Clark, Walter, ed., *Histories of Several Regiments*, Vol. 3, p. 94.
103. Morrison, James L., *The Memoirs of Henry Heth*, 188.
104. Chapman, Craig S., *More Terrible Than Victory*, 164.
105. Freeman, Douglas, *Lee's Lieutenants*, Vol. 3, p. 397.
106. Chapman, Craig S., *More Terrible Than Victory*, 167.
107. Moore, John, "The Battle of Spotsylvania," *Weekly Philadelphia Times*, 26 November 1882.
108. Underwood, George, "Twenty-Sixth Regiment," in Clark, Walter, ed., *Histories of Several Regiments*, Vol. 2, 384.
109. Freeman, Douglas, *Lee's Lieutenants*, Vol. 3, p. 398.
110. *Ibid.*, 404.
111. *Ibid.*, 398.
112. Venner, William T., *The Seventh Tennessee Infantry*, 130.
113. Moore, John, "The Battle of Spotsylvania," *Weekly Philadelphia Times*, 26 November 1882.
114. Burnside, Ambrose, report, 26 November 1864.
115. Morrison, James L., *The Memoirs of Henry Heth*, 186.
116. Moore, John, "The Battle of Spotsylvania," *Weekly Philadelphia Times*, 26 November 1882.
117. Venner, William T., *The Seventh Tennessee Infantry*, 130.
118. Morrison, James L., *The Memoirs of Henry Heth*, 186.
119. J.W. Crawley, Joseph Lenhardt and Nathan Myers, *CSRC*.
120. Bird, Francis, letter, 13 May 1864, Southern Historical Collection, Wilson Library, University of North Carolina at Chapel Hill.
121. Burnside, Ambrose, report, 26 November 1864.
122. Moore, John, "The Battle of Spotsylvania," *Weekly Philadelphia Times*, 26 November 1882.
123. Lucas Gash, Monroe Hovis, Allen Davis and Logan Warlick, *CSRC*.
124. Hess, Earl J., *Lee's Tar Heels*, 223.
125. Craig, Joel, and Baker, Sharlene. *As You May Never See Us Again*, 76.
126. Day, William A., *The History of Company I* (Sherrill's Ford, NC: Catawba County, 1893), 22.
127. Warlick letter, 19 May 1864.
128. Bird, Francis, letter, 13 May 1864, Southern Historical Collection, Wilson Library, University of North Carolina at Chapel Hill.
129. Venner, William T., *The Seventh Tennessee Infantry*, 132.
130. Moore, John, "The Battle of Spotsylvania," *Weekly Philadelphia Times*, 26 November 1882.
131. 11th North Carolina Infantry, *CSRC*.
132. Freeman, Douglas, *Lee's Lieutenants*, Vol. 3, p. 434.
133. Warlick letter, 19 May 1864.
134. Freeman, Douglas, *Lee's Lieutenants*, Vol. 3, p. 437.
135. Warlick letter, 19 May 1864.
136. Hess, Earl J., *Lee's Tar Heels*, 224.
137. Outlaw, Edward, and Martin, William, in Clark, Walter, ed., *Histories of Several Regiments*, 596.
138. Bird, Francis, letter, 20 May 1864, Southern Historical Collection, Wilson Library, University of North Carolina at Chapel Hill.

Chapter 13

1. Robinson, John H., "Fifty-Second Regiment," in Clark, Walter, ed., *Histories of Several Regiments*, Vol. 3, p. 246.
2. Hess, Earl J., *Lee's Tar Heels*, 232.
3. Chapman, Craig S., *More Terrible Than Victory*, 171.
4. *Ibid.*, 172.
5. Warlick letter, 25 May 1864.
6. *Ibid.*
7. Hess, Earl J., *Lee's Tar Heels*, 226.
8. Chapman, Craig S., *More Terrible Than Victory*, 173.
9. Venner, William T., *The Seventh Tennessee Infantry*, 133.
10. Furguson, Ernest, B., *Not War but Murder: Cold Harbor, 1864* (New York: Alfred A. Knopf, 2000), 86.
11. Hill, Ambrose P., Correspondence, 30 May 1864, *Official Records*, Vol. 51, Pt. 2, p. 969.
12. Robinson, John H., "Fifty-Second Regiment," in Clark, Walter, ed., *Histories of Several Regiments*, Vol. 3, p. 246.
13. Chapman, Craig S., *More Terrible Than Victory*, 176.
14. Hess, Earl J., *Lee's Tar Heels*, 227.
15. *Ibid.*, 226–7.
16. Thorp, John H., "Forty-Seventh Regiment," in Clark, Walter, ed., *Histories of Several Regiments*, Vol. 3, p. 95.
17. *Ibid.*
18. Furguson, Ernest, B., *Not War but Murder*, 149.
19. Chapman, Craig S., *More Terrible Than Victory*, 177.

20. Thorp, John H., "Forty-Seventh Regiment," in Clark, Walter, ed., *Histories of Several Regiments*, Vol. 3, p. 95.
21. Henry, J.L., letter, 2 June 1864.
22. Aubery, James M., *The Thirty-Sixth Wisconsin Infantry, 1st brigade, 2d Division, 2d Army Corps, Army of the Potomac* (Wisconsin: Fantine Aubery McCleary, 1900), 71.
23. William Wilkerson, James Burden, Michael Craft, Theodore Ramsour and Robert Roseman, *CSRC*.
24. 11th North Carolina Infantry, *CSRC*.
25. Hess, Earl J., *Lee's Tar Heels*, 228.
26. Outlaw, Edward, and Martin, William, in Clark, Walter, ed., *Histories of Several Regiments*, 598.
27. Chapman, Craig S., *More Terrible Than Victory*, 181.
28. Robinson, John H., "Fifty-Second Regiment," in Clark, Walter, ed., *Histories of Several Regiments*, Vol. 3, p. 246.
29. Long, Breckinridge, "Reminiscences," no date.
30. *Ibid*.
31. Davis, Thomas, *CSRC*.
32. William Taylor, Robert Hall and Barry Henry, *CSRC*.
33. Harbison, William, *CSRC*.
34. *Western Democrat*, 20 December 1864.
35. Thorp, John H., "Forty-Seventh Regiment," in Clark, Walter, ed., *Histories of Several Regiments*, Vol. 3, p. 95.
36. *Ibid.*, 246.
37. Hess, Earl J., *Lee's Tar Heels*, 229.
38. Thorp, John H., "Forty-Seventh Regiment," in Clark, Walter, ed., *Histories of Several Regiments*, Vol. 3, p. 96.
39. *Ibid*.
40. Albright, Henry, diary, 2 June 1864.
41. King, Campbell, *CSRC*.
42. Chapman, Craig S., *More Terrible Than Victory*, 184.
43. Thorp, John H., "Forty-Seventh Regiment," in Clark, Walter, ed., *Histories of Several Regiments*, Vol. 3, p. 96.
44. 11th North Carolina Infantry, *CSRC*.
45. McMahon, Martin T., "Cold Harbor," in Buel, Clarence C., and Robert U. Johnson. *Battles and Leaders of the Civil War*, Vol. 4, p. 220.
46. Robinson, John H., "Fifty-Second Regiment," in Clark, Walter, ed., *Histories of Several Regiments*, Vol. 3, p. 246.
47. *Ibid.*, 247.
48. Hess, Earl J., *Lee's Tar Heels*, 230.
49. *Ibid.*, 231.
50. Robinson, John H., "Fifty-Second Regiment," in Clark, Walter, ed., *Histories of Several Regiments*, Vol. 3, p. 247.
51. Wright, James, letter, 12 June 1864.
52. Warlick letter, 12 June 1864.
53. Warlick letter, 16 June 1864.
54. Bird, Francis, letter, 17 June 1864, Southern Historical Collection, Wilson Library, University of North Carolina at Chapel Hill.
55. Robinson, John H., "Fifty-Second Regiment," in Clark, Walter, ed., *Histories of Several Regiments*, Vol. 3, p. 247.
56. Venner, William T., *The Seventh Tennessee Infantry*, 135.
57. Robinson, John H., "Fifty-Second Regiment," in Clark, Walter, ed., *Histories of Several Regiments*, Vol. 3, p. 247.
58. Murdock, John, letter, 30 July 1864.
59. Furgurson, Ernest, B., *Not War but Murder*, 84.

60. Albright, Henry, diary, 17 June 1864.
61. Freeman, Douglas, *Lee's Lieutenants*, Vol. 3, p. 537.
62. Venner, William T., *The Seventh Tennessee Infantry*, 135.
63. *Ibid*.
64. Stedman, Charles, "Forty-Fourth Regiment," in Clark, Walter, ed., *Histories of Several Regiments*, Vol. 3, p. 29.
65. Livingston, Larkin, *CSRC*.
66. Sprunt, James, "General William MacRae: Lee's Fighting Brigadier," in *Confederate Military History* (Cape Fear Historical Institute, 2006), Vol. 5, pp. 330–31.
67. Underwood, George, "Twenty-Sixth Regiment," in Clark, Walter, ed., *Histories of Several Regiments*, Vol. 2, 385.
68. *Ibid*.
69. Outlaw, Edward, and Martin, William, in Clark, Walter, ed., *Histories of Several Regiments*, 597.
70. Chapman, Craig S., *More Terrible Than Victory*, 208.
71. *Ibid*.
72. Hess, Earl J., *Lee's Tar Heels*, 237.
73. Chapman, Craig S., *More Terrible Than Victory*, 208.
74. Bird, Francis, letter 9 July 1864, Southern Historical Collection, Wilson Library, University of North Carolina at Chapel Hill.
75. Warlick Lewis, letter, 8 July 1864.
76. Edwards, William W., letter, 15 July 1864.
77. Underwood, George, "Twenty-Sixth Regiment," in Clark, Walter, ed., *Histories of Several Regiments*, Vol. 2, 385.
78. Edwards, William W., letter, 15 July 1864.
79. Kerr, William, *CSRC*.
80. Hess, Earl J., *Lee's Tar Heels*, 239.
81. Robinson, John H., "Fifty-Second Regiment," in Clark, Walter, ed., *Histories of Several Regiments*, Vol. 3, p. 247.
82. *Ibid*.
83. Moore, Thomas, *CSRC*.
84. Powell, William H., "The Battle of the Petersburg Crater," in Buel, Clarence C., and Robert U. Johnson. *Battles and Leaders of the Civil War*, Vol. 4, p. 551.
85. *Ibid*.
86. *Ibid.*, pp. 551–5.
87. Catton, Bruce, *Grant Takes Command* (Boston: Little, Brown, 1969), 325.
88. Chapman, Craig S., *More Terrible Than Victory*, 211.
89. Bartlett, Jacob, "Recollections," Southern Historical Collection, Wilson Library, University of North Carolina at Chapel Hill.
90. Hess, Earl J., *Lee's Tar Heels*, 241.
91. Bartlett, Jacob, "Recollections," Southern Historical Collection, Wilson Library, University of North Carolina at Chapel Hill.
92. Warlick Lewis, letter, 8 August 1864.
93. Robinson, John H., "Fifty-Second Regiment," in Clark, Walter, ed., *Histories of Several Regiments*, Vol. 3, p. 247.
94. Warlick Lewis, letter, 8 August 1864.

Chapter 14

1. Robinson, John H., "Fifty-Second Regiment," in Clark, Walter, ed., *Histories of Several Regiments*, Vol. 3, p. 247–8.

2. Outlaw, Edward, and Martin, William, in Clark, Walter, ed., *Histories of Several Regiments*, 597.
3. Hess, Earl J., *Lee's Tar Heels*, 241.
4. Outlaw, Edward, and Martin, William, in Clark, Walter, ed., *Histories of Several Regiments*, 597–8.
5. Venner, William T., *The Seventh Tennessee Infantry*, 136.
6. Hess, Earl J., *Lee's Tar Heels*, 241.
7. Venner, William T., *The Seventh Tennessee Infantry*, 136.
8. McMahon, Martin, "The Battle of the Petersburg Crater," in Buel, Clarence C., and Robert U. Johnson, *Battles and Leaders of the Civil War*, Vol. 4, p. 219.
9. Furguson, Ernest, B., *Not War but Murder*, 126.
10. Bartlett, Jacob, "Recollections," Southern Historical Collection, Wilson Library, University of North Carolina at Chapel Hill.
11. Robinson, John H., "Fifty-Second Regiment," in Clark, Walter, ed., *Histories of Several Regiments*, Vol. 3, p. 248.
12. 11th North Carolina Infantry, *CSRC*.
13. Hess, Earl J., *Lee's Tar Heels*, 241.
14. Setser, William, letter, 28 August 1864.
15. Cates, John, *CSRC*.
16. Murdock, John, *Confederate Incognito*, 220.
17. Morrison, James L., *The Memoirs of Henry Heth*, 190.
18. Murdock, John, *Confederate Incognito*, 220.
19. Robinson, John H., "Fifty-Second Regiment," in Clark, Walter, ed., *Histories of Several Regiments*, Vol. 3, p. 248.
20. Bartlett, Jacob, "Recollections," Southern Historical Collection, Wilson Library, University of North Carolina at Chapel Hill.
21. Outlaw, Edward, and Martin, William, in Clark, Walter, ed., *Histories of Several Regiments*, 599.
22. Robinson, John H., "Fifty-Second Regiment," in Clark, Walter, ed., *Histories of Several Regiments*, Vol. 3, p. 248.
23. Waddell, Duncan, "Sketch of Woodston Garrett," North Carolina Department of Archives and History, Raleigh.
24. Murdock, John, *Confederate Incognito*, 220.
25. John Smith, Henry Kiser and Robert Bell, *CSRC*.
26. Styles, Marshall, personal communication, 26 March 2014.
27. Setser, William, letter, 28 August 1864.
28. Chapman, Craig S., *More Terrible Than Victory*, 218.
29. William Rea, John Long and Thomas Benfield, *CSRC*.
30. Furguson, Ernest, B., *Not War but Murder*, 128.
31. Murdock, John, *Confederate Incognito*, 220.
32. Bartlett, Jacob, "Recollections," Southern Historical Collection, Wilson Library, University of North Carolina at Chapel Hill.
33. *Wilmington Star*, 12 March 1897.
34. Outlaw, Edward, and Martin, William, in Clark, Walter, ed., *Histories of Several Regiments*, 599.
35. 11th North Carolina Infantry, *CSRC*.
36. Morrison, James L., *The Memoirs of Henry Heth*, 191.
37. Waddell, Duncan, "Sketch of Woodston Garrett."
38. Trudeau, Noah Andre, *The Last Citadel* (Baton Rouge: Louisiana State University Press, 1991), 179.
39. Justice, Ephraim, letter, 30 August 1864. Ephraim Justice Collection, Emory University, Atlanta, GA.
40. Jordan, Weymouth, *North Carolina Troops, 1861–1865* (Raleigh: North Carolina Office of Archives and History, 1975), Vol. 5, pp. 1–105.
41. Thuersam, Bernhard, "General William MacRae, Wilmington's Fighting Brigadier," Cape Fear Historical Institute Papers, 2006.
42. Hess, Earl J., *Lee's Tar Heels*, 248.
43. Rinck, Andrew, letter, 5 September 1864.
44. Young, Louis G., "Pettigrew-Kirkland-MacRae Brigade," in, Clark, Walter, ed., *Histories of the Several Regiments and Battalions from North Carolina*, 565.
45. Bird, Francis, letter, 22 August 1864, Southern Historical Collection, Wilson Library, University of North Carolina at Chapel Hill.
46. McDonald, David, letter, 29 August 1864.
47. Young, Louis G., "Pettigrew-Kirkland-MacRae Brigade," in, Clark, Walter, ed., *Histories of the Several Regiments and Battalions from North Carolina*, 565.
48. Caldwell, J.F., *The History of a Brigade of South Carolinians: Known First as Gregg's, and Subsequently as McGowan's Brigade* (Philadelphia: King and Bird, 1866), 181.
49. Young, Louis G., "Pettigrew-Kirkland-MacRae Brigade," in, Clark, Walter, ed., *Histories of the Several Regiments and Battalions from North Carolina*, 565.
50. Rogers, George T., "Retaking Railroad at Reams Station," *Confederate Veteran* 5 (1897), 580.
51. Carmichael, Peter S., *Lee's Young Artillerist, William R.J. Pegram* (Charlottesville: University of Virginia Press, 1995), 138.
52. Miller, Richard F., *Harvard's Civil War: A History of the Twentieth Massachusetts Volunteer Infantry* (Lebanon, NH: University Press of New England, 2005), 415.
53. Jordan, Weymouth, *North Carolina Troops: 1861–1865*, Vol. 5, pp. 1–105.
54. Young, Louis G., "Pettigrew-Kirkland-MacRae Brigade," in Clark, Walter, ed., *Histories of the Several Regiments and Battalions from North Carolina*, 566.
55. *Ibid*.
56. Husk, Martin W., *The 111th New York Volunteer Infantry: A Civil War History* (Jefferson, NC: McFarland, 2009), 158.
57. Young, Louis G., "Pettigrew-Kirkland-MacRae Brigade," in, Clark, Walter, ed., *Histories of the Several Regiments and Battalions from North Carolina*, 566.
58. Outlaw, Edward, and Martin, William, in Clark, Walter, ed., *Histories of Several Regiments*, 599.
59. *Wilmington Star*, 12 March 1897.
60. Husk, Martin W., *The 111th New York Volunteer Infantry*, 158.
61. *Wilmington Star*, 12 March 1897.
62. Rogers, George T., "Retaking Railroad at Reams Station," *Confederate Veteran* 5 (1897), 580.
63. James Montgomery, John Warlick and John Morefield, *CSRC*.
64. Rogers, George T., "Retaking Railroad at Reams Station," *Confederate Veteran* 5 (1897), 580.
65. Hubbard, David. Alexander, John, *CSRC*.
66. Rinck, Andrew, letter, 5 September 1864.
67. Husk, Martin W., *The 111th New York Volunteer Infantry*, 158.
68. Thomas, Gerald W. Thomas, *Experiences of Bertie County's Confederate Soldiers*, 166.
69. Carter, Joseph. Glenn, Robert, *CSRC*.
70. Underwood, George, "Twenty-Sixth Regiment," in Clark, Walter, ed., *Histories of Several Regiments*, Vol. 2, p. 389.
71. Husk, Martin W., *The 111th New York Volunteer Infantry*, 158.
72. James Hill, Miles Askew, Joseph Humphreys and James Young, *CSRC*.
73. Rogers, George T., "Retaking Railroad at Reams Station," *Confederate Veteran* 5 (1897), 580.

74. *Wilmington Star*, 12 March 1897.
75. Husk, Martin W., *The 111th New York Volunteer Infantry*, 158.
76. Chapman, Craig S., *More Terrible Than Victory*, 228.
77. Thorp, John H., "Forty-Seventh Regiment," in Clark, Walter, ed., *Histories of Several Regiments*, Vol. 3, p. 97.
78. Hart, Walter Osgood, "Plodding and Thinking" (Madison, WI: Privately published, 1900), 29.
79. Robinson, John H., "Fifty-Second Regiment," in Clark, Walter, ed., *Histories of Several Regiments*, Vol. 3, p. 249.
80. Chapman, Craig S., *More Terrible Than Victory*, 230.
81. Wright, James, letter, 27 August 1864.
82. Justice, Benjamin, letter, 30 August 1864.
83. Todd, William, *CSRC*.
84. Hart, Walter Osgood, "Plodding and Thinking," 30.
85. Rogers, George T., "Retaking Railroad at Reams Station," *Confederate Veteran* 5 (1897), 580.
86. Webb, A.S., letter, 27 August 1864.
87. Hart, Walter Osgood, "Plodding and Thinking," 30.
88. Underwood, George, "Twenty-Sixth Regiment," in Clark, Walter, ed., *Histories of Several Regiments*, Vol. 2, p. 388.
89. Lee, Robert E., *Official Records*. Vol. 42, Part 2, p. 1207.
90. Henry Heth Report, 30 August 1864.
91. Outlaw, Edward, and Martin, William, in Clark, Walter, ed., *Histories of Several Regiments*, 599.
92. Hoyle, Lemuel, letter, 29 August 1864.
93. Welch, Spencer, *A Confederate Surgeon's Letters to His Wife*, 107.
94. James Montgomery and David Hubbard, *CSRC*.
95. Waddell, Duncan, *CSRC*.
96. Warlick, John C., letter, 1 December 1901.
97. Rinck, Andrew, letter, 5 September 1864.
98. *Ibid.*
99. Talbert, James A., letter, 29 September 1864.
100. Wright, James W., letter, 2 September 1864.
101. Rinck, Andrew, letter, 5 September 1864.
102. Wright, James, letter, 27 August 1864.
103. Venner, William T., *The Seventh Tennessee Infantry*, 137.
104. Warlick letter, 13 September 1864.
105. Chapman, Craig S., *More Terrible Than Victory*, 223; Hess, Earl J., *Lee's Tar Heels*, 259; Watson, Jones, *CSRC*.
106. Robinson, John H., "Fifty-Second Regiment," in Clark, Walter, ed., *Histories of Several Regiments*, Vol. 3, p. 249.
107. Ramsey, Evan, letter, 25 September 1864.

Chapter 15

1. Hess, Earl J., *Lee's Tar Heels*, 260.
2. 11th North Carolina Infantry, *CSRC*.
3. *Ibid.*
4. Underwood, George, "Twenty-Sixth Regiment," in Clark, Walter, ed., *Histories of Several Regiments*, Vol. 2, 389.
5. Chapman, Craig S., *More Terrible Than Victory*, 243.
6. *History of the Thirty-Sixth Regiment Massachusetts Volunteers, 1861–1865* (Boston: Press of Rockwell and Churchill, 1884), 255.
7. Hess, Earl J., *Lee's Tar Heels*, 262.
8. *History of the Thirty-Fifth Regiment Massachusetts Volunteers, 1862–1865* (Boston: Mills, Knight, 1884), 297–8.
9. *History of the Thirty-Fifth Regiment Massachusetts Volunteers*, 297–8.
10. Outlaw, Edward, and Martin, William, in Clark, Walter, ed., *Histories of Several Regiments*, 600.
11. Means, Paul B., "Colonel William Joseph Martin: University of North Carolina, 1868," Davidson College Collection, Davidson, NC, 24 November 1905, p. 1.
12. Samuel McElroy and David McDonald, *CSRC*.
13. *History of the Thirty-Sixth Regiment Massachusetts Volunteers*, 261.
14. Chapman, Craig S., *More Terrible Than Victory*, 244.
15. Henry Hill, Alva Smith and Abraham Huffman, *CSRC*.
16. *History of the Thirty-Fifth Regiment Massachusetts Volunteers*, 298.
17. *Ibid.*, 299.
18. Chapman, Craig S., *More Terrible Than Victory*, 244.
19. *History of the Thirty-Sixth Regiment Massachusetts Volunteers*, 262.
20. *Ibid.*, 298.
21. James Saville, Thomas Holmes, William Blain and William Flintoff, *CSRC*.
22. *History of the Thirty-Sixth Regiment Massachusetts Volunteers*, 262.
23. Outlaw, Edward, and Martin, William, in Clark, Walter, ed., *Histories of Several Regiments*, 600.
24. *History of the Thirty-Sixth Regiment Massachusetts Volunteers*, 264.
25. Freeman, Douglas, *Lee's Lieutenants*, Vol. 4, p. 592.
26. Outlaw, Edward, and Martin, William, in Clark, Walter, ed., *Histories of Several Regiments*, 600.
27. *Ibid.*
28. Hess, Earl J., *Lee's Tar Heels*, 260.
29. 11th North Carolina Infantry, *CSRC*.
30. Hess, Earl J., *Lee's Tar Heels*, 266.
31. *Ibid.*
32. 11th North Carolina Infantry, *CSRC*.
33. Cornwell, Sidney. Bridges, Rosward, *CSRC*.
34. Chapman, Craig S., *More Terrible Than Victory*, 246.
35. Murdock, John, *Confederate Incognito*, 222.
36. Webb, R.S., letter, 3 October 1864.
37. Albright, William and Upton, Daniel, *CSRC*.
38. Heth, Henry, Report, 11 April 1865.
39. Webb, R.S., letter, 3 October 1864.
40. *Ibid.*
41. Hess, Earl J., *Lee's Tar Heels*, 267.
42. Young, Louis G., "Pettigrew-Kirkland-MacRae Brigade," in Clark, Walter, ed., *Histories of the Several Regiments and Battalions from North Carolina*, 393.
43. Hess, Earl J., *Lee's Tar Heels*, 267.
44. 11th North Carolina Infantry, *CSRC*.
45. Pierce, Byron, *Official Records*, Vol. 42: No. 83.
46. Thomas Neily, James Gribble and George Ewing, *CSRC*.
47. Warlick letter, 6 October 1864.
48. *Ibid.*
49. Pierce, Byron, *Official Records*, Vol. 42, No. 83.
50. Young, Louis G., "Pettigrew-Kirkland-MacRae

Brigade," in Clark, Walter, ed., *Histories of the Several Regiments*.
51. 11th North Carolina Infantry, *CSRC*.
52. Hoyle, Lemuel, letter, 20 October 1864.
53. Black, Michael, personal communication, 13 August 2014.
54. Warlick letter, 10 October 1864.
55. Welch, Spencer, *A Confederate Surgeon's Letters to His Wife*, 110.
56. Freeman, Douglas, *Lee's Lieutenants*, Vol. 4, p. 612.
57. Welch, Spencer, *A Confederate Surgeon's Letters to His Wife*, 110.
58. Freeman, Douglas, *Lee's Lieutenants*, Vol. 4, p. 609.
59. Hess, Earl J., *Lee's Tar Heels*, 270.
60. 11th North Carolina Infantry, *CSRC*.
61. Hess, Earl J., *Lee's Tar Heels*, 270.
62. 11th North Carolina Infantry, *CSRC*.
63. Bearss, Edwin, and Suderow, Bryce, *Petersburg Campaign: The Western Front Battles* (El Dorado Hills, CA: Savsa Beatie, 2014), 121.
64. Hess, Earl J., *Lee's Tar Heels*, 270.
65. Heth, Henry, Report, 11 April 1865.
66. Murdock, John, *Confederate Incognito*, 223.
67. Bearss, Edwin, and Suderow, Bryce, *Petersburg Campaign*, 135; B. Wilson Ruddick, George Keller and Luico Ferrell, *CSRC*.
68. Roe, Alfred S., and Nutt, Charles, *History of the First Regiment of Heavy Artillery Massachusetts Volunteers, 1861–1865* (Boston: Regimental Association, 1917), 193.
69. Suderow, Bryce, "The Battle of Burgess Mill, October 27, 1864 (First Day of Battle of Boydton Plank Road)," The Siege of Petersburg Online, 2011.
70. R. Benjamin Whisenhunt and John Pendergrass, *CSRC*.
71. Hess, Earl J., *Lee's Tar Heels*, 272.
72. Trudeau, Noah Andre, *The Last Citadel*, 245.
73. Hess, Earl J., *Lee's Tar Heels*, 273.
74. Bartlett, Jacob, "Recollections," Southern Historical Collection, Wilson Library, University of North Carolina at Chapel Hill.
75. Trudeau, Noah Andre, *The Last Citadel*, 245.
76. Bearss, Edwin, and Suderow, Bryce, *Petersburg Campaign*, 138.
77. Warlick letter, 29 October 1864.
78. Evans, Tim, personal communication, 18 October 1864.
79. Abernathy, James. Cordell, John, *CSCR*.
80. McAllister, Robert, letter, no date.
81. Hess, Earl J., *Lee's Tar Heels*, 273.
82. Robinson, John H., "Fifty-Second Regiment," in Clark, Walter, ed., *Histories of Several Regiments*, Vol. 3, p. 250.
83. Hess, Earl J., *Lee's Tar Heels*, 273.
84. Robert Flow, William Butler, George Summeron and Ezekiel Henderson, *CSRC*.
85. Stedman, Charles, "Forty-Fourth Regiment," in Clark, Walter, ed., *Histories of Several Regiments*, Vol. 3, p. 32.
86. Stedman, Charles, "Forty-Fourth Regiment," in Clark, Walter, ed., *Histories of Several Regiments*, Vol. 3, p. 32.
87. Bartlett, Jacob, "Recollections," Southern Historical Collection, Wilson Library, University of North Carolina at Chapel Hill.
88. Hoyle, Lemuel, letter, 5 November 1864.
89. McAllister, Robert, letter, no date.
90. Hoyle, Lemuel, letter, 5 November 1864.
91. *Raleigh Daily Confederate*, 29 October 1864.
92. Jarratt, Gus, letter, 14 November 1864.
93. Thorp, John H., "Forty-Seventh Regiment," in Clark, Walter, ed., *Histories of Several Regiments*, Vol. 3, p. 98.
94. De Trobriand, Regis, *Four Years with the Army of the Potomac* (Boston: Ticknor, 1889), 663.
95. Stedman, Charles, "Forty-Fourth Regiment," in Clark, Walter, ed., *Histories of Several Regiments*, Vol. 3, p. 32.
96. Horn, John, *The Petersburg Campaign, June 1864–April 1865* (Conshohocken, PA: Combined Books, 1993), 179.
97. De Trobriand, Regis, *Four Years with the Army of the Potomac*, 663.
98. Joseph Pennix and John W. Campbell, *CSRC*.
99. Horn, John, *The Petersburg Campaign*, 179.
100. Hess, Earl J., *Lee's Tar Heels*, 275.
101. 11th North Carolina Infantry, *CSRC*.
102. Hoyle, Lemuel, letter, 5 November 1864.
103. Suderow, Bryce, "The Battle of Burgess Mill," 24.
104. Warlick letter, 29 October 1864.

Chapter 16

1. 11th North Carolina Infantry, *CSRC*.
2. Freeman, Benjamin, letter, 6 January 1865.
3. Hephner, Richard H., "Where Youth and Laughter Go: The Experience of Trench Warfare from Petersburg to the Western Front," Virginia Polytechnic Institute and State University, 1997.
4. Hess, Earl J., *In the Trenches at Petersburg: Field Fortifications and Confederate Defeat* (Chapel Hill: University of North Carolina, 2009), 215–29.
5. Morrison, James L., *The Memoirs of Henry Heth*, 192.
6. Day, William A., diary, 2 November 1864.
7. Venner, William T., *The Seventh Tennessee Infantry*, 145.
8. Day, William A., diary, 5 November 1864.
9. Venner, William T., *The Seventh Tennessee Infantry*, 145.
10. Trudeau, Noah Andre, *The Last Citadel*, 292.
11. 11th North Carolina Infantry, *CSRC*.
12. Hoyle, Lemuel, letter, 22 November 1864.
13. 11th North Carolina Infantry, *CSRC*.
14. Sale, John, letter (n.d.) November 1864.
15. Warlick letter, 29 November 1864.
16. Welch, Spencer, *A Confederate Surgeon's Letters to His Wife*, 116.
17. Perry, Aldo S., *Civil War Courts-Martial of North Carolina Troops* (Jefferson, NC: McFarland, 2012), 84.
18. Warlick, John, letter 1 November 1901.
19. Warlick letter, 3 December 1864.
20. Freeman, Douglas, *Lee's Lieutenants*, Vol. 4, p. 619.
21. Warlick letter, 27 November 1864.
22. Battle, Walter, letter, 25 December 1864.
23. Day, William A., diary, winter 1864.
24. Kendrick, Thomas, letter, 25 December 1864.
25. Battle, Walter, letter, 25 December 1864.
26. Chambers, Henry, diary, 31 December 1864.
27. Venner, William T., *The Seventh Tennessee Infantry*, 147.
28. Hephner, Richard H., "Where Youth and Laughter Go," 39.
29. Day, William, "Life Among Bullets—In the Rifle Pits," *Confederate Veteran* 29 (1921), p. 217.

30. Battle, Walter, letter, 25 December 1864.
31. Chambers, Henry, diary, 31 December 1864.
32. 11th North Carolina Infantry, *CSRC*.
33. Freeman, Douglas, *Lee's Lieutenants*, Vol. 4, p. 620.
34. Chapman, Craig S., *More Terrible Than Victory*, 267.
35. Freeman, Douglas, *Lee's Lieutenants*, Vol. 4, p. 621.
36. Warlick letter, 11 January 1865.
37. Day, William A., diary, winter 1864.
38. Hess, Earl J., *Lee's Tar Heels*, 282.
39. Trudeau, Noah Andre, *The Last Citadel*, 289.
40. Hephner, Richard H., "Where Youth and Laughter Go," 19.
41. Day, William, "Life Among Bullets—In the Rifle Pits," *Confederate Veteran* 29 (1921), p. 217.
42. Warlick letter, 27 January 1865.
43. Thorp, John H., "Forty-Seventh Regiment," in Clark, Walter, ed., *Histories of Several Regiments*, Vol. 3, p. 98.
44. Battle, Walter, letter, 25 December 1864.
45. Armfield, John, letter, 17 February 1865.
46. Freeman, Benjamin, letter, 1 February 1865.
47. Freeman, Benjamin, letter, 28 January 1865.
48. Warlick letter, 27 January 1865.
49. Battle, Walter, letter, 18 January 1865.
50. Freeman, Benjamin, letter, 1 February 1865.
51. Day, William, "Life Among Bullets—In the Rifle Pits," *Confederate Veteran* 29 (1921), p. 218.
52. Venner, William T., *The Seventh Tennessee Infantry*, 148.
53. Day, William, "Life Among Bullets—In the Rifle Pits," *Confederate Veteran* 29 (1921), p. 218.
54. 11th North Carolina regiment, *CSRC*.
55. Battle, Walter, letter, 18 January 1865.
56. Thorp, John H., "Forty-Seventh Regiment," in Clark, Walter, ed., *Histories of Several Regiments*, Vol. 3, p. 99.
57. Bearss, Edwin, and Suderow, Bryce, *Petersburg Campaign*, 187.
58. Chapman, Craig S., *More Terrible Than Victory*, 272.
59. McAllister, Robert, *Official Records*, Vol. 46, pp. 238–240.
60. Bearss, Edwin, and Suderow, Bryce, *Petersburg Campaign*, 188.
61. Chapman, Craig S., *More Terrible Than Victory*, 272.
62. William Whitted, John Gattis, John Pepper and James Marshall, *CSRC*.
63. Gabriel Miller, James Miller, Edward Martin, John Mardre, *CSRC*.
64. McAllister, Robert, *Official Records*, Vol. 46, pp. 238–240.
65. 11th North Carolina Infantry, *CSRC*.
66. Nathaniel Mardre and Charles Davenport, *CSRC*.
67. Murdock, John, *Confederate Incognito*, 230.
68. Freeman, Douglas, *Lee's Lieutenants*, Vol. 4, p. 620.
69. Hephner, Richard H., "Where Youth and Laughter Go," 18.
70. Armfield, John, letter, 17 February 1865.
71. Venner, William T., *The Seventh Tennessee Infantry*, 148.
72. Hephner, Richard H., "Where Youth and Laughter Go," 18.
73. Sollers, Somerville, letter, no date.
74. Trudeau, Noah Andre, *The Last Citadel*, 291.
75. Hunter, Andrew, Court-martial document, 25 February 1865, *CSRC*.
76. Hunter, Andrew, *CSRC*.
77. Chambers, Henry, diary, 26 February 1865.
78. Freeman, Benjamin, letter, 26 February 1865.
79. Martin, William, *CSRC*.
80. 11th North Carolina Infantry, *CSRC*.
81. Day, William, "Life Among Bullets—In the Rifle Pits," *Confederate Veteran* 29 (1921), 217.
82. Battle, Walter, letter, 18 January 1865.
83. Gaither, J.B., letter, no date.
84. 11th North Carolina Infantry, *CSRC*.
85. Justice, Benjamin, letter, 11 March 1865.
86. Trudeau, Noah Andre, *The Last Citadel*, 295.
87. Murdock, John, *Confederate Incognito*, 9 March 1865.
88. Freeman, Benjamin, letter, 15 March 1865.
89. Gibson, James, letter, 5 February 1865.
90. Venner, William T., *The Seventh Tennessee Infantry*, 148.
91. Stevens, Hazard, "The Storming of the Lines of Petersburg by the Sixth Corps, April 2, 1865," Military Historical Society of Massachusetts, Papers (1907), Vol. 6, p. 415.
92. Hill, Joseph C., "Report of Lieut. Col. Joseph C. Hill, Sixth Maryland Infantry, of Operations March 25, 1865," *Official Records*, Vol. 46, No. 140, p. 1000.
93. Stevens, Hazard, "The Storming of the Lines of Petersburg," 415.
94. Hill, Joseph C., *Official Records*, Vol. 46, No. 140.
95. Dudley Burch and David Smith, *CSRC*.
96. James Saville and Charles Watt, *CSRC*.
97. Hess, Earl J., *Lee's Tar Heels*, 290.
98. Hoyle, Joseph J., *"Deliver Us from This Cruel War": The Civil War Letters of Lieutenant Joseph J. Hoyle, 55th North Carolina Infantry*, Jeffrey M. Girvan, ed. (Jefferson, NC: McFarland, 2010), 217.
99. Chapman, Craig S., *More Terrible Than Victory*, 282.
100. Hess, Earl J., *Lee's Tar Heels*, 290.

Chapter 17

1. 11th North Carolina Infantry, *CSRC*.
2. *Ibid.*, *CSRC*.
3. Bearss, Edwin, and Suderow, Bryce, *Petersburg Campaign*, 449.
4. Freeman, Douglas, *Lee's Lieutenants*, Vol. 3, p. 663.
5. *Ibid.*, 671.
6. *Ibid.*, 675.
7. Chapman, Craig S., *More Terrible Than Victory*, 286.
8. Erson, Eric, Official Report, 11 April 1865.
9. MacRae, William, Official Report, 11 April 1865.
10. Greene, A. Wilson, *The Final Battles of the Petersburg Campaign: Breaking the Backbone of the Rebellion* (Knoxville: University of Tennessee Press, 2008), 211.
11. Greene, A. Wilson, *The Final Battles of the Petersburg Campaign*, 209.
12. Venner, William T., *The Seventh Tennessee Infantry*, 149.
13. Outlaw, Edward, and Martin, William, in Clark, Walter, ed., *Histories of Several Regiments*, 602.
14. Bearss, Edwin, and Suderow, Bryce, *Petersburg Campaign*, 525.
15. *Ibid.*, 529.
16. Venner, William T., *The Seventh Tennessee Infantry*, 150.
17. Greene, A. Wilson, *The Final Battles of the Petersburg Campaign*, 282.

18. Trudeau, Noah Andre, *The Last Citadel*, 370.
19. Bearss, Edwin, and Suderow, Bryce, *Petersburg Campaign*, 542.
20. Truex, William, *Official Records*. Vol. 46, No. 132.
21. Trudeau, Noah Andre, *The Last Citadel*, 371.
22. Casstevens, Frances H., *The 28th North Carolina Infantry*, 157.
23. Greene, A. Wilson, *The Final Battles of the Petersburg Campaign*, 322.
24. McDonald, Andrew, *Official Records*, Vol. 46, No. 135, p. 987.
25. Bogardes, Charles, *Official Records*, Vol. 46, No. 136, p. 989.
26. Greene, A. Wilson, *The Final Battles of the Petersburg Campaign*, 209.
27. Bartlett, Jacob, "Recollections," Southern Historical Collection, Wilson Library, University of North Carolina at Chapel Hill.
28. Greene, A. Wilson, *The Final Battles of the Petersburg Campaign*, 329.
29. Day, William A., "Don't Shoot," Lincolnton Library, 1893.
30. Greene, A. Wilson, *The Final Battles of the Petersburg Campaign*, 329.
31. Warlick, John C., letter, n.d.
32. Bearss, Edwin, and Suderow, Bryce, *Petersburg Campaign*, 513.
33. Jacob Miller and Andrew Rinck, *CSRC*.
34. Bartlett, Jacob, "Recollections," Southern Historical Collection, Wilson Library, University of North Carolina at Chapel Hill.
35. Bogardes, Charles, *Official Records*, Vol. 46, No. 136, p. 989.
36. Janeway, Jacob, *Official Records*, Vol. 46, No. 134, p. 986.
37. John Land, Jordan Landis, William Brogden, *CSRC*.
38. Wiggins, Octavius, letter, 2 April 1865.
39. Greene, A. Wilson, *The Final Battles of the Petersburg Campaign*, 329.
40. Schoen, Gary, *14th New Jersey History* (self-published, 2013).
41. Outlaw, Edward, and Martin, William, in Clark, Walter, ed., *Histories of Several Regiments*, 602.
42. Joseph Pennix and William Benbury, *CSRC*.
43. Bearss, Edwin, and Suderow, Bryce, *Petersburg Campaign*, 546.
44. Greene, A. Wilson, *The Final Battles of the Petersburg Campaign*, 246.
45. Ibid.
46. Venner, William T., *The Seventh Tennessee Infantry*, 150.
47. Chapman, Craig S., *More Terrible Than Victory*, 292.
48. Trudeau, Noah Andre, *The Last Citadel*, 375.
49. 11th North Carolina Infantry, *CSRC*.
50. Ibid.
51. Greene, A. Wilson, *The Final Battles of the Petersburg Campaign*, 433.
52. Robinson, John H., "Fifty-Second Regiment," in Clark, Walter, ed., *Histories of Several Regiments*, Vol. 3, p. 251.
53. Hess, Earl J., *Lee's Tar Heels*, 295.
54. Venner, William T., *The Seventh Tennessee Infantry*, 155.
55. Freeman, Douglas, *Lee's Lieutenants*, Vol. 3, p. 679.
56. Caldwell, J.F., *The History of a Brigade of South Carolinians: Known First as Gregg's and Subsequently as McGowan's Brigade* (Philadelphia: King and Baird, 1866), 220.
57. Robinson, John H., "Fifty-Second Regiment," in Clark, Walter, ed., *Histories of Several Regiments*, Vol. 3, p. 251.
58. Greene, A. Wilson, *The Final Battles of the Petersburg Campaign*, 437.
59. Trudeau, Noah Andre, *The Last Citadel*, 395.
60. Ibid.
61. Robinson, John H., "Fifty-Second Regiment," in Clark, Walter, ed., *Histories of Several Regiments*, Vol. 3, p. 251.
62. Greene, A. Wilson, *The Final Battles of the Petersburg Campaign*, 439.
63. Trudeau, Noah Andre, *The Last Citadel*, 396.
64. Caldwell, J. F., *The History of a Brigade of South Carolinians*, 220, 223.
65. Trudeau, Noah Andre, *The Last Citadel*, 396.
66. Stedman, Charles, "Forty-Fourth Regiment," in Clark, Walter, ed., *Histories of Several Regiments*, Vol. 3, p. 32.
67. John Butler and James Smith, *CSRC*.
68. Greene, A. Wilson, *The Final Battles of the Petersburg Campaign*, 329.
69. Venner, William T., *The Seventh Tennessee Infantry*, 155.
70. MacRae, William, Official Report, 11 April 1865.
71. Freeman, Douglas, *Lee's Lieutenants*, Vol. 3, p. 688.
72. Caldwell, J.F., *The History of a Brigade of South Carolinians*, 223.
73. 11th North Carolina Infantry, *CSRC*.
74. Greene, A. Wilson, *The Final Battles of the Petersburg Campaign*, 440.
75. Bartlett, Jacob, "Recollections," Southern Historical Collection, Wilson Library, University of North Carolina at Chapel Hill.
76. 11th North Carolina Infantry, *CSRC*.
77. Ibid.
78. Caldwell, J.F., *The History of a Brigade of South Carolinians*, 226.
79. Freeman, Douglas, *Lee's Lieutenants*, Vol. 3, p. 688.
80. Ibid., 689.
81. Hess, Earl J., *Lee's Tar Heels*, 299.
82. Freeman, Douglas, *Lee's Lieutenants*, Vol. 3. p. 689.
83. Robinson, John H., "Fifty-Second Regiment," in Clark, Walter, ed., *Histories of Several Regiments*, Vol. 3, p. 252.
84. Venner, William T., *The Seventh Tennessee Infantry*, 156.
85. Caldwell, J.F., *The History of a Brigade of South Carolinians*, 226. 86. Freeman, Douglas, *Lee's Lieutenants*, Vol. 3, p. 691.
87. Chapman, Craig S., *More Terrible Than Victory*, 300.
88. Freeman, Douglas, *Lee's Lieutenants*, Vol. 3, p. 692.
89. Venner, William T., *The Seventh Tennessee Infantry*, 156.
90. Caldwell, J.F., *The History of a Brigade of South Carolinians*, 229.
91. Bearss, Edwin, and Suderow, Bryce, *Petersburg Campaign*, 550.
92. Caldwell, J.F., *The History of a Brigade of South Carolinians*, 229.
93. Freeman, Douglas, *Lee's Lieutenants*, Vol. 3, p. 694.
94. Caldwell, J.F., *The History of a Brigade of South Carolinians*, 230.
95. Stoeks, Gaston, *CSRC*.
96. Caldwell, J.F., *The History of a Brigade of South Carolinians*, 230.
97. Freeman, Douglas, *Lee's Lieutenants*, Vol. 3, p. 707.

98. Chapman, Craig S., *More Terrible Than Victory*, 305.
99. Thorp, John H., "Forty-Seventh Regiment," in Clark, Walter, ed., *Histories of Several Regiments*, Vol. 3, p. 100.
100. 11th North Carolina Infantry, *CSRC*.
101. Outlaw, Edward, and Martin, William, in Clark, Walter, ed., *Histories of Several Regiments*, 603.
102. Chapman, Craig S., *More Terrible Than Victory*, 310.
103. Venner, William T., *The Seventh Tennessee Infantry*, 156.
104. Bearss, Edwin, and Suderow, Bryce, *Petersburg Campaign*, 553.
105. Haskell, John C, ed., *The Haskell Memoirs* (New York: G.P. Putnam's Sons, 1960), 91.
106. Hess, Earl J., *Lee's Tar Heels*, 302.
107. Outlaw, Edward, and Martin, William, in Clark, Walter, ed., *Histories of Several Regiments*, 603.
108. Warlick, William, *CSRC*.
109. 11th North Carolina Infantry, *CSRC*.
110. Venner, William T., *The Seventh Tennessee Infantry*, 157.
111. Hess, Earl J., *Lee's Tar Heels*, 302.
112. Caldwell, J.F., *The History of a Brigade of South Carolinians*, 235.
113. 11th North Carolina Infantry, *CSRC*.
114. Bearss, Edwin, and Suderow, Bryce, *Petersburg Campaign*, 554.
115. Caldwell, J.F., *The History of a Brigade of South Carolinians*, 235.
116. Thorp, John H., "Forty-Seventh Regiment," in Clark, Walter, ed., *Histories of Several Regiments*, Vol. 3, p. 100.
117. Caldwell, J.F., *The History of a Brigade of South Carolinians*, 236.
118. Thorp, John H., "Forty-Seventh Regiment," in Clark, Walter, ed., *Histories of Several Regiments*, Vol. 3, p. 100.
119. Caldwell, J. F., *The History of a Brigade of South Carolinians*, 236.
120. *Ibid*.
121. Freeman, Douglas, *Lee's Lieutenants*, Vol. 3, p. 740.
122. Outlaw, Edward, and Martin, William, in Clark, Walter, ed., *Histories of Several Regiments*, 603.
123. *Ibid*.
124. Freeman, Douglas, *Lee's Lieutenants*, Vol. 3, p. 741.
125. *Ibid.*, 741.
126. *Ibid.*, 745.
127. Hess, Earl J., *Lee's Tar Heels*, 304.
128. *Ibid.*, 305.
129. Venner, William T., *The Seventh Tennessee Infantry*, 157.
130. Underwood, George, *The 26th Regiment N.C. Troops: Pettigrew's Brigade, Heth's Division*, 393.
131. Venner, William T., *The Seventh Tennessee Infantry*, 157.

Bibliography

Books

Alleman, Tillie Pierce. *At Gettysburg; or, What a Girl Saw and Heard of the Battle.* New York: W. Lake Borland, 1889.

Aubery, James M. *The Thirty-Sixth Wisconsin Infantry, 1st Brigade, 2d Division, 2d Army Corps, Army of the Potomac.* Wisconsin: Fantine Aubery McCleary, 1900.

Barrett, John G. *North Carolina as a Civil War Battleground, 1861–1865.* Raleigh: North Carolina State Department of Archives and History, 1960.

Bearss, Edwin, and Suderow, Bryce. *Petersburg Campaign: The Western Front Battles.* El Dorado Hills, CA: Savsa Beatie, 2014.

Benedict, George G. *Vermont in the Civil War.* Burlington: Free Press Association, 1888.

Black, Robert C. *The Railroads of the Confederacy.* Chapel Hill: University of North Carolina Press, 1952.

Bond, William R. *Pettigrew or Pickett?: An Historical Essay.* Scotland Neck, NC: W.L.L. Hall, 1888.

Bridges, Hal. *Lee's Maverick General: Daniel Harvey Hill.* New York: McGraw Hill, 1961.

Bright, Leslie S. *The Blockade Runner Modern Greece and Her Cargo.* Raleigh: Underwater Archaeology Branch, North Carolina Department of Cultural Resources, 1977.

_____, William H. Rowland, and James C. Bardon. *The CSS Neuse: A Question of Iron and Time.* Raleigh: North Carolina Office of Archives and History, 1981.

Brock, R.A. *The Appomattox Roster: A List of the Paroles of the Army of Northern Virginia Issued at Appomattox Court House on April 9, 1865.* New York: Antiquarian Press, 1962.

Brown, Kent M. *Retreat from Gettysburg: Lee, Logistics, and the Pennsylvania Campaign.* Chapel Hill: University of North Carolina Press, 2005.

Buel, Clarence C., and Robert U. Johnson. *Battles and Leaders of the Civil War.* New York: Century, 1914. 4 volumes.

Burke County Historical Society. *The Heritage of Burke County.* Morganton, NC, 1981.

Burke, James C. *The Wilmington and Weldon Railroad in the Civil War.* Jefferson, NC: McFarland, 2012.

Caldwell, J.F. *The History of a Brigade of South Carolinians First Known as Gregg's and Subsequently as McGowan's Brigade.* Philadelphia: King & Bird, 1866.

Carbone, John. *The Civil War in Coastal North Carolina.* Raleigh: Officer of Archives and History, North Carolina Department of Cultural Resources, 2001.

Carmichael, Peter S. *Lee's Young Artillerist: William R.J. Pegram.* Charlottesville: University of Virginia Press, 1995.

Casey, Silas. *Infantry Tactics for the Instruction, Exercise, and Maneuvers of the Soldier, a Company, Line of Skirmishers, Battalion, Brigade or Corps D'Armie.* New York: D. Van Nostrand, 1862.

Casstevens, Frances H. *The 28th North Carolina Infantry: A Civil War History and Roster.* Jefferson, NC: McFarland, 2008.

Catton, Bruce. *Grant Takes Command.* Boston: Little, Brown, 1969.

Chapman, Craig S. *More Terrible Than Victory: North Carolina's Bloody Bethel Regiment, 1861–1865.* Dulles, VA: Brassey's, 1998.

Chestnut, Mary B. *A Diary from Dixie.* New York: D. Appleton, 1905.

Clark, Walter, ed. *Histories of the Several Regiments and Battalions from North Carolina in the Great War, 1861–65.* Raleigh, NC: E.M. Uzzell, 1901.

Coddington, Edwin B. *The Gettysburg Campaign: A Study in Command.* New York: Touchstone, 1997.

Coffin, Charles, C. *Marching to Victory.* New York: Harper, 1902.

Craig, Joel, and Sharlene Baker. *As You May Never See Us Again: The Civil War Letters of George and Walter Battle, 4th North Carolina Infantry.* Wake Forest, NC: Scuppernong, 2004.

Crocker, James F. *Gettysburg: Pickett's Charge and Other War Addresses.* Portsmouth, VA: W.A. Fisk, 1915.

Curtis, Orson B. *History of the Twenty-Fourth Michigan of the Iron Brigade.* Detroit: Winn and Hammond, 1891.

Davis, Archie K. *Boy Colonel of the Confederacy: The Life and Times of Henry King Burgwyn, Jr.* Chapel Hill: University of North Carolina Press, 1985.

Davis, George B., Leslie J. Perry and Joseph W. Kirkley. *The Official Military Atlas of the Civil War.* New York: Fairfax Press, 1978.

Day, W.A. *The History of Company I*. Sherrill's Ford, NC: Catawba County, 1893.

Day, William A. *A True History of Company I, 49th Regiment, North Carolina Troops, in the Great Civil War Between the North and the South*. Newton, NC: Enterprise Job Office, 1898.

De Trobriand, Regis. *Four Years with the Army of the Potomac*. Boston: Ticknor, 1889.

Ernsberger, Don. *Also for Glory: The Pettigrew-Trimble Charge at Gettysburg, July 3, 1863*. Bloomington, IN: Xlibris, 2008.

Franks, George F. *Battle of Falling Waters, 1863*. North Charleston, SC: Create Space, 2013.

Freeman, Douglas S. *Lee's Lieutenants*. New York: Scribner's, 1942. 4 volumes.

Furgurson, Ernest B. *Not but Murder: Cold Harbor, 1864*. New York: Alfred A. Knopf, 2000.

Gardner, James B. *Record of the Service of the Forty-fourth Massachusetts Volunteer Militia in North Carolina, August 1862 to May 1863*. Boston: Privately printed, 1887.

Gragg, Rod. *Covered with Glory: The 26th North Carolina Infantry at the Battle of Gettysburg*. New York: HarperCollins, 2000.

Greene, A. Wilson. *The Final Battles of the Petersburg Campaign: Breaking the Backbone of the Rebellion*. Knoxville: University of Tennessee Press, 2000.

Hamilton, J.G. de Roulhac, ed. *The Papers of Randolph Abbott Shotwell*. Raleigh: North Carolina Historical Commission, 1929.

Hardy, Michael C. *Civil War Charlotte: Last Capital of the Confederacy*. Charleston, SC: History, 2012.

_____. *North Carolina in the Civil War*. Charleston, SC: History, 2011.

Haskell, John C., ed. *The Haskell Memoirs*. New York: G.P. Putnam's Sons, 1960.

Henderson, William D. *The Road to Bristoe Station: Campaigning with Lee and Meade, August 1–October 20, 1863*. Lynchburg, VA: H.E. Howard, 1987.

Hess, Earl J. *In the Trenches at Petersburg: Field Fortifications and Confederate Defeat*. Chapel Hill: University of North Carolina, 2009.

_____. *Lee's Tar Heels: The Pettigrew-Kirkland-MacRae Brigade*. Chapel Hill: University of North Carolina Press, 2002.

Hill, Daniel H., Jr. *Confederate Military History: First at Bethel, Farthest at Gettysburg and Chickamauga, Last at Appomattox*. Atlanta: Confederate, 1899.

History of the Thirty-Fifth Regiment Massachusetts Volunteers, 1862–1865. Boston: Mills, Knight, 1884.

History of the Thirty-Sixth Regiment Massachusetts Volunteers, 1861–1865. Boston: Press of Rockwell and Churchill, 1884.

Horn, John. *The Petersburg Campaign, June 1864–April 1865*. Conshohocken, PA: Combined, 1993.

Hotchkins, Jedediah. *Make Me a Map of the Valley: The Civil War Journal of Stonewall Jackson's Topographer*. Dallas: Southern Methodist University Press, 1973.

Hoyle, Joseph J. *"Deliver Us from This Cruel War": The Civil War Letters of Lieutenant Joseph J. Hoyle, 55th North Carolina Infantry*. Edited by Jeffrey M. Girvan. Jefferson, NC: McFarland, 2010.

Husk, Martin W. *The 111th New York Volunteer Infantry: A Civil War History*. Jefferson, NC: McFarland, 2009.

Johnson, Robert U., and Clarence C. Buel. *Battles and Leaders of the Civil War*. New York: Century, 1887.

Jordan, Weymouth. *North Carolina Troops, 1861–1865*. Raleigh: North Carolina Office of Archives and History, 1975.

Keegan, John. *The Face of Battle*. New York: Penguin, 1976.

Kirwan, Thomas. *Memorial History of the Seventeenth Regiment Massachusetts Volunteer Infantry in the Civil War from 1861–1865*. Salem, MA: Salem Press, 1911.

Lawing, Mike, and Carolyn Lawing, ed. *My Dearest Friend: The Civil War Correspondence of Cornelia McGrimsey and Lewis Warlick*. Durham, NC: Carolina Academic Press, 2000.

Leon, Louis. *Diary of a Tar Heel Confederate Soldier*. Charlotte, NC: Stone, 1913.

Mast, Greg. *State Troops and Volunteers: A Photographic Record of North Carolina's Soldiers*. Raleigh: North Carolina Department of Cultural Resources, Division of Archives and History, 1995.

Miller, Richard F. *Harvard's Civil War: A History of the Twentieth Massachusetts Volunteer Infantry*. Lebanon, NH: University Press of New England, 2005.

Miller, Trevelyan, and Robert S. Lanier. *The Photographic History of the Civil War*. New York: Review of Reviews, 1910.

Moore, John W. *History of North Carolina*. Raleigh, NC: Alfred Williams, 1880.

Morrison, James, ed. *The Memoirs of Henry Heth*. Westport, CT: Greenwood, 1974.

Munson, E.B. *Confederate Incognito: The Civil War Reports of "Long Grabs," a.k.a. Murdoch John McSween, 26th and 35th North Carolina Infantry*. Jefferson, NC: McFarland, 2013.

Nolan, Alan T. *The Iron Brigade*. Ann Arbor, MI: Hardscrabble, 1983.

North Carolina Literary and Historical Association. *Report of the Committee in 1904: Five Points in the Record of North Carolina in the Great War of 1861–1865*. Goldsboro, NC: Nash Brothers, 1905.

Page, Charles D. *History of the Fourteenth Regiment, Connecticut Vol. Infantry*. Meriden, CT: Horton, 1906.

Perry, Aldo S. *Civil War Courts-Martial of North Carolina Troops*. Jefferson, NC: McFarland, 2012.

Photographic History of the Civil War in Ten Volumes. Volume Five, *Forts and Artillery*. New York: Review of Reviews, 1911.

Priest, John M. *Into the Fight: Pickett's Charge at Gettysburg*. Shippensburg, PA: White Mane, 1998.

Roe, Alfred S., and Charles Nutt. *History of the First Regiment of Heavy Artillery Massachusetts Volunteers, 1861–1865*. Boston: Regimental Association, 1917.

Rollins, Richard, ed. *Pickett's Charge: Eyewitness Accounts*. Redondo Beach, CA: Rank and File, 1994.

Stewart, George R. *Pickett's Charge: A Microhistory of the Final Attack at Gettysburg, July 3, 1863*. Boston: Houghton Mifflin, 1959.

Tompkins, D.A. *History of Mecklenburg County and the City of Charlotte*. Charlotte, NC: Observer Printing House, 1903.

Trudeau, Noah Andre. *The Last Citadel*. Baton Rouge: Louisiana State University Press, 1991.
Tuther, T., Jr., comp. *Kelley's Wilmington Directory: Business Directory for 1860–61*. Wilmington, NC: Geo. H. Kelley, 1860.
Underwood, George. *The 26th Regiment N.C. Troops: Pettigrew's Brigade, Heth's Division, Hill's Corps, A.N.V.* Goldsboro, NC: Nash and Brothers, 1901.
Venner, William T. *The 19th Indiana Infantry at Gettysburg: Hoosiers' Courage*. Shippensburg, PA: Burd Street, 1998.
_____. *The 7th Tennessee Infantry in the Civil War*. Jefferson, NC: McFarland, 2013.
_____, ed. *Queen City Lady: The 1861 Journal of Amanda Wilson*. Cincinnati: Larrea, 1996.
The War of the Rebellion: A Compilation of the Official Records of the Union and Confederate Armies. Washington, DC: U.S. Government Printing Office, 1880–1901.
Warner, Ezra J. *Generals in Gray: Lives of the Confederate Commanders*. Baton Rouge: Louisiana State University Press, 1959.
Watford, Christopher, ed. *The Civil War in North Carolina: Soldiers and Civilians' Letters and Diaries, 1861–1865*. Jefferson, NC: McFarland, 2003.
Welch, Spencer. *A Confederate Surgeon's Letters to His Wife*. New York: Neale, 1911.

Diaries and Journals

Carpenter, Kinchen J., Diary. In Julie C. Williams (ed.), *War Diary of Kinchen Jahu Carpenter, Company I, 50th North Carolina Regiment, War Between the States*. Rutherford, NC: Self published, 1955.
Day, William A., Diary. In Lincolnton, NC, Library.
Leon, Luis. "From Start to Finish. A Diary of a Confederate Soldier." Charlotte: *Charlotte Observer*, 1926.
Whitney, Dana. Memoir. Hartford, CT.

Family History Collections

Burke County Library, Morganton, NC.
Arrowood, Gerald. Family collection
Bristol, Elam. Letters
Davidson College Archives. Davidson, NC.
Martin, William J. Collection
Denison Homestead, Mystic, CT.
Bentley, Franklin. Letters
Duke University. David M. Rubenstein Rare Book & Manuscript Library. Durham, NC.
Biddle, Samuel. Collection
Henry, Jessie L. Collection
Leventhorpe, Collett. Collection
Emory University, Atlanta, GA.
Justice, Ephraim. Collection
Greensboro Historical Museum, Greensboro, NC.
Albright, Henry. Collection
Lincoln County Library, Local History Room. Lincolnton, NC.
Brown, John J. family collection
Dellinger, F. W. family collection
Farmer, John H. family collection
Heil, M. F. family collection
Kendrick, Thomas L. family collection
North Carolina Department of Archives and History, Raleigh, NC.
Burgwyn, William H. Papers
Daniels, Dennis F. Manuscript
Huske, Henry. Letters
Leventhorpe, Louise Bryan. Reminiscences
Myers, Ambrose. Letters
Waddell, Duncan, "Sketch of Woodston Garrett"
Wilkes, John. Letters
University of North Carolina. Southern Historical Collection. Chapel Hill, NC.
Bartlett, Jacob. Reminiscences
Bird, Francis. Papers
Cain, William. Letters
Foxhall, Lindsay H. Family papers
Lineback, Julius. Papers
Ross, Egbert A. Letters
Saunders, Joseph H. Papers
Vermont Historical Society. Barre, VT.
Barney, Valentine G. Letters

Manuscripts

Adjutant-General's Office. Raleigh, NC.
Compiled Service Records of Confederate Soldiers Who Served in Organizations from the State of North Carolina. Washington, DC.
Cooke, R.J. "General Hospital No. 4," 2005.
General Order Book, 1862–1863. "11th 'Bethel' Regiment, North Carolina Troops." Transcribed by Ellen Poteet. Olde Mecklenburg Genealogical Society, Charlotte, NC.
Hart, Walter Osgood. *Plodding and Thinking*. Madison, WI: Privately published, 1900.
Hephner, Richard H. "Where Youth and Laughter Go: The Experience of Trench Warfare from Petersburg to the Western Front." Virginia Polytechnic Institute and State University, 1997.
North Carolina State Convention Resolutions. Raleigh, NC.
Peake, Heather K., "General John D. Imboden and the Confederate retreat from Gettysburg." Huntingdon, TN: Civil War Interactive, no date.
Schoen, Gary, "14th New Jersey History." Self-published manuscript, 2013.
Sprunt, James, "General William MacRae: Lee's Fighting Brigadier." Cape Fear Historical Institute, 2006.
Suderow, Bryce, "The Battle of Burgess Mill: October 27, 1864, (First Day of Battle of Boydton Plank Road)," The Siege of Petersburg Online, 2011.
Thomas, Gerald, "Experiences of Bertie County's Confederate Soldiers," Windsor, NC, 1996.
Thuersam, Bernhard, "General William MacRae; Wilmington's Fighting Brigadier." The Cape Fear Historical Institute Papers, 2006.

Newspapers and Periodicals

Charlotte (NC) *Observer.* 23 September 1894, 7 February 1895.
Charlotte (NC) *Western Democrat.* 21 May 1861, 16 September 1862, 29 December 1863, 6 October 1863, 20 December 1864.
Charlotte North Carolina Whig. 7 May 1861.
Confederate Veteran. Volumes: 3 (1895), 4 (1896), 5 (1897), 6 (1898), 8 (1900), 12 (1904), 17, (1909), 18 (1910), 24 (1916), 26 (1918), 27 (1919), 29 (1921), 31 (1923), 32 (1924), 37 (1931), 38 (1932).
Davidson (NC) *Monthly.* April 1896.
Edenton (NC) *Chowan Herald.* 8 March 2000.
Fayetteville (NC) *Observer.* 7 September 1863, 17 September 1863.
Frank Leslie's Illustrated Newspaper. New York. May 16, 1863.
Greensboro (NC) *Patriot.* 23 July 1863.
Harper's New Monthly Magazine. New York. May 1857.
Harper's Weekly. New York. 28 December 1861, 3 December 1864.
Hyde Oark (VT) *Lamoille Newsdealer.* 21 June 1861.
Lenoir (NC) *Topic.* 25 March 1922.
Military Historical Society of Massachusetts, Boston. 1907.
New Bern (NC) *Daily Progress.* 22 May 1861.
New York Tribune. 9 May 1864, 31 May 1864.
Petersburg (VA) *Express.* 20 May 1861, 22 May 1861.
Raleigh (NC) *Daily Confederate.* 29 October 1864.
Raleigh (NC) *Eastern Democrat.* 26 April 1861.
Raleigh (NC) *News and Observer.* 16 September 1851.
Raleigh (NC) *Observer.* 30 November 1877.
Raleigh (NC) *Register.* 18 August 1863.
Raleigh (NC) *State Journal.* 8 May 1861.
Raleigh (NC) *Weekly.* 21 April 1862.
Raleigh North Carolina Standard. 1 October 1862, 24 December 1862, 8 July 1863, 22 July 1863.
Richmond (VA) *Daily Dispatch.* 11 June 1861.
Richmond (VA) *Examiner.* 23 May 1861.
Rutherford (NC) *Company Front.* October 1993.
Salisbury (NC) *Carolina Watchman.* 27 July 1863, 5 August 1863, 6 September 1883.
Scribner's Monthly. New York. Vol. 22 (September 1881).
Southern Historical Society Papers. Richmond, VA. Vol. 7 (1879), Vol. 20 (1892), Vol. 29 (1901).
Strategy and Tactics. Bakersfield, CA. October/November 2007.
Washington (NC) *Palmico's Past.* 7 April 2013.
Weekly Philadelphia Times. 26 November 1882.
Weekly Raleigh (NC) *Register.* 19 June 1861.
Wilmington (NC) *Journal.* 10 July 1862.
Wilmington (NC) *Journal Office.* 16 October 1862.
Wilmington (NC) *Star.* 12 March 1897.

Personal Communications

Black, Michael, 24 July 2014.
Evans, Tim, 18 October 2014.
Hennessee, Nick, 31 March 2014.
Lassiter, Kelly, 4 February 2014.
Lewis, Gil, 25 March 2014.
Martin, Hall. 30 January 2014
Perry, Darren, 8 August 2014.
Smith, Skip, 19 August 2014.
Styles, Marshall, 26 March 2014.
Whisnant, Anthony, 25 March 2014.

Index

Abee, Andrew J. (Co. D) 247, 286
Abernathy, Enoch R. (Co. E) 288
Abernathy, Ezekial (Co. H) 223, 308
Abernathy, James A. (Co. I) 316
Abernathy, James B. (Co. I) 185, 231, 249, 323
Abernathy, William A. (Co. I) 224, 235, 316
Adams, Baird (Co. K) 223, 325
Adams, Hannibal A. (Co. E) 250, 292
Adams, James (26th NC) 175, 180, 196, 197
Adams, James H. (Co. C) 112, 223, 240, 275
Aderholdt, John A. (Co. I) 217, 249, 256, 321
Albright, William S. (Co. D) 180, 246, 286
Alexander, Charles W. (Co. A) 260
Alexander, James F. (Co. E) 164, 190, 202, 208, 213, 252, 288
Alexander, James N. (Co. A) 219, 245, 255, 260
Alexander, John A. (Co. H) 243, 312
Alexander, John G. (Co. A) 169, 245, 260
Alexander, Marshall R. (Co. A) 227, 247, 250, 260
Alexander, Miles A. (Co. A) 232, 260
Alexander, Milton M. (Co. A) 232, 260
Alexander, Peter (Co. E) 288
Alexander, Richard B. (Co. A) 208, 226, 250, 260
Alexander, Robert C. (Co. A) 232, 260
Alexander, Webster S. (Co. A) 250, 266
Allen, Cyrus A. (Co. A) 75, 98, 232, 250, 265
Allen, Hamilton W. (Co. A) 227, 239, 264
Allen, Jacob C. (Co. A) 264
Allen, Ruffin (Co. G) 225, 242, 305

Allen, William (1st NY) 14
Allison, Thomas J. (Co. K) 325
Allran, Jacob (Co. I) 223, 231, 316
Allran, John P. (Co. I) 222, 316
Amelia Court House, VA 214
Anderson, William W. (Co. K) 232, 324
Andrew, Wesley (Co. G) 234, 237
Andrews, E. M. (Co. H) 256, 313
Andrews, George (Co. G) 306
Andrews, George W. (Co. B) 227, 236, 267
Andrews, James (Co. B) 239, 251, 267
Andrews, Wesley (Co. G) 305
Andrews, William (Co. B) 267
Anthony, Joseph J. (Co. B) 268
Anthony, Philip B. (Co. B) 80, 81, 223, 227, 268
Appomattox Court House, VA 216, 217
Appomattox River, VA 212, 213
Appomattox train station, VA 216
Archer, James (CS) 76
Archer's Brigade 76, 77, 78, 94, 108, 110, 176, 180
Armfield, Mark D. (Co. B) 21, 22, 40, 71, 76, 78, 81, 82, 86, 87, 89, 90, 91, 94, 96, 101, 128, 224, 232, 236, 267
Army of Northern Virginia 62
Army of Northern Virginia battle flag 66
Ashe, Richard J. (1st NC) 7
Asheville, NC 16, 22, 192
Ashley, Benbury (Co. F) 295
Ashley, Bryant (Co. F) 295
Ashley, Enos (Co. F) 295
Ashley, Joshua (Co. F) 295
Ashley, Lee T. (Co. H) 223, 308
Ashley, Moses (Co. E) 292
Ashley, William (Co. H) 248, 308, 313
Askew, Bryant (Co. F) 252
Askew, Enos (Co. F) 221
Askew, Joshua (Co. F) 254, 295
Askew, Miles (Co. F) 171, 230, 237, 246, 295

Atkin, Thomas S. (Co. K) 225, 249, 325
Atlanta, GA 173
Aubery, James (U.S.) 154
Auten, P. S. (Co. A) 232, 236, 264
Auton, Samuel W. (Co. E) 252, 288
Averett, David T. (Co. G) 252, 306
Avery, Absalon (Co. I) 231, 249, 321
Avery, Clark M. (1st NC) 7, 11

Backus, Thomas (Co. F) 223, 296
Bagley, Thomas C. (Co. F) 240, 300
Bailey, Richard (Co. F) 296
Bailey, William (Co. H) 313
Baird, Thomas (U.S.) 122
Baker, Aaron W. (Co. E) 292
Baker, Gilbert (Co. C) 275
Baker, Joel M. (Co. E) 288
Baker, Joseph (Co. K) 223, 325
Baker, Lucius (Co. D) 122, 241, 281
Baker, Martin (Co. B) 268
Baker, William M. (Co. E) 252, 292
Ball, Jeremiah C. (Co. K) 325
Ballard, Benjamin H. (Co. E) 292
Ballard, Thomas J. (Co. I) 223, 316
Baltimore, MD 70, 71
Barnett, Elam L. (Co. A) 260
Barnett, James F. (Co. A) 260
Barnett, John L. (Co. A) 227, 236, 261
Bartlett, Jacob S. (Co. K) 62, 121, 161, 162, 163, 164, 166, 185, 187, 190, 202, 206, 213, 256, 325
Bartlett, James P. (Co. K) 225, 241, 328
Bartlett, John H. (Co. K) 243, 328
Barts, Allen (Co. G) 306
Bass, Burton (Co. E) 225, 248, 288
Bass, James A. (Co. E) 229, 288
Bateman, Timothy C. (Co. F) 240, 296
Bates, Frederick W. (Co. F) 230, 237, 296
Battalion drill 23

357

Index

Bazemore, Armstead L. (Co. C) 275
Bazemore, Henry (Co. C) 22, 226, 251, 275
Bazemore, William H. (Co. C) 42, 51, 226, 275
Bazemore, William J. (Co. C) 223, 275
Beach, James C. (Co. D) 222, 281
Beal, Charles (Co. E) 225, 248, 292
Beal, John (Co. E) 225, 248, 292
Beatty, John W. (Co. E) 248, 288
Belk, William (Co. H) 253, 313
Belk, William A. (Co. E) 241, 288
Bell, David B. (1st NC) 7
Bell, E. Charles (Co. H) 308
Bell, George H. (Co. K) 244, 325
Bell, James A. (Co. K) 235, 238, 328
Bell, Martin (Co. I) 316
Bell, Robert M. (Co. I) 165, 235, 245, 316
Benbury, William E. (Co. F) 22, 202, 207, 213, 234, 252, 296
Bendix, John (7th NY) 9
Benfield, Martin (Co. D) 246, 286
Benfield, Thomas W. (Co. D) 113, 166, 240, 245, 281
Bennett, Harold M. (Co. G) 306
Berryville, VA 67
Bertie County, NC 18, 21
Bertie Volunteers 18
Bethel Church (battle) 9–15
Bethel Church, VA 9, 10
Bethel Regiment 16, 17, 18, 20, 22, 23, 25, 27, 29, 30, 31, 34, 35, 37, 44, 49, 52, 55, 61, 66, 73, 89, 167, 169, 191, 204
Big Bethel, VA (battle) 12, 23
Biggart, James (Co. H) 308
Bigham, James W. (Co. A) 232, 255, 264
Bigham, John H. (Co. A) 264
Bigham, John R. (Co. A) 232, 261
Bingham, Robert W. (Co. D) 225, 241, 281
Bird, Francis W. (Co. C) 21, 23, 28, 29, 30, 31, 35, 40, 63, 66, 71, 75, 76, 82, 86, 88, 90, 96, 97, 98, 100, 101, 102, 103, 104, 105, 106, 109, 110, 112, 113, 114, 115, 116, 118, 122, 124, 125, 126, 128, 131, 132, 134, 148, 150, 153, 154, 157, 158, 160, 164, 167, 168, 169, 171, 172, 173, 175, 180, 245, 259, 274
Bird, George W. (Co. K) 243, 325
Bird, Thomas J. (Co. K) 254, 329
Bird, William L. (Co. E) 226, 229, 237, 252, 288
Bird, Wilson R. (Co. K) 254, 328
Bisaner, Jacob H. (Co. I) 97, 235, 238, 254, 317
Black, Clinton M. (Co. D) 286
Black, Ezekiel (Co. A) 250, 266
Black, James M. (Co. A) 254, 261
Black, John B. (Co. H) 308
Black, Michael 3
Black, Patrick (Co. K) 58, 325

Black, Samuel (Co. D) 3, 84, 113, 182, 229, 240, 281
Black, Thomas J. (Co. A) 250, 261
Blackburn, A. Lafayette (Co. I) 231, 238, 246, 317
Blackstone, William R. (Co. C) 256, 275
Blackwater River, VA 35, 36, 37, 40
Blackwood, Edmund (Co. G) 145, 244, 306
Blackwood, Philo (Co. G) 230, 300
Blackwood, Robert (Co. G) 301
Blain, William M. (Co. D) 178, 246, 281
Blair, Stephen W. (Co. H) 256, 308
Blakeley, James J. (Co. A) 239, 265
Blakely, Monroe (Co. A) 221, 261
Blankenship, J. N. (Co. H) 311
Blankenship, Stephen P. (Co. H) 102, 114, 115, 248, 311
Blankenship, Thomas G. (Co. H) 312
Blount's Creek, NC 55, 56, 57, 58
Blue, David (Co. D) 240, 281
Bogardes, Charles (U.S.) 206
Bogue, Jesse (Co. F) 217, 256, 296
Bolick, B. Sidney (Co. I) 225, 235, 317
Booker, James C. (Co. G) 306
Boon, James H. (Co. G) 252, 306
Bowman, Jacob (Co. B) 239, 268
Bowman, Samuel (Co. B) 251, 273
Boyce, Charles B. (Co. H) 222, 308
Boyce, Hugh (Co. H) 308
Boyce, Kenny (Co. F) 223, 296
Boyd, Benjamin F. (Co. K) 137, 243, 328
Boyd, David (Co. H) 253, 315
Boyd, Jesse A. (Co. H) 225, 253, 313
Boyd, John J. (Co. H) 225, 253, 313
Boydton plank road, VA 174, 176, 182, 183
Boyles, Alexander (Co. I) 321
Boyles, Frank J. (Co. I) 223, 317
Boyles, John (Co. I) 230, 238, 321
Boyles, Joseph (Co. I) 113, 241, 249, 321
Boyles, William S. (Co. I) 317
Bradley, John L. (Co. E) 234, 288
Bradshaw, John F. (Co. E) 250, 292
Branch, Anderson (Co. B) 268
Branch, Anthony C. (Co. B) 233, 236
Branch, Green A. (Co. B) 224, 274
Branch, Martin (Co. B) 84, 227, 236, 251, 268
Branch, Reuben (Co. B) 59, 251, 268
Bratton, William J. (Co. F) 241, 296
Brewer, William (Co. B) 239, 272
Bridgers, John (1st NC) 5, 7, 10, 12, 15

Bridges, Roswald D. (Co. F) 180, 247, 252, 296
Brigade Sharpshooters 160, 165, 168, 175, 184, 202
Briggs, Andrew (Co. F) 248, 296
Briggs, James (Co. F) 242, 248, 296
Brigmam, Columbus C. (Co. A) 226, 232, 261
Brimmer, John (Co. E) 229, 288
Briscoe, Robert (Co. F) 97, 234, 295
Bristoe Station (battle) 119–125, 142
Bristoe Station, VA 119
Bristol, Elam B. (Co. B) 34, 46, 47, 226, 267
Bristol, Lambert A. (Co. B) 22, 46, 129, 227, 268
Brittain, Julius T. (Co. D) 240, 282
Brittain, O. Joseph (Co. D) 113, 240, 281
Brittain, Samuel (Co. D) 255, 282
Brittain, William T. (Co. K) 243, 328
Britton, Daniel W. (Co. C) 275
Broad Run, VA 121, 122, 124
Brock, A. John (Co. G) 252
Brockenbrough's Brigade 76, 107, 108, 110, 111, 112, 113
Brockwell, A. John (Co. G) 305
Brockwell, Anderson (Co. G) 301
Brogden, William G. (Co. C) 207, 244, 251, 279
Brook, John (U.S.) 143
Brower, Alfred M. (Co. H) 253, 313
Brown, Calvin S. (Co. D) 21, 23, 40, 281
Brown, James W. (Co. H) 308
Brown, John A. (Co. I) 222, 317
Brown, Thomas K. (Co. K) 325
Brown, William J. (Co. A) 145, 226, 236, 243, 261
Bryan, Louise 25
Bryant, Sidney A. (Co. H) 248, 309
Buford, John (U.S.) 111, 113
Buncombe County, NC 21
Buncombe Riflemen 7
Bunker Hill, VA 114, 116
Burch, Dudley Y. (Co. G) 201, 250, 301
Burden, James M. (Co. C) 154, 244, 255, 275
Burgess, Henry T. (Co. G) 222, 301
Burgess, Washington (Co. G) 252, 301
Burgess Mill (battle) 183–188, 190, 196
Burgess Mill, VA 202, 204
Burgin, Benjamin J. (Co. K) 249, 325
Burgin, John A. (Co. K) 324
Burgwyn, Henry K. (26th NC) 48, 79
Burke County, NC 21, 51, 113, 192
Burke Rifles 7, 22, 23
Burnett, Thomas W. (Co. K) 81, 232, 325
Burnett, William A. (Co. K) 325
Burns, Elisha P. (Co. K) 223, 325
Burns, Henry F. (Co. H) 223, 313

Burns, John J. (Co. K) 225, 226, 235, 325
Burns, Robert (Co. H) 309
Burnside, Ambrose E. (U.S.) 29, 146, 147, 161
Butler, Benjamin (U.S.) 9, 18
Butler, Erwin (Co. D) 285
Butler, John (Co. B) 251, 272
Butler, John (Co. C) 275
Butler, John (Co. D) 212
Butler, John M. (Co. D) 252, 255, 282
Butler, Levin E. (Co. C) 241, 275
Butler, Thaddeus W. (Co. C) 276
Butler, Thomas P. (Co. D) 224, 286
Butler, William (Co. D) 18
Butler, William H. (Co. C) 246, 276
Butler, William H. (Co. D) 247, 255, 285
Bynum, Benjamin S. (Co. I) 224, 322
Byram, James (Co. A) 222, 261
Byron, John (U.S.) 169
Byrum, A. J. (Co. F) 234, 296
Byrum, George F. (Co. F) 296
Byrum, Isaac (Co. F) 95, 102, 103, 234, 237, 296
Byrum, Jesse B. (Co. C) 251, 276
Byrum, Reuben L. (Co. C) 240, 251, 276

Caldwell, John S. (Co. H) 240, 253, 308
Caldwell County, NC 21
Cale, Thomas F. (Co. C) 276
Cale, William H. (Co. C) 276
Cambridge 31
Camp Davis, NC 32, 33, 34, 35
Camp Holmes, NC 28
Camp Mangum, NC 20, 23, 24, 26, 27
Camp Wilson, VA 35
Campbell, A. Lorenzo (Co. I) 224, 322
Campbell, John C. (Co. H) 311
Campbell, John W. (Co. E) 188, 248, 293
Campbell, Milton (Co. E) 293
Campbell, Robert (Co. G) 245, 301
Campbell, Thomas J. (Co. H) 230, 309
Campbell, William H. (Co. A) 264
Canady, Gideon (Co. G) 301
Canady, Ruffin (Co. G) 306
Cannon, James (Co. B) 227, 245, 268
Cantwell, John (51st NC) 28
Cape Fear River, NC 28
Cape Hatteras, NC 18, 19
Carlton, Robert W. (Co. B) 224, 227, 236, 267
Carmichael, William (52nd NC) 175, 180
Carothers, James (Co. H) 313
Carothers, James A. (Co. H) 224, 244, 253, 309

Carothers, John D. (Co. H) 223, 312
Carpenter, Albert (Co. I) 222, 317
Carpenter, David (Co. I) 225, 231, 317
Carpenter, Henry (Co. I) 322
Carpenter, Henry S. (Co. I) 231, 238, 249, 317
Carpenter, Jacob J. (Co. I) 231, 238, 317
Carpenter, Joseph C. (Co. H) 250, 313, 317
Carpenter, Michael (Co. I) 122, 123, 242, 254, 317
Carpenter, William B. (Co. H) 248, 313
Carpenter, William F. (Co. I) 231, 238, 249, 317
Carr, Joseph (2nd NY) 14
Carroll, John (Co. B) 226, 267
Carswell, Nathan (Co. B) 272
Carswell, Rankin R. (Co. B) 227, 236, 272
Carswell, Thomas H. (Co. B) 272
Carter, Benjamin (Co. C) 97, 228, 279
Carter, Joseph B. (Co. C) 171, 233, 245, 275
Carter, R. J. (Co. H) 313
Cashtown, PA 71
Casper, George M. (Co. C) 279
Casper, James H. (Co. C) 240, 276
Casper, Joseph W. (Co. C) 78, 228, 276
Casper, Justin (Co. C) 222, 276
Casper, Thomas (Co. C) 280
Casper, William J. (Co. C) 276
Castellaw, James C. (Co. C) 26, 221, 276
Castellaw, Sarah 26, 27
Catawba County, NC 22
Cates, John W. (Co. G) 164, 245, 301
Cates, Stephen P. (Co. G) 301
Cates, Thomas (Co. G) 306
Cates, William (Co. G) 30, 51, 223, 301
Cates, William B. (Co. G) 223, 301
Cathey, Robert A. (Co. I) 235, 317
Cathey, William C. (Co. E) 79, 86, 229, 237, 289
Causby, David A. (Co. B) 225, 239, 268
Causby, George (Co. D) 226, 239, 252, 282
Causby, John N. (Co. D) 32, 222, 281
Causby, William (Co. D) 229, 245, 255, 282
Cedar Creek (battle) 183
Ceres 57
Chambers, John (U.S.) 43, 44
Chapel Hill, NC 22, 33, 173, 192
Chapman, William (Co. B) 272
Charlestown, SC 25
Charlestown, VA 67
Charlotte, NC 5, 7, 21, 22, 23, 32, 131, 173, 192, 193

Charlotte Grays 7
Chatham County, NC 21, 59
Cheek, John A. (Co. G) 240, 301
Cheek, Nathaniel J. (Co. G) 252, 301
Cheek, Thomas F. (Co. G) 248, 305
Cheek, Virgil C. (Co. G) 252, 305
Chesnut, Mary 48
Chester, John M. (Co. B) 251, 273
Chester, Milton E. (Co. A) 224, 261
Chester Gap, VA 66
Chickahominy River, VA 158
Chisenhall, Samuel (Co. G) 225, 249, 252, 301
Chowan County, NC 18, 21, 22
Chrisenbery, Caleb E. (Co. H) 223, 311
Chrisenbery, Thomas C. (Co. D) 229, 285
Christy, James F. (Co. E) 83, 229, 289
Clanton, John B. (Co. E) 75, 79, 229, 237, 287
Clanton, William L. (Co. I) 253, 322
Clark, B. B. (Co. B) 268
Clark, Benjamin A. (Co. D) 222, 241, 281, 282
Clark, Henry T. (Gov. candidate) 19, 34
Clark, James A. (Co. E) 81, 229, 292
Clark, James C. (Co. D) 224, 286
Clark, James M. (Co. I) 239, 317
Clark, John M. (Co. B) 239, 268
Clark, Mitchell (Co. D) 233, 237, 282
Clark, Patrick M. (Co. H) 226, 230, 253, 308
Clark, William A. (Co. H) 222, 309
Clarke, Mitchell (Co. D) 237, 255
Clauntz, Jones (Co. B) 273
Clay, James H. (Co. D) 255, 286
Clay, Joseph M. (Co. D) 97, 233, 282
Clayton, William L. (Co. K) 254, 329
Clemens, John (Co. G) 95
Clements, George R. (Co. G) 306
Clements, James H. (Co. G) 248, 301
Clements, John R. (Co. G) 145, 234, 244, 301
Clements, William G. (Co. G) 244, 252, 301
Clemmens, Robert R. (Co. E) 293
Cline, William A. (Co. I) 239, 257, 321
Clingman, Craige (Co. C) 81
Clingman, Thomas (CS) 34
Cobb, Calvin R. (Co. H) 253, 313
Cobb, Charles E. (Co. H) 309
Cochrane, John F. (Co. A) 241, 250, 261
Codman, Charles (U.S.) 44
Cody, Absalom G. (Co. I) 231, 322
Cody, James (Co. I) 243, 256, 317

Cody, John (Co. I) 256, 323
Cody, W. A. (Co. D) 282
Coffey, Benjamin M. (Co. H) 78, 230, 309
Coffey, John C. (Co. B) 273
Cold Harbor (battle) 153–157
Cole, George (Co. G) 222, 301
Coleman, Columbus A. (Co. B) 251, 274
Coleman, H. G. (Co. H) 313
Coleman, Robert L. (Co. K) 324
Commodore Hill 57
Confederate Pike 20
Connecticut Infantry (10th) 44, 45
Conner, James R. (Co. F) 230, 237, 296
Conner's Brigade 168
Cook, David (Co. B) 272
Cook, John (Co. B) 81, 228, 236, 251, 272
Cook, John D. (Co. D) 112, 122, 240, 241, 285
Cook, Thomas (Co. B) 241, 268
Cooke, John (CS) 119, 121, 130, 133, 196, 210, 212
Cooke's Brigade 119, 120, 121, 122, 123, 124, 125, 129, 130, 131, 135, 136, 143, 145, 154, 159, 161, 163, 165, 168, 169, 172, 180, 196, 197, 209, 210, 211, 212
Coon, Adolphus S. (Co. I) 239, 257, 317
Coon, David A. (Co. I) 75, 88, 96, 103, 105, 235, 316
Cooper, Asa (Co. C) 279
Cooper, James M. (Co. H) 241, 309
Cooper, Thomas W. (Co. C) 81, 228, 275
Cooper, William E. (Co. B) 251, 273
Copeland, Timothy (Co. F) 224, 296
Copeland, William D. (Co. C) 221, 276
Cordell, David L. (Co. K) 235, 328
Cordell, James M. (Co. K) 241, 328
Cordell, John H. (Co. K) 185, 249, 254, 325
Cordell, Joseph (Co. K) 326
Cornwell, Sidney (Co. I) 180, 235, 247, 317
Corprew, Jonathan (Co. C) 226, 228, 276
Costin, Letitia 52
Costin, Miles 52
Couch, William H. (Co. G) 225, 248, 304
Courtney, James (Co. B) 239, 268
Cox, Eli (Co. H) 253, 313
Cox, Henry V. (Co. I) 256, 317
Crabtree, William E. (28th NC) 99
Craft, Michael J. (Co. I) 42, 154, 226, 244, 317
Craig, John W. (Co. G) 224, 304
Craige, Clingman (Co. C) 228, 275
The Crater (battle) 161–162
Crawley, J. W. (Co. B) 148, 239, 243, 247, 268

Creaseman, Joseph (Co. A) 221, 261
Creaseman, Joseph (Co. K) 82, 232
Creasman, Abraham, Jr. (Co. K) 256, 326
Creasman, Abraham, Sr. (Co. K) 249, 328
Creasman, Jacob (Co. K) 328
Creasman, Joseph (Co. K) 328
Creasman, William L. (Co. K) 326
Creecy, Henry L. (Co. F) 242, 296
Creecy, James E. (Co. F) 225, 240, 295
Crittenden, Thomas (U.S.) 146
Cromwell, Elias M. (Co. H) 311
Crook, Jasper A. (Co. K) 326
Crouch, Eliphus (Co. B) 251, 268
Crouch, Peyton (Co. B) 223, 268
Crow, Joseph W. (Co. K) 243, 255, 326
Crow, Levi (Co. K) 83, 326
Crump, Elijah H. (Co. B) 268
Crumpler, H. C. (Co. G) 306
Cryst, Henry J. (Co. I) 223, 317
Culberson, John W. (Co. E) 225, 248, 293
Culbert, Daniel (Co. I) 253, 324
Cullifer, John C. (Co. C) 276
Cullifer, Simon (Co. C) 223, 279
Cullifer, William T. (Co. C) 276
Culpeper, VA 65, 116, 132
Curtin, John (U.S.) 176, 177, 178, 179
Custer, George A. (U.S.) 109, 216
Custer's Brigade 110
Cutler, Lysander (U.S.) 76

Dail, Joseph (Co. F) 300
Dail, Joshua (Co. F) 222, 252, 296
Dale, David (Co. B) 268
Daniel, Algernon (Co. G) 234, 237, 301
Daniel, Alvis (Co. G) 301
Daniel, Robert (Co. G) 240, 301
Darnell, Jackson J. (Co. A) 227, 265
Darnold, James C. (Co. K) 232, 239, 327
Davenport Charles G. (Co. F) 197, 295
David, Augustus (Co. C) 276
David, Edward (Co. C) 223
David, James T. (Co. G) 257, 302
Davidson, John M. (Co. K) 242, 326
Davidson, Louis "Lewis" (Co. F) 234, 296
Davidson College, NC 5
Davis, Alfred (Co. C) 222, 276
Davis, Allen (Co. C) 148, 244, 255, 276
Davis, Barry L. (Co. B) 228, 251, 268
Davis, Benjamin (Co. G) 302
Davis, Demarcus (Co. G) 302
Davis, Duncan (Co. G) 248, 305
Davis, Edward (Co. C) 222, 276
Davis, F. M. (Co. K) 328
Davis, Fendall (Co. G) 230, 302

Davis, Henry A. (Co. G) 242, 252, 302
Davis, Jefferson (CS President) 48, 117, 202
Davis, John (Co. C) 247, 279
Davis, Joseph (CS) 133, 202
Davis, Marcus (Co. G) 302
Davis, Samuel (Co. I) 231, 318
Davis, Thomas (Co. G) 156, 230, 237, 244, 252, 300
Davis' Brigade 76, 91, 93, 94, 108, 111, 112, 113, 143, 145, 154, 164, 180, 181
Day, Samuel M. (Co. B) 228, 236, 268
Deans, William D. (Co. F) 296
Deaton, James C. (Co. A) 261
Deggerhart, Jacob L. (Co. H) 248, 312
Deggerhart, L. D. (Co. H) 309
Deggerheart, John V. (Co. K) 225, 249, 326
Dellinger, Frederick W. (Co. I) 50, 104, 136, 231, 238, 243, 318
Dellinger, John F. (Co. I) 226, 318
Dellinger, P. Franklin (Co. I) 30, 49, 50, 65, 96, 136, 231, 235, 238, 243, 318
Dellinger, Phillip (Co. I) 318
Denton, John (Co. E) 293
de Trobriand, Regis (U.S.) 185, 186, 187, 188
Dickerson, J. R. (Co. K) 256, 329
Dickerson, William T. (Co. K) 116, 183, 188, 249, 259, 324
Dishman, William (Co. K) 329
Dixie Rebels 18
Dixon, Hugh M. (Co. H) 309
Dixon, William W. (Co. E) 229, 289
Dollihite, W. H. (Co. H) 312
Donaldson, Stanhope L. (Co. D) 286
Dorsey, Elisha W. (Co. B) 227, 236, 267
Dorsey, Thomas A. (Co. B) 233, 269
Douglas, Ashley (Co. G) 302
Drewey, Andres G. (Co. G) 309
Duckworth, Henry D. (Co. A) 250, 261
Duckworth, James A. (Co. A) 266
Duckworth, John A. (Co. H) 253, 313
Duckworth, Jonathan N. (Co. B) 233, 236, 269
Duckworth, Walter (Co. B) 44, 226, 269
Duckworth, William (Co. B) 84, 228, 272
Dulin, Daniel (Co. A) 97, 232, 261
Durham, William S. (Co. G) 230, 300
Durham, NC 22
Durhamsville, NC 84
Duryea, Hiram (5th NY) 9, 11, 12, 15

Index

Duryea's Zouaves (5th NY) 9, 10, 11, 12, 13, 15
Duval, John M. (Co. B) 79, 227, 236, 267

Early, Jubal (CS) 142, 143, 145, 154, 183
Earnhardt, Joseph M. (Co. A) 207, 232, 250, 261
Earnhardt, William C. (Co. A) 232, 265
Earnhart, George (Co. H) 253, 313
Earnhart, J. H. (Co. A) 227, 261
Earnhart, Joseph M. (Co. A) 261
Earnhart, S. O. (Co. A) 239, 265
Earnhart, William (Co. D) 222, 282
Eaton, James H. (Co. B) 273
Edenton, NC 22
Edgecombe County, NC 19
Edgecombe Guards 5, 7
Edwards, Cornelius (Co. G) 230, 302
Edwards, James M. (Co. H) 225, 248, 313
Edwards, Marshall (Co. E) 225, 248, 293
Edwards, Shepherd (Co. E) 252, 293
18th Regiment of Foot (British) 25
Elias, Lewis (Co. D) 100, 102, 114, 115, 118, 125, 128, 134, 141, 149, 154, 157, 175, 179, 180, 181, 182, 183, 188, 190, 281
Eliason, William A. (F & S) 258
Eller, Alexander (Co. E) 289
Eller, Samuel W. (Co. E) 289
Elliott, Charles W. (Co. F) 221, 296
Elliott, Daniel (Co. H) 248
Elliott, Hiram C. (Co. B) 255, 273
Elliott, William A. (Co. A) 49, 50, 51, 52, 53, 54, 57, 59, 60, 61, 62, 63, 64, 65, 75, 227, 264
Ellis, Daniel (Co. H) 313
Ellis, John W. (Governor) 7, 19, 34
Ellwood, John J. (Co. E) 293
Elmira prison, NY 182
Elms, James A. (Co. H) 311
Elms, John P. (Co. A) 264
Enfield Blues 7, 23
Ernest, Hamilton (Co. B) 269
Erson, Eric (52nd NC) 204, 205, 209
Erwin, George P. (Co. B) 37, 47, 57, 58, 87, 100, 267
Erwin, Joseph J. (Co. E) 292
Escort 58
Etters, James H. (Co. H) 222, 309
Evans, Aaron J. (Co. C) 241, 276
Evans, John (Co. I) 256, 324
Everett, James H. (Co. K) 329
Ewell, Richard (CS) 107, 214, 215
Ewing, George R. (Co. A) 181, 232, 236, 247, 261
Ewing, William E. (Co. A) 232, 236, 265

Fair, Henry (Co. D) 225, 247, 284
Fair, Hezekiah (Co. D) 240, 285

Falling Waters (battle) 108–114, 142
Falling Waters, MD 107
Faribault, George (47th NC) 133, 156, 157, 158
Farmer, Joseph J. (Co. F) 242, 296
Farmville, VA 215
Farthing, Paul (Co. A) 261
Fayetteville Arsenal 6, 24
Fayetteville Independent Light Infantry 7
Ferree, Thomas C. (Co. B) 224, 269
Ferrell, Luico (Co. G) 184, 248, 304
Ferrero, Edward (U.S.) 161
Fillmore, Millard (President) 52
Fincannon, John (Co. B) 228, 269
Finger, Calvin D. (Co. I) 316
Finger, Henry F. (Co. H) 224, 314
Finger, John (Co. E) 234, 241, 289
Finger, John (Co. F) 95
Finger, Robert P. (Co. I) 235, 318
Finger, Sidney M. (F & S) 259, 316
Fisher, James W. (Co. A) 250, 261
Fite, William J. (Co. H) 253, 314
Five Forks (battle) 204, 210
Fleetwood, Joseph (Co. F) 296
Flintoff, William D. (Co. G) 178, 234, 246, 302
Flow, Robert H. (Co. A) 187, 247, 261
Floyd, Henry (Co. F) 224, 234, 297
Floyd, James R. (Co. C) 233, 276
Floyd, John G. (Co. C) 188, 247, 276
Ford, William C. (Co. A) 261
Forehand, Adam (Co. F) 240, 248, 297
Fort Archer, VA 176
Fort Caswell, NC 28
Fort Delaware Prison, DE 49, 130, 182
Fort Fisher, NC 28, 29, 30, 31, 33
Fort McHenry prison, MD 105
Fort Stedman, VA 201
Fort Sumter, SC 48
Fort Wagner, NC 32
Foster, John (U.S.) 39, 41, 42, 44, 45
14th Regiment of Foot (British) 25
Fowler, Washington (Co. G) 256, 304
Fox, William J. (Co. B) 269
Franklin, William R. (Co. G) 302
Franklin, VA 39
Frazier, Isaac S. (Co. A) 37, 261
Fredericksburg Battery 92, 93
Freeland, John F. (Co. G) 37, 40, 71, 75, 88, 90, 94, 99, 101, 102, 115, 118, 125, 134, 141, 149, 154, 157, 164, 175, 176, 179, 183, 188, 190, 191, 202, 213, 217, 256, 300
Freeman, Jacob W. (Co. C) 277
Front Royal, VA 66

Fry, Birkett (CS) 94
Fugua, William M. (F & S) 259

Galloway, H. H. (Co. B) 102, 114, 239, 251, 267
Galloway, James S. (Co. A) 86, 227, 261
Garner, Elias (Co. C) 280
Garrard, Jeptha (U.S.) 40, 41
Garrett, Esau (Co. G) 95, 234, 302
Garrett, Stephen (Co. F) 224, 242, 297
Garrett, Woodston (Co. G) 136, 137, 160, 166, 248, 302
Garrison, Alfred (Co. E) 225, 248, 293
Garrison, J. S. (Co. A) 232, 265
Garrison, Lorenzo D. (Co. B) 273
Gash, Lucius W. (Co. K) 83, 148, 232, 244, 326
Gaston County, NC 21
Gatling, William J. (Co. F) 297
Gattis, James B. (Co. G) 252, 305
Gattis, James K. (Co. G) 223, 304
Gattis, John T. (Co. G) 197, 249, 306
Gault, Albert R. (Co. I) 249, 256, 324
Gault, James (Co. I) 44, 226, 318
Getty, George (U.S.) 135, 136
Gettysburg (battle) 75–101
Gettysburg, PA 72, 73, 74
Gibson, James A. (Co. A) 261
Gilbert, J. Franklin (Co. I) 33, 222, 318
Gilbert, Johnson F. (Co. B) 247, 269
Gilbert, Marcus (Co. I) 223, 322
Giles, Alexander (Co. D) 255, 285
Giles, Sidney L. (Co. D) 86, 229, 282
Giles, William W. (Co. D) 224, 233, 239, 285
Gilliam, Francis (Co. C) 21, 33, 275
Gilliam, John H. (Co. C) 277
Glasscock, Spencer S. (Co. I) 318
Glasscock, Stanhope A. (Co. I) 235, 238, 318
Glendown, Joseph B. (Co. K) 326
Glenn, David M. (Co. I) 231, 243, 253, 318
Glenn, David P. (Co. A) 95, 232, 262
Glenn, Franklin C. (Co. A) 262
Glenn, Robert J. (Co. I) 171, 246, 254, 318
Glover, Joshua (Co. A) 232, 266
Goldsboro, NC 24, 45
Good, George (Co. D) 282
Goodman, John E. (Co. E) 79, 229, 288
Goodman, William J. (Co. A) 86, 227, 266
Goodrum, Charles H. (Co. A) 223, 266
Goodrum, William J. (Co. A) 266
Goodson, Henry (Co. K) 328

Goodson, John L. (Co. K) 326
Goodson, Thomas (Co. K) 241, 326
Goodwin, Amariah (Co. F) 297
Goodwin, Benjamin F. (Co. F) 225, 240, 297
Goodwin, Eli (Co. F) 51, 223, 297
Gordon, John (CS) 217
Grant, Ulysses S. (U.S.) 133, 142, 150, 151, 152, 157, 158, 162, 183, 218
Graves, C. J. (Co. G) 307
Gray, Walter W. (Co. A) 262
Green, Samuel (Co. F) 221, 297
Greencastle, PA 68, 105
Greenville, NC 53, 54, 59
Greenwich, VA 119
Greer, Edward (Co. H) 311
Greer, Z. B. (Co. H) 222, 309
Gregory, John T. (Co. C) 225, 233, 277
Gregory, Lemuel D. (Co. C) 222, 277
Gregory, William L. (Co. C) 79, 228, 277
Gribble, James R. (Co. A) 181, 247, 250, 260
Grier, Paul B. (Co. E) 116, 124, 241, 292
Grier, Thomas H. (Co. E) 289
Grier, William (Co. H) 21, 71, 118, 125, 131, 154, 166, 175, 176, 179, 180, 181, 182, 183, 187, 188, 190, 191, 192, 307
Griffin, David (Co. B) 240, 269
Griffin, Edmund (Co. D) 250, 286
Griffin, George (Co. E) 222, 289
Griffin, James (Co. B) 240, 269
Griffin, Joshua (Co. F) 297
Griffin, Simon (U.S.) 156, 176
Griffin, William L. (Co. B) 27, 247, 269
Groves, Robert A. (Co. A) 239, 250, 262
Guards of Southern Independence 24
Gudger, John P. (Co. K) 226, 326

Hagerstown, MD 68, 106
Hall, John P. (Co. K) 241, 256, 326
Hall, N. C. (Co. H) 244, 314
Hall, Robert B. (Co. H) 156, 244, 314
Hallman, Abel (Co. I) 253, 318
Hallman, Andrew (Co. I) 318
Hallman, Michael (Co. I) 318
Hamel, Alexander R. (Co. H) 235, 311
Hamilton, NC 23
Hampton, Wade (CS) 179
Hampton Roads, VA 195
Hampton's Legion 48
Hancock, Winfield (U.S.) 140, 185, 189
Hand, Andrew J. (Co. A) 232, 247, 262
Hand, Robert H. (Co. A) 226, 239, 260
Hand, William L. (Co. A) 31, 32, 37, 40, 61, 71, 75, 86, 88, 90, 95, 101, 232, 260
Hanna, John N. (Co. H) 248, 311
Hanover Junction, VA 62, 64
Harbison, Tolbert (Co. B) 222, 269
Harbison, William T. (Co. B) 156, 244, 269
Harget, Aley (Co. H) 223, 311
Hargroves, Israel (Co. C) 280
Hargroves, Richard (Co. C) 224, 242, 280
Harmon, James F. (Co. C) 247, 279
Harmon, Levi (Co. H) 249, 309
Harrell, George B. (Co. C) 251, 277
Harrelson, James F. (Co. I) 143, 244, 316
Harris, Abel F. (Co. K) 222, 324
Harris, Charles C. (Co. E) 293
Harris, Frank C. (Co. H) 80, 95, 235, 238, 309
Harris, James H. (Co. H) 309
Harris, John C. (Co. H) 309
Harris, Lewis B. (Co. B) 240, 247, 251, 269
Harris, Nathan O. (Co. A) 95, 232, 250, 265
Harris, Robert H. (Co. H) 309
Harris, Thomas C. (Co. F) 225, 234, 248, 297
Harris, Thomas L. (Co. K) 235, 326
Harris, Warren C. (Co. A) 250, 265
Harrisburg, PA 70
Harris's Brigade 165
Hartgrove, Richard (Co. E) 226
Hartgrove, Richard D. (Co. E) 225, 229, 248, 289
Hartgrove, William W. (Co. E) 226, 229, 243, 255, 289
Hartline, Adam (Co. E) 255, 293
Hartline, Andrew (Co. E) 252, 293
Hartline, David 3
Hartline, David L. (Co. E) 88, 229, 244, 257, 289
Hartline, George H. (Co. H) 289
Hartline, Paul (Co. E) 226, 252, 289
Hartranft, John (U.S.) 178
Harvey, Nelson (Co. I) 318
Harwood, Wesley J. (Co. G) 256, 300
Haskett, Thomas T. (Co. F) 234, 297
Hatcher's Run, VA 184, 185, 188, 196, 198, 209
Hathcock, Carney (Co. G) 222, 302
Hathcock, Franklin (Co. G) 302
Haun, Christy S. (Co. I) 235, 318
Hauser, Henry (Co. I) 231, 238, 244, 318
Havner, Adolphus J. (Co. I) 235, 318
Havner, Daniel M. (Co. I) 222, 318
Havner, George H. (Co. I) 235, 321
Havner, Hosea (Co. I) 231, 318
Havner, Jacob L. (Co. I) 231, 238, 319

Havner, John (Co. I) 231, 319
Havner, Julius A. (Co. I) 244, 250, 319
Havner, Michael (Co. I) 222, 319
Hawkins, William P. (Co. D) 244, 252, 286
Hawks, James W. (Co. C) 280
Hawks, Reuben (Co. B) 269
Hayes, Jesse B. (Co. H) 249, 309
Haynes, Albert S. (Co. I) 21, 31, 32, 33, 40, 71, 82, 90, 91, 93, 95, 97, 100, 101, 104, 131, 235, 238, 316
Haynes, Andrew R. (Co. I) 235, 316
Haynes, Daniel (Co. I) 319
Haynes, Daniel H. (Co. I) 79, 231, 319
Haynes, David A. (Co. I) 256
Haynes, John F. (Co. I) 235, 239, 319
Haynes, R. Workman (Co. I) 222, 319
Haynes, Ryan W. (Co. I) 145, 244, 253, 324
Hazel River, VA 66
Heckman, Charles (U.S.) 42
Hedricks, Thomas (Co. F) 297
Helms, Ezekiel T. (Co. E) 79, 229, 292
Henderson, Ezekiel (Co. K) 225, 235, 239, 249, 328
Henderson, Isaac S. (Co. A) 262
Henderson, Thomas M. (Co. A) 225, 239, 262
Henderson, Wright (Co. H) 314
Hendrix, Nathan (Co. F) 297
Hennessa, Robert J. (Co. B) 267
Hennessee, Emanuel (Co. D) 182, 247, 282
Hennessee, Patrick W. (Co. D) 233, 252, 281
Hennessee, Robert J. (Co. B) 97, 233, 255, 267
Henry, Barry G. (Co. H) 156, 244, 314
Henry, Tyrell B. (Co. H) 244, 249, 314
Henson, Adam (Co. D) 282
Hereford County, NC 21
Hern, W. Ranson (Co. D) 282
Herring, George T. (Co. A) 232, 256, 262
Herron, James M. (Co. A) 266
Herron, John W. (Co. H) 311
Hertford, NC 22
Hester, John W. (Co. G) 252, 302
Heth, Henry (CS) 63, 65, 72, 73, 74, 77, 84, 106, 107, 108, 109, 110, 112, 116, 117, 119, 120, 125, 128, 134, 135, 136, 137, 138, 141, 142, 143, 145, 146, 148, 151, 154, 158, 159, 161, 164, 165, 166, 167, 168, 172, 180, 181, 183, 191, 196, 202, 209, 210, 214
Heth's Division 63, 65, 76, 105, 107, 108, 113, 119, 127, 133, 134,

135, 136, 138, 139, 140, 141, 145, 173, 176, 191, 204, 205, 214
Heth's Salient 146
Hicks, Joseph S. (Co. D) 254, 282
Hicks, Rufus (Co. D) 244, 285
Hill, Ambrose P. (CS) 62, 63, 64, 73, 74, 77, 100, 107, 112, 119, 120, 125, 133, 135, 137, 138, 140, 142, 152, 154, 167, 176, 183, 210
Hill, Cornelius H. (Co. H) 311
Hill, Daniel H. (1st NC) 5, 6, 7, 8, 9, 10, 12, 14, 15, 17, 18, 54, 55, 57, 58, 88
Hill, Henry H. (Co. A) 54, 177, 246, 250, 262
Hill, James W. (Co. E) 171, 229, 237, 246, 289
Hill, Joseph (U.S.) 201
Hill, Miles (Co. A) 265
Hill, Milton (Co. A) 227, 262
Hill, William L. (Co. I) 253, 324
Hillsboro, NC 117
Hinnant, Henry (Co. H) 246, 312
Hipp, Stephen (Co. E) 289
Hobbs, Ferdinand (Co. A) 232, 250, 265
Hoffman, Miles (Co. H) 253, 314
Hoggard, William (Co. C) 51, 222, 277
Hoggard, William M. (Co. C) 223, 275
Hoke, William J. (1st NC) 7, 14, 19
Holder, Thomas (Co. C) 233, 277
Holdsclaw, Robert H. (Co. E) 293
Holland, Robert (Co. H) 256, 314
Hollingsworth, John B. (Co. E) 252, 289
Holloway, William H. (Co. G) 307
Holmes, Thomas L. (Co. A) 178, 246, 262
Holton, Harrison (Co. E) 255, 293
Hood, James C. (Co. D) 222, 282
Hoover, Daniel R. (Co. I) 235, 321
Hoover, David M. (Co. I) 226, 231, 319
Hoover, Samuel L. (Co. H) 249, 311
The Hornets' Nest 7
Hoskins, Blake B. (Co. F) 234, 295
Hotchkiss, Seth A. (Co. H) 310
Hovis, B. Monroe (Co. I) 225, 235, 262, 319
Hovis, Laban L. (Co. I) 235, 238, 253, 316
Hovis, Monroe (Co. A) 148, 243, 255
Hovis, Moses (Co. H) 253, 314
Howard, Anderson Z. (Co. K) 223, 326
Howard, Thomas M. (Co. A) 242, 250, 265
Hoyle, Lemuel J. (Co. I) 51, 70, 95, 100, 104, 105, 115, 117, 118, 125, 130, 132, 134, 141, 149, 154, 157, 164, 172, 175, 179, 182, 183, 187, 188, 190, 192, 235, 316
Hubbard, Daniel (Co. I) 253, 322
Hubbard, David (Co. I) 169, 173, 319

Hubbart, Charles (Co. I) 242, 319
Hubbart, David (Co. I) 231, 246
Hubbert, Charles (Co. I) 319
Hubbert, Daniel (Co. I) 322
Hubbert, David (Co. I) 319
Hubbert, Matthew (Co. I) 22, 319
Hudson, John W. (Co. F) 223, 297
Hudspeth, George (Co. H) 243, 253, 314
Hudspeth, John T. (Co. I) 145, 244, 256, 319
Hudspeth, Lewis (Co. A) 222, 262
Huffman, Abraham (Co. D) 177, 240, 246, 285
Hughes, Henry (Co. C) 277
Humphreys, David (Co. H) 314
Humphreys, Joseph L. (Co. H) 171, 246, 256, 310
Humphreys, Thomas L. (Co. H) 253, 311
Hunter, Anderson (Co. G) 253, 305
Hunter, Andrew J. (Co. A) 266
Hunter, Andrew J. (Co. E) 199, 293
Hunter, David P. (Co. A) 227, 250, 262
Hunter, Madison (Co. A) 256, 262
Hunter, Robert (CS Senator) 195
Hunter, Thomas H. (Co. A) 224, 262
Huske, Benjamin (1st NC) 15
Huske, Wright (1st NC) 7
Huskey, William (Co. G) 302
Huss, Jacob (Co. I) 123, 242, 319
Huss, John (Co. I) 241, 253, 319
Hutchison, James H. (Co. A) 227, 262

Icehower, William S. (Co. A) 156, 226, 236, 244, 260
Imboden, John (CS) 105
Indiana Infantry (19th) 79, 80, 82, 84, 85, 86, 88, 89
Ingle, Peter (Co. H) 230, 249, 310
Iredell County, NC 21
Iron Brigade 76, 80, 86
Ivey, Edward (Co. G) 302
Ivey, Thomas (Co. G) 302
Ivey, William G. (Co. G) 84, 230, 238, 302

Jackson, Joseph (Co. C) 225, 240, 277
Jackson, Thomas "Stonewall" (CS) 62, 64
James River, VA 158, 161
Jameson, James W. (Co. E) 248, 292
Jameson, Jones W. (Co. E) 240, 248, 292
Jameson, Thomas J. (Co. E) 226, 234, 252, 289
Jamison, James W. (Co. E) 225, 292
Jamison, Jones W. (Co. E) 292
Jamison, Thomas J. (Co. E) 289
Jenkins, David (Co. A) 227, 262
Jenkins, Doctrine (Co. C) 221, 277
Jenkins, Hiram (Co. D) 286

Jenkins, Jacob (Co. A) 239, 265
Jenney, Edwin (U.S.) 41, 44, 45
Jennings, James "Jesse" R. (Co. G) 21, 23, 32, 33, 222, 300
Jericho Mills, VA 151
Jernigan, Samuel (Co. C) 221, 277
Jetton, Taylor B. (Co. I) 241, 253, 321
Jetton, William H. (Co. I) 41, 96, 235, 316
Johnson, Alfred (Co. A) 61
Johnson, Bushrod (CS) 161
Johnson, Daniel L. (Co. D) 245, 282
Johnson, David (Co. B) 224, 274
Johnson, Harvey M. (Co. I) 253, 324
Johnson, John (Co. B) 273
Johnson, John W. (Co. D) 240, 282
Johnson, John W. (Co. H) 312
Johnson, Lee (Co. I) 96, 322
Johnson, Leonidas (Co. I) 235
Johnson, Robert (Co. I) 224, 322
Johnson, Robert N. (Co. D) 171, 247, 282
Johnson, Solomon (Co. B) 273
Johnson, Thomas N. (Co. A) 61, 227, 262
Johnson's Island Prison, IL 128
Johnston, Alfred (Co. A) 262
Johnston, J. W. (Co. E) 248
Johnston, John F. (Co. K) 329
Johnston, William J. (Governor candidate) 34
Jolly, William (Co. G) 225, 240, 302
Jones, Abraham (U.S.) 105
Jones, John (26th NC) 96, 101, 103, 104, 106, 107, 110, 112, 114
Jones, Theophilus (Co. F) 234, 297
Jones, Wiley (Co. C) 280
Jones Farm (battle) 176–179
Jones Farm, VA 176
Jordan, Hance (Co. F) 139, 243, 297
Jordan, John (31st NC) 41
Jordan, Nathan C. (Co. F) 230, 237, 297
Jordan, Noah W. (Co. D) 252, 282
Jordan, Robert S. (Co. F) 252, 297
Justice, Ephraim (Co. K) 167, 329
Justice, Foster (Co. K) 242, 326
Justice, Samuel (Co. B) 223, 269

Keener, Peter (Co. H) 256, 314
Keever, George P. (Co. I) 231, 238, 319
Keith, John C. (Co. D) 35, 283
Keller, David (Co. B) 222, 269
Keller, George (Co. B) 184, 247, 269
Keller, John J. (Co. B) 224, 228, 236, 273
Kelly, Alfred B. (Co. K) 224, 326
Kelly, Patrick (Co. K) 326
Kenan, Thomas (43rd NC) 28

Kennedy, William (Co. A) 242, 256, 262
Kerns, John D. (Co. A) 250, 262
Kerns, Thomas J. (Co. A) 251, 263
Kerr, Rufus David (Co. H) 32, 222, 310
Kerr, Thomas 32
Kerr, William J. (Co. E) 40, 71, 75, 80, 88, 90, 100, 101, 102, 114, 115, 118, 125, 134, 141, 149, 154, 157, 161, 193, 195, 199, 245, 287
Key, Abel (Co. H) 230, 310
Kilpatrick, Judson (U.S.) 13, 109, 110, 112, 113
Kilpatrick, William F. (Co. H) 253, 314
Kincaid, Cephas G. (Co. I) 249, 322
Kincaid, George W. (Co. D) 97, 233, 281
Kincaid, James W. (Co. D) 229, 283
Kincaid, Robert (Co. B) 225, 255, 274
Kincaid, William (Co. B) 251, 274
Kincaid, William J. (Co. D) 233, 237, 281
Kincaid, William W. (Co. D) 71, 75, 88, 90, 95, 101, 139, 140, 225, 242, 283
King, Arguile (Co. E) 290
King, Baxter (Co. G) 81, 230, 250, 302
King, Bellfield (Co. G) 129, 253, 304
King, Campbell (Co. A) 157, 241, 244, 251, 265
King, James (Co. G) 253, 307
King, John (Co. G) 253, 302
King, John A. (Co. A) 61, 265
King, Joseph (Co. C) 112, 240, 277
King, Rufus (Co. G) 240, 303
King, Whitfield (Co. G) 305
King, William D. (Co. G) 248, 253, 307
King, William H. (Co. G) 305
King, Willis (Co. G) 305
Kingston, NC 38, 59, 61
Kinney, Alexander D. (Co. D) 244, 286
Kinney, Benjamin (Co. A) 265
Kinston, M. (Co. B) 251, 274
Kirkland, William W. (CS) 117, 118, 120, 121, 122, 129, 130, 132, 133, 134, 135, 136, 139, 142, 144, 145, 146, 151, 152, 155, 156, 159, 165
Kirkland's Brigade 119, 120, 121, 122, 123, 124, 125, 130, 131, 133, 134, 135, 139, 140, 143, 145, 148, 151, 154, 165
Kiser, Henry (Co. I) 245, 324
Kiser, Hiram A. (Co. I) 3, 86, 231, 319
Kiser, Jacob (Co. I) 319
Kiser, John A. (Co. I) 242
Kiser-Whitesides, Pam 3
Kistler, Paul H. (Co. E) 291
Knapp, Theodore J. (Co. F) 295
Knipper, Thomas (Co. A) 251, 263

Knox William H. (Co. H) 241, 246, 250, 310
Knox, John H. (Co. H) 230, 243, 308
Kuter, James L. (Co. C) 277
Kyle, William (52nd NC) 202
Kyles, Fielding (Co. E) 248, 290
Kyles, James (Co. K) 225, 241, 329
Kyles, John (Co. E) 250, 293
Kyles, William (Co. E) 224, 290

Lafayette Light Infantry 7
Lambert, Jonathan M. (Co. E) 223, 290
Lambert, William T. (Co. E) 252, 293
Land, John (Co. B) 207, 251, 274
Landis, Jordan N. (Co. B) 207, 233, 251, 255, 269
Landis, William T. (Co. B) 228, 269
Lane, Caleb (Co. F) 234, 297
Lane, James H. (1st NC) 6, 7, 18, 19, 176
Lane, John (26th NC) 133
Lane, John E. (Co. D) 136, 242, 281
Lane, Samuel (Co. D) 223, 283
Lane, Thomas H. (Co. B) 269
Lane, William (Co. F) 225, 234, 297
Lane's Brigade 96, 177, 178, 205, 209, 210
Lankford, William (47th NC) 175, 180
Largent, John P. (Co. D) 229, 237, 285
Lassiter, George W. (Co. F) 98, 252, 298
Lassiter, Kelly 3
Lawmon, William L. (Co. D) 252, 286
Lawson, Hudson (Co. E) 224, 293
Leary, Quinton L. (Co. F) 298
Leary, William H. (Co. F) 254, 295
Ledford, William (Co. B) 274
Ledlie, James (U.S.) 41, 45, 161
Ledwell, David (Co. E) 293
Lee, Charles C. (1st NC) 6, 7, 18
Lee, Robert E. (CS) 62, 63, 64, 70, 77, 78, 90, 91, 99, 105, 106, 107, 108, 115, 116, 117, 125, 127, 132, 133, 146, 148, 166, 172, 176, 191, 194, 201, 210, 214, 215, 216, 217
Leggett, Robert (U.S.) 44
Leggett, William (Co. C) 277
Lenhardt, Cameron L. (Co. I) 235, 319
Lenhardt, Jacob M. (Co. I) 235, 322
Lenhardt, Joseph M. (Co. I) 148, 231, 242, 244, 256, 319
Leon, Louis (1st NC) 6, 7, 8, 12, 15, 16, 17, 18, 20
Leventhorpe, Collett (F & S) 25, 26, 27, 28, 29, 30, 32, 33, 34, 35, 37, 38, 40, 41, 42, 45, 46, 47, 49, 50, 51, 52, 53, 54, 55, 56, 57, 58, 59, 60, 61, 62, 63, 64, 65, 66, 70, 71, 73, 75, 76, 78, 81, 82, 88, 103, 105, 131, 187, 226, 239, 258

Lewis, Emanuel (Co. A) 135, 242, 263
Lewis, Lindsay (Co. E) 229, 290
Lewter, Charles M. (Co. G) 248, 305
Lilly, Thomas (26th NC) 160, 175, 180
Lincoln, Abraham (President) 7, 195
Lincoln County, NC 21, 33
Lincolnton, NC 22
Lindsay, Andrew J. (Co. K) 254, 329
Linebarger, Marshall "Manassas" (Co. E) 246, 294
Little, Benjamin (52nd NC) 133
Livingston, Jordan (Co. B) 228, 236, 269
Livingston, Larkin (Co. B) 159, 241, 245, 255, 270
Lloyd, John W. (Co. G) 221, 303
Lloyd, Thadeus (Co. G) 230, 303
Lloyd, Whitnel (1st NC) 17
Lloyd, William (Co. G) 248, 305
Loftin, Martin (Co. E) 225, 248, 294
Lohr, Samuel farm, PA 103
London, James W. (Co. B) 270
Long, John (Co. F) 166, 245, 298
Long, Joseph S. (Co. F) 97, 234, 298
Long, Richard (Co. F) 298
Longee, Augustus H. (Co. C) 242, 280
Longstreet, James (CS) 62, 107, 137, 139, 140, 141, 142, 214, 215, 216
Loudermilk, George (Co. B) 145, 243, 251, 270
Loudon, Thomas (Co. D) 285
Loven, George A. (Co. B) 226, 272
Lowrie, James B. (Co. H) 40, 75, 86, 88, 230, 259, 308
Lowrie, Patrick J. (F & S) 222, 259, 308
Lowrie, Robert (Co. H) 116, 118, 125, 131, 134, 141, 149, 154, 157, 164, 175, 179, 183, 188, 190, 202, 213, 217, 256, 311
Lucas, Augustus G. (Co. C) 143, 244, 280
Lucas, Henderson (F & S) 76, 82, 88, 117, 226, 258
Luther, Washington (Co. K) 256, 330

MacDougal, Clinton (U.S.) 210
Mace, Abraham (Co. D) 225, 240, 285
Mace, William H. (Co. D) 233, 241, 270
MacRae, William (CS) 159, 160, 161, 164, 166, 167, 168, 173, 175, 176, 178, 180, 181, 182, 184, 185, 187, 188, 190, 192, 196, 204, 212, 215, 217, 218
MacRae's Brigade 161, 163, 164, 165, 166, 168, 169, 171, 172, 175, 178, 180, 181, 182, 183, 185, 186,

188, 191, 196, 201, 209, 210, 214, 215, 216
Madden, James P. (Co. H) 223, 310
Maddox, George W. (Co. E) 294
Madill, Henry (U.S.) 210
Madison Court House, VA 118
Magnolia, NC 52
Magruder, John (CS Infantry) 15
Mahone, William (CS) 161
Mahone's Division 214
Manassas (1st battle) 20
Mangum, William (Co. G) 256, 305
Mann, Caswell S. (Co. G) 307
Mann, William S. (Co. G) 307
Mansfield, Calvin (Co. F) 298
Marcon, Henderson (Co. G) 303
Mardre, Nathanial (Co. F) 102, 114, 183, 188, 190, 191, 197, 240, 243, 249, 295
Mardre, William B. (F & S) 256, 259, 277
Marine Hospital, NC 32
Marshall, James K. (52nd NC) 48, 87, 90, 91, 93, 95, 96
Marshall, James M. (Co. H) 197, 249, 314
Marshall, John (Co. H) 314
Martin, Edward (F & S) 117, 118, 141, 176, 197, 249, 259, 329
Martin, Joseph (Co. D) 247, 286
Martin, William (Co. E) 234, 290
Martin, William E. (Co. I) 224, 320
Martin, William J. (F & S) 24, 39, 42, 52, 58, 62, 63, 75, 116, 117, 118, 119, 121, 122, 123, 124, 125, 128, 129, 130, 131, 132, 133, 134, 135, 136, 137, 139, 140, 141, 142, 143, 144, 145, 146, 148, 149, 150, 151, 152, 153, 154, 155, 156, 157, 158, 159, 161, 163, 164, 165, 166, 167, 168, 169, 171, 172, 173, 175, 176, 177, 179, 180, 187, 200, 202, 204, 205, 207, 209, 212, 213, 214, 215, 216, 217, 218, 241, 243, 245, 246, 255, 258
Maryland Infantry (6th) 201
Mason, Elias (Co. K) 224, 329
Massachusetts Infantry (3rd) 58
Massachusetts Infantry (4th) 14
Massachusetts Infantry (17th) 43, 44, 58
Massachusetts Infantry (23rd) 43, 44
Massachusetts Infantry (36th) 177
Massachusetts Infantry (44th) 44, 45
Massachusetts Infantry (45th) 44, 45
Massachusetts Infantry (49th) 58
Matheson, John (Co. E) 294
McAllister, Robert (U.S.) 185, 187, 196, 197
McAnear, Tom 3
McCall, Jacob A. (Co. A) 266
McCall, William W. (Co. B) 270
McCarmick, John (Co. E) 290
McClure, Ottway B. (Co. K) 244, 254, 330

McComb, William (CS) 191, 196, 204
McCombs, James P. (11th Regt. Surg.) 87, 103, 172, 173, 174, 179, 256, 258
McCombs' Brigade 191, 196, 197, 209, 210, 214
McConnell, James H. (Co. H) 314
McConnell, John F. (Co. A) 227, 263
McConnell, John H. (Co. A) 227, 251, 263
McConnell, Thomas Y. (Co. A) 263
McCorkle, Hugh P. (Co. E) 240, 252, 290
McCorkle, James G. (F & S) 96, 164, 232, 247, 259, 260, 285
McCoy, William H. (Co. I) 256, 321
McDade, Henry L. (Co. G) 256, 300
McDade, John H. (Co. G) 79, 230, 288, 300
McDonald, David W. (Co. E) 168, 177, 229, 246, 288
McDonald, John H. (Co. E) 217, 255
McDowell, George B. (Co. F) 84, 230, 295
McElroy, Samuel J. (Co. A) 177, 232, 246, 260
McGimsey, Walter W. (Co. B) 272
McGinn, Robert F. (Co. A) 225, 239, 265
McGinnis, Sidney A. (Co. A) 225, 233, 266
McGowan, Samuel (CS) 176
McGowan's Brigade 209, 212
McGrimsey, Walter (Co. B) 81, 227, 255, 272
McKee, William H. (Co. K) 249, 325
McKeen, H. Boyd (U.S.) 153
McKesson, James C. (Co. D) 233, 285
McLellan, William (Co. E) 255, 291
McLure, Cyrus A. (Co. E) 61, 234, 240, 248, 290
McLure, James D. (Co. E) 222, 290
McMillan, James E. (Co. H) 243, 310
McMillon, Pleasant (Co. D) 225, 252, 287
McQuaige, James W. (Co. H) 249, 311
McQuaige, W. D. (Co. H) 311
McQuay, James (Co. E) 97, 234, 290
McQuay, Seaborn (Co. E) 222, 290
McQuay, William H. (Co. E) 229, 237, 290
McReed, William (Co. K) 232, 329
McWhirter, James (Co. K) 266
McWhirter, John (Co. A) 233, 263
Meade, George (U.S.) 127, 128, 205
Means, John (Co. E) 32, 248, 294
Means, John S. (Co. E) 222, 288

Means, William N. (Co. E) 42, 47, 226, 287
Mecklenburg County, NC 21
Melton, Eugene A. (Co. D) 136, 233, 242, 283
Melton, William (Co. D) 223, 226, 283
Meredith, Solomon (U.S.) 76
Merritt, James Y. (Co. G) 307
Merritt, Samuel N. (Co. H) 311
Mexican War 5, 33, 63, 64
Michaux, John P. (Co. B) 171, 227, 267
Michigan Cavalry (6th) 109
Michigan Infantry (5th) 184
Michigan Infantry (7th) 153
Michigan Infantry (24th) 79
Miles, Nelson (U.S.) 210, 211, 212
Military General Hospital No. 4 32, 33
Miller, David U. (Co. K) 327
Miller, Gabriel (Co. K) 197, 249, 329
Miller, Jackson (Co. D) 229, 237, 242, 250, 283
Miller, Jacob A. (Co. I) 206, 253, 321
Miller, James (Co. F) 243, 254, 298
Miller, James M. (Co. K) 197, 249, 330
Miller, John E. (Co. E) 290
Miller, Joseph A. (Co. K) 249, 330
Miller, Marshall (Co. D) 240, 246, 283
Miller, William A. (Co. K) 329
Mincey, John (Co. G) 230, 253, 303
Mincey, Kinchen (Co. B) 247, 273
Mincey, Wiley (Co. H) 241, 253, 310
Mine Run, VA 127
Mississippi Infantry (2nd) 202
Mitchell, Jackson (Co. D) 285
Mitchell, James E. (Co. C) 130, 241, 251, 277
Mitchell, Jeremiah (Co. C) 228, 277
Mitchell, John (Co. D) 252, 285
Mitschka, John (Co. E) 290
Mizell, John N. (Co. C) 222, 277
Modern Greece 31
Modlin, Elisha (Co. F) 298
Monday, Osborne M. (Co. E)
Montegue, Edgar (CS Infantry) 11
Monteith, Moses O. (Co. A) 242, 250, 265
Montgomery, James H. (Co. A) 169, 174, 233, 245, 263
Montieth, Henry L. (Co. A) 263
Montieth, R.obert J. (Co. A) 256, 263
Moody, David E. (Co. B) 270
Mooney, McCameron (Co. I) 249, 320
Moore, Joseph A. (Co. B) 270
Moore, Levi (Co. F) 222, 298
Moore, Thomas B. (Co. B) 161, 228, 236, 245, 267
Morefield, John (Co. D) 169, 245, 287

Morgan, Andrew A. (Co. B) 228, 236, 270
Morgan, John (Co. B) 222, 270
Morgan, Perry W. (Co. B) 240, 270
Morganton, NC 22, 47, 161
Morris, Archibald G. (Co. K) 222, 326
Morris, Charles (Co. K) 42, 226, 241, 326
Morris, Cornelius (Co. K) 224, 226, 241, 326
Morris, Monroe (Co. K) 225, 235, 327
Morris, William D. (Co. C) 277
Morris, Zebedee W. (Co. K) 137, 165, 232, 245, 329
Morrison, A. H. (Co. B) 226, 228, 270
Morrison, William T. (Co. H) 235, 312
Morrison, William V. (Co. K) 327
Morrow, Henry (U.S.) 79
Moses, S. Alfred (Co. B) 251, 270
Mosteller, Isaiah (Co. D) 243, 250, 285
Mosteller, John (Co. D) 252, 287
Mott, Gershom (U.S.) 135
Motz, Charles (Co. I) 321
Motz, George (Co. I) 255, 259, 321
Mull, Henry (Co. B) 241, 270
Mullin, Alfred E. (Co. I) 242, 256, 321
Munds, Thomas (Co. F) 252, 277, 298
Murdock, William D. (Co. E) 290
Myers, Nathan (Co. C) 148, 244, 255, 277
Myers, Thomas L. (Co. C) 222

Nance, William W. (Co. I) 223, 322
Narron, John G. (Co. E) 225, 248, 294
Nashville 29
Naval Blockade 28, 31
Naval Hospital, NC 32
Neal, George A. (Co. A) 227, 263
Neal, George A. (Co. E) 229, 237, 292
Neely, John W. (Co. H) 253, 310
Neighbour, Ferdinand (Co. K) 235, 329
Neily, Thomas W. (Co. A) 181, 232, 247, 255, 260
CSS Neuse 39, 40
Neuse River, NC 39, 42, 45
Neville, John (Co. G) 305
Neville, John S. (Co. G) 248, 303
New Bern, NC 47, 53, 55, 57
New Jersey Infantry (9th) 41, 42
New Jersey Infantry (12th) 96, 97
New Jersey Infantry (14th) 207
New York Artillery (3rd Light) 41, 44, 45
New York Cavalry (1st) 105
New York Cavalry (3rd) 58
New York Cavalry (5th) 134, 135
New York Infantry (1st) 14
New York Infantry (2nd) 14

New York Infantry (3rd) 9, 13, 14
New York Infantry (5th) 9, 13, 14
New York Infantry (7th) 5, 9, 169
New York Infantry (39th) 169
New York Infantry (42nd) 153
New York Infantry (52nd) 169
New York Infantry (57th) 169
New York Infantry (82nd) 122
New York Infantry (88th) 169
New York Infantry (93rd) 184
New York Infantry (111th) 169
New York Infantry (125th) 169
New York Infantry (126th) 169
New York Infantry (151st) 206
Newell, Alexander H. (Co. A) 95, 233, 263
Newman, Elias (Co. H) 253, 310
Nichols, John S. (Co. E) 21, 222, 287
Nisbet, John G. (Co. E) 223, 290
Nixon, Thomas W. (Co. F) 298
Norment, Isaac (Co. A) 233, 254, 263
Norment, John (Co. A) 263
North Carolina Infantry (1st) 5, 7, 8, 16, 19, 20, 21, 22, 23, 40
North Carolina Infantry (11th) 16, 20, 21, 22, 24, 27, 28, 37, 39, 42, 47, 50, 51, 55, 58, 59, 62, 63, 65, 66, 67, 70, 71, 72, 77, 78, 79, 80, 85, 86, 87, 90, 91, 92, 93, 97, 103, 106, 108, 112, 114, 117, 122, 124, 133, 140, 143, 148, 152, 153, 154, 157, 164, 166, 167, 168, 171, 173, 175, 176, 177, 178, 181, 183, 184, 187, 188, 190, 192, 193, 195, 200, 201, 203, 204, 205, 206, 207, 209, 213, 216, 217, 219
North Carolina Infantry (15th) 159, 169
North Carolina Infantry (21st) 117
North Carolina Infantry (22nd) 48
North Carolina Infantry (26th) 35, 48, 49, 50, 55, 61, 62, 72, 77, 78, 79, 80, 87, 91, 93, 94, 96, 101, 106, 108, 114, 122, 123, 133, 134, 146, 160, 164, 167, 175, 176, 180, 196, 197
North Carolina Infantry (28th) 19, 117, 204, 205
North Carolina Infantry (29th) 99
North Carolina Infantry (31st) 41
North Carolina Infantry (34th) 24, 25
North Carolina Infantry (43rd) 28
North Carolina Infantry (44th) 48, 49, 116, 122, 129, 133, 134, 139, 140, 148, 164, 167, 175, 176, 180, 181, 187
North Carolina Infantry (46th) 120, 169
North Carolina Infantry (47th) 48, 49, 72, 77, 78, 87, 94, 122, 123, 133, 134, 139, 146, 153, 156, 164, 167, 175, 176, 180, 187, 217
North Carolina Infantry (51st) 28
North Carolina Infantry (52nd) 48, 49, 77, 87, 90, 94, 122, 123,

133, 134, 139, 140, 146, 164, 167, 175, 176, 177, 180, 181, 202, 204, 209, 210, 214
North Carolina Infantry (53rd) 26
North Carolina Infantry (55th) 91, 92, 93
North Carolina Infantry (59th) 41
North Carolina Infantry (63rd) 41
North Carolina Military Institute 5, 6
Norwood, David J. (Co. G) 224, 234, 303
Norwood, Thomas F. (Co. G) 300
Nowell, Jacob (Co. F) 298
Nugent, Robert (U.S.) 210
Null, John S. (Co. E) 294
Nutt, Erasmus D. (Co. G) 307

Oaks, John (Co. I) 235, 239, 253, 323
Ohio Infantry (126th) 201
Orange County, NC 21
Orange Court House, VA 117, 126, 127, 133, 158
Orange Light Infantry 7, 23
Orange Plank Rd. (VA) 133, 140
Orman, J E. (Co. A) 255, 263
Orr, James F. (Co. A) 247, 254, 263
Orr, N. C. (Co. A) 241, 263
Ostwalt, Francis H. (Co. E) 98, 224, 234, 290
Outer Banks, NC 18
Outlaw, Edward R. (Co. C) 29, 96, 98, 99, 109, 110, 114, 115, 118, 124, 125, 128, 132, 134, 137, 139, 141, 145, 149, 163, 165, 175, 178, 179, 183, 188, 190, 202, 213, 215, 216, 217, 218, 255, 275
Owens, Richard A. (Co. A) 277
Owens, William (1st NC) 14
Owens, William A. (F & S) 23, 24, 26, 259

Page, John D. (Co. H) 314
Page, Lemuel (Co. I) 320
Pamlico River 54, 55, 57
Parker, Asa (Co. I) 254, 320
Parker, John H. (Co. C) 240, 278
Parker, Thomas H. (Co. C) 247, 255, 278
Parker, William G. (Co. C) 51, 52, 53, 54, 59, 62, 64, 65, 228, 278
Parker's Store, VA 134
Parks, Austin L. (Co. B) 251, 274
Parks, H. H. (Co. B) 233, 270
Parks, James P. (Co. B) 228, 240, 251, 272
Parks, Thomas (1st NC) 6
Parks, Thomas B. (Co. H) 314
Parks, Thomas R. (Co. B) 75, 88, 90, 101, 128, 134, 141, 149, 154, 157, 164, 175, 179, 183, 188, 202, 213, 215, 217, 233, 239, 255, 267
Parris, William E. (Co. F) 224
Parrish, Stephen (Co. F) 247, 298
Parrish, William E. (Co. F) 230, 298
Patterson, Samuel (1st NC) 13, 221
Patton, Calvin (Co. K) 330

Patton, George (Co. B) 27, 221, 270
Patton, George A. (Co. K) 136, 243, 254, 327
Patton, James L. (Co. K) 254, 329
Patton, John (Co. B) 221, 270
Patton, John M. (Co. K) 232, 238, 325
Patton, Robert C. (Co. K) 327
Patton, William S. (Co. B) 228, 241, 251, 270
Paysour, Caleb (Co. A) 233, 250, 266
Paysour, S. Peter (Co. A) 254, 266
Peace Commission (1865) 195
Pearson, Edward (Co. G) 222, 303
Pearson, Forest (Co. G) 221, 303
Pearson, Henry C. (Co. G) 303
Pearson, John (Co. D) 229, 252, 283
Pearson, Michael (Co. B) 228, 270
Pearson, Robert G. (Co. D) 285
Pearson, Robert H. (Co. D) 250
Pearson, Thomas (Co. B) 112, 240, 245, 251, 270
Peeble's farm, VA 182
Peele, Thomas H. (Co. C) 82, 228, 278
Pegram, William (CS) 168
Pegram's farm, VA 182
Pender, William (CS) 49
Pender's Division 87
Pendergrass, Alvis (Co. G) 253, 303
Pendergrass, Charles H. (Co. G) 230, 248, 306
Pendergrass, George (Co. G) 242, 303
Pendergrass, George W. (Co. G) 305
Pendergrass, James A. (Co. G) 303
Pendergrass, James M. (Co. G) 224, 305
Pendergrass, John L. (Co. G) 184, 234, 248, 303
Pendergrass, Thompson (Co. G) 303
Pendergrass, William (Co. G) 230, 303
Pendergrass, William H. (Co. G) 305
Pendigrant, Alvis (Co. G) 171
Pendley, Adolphus (Co. B) 251, 274
Pennix, John A. (Co. E) 255, 294
Pennix, Joseph W. (Co. E) 188, 207, 248, 252, 294
Pennsylvania Cavalry (12th) 105
Pennsylvania Infantry (53rd) 113
Pennsylvania Infantry (67th) 201
Pepper, John (Co. H) 197, 249, 315
Perquimans County, NC 21
Perry, Alfred (Co. B) 240, 270
Perry, Timothy (Co. F) 224, 298
Petersburg, VA 62, 158, 159, 193
Petersburg breakthrough 204–209
Petersburg trenches 190, 191, 192, 194, 199, 202, 204, 213
Pettigrew, James J. (CS) 48, 49, 51, 52, 53, 59, 62, 63, 64, 70, 72, 73, 74, 75, 77, 78, 84, 86, 87, 93, 94, 95, 100, 106, 107, 108, 109, 110, 115, 118, 133, 159
Pettigrew's Brigade 50, 64, 69, 76, 105, 107, 110, 114
Pettis, Stephen J. (Co. A) 251, 266
Pettus, H. M. (Co. A) 255, 265
Pettus, John W. (Co. A) 242, 251, 266
Petty, Henry (Co. G) 242, 253, 303
Petty, John W. (Co. G) 223, 303
Peysour, Caleb (Co. A) 266
Peysour, S. Peter (Co. A) 266
Phelps, Thomas (Co. C) 278
Phelps, William J. (Co. C) 278
Phillips, C. S. (Co. B) 256, 270
Phillips, Elijah (Co. B) 224, 270
Pickens, George A. (Co. K) 243, 254, 328
Pickeral House, VA 191
Pickett, George (CS) 63
Pickett's Charge 91–101, 142
Pickett's Division 93, 94, 203, 214
Pierce, Byron (U.S.) 181, 184
Pierce, James H. (Co. C) 228, 278
Pierce, Job (Co. F) 247, 298
Pierce, Richard (Co. F) 298
Pittman, John N. (Co. K) 96, 235, 327
Plymouth, NC 21, 22, 53
Po River, VA 143, 145
Poindexter, Denson F. (Co. D) 287
Point Lookout prison, MD 105, 130, 182
Polk, James (President) 48
Pollocksville, NC 34
Pool, Albert J. (Co. I) 231, 244, 320
Pool, George S. (Co. E) 143, 244, 290
Poor, William H. (Co. K) 241, 327
Porter, Robert C. (Co. H) 84, 230, 238, 312
Poteet, John (Co. D) 240, 286
Poteet, Peter (1st NC) 11, 221
Poteet, Samuel (Co. D) 223, 283
Potomac River, VA 67, 106, 107, 109, 113, 114
Potter, John (Co. F) 242, 298
Potter, Robert (U.S.) 146
Potter, Samuel (Co. F) 242, 298
Potts, John W. (Co. G) 224, 248, 306
Powell, Daniel (Co. A) 80, 227, 263
Powell, Joseph H. (Co. D) 252, 287
Powell, Kemp W. (Co. D) 222, 283
Powell, Moses (Co. D) 283
Powell, William (Co. D) 22
Powell, William A. (Co. C) 280
Powell, William H. (Co. F) 222, 298
Powell, William P. (Co. D) 241, 252, 283
Powell, William W. (Co. C) 228, 236, 251, 278
Powers, Daniel (Co. A) 86
Powers, James R. (Co. K) 241, 327
Powers, Jesse A. (Co. C) 251, 280
Price, J. A. (Co. H) 223, 315

Prim, Thomas (Co. A) 227, 266
Pritchard, Andrew J. (Co. C) 78, 228, 278
Pritchard, James W. (Co. C) 278
Pritchard, Joseph J. (Co. C) 278
Proctor, John R. (Co. F) 230, 237, 298
Propst, L. H. (Co. K) 330
Pruett, Ransom (Co. D) 223, 286
Pryor, Roger (CS) 37, 38
Puckett, Elias W. (Co. B) 225, 233, 271
Puckett, Julius J. (Co. D) 229, 247, 291
Puckett, William C. (Co. D) 229, 255, 291
Puett, John W. (Co. B) 222, 271

Query, Robert L. (Co. A) 251, 263
Query, Samuel F. (Co. A) 42, 226, 263
Quickel, Levi H. (Co. I) 254, 323

Raborn, M. D. (Co. A) 265
Raleigh, NC 5, 6, 7, 20, 22, 24, 27
Ramsaur, Oliver (Co. I) 97, 316
Ramsaur, John F. (Co. I) 202, 213, 320
Ramsaur, John M. (Co. I) 323
Ramsaur, Oliver A. (Co. I) 316
Ramsaur, Walter G. (Co. I) 115, 242, 316
Ramsaur, William (Co. I) 102, 114, 122
Ramsey, John (U.S.) 212
Ramsey, Jonas (Co. D) 286
Ramsey, R. Nelson (Co. I) 231, 320
Ramsour, John F. (Co. I) 253
Ramsour, John M. (Co. I) 242, 323
Ramsour, Oliver A. (Co. I) 235, 316
Ramsour, Theodore J. (Co. I) 154, 244, 320
Randalsburg Rifles 6
Randolph, George (CS Artillery) 11
Randolph County, NC 59
Rapidan River, VA 117, 129, 133
Ratchford, Ezekiel C. (Co. A) 51, 222, 263
Ratchford, J. W. (1st NC) 13, 221
Rawls, James R. (Co. C) 241, 278
Rayner, James T. (Co. C) 82, 164, 176, 202, 228, 236, 254, 259, 275
Rea, William D. (Co. F) 95, 154, 157, 166, 234, 245, 295
Ream's Station (battle) 168–173, 174, 180
Ream's Station, VA 167
Reap, Thomas (Co. I) 224, 320
Red Stick War 25
Reeves, Edward (Co. G) 225, 240, 303
Reid, James C. (Co. E) 248, 252, 294
Reid, William M. (Co. H) 312
Reinhardt, Charles (Co. I) 224, 323
Reinhardt, Robert (Co. I) 231, 323

Rhine, Arthur M. (Co. H) 253, 315
Rhodes, Edward A. (Co. C) 86, 228, 275
Rhodes, Jacob B. (Co. I) 253, 322
Rhodes, Robert H. (F & S) 208, 250, 259, 280
Rhyne, David (Co. E) 248, 294
Rice, John S. (Co. H) 312
Rice, Napoleon B. (Co. C) 228, 278
Richey, Joseph C. (Co. I) 136, 231, 243, 320
Richey, William F. (Co. E) 229, 237, 292
Richmond, Silas (U.S.) 58
Richmond, VA 8, 18, 19, 28, 48, 62, 193
Ridley, J. S. (F & S) 258
Rievs, John (Co. K) 249
Rievs, William R. (Co. E) 229, 294
Riggsbee, Hawkins (Co. G) 253, 306
Rinck, Andrew (Co. I) 128, 129, 132, 167, 169, 173, 206, 207, 246, 254, 323
Rinck, Daniel (Co. I) 241, 320
Rinck, Noah (Co. I) 320
River Queen 195, 196
Roanoke Island (battle) 41, 42
Roanoke Island, NC 19
Roberts, Martin P. (Co. K) 241, 329
Roberts, Peyton (Co. A) 227, 263
Roberts, Stephen W. (Co. F) 82, 84, 118, 125, 134, 136, 141, 149, 230, 243, 295
Robertson, Beverly (CS) 40, 41, 42, 45
Robinson, Henry D. (Co. F) 222, 298
Robinson, John (Co. F) 299
Rochelle, Thomas B. (Co. H) 253, 315
Rodgers, Council (1st NC) 13, 221
Rodgers, William H. (Co. G) 248, 307
Rogers, Sion (47th NC) 48
Rollins, Thomas B. (Co. G) 307
Roseman, Robert M. (Co. I) 154, 244, 324
Ross, Egbert (1st NC) 6, 7, 12, 13, 15, 17, 18, 25
Ross, Egbert A. (Co. A) 21, 23, 26, 31, 33, 34, 57, 58, 72, 73, 76, 78, 81, 82, 84, 88, 226, 259
Ross, Robert A. (Co. H) 223, 263, 312
Ross, Stephen A. (Co. D) 243, 287
Roundtree, Noah (Co. F) 42, 226, 299
Rozzell, James T. (Co. E) 137, 243, 294
Rozzell, William F. (Co. E) 47, 116, 229, 237, 287
Ruddick, B. William (Co. A) 247, 264
Ruddick, Burl M. (Co. A) 247, 264
Ruddick, Theo C. (Co. A) 239, 247, 260
Ruddick, Wilson (Co. A) 184

Rudisill, Absalom (Co. D) 139, 243, 247, 287
Ruggs, Horace (U.S.) 172
Russell, John C. (Co. H) 239, 310
Rutherford, NC 25

Sadler, Julius (1st NC) 8
Sanders, Jacob (Co. H) 256, 315
Sartain, Zera (Co. G) 303
Saulman, James W. (Co. D) 254, 283
Saulman, John M. (Co. D) 229, 286
Saunders, George R. (Co. F) 299
Saunders, Joseph (1st NC) 9
Saunders, William F. (Co. F) 254, 299
Saville, James M. (Co. H) 90, 101, 164, 179, 201, 235, 246, 250, 308
Saville, Robert D. (Co. H) 230, 308
Sayler's Creek, VA 215
Scales' Brigade 209
Scott, Rayford S. (Co. H) 225, 315
Seagle, Andrew (Co. I) 256, 320
Seagle, Monroe (Co. I) 322
Seagler, Alfred A. (Co. I) 231, 320
Seagraves, Charles J. (Co. G) 307
Seaman's Home, NC 32
Seminole Indians 64
Settlemire, David (Co. D) 86, 229, 286
Seven Pines (battle) 49
Seward, William (Sec. of State) 195
Shelton, James (Co. B) 246, 250, 274
Shenandoah River, VA 66, 116
Shenandoah Valley, VA 66, 67
Shepard, Samuel (7th TN) 112
Shepherdstown, VA 67
Sherman, William T. (U.S.) 173, 199, 200
Sherrill, Wilburn (Co. E) 291
Sherrill, William A. (Co. I) 243, 249, 320
Ship Point, VA 18
Shope, Thomas J. (Co. K) 254, 330
Short, Daniel (Co. B) 247, 273
Short, William W. (Co. B) 222, 271
Shroat, Alfred B. (Co. K) 329
Shrum, J. Frank (Co. I) 223, 320
Shuffler, Harvey (Co. B) 226, 240, 271
Shuffler, John (Co. B) 124, 228, 241, 251, 271
Shuffler, Sidney (Co. B) 240, 247, 271
Shuffler, William (Co. B) 226, 240, 251, 271
Shuford, Noah P. (Co. I) 231, 323
Shuford, Sidney (Co. I) 254, 322
Shull, Anthony (Co. I) 225, 226, 241, 320
Sigmore, Elijah (Co. I) 224, 231, 238, 323
Sigmore, Noah (Co. I) 124, 242, 323
Simpson, Frederick (Co. F) 250, 299
Simpson, John E. (Co. D) 233, 283
Simpson, John W. (Co. A) 266

Simpson, Robert F. (Co. A) 233, 264
Simpson, Thomas A. (Co. D) 252, 287
Sims, James M. (Co. A) 239, 254, 259, 260
Sims, Samuel (Co. B) 271
Singletary, George (44th NC) 48, 116, 122, 126, 128, 133, 146
Singleton, James V. (Co. B) 255, 271
Singleton, Lucius (Co. B) 228, 254, 271
Singleton, Marcus D. (Co. B) 223, 271
Singleton, Rufus W. (Co. B) 251, 274
Singleton, Silas S. (Co. B) 240, 271
Sioux Indians 63
Skiles, Henry (Co. C) 279
Skiles, James W. (Co. C) 279
Skiles, Robert M. (Co. C) 240, 278
Sledge, William P. (Co. G) 253, 307
Sloop, Alexander (Co. H) 238, 310
Small, Edward A. (Co. F) 21, 23, 40, 71, 75, 82, 83, 84, 88, 90, 101, 234, 295
Small, Thomas M. (Co. F) 115, 245, 295
Smith, Albert J. (Co. H) 310
Smith, Alexander (Co. B) 273
Smith, Alfred B. (Co. K) 235, 239, 327
Smith, Alva (Co. B) 177, 240, 126, 271
Smith, Anderson (Co. B) 251, 271
Smith, Aristides S. (F & S) 259
Smith, Carney (Co. G) 252, 303
Smith, Charlton (Co. F) 234, 299
Smith, David D. (Co. I) 231, 238
Smith, David H. (Co. C) 251, 280
Smith, David H. (Co. I) 323
Smith, David J. (Co. E) 201, 250, 291
Smith, Elam C. (Co. B) 274
Smith, Elijah C. (Co. B) 251
Smith, Henry (Co. B) 228, 240, 247, 251, 273
Smith, James C. (Co. B) 240, 271
Smith, James J. (Co. F) 212, 252, 299
Smith, James W. (Co. H) 242, 243, 249, 310
Smith, John (Co. A) 95
Smith, John (Co. G) 244, 252, 306
Smith, John B. (Co. K) 223, 327
Smith, John J. (Co. I) 136, 165, 243, 245, 323
Smith, John S. (Co. A) 233, 266
Smith, John T. (Co. H) 256, 310
Smith, Richard (Co. K) 246, 327
Smith, Thomas (Co. B) 271
Smith, Thomas (Co. K) 222, 327
Smith, Thomas J. (Co. H) 225, 241, 310
Smith, William (Co. F) 95
Smith, William A. (Co. B) 228, 236, 271

Smith, William E. (Co. K) 243, 329
Smith, William J. (Co. F) 234, 299
Smithwick, Alfred (Co. C) 279
Snead, Franklin (Co. H) 253, 315
Snider, Heremiah A. (Co. H) 312
Snider, John A. (Co. H) 235
Snipes, Jeter J. (Co. G) 82, 230, 305
Southern Stars 7, 23
Spain, H. P. (Co. D) 243, 287, 315
Spake, Christopher (Co. K) 250, 330
Sparrow, George W. (Co. G) 303
Sparrow, Helory (Co. G) 307
Sparrow, Houston (Co. G) 303
Sparrow, Hutson (Co. G) 307
Sparrow, Van B. (Co. G) 230, 242, 304
Sparrow, William T. (Co. G) 240, 304
Speagle, Aaron (Co. I) 224, 231, 323
Speagle, Cain (Co. I) 249
Speagle, Calvin (Co. I) 225, 324
Speagle, L. Monroe (Co. I) 231, 323
Speagle, William P. (Co. I) 231, 320
Spence, Robert (U.S.) 201
Sperryville, VA 66, 118
Spinola, Francis (U.S.) 57, 58
Spotsylvania (battle) 143–149
Spotsylvania, VA 142
Spotsylvania Court House, VA 142
Sprinkle, J. I. (Co. E) 256, 294
Squires, John A. (Co. H) 249, 315
Squirrel Rd., VA 167
Stacy, George L. (Co. B) 233, 271
Stanford, James L. (Co. H) 243, 253, 315
Starney, Joshua (Co. D) 192, 287
Starr, Joseph B. (1st NC) 7, 18
Stars and Stripes 31
Stearns, David M. (Co. F) 242, 299
Stearns, James W. (Co. F) 299
Stearns, John (Co. F) 299
Stedman, Charles (44th NC) 175, 180
Stephens, T. Gaston (Co. G) 307
Stepp, Joseph M. (Co. K) 254, 330
Sterling, Edward (NC recruit) 24
Stewart, Sarah 26
Stewart, Thaddeus C. (Co. C) 26, 221, 278
Stinson, John B. (Co. E) 291
Stokes, Gaston (Co. C) 215, 255, 280
Stone, Alexander (Co. E) 225, 291
Stone, David G. (Co. C) 228, 278
Stone, John (Co. C) 241, 279
Stone, John (CS) 202
Stowe, Jacob C. (Co. A) 246, 264
Stowe, James M. (Co. A) 227, 264
Strain, James A. (Co. G) 225, 248, 304
Strain, Thomas (Co. G) 230, 248, 306
Stroup, Daniel S. (Co. I) 235, 254, 320

Stroup, S. F. (Co. K) 254, 330
Stroup, William J. (Co. K) 235, 327
Strutt, Pinkney S. (Co. I) 224, 231, 238, 320
Stuart, J. E. B. (CS) 149
Sudderth, Elam M. (Co. D) 233, 283
Sudderth, Robert W. (Co. B) 254, 274
Suggs, William M. (Co. G) 98, 99, 234, 305
Suit, Brantly (Co. G) 230, 304
Sullivan, Coatsworth (Co. I) 320
Summeron, George (Co. H) 187, 249, 315
Summerow, Peter J. (Co. I) 254, 322
Summers, Perry (Co. D) 122, 233, 241, 283
Summey, John S. (F & S) 258
Summy, John B. (Co. H) 253, 315
Sutherland Station (battle) 209–213
Suttles, John (Co. K) 327
Sutton, Seth S. (Co. F) 234, 242, 248, 299
Swain, James W. (Co. F) 242, 299
Swannanoa, NC 22, 58
Swink, Archibald (Co. B) 247, 273

Taggert, John C. (Co. H) 244, 253, 312
Tallant, Aaron (Co. I) 231, 323
Tar River 53
Tarboro, NC 52
Tate, Hugh (Co. D) 97, 233, 237, 281
Tate, John M. (F & S) 129, 132, 258, 259, 281
Taylor, Charles (Co. D) 233, 240, 283
Taylor, George W. (Co. D) 223, 283
Taylor, Harvey S. (Co. A) 264
Taylor, Houston S. (Co. A) 247
Taylor, J. Q. (Co. A) 245, 267
Taylor, Joel (Co. D) 283
Taylor, Joseph W. (Co. F) 234, 247, 299
Taylor, Robert C. (Co. A) 251, 264
Taylor, William B. (Co. A) 67, 83, 84, 86, 88, 102, 114, 115, 118, 125, 132, 134, 141, 149, 154, 156, 175, 179, 181, 183, 188, 190, 202, 213, 217, 244, 255, 260
Taylor, William H. (Co. C) 223, 278
Teem, John P. (Co. B) 233, 271
Teem, William C. (Co. B) 246, 251, 273
Tennessee Infantry (7th) 112
Tenney, Nathaniel B. (Co. G) 81, 230, 300
Tenney, William C. (Co. G) 306
Thatch, Henry C. (Co. F) 234, 299
Thatch, Stephen (Co. C) 225, 278
Thomas, Joseph T. (Co. C) 279
Thomasson, James B. (Co. A) 251, 267

Thompson, D. B. (CS) 50
Thompson, David (Co. C) 275
Thompson, J. B. (Co. A) 264
Thompson, James J. (Co. G) 304
Thorpe, John (1st NC) 13, 15, 202
Thrift, Pinkney (Co. G) 248, 304
Thrift, William (Co. G) 234, 304
Thrower, Alex (Co. H) 243, 245, 310
Thrower, Jefferson T. (Co. H) 42, 226, 242, 246, 312
Tilly, John M. (Co. G) 307
Tilly, William A. (Co. G) 304
Todd, Augustus (Co. C) 278
Todd, Elisha (Co. C) 254, 278
Todd, Lewis (Co. C) 254, 279
Todd, Nehemiah J. (Co. C) 279
Todd, R. L. (Co. D) 234, 284
Todd, William H. (Co. C) 90, 101, 102, 113, 128, 154, 157, 171, 172, 175, 183, 202, 240, 245, 250, 275
Topsail Inlet, NC 33
Totherow, George (Co. I) 320
Totopotomoy Creek, VA 152
Townsend, Frederick (3rd NY) 9, 11, 12
Trantham, John (Co. K) 242, 327
Trantham, Joseph (Co. K) 242, 327
Tredenick, Richard (Co. H) 312
Triplett, James H. (Co. K) 83, 232, 324
Tripp, Jerry (Co. G) 78, 230, 304
Tripp, William (Co. G) 253, 307
Troutman, Joseph W. (Co. F) 234, 245, 295
Truex, William (U.S.) 205, 206, 207
Trumbull, John D. (Co. C) 279
Turberfield, James (Co. H) 315
Turner, Jeremiah (7th TN) 3
Turner, John W. (Co. E) 294
Turner, Richard (Co. G) 223, 306
Turner, William S. (Co. E) 47, 116, 161, 164, 175, 179, 183, 187, 188, 225, 247, 288
Tyrrell County, NC 48

United States Naval Observatory 48
University of North Carolina, Chapel Hill 24, 48, 51
University of Virginia, VA 24
Upton, Daniel H. (Co. D) 180, 246, 287

Vance, Zebulon (Governor) 34, 35
Vann, Lemuel D. (Co. G) 304
Vermont Infantry (1st) 14
Virginia Cavalry (18th) 105
Virginia Infantry (13th) 64
Virginia Military Institute, VA 6

Wacaster, Abraham (Co. I) 224, 320
Wacaster, Adolphus (Co. I) 232, 238, 243, 321
Waddell, Duncan C. (Co. G) 51, 84, 86, 160, 165, 166, 168, 173, 175, 234, 238, 246, 306

Wade, Lamont 3
Wadkins, John B. (Co. D) 229, 256, 284
Wadsworth, James (U.S.) 139
Wakefield, Sidney D. (Co. B) 224, 228, 236, 271
Walker, Benjamin H. (Co. E) 42, 226, 291
Walker, Elisha F. (Co. B) 22, 233, 247, 272
Walker, Henry (CS) 119, 120, 133
Walker, J. H. (Co. E) 26, 221, 291
Walker, James H. (Co. E) 248, 291
Walker, James R. (Co. B) 247, 273
Walker, John H. (Co. E) 252, 291
Walker, Joseph (Co. B) 251, 273
Walker, Landsey L. (Co. E) 254, 294
Walker, Levi L. (Co. E) 145, 230, 237, 244, 291
Walker's Brigade 119, 124, 125, 135, 143, 145, 146, 148, 164
Wallace, William A. (Co. A) 233, 251, 264
Waller, Phoenix L. (Co. H) 249, 315
Wallis, William (1st NC) 7
Walls, M. Lafayette (Co. D) 226, 229, 284
Walters, George F. (Co. G) 306
Walters, Sidney (Co. G) 253, 307
Ward, Aaron (Co. F) 250, 299
Ward, Anderson S. (Co. F) 95, 234, 254, 299
Ward, Warren J. (Co. C) 279
Ward, Whitmel T. (Co. C) 279
Ward, William C. (Co. C) 225, 247, 280
Ward, William T. (Co. C) 279
Warlick, A. P. (Co. B) 228, 272
Warlick, D. Logan (Co. B) 243, 273
Warlick, John C. (Co. I) 40, 41, 42, 45, 169, 173, 206, 235, 246, 254, 322
Warlick, John L. (Co. B) 192, 227, 236
Warlick, Lewis (Co. B) 22, 28, 30, 31, 32, 34, 35, 37, 38, 39, 40, 42, 44, 45, 46, 47, 49, 50, 51, 52, 57, 59, 63, 64, 65, 117, 130, 131, 132, 135, 148, 149, 152, 158, 160, 162, 164, 173, 175, 179, 182, 185, 188, 190, 192, 194, 195, 242, 272
Warlick, Lewis (1st NC) 6, 7, 8, 9, 11, 15, 17, 18, 19
Warlick, Logan (Co. B) 148
Warlick, Patrick (Co. B) 95
Warlick, Pinkney (Co. B) 44, 245, 272
Warlick, Portland A. (Co. B) 223, 233, 267
Warlick, William J. (Co. B) 216, 255, 274
Warren, Thomas M. (Co. H) 249, 315
Washburn, Peter (4th MA) 14
Washington, NC 54, 55, 57
Washington College, MD 5

Waters, Allen (Co. H) 315
Watkins, Jesse M. (Co. K) 243, 327
Watkins, Miniard (Co. K) 224, 328
Watkins, Uriah P. (Co. K) 241, 328
Watson, John (Co. E) 100
Watson, Jones (Co. G) 102, 114, 173, 174, 300
Watt, John Charles B. (Co. H) 201, 250, 312
Watts, Hosea (Co. B) 273
Watts, James I. (Co. I) 222, 321
Watts, John (Co. B) 225, 251, 274
Weathers, Richard (Co. G) 307
Weaver, Phillip C. (Co. I) 242, 249, 322
Webb, Alexander (U.S.) 120, 124
Weber, Peter (U.S.) 109, 110
Webster, Daniel 52
Weisiger, David (CS) 183, 184, 185, 187, 188
Welch, William B. (Co. F) 222, 299
Welch, William G. (Co. F) 224, 299
Weldon, NC 47, 49, 51, 61
Weldon & Petersburg Railroad, VA 164, 165, 166, 167, 171, 173, 182, 192
Wells, Oliver (Co. K) 325
West, Jack L. (Co. A) 265
West, John P., Jr. (Co. K) 145, 327
West, John P., Sr. (Co. K) 244, 324
West, William R. (Co. K) 232, 324
West Point, NY 6, 63, 64, 117
Whedbee, George W. (Co. F) 234, 299
Whisenhunt, Alexander (Co. D) 27, 211, 284
Whisenhunt, Benjamin (Co. D) 184, 240, 247, 252, 284
Whisenhunt, James (Co. D) 27, 221, 284
Whisenhunt, Stanhope (Co. D) 27, 221, 284
Whisenhunt, Wilburn (Co. D) 223, 284
Whitaker, James R. (Co. G) 116, 175, 179, 252, 300
Whitaker, Thomas J. (Co. G) 224, 240, 246, 304
White, Isaac N. (Co. F) 234, 252, 299
White, James (Co. F) 299
White, James B. (Co. F) 230, 234, 252, 299
White, Riddick (Co. C) 222, 279
White, Robert (Co. F) 240, 300
White, William (1st NC) 14, 221
White Hall (battle) 39–46, 47
White Hall, NC 39, 40, 41, 43, 45
Whitted, William G. (Co. G) 197, 249, 300
Whitters, B. A. (Co. A) 246, 264
Wikerson, John (Co. H) 315
Wilcox, Cadmus (CS) 136, 137, 167
Wilcox's Division 136, 138, 139, 140, 141, 151, 167, 205, 214
The Wilderness (battle) 134–141
The Wilderness 133
Wilkerson, James F. (Co. H) 315

Wilkerson, William H. (Co. H) 154, 244, 310
Wilkes County, NC 21
Willcox, Orlando (U.S.) 148
Williams William M. (Co. D) 240
Williams, Baird (Co. D) 224, 287
Williams, Charles (1st NC) 13, 221
Williams, Elijah H. (Co. D) 229, 237
Williams, Forrest (Co. G) 224, 304
Williams, J. L. (Co. D) 284
Williams, James (Co. F) 300
Williams, James H. (Co. C) 228, 233, 279
Williams, James W. (Co. G) 230, 304
Williams, Jane 27
Williams, John (Co. D) 252, 284
Williams, John A. (Co. B) 27, 221, 272
Williams, John A. (Co. D) 225, 284
Williams, Johnson (Co. G) 253, 307
Williams, Joseph (Co. D) 223, 284
Williams, Joseph B. (Co. B) 228, 247, 272
Williams, Lewis S. (1st NC) 7, 23
Williams, Marcus (Co. D) 286
Williams, Martin (Co. B) 274
Williams, Moulton (Co. D) 240, 250, 284
Williams, Norris (Co. G) 253, 304
Williams, Oliver M. (Co. C) 251, 280
Williams, Robert G. (Co. B) 244, 250, 272
Williams, Samuel (Co. G) 230, 304
Williams, Solomon (U.S.) 80
Williams, Spain H. (Co. A) 264
Williams, W. A. (Co. D) 287
Williams, William (Co. C) 279
Williams, William H. (Co. D) 113, 229, 239, 284
Williams, William M. (Co. D) 284
Williamson, Edward Y. (Co. E) 234, 291
Williamson, Henry C. (Co. C) 280
Williamsport, MD 106, 107
Willis, William (Reverend) 17
Willoughby's Run, PA 79, 80, 91
Wilmington, NC 24, 28, 29, 30, 31, 32, 33, 34, 35, 41, 52, 159
Wilmington & Weldon RR 28, 39
Wilson, Harrison S. (Co. I) 254, 324
Wilson, J. F. (Co. H) 315
Wilson, John (11th NC Regt. Surg.) 29, 32, 87, 103, 104, 156, 179, 258
Wilson, John R. (Co. E) 294
Wilson, Robert L. (Co. E) 248, 288
Wilson, W. H. (Co. H) 256
Wilson, William M. (F & S) 256, 259, 266
Winchester, VA 88
Windsor, NC 22, 27, 216
Wingate, Angus (Co. A) 97, 233, 264

Wingate, Charles (Co. A) 254, 264
Wingate, James (Co. E) 224, 230, 237, 291
Wingate, Joseph W. (Co. F) 124, 242, 300
Wingate, Murchison (Co. A) 251, 264
Wingate, R. James (Co. H) 135, 243, 310
Wingate, Thomas (Co. E) 230, 248, 291
Winston, Patrick H. (Co. C) 247, 280
Winters, Moulton (Co. D) 229, 281
Winthrope, Theodore (U.S.) 14
Wisconsin Infantry (36th) 153, 154, 172
Wise, Zenas (Co. I) 256, 321
Womack, William T. (Co. D) 202, 213, 217, 255, 284
Womble, J. M. (Co. H) 316
Wood, John H. (Co. I) 222, 321
Wood, Perry (Co. I) 235, 249, 321
Wood, William (Co. D) 229, 237, 284
Wooten, Bryant H. (Co. H) 316
Wright, John (Co. C) 280
Wright, Taylor (Co. A) 97, 233, 246, 266
Wyant, David (Co. I) 249, 323
Wyatt, Henry (1st NC) 15, 202, 221
Wyont, David (Co. I) 235

Yaunts, Reuben C. (Co. E) 25, 80, 230, 291
Yoder, David (Co. I) 242, 323
York, George W. (Co. E) 248, 294
York, William (Co. B) 273
Yorktown, VA (fortifications) 8, 17, 18
Young, James H. (Co. H) 223, 311
Young, James M. (Co. K) 21, 40, 71, 75, 88, 90, 101, 102, 114, 115, 118, 125, 134, 141, 149, 154, 157, 166, 171, 183, 190, 192, 193, 195, 196, 197, 202, 209, 217, 218, 246, 256, 324
Young, Louis (CS) 73, 167, 197
Young, Samuel M. (Co. K) 232, 238, 327

Zabriskie, Adam (U.S.) 42
Zeke's Island, NC 30

www.ingramcontent.com/pod-product-compliance
Lightning Source LLC
Chambersburg PA
CBHW081535300426
44116CB00015B/2636